T0189414

# Lecture Notes in Computer Science    12892

More information about this subseries at http://www.springer.com/series/7407

Igor Farkaš · Paolo Masulli ·
Sebastian Otte · Stefan Wermter (Eds.)

# Artificial Neural Networks and Machine Learning – ICANN 2021

30th International Conference on Artificial Neural Networks
Bratislava, Slovakia, September 14–17, 2021
Proceedings, Part II

 Springer

*Editors*
Igor Farkaš ⓘD
Comenius University in Bratislava
Bratislava, Slovakia

Paolo Masulli ⓘD
iMotions A/S
Copenhagen, Denmark

Sebastian Otte ⓘD
University of Tübingen
Tübingen, Baden-Württemberg, Germany

Stefan Wermter ⓘD
Universität Hamburg
Hamburg, Germany

ISSN 0302-9743          ISSN 1611-3349 (electronic)
Lecture Notes in Computer Science
ISBN 978-3-030-86339-5          ISBN 978-3-030-86340-1 (eBook)
https://doi.org/10.1007/978-3-030-86340-1

LNCS Sublibrary: SL1 – Theoretical Computer Science and General Issues

This Springer imprint is published by the registered company Springer Nature Switzerland AG
The registered company address is: Gewerbestrasse 11, 6330 Cham, Switzerland

# Preface

Research on artificial neural networks has progressed over decades, in recent years being fueled especially by deep learning that has proven, albeit data-greedy, efficient in solving various, mostly supervised, tasks. Applications of artificial neural networks, especially related to artificial intelligence, affect our lives, providing new horizons. Examples range from autonomous car driving, virtual assistants, and decision support systems to healthcare data analytics, financial forecasting, and smart devices in our homes, just to name a few. These developments, however, also provide challenges, which were not imaginable previously, e.g., verification of raw data, explaining the contents of neural networks, and adversarial machine learning.

The International Conference on Artificial Neural Networks (ICANN) is the annual flagship conference of the European Neural Network Society (ENNS). Last year, due to the COVID-19 pandemic, we decided not to hold the conference but to prepare the ICANN proceedings in written form. This year, due to the still unresolved pandemic, the Organizing Committee, together with the Executive Committee of ENNS decided to organize ICANN 2021 online, since we felt the urge to allow research presentations and live discussions, following the now available alternatives of online conference organization. So for the first time, ENNS and the Organizing Committee prepared ICANN as an online event with all its challenges and sometimes unforeseeable events!

Following a long-standing successful collaboration, the proceedings of ICANN are published as volumes within the Lecture Notes in Computer Science Springer series. The response to this year's call for papers resulted, unexpectedly, in a record number of 557 article submissions (a 46% rise compared to previous year), of which almost all were full papers. The paper selection and review process that followed was decided during the online meeting of the Bratislava organizing team and the ENNS Executive Committee. The 40 Program Committee (PC) members agreed to check the submissions for the formal requirements and 64 papers were excluded from the subsequent reviews. The majority of the PC members have doctoral degrees (80%) and 75% of them are also professors. We also took advantage of filled-in online questionnaires providing the reviewers' areas of expertise. The reviewers were assigned one to four papers, and the papers with undecided scores also received reports from PC members which helped in making a final decision.

In total, 265 articles were accepted for the proceedings and the authors were requested to submit final versions. The acceptance rate was hence about 47% when calculated from all initial submissions. A list of PC members and reviewers who agreed to publish their names is included in the proceedings. With these procedures we tried to keep the quality of the proceedings high while still having a critical mass of contributions reflecting the progress of the field. Overall we hope that these proceedings will contribute to the dissemination of new results by the neural network community during these challenging times and we hope that we can have a physical ICANN in 2022.

Finally, we very much thank the Program Committee and the reviewers for their invaluable work.

September 2021

Igor Farkaš
Paolo Masulli
Sebastian Otte
Stefan Wermter

# Organization

## Organizing Committee

Cabessa Jérémie     Université Paris 2 Panthéon-Assas, France
Kerzel Matthias     University of Hamburg, Germany
Lintas Alessandra     University of Lausanne, Switzerland
Malinovská Kristína     Comenius University in Bratislava, Slovakia
Masulli Paolo     iMotions A/S, Copenhagen, Denmark
Otte Sebastian     University of Tübingen, Germany
Wedeman Roseli     Universidade do Estado do Rio de Janeiro, Brazil

## Program Committee Chairs

Igor Farkaš     Comenius University in Bratislava, Slovakia
Paolo Masulli     iMotions A/S, Denmark
Sebastian Otte     University of Tübingen, Germany
Stefan Wermter     University of Hamburg, Germany

## Program Committee

Andrejková Gabriela     Pavol Jozef Šafárik University in Košice, Slovakia
Atencia Miguel     Universidad de Malaga, Spain
Bodapati Jyostna Devi     Indian Institute of Technology, Madras, India
Bougie Nicolas     Sokendai/National Institute of Informatics, Japan
Boža Vladimír     Comenius University in Bratislava, Slovakia
Cabessa Jérémie     Université Paris 2 Panthéon-Assas, France
Di Nuovo Alessandro     Sheffield Hallam University, UK
Duch Włodzisław     Nicolaus Copernicus University, Poland
Eppe Manfred     Universität Hamburg, Germany
Fang Yuchun     Shanghai University, China
Garcke Jochen     Universität Bonn, Germany
Gregor Michal     University of Žilina, Slovakia
Guckert Michael     Technische Hochschule Mittelhessen, Germany
Guillén Alberto     University of Granada, Spain
Heinrich Stefan     University of Tokyo, Japan
Hinaut Xavier     Inria, France
Humaidan Dania     University of Tübingen, Germany
Jolivet Renaud     University of Geneva, Switzerland
Koprinkova-Hristova Petia     Bulgarian Academy of Sciences, Bulgaria
Lintas Alessandra     University of Lausanne, Switzerland
Lü Shuai     Jilin University, China
Micheli Alessio     Università di Pisa, Italy

| | |
|---|---|
| Oravec Miloš | Slovak University of Technology in Bratislava, Slovakia |
| Otte Sebastian | University of Tübingen, Germany |
| Peltonen Jaakko | Tampere University, Finland |
| Piuri Vincenzo | University of Milan, Italy |
| Pons Rivero Antonio Javier | Universitat Politècnica de Catalunya, Barcelona, Spain |
| Schmidt Jochen | TH Rosenheim, Germany |
| Schockaert Cedric | Paul Wurth S.A., Luxembourg |
| Schwenker Friedhelm | University of Ulm, Germany |
| Takáč Martin | Comenius University in Bratislava, Slovakia |
| Tartaglione Enzo | Università degli Studi di Torino, Italy |
| Tetko Igor | Helmholtz Zentrum München, Germany |
| Triesch Jochen | Frankfurt Institute for Advanced Studies, Germany |
| Vavrečka Michal | Czech Technical University in Prague, Czech Republic |
| Verma Sagar | CentraleSupélec, Université Paris-Saclay, France |
| Vigário Ricardo | Nova School of Science and Technology, Portugal |
| Wedemann Roseli | Universidade do Estado do Rio de Janeiro, Brazil |
| Wennekers Thomas | Plymouth University, UK |

## Reviewers

| | |
|---|---|
| Abawi Fares | University of Hamburg, Germany |
| Aganian Dustin | Technical University Ilmenau, Germany |
| Ahrens Kyra | University of Hamburg, Germany |
| Alexandre Frederic | Inria Bordeaux, France |
| Alexandre Luís | University of Beira Interior, Portugal |
| Ali Hazrat | Umeå University, Sweden |
| Alkhamaiseh Koloud | Western Michigan University, USA |
| Amaba Takafumi | Fukuoka University, Japan |
| Ambita Ara Abigail | University of the Philippines Diliman, Philippines |
| Ameur Hanen | University of Sfax, Tunisia |
| Amigo Galán Glauco A. | Baylor University, USA |
| An Shuqi | Chongqing University, China |
| Aouiti Chaouki | Université de Carthage, Tunisia |
| Arany Adam | Katholieke Universiteit Leuven, Belgium |
| Arnold Joshua | University of Queensland, Australia |
| Artelt André | Bielefeld University, Germany |
| Auge Daniel | Technical University of Munich, Germany |
| Bac Le Hoai | University of Science, Vietnam |
| Bacaicoa-Barber Daniel | University Carlos III of Madrid, Spain |
| Bai Xinyi | National University of Defense Technology, China |
| Banka Asif | Islamic University of Science & Technology, India |
| Basalla Marcus | University of Liechtenstein, Liechtenstein |
| Basterrech Sebastian | Technical University of Ostrava, Czech Republic |
| Bauckhage Christian | Fraunhofer IAIS, Germany |
| Bayer Markus | Technical University of Darmstadt, Germany |

| | |
|---|---|
| Bečková Iveta | Comenius University in Bratislava, Slovakia |
| Benalcázar Marco | Escuela Politécnica Nacional, Ecuador |
| Bennis Achraf | Institut de Recherche en Informatique de Toulouse, France |
| Berlemont Samuel | Orange Labs, Grenoble, France |
| Bermeitinger Bernhard | Universität St. Gallen, Switzerland |
| Bhoi Suman | National University of Singapore, Singapore |
| Biesner David | Fraunhofer IAIS, Germany |
| Bilbrey Jenna | Pacific Northwest National Lab, USA |
| Blasingame Zander | Clarkson University, USA |
| Bochkarev Vladimir | Kazan Federal University, Russia |
| Bohte Sander | Universiteit van Amsterdam, The Netherlands |
| Bouchachia Abdelhamid | Bournemouth University, UK |
| Bourguin Grégory | Université du Littoral Côte d'Opale, France |
| Breckon Toby | Durham University, UK |
| Buhl Fred | University of Florida, USA |
| Butz Martin V. | University of Tübingen, Germany |
| Caillon Paul | Université de Lorraine, Nancy, France |
| Camacho Hugo C. E. | Universidad Autónoma de Tamaulipas, Mexico |
| Camurri Antonio | Università di Genova, Italy |
| Cao Hexin | OneConnect Financial Technology, China |
| Cao Tianyang | Peking University, China |
| Cao Zhijie | Shanghai Jiao Tong University, China |
| Carneiro Hugo | Universität Hamburg, Germany |
| Chadha Gavneet Singh | South Westphalia University of Applied Sciences, Germany |
| Chakraborty Saikat | C. V. Raman Global University, India |
| Chang Hao-Yuan | University of California, Los Angeles, USA |
| Chang Haodong | University of Technology Sydney, Australia |
| Chen Cheng | Tsinghua University, China |
| Chen Haopeng | Shanghai Jiao Tong University, China |
| Chen Junliang | Shenzhen University, China |
| Chen Tianyu | Northwest Normal University, China |
| Chen Wenjie | Communication University of China, China |
| Cheng Zhanglin | Chinese Academy of Sciences, China |
| Chenu Alexandre | Sorbonne Université, France |
| Choi Heeyoul | Handong Global University, South Korea |
| Christa Sharon | RV Institute of Technology and Management, India |
| Cîtea Ingrid | Bitdefender Central, Romania |
| Colliri Tiago | Universidade de São Paulo, Brazil |
| Cong Cong | Chinese Academy of Sciences, China |
| Coroiu Adriana Mihaela | Babes-Bolyai University, Romania |
| Cortez Paulo | University of Minho, Portugal |
| Cuayáhuitl Heriberto | University of Lincoln, UK |
| Cui Xiaohui | Wuhan University, China |
| Cutsuridis Vassilis | University of Lincoln, UK |

| | |
|---|---|
| Cvejoski Kostadin | Fraunhofer IAIS, Germany |
| D'Souza Meenakshi | International Institute of Information Technology, Bangalore, India |
| Dai Feifei | Chinese Academy of Sciences, China |
| Dai Peilun | Boston University, USA |
| Dai Ruiqi | INSA Lyon, France |
| Dang Kai | Nankai University, China |
| Dang Xuan | Tsinghua University, China |
| Dash Tirtharaj | Birla Institute of Technology and Science, Pilani, India |
| Davalas Charalampos | Harokopio University of Athens, Greece |
| De Brouwer Edward | Katholieke Universiteit Leuven, Belgium |
| Deng Minghua | Peking University, China |
| Devamane Shridhar | KLE Institute of Technology, Hubballi, India |
| Di Caterina Gaetano | University of Strathclyde, UK |
| Di Sarli Daniele | Università di Pisa, Italy |
| Ding Juncheng | University of North Texas, USA |
| Ding Zhaoyun | National University of Defense Technology, China |
| Dold Dominik | Siemens, Munich, Germany |
| Dong Zihao | Jinan University, China |
| Du Songlin | Southeast University, China |
| Edwards Joshua | University of North Carolina Wilmington, USA |
| Eguchi Shu | Fukuoka University, Japan |
| Eisenbach Markus | Ilmenau University of Technology, Germany |
| Erlhagen Wolfram | University of Minho, Portugal |
| Fang Tiyu | University of Jinan, China |
| Feldager Cilie | Technical University of Denmark, Denmark |
| Ferianc Martin | University College London, UK |
| Ferreira Flora | University of Minho, Portugal |
| Fevens Thomas | Concordia University, Canada |
| Friedjungová Magda | Czech Technical University in Prague, Czech Republic |
| Fu Xianghua | Shenzhen University, China |
| Fuhl Wolfgang | Universität Tübingen, Germany |
| Gamage Vihanga | Technological University Dublin, Ireland |
| Ganguly Udayan | Indian Institute of Technology, Bombay, India |
| Gao Ruijun | Tianjin University, China |
| Gao Yapeng | University of Tübingen, Germany |
| Gao Yue | Beijing University of Posts and Telecommunications, China |
| Gao Zikai | National University of Defense Technology, China |
| Gault Richard | Queen's University Belfast, UK |
| Ge Liang | Chongqing University, China |
| Geissler Dominik | Relayr GmbH, Munich, Germany |
| Gepperth Alexander | ENSTA ParisTech, France |
| Gerum Christoph | University of Tübingen, Germany |
| Giancaterino Claudio G. | Catholic University of Milan, Italy |
| Giese Martin | University Clinic Tübingen, Germany |

| | |
|---|---|
| Jia Qiaomei | Northwest University, China |
| Jia Xiaoning | Inner Mongolia University, China |
| Jin Peiquan | University of Science and Technology of China, China |
| Jirak Doreen | Istituto Italiano di Tecnologia, Italy |
| Jodelet Quentin | Tokyo Institute of Technology, Japan |
| Kai Tang | Toshiba, China |
| Karam Ralph | Université Franche-Comté, France |
| Karlbauer Matthias | University of Tübingen, Germany |
| Kaufhold Marc-André | Technical University of Darmstadt, Germany |
| Kerzel Matthias | University of Hamburg, Germany |
| Keurulainen Antti | Bitville Oy, Finland |
| Kitamura Takuya | National Institute of Technology, Japan |
| Kocur Viktor | Comenius University in Bratislava, Slovakia |
| Koike Atsushi | National Institute of Technology, Japan |
| Kotropoulos Constantine | Aristotle University of Thessaloniki, Greece |
| Kovalenko Alexander | Czech Technical University, Czech Republic |
| Krzyzak Adam | Concordia University, Canada |
| Kurikawa Tomoki | Kansai Medical University, Japan |
| Kurpiewski Evan | University of North Carolina Wilmington, USA |
| Kurt Mehmet Necip | Columbia University, USA |
| Kushwaha Sumit | Kamla Nehru Institute of Technology, India |
| Lai Zhiping | Fudan University, China |
| Lang Jana | Hertie Institute for Clinical Brain Research, Germany |
| Le Hieu | Boston University, USA |
| Le Ngoc | Hanoi University of Science and Technology, Vietnam |
| Le Thanh | University of Science, Hochiminh City, Vietnam |
| Lee Jinho | Yonsei University, South Korea |
| Lefebvre Grégoire | Orange Labs, France |
| Lehmann Daniel | University of Greifswald, Germany |
| Lei Fang | University of Lincoln, UK |
| Léonardon Mathieu | IMT Atlantique, France |
| Lewandowski Arnaud | Université du Littoral Côte d'Opale, Calais, France |
| Li Caiyuan | Shanghai Jiao Tong University, China |
| Li Chuang | Xi'an Jiaotong University, China |
| Li Ming-Fan | Ping An Life Insurance of China, Ltd., China |
| Li Qing | The Hong Kong Polytechnic University, China |
| Li Tao | Peking University, China |
| Li Xinyi | Southwest University, China |
| Li Xiumei | Hangzhou Normal University, China |
| Li Yanqi | University of Jinan, China |
| Li Yuan | Defence Innovation Institute, China |
| Li Zhixin | Guangxi Normal University, China |
| Lian Yahong | Dalian University of Technology, China |
| Liang Nie | Southwest University of Science and Technology, China |
| Liang Qi | Chinese Academy of Sciences, Beijing, China |

| | |
|---|---|
| Liang Senwei | Purdue University, USA |
| Liang Yuxin | Northwest University, China |
| Lim Nengli | Singapore University of Technology and Design, Singapore |
| Liu Gongshen | Shanghai Jiao Tong University, China |
| Liu Haolin | Chinese Academy of Sciences, China |
| Liu Jian-Wei | China University of Petroleum, China |
| Liu Juan | Wuhan University, China |
| Liu Junxiu | Guangxi Normal University, China |
| Liu Qi | Chongqing University, China |
| Liu Shuang | Huazhong University of Science and Technology, China |
| Liu Shuting | University of Shanghai for Science and Technology, China |
| Liu Weifeng | China University of Petroleum, China |
| Liu Yan | University of Shanghai for Science and Technology, China |
| Liu Yang | Fudan University, China |
| Liu Yi-Ling | Imperial College London, UK |
| Liu Zhu | University of Electronic Science and Technology of China, China |
| Long Zi | Shenzhen Technology University, China |
| Lopes Vasco | Universidade da Beira Interior, Portugal |
| Lu Siwei | Guangdong University of Technology, China |
| Lu Weizeng | Shenzhen University, China |
| Lukyanova Olga | Russian Academy of Sciences, Russia |
| Luo Lei | Kansas State University, USA |
| Luo Xiao | Peking University, China |
| Luo Yihao | Huazhong University of Science and Technology, China |
| Ma Chao | Wuhan University, China |
| Ma Zeyu | Harbin Institute of Technology, China |
| Malialis Kleanthis | University of Cyprus, Cyprus |
| Manoonpong Poramate | Vidyasirimedhi Institute of Science and Technology, Thailand |
| Martinez Rego David | Data Spartan Ltd., UK |
| Matsumura Tadayuki | Hitachi, Ltd., Tokyo, Japan |
| Mekki Asma | Université de Sfax, Tunisia |
| Merkel Cory | Rochester Institute of Technology, USA |
| Mirus Florian | Intel Labs, Germany |
| Mizuno Hideyuki | Suwa University of Science, Japan |
| Moh Teng-Sheng | San Jose State University, USA |
| Mohammed Elmahdi K. | Kasdi Merbah university, Algeria |
| Monshi Maram | University of Sydney, Australia |
| Moreno Felipe | Universidad Católica San Pablo, Peru |
| Morra Lia | Politecnico di Torino, Italy |

| | |
|---|---|
| Morzy Mikołaj | Poznań University of Technology, Poland |
| Mouček Roman | University of West Bohemia, Czech Republic |
| Moukafih Youness | International University of Rabat, Morocco |
| Mouysset Sandrine | University of Toulouse, France |
| Müller Robert | Ludwig-Maximilians-Universität München, Germany |
| Mutschler Maximus | University of Tübingen, Germany |
| Najari Naji | Orange Labs, France |
| Nanda Abhilasha | Vellore Institute of Technology, India |
| Nguyen Thi Nguyet Que | Technological University Dublin, Ireland |
| Nikitin Oleg | Russian Academy of Sciences, Russia |
| Njah Hasna | University of Sfax, Tunisia |
| Nyabuga Douglas | Donghua University, China |
| Obafemi-Ajayi Tayo | Missouri State University, USA |
| Ojha Varun | University of Reading, UK |
| Oldenhof Martijn | Katholieke Universiteit Leuven, Belgium |
| Oneto Luca | Università di Genova, Italy |
| Oota Subba Reddy | Inria, Bordeaux, France |
| Oprea Mihaela | Petroleum-Gas University of Ploiesti, Romania |
| Osorio John | Barcelona Supercomputing Center, Spain |
| Ouni Achref | Institut Pascal UCA, France |
| Pan Yongping | Sun Yat-sen University, China |
| Park Hyeyoung | Kyungpook National University, South Korea |
| Pateux Stéphane | Orange Labs, France |
| Pecháč Matej | Comenius University in Bratislava, Slovakia |
| Pecyna Leszek | University of Liverpool, UK |
| Peng Xuyang | China University of Petroleum, China |
| Pham Viet | Toshiba, Japan |
| Pietroń Marcin | AGH University of Science and Technology, Poland |
| Pócoš Štefan | Comenius University in Bratislava, Slovakia |
| Posocco Nicolas | Eura Nova, Belgium |
| Prasojo Radityo Eko | Universitas Indonesia, Indonesia |
| Preuss Mike | Universiteit Leiden, The Netherlands |
| Qiao Peng | National University of Defense Technology, China |
| Qiu Shoumeng | Shanghai Institute of Microsystem and Information Technology, China |
| Quan Hongyan | East China Normal University, China |
| Rafiee Laya | Concordia University, Canada |
| Rangarajan Anand | University of Florida, USA |
| Ravichandran Naresh Balaji | KTH Royal Institute of Technology, Sweden |
| Renzulli Riccardo | University of Turin, Italy |
| Richter Mats | Universität Osnabrück, Germany |
| Robine Jan | Heinrich Heine University Düsseldorf, Germany |
| Rocha Gil | University of Porto, Portugal |
| Rodriguez-Sanchez Antonio | Universität Innsbruck, Austria |
| Rosipal Roman | Slovak Academy of Sciences, Slovakia |

| | |
|---|---|
| Rusiecki Andrzej | Wroclaw University of Science and Technology, Poland |
| Salomon Michel | Université Bourgogne Franche-Comté, France |
| Sarishvili Alex | Fraunhofer ITWM, Germany |
| Sasi Swapna | Birla Institute of Technology and Science, India |
| Sataer Yikemaiti | Southeast University, China |
| Schaaf Nina | Fraunhofer IPA, Germany |
| Schak Monika | University of Applied Sciences, Fulda, Germany |
| Schilling Malte | Bielefeld University, Germany |
| Schmid Kyrill | Ludwig-Maximilians-Universität München, Germany |
| Schneider Johannes | University of Liechtenstein, Liechtenstein |
| Schwab Malgorzata | University of Colorado at Denver, USA |
| Sedlmeier Andreas | Ludwig-Maximilians-Universität München, Germany |
| Sendera Marcin | Jagiellonian University, Poland |
| Shahriyar Rifat | Bangladesh University of Engineering and Technology, Bangladesh |
| Shang Cheng | Fudan University, China |
| Shao Jie | University of Electronic Science and Technology of China, China |
| Shao Yang | Hitachi Ltd., Japan |
| Shehu Amarda | George Mason University, USA |
| Shen Linlin | Shenzhen University, China |
| Shenfield Alex | Sheffield Hallam University, UK |
| Shi Ying | Chongqing University, China |
| Shrestha Roman | Intelligent Voice Ltd., UK |
| Sifa Rafet | Fraunhofer IAIS, Germany |
| Sinha Aman | CNRS and University of Lorraine, France |
| Soltani Zarrin Pouya | Institute for High Performance Microelectronics, Germany |
| Song Xiaozhuang | Southern University of Science and Technology, China |
| Song Yuheng | Shanghai Jiao Tong University, China |
| Song Ziyue | Shanghai Jiao Tong University, China |
| Sowinski-Mydlarz Viktor | London Metropolitan University, UK |
| Steiner Peter | Technische Universität Dresden, Germany |
| Stettler Michael | University of Tübingen, Germany |
| Stoean Ruxandra | University of Craiova, Romania |
| Su Di | Beijing Institute of Technology, China |
| Suarez Oscar J. | Instituto Politécnico Nacional, México |
| Sublime Jérémie | Institut supérieur d'électronique de Paris, France |
| Sudharsan Bharath | National University of Ireland, Galway, Ireland |
| Sugawara Toshiharu | Waseda University, Japan |
| Sui Yongduo | University of Science and Technology of China, China |
| Sui Zhentao | Soochow University, China |
| Swiderska-Chadaj Zaneta | Warsaw University of Technology, Poland |
| Szandała Tomasz | Wroclaw University of Science and Technology, Poland |

| Šejnová Gabriela | Czech Technical University in Prague, Czech Republic |
| Tang Chenwei | Sichuan University, China |
| Tang Jialiang | Southwest University of Science and Technology, China |
| Taubert Nick | University Clinic Tübingen, Germany |
| Tek Faik Boray | Isik University, Turkey |
| Tessier Hugo | Stellantis, France |
| Tian Zhihong | Guangzhou University, China |
| Tianze Zhou | Beijing Institute of Technology, China |
| Tihon Simon | Eura Nova, Belgium |
| Tingwen Liu | Chinese Academy of Sciences, China |
| Tong Hao | Southern University of Science and Technology, China |
| Torres-Moreno Juan-Manuel | Université d'Avignon, France |
| Towobola Oluyemisi Folake | Obafemi Awolowo University, Nigeria |
| Trinh Anh Duong | Technological University Dublin, Ireland |
| Tuna Matúš | Comenius University in Bratislava, Slovakia |
| Uelwer Tobias | Heinrich Heine University Düsseldorf, Germany |
| Van Rullen Rufin | CNRS, Toulouse, France |
| Varlamis Iraklis | Harokopio University of Athens, Greece |
| Vašata Daniel | Czech Technical University in Prague, Czech Republic |
| Vásconez Juan | Escuela Politécnica Nacional, Ecuador |
| Vatai Emil | RIKEN, Japan |
| Viéville Thierry | Inria, Antibes, France |
| Wagner Stefan | Heinrich Heine University Düsseldorf, Germany |
| Wan Kejia | Defence Innovation Institute, China |
| Wang Huiling | Tampere University, Finland |
| Wang Jiaan | Soochow University, China |
| Wang Jinling | Ulster University, UK |
| Wang Junli | Tongji University, China |
| Wang Qian | Durham University, UK |
| Wang Xing | Ningxia University, China |
| Wang Yongguang | Beihang University, China |
| Wang Ziming | Shanghai Jiao Tong University, China |
| Wanigasekara Chathura | University of Auckland, New Zealand |
| Watson Patrick | Minerva KGI, USA |
| Wei Baole | Chinese Academy of Sciences, China |
| Wei Feng | York University, Canada |
| Wenninger Marc | Rosenheim Technical University of Applied Sciences, Germany |
| Wieczorek Tadeusz | Silesian University of Technology, Poland |
| Wiles Janet | University of Queensland, Australia |
| Windheuser Christoph | ThoughtWorks Inc., Germany |
| Wolter Moritz | Rheinische Friedrich-Wilhelms-Universität Bonn, Germany |

| | |
|---|---|
| Wu Ancheng | Pingan Insurance, China |
| Wu Dayan | Chinese Academy of Sciences, China |
| Wu Jingzheng | Chinese Academy of Sciences, China |
| Wu Nier | Inner Mongolia University, China |
| Wu Song | Southwest University, China |
| Xie Yuanlun | University of Electronic Science and Technology of China, China |
| Xu Dongsheng | National University of Defense Technology, China |
| Xu Jianhua | Nanjing Normal University, China |
| Xu Peng | Technical University of Munich, Germany |
| Yaguchi Takaharu | Kobe University, Japan |
| Yamamoto Hideaki | Tohoku University, Japan |
| Yang Gang | Renmin University of China, China |
| Yang Haizhao | Purdue University, USA |
| Yang Jing | Guangxi Normal University, China |
| Yang Jing | Hefei University of Technology, China |
| Yang Liu | Tianjin University, China |
| Yang Sidi | Concordia University, Canada |
| Yang Sun | Soochow University, China |
| Yang Wanli | Harbin Institute of Technology, China |
| Yang XiaoChen | Tianjin University of Technology, China |
| Yang Xuan | Shenzhen University, China |
| Yang Zhao | Leiden University, The Netherlands |
| Yang Zhengfeng | East China Normal University, China |
| Yang Zhiguang | Chinese Academy of Sciences, China |
| Yao Zhenjie | Chinese Academy of Sciences, China |
| Ye Kai | Wuhan University, China |
| Yin Bojian | Centrum Wiskunde & Informatica, The Netherlands |
| Yu James | Southern University of Science and Technology, China |
| Yu Wenxin | Southwest University of Science and Technology, China |
| Yu Yipeng | Tencent, China |
| Yu Yue | BNU-HKBU United International College, China |
| Yuan Limengzi | Tianjin University, China |
| Yuchen Ge | Hefei University of Technology, China |
| Yuhang Guo | Peking University, China |
| Yury Tsoy | Solidware, South Korea |
| Zeng Jia | Jilin University, China |
| Zeng Jiayuan | University of Shanghai for Science and Technology, China |
| Zhang Dongyang | University of Electronic Science and Technology of China, China |
| Zhang Jiacheng | Beijing University of Posts and Telecommunications, China |
| Zhang Jie | Nanjing University, China |
| Zhang Kai | Chinese Academy of Sciences, China |

| | |
|---|---|
| Zhang Kaifeng | Independent Researcher, China |
| Zhang Kun | Chinese Academy of Sciences, China |
| Zhang Luning | China University of Petroleum, China |
| Zhang Panpan | Chinese Academy of Sciences, China |
| Zhang Peng | Chinese Academy of Sciences, China |
| Zhang Wenbin | Carnegie Mellon University, USA |
| Zhang Xiang | National University of Defense Technology, China |
| Zhang Xuewen | Southwest University of Science and Technology, China |
| Zhang Yicheng | University of Lincoln, UK |
| Zhang Yingjie | Hunan University, China |
| Zhang Yunchen | University of Electronic Science and Technology of China, China |
| Zhang Zhiqiang | Southwest University of Science and Technology, China |
| Zhao Liang | University of São Paulo, Brazil |
| Zhao Liang | Dalian University of Technology, China |
| Zhao Qingchao | Harbin Engineering University, China |
| Zhao Ying | University of Shanghai for Science and Technology, China |
| Zhao Yuekai | National University of Defense Technology, China |
| Zheng Yuchen | Kyushu University, Japan |
| Zhong Junpei | Plymouth University, UK |
| Zhou Shiyang | Defense Innovation Institute, China |
| Zhou Xiaomao | Harbin Engineering University, China |
| Zhou Yucan | Chinese Academy of Sciences, China |
| Zhu Haijiang | Beijing University of Chemical Technology, China |
| Zhu Mengting | National University of Defense Technology, China |
| Zhu Shaolin | Zhengzhou University of Light Industry, China |
| Zhu Shuying | The University of Hong Kong, China |
| Zugarini Andrea | University of Florence, Italy |

# Contents – Part II

**Convolutional Neural Networks and Kernel Methods**

**Deep Learning and Optimization I**

## Explainable Methods

## Few-shot Learning

## Generative Adversarial Networks

# Computer Vision and Object Detection

# Selective Multi-scale Learning for Object Detection

Junliang Chen[1,2,3], Weizeng Lu[1,2,3], and Linlin Shen[1,2,3(✉)]

[1] Computer Vision Institute, School of Computer Science and Software Engineering, Shenzhen University, Shenzhen, China
[2] Shenzhen Institute of Artificial Intelligence of Robotics of Society, Shenzhen, China
[3] Guangdong Key Laboratory of Intelligent Information Processing, Shenzhen University, Shenzhen 518060, China
{chenjunliang2016,luweizeng2018}@email.szu.edu.cn, llshen@szu.edu.cn

**Abstract.** Pyramidal networks are standard methods for multi-scale object detection. Current researches on feature pyramid networks usually adopt layer connections to collect features from certain levels of the feature hierarchy, and do not consider the significant differences among them. We propose a better architecture of feature pyramid networks, named selective multi-scale learning (SMSL), to address this issue. SMSL is efficient and general, which can be integrated in both single-stage and two-stage detectors to boost detection performance, with nearly no extra inference cost. RetinaNet combined with SMSL obtains 1.8% improvement in AP (from 39.1% to 40.9%) on COCO dataset. When integrated with SMSL, two-stage detectors can get around 1.0% improvement in AP.

**Keywords:** Multi-scale · Object detection

## 1 Introduction

Object detection is a fundamental task in computer vision, whose target is to classify and locate all objects in an image. Image recognition aims to predict the probability of all classes for an image, and adopt the top probabilities and their corresponding classes as final result. Unlike image recognition where there is usually only one object in an image, in object detection, there usually exists various objects in the same image, with a wide range of scales. Therefore, it is difficult to represent different kinds of objects at the same feature representation level. To achieve this goal, a solution is to use multi-level feature representations. The features at higher levels are semantically strong with lower resolutions. While the low-level features are spatially finer with higher resolutions. Hence, the high-level features are more suitable for large-object detection while the low-level features are more beneficial for detecting smaller objects. The pyramidal architecture with multi-scale feature representations is widely used by many powerful object detectors [16,22,23].

I. Farkaš et al. (Eds.): ICANN 2021, LNCS 12892, pp. 3–14, 2021.
https://doi.org/10.1007/978-3-030-86340-1_1

One of the widely used pyramidal architecture is Feature Pyramid Networks (FPN) [15]. FPN takes inputs from a backbone model, which is usually constructed for image recognition. The backbone model generates feature representations in different hierarchies with decreasing resolutions. FPN sequentially takes two adjacent layers from different levels in backbone as inputs, and combines them with a top-down pathway and lateral connections. The high-level features, with stronger semantic but lower resolution, are upsampled to fit the spatial size of the low-level features with higher resolution. Then a binary operation, usually element-wise summation, is conducted to aggregate the features. The low-level finer features are semantically enhanced after combination with high-level features from top-down pathway.

Although FPN is simple and effective for many detectors, there are some aspects to be improved. Path Aggregation Network (PANet) [18] adds an additional bottom-up pathway on the base of FPN. This additional branch can strengthen the semantically enhanced features after FPN, with finer spatial features at lower levels. Balanced Feature Pyramid (BFP) [21] gathers cross-level features from FPN or other pyramidal architectures to the same level. Then a refinement module is carried out after element-wise average of the gathered features. The averaged features, a fusion of features cross all levels, can be considered as global information. The fused features are then scattered to all levels and summed up with the original input features. This process merges the original features with features from all other levels, enabling detectors to perceive information from all levels. Recent researches [9,11] explore better connections of cross-scale features to produce a pyramidal architecture for feature representations.

However, the above works ignore the variances among features from different scales and give them the same weights for combination, or only merge features from partial scales. Inspired by these, we propose an architecture, named selective multi-scale learning (SMSL), to dynamically learn a better feature representation for each level from multi-scale features. SMSL can efficiently improve the detection performance of both single-stage and two-stage detectors with only a small increase of inference cost.

In this study, we make the following contributions:

- We propose the selective multi-scale learning (SMSL) to generate specific features for each level by selectively merge features from multi scales.
- Combined with SMSL, RetinaNet achieves performance of 44.3% AP on COCO dataset.
- The proposed framework can also be applied to two-stage object detectors to improve the detection performance.

# 2   Related Work

Recognizing multi-scale objects is a fundamental but challenging task in computer vision. Pyramidal feature representations is a general technique [1] in this area. A simple method is to use convolutional networks (ConvNets) to extract features from image pyramids. However, this method brings huge computation burden, as the ConvNets forward repeatedly for the same image. To solve the problem, an effective solution is to directly take advantage of the features generated by the ConvNets, instead of using image pyramids. Recent researches [3,7,16,20] propose many cross-scale connections to connect multi-level features from the ConvNets. Though keep the original resolution, the connected features are semantically enhanced.

**Partial Connections.** Partial connections are one of the standard pyramidal architectures. FPN [15] connects two adjacent layers in the top-down pathway by upsampling the high-level features to fit the size of the features at lower level and element-wisely sum up them. This architecture enhances the low-level features with stronger semantic information from higher levels. Although FPN is simple and effective to improve feature representations, the features still lack information from lower levels. To address this problem, Liu et al. [18] propose Path Aggregation Network (PANet) to add an accessional bottom-up pathway on the basis of FPN. In PANet, low-level features are downsampled and summed up with features at higher level. Therefore, the semantically enhanced features after FPN can obtain finer spatial information. NAS-FPN [6] uses Neural Architecture Search (NAS) algorithm to discover a better pyramidal architecture covering all cross-scale connections.

**Full Connections.** Another way to integrate multi-level features is to gather features and fuse them to generate features for different levels and scatter the fused features to the corresponding level. Kong et al. [11] first gather multi-level features and combine them, then use global attention for further refinement. After that, the local reconfiguration module is employed to further capture local information. The produced features are resized and element-wisely summed up with the original input which is linearly projected by a $1 \times 1$ convolution. Balanced Feature Pyramid (BFP) [21] gathers features to a level and applies element-wise averaging. Then a non-local module is utilized to refine the integrated features, which are then scattered to all levels. The refined features are element-wisely summed up with the original input features at each level.

The above methods obtain features from partial scales, and usually merge them through linear operation (such as element-wise summation) which gives features from different scales the same weights. However, for a specific level, the features from different scales have different importance. Therefore, the detector should learn to selectively merge the multi-scale features.

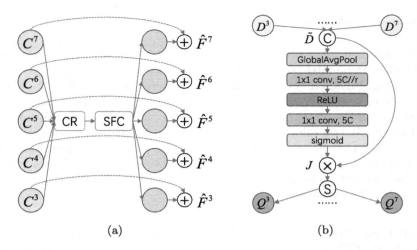

(a)                             (b)

**Fig. 1.** (a) The overview of the proposed selective multi-scale learning. (b) The channel rescaling module. "Ⓒ" and "Ⓢ" denote channel concatenation and channel splitting, respectively.

## 3  Selective Multi-scale Learning

### 3.1  Network Architecture

**Overview.** Figure 1(a) shows the architecture of selective multi-scale learning. We use the $\{C^3, C^4, C^5\}$ layers from ResNet [8] backbone. Then we generate $C^6$ and $C^7$ layers by separately applying a $3 \times 3$ convolution with stride 2 on $C^5$ and $C^6$ layers. Therefore, the original inputs are $\{C^3, C^4, C^5, C^6, C^7\}$, which are gathered to a level and then passed to channel rescaling (CR) module shown in Fig. 1(b) and selective feature combination (SFC) module (Fig. 2(a)) to generate level-specific features. At each level, the generated features are then element-wisely summed up with the corresponding input as the final output.

**Channel Rescaling.** The features at level $l$ after resizing are denoted as $\mathbf{D}^l \in \mathbb{R}^{C \times H \times W}$ with a resolution $H \times W$, and the indexes of the input levels with lowest and highest resolution are denoted as $l_{min}$ and $l_{max}$. Let $L$ be the number of levels, then $L = l_{max} - l_{min} + 1$. In our experiments, the gather level is set to $(l_{min} + l_{max})/2$.

The context of the multi-level features at each channel is different, so the importance of features at each channel is as well different. Therefore, we aim to emphasize the important features and suppress the less useful features, which can be regarded to select the information via a gate. To achieve this goal, we propose channel rescaling module to rescale the features at different channels of the multi-level features. After gathering the multi-level features, we first concat them as:

$$\tilde{\mathbf{D}} = \left[ \mathbf{D}^{l_{min}}, \dots, \mathbf{D}^l, \dots, \mathbf{D}^{l_{max}} \right] \tag{1}$$

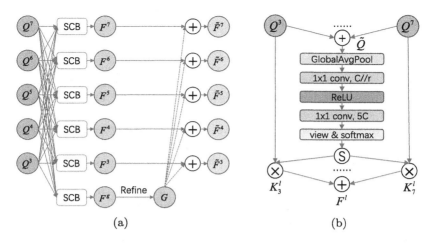

**Fig. 2.** (a) The selective feature combination module. "SCB" denotes the selective combination module. (b) An selective combination module for the $l$-th level. "Ⓢ" denotes channel spliting.

where $\widetilde{\mathbf{D}} \in \mathbb{R}^{LC \times H \times W}$. Then channel rescaling (CR) is accomplished by the following steps.

For a specific channel of $\widetilde{\mathbf{D}}$, we get the global information by using global average pooling (GAP). We denote the result after GAP as $\mathbf{x}$. The result of the $c'$-th channel can be calculated as:

$$x_{c'} = \frac{1}{HW} \sum_{i=1}^{H} \sum_{j=1}^{W} \widetilde{D}_{c',i,j} \tag{2}$$

We then generate the weights for each channel by two fully connected (FC) layers followed by the sigmoid function:

$$\mathbf{s} = \sigma(\mathbf{W_2}\delta(\mathbf{W_1 x})) \tag{3}$$

where $\mathbf{W_1} \in \mathbb{R}^{\frac{LC}{r} \times LC}$, $\mathbf{W_2} \in \mathbb{R}^{LC \times \frac{LC}{r}}$, $\delta$ is the ReLU function and $\sigma$ denotes the sigmoid function. $r$ is the reduction ratio, and is set to 8 in our experiments.

We denote the output after channel rescaling module as $\mathbf{J}$. For the $c'$-th channel, the output $\mathbf{J}_{c'}$ is generated by rescaling $\widetilde{\mathbf{D}}_{c'}$ with $s_{c'}$:

$$\mathbf{J}_{c'} = s_{c'} \otimes \widetilde{\mathbf{D}}_{c'} \tag{4}$$

where $\otimes$ denotes the channel-wise multiplication.

Then we split $\mathbf{J}$ into $L$ groups:

$$\mathbf{J} = \left[ \mathbf{Q}^{l_{min}}, \dots, \mathbf{Q}^l, \dots, \mathbf{Q}^{l_{max}} \right] \tag{5}$$

$$\mathbf{Q}^l = \mathbf{J}_{1+(l-1)C:lC,:,:} \tag{6}$$

where $l \in \{l_{min}, \dots, l_{max}\}$.

**Selective Feature Combination.**

**Local Feature.** A simple approach is to scatter the $L$ rescaled features $\mathbf{Q} = \{\mathbf{Q}^{l_{min}}, \ldots, \mathbf{Q}^{l_{max}}\}$ to all levels. However, as mentioned before, features at different levels have various semantic contexts and are thus suitable to detect objects with different sizes. In addition, the features scattered to $l$-th level shall put more emphasis on the neighboring levels, i.e. $\{\mathbf{Q}^{l-1}, \mathbf{Q}^l, \mathbf{Q}^{l+1}\}$, as they have more similar semantic contexts.

Motivated by these observations, we design a selective combination (SFC) module (Fig. 2(b)) to combine the set of $\mathbf{Q}$ features to generate local feature $\mathbf{F}^l$, which is to be scattered to the $l$-th level. The $C$ channel feature $\mathbf{F}^l = \{\mathbf{F}_1^l, \ldots, \mathbf{F}_c^l, \ldots, \mathbf{F}_C^l\}$ is a weighted combination of $\mathbf{Q}$. The weights are different for each target level and learned by the following steps.

Our goal is to adaptively select features from different levels. An effective idea is to use gate to control the information flow from multiple levels. To achieve this goal, we should aggregate the features from multiple levels. A simple way is to use concatenation to merge the features, but this requires more parameters. Therefore, we use element-wise summation to merge features from multiple levels:

$$\widetilde{\mathbf{Q}} = \sum_{i=l_{min}}^{l_{\max}} \mathbf{Q}^i \tag{7}$$

then we create the global context $\mathbf{g} \in \mathbb{R}^C$ by simply using average pooling, the $c$-th element of the global context can be formulated as:

$$g_c = \frac{1}{H \times W} \sum_{i=1}^{H} \sum_{j=1}^{W} \widetilde{Q}_{c,i,j} \tag{8}$$

Next, we compact the global context into feature $\mathbf{z}^l \in \mathbb{R}^{\frac{C}{r}}$ to guide the adaptive selection. $r$ is the reduction ratio, and is set as 8 in our experiments. To achieve this, we apply a fully connected (FC) layer to generate the result:

$$\mathbf{z}^l = \delta(\mathcal{L}(\mathcal{FC}_1^l(\mathbf{g}))) = \delta(\mathcal{L}(\mathbf{W}^l\mathbf{g})) \tag{9}$$

where $\mathbf{W}^l \in \mathbb{R}^{\frac{C}{r} \times C}$, $\mathcal{L}$ denotes the Layer Normalization [2] and $\delta$ is the ReLU function [19].

To adaptively select features from different levels, a soft attention across channels is employed. The soft attention is a channel-wise weight generated under the guidance of the compacted global context $\mathbf{z}^l$. We first generate the original weight $\mathbf{U}^l \in \mathbb{R}^{LC}$ using an FC layer:

$$\mathbf{U}^l = \mathcal{FC}_2^l(\mathbf{z}^l) = \mathbf{V}^l\mathbf{z}^l \tag{10}$$

where $\mathbf{V}^l \in \mathbb{R}^{C \times LC}$. Then we reshape the weight $\mathbf{U}^l \in \mathbb{R}^{LC}$ into $\mathbf{M}^l \in \mathbb{R}^{L \times C}$. Let $\mathbf{A}^l \in \mathbb{R}^{L \times C}$ be the soft attention weight for $\{\mathbf{Q}^{l_{min}}, \ldots, \mathbf{Q}^{l_{max}}\}$.

For a specific level $i$ and channel $c$, the soft attention weight $A_{i,c}^l$ can be computed as:

$$A_{i,c}^l = \frac{e^{\mathbf{M}_{i,c}^l}}{\sum_{j=l_{min}}^{l_{max}} e^{\mathbf{M}_{j,c}^l}} \tag{11}$$

After adaptive selection, all the features from different levels own their specific weights in the channel-wise aspect. The final output $\mathbf{F}^l \in \mathbb{R}^C$ are the weighted summation of multi-level features via the soft attention weights. For the $c$-th channel, the output $\mathbf{F}^l_c$ can be calculated as:

$$\mathbf{K}^l_{i,c} = A^l_{i,c} \otimes \mathbf{Q}^i_c, \ i \in \{l_{min}, \dots, l_{max}\} \tag{12}$$

$$\mathbf{F}^l_c = \sum_{i=l_{min}}^{l_{max}} \mathbf{K}^l_{i,c} \tag{13}$$

where $\otimes$ denotes the channel-wise multiplication.

**Global Feature.** As global context has been widely used in rescaling and weight features of different levels, we argue that a global feature represents the overall information of all levels shall also be learned and injected into the $L$ local features $\mathbf{F}^l$, before they are scattered to the target levels. The same combination process described above can be used to learn the weights of $\mathbf{Q}$, which can be used to calculate the global feature $\mathbf{F}^g$. We use the non-local [24] module with embed Gaussian attention to further refine $\mathbf{F}^g$ to $\mathbf{G}$. As justified by the ablation study in experimental section, the inclusion of $\mathbf{G}$ can further increase the performance of the feature pyramid network.

The $L$ local features to be scattered to the $l$-th target level, $\widetilde{\mathbf{F}}^l$, can now be calculated as the element-wise summation of $\mathbf{F}^l$ and global feature $\mathbf{G}$:

$$\widetilde{\mathbf{F}}^l = \mathbf{F}^l \oplus \mathbf{G} \tag{14}$$

where $\oplus$ denotes the element-wise summation.

After feature fusion, the fused features are then scattered to the same size as the input of the corresponding level via resizing. For the $l$-th level, the final features $\hat{\mathbf{F}}^l$ can be computed as:

$$\hat{\mathbf{F}}^l = Resize(\widetilde{\mathbf{F}}^l) \oplus \mathbf{C}^l \tag{15}$$

where $Resize$ denotes the resizing function, $\oplus$ denotes the element-wise summation.

## 4   Experiments

### 4.1   Dataset and Evaluation Metrics

We conduct our experiments on the COCO dataset [17]. For training, we use the data in *train-2017* split, which contains 115k images. For ablation study, we use the data in the *val-2017* split consisting of 5k images as validation. We report our main results on the *test-dev* (20k images without public annotations available) split. All the results are reported in the standard COCO-style Average Precision (*AP*) metrics.

**Table 1.** Ablation studies on component effectiveness on COCO *val-2017*, with ResNet-50 [8] backbone. "LF", "GF", and "CR" denote local features, global feature, and channel rescaling respectively.

| LF | GF | CR | $AP$ | $AP_{50}$ | $AP_{75}$ | $AP_S$ | $AP_M$ | $AP_L$ |
|----|----|----|------|-----------|-----------|--------|--------|--------|
| ✓ |   |   | 35.5 | 55.5 | 37.7 | 20.8 | 39.7 | 46.2 |
| ✓ |   | ✓ | 35.8 | 56.5 | 37.9 | 21.1 | 40.2 | 46.4 |
| ✓ | ✓ |   | 35.8 | 56.0 | 38.0 | 20.5 | 40.0 | 47.1 |
| ✓ | ✓ | ✓ | **36.1** | **56.6** | **38.4** | **21.2** | **40.3** | **47.3** |

**Table 2.** Application in other pyramidal architectures based on RetinaNet detector (1st group) and two-stage detectors (2nd group) on COCO *val-2017*. "*" denotes our re-implementation. "Params" denotes the number of total parameters (M) and "Time" denotes the inference time (ms) on single Tesla P100.

|  | SMSL | $AP$ | $AP_{50}$ | $AP_{75}$ | Params (M) | Time (ms) |
|--|------|------|-----------|-----------|------------|-----------|
| Arch |  |  |  |  |  |  |
| FPN |   | 35.5 | 55.3 | 37.9 | 37.74 | 96.8 |
| FPN | ✓ | 36.4[+0.9] | 56.9 | 38.9 | 38.72 | 99.0 |
| PANet* |   | 35.9 | 55.8 | 38.4 | 39.51 | 100.6 |
| PANet* | ✓ | 37.0[+1.1] | 57.6 | 39.4 | 40.49 | 101.6 |
| Detector |  |  |  |  |  |  |
| Mask |   | 35.2 | 56.4 | 37.9 | 44.18 | 92.6 |
| Mask | ✓ | 36.0[+0.8] | 57.6 | 38.6 | 45.15 | 97.2 |
| Cascade |   | 38.1 | 55.9 | 41.1 | 69.17 | 84.0 |
| Cascade | ✓ | 39.1[+1.0] | 57.5 | 42.2 | 70.15 | 88.0 |

### 4.2    Implementation Details

For fair comparisons, all the experiments are conducted on the MMDetection [4] platform. If not specified, for all other hyper-parameters, we follow the same settings in MMDetection [4] for fair comparison.

**Training Details.** The training settings are as follows if not specified. We use ResNet-50 [8] as our backbone networks, and RetinaNet [16] as our detector. The backbone network is initialized with the pretrained model on ImageNet [5]. We use the stochastic gradient descent (SGD) optimizer to train our networks for 12 epochs with batch size 16. The initial learning rate is 0.01 and divided by 10 after 8 and 11 epochs. The input images are resized to have a resolution of $\sim 1333 \times 800$.

**Table 3.** Comparisons with mainstream methods on COCO *test-dev*. "†" denotes results under multi-scale testing.

| Method | Backbone | $AP$ | $AP_{50}$ | $AP_{75}$ | $AP_S$ | $AP_M$ | $AP_L$ |
|---|---|---|---|---|---|---|---|
| Two-stage methods | | | | | | | |
| Faster R-CNN [15] | ResNet-101 | 36.2 | 59.1 | 39.0 | 18.2 | 39.0 | 48.2 |
| Mask R-CNN [7] | ResNeXt-101 | 39.8 | 62.3 | 43.4 | 22.1 | 43.2 | 51.2 |
| LH R-CNN [14] | ResNet-101 | 41.5 | – | – | 25.2 | 45.3 | 53.1 |
| Cascade R-CNN [3] | ResNet-101 | 42.8 | 62.1 | 46.3 | 23.7 | 45.5 | 55.2 |
| TridentNet [13] | ResNet-101-DCN | 48.4 | 69.7 | 53.5 | 31.8 | 51.3 | 60.3 |
| Single-stage methods | | | | | | | |
| ExtremeNet [28] | Hourglass-104 | 40.2 | 55.5 | 43.2 | 20.4 | 43.2 | 53.1 |
| FoveaBox [10] | ResNet-101 | 40.6 | 60.1 | 43.5 | 23.3 | 45.2 | 54.5 |
| FoveaBox [10] | ResNeXt-101 | 42.1 | 61.9 | 45.2 | 24.9 | 46.8 | 55.6 |
| CornerNet [12] | Hourglass-104 | 40.5 | 56.5 | 43.1 | 19.4 | 42.7 | 53.9 |
| CornerNet [12]† | Hourglass-104 | 42.2 | 57.8 | 45.2 | 20.7 | 44.8 | 56.6 |
| FreeAnchor [27] | ResNet-101 | 43.1 | 62.2 | 46.4 | 24.5 | 46.1 | 54.8 |
| FreeAnchor [27] | ResNeXt-101 | 44.9 | 64.3 | 48.5 | 26.8 | 48.3 | 55.9 |
| FSAF [29] | ResNet-101 | 40.9 | 61.5 | 44.0 | 24.0 | 44.2 | 51.3 |
| FSAF [29] | ResNeXt-101 | 42.9 | 63.8 | 46.3 | 26.6 | 46.2 | 52.7 |
| FCOS [23] | ResNet-101 | 41.5 | 60.7 | 45.0 | 24.4 | 44.8 | 51.6 |
| FCOS [23] | ResNeXt-101 | 44.7 | 64.1 | 48.4 | 27.6 | 47.5 | 55.6 |
| ATSS [26] | ResNet-101 | 43.6 | 62.1 | 47.4 | 26.1 | 47.0 | 53.6 |
| Dense RepPoints [25] | ResNeXt-101-DCN | 48.9 | 69.2 | 53.4 | 30.5 | 51.9 | 61.2 |
| RetinaNet [16] | ResNet-101 | 39.1 | 59.1 | 42.3 | 21.8 | 42.7 | 50.2 |
| RetinaNet (ours) | ResNet-101 | 40.9 | 62.3 | 44.1 | 25.1 | 44.7 | 49.9 |
| RetinaNet (ours)† | ResNet-101 | 42.7 | 63.8 | 46.3 | 27.8 | 45.1 | 52.5 |
| RetinaNet [16] | ResNeXt-101 | 40.8 | 61.1 | 44.1 | 24.1 | 44.2 | 51.2 |
| RetinaNet (ours) | ResNeXt-101 | 42.6 | 64.4 | 45.7 | 26.7 | 46.3 | 51.8 |
| RetinaNet (ours)† | ResNeXt-101 | 44.3 | 65.5 | 48.2 | 29.4 | 46.9 | 54.5 |

**Inference Details.** The inference settings are as follows if not specified. For inference, we first select the top 1000 confidence predictions from each prediction layer. Then, we use a confidence threshold of 0.05 to filter out the predictions with low confidence for each class. Then, we apply non-maximum suppression (NMS) to the filtered predictions for each class separately with a threshold of 0.5. Finally, we adopt the predictions with top 100 confidences for each image as the final results.

## 4.3   Ablation Study

As our selective multi-scale learning approach mainly consists of two steps, i.e. CR and SFC, we firstly justify the importance of the proposed module using ablation study. As the local features (LF) are necessary to scatter to the feature pyramid, we only perform an ablation study on the global feature (GF) included in the combination module. The two modules, i.e. CR and GF are removed to see their effects on the performance of the baseline, which are shown in Table 1.

The second row in the table suggests that the CR module improve the overall AP of baseline from 35.5% to 35.8%. Compared to the baseline, the adoption of GF improves $AP$ and $AP_{50}$ by 0.3% and 1.1%, respectively. When both modules are used, the $AP$ is further improved to 36.1%. In summary, both CR and GF can enhance the features and effectively boost the detection performance, which justify the usefulness of our approach.

## 4.4   Application in Pyramid Architectures

In this section, we evaluate the effectiveness of our method on different pyramidal architectures by combining them with our method. As shown in the 1st group of Table 2, when combined with SMSL, FPN [15] and PANet [21] get 0.9% and 1.1% improvement in AP respectively, with only a small increase of parameters and little extra inference time (+2.2 ms and +1.0 ms, respectively).

## 4.5   Application in Two-Stage Detectors

In this section, we conduct experiments to evaluate the effectiveness of our method on two-stage detectors, including Mask R-CNN [7] and Cascade R-CNN [3]. The resolution of the input image is set to 640 × 640. The batch size is adjusted according to the memory limitation with a linearly scaled learning rate. As shown in the 2nd group of Table 2, when combined with SMSL, Mask R-CNN and Cascade R-CNN get 0.8% and 1.0% improvement in AP, with nearly no extra inference time (+4.6 ms and +4.0 ms, respectively). The results justify the effectiveness of our method on two-stage detectors.

## 4.6   Comparisons with Mainstream Methods

After ablation study and comparison with pyramidal networks, we now compare our approach with mainstream methods in Table 3. Both single-stage and two-stage detectors are included for comparison. We report the performance of our SFPN using both ResNet-101 and ResNeXt-101 backbones. We adopt 2× longer training with scale-jitter. For ResNeXt-101 backbone, due to memory limitation, we train the detector using batch size 12 with a linearly scaled learning rate.

As shown in Table 3, combined with our method, RetinaNet with ResNet-101 backbone get 1.8% improvement in AP. With ResNeXt-101 backbone and single-scale setting, RetinaNet with our method achieves 42.6% AP, which is close to two-stage detectors, such as Cascade R-CNN (42.8% AP). If multi-scale test is adopted, the best performance of RetinaNet can be further boosted to 44.3% AP, which surpasses many mainstream object detectors.

## 5  Conclusions

In this paper, we propose selective multi-scale learning, which considers the different importance of the cross-scale features and selectively combine multi-scale features. SMSL can effectively improve the detection performance of single-stage detector, with almost no extra inference cost. The experimental results shows that SMSL can also be applied to two-stage detectors to boost the detection performance.

**Acknowledgments.** This work was supported by National Natural Science Foundation of China under Grant 91959108.

## References

1. Adelson, E.H., Anderson, C.H., Bergen, J.R., Burt, P.J., Ogden, J.M.: Pyramid methods in image processing. RCA Engineer **29**(6), 33–41 (1984)
2. Ba, J., Kiros, J.R., Hinton, G.E.: Layer normalization. arXiv preprint arXiv:1607.06450 (2016)
3. Cai, Z., Vasconcelos, N.: Cascade R-CNN: delving into high quality object detection. In: The IEEE Conference on Computer Vision and Pattern Recognition, pp. 6154–6162 (2018)
4. Chen, K., et al.: MMDetection: open MMLab detection toolbox and benchmark. arXiv preprint arXiv:1906.07155 (2019)
5. Deng, J., Dong, W., Socher, R., Li, L., Kai, L., Li, F.-F.: ImageNet: a large-scale hierarchical image database. In: The IEEE Conference on Computer Vision and Pattern Recognition, pp. 248–255 (2009)
6. Ghiasi, G., Lin, T.Y., Le, Q.V.: NAS-FPN: learning scalable feature pyramid architecture for object detection. In: The IEEE Conference on Computer Vision and Pattern Recognition, pp. 7036–7045 (2019)
7. He, K., Gkioxari, G., Dollar, P., Girshick, R.: Mask R-CNN. In: The IEEE International Conference on Computer Vision, pp. 2961–2969 (2017)
8. He, K., Zhang, X., Ren, S., Sun, J.: Deep residual learning for image recognition. In: The IEEE Conference on Computer Vision and Pattern Recognition, pp. 770–778 (2016)
9. Kim, S.-W., Kook, H.-K., Sun, J.-Y., Kang, M.-C., Ko, S.-J.: Parallel feature pyramid network for object detection. In: Ferrari, V., Hebert, M., Sminchisescu, C., Weiss, Y. (eds.) ECCV 2018. LNCS, vol. 11209, pp. 239–256. Springer, Cham (2018). https://doi.org/10.1007/978-3-030-01228-1_15
10. Kong, T., Sun, F., Liu, H., Jiang, Y., Li, L., Shi, J.: FoveaBox: beyond anchor-based object detector. IEEE Trans. Image Process. **29**, 7389–7398 (2020)
11. Kong, T., Sun, F., Huang, W., Liu, H.: Deep feature pyramid reconfiguration for object detection. In: Ferrari, V., Hebert, M., Sminchisescu, C., Weiss, Y. (eds.) ECCV 2018. LNCS, vol. 11209, pp. 172–188. Springer, Cham (2018). https://doi.org/10.1007/978-3-030-01228-1_11
12. Law, H., Deng, J.: CornerNet: detecting objects as paired keypoints. In: Ferrari, V., Hebert, M., Sminchisescu, C., Weiss, Y. (eds.) Computer Vision – ECCV 2018. LNCS, vol. 11218, pp. 765–781. Springer, Cham (2018). https://doi.org/10.1007/978-3-030-01264-9_45

13. Li, Y., Chen, Y., Wang, N., Zhang, Z.: Scale-aware trident networks for object detection. In: The IEEE International Conference on Computer Vision, pp. 6054–6063 (2019)
14. Li, Z., Peng, C., Yu, G., Zhang, X., Deng, Y., Sun, J.: Light-head R-CNN: in defense of two-stage object detector. arXiv preprint arXiv:1711.07264 (2017)
15. Lin, T.Y., Dollar, P., Girshick, R., He, K., Hariharan, B., Belongie, S.: Feature pyramid networks for object detection. In: The IEEE Conference on Computer Vision and Pattern Recognition, pp. 2117–2125 (2017)
16. Lin, T.Y., Goyal, P., Girshick, R., He, K., Dollar, P.: Focal loss for dense object detection. In: The IEEE International Conference on Computer Vision, pp. 318–327 (2017)
17. Lin, T.-Y., et al.: Microsoft COCO: common objects in context. In: Fleet, D., Pajdla, T., Schiele, B., Tuytelaars, T. (eds.) ECCV 2014. LNCS, vol. 8693, pp. 740–755. Springer, Cham (2014). https://doi.org/10.1007/978-3-319-10602-1_48
18. Liu, S., Qi, L., Qin, H., Shi, J., Jia, J.: Path aggregation network for instance segmentation. In: The IEEE Conference on Computer Vision and Pattern Recognition, pp. 8759–8768 (2018)
19. Nair, V., Hinton, G.E.: Rectified linear units improve restricted Boltzmann machines. In: International Conference on Machine Learning (2010)
20. Newell, A., Yang, K., Deng, J.: Stacked hourglass networks for human pose estimation. In: Leibe, B., Matas, J., Sebe, N., Welling, M. (eds.) ECCV 2016. LNCS, vol. 9912, pp. 483–499. Springer, Cham (2016). https://doi.org/10.1007/978-3-319-46484-8_29
21. Pang, J., Chen, K., Shi, J., Feng, H., Ouyang, W., Lin, D.: Libra R-CNN: towards balanced learning for object detection. In: The IEEE Conference on Computer Vision and Pattern Recognition, pp. 821–830 (2019)
22. Ren, S., He, K., Girshick, R., Sun, J.: Faster R-CNN: towards real-time object detection with region proposal networks. In: Advances in Neural Information Processing Systems, pp. 91–99 (2015)
23. Tian, Z., Shen, C., Chen, H., He, T.: FCOS: fully convolutional one-stage object detection. In: The IEEE International Conference on Computer Vision, pp. 9627–9636 (2019)
24. Wang, X., Girshick, R., Gupta, A., He, K.: Non-local neural networks. In: The IEEE Conference on Computer Vision and Pattern Recognition, pp. 7794–7803 (2018)
25. Yang, Z., et al.: Dense RepPoints: representing visual objects with dense point sets. In: Vedaldi, A., Bischof, H., Brox, T., Frahm, J.-M. (eds.) ECCV 2020. LNCS, vol. 12366, pp. 227–244. Springer, Cham (2020). https://doi.org/10.1007/978-3-030-58589-1_14
26. Zhang, S., Chi, C., Yao, Y., Lei, Z., Li, S.Z.: Bridging the gap between anchor-based and anchor-free detection via adaptive training sample selection. In: CVPR, pp. 840–849 (2020)
27. Zhang, X., Wan, F., Liu, C., Ji, R., Ye, Q.: FreeAnchor: learning to match anchors for visual object detection. In: NeurIPS (2019)
28. Zhou, X., Zhuo, J., Krahenbuhl, P.: Bottom-up object detection by grouping extreme and center points. In: The IEEE Conference on Computer Vision and Pattern Recognition, pp. 850–859 (2019)
29. Zhu, C., He, Y., Savvides, M.: Feature selective anchor-free module for single-shot object detection. In: Proceedings of the IEEE/CVF Conference on Computer Vision and Pattern Recognition, pp. 840–849 (2019)

# DRENet: Giving Full Scope to Detection and Regression-Based Estimation for Video Crowd Counting

Changsheng Liu[1,2] , Yuan Huang[3] , Yadong Mu[1(✉)] , and Xiaoming Yu[3]

[1] Wangxuan Institute of Computer Technology, Peking University, Beijing 100080, China
myd@pku.edu.cn
[2] Peking University Founder Group Co. Ltd, Beijing 100871, China
[3] Beijing Founder Electronics Co. Ltd, Beijing 100085, China

**Abstract.** Currently existing deep learning-based video crowd counting methods mainly involve leveraging the temporal correlation to improve the model. Despite their comparable results, most of these counting methods disregard the fact that crowd density varies enormously in the spatial and temporal domains of videos. This thus hinders the improvement in performance of video crowd counting. To overcome that issue, a new detection and regression estimation network, named DRENet, is proposed, which starts with estimating the crowd density by generating a video object detection-, and a mixed 3D-2D convolution-based (regression-based) density maps separately, in which the detection- and regression-based methods function well in sparse and congested scenes, respectively. Moreover, a multi-column attention-based fusion block is proposed to perceive the crowd density in a frame, and to adaptively allocate the relative weights for the video detection- and regression-based estimations. Furthermore, the optimal crowd counts are obtained with guidance from the attention block. The experimental results demonstrate that our method achieves state-of-the-art performance on three public video crowd counting datasets.

**Keywords:** Video object detection · Mixed 3D-2D convolutions · Multi-column attention-based fusion

## 1 Introduction

Crowd counting, aiming to estimate the crowd density or count the number of people in an image or a video, plays an important role in computer vision; it facilitates a variety of fundamental applications such as public safety management [1] and video surveillance [2], and scene understanding [3].

To achieve this, a variety of methods have been proposed and can generally be divided into detection- and regression-based approaches. Early crowd counting studies were based on detection frameworks [4–6]. Object detectors were applied to localize the position of each individual, and the number of detections was treated as the crowd count. Benefiting from the recent progress in object detection via deep convolutional neural

© Springer Nature Switzerland AG 2021
I. Farkaš et al. (Eds.): ICANN 2021, LNCS 12892, pp. 15–27, 2021.
https://doi.org/10.1007/978-3-030-86340-1_2

networks (CNNs), detection-based crowd counting for ideal images with sparse crowd densities could surpass human performance [7, 8]. Unlike the crowd counting methods based on detection, the regression-based methods estimate the crowd count by directly learning the mapping between features of the image and crowd count [9–15]. When compared with detection-based methods, regression-based methods usually function well for crowded patches; this is because, by benefiting from the rich context in local patches, regression-based methods can capture the general density information [16–18]. Although great achievements have been made in this field, most existing approaches still employ image-based methods for crowd counting while failing to exploit the temporal information in a video sequence. This hinders the improvement in performance of video crowd counting. In contrast, some recent studies have attempted to leverage the temporal correlation in a video sequence to improve the performance of crowd counting [9, 10, 17, 19, 20].

**Table 1.** Statistical information of crowd count differences in the spatial and temporal domains of three video crowd counting datasets used in the study.

| Dataset | Max/Min number of the crowd | |
|---|---|---|
| | Spatial domain | Temporal domain |
| UCSD [21] | 17/0 | 46/11 |
| Mall [22] | 15/0 | 53/13 |
| FDST [10] | 43/0 | 57/9 |

Despite their promising results, such methods utilizing temporal information have two drawbacks. First, the model sizes of the enhanced 3D CNNs [20] and the 3D CNNs [19] are usually much larger than those of the 2D CNNs to capture the temporal information in videos. However, the development of a very deep 3D CNN from scratch results in very high computational costs and memory demands [23]. Second, previous study [8] on image-based methods for crowd counting indicates that, although density-map-based regression techniques have the advantage of being able to model highly occluded scenes, they are prone to high false-positive rates and may lead to overestimated results for low-density scenes; Detection-based approaches exhibit fewer false positives for low-density scenes, but they do not perform well in occluded scenarios. Herein, we obtained statistical information of the crowd count differences in the spatial and temporal domains of three video crowd counting datasets. These differences are shown in Table 1. In the temporal domain of videos, the max/min number of the crowd is the number of the crowd in a frame with maximum crowd density compared to that in a frame with minimum crowd density. Further, in the spatial domain, a frame is cropped into $4 \times 3$ patches; the max/min number of the crowd shows the number of the crowd in a patch with maximum crowd density, compared to that in a patch with minimum crowd density. From Table 1, it is apparent that crowd densities in the real world vary enormously in the temporal and spatial domains. However, existing studies on crowd counting in videos are exclusively based on regression-based methods to simultaneously handle low- and high-density scenes, which thus hinders the improvement in performance.

In this study, a novel detection and regression estimation network named DRENet is therefore proposed to address these issues. It not only efficiently extracts temporal information from videos but also adaptively combines the advantages of the detection- and regression-based estimations for crowd counting. Specifically, to address the first issue regarding regression estimates, we build on the method [24] and replace the fifth convolution group in the 2D ResNets with 3D convolutions, to make use of 3D CNNs with limited convolution layers whilst improving the depth of the CNNs. Moreover, to solve the second issue, unlike most existing approaches to crowd counting in videos [9, 10, 17, 19, 20], our method takes both detection- and regression-based methods into consideration. Given this fusion of models, our method behaves like regression-based methods in low-density scenes but like detection-based methods in congested scenes. This, theoretically, should work better than any other model using just one approach. In summary, this study makes the following contributions:

1. We found that real-world crowd counting situations in videos vary enormously in both the spatial and temporal domains.
2. A novel framework named DRENet is proposed herein; it integrates video object detection-based and regression-based methods into the framework to capture the variation of crowd density in a scene. It further estimates the optimal counts based on a multi-column, attention-based fusion block. Experimental results demonstrate that our method achieves state-of-the-art performance on three public video datasets with varying crowd densities.
3. The temporal information is extracted from the regression block via the mixed 3D-2D convolutions. To the best of our knowledge, this is the first time an attempt is being made to utilize mixed 3D-2D convolution for crowd counting in videos.

## 2  Related Works

**Crowd Counting by Detection.** Early work on crowd counting mainly involved detection frameworks [4–6]; a sliding-window detector incorporating local and global features was applied to detect pedestrians in the scene [25] and count the number of people in the crowd, based on the summation of the results over all the detectors. Although detection-based methods achieve a satisfying count result in a scene with low density, the performance of those methods degrades in crowded scenes owing to perspective distortion and occlusion [8, 16].

**Crowd Counting by Regression.** Considering the failure of detection-based methods in extremely congested scenes, some studies were proposed to directly estimate the total number of the crowd by means of the extracted local [26] and global [21] image features. Recently, inspired by the great success of deep CNNs in feature extraction, the deep learning-based methods have become the mainstream methods for crowd counting. Alternatively, an appropriate counting method that combines the detection-based methods and regression-based methods was proposed [16]; it is based on the density conditions in an image and results in more accurate estimations. However, DecideNet [16] fails to explore the temporal information in a video sequence for both the detection model and the regression model.

**Mixed 3D-2D Convolutions for Spatiotemporal Modeling.** Mixed convolutions (MC), integrating 2D and 3D convolutions into a framework, are a new form of spatiotemporal convolutions [24]. MCs were first exploited by Tran et al. [24] in action recognition and achieve good performance, in which MC ResNets yield significant gain over 2D ResNets of comparable capacity, and they match the performance of 3D ResNets with three times as many parameters. However, mixed 3D-2D convolutions have not yet been applied in video crowd counting, which inspires the study in the field.

**Video Object Detection.** Current leading object detectors for images are built upon deep CNNs [27, 28]. Owing to the complex nature of video variation, e.g., occlusion, motion blur, and out-of-focus issues, it is not a trivial matter to transfer the success of image object detectors [8, 29, 30] into the video domain. When compared with image object detectors, video object detectors [31–33] achieve promising performance for per-frame detection by applying the temporal information in the video sequence. This inspires us to exploit object detectors in videos for crowd counting in our framework.

## 3   Crowd Counting by DRENet

### 3.1   Problem Formulation

The crowd counting task is regarded as a regression problem between the extracted crowd features and the crowd density map in our solution. Let us suppose the center pixel location of the head of a person, $p_i$, is provided for each frame, $I_t$, in the videos. The ground-truth crowd density map, $D_t^g$, is produced by a Gaussian kernel following the method [12]. The ground-truth crowd count, $C_t^g$, is generated by integrating the $D_t^g$ term as shown in Eq. 1.

$$C_t^g = \int D_t^g. \tag{1}$$

For the task of crowd counting in videos, a non-linear regression function is trained by minimizing the Euclidean loss between the ground-truth and the estimated crowd density generated by DRENet.

### 3.2   Network Architecture

The overall architecture of DRENet is shown in Fig. 1. As shown in Fig. 1, DRENet simultaneously estimates crowd counts with both video object detection and regression models. Finally, a multi-column attention-based fusion block is exploited to decide which estimation result should be adopted for a specific pixel in a frame of the video, and the final density map is output. Our framework includes three CNN blocks: the regression block (RegNet), the video detection block (VDNet), and the multi-column attention-based fusion block (AFNet).

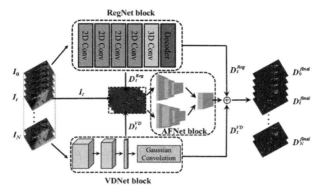

**Fig. 1.** The architecture of our proposed DRENet. $N$ frames in a video are sent to the VDNet and RegNet blocks for generating two kinds of crowd density map estimations. The optimal crowd density map $D_t^{final}$ is generated by the AFNet block.

**The RegNet Block.** The mixed 3D-2D convolutions are utilized in the RegNet block for video crowd counting, which is shown as the RegNet block branch in Fig. 1. Specifically, we utilize an existing pre-trained model, ResNet-34, with five convolution groups [27] as our base model for our architecture. First, we replace the classification part of ResNet-34, with two 2D convolution layers as the decoder to output the regression-based crowd density map, $D_t^{Reg}$, for a given frame, $I_t$, in a video. The value of each pixel represents the estimated count at that point. In addition, a rectified linear unit (ReLU) is applied after the decoder to ensure that the output density map contains positive values. Second, all 2D convolutions in the fifth group are replaced by 3D convolutions, and the remaining groups maintain their 2D convolutions. Third, the kernel size of the convolutions in groups 1 and 5 changes from 2 to 1, which results in the output sizes of our framework being 1/8 of the original input sizes.

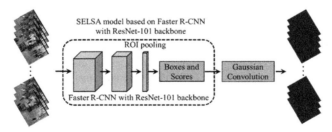

**Fig. 2.** The proposed VDNet block is built upon the SELSA model [31]. A Gaussian convolution is plugged following the bounding box outputs to generate the $N$ detection-based crowd density maps with the input of $N$ frames in a video.

**The VDNet Block.** Based on the motivations that sparse scenes are the expected settings for object detectors and object detection in videos is capable of improving the performance of per-frame detection by exploiting information in the temporal dimension [31–33], the VDNet block, shown in Fig. 2, is proposed and built. It could be viewed as an extension of the SELSA network [31] for head detection in videos, which is based on the ResNet-101 backbone [27]. More specifically, a Gaussian convolutional layer is designed and plugged after the bounding box outputs of the SELSA network, in which a constant Gaussian function, $N^{VD}(p|\mu = P, \sigma^2)$, is applied to convolve over the center points of the detected bounding boxes, $\mathbf{P}_t^{VD}$, on the original image patch. The detection density map, $D_t^{VD}$, generated by the layer is given as Eq. 2.

$$D_t^{VD}(p|\,\Omega_{VD}, I_t) = \sum_{P \in \mathbf{P}_t^{VD}} N^{VD}(p|\mu = P, \sigma^2). \tag{2}$$

**Multi-Column Attention-Based Fusion Block.** To obtain an accurate estimation result based on $D_t^{Reg}$ and $D_t^{VD}$, single-column fully connected convolutional networks are proposed that merge the estimated crowd counting results from different branches, with promising results [16, 19]. Inspired by the multi-column deep neural networks promising performance on different tasks [34], multi-column fully connected convolutional networks are used to adaptively merge both the estimation results from the regression-based method and the detection-based method—this obviously differs from existing methods [16, 19]. Given this fusion of models, our multi-column, attention-based fusion block AFNet can be interpreted as the integration of multi-column fusion branches. This is theoretically better than any fusion block applied on only a single branch and shown in Fig. 3.

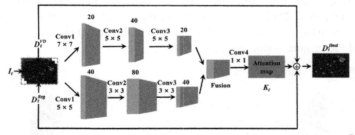

**Fig. 3.** The AFNet block: stacking two kinds of crowd density maps $D_t^{VD}$ and $D_t^{Reg}$, and the original frame $I_t$ as an input, it generates a probabilistic attention map $K_t$. The final crowd density map $D_t^{final}$ is jointly determined by $D_t^{VD}$, $D_t^{Reg}$, and $K_t$.

For a given frame $I_t$, the AFNet block firstly upsamples $D_t^{VD}$ and $D_t^{Reg}$ to the same size of $I_t$. Then $I_t$, $D_t^{VD}$, and $D_t^{Reg}$ are stacked together as inputs for the two AFNet fusion branches. Note that each branch in the AFNet consists of four fully connected convolutional layers, followed by a pixel-wise sigmoid layer to output a probabilistic attention map $K_t(p|\,\Omega_{AF}, I_t)$. The specific value in probabilistic attention map at the pixel $p$, reflects the importance of the detection-based density map $D_t^{VD}$, compared to the regression-based counterpart $D_t^{Reg}$. A higher $K_t$, at pixel $p$, means a higher attention we should rely on the detection-based estimation, rather than the regression-based estimation for $p$. The final density map estimation, $D_t^{final}(p \mid I_t)$, is therefore defined as the weighted sum between two density maps $D_t^{VD}$ and $D_t^{Reg}$, which is guided by the attention map $K_t$:

$$
\begin{aligned}
D_t^{final}(p \mid I_t) = {} & K_t(p \mid \Omega_{AF}, I_t) \odot D_t^{VD}(p \mid \Omega_{VD}, I_t) + \\
& (\mathbf{J} - K_t(p \mid \Omega_{AF}, I_t)) \odot D_t^{Reg}(p \mid \Omega_{Reg}, I_t),
\end{aligned}
\tag{3}
$$

where $\mathbf{J}$ is an all-ones-matrix with the same size of $K_t$, and $\odot$ is the Hadamard product for two matrices.

## 4  Experimental Results

Our method was evaluated on three major video crowd counting datasets collected from real-world surveillance cameras. These are the UCSD dataset [21], the Mall dataset [22], and the FDST dataset [10]. For all datasets, our strategy for the implementation of DRENet consisted of two stages. First, RegNet and VDNet were trained on the different datasets respectively. Second, the AFNet was trained based on the two kinds of crowd density maps generated by the trained RegNet and VDNet on different datasets. In training the VDNet, the backbone of the network was initialized with ImageNet pre-trained weights. A total of 250,000 iterations of stochastic gradient descent (SGD) training were performed using two GPUs. The initial learning rate was $1.0 \times 10^{-4}$ and was divided by 10 at the 125,000th, and 180,000th iteration. The RegNet and AFNet training processes were similar. In training both networks, the Adam optimizer was used. The initial decay rates were $\beta_1 = 0.9$ and $\beta_2 = 0.999$, and a tolerance of 1e−8 was used. Further, a fixed learning rate of 1e−5 was utilized. The pixel-wise mean square error (MSE) between the estimated density map $D_t^{Reg}$ and the ground-truth density map $D_t^{gt}$ was used as the loss function for the AFNet. For the loss of the VDNet, inspired by the method [16], the bounding boxes were applied as the supervision and the classification and localization error in the original SELSA [31] was used as the loss for the VDNet. For the loss function of the AFNet, two kinds of errors were considered: one of them was the MSE between $D_t^{final}$, and $D_t^{gt}$; the second error measured the quality of the output probabilistic map $K_t$ in AFNet. Following the setting proposed in method [16], the Euclidean distances between the probabilistic attention map, and the video object detection score map was used as the second error component. Following the convention of existing study [17], the mean absolute error (MAE) and the MSE were used as the evaluation metrics.

### 4.1  The Mall Dataset

The Mall dataset [22] is composed of 2,000 frames, each with a resolution of $640 \times 480$. For a fair comparison with previous studies, the first 800 frames were used for training, and the remaining part was used for testing. We sent sixteen frames to the network at a time. Table 2 compares the DRENet with previous studies [9, 10, 15–17, 20, 35, 36], which demonstrates that DRENet outperforms the image-based methods by at least

7.9% in terms of MAE (compared with DecideNet [16]). In addition, DRENet also outperforms the video-based methods by at least 4.8% in terms of MAE (compared with STDNet [17]). We found that the crowd in the Mall dataset is sparse. In this case, the estimated results of crowd density based on regression are usually overestimated. The VDNet, however, estimates crowd density accurately, which results in it outperforming state-of-the-art methods.

Table 2. Comparisons of different methods on the Mall dataset [22].

|  | Method | MAE | MSE |
|---|---|---|---|
| Image-based | MoC-CNN [35] | 2.75 | 13.4 |
|  | HSRNet [15] | 1.80 | 2.28 |
|  | DRSAN [36] | 1.72 | 2.10 |
|  | DecideNet [16] | 1.52 | 1.90 |
| Video-based | Bi-ConvLSTM [9] | 2.10 | 7.60 |
|  | LSTN [10] | 2.00 | 2.50 |
|  | E3D [20] | 1.64 | 2.13 |
|  | STDNet [17] | 1.47 | 1.88 |
|  | **DRENet (ours)** | **1.40** | **1.81** |

### 4.2 The UCSD Dataset

The UCSD dataset [21] is also a publicly available video-based dataset, which consists of 2,000 Gy-level frames with the frame rate per second of 10 fps. Following the settings mentioned in the study, we used the 601–1,400th frames as training data, and the remaining 1200 frames were selected as the test set. Moreover, sixteen frames were sent to the network simultaneously. Table 3 compares the proposed DRENet with state-of-the-art image- and video-based methods. The results demonstrate that the DRENet outperforms all of the previous image-based methods [11, 13, 14, 18] in terms of MAE and MSE by at least 20% and 9.4% (compared to PaDNet) respectively. In addition, our proposed DRENet also outperforms video-based methods; such as, LSTN [10], ConvLSTM [9], E3D [20], and STDNet [17].

## 5   The FDST Dataset

To better evaluate our DRENet in video crowd counting, a large-scale video crowd counting dataset—the FDST dataset [10]—is used to evaluate our method in the study. The FDST dataset contains 15,000 frames, with 394,081 annotated heads. Following the settings in the study [10]; 9,000 frames were used for training, and the remaining 6,000

**Table 3.** Comparisons of different methods on the UCSD dataset [21].

|             | Method            | MAE  | MSE  |
|-------------|-------------------|------|------|
| Image-based | CSRNet [13]       | 1.16 | 1.47 |
|             | ADCrowdNet [18]   | 0.98 | 1.25 |
|             | PACNN [14]        | 0.89 | 1.18 |
|             | PaDNet [11]       | 0.85 | 1.06 |
| Video-based | Bi-ConvLSTM [9]   | 1.13 | 1.43 |
|             | LSTN [10]         | 1.07 | 1.39 |
|             | E3D [20]          | 0.93 | 1.17 |
|             | STDNet [17]       | 0.76 | 1.01 |
|             | **DRENet (ours)** | **0.68** | **0.96** |

frames were used for testing. Sixteen frames are sent to the network simultaneously. Table 4 shows the comparison results between the DRENet and existing methods [9, 10, 12]. Similar to the comparison results on the UCSD dataset, the DRENet outperforms the image-based method by 46.4% in terms of MAE (compared with MCNN [12]). The DRENet also outperforms the five video-based methods by at least 14% in terms of MAE (compared with MLSTN [37]). It is worth noting that the improvement on the FDST dataset is significant because the frame rate per second of the FDST dataset is 30 fps. Further, it is much more suitable for both the VDNet and the RegNet in extracting effective temporal features, since there are high correlations between consecutive frames. These comparison results also demonstrate the effectiveness of the powerful temporal information in video crowd counting.

**Table 4.** Comparisons of different methods on the FDST dataset [10].

| Method            | MAE  | MSE  |
|-------------------|------|------|
| ConvLSTM [9]      | 4.48 | 5.82 |
| MCNN [12]         | 3.77 | 4.88 |
| LSTN [10]         | 3.35 | 4.45 |
| COMBI [38]        | 2.92 | 3.76 |
| ALL-EST [38]      | 2.84 | 3.57 |
| MLSTN [37]        | 2.35 | 3.02 |
| **DRENet (ours)** | **2.02** | **2.67** |

## 5.1    Effects of Different Components in the DRENet

To get more insights into each component of the proposed DRENet, ablation studies are conducted on the UCSD dataset and the qualitative results are listed in Table 5, which shows several interesting observations.

Firstly, we evaluated the performance of the method based on the 2D ResNet-34 [27]. Compared to the 2D ResNet-34 [27], the RegNet used in our study obtains lower estimation errors for both the MAE and the MSE. This can be regarded as a verification that the mixed 3D-2D convolutions can boost the performance on the task of video crowd counting. This, of course, results from the use of the temporal information in videos.

Secondly, the estimation results from only using either the RegNet ("RegNet only") or the VDNet ("VDNet only") have higher errors compared to using the DRENet. This demonstrates the effectiveness of making use of both detection- and regression-based methods in video crowd counting.

Thirdly, performing late fusion by averaging two classes of crowd density maps ("RegNet + VDNet + Late Fusion") achieves only a mediocre performance on two kinds of crowd density estimations. However, with the AFNet, we obtain a significant decrease in both MAE and MSE metrics, as compared with those performing the late fusion. This demonstrates the effectiveness of our proposed multi-column attention-based fusion block in DRENet.

**Table 5.** Qualitative results of different DRENet components on the UCSD dataset [21].

| Method | MAE | MSE |
|---|---|---|
| ResNet-34 [27] | 0.96 | 1.25 |
| RegNet only | 0.85 | 1.09 |
| VDNet only | 0.79 | 1.03 |
| RegNet + VDNet + Late Fusion | 0.82 | 1.06 |
| RegNet + VDNet + AFNet | 0.68 | 0.96 |

## 6    Conclusion

In this paper, a novel video crowd counting architecture named DRENet has been proposed. It was motivated by the fact that crowd density varies enormously in the spatial and temporal domains in videos. Further, the detection- and regression-based counting methods achieve complementary performance under situations with time-varying, and space-varying crowd densities in videos. To the best of our knowledge, DRENet is the first framework to estimate crowd counts in videos, under the guidance of an attention-based block. This attention mechanism adaptively applies attention weights for video object detection-, and regression-based count estimations. Furthermore, both mixed 3D-2D convolutions and video object detection are the first to be used in video crowd counting. Our architecture is evaluated on three challenging video crowd counting benchmarks, collected from real-world scenes with high variation in complex background and crowd densities. Experimental results confirm that our architecture achieves state-of-the-art performance on the three public datasets.

# References

1. Xu, M.L., Li, C.X., Lv, P., Lin, N., Hou, R., Zhou, B.: An efficient method of crowd aggregation computation in public areas. IEEE Trans. Circuits Syst. Video Technol. **28**(10), 2814–2825 (2018)
2. Zhang, Z., Wang, M., Geng, X.: Crowd counting in public video surveillance by label distribution learning. Neurocomputing **166**, 151–163 (2015)
3. Cong, Z., Hongsheng, L., Wang, X., Xiaokang, Y.: Cross-scene crowd counting via deep convolutional neural networks. In: 2015 IEEE Conference on Computer Vision and Pattern Recognition (CVPR), Boston, pp. 833–841. IEEE (2015)
4. Leibe, B., Seemann, E., Schiele, B.: Pedestrian detection in crowded scenes. In: 2005 IEEE Computer Society Conference on Computer Vision and Pattern Recognition (CVPR 2005), San Diego, pp. 878–885. IEEE (2005)
5. Dalal, N., Triggs, B.: Histograms of oriented gradients for human detection. In: 2005 IEEE Computer Society Conference on Computer Vision and Pattern Recognition (CVPR 2005), San Diego, vol. 1, pp. 886–893. IEEE (2005)
6. Viola, P., Jones, M.J., Snow, D.: Detecting pedestrians using patterns of motion and appearance. In: Proceedings Ninth IEEE International Conference on Computer Vision, Nice, pp. 734–741. IEEE (2003)
7. Gao, C., Li, P., Zhang, Y., Liu, J., Wang, L.: People counting based on head detection combining Adaboost and CNN in crowded surveillance environment. Neurocomputing **208**, 108–116 (2016)
8. Vora, A., Chilaka, V.: FCHD: a fast and accurate head detector. arXiv preprint arXiv:1809.08766 (2019)
9. Xiong, F., Shi, X., Yeung, D.: Spatiotemporal modeling for crowd counting in videos. In: 2017 IEEE International Conference on Computer Vision (ICCV), Venice, pp. 5161–5169. IEEE (2017)
10. Fang, Y., Zhan, B., Cai, W., Gao, S., Hu, B.: Locality-constrained spatial transformer network for video crowd counting. In: 2019 IEEE International Conference on Multimedia and Expo (ICME), Shanghai, pp. 814–819. IEEE (2019)
11. Tian, Y., Lei, Y., Zhang, J., Wang, J.Z.: PaDNet: pan-density crowd counting. IEEE Trans. Image Process. **29**, 2714–2727 (2020)
12. Zhang, Y., Zhou, D., Chen, S., Gao, S., Ma, Y.: Single-image crowd counting via multi-column convolutional neural network. In: 2016 IEEE Conference on Computer Vision and Pattern Recognition (CVPR), Los Alamitos, vol. 1, pp. 589–597. IEEE Computer Society (2016)
13. Li, Y., Zhang, X., Chen, D.: CSRNet: dilated convolutional neural networks for understanding the highly congested scenes. In: 2018 IEEE/CVF Conference on Computer Vision and Pattern Recognition, Salt Lake City, pp. 1091–1100. IEEE (2018)
14. Shi, M., Yang, Z., Xu, C., Chen, Q.: Revisiting perspective information for efficient crowd counting. In: 2019 IEEE/CVF Conference on Computer Vision and Pattern Recognition (CVPR), Long Beach, pp. 7271–7280. IEEE (2019)
15. Zou, Z., Liu, Y., Xu, S., Wei, W., Wen, S., Zhou, P.: Crowd counting via hierarchical scale recalibration network. In: 2020 IEEE/CVF Conference on Computer Vision and Pattern Recognition (CVPR), Seattle, pp. 2864–2871. IEEE (2020)

16. Liu, J., Gao, C., Meng, D., Hauptmann, A.G.: DecideNet: counting varying density crowds through attention guided detection and density estimation. In: 2018 IEEE/CVF Conference on Computer Vision and Pattern Recognition, Salt Lake City, pp. 5197–5206. IEEE (2018)

17. Ma, Y.J., Shuai, H.H., Cheng, W.H.: Spatiotemporal dilated convolution with uncertain matching for video-based crowd estimation. IEEE Trans. Multimedia, 1–1 (2021)

18. Liu, N., Long, Y., Zou, C., Niu, Q., Pan, L., Wu, H.: ADCrowdNet: an attention-injective deformable convolutional network for crowd understanding. In: 2019 IEEE/CVF Conference on Computer Vision and Pattern Recognition (CVPR), Long Beach, pp. 3220–3229. IEEE (2019)

19. Miao, Y., Han, J., Gao, Y., Zhang, B.: ST-CNN: spatial-temporal convolutional neural network for crowd counting in videos. Pattern Recognit. Lett. **125**, 113–118 (2019)

20. Zou, Z., Shao, H., Qu, X., Wei, W., Zhou, P.: Enhanced 3D convolutional networks for crowd counting. arXiv preprint arXiv:1908.04121 (2019)

21. Chan, A.B., Zhang-Sheng John, L., Vasconcelos, N.: Privacy preserving crowd monitoring: counting people without people models or tracking. In: 2008 IEEE Conference on Computer Vision and Pattern Recognition, Anchorage, pp. 1–7. IEEE (2008)

22. Chen, K., Chen, C.L., Gong, S., Xiang, T.: Feature mining for localised crowd counting. In: 24th British Machine Vision Conference, Bristol, pp. 1–11 (2013)

23. Qiu, Z., Yao, T., Mei, T.: Learning spatio-temporal representation with pseudo-3D residual networks. In: 2017 IEEE International Conference on Computer Vision (ICCV), Venice, vol. 1, pp. 5534–5542. IEEE (2017)

24. Tran, D., Wang, H., Torresani, L., Ray, J., LeCun, Y., Paluri, M.: A closer look at spatiotemporal convolutions for action recognition. arXiv preprint arXiv:1711.11248v3 (2018)

25. Dollar, P., Wojek, C., Schiele, B., Perona, P.: Pedestrian detection: an evaluation of the state of the art. IEEE Trans. Pattern Anal. Mach. Intell. **34**(4), 743–761 (2012)

26. Chan, A.B., Vasconcelos, N.: Counting people with low-level features and bayesian regression. IEEE Trans. Image Process. **21**(4), 2160–2177 (2012)

27. He, K., Zhang, X., Ren, S., Sun, J.: Deep residual learning for image recognition. In: 2016 IEEE Conference on Computer Vision and Pattern Recognition (CVPR), Las Vegas, pp. 770–778. IEEE (2016)

28. Simonyan, K., Zisserman, A.: Very deep convolutional networks for large-scale image recognition. arXiv preprint arXiv:1409.1556 (2014)

29. Ren, S., He, K., Girshick, R., Sun, J.: Faster R-CNN: towards real-time object detection with region proposal networks. In: Proceedings of the 28th International Conference on Neural Information Processing Systems, Montreal, Canada, vol. 1, pp. 91–99. MIT Press (2015)

30. Cai, Z., Vasconcelos, N.: Cascade R-CNN: delving into high quality object detection. In: 2018 IEEE/CVF Conference on Computer Vision and Pattern Recognition, Salt Lake City, pp. 6154–6162. IEEE (2018)

31. Wu, H., Chen, Y., Wang, N., Zhang, Z.: Sequence level semantics aggregation for video object detection. In: 2019 IEEE/CVF International Conference on Computer Vision (ICCV), Seoul, pp. 9216–9224. IEEE (2019)

32. Wu, C., Feichtenhofer, C., Fan, H., He, K., Krähenbühl, P., Girshick, R.: Long-term feature banks for detailed video understanding. In: 2019 IEEE/CVF Conference on Computer Vision and Pattern Recognition (CVPR), Long Beach, pp. 284–293. IEEE (2019)

33. Deng, J., Pan, Y., Yao, T., Zhou, W., Li, H., Mei, T.: Relation distillation networks for video object detection. In: 2019 IEEE/CVF International Conference on Computer Vision (ICCV), Seoul, pp. 7022–7031. IEEE (2019)

34. Ciregan, D., Meier, U., Schmidhuber, J.: Multi-column deep neural networks for image classification. In: 2012 IEEE Conference on Computer Vision and Pattern Recognition, Providence, pp. 3642–3649. IEEE (2012)

35. Kumagai, S., Hotta, K., Kurita, T.: Mixture of counting CNNs: adaptive integration of CNNs specialized to specific appearance for crowd counting. arXiv preprint arXiv:1703.09393 (2017)

36. Liu, L., Wang, H., Li, G., Ouyang, W., Lin, L.: Crowd counting using deep recurrent spatial-aware network. In: Twenty-Seventh International Joint Conference on Artificial Intelligence (IJCAI), Palo Alto, pp. 849–855. AAAI Press/IJCAI (2018)

37. Fang, Y., Gao, S., Li, J., Luo, W., He, L., Hu, B.: Multi-level feature fusion based locality-constrained spatial transformer network for video crowd counting. Neurocomputing **392**, 98–107 (2020)

38. Liu, W., Salzmann, M., Fua, P.: Estimating people flows to better count them in crowded scenes. arXiv preprint arXiv:1911.10782 (2019)

# Sisfrutos Papaya: A Dataset for Detection and Classification of Diseases in Papaya

Jairo Lucas de Moraes[(✉)] [iD], Jorcy de Oliveira Neto[(✉)], Jacson R. Correia-Silva[(✉)],
Thiago M. Paixão[(✉)], Claudine Badue[(✉)], Thiago Oliveira-Santos[(✉)],
and Alberto F. De Souza[(✉)]

Universidade Federal do Estado do Espírito Santo, Vitória, ES, Brazil
artsoft.lucas@terra.com.br, {jorcyd,jacson,thiagopx,claudine,
todsantos,alberto}@lcad.inf.ufes.br

**Abstract.** In recent years, approaches based on machine learning, more specifically Deep Neural Networks (DNN), have gained prominence as a solution to computer vision problems in the most diverse areas. However, this type of approach requires a large number of samples of the problem to be treated, which often makes this type of approach difficult. In computer vision applications aimed at fruit growing, this problem is even more noticeable, as the performance of computer vision approaches in this segment is still well below the performance achieved in other areas. One of the main reasons listed by the literature for the little evolution in this area is the lack of large data sets duly and manually annotated, which are mandatory for applications that use cutting-edge computer vision techniques such as DNNs. The present work aims to leverage research in this domain, creating a new dataset of images, of an unparalleled size in the literature, with the main diseases and damages of papaya fruit (*Carica Papaya*). The proposed data set in this work consists of 15,179 RGB images duly and manually annotated with the position of the fruit and the disease/damage found within it.

In order to validate our dataset, we used it to train a DNN-based classifier in the task of detecting diseases and defects in a papaya image. We recreated the old challenge "Man vs. Machine" comparing our classifier with a human expert in a real environment. Our model reached an f1-score of 80.01%, while the overall performance obtained by the human expert was 67.3%. The project is available at https://github.com/jairolucas/Sisfrutos-Papaya.

**Keywords:** Papaya · Fruit diseases · Dataset · Detection and classification · Deep learning · Computer vision

## 1 Introduction

Fruit production in general, and more specifically in Brazil, has achieved great prominence mainly because it is an important source of crop diversification and increased income for small farmers, as well as the fact that it is a highly labor-aggregating activity. Considering this scenario, the agriculture of papaya (*Carica Papaya*) is one of the most outstanding examples of worldwide fruit production, as it is produced in more than 40

© Springer Nature Switzerland AG 2021
I. Farkaš et al. (Eds.): ICANN 2021, LNCS 12892, pp. 28–39, 2021.
https://doi.org/10.1007/978-3-030-86340-1_3

countries, with a special part played by Brazil, which is the 2nd largest world producer [27], with an annual production of more than 1.5 million tons, second only to India. In addition, due to the high quality of the fruit produced in Brazil, it ranks as the second largest exporter in the world, just behind Mexico [27, 28]. At the national level, the Brazilian states of Espirito Santo and Bahia account for more than 70% of the fruits produced and for more than 95% of the exported fruits, this culture being extremely important for the economy of the region and the country [27].

This work is focused on leveraging artificial vision research using Deep Learning techniques with a focus on Papaya's quality control.

In the past few years, Convolutional Neural Networks (CNNs) have been employed to solve several tasks in computer vision, such as classification, detection and segmentation. But CNNs need a large amount of data to achieve a good performance, which can make its application unfeasible in some tasks. In agriculture, there are few CNN-based approaches to detection, classification and computer vision based quality control measures (disease recognition, ripening and damage to fruit) [1, 2]. One of the main reasons listed by [1] is the lack of large annotated datasets needed to train these networks. In a survey published by Li [3] in 2018, 45 papers were reported, but only two of them used CNNs for non-destructive approaches on quality control automation in blueberry and strawberry crops.

Despite this, the future scenario is very promising. Naranjo [4] published in 2020 a comprehensive review on the use of CNN networks applied to the tasks of detection, classification and quality control of fruits in general (i.e. without being specific to a certain crop). In this study the authors shows that, in the last two years, the amount of research using this type of approach in this field has increased considerably.

This increase has occurred mainly in the tasks of detection and classification of fruits [14–17], and coincides with the creation of large data sets such as Fruits-360 [5], which at the time of its publication (2018) had 38,409 images regarding 60 different fruits duly and manually annotated. This allowed for generating a good training dataset for a CNN network.

An early detection and correct classification of diseases or defects in a fruit are essential for the adoption of correct measures to control and mitigate losses [7]. However, this task is inherently manual and requires technical expertise that is not always available. Moreover, manual classification s highly dependent on the evaluator's experience and psychological status, which can lead to incorrect interpretations about the type of disease or defects found in the fruit.

An autonomous system to detect and classify diseases in a fruit is a challenging problem for computer vision research. Some topics to be covered in this field are: (i) is there an expected fruit in the image? (ii) what are the coordinates of the fruit? (iii) is there any disease of mechanical damage in the fruit? (iv) what are the coordinates of the disease or mechanical damage?

As exposed in the literature, one of the main obstacles to detect and classify diseases in fruits using CNNs is the hard work of gathering and annotating a large dataset with these images. Up to the scope of our research (as of 2021), we did not find in the literature a large set of public data that offered these samples, in any culture, making the researcher himself have to acquire and annotate the images to assemble his own data set, an extremely expensive task. Regarding this, the published research for the task of detecting and classifying diseases ends up using small data sets and without any defined standard. This lack of standardization in the evaluated datasets makes it difficult to compare the results of the techniques proposed in each work, as well as the validation of these techniques in real environments, where thousands of images, in different scenarios, need to be evaluated.

We have created a data set with more than 15,000 duly and manually annotated images of the main diseases that affect this fruit culture (i.e. the *Carica Papaya*). Our data set should help to leverage research in this field and could stand as a standardized benchmark for evaluating future works. As a second contribution, we use a classifier model based on deep learning to train and evaluate our data set, achieving excellent results.

This paper is organized as follows. In Sect. 2 we will discuss the most recent relevant works for the domain covered. In Sect. 3 we describe in detail the data set created. In Sect. 4 we describe the methodology used by our classifier, detailing the subsets of data, the network parameters and the approach used. In Sect. 5 the results obtained are detailed and in Sect. 6 the main conclusions of the work are presented, as well as suggestions for future works for the same domain.

## 2 Related Works

In this section, we describe the work related to the detection and classification of diseases and damage to fruits in different crops.

In one of the latest works published in the area, Kukreja [6] proposed a CNN to detect the main diseases (Blackspot, Melanose Canker, Scab and Anthracnose) and noticeable damage in citrus fruits. Initially, the author used a data set with 150 RGB images of size $256 \times 256$, composed by 128 images of defective fruits and 22 images of healthy fruits. The experiments obtained an accuracy of 67%. Next, the author used several data augmentation techniques for generating a total of 1,200 images, such as rotation, resizing, resizing and changing the luminosity. The images were also enhanced by pre-processing. Therefore, an accuracy of 89.1% was achieved. In addition, they concluded that a large number of samples is essential in Convolutional Neural Networks and that data augmentation techniques can be used to significantly improve networks when only few samples are available for the training step. Yunong [7] proposed a method for detecting Anthracnose disease in apples. The authors used 500 images of healthy apples and 140 images of apples affected by anthracnose. The data augmentation was used to increase the number of images in the dataset. In addition, they also used an Adversarial Cycle-Consistent (CycleGAN) [8] to generate similar synthetic images. After increasing the dataset size, the authors used a densely connected neural network (DenseNet) [9] to optimize the Yolo-V3 model [10]. They achieved an accuracy of 86.9% using the dataset without synthetic images and 91.7% of accuracy using the synthetic images.

Tarek et al. [11, 12] published two studies related to the use of computer vision to detect diseases in Papaya. In the first [11], they proposed a specialist system to detect and classify diseases in images captured by a mobile device. The method consists of converting the input image to a standard size of $300 \times 300$ using bicubic interpolation, followed by applying a histogram equalization to improve its contrast, and converting the image from RGB to l * a * B color space. After these steps, they used K-means to segment the images and SVM to detect and classify the disease. They used 129 images of Papaya for training and testing sets, 84 and 45 images respectively. The author obtained an accuracy of 90.15%.

In the second work, Tarek et al. [12] compared nine distinct classifiers for detection and classification of Papaya diseases: K-Nearest Neighbors (KNN), Logistic Regression, Repeated Incremental Pruning to Produce Error Reduction (RIPPER), Naive Bayes, Random Forests, Support Vector Machine (SVM), Back Propagation Neural Network (BPN) and Counter Propagation Network (CPN). The classifiers were trained and tested on the same data used in [11]. The authors reported that the best accuracy was 95.2% obtained by the SVM. However, the same classifier obtained only 90.15% in the first work [11], but they did not provide more details about this improvement.

Abirami [13] proposed a method to detect and classify diseases in fruits, caused by fungi and bacteria. They first used a threshold to segment the affected part of the fruit, then a Local Binary Standard (LBP) to extract features, and finally a feedforward neural network for classification. The dataset has 100 images, but they did not provide details on the division of the training and testing sets and the kind of fruits used. They achieved 92% accuracy in bacterial diseases and 86% in viral diseases. They also did not specified what types of diseases have been detected.

As it can be seen from, the studies mentioned above all use distinct data sets, with small amounts of samples, and some studies do not clearly categorize the data set used. This lack of standardization makes it impossible to compare the techniques listed in each work, as well as their replication in a real environment. In this work, we propose to overcome these limitations with the creation of the Sisfrutos Papaya data set.

# 3 The Sisfrutos Papaya DataSet

The dataset introduced in this work leverages the research on computer vision techniques for detection and classification of Papaya's (*Carica Papaya*) diseases, mainly those techniques based on deep learning. The creation of this dataset was motivated by the lack of collections with (i) many annotated samples and (ii) covering a large range of diseases, which has caused the researchers to produce their own (unstandardized) collections. The lack of comprehensive and standardized benchmarks makes difficult to compare the different approaches in the literature, therefore it is not trivial to establish the state-of-the-art in automatic detection and/or classification of fruits diseases. This issue is not exclusive for the Papaya culture, being also observed for several other fruit cultures [12].

## 3.1 Image Acquisition

The images used in the work were acquired over 5 months in a real production environment and in different fruit packaging facilities in the Brazilian states of Espírito Santo and Bahia. Those agreed to participate in this work anonymously due to industrial information security reasons. All images were evaluated by trained professionals, with extensive experience in evaluating fruit diseases, and who worked in the fruit quality control sector in the partner companies at the time of this evaluation. The acquisition followed the following protocol:

- In real time, the first evaluator randomly selects the fruit during its passage through the production conveyor (after washing and before packaging).
- Using a mobile device and specific software for the annotations, the expert photographs the fruit and selects the region of interest (ROI), marking the region of the fruit, and when applicable, the region of the disease or defect. The image and the respective annotations are stored in a database.
- In the second evaluation, usually carried out on a different date than the first, a second expert, with more experience, randomly visualizes, without access to the first evaluation, the images of the fruits that have already undergone the first evaluation and carries out their own evaluation.
- The second expert and his evaluation has definitive weight in case of disagreement with the first expert (i.e. considered the Ground Truth).
- Whenever there is a discrepancy between the human evaluations, an error is computed for the first human evaluator, thus being considered an "human expert evaluation error".

Figure 1 shows the evaluation being carried out by the first expert and the software used by the 2nd expert to do his evaluation. The Fig. 2 shows examples of the diseases and defects included in the Dataset.

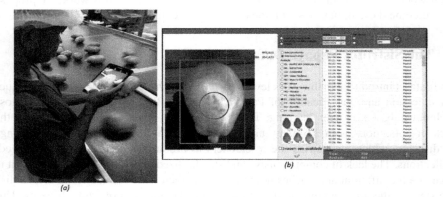

**Fig. 1.** (a) - Evaluation being carried out by the 1st. expert. (b) - Software used by the 2nd. Expert to take notes.

Our final dataset included 6 types of diseases, in addition to mechanical damage to the fruit. The diseases were selected because they are part of those that cause the greatest financial losses [28], and that have a significant degree of occurrence. The dataset is not balanced, thus having different amounts of samples of each fruit disease. Diseases such as Anthracnose and Phytophthora have few samples due to their low occurrence compared to the others. The diseases/damage included in the dataset were:

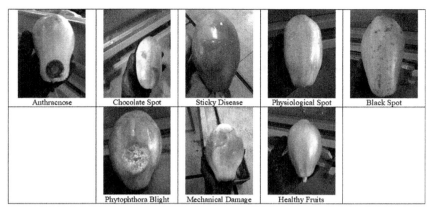

**Fig. 2.** Examples of diseases and damages included in the dataset

- Anthracnose;
- Chocolate Spot;
- Sticky Disease;
- Physiological Spot;
- Black Spot;
- Phytophthora Blight;
- Mechanical Damage;

### 3.2 Specification of Images and Annotations

The DataSet consists of 15,179 images in the RGB standard, with a resolution of 503 × 672 (width × height), a complex background, and significant variation in brightness, pose (rotation and translation) and capture distance.

The images are annotated with the coordinates (x, y) of the central point of the fruit with its respective width and height, and the coordinate of the central point of the disease (xd, yd) with its width and height. These values are given in relation to the image size, thus allowing the image to be resized without losing the regions of interest. These annotations follow the pattern of the YoloV4 network [20]. Table 1 shows the distribution of each class and its respective representation in the Dataset.

**Table 1.** Sisfrutos Papaya dataset

| Class | Sample quantity | (%) |
|---|---|---|
| Healthy Fruits | 4.352 | 28,67% |
| Anthracnose | 156 | 1,03% |
| Phytophthora Blight | 170 | 1,12% |

(continued)

**Table 1.** (*continued*)

| Class | Sample quantity | (%) |
|---|---|---|
| Mechanical Damage | 1.513 | 9,97% |
| Chocolate Spot | 2.040 | 13,44% |
| Sticky Disease | 1.308 | 8,62% |
| Physiological Spot | 2.728 | 17,97% |
| Black Spot | 2.912 | 19,18% |
| Total | 15.179 | 100,00% |

# 4 Methodology

The dataset introduced in this work enables the evaluation of DNNs in papaya fruit diseases/damages detection and classification. The conducted experiments aim to compare the performance of a DNN against a human expert. This section details the DNN architecture, the performance metrics, the datasets, and the carried experiment.

## 4.1 Detection Model

In this work, we adopted YOLOv4 [20] as the detection model for detection of diseases/damage on papaya fruit. The choice of YOLOv4 was motivated by the fact it has achieved the state-of-the-art in several object detection dataset (e.g., [21 and 22]). The most recent version of YOLO has incorporated techniques, such as PAN (Path Aggregation Network), CBAM (Convolutional Block Attention Module), and CBN (Cross-iteration Batch Normalization) that enable efficient training on large datasets using a single GPU without loss of accuracy. A more detailed description of these techniques can be found in [23–25].

## 4.2 Sub Dataset

The original dataset was segmented into 3 different subsets, the first one being used to train the model (training set) comprising approximately 80% of the images, the second for model adjustments (validation set) with approximately 10% of the total images and the last one for the actual model tests (test set), with approximately 10% of the remaining images. Table 2 shows the distribution of classes in the respective data sets.

Using the validation set, a tunning procedure was applied over several hyperparameters in order to obtain the best set of weights for the model. The best performance was achieved in the 15,000th iteration, using a batch $= 64$, subdivisions $= 32$, learning_rate $= 0.0002$, decay $= 0.0005$, $416 \times 416$ network size, policy $=$ sgdr (sgdr_cycle $= 1000$ and sgdr_mult $= 2$), saturation $= 0$, exposure $= 0$, hue $= 0$. The other parameters follow the pattern suggested in [20]. Figure 3 shows the evolution of the F1-Score metric (over the iterations during model training. For more details on the metrics used, see [17, 26].

After training and validation, the model was evaluated using the Test set. The results are presented in Sect. 5.

**Table 2.** Distribution of classes in the respective data sets.

| Class | Sample quantity in the **Training** set | Sample quantity in the **Validation** set | Sample quantity in the **Test** set |
|---|---|---|---|
| Healthy Fruits | 3,452 | 449 | 451 |
| Anthracnose | 131 | 13 | 12 |
| Phytophthora Blight | 144 | 13 | 13 |
| Mechanical Damage | 1,150 | 182 | 181 |
| Chocolate Spot | 1,636 | 202 | 202 |
| Sticky Disease | 1,078 | 115 | 115 |
| Physiological Spot | 2,148 | 290 | 290 |
| Black Spot | 2,332 | 290 | 290 |
| Total | 12,071 | 1,554 | 1,554 |

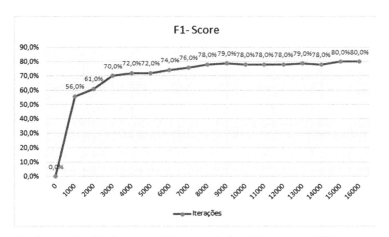

**Fig. 3.** Graph with the metric F1-score calculated for every 1,000 iterations

### 4.3 Hardware Specification

The experiment was conducted on a machine equipped with an Intel Xeon CPU E5606 (2,13 GHz), 24 GB RAM, and a NVIDIA TITAN XP gpu (12 GB). The model was trained over 16,000 iterations, taking approximately 78 h.

## 5 Results and Discussion

As the main objective of this work is to create a large dataset of disease samples in Papaya and use it as a baseline for detection and classification for future work, we need to evaluate its performance correctly and effectively. For that purpose, we performed the classical "Man vs. Machine" accuracy challenge.

In this experiment, we compared the precision of the presented model against the one achieved by human experts. For this, we consider the entire test portion of the dataset (1,554 images) and its respective human expert evaluations. Table 3 shows the confusion matrix generated by the evaluation of human experts.

**Table 3.** Confusion matrix of human experts (HF - Healthy Fruits; AN - Anthracnose; MD - Mechanical Damage; SP - Chocolate Spot; SD - Sticky Disease; FS - Physiological Spot; BS - Black Spot; PT - Phytophthora Blight).

| Ground Truth | Human Expert | | | | | | | | |
|---|---|---|---|---|---|---|---|---|---|
| | HF | AN | MD | CS | SD | PS | BS | PT | Total |
| HF | 331 | | 50 | | 23 | 28 | 19 | | 451 |
| AN | | 11 | | | | | 1 | | 12 |
| MD | 110 | | 69 | | | | | 2 | 181 |
| CS | | | | 183 | | 12 | 7 | | 202 |
| SD | 62 | | | | 44 | 9 | | | 115 |
| PS | | | 39 | 17 | 0 | 155 | 79 | | 290 |
| BS | | 4 | | 52 | | 1 | 233 | | 290 |
| PT | | 3 | | | | | 0 | 10 | 13 |
| Total | 503 | 18 | 158 | 252 | 67 | 205 | 339 | 12 | 1554 |

As can be seen, fruit disease detection and classification is a quite challenging task, even for human experts specifically trained for this function. The performance of these experts proved to be somewhat weak in this task, when compared against the automated system, reaching an overall average of f1-score of just 67.3% in the evaluated examples, even being below 50% for two of the evaluated diseases. This data reflects the actual reality of the quality control department of most fruit processing facilities, where the expert's assessment is subject to human intrinsic, such as stress, tiredness, mood changes and other psychological conditions. In addition, some defects, such as sticky disease and mechanical damage (especially when in the early fruit stages), requires a more in-depth visual inspection to be detected, which the human expert is not always willing to do. It is also worth mentioning that the annotations of the human experts were acquired in an actual quality control environment of the partner facilities, being performed by properly trained professionals who were in charge of quality control inspections at the time of this evaluation.

Our model surpassed the general human expert performance by obtaining an f1-score of 80.1%. The model was also shown to be superior in technically all the evaluated classes. Figure 4 shows a graph that depicts the performance by class of the human experts in relation to our classifier. Figure 5 shows examples of correct and incorrect assessments generated by our model.

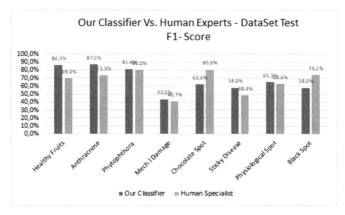

**Fig. 4.** Graph with the performance of our model vs. human expert, in each class

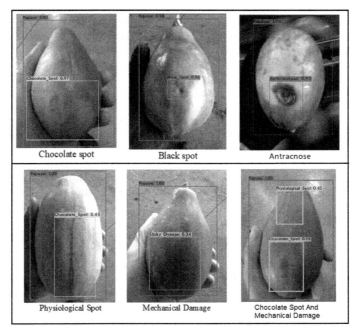

**Fig. 5.** Ground truth and the respective model prediction.

# 6   Conclusion and Future Works

The approaches based on CNN and DNN for solving problems in the area of computer vision have advanced successfully in the most diverse areas, however, this type of approach requires a large set of data with samples of the desired domain duly noted. The area of detection and classification of diseases in fruits, of the most diverse cultures, does not have a public data set with such characteristics. As a result, all published works use databases with few samples that are generally gathered by the researchers themselves, which makes it difficult to be able to compare or even validate the performance of each algorithm.

In this work, we successfully attacked this problem and created a dataset with more than 15,000 images with the main diseases and damages of the Papaya culture. This data set should leverage research in this area, in addition to being a benchmark for evaluating the results of future work.

The tests with our model showed that it obtained a superior performance to a human expert, achieving an f1-score of 80.1% and proving that the dataset created can be used by models that use deep learning to create real-world solutions for automation of the quality control process.

For future works, samples of new diseases will be included in this data set, thus making it even more comprehensive. Still, in the domain of Papaya quality control, it is desirable to have a large dataset that offers samples with distinct and labeled fruit ripening degrees. Current studies on the classification of Papaya ripeness [18, 19], report a good accuracy, but use extremely small sample datasets (300 samples) and classify the fruit based on 3 discrete maturation stages (green, partially ripe and ripe), which isn't suited for real-world applications.

## References

1. Barth, R., Ijsselmuidem, J., Hemming, J., Henten, E.J.: Data synthesis methods for semantic segmentation in agriculture: a capsicum annuum dataset. Comput. Electron. Agric. **144**, 284–296 (2018)
2. Gongal, A., Amatya, S., Karkee, M., Zhang, Q., Lewis, K.: Sensors and systems for fruit detection and localization: a review. Comput. Electron. Agric. **116**, 8–16 (2015)
3. Li, S., et al.: Optical non-destructive techniques for small berry fruits: a review. Artif. Intell. Agric. **2**, 85–98 (2019)
4. Naranjo-Torres, J., Mora, M., García, R., Barrientos, R.J., Fredes, C., Valenzuela, A.: A review of convolutional neural network applied to fruit image processing. MDPI ACS Style. **10**, 3443 (2020)
5. Mure, H.S., Oltean, M.: Fruit recognition from images using deep learning. Acta Univ. Sapientiae, Informatica **10**(1), 26–42 (2018)
6. Kukreja, V., Dhiman, P.: A deep neural network based disease detection scheme for Citrus fruits. In: International Conference on Smart Electronics and Communication (ICOSEC), Trichy, India, pp. 97–101 (2020)
7. Yunong, T., Guodong, Y., Zhe, W., Zize, L.: Detection of apple lesions in orchards based on deep learning methods of CycleGAN and YOLOV3-dense. J. Sens. **2019**, 13 (2019)
8. Goodfellow, L., Pouget-Abadie, J., Mirza, M., et al.: Generative adversarial nets. In: International Conference on Neural Information Processing Systems, Montréal, Canada, pp. 2672–2680 (2014)
9. Huang, G., Liu, Z., Van, M.L., Weinberger, K.Q.: Densely connected convolutional networks. In: IEEE-Conference on Computer Vision and Pattern Recognition (CVPR), Honolulu, USA, pp. 2261–2269 (2017)
10. Redmon, J., Farhadi, A.: YOLOv3: an incremental improvement. https://arxiv.org/abs/1804. 02767 (2018)

11. Habib, M.T., Majumder, A., Jakaria, A.Z.M, Akter, M., Uddin, M.S., Ahmed, F.: Machine vision based papaya disease recognition. J. King Saud Univ. Comput. Inf. Sci. **32**(3), 300–309 (2020). ISSN 1319-1578

12. Habib, M.T., Majumder, A., Nandi, R.N., Ahmed, F., Uddin, M.S.: A comparative study of classifiers in the context of papaya disease recognition. In: Uddin, M.S., Bansal, J.C. (eds.) Proceedings of International Joint Conference on Computational Intelligence. AIS, pp. 417–429. Springer, Singapore (2020). https://doi.org/10.1007/978-981-13-7564-4_36

13. Abirami, S., Thilagavathi, M.: Classification of fruit diseases using feed forward back propagation neural network. In: International Conference on Communication and Signal Processing (ICCSP), 0765–0768 (2019)

14. Koirala, A., Walsh, K.B., Wang, Z., McCarthy, C.: Deep learning–method overview and review of use for fruit detection and yield estimation. Comput. Electron. Agric. **162**, 219–234 (2019)

15. Park, Y., Yang, H.S.: Convolutional neural network based on an extreme learning machine for image classification. Neurocomputing **339**, 66–76 (2019)

16. Mohit, D., Narinder, S.P., Sanjay, K.S., Sonali, A.: Fruit classification using deep feature maps in the presence of deceptive similar classes. Comput. Vis. Pattern Recogn. arXiv:2007.05942 (2020)

17. Margherita, G., Enrico, B., Giorgio, V.: Metrics for multi-class classification: an overview. arXiv:2008.05756 (2020)

18. Santi, K.B., Amiya, K.R., Prabira, K.S.: Status classification of papaya fruits based on machine learning and transfer learning approach. Inf. Proc. Agric. (2020)

19. Simbolon, Z. K., Syakry, S. A., Syahroni, M.: Separation of the mature level of papaya callina fruit automatically based on color (RGB) uses digital image processing. In: International Conference on Science and Innovated Engineering (I-COSINE), p. 536 (2020)

20. Alexey, B., Chien-Yao, W., Hong-Yuan, M.: YOLOv4: optimal speed and accuracy of object detection. https://arxiv.org/abs/2004.10934 (2020)

21. Lin, T.-Y., et al.: Microsoft COCO: common objects in context. In: Fleet, D., Pajdla, T., Schiele, B., Tuytelaars, T. (eds.) ECCV 2014. LNCS, vol. 8693, pp. 740–755. Springer, Cham (2014). https://doi.org/10.1007/978-3-319-10602-1_48

22. Everingham, M., Van, L.G., Williams, C.K., Winn, J.,Zisserman, A.: The PASCAL visual object classes challenge 2012 (VOC2012) results (2012). http://www.pascalnetwork.org/challenges/VOC/voc2012/workshop/index.html

23. Shu, L., Lu, Q., Haifang, Q., Jianping S. and Jiaya, J.: Path aggregation network for instance segmentation. In: Proceedings of the IEEE Conference on Computer Vision and Pattern Recognition (CVPR), pp. 8759–8768 (2018)

24. Woo, S., Park, J., Lee, J.-Y., Kweon, I.S.: CBAM: convolutional block attention module. In: Ferrari, V., Hebert, M., Sminchisescu, C., Weiss, Y. (eds.) ECCV 2018. LNCS, vol. 11211, pp. 3–19. Springer, Cham (2018). https://doi.org/10.1007/978-3-030-01234-2_1

25. Zhuliang, Y., Yue, C., Shuxin, Z., Gao, H.: Cross-iteration batch normalization. arXiv:2002.05712 (2020)

26. Padilla, R., Netto, S.L., Silva, E.A.B.: A survey on performance metrics for object-detection algorithms. In: 2020 International Conference on Systems, Signals and Image Processing (IWSSIP), Niterói, Brazil, pp. 237–242 (2020)

27. Comex Stat - Portal de Comércio Exterior do Ministério do Desenvolvimento, Indústria e Comércio. http://comexstat.mdic.gov.br/pt/home. Accessed 10 Jan 2021

28. Dantas, J., Junghans, D., Lima, J.: O produtor pergunta, a Embrapa responde" – 2ª. Edição, Embrapa, Brasília (2013)

29. Tan, M., Pang, R., Le, Q.V.: EfficientDet: scalable and efficient object detection. In: Proceedings of the IEEE Conference on Computer Vision and Pattern Recognition (2020)

# Faster-LTN: A Neuro-Symbolic, End-to-End Object Detection Architecture

Francesco Manigrasso[ID], Filomeno Davide Miro, Lia Morra[(✉)][ID], and Fabrizio Lamberti[ID]

Dipartimento di Automatica e Informatica, Politecnico di Torino, Torino, Italy
{francesco.manigrasso,lia.morra,fabrizio.lamberti}@polito.it,
filomenodavide.miro@studenti.polito.it

**Abstract.** The detection of semantic relationships between objects represented in an image is one of the fundamental challenges in image interpretation. Neural-Symbolic techniques, such as Logic Tensor Networks (LTNs), allow the combination of semantic knowledge representation and reasoning with the ability to efficiently learn from examples typical of neural networks. We here propose Faster-LTN, an object detector composed of a convolutional backbone and an LTN. To the best of our knowledge, this is the first attempt to combine both frameworks in an end-to-end training setting. This architecture is trained by optimizing a grounded theory which combines labelled examples with prior knowledge, in the form of logical axioms. Experimental comparisons show competitive performance with respect to the traditional Faster R-CNN architecture.

**Keywords:** Object detection · NeuroSymbolic AI · Convolutional neural network · Logic tensor networks

## 1 Introduction

A long-standing problem in Semantic Image Interpretation (SII) and related tasks is how to combine learning from data with existing background knowledge in the form of relational knowledge or logical axioms [1]. Neural-Symbolic (NeSy) integration, which aims at integrating symbolic knowledge representation and learning with machine learning techniques [2], can provide an elegant and principled solution to augment state-of-the-art deep neural networks with these novel capabilities, increasing their performance, robustness and explainability.

The present work leverages the Logic Tensor Network (LTN) paradigm that was proposed by Serafini, Donadello and d'Avila Garcez [3,4]. In very simple terms, LTNs operate by interpreting (or *grounding*) a First-Order Logic (FOL) as functions on real vectors, which parameters can be trained via stochastic gradient descents to maximize the satisfiability of a given theory. LTNs have been successfully applied to the tasks of part-of relationship detection [3] and visual

© Springer Nature Switzerland AG 2021
I. Farkaš et al. (Eds.): ICANN 2021, LNCS 12892, pp. 40–52, 2021.
https://doi.org/10.1007/978-3-030-86340-1_4

relationship detection [5]. Previous works have shown how LTNs can compensate the lack of supervision (e.g., in few-shot learning scenarios) by relying on logical axioms derived from pre-existing knowledge bases.

To close the semantic gap between the symbolic (concept) and subsymbolic (pixel) levels, LTNs for SII rely on convolutional neural networks (CNNs) to extract semantic features which form the basis for grounding object instances in a real vector. Previous works [3,5] relied on pre-trained CNNs, which however suffer from all the limitations traditionally associated with deep learning, namely, the need for a large-scale annotated dataset for training, and lack of interpretability. To fully reap the benefits of NeSy techniques in SII, end-to-end architectures in which the LTN is jointly trained with the feature extraction CNN are needed.

In this work, we propose Faster-LTN, an object detector which unifies the Faster R-CNN object detector with a LTN-based classification head. Differently from previous works [3,5], both modules are jointly trained in an end-to-end fashion. The logical constraints imposed by the LTN can thus shape the training of the convolutional layers, that are no longer purely data-driven. To achieve this objective, we propose several modifications to the original LTN formulation to increase the architecture scalability and deal with data imbalance. Experimental results on the PASCAL VOC and PASCAL PART datasets show that Faster-LTN converges to competitive performance with respect to purely neural architectures, thus proving the feasibility of this approach. The Faster-LTN was implemented in Keras and is available at https://gitlab.com/grains2/Faster-LTN.

The rest of the paper is organized as follows. In Sect. 2, related work is presented. In Sect. 3, different variations of the Faster-LTN architecture are presented, after a brief introduction to the theory behind LTNs. Section 4 presents the experimental setting and results. Finally, conclusions are drawn.

## 2 Related Work

A natural image is comprised of scenes, objects and parts, all interconnected by a complex network of spatial and semantic relationships. Thus, developing semantic image interpretation (SII) components requires to recognize a hierarchy of components, and entails both robust visual perception and the ability to encode and (reason about) visual relationships. Several techniques have been proposed to augment Convolutional Neural Networks (CNNs) with relationship representation and reasoning capabilities, including Relational Network [6], Graph Neural Networks [7] and Neural-Symbolic (NeSy) techniques [3,5,8]. For a more general introduction to NeSy techniques, the reader is referred to recent surveys [9,10].

Many recent approaches extract features from CNNs to a subsequent symbolic or neuro-symbolic module [3,5,11,12]. Yuke Zhu et al. [11] use a Markov Logic Network (MLN) to process text information with associated visual features; a knowledge base is used to represent relations between objects using visual, physical, and categorical attributes. Kenneth Marino et al. [13] incorporate a Graph Search Neural Network (GSNN) into a classification network.

Donatello et al. [3] and Cewu Lu et al. [12] have demonstrated the use of visual features to train LTNs for visual relationship detection, in form of *subject-verb-object* triplets or *part of* relationships. These works demonstrate how NeSy techniques enable the definition of logical axioms that serve as high-level inductive biases, driving the network to find the optimal solution that is compatible with said inductive biases. However, since in the above-mentioned cases the feature extraction and the classification networks are trained separately, the CNN cannot leverage these additional inductive biases during training.

There are, however, some practical hurdles associated with the training of NeSy architectures. Scalability, when dealing with large amounts of data, is a known issue associated with symbolic AI [14]. For this reason, many NeSy architectures rely on a conventional object detector to provide an initial list of candidate objects [3], thus disregarding the effect of the background and simplifying (i.e., reducing) the scale of the problem. In this work, we compare several strategies that are effectively capable of training a LTN-based object detector from scratch, taking into account the effect of the background and the resulting data imbalance.

Another aspect related to scalability is the choice of aggregation function and fuzzy logic operators. Emilie van Krieken et al. [14] and Samy Badreddine [4] found substantial differences between differential fuzzy logic operators in terms of computational efficiency, scalability, gradients, and ability to handle exceptions, which are important characteristics in a learning setting. Their analysis lays the groundwork for the present FasterLTN architecture, which incorporates and extends the log-product aggregator analyzed in [14].

## 3    The Faster-LTN Architecture

This section describes the Faster-LTN architecture and training procedure in detail. An overview of the overall architecture is presented in Fig. 1. We first summarize the Faster R-CNN overall architecture (Sect. 3.1). Then, we introduce the main concepts behind LTNs (Sect. 3.2) and their application to object detection (Sect. 3.3), referring the reader to [3,4] for additional details. Finally, the joint training procedure of Faster-LTN is explained in Sect. 3.4, highlighting the main changes introduced to make end-to-end training feasible.

### 3.1    Faster R-CNN

Faster R-CNN is a two-stage object detector composed of a Region Proposal Network (RPN) and a classification network with a shared backbone [15]. For each anchor, the RPN generates a binary classification label (Background vs. foreground), while a regression layer computes the bounding box coordinates. Regions of Interest (ROIs) selected by the RPN are fed to an ROI Pooling layer, which extracts and resizes each proposal bounding box's features from the shared backbone. Feature maps of equal size are passed to the classifier. The classifier comprises two convolutional heads, a classification layer (with softmax

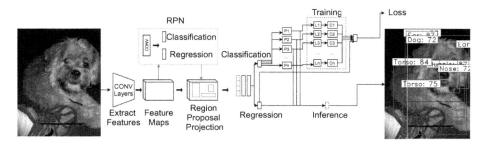

**Fig. 1.** Faster-LTN architecture. The first part of the architecture, up to the RPN, is the same as in the Faster R-CNN network [15]. The feature maps associated to the RPN proposals are extracted by the backbone, concatenated and passed to the LTN, which includes a collection of predicates $P_i$, each corresponding to a specific class. At training time, a batch of labelled examples in the training dataset are used to define a partial theory $\mathcal{T}_{expl}$. Each positive or negative example corresponds to a positive or negative literal (L) for the corresponding predicates. The truth value of the aggregated clauses (C) is maximized to find the optimal grounding $\mathcal{G}^*$. At inference time, the truth value of the predicates $P_i$ is computed.

activation) that computes the final object classification and a regression layer (with linear activation) that computes the bounding box.

Training of the RPN and classifier heads is performed jointly in an alternating fashion. At each forward pass (corresponding to one image), the RPN is trained and updated; then, the RPN output is kept fixed, and the detector head is updated. A fixed number of positive (object) and negative (Background) examples are selected at each step to train the classifier head.

The loss is as a combination of regression and classification loss:

$$L(\{p_i\}, \{b_i\}) = \frac{1}{n_c} \sum_i L_{cls}(p_i, p_i') + \lambda \frac{1}{n_r} \sum_i p_i * L_{reg}(b_i, b_i') \qquad (1)$$

In the Faster-LTN, we keep the RPN module intact and substitute the classifier head with an LTN.

### 3.2  Logic Tensor Network

**Grounding.** In the LTN framework, it is possible to encode a FOL language $\mathcal{L}$ by defining its interpretation domain as a subset of $\mathbb{R}^n$. In the LTN formalism, this process is called *grounding*.

Given the vector space $\mathbb{R}^n$, a grounding $\mathcal{G}$ for $\mathcal{L}$ has the following properties:

1. $\mathcal{G}(c) \in \mathbb{R}^n$, for every $c \in \mathcal{C}$;
2. $\mathcal{G}(P) \in \mathbb{R}^{n*k} \to [0, 1]$, for every $p \in \mathcal{P}$

The grounding of a set of **closed terms** $t_1, .., t_m$ of $\mathcal{L}$ in an atomic formula is defined as:

$$\mathcal{G}(\mathcal{P}(t_1, ...t_m)) = \mathcal{G}(P)(\mathcal{G}(t_1), ..., \mathcal{G}(t_m)) \qquad (2)$$

Formulas can be connected with fuzzy logic *operators* such as conjunctions ($\wedge$), disjunctions ($\vee$), and implications ($\implies$), including logical quantifiers ($\forall$ and $\exists$). Several real-valued, differentiable implementations are available in the fuzzy logic domain [14]. Our implementation, as in [3], is based on the Lukasiewicz [16] formulation:

$$\mathcal{G}(\neg\phi) = 1 - \mathcal{G}(\phi) \tag{3}$$
$$\mathcal{G}(\phi \vee \psi) = min(1, \mathcal{G}(\phi) + \mathcal{G}(\psi)) \tag{4}$$

Predicate symbols are interpreted as functions that map real vectors to the interval $[0, 1]$, which can be interpreted as the predicate's degree of truth. A typical example is the *is-a* predicate, which quantifies the existence of a given object. For instance, if $b = \mathcal{G}(x)$ is the grounding of a dog bounding box, than $\mathcal{G}(\mathsf{Dog})(v) \simeq 1$. A logical constraint expressed in FOL allows to define its properties, i.e., $\forall x \, (\mathsf{Dog}(x) \rightarrow \mathsf{hasMuzzle}\,(x))$.

In LTNs, predicates are typically defined as the generalization of the neural tensor network:

$$\mathcal{G}(\mathcal{P})(\mathbf{v}) = \sigma\left(u_P^T \tanh\left(\mathbf{v_T} W_P^{[1:k]}\mathbf{v} + V_P\mathbf{v} + b_p\right)\right) \tag{5}$$

where $\sigma$ is the sigmoid function, $W[1:k] \in \mathbb{R}^{k \times mn \times mn}$, $V_p \in \mathbb{R}^{k \times mn}$, $u_p \in \mathbb{R}^k$ and $b_p \in \mathbb{R}$ are learnable tensors of parameters. With this formulation, the truth value of a clause can be determined by a neural network which first computes the grounding of the *literals* (i.e., atomic objects) contained in the clause, and then combines them using fuzzy logical operators, as defined by Eqs. 3–4.

**Grounded Theory.** A Grounded Theory (GT) $\mathcal{T}$ is defined by a pair $\langle \mathcal{K}, \hat{\mathcal{G}} \rangle$, where the knowledge base $\mathcal{K}$ is a set of closed formulas, and $\hat{\mathcal{G}}$ is a partial grounding. $\mathcal{K}$ is constructed from labelled examples, as well as logical axioms, as defined in Section 3.3. In practice, a partial grounding is optimized since, qualitatively, our set $\mathcal{K}$ represents a limited and finite set of examples. A grounding $G$ **satisfies** a GT $\langle \mathcal{K}, \hat{\mathcal{G}} \rangle$ if $\mathcal{G}$ completes $\hat{\mathcal{G}}$ and $\mathcal{G}(\phi) = 1 \, \forall \, \phi \in \mathcal{K}$.

**Best Satisfability Problem.** Given a grounding $\hat{\mathcal{G}}_\theta$, where $\theta$ is the set of parameters of all predicates, the learning problem in LTNs is framed as a *best satisfability problem* which consists in determining the values of $\Theta^*$ that maximize the truth values of the conjunction of all clauses $\phi \in \mathcal{K}$:

$$\Theta^* = argmax_\Theta \hat{\mathcal{G}}_\theta \left(\bigwedge_{\phi \in \mathcal{K}} \phi\right) - \lambda ||\Theta||_2^2 \tag{6}$$

where $\lambda ||\Theta||_2^2$ is a regularization term. In practical problems, it is unlikely that a grounded theory can be satisfiable in the classical sense. Hence, we opt instead to find the grounding which achieves the best possible satisfaction, while accounting for the inevitable exception to the rule. Such exceptions can easily arise in the visual domain not only to account to allow the occasional deviation from the norm, but also to account for properties that are not visible. For instance, a cat has (usually) a tail, but a few cats may be tail-less; more frequently, the tail will be occluded or cut from the image.

## 3.3 LTN for Object Detection

**A Grounded Theory for Object Detection.** Let us consider a set of bounding boxes $b \in \mathcal{B}$ with known class $c \in \mathcal{C}$. An object with bounding box $b_n$ is grounded by the vector:

$$\mathbf{v_{b_n}} = < \mathbf{z}_{b_n}, b_n > \tag{7}$$

where $\mathbf{z}_{b_n} = f(I, b_n)$ is an embedding feature vector, calculated by a convolutional neural network $f$, given an image $I$ and the bounding box coordinates $b_n$ predicted by the RPN layer. This is slightly different from previous works [3], where the grounding of a bounding box was defined by the probability vector predicted by a pre-trained Faster R-CNN, and allows to effectively connect the convolutional layers and the LTN.

We set the embedding $f(I, b_n)$ to the output of the last fully connected layer of the classifier head, without softmax activation. Other choices are possible, e.g., by sum pooling the output of an earlier convolutional layer.

The *is-a* predicate for class $c \in \mathcal{C}$ is grounded by a tensor network, defined as in Eq. 5, which implements a one-vs-all classifier. It must be noticed that, differently from [3], the *is-a* predicate takes as input only the embedding features $\mathbf{z}_{b_n}$, excluding the bounding box coordinates. This allows to retain one of the basic properties of object detectors, i.e., invariance to translation.

The *part-of* predicate is defined over pairs of bounding boxes [3]. A pair of two generic bounding boxes $b_m$ and $b_l$ is grounded by the vector:

$$\mathbf{v_{b_{m,l}}} = < \mathbf{z}_{b_m}, b_m, \mathbf{z}_{b_l}, b_l, ir_{m,l} > \tag{8}$$

where $ir_{m,l}$ is the *containment ratio* defined as:

$$ir_{m,l} = \frac{Area\left(b_m \cap b_l\right)}{Area\left(b_m\right)} \tag{9}$$

The grounding $\mathcal{G}\left(\mathsf{part} - \mathsf{of}\right)\left(\mathbf{v_{b_{m,l}}}\right)$ is a neural tensor network as in Eq. 5.

**Defining a Theory from Labelled Examples.** Let us now consider how a GT is constructed to solve the best satisfiability problem defined in Eq. 6 for object detection. As in [3], two grounded theories $\mathcal{T}_{expl}$ and $\mathcal{T}_{prior}$ are defined. The former, $\mathcal{T}_{expl}$, aggregates all the clauses derived from the labelled training set, essentially replicating the classical learning-by-example setting. The theory

$\mathcal{T}_{prior}$, on the contrary, introduces *logical* and *mereological* constraints that represent prior knowledge or, in a more general sense, desirable properties of the final solution.

In this work, two types of constraints are defined. First, we enforce *mutual exclusion* through the clause:

$$\forall x (P_1(x) \implies (\neg P_2(x) \wedge ... \wedge \neg P_n(x))) \tag{10}$$

Equation 10 is translated into $K(K-1))/2$ clauses, corresponding to all unordered class pairs over $K$ classes, e.g., $\mathsf{Cat}(x) \implies \neg \mathsf{Person}(x)$.

Secondly, we impose *mereological constraints* on the grounding of *part-of* and *is-a* predicates derived from an existing ontology (e.g., Wordnet) which includes *meronimy* (i.e., *part-whole*) relationships. Axioms are included to specify that a *part* cannot include another *part*, that a *whole* object cannot include another *whole* object, and that each *whole* is generally associated with a set of given *parts*. An example of such axioms is as follows:

$$\forall x, y \, (\mathsf{Cat}(x) \wedge \mathsf{partOf}(y, x) \rightarrow \mathsf{Tail}\,(y) \vee \mathsf{Head}\,(y) ... \vee \mathsf{Eye}\,(y)) \tag{11}$$

to indicate that if an object $y$ is classified as part of $x$ and $x$ is a cat, than $y$ can be only an object that we know is a part of the whole cat. Mereological constraints were enforced exploiting the KB developed in [3], to which the reader is referred for further information.

## 3.4   Faster-LTN

The overall architecture, illustrated in Fig. 1, is an end-to-end system connecting a convolutional object detector with an LTN. Specifically, the classifier head is modified, by removing the softmax activation, and feeding the output to the LTN. At training time, a GT is constructed as defined in Sect. 3.4. The LTN is implemented by defining three additional layers: *Predicate*, *Literal* and *Clause* layers. For each class $c$, the corresponding literal computes the truth value of all positive (i.e., belonging to class $c$) and negative (i.e., not belonging to class $c$) examples. The Clause layer aggregates all literals for a given class, using the selected aggregation function. Additionally, it is possible to define clauses (e.g., for *part-of* predicates) that take as input multiple literals. For the sake of simplicity, in Fig. 1 only $\mathcal{T}_{expl}$ is shown. The final loss of the LTN is given by summing $L_{LTN}$ with the regression loss, as for the RPN layer.

**Training.** In order to deal with memory constraints, a partial $\mathcal{T}_{expl}$ needs to be rebuilt with every batch of examples. In the original implementation [3], the LTN was trained on the predictions of a pre-trained object detector, allowing for a relatively large batch size. In our setting, the LTN is trained on all proposals extracted by the RPN, and a separate batch is constructed for each image, taking into account background as well as foreground examples. It is worth noticing that one-vs-all classification amplifies the data imbalance between positive and negative examples for each class, even when the training batch consists of an equal number of objects and background proposals.

**Aggregation Function.** The chosen aggregator function is the log-product, which was shown in [14] to scale well with the number of inputs, and which formulation is equivalent to the cross-entropy loss. However, in our case, this choice does not weight adequately the contribution of positive examples, given the high level of class imbalance. Hence, inspired by [17], we introduce the focal log-product aggregation defined as:

$$L_{LTN} = -\sum_{j=0}^{K}\sum_{i=0}^{N} \alpha_c(1 - x_{i,j})^{\gamma} log\,(x_{i,j}) \tag{12}$$

where $\alpha_c$ is a class-dependent weight factor, $\gamma$ enhances the contribution of literals with low truth value (i.e., misclassified examples), $x_i$ is the literal of the $i$-th ROI in the $j$-th class, $K$ is the number of classes and $N$ is the batch size.

To set the value of $\alpha_c$, we simply observe that for each training batch and each class $c$, the number of negative examples is given by the number of background examples (which is fixed during training), plus the positive examples that belong to other classes. Hence, we set $\alpha_c = \frac{1-\beta}{1-\beta^{pos_c}}$ and $\alpha_c = \frac{1-\beta}{1-\beta^{neg_c}}$, for positive and negative examples respectively. Let $p(c)$ be the fraction of bounding boxes in the training set belonging to class $c$. Then, for a given batch the percentage of positive and negative examples becomes $pos_c = \frac{N}{2}p(c)$ and $neg_c = \frac{N}{2} + \frac{N}{2}(1 - p(c))$, respectively.

## 4 Experiments

### 4.1 Dataset

Experiments were performed on the PASCAL VOC 2010 [18] and PASCAL PART [19] benchmarks. For the latter, we selected 20 classes for whole objects and 39 classes for parts. All experiments are conducted on the trainval partition with 80:20 split. For PASCAL PART (10K images), we further experiment reducing the training set by 50% by random selection: the number of images is thus roughly 8K for PASCAL PART and 4K for PASCAL PART REDUCED.

### 4.2 Experimental Setup

**Faster R-CNN.** The architecture of the Faster R-CNN follows quite closely the original implementation [15]. The backbone architecture was ResNet50 pre-trained on ImageNet; the anchor scales were set to $128^2$, $256^2$, and $512^2$, with aspect ratios of 1:1, 1:2, and 2:1. The number of RPN proposals is set to 300. For training the classifier head, 128 bounding boxes were randomly selected, with a ratio of 32:96 positive and negative examples, for the PASCAL VOC dataset; for PASCAL PART, 32 bounding boxes with 16:16 ratio. The network was trained for 100 epochs with the Adam optimizer; the learning rate was set to $10^{-5}$ for the first 60 epochs, and then reduced to $10^{-6}$. Regularization techniques included data augmentation (horizontal flip) and weight decay (with rate $5 \times 10^{-4}$).

**Table 1.** Results of the Faster R-CNN (FR-CNN), Faster R-CNN with focal loss (FR-CNN FL), and Faster-LTN (F-LTN) on PASCAL VOC.

| Class | FR-CNN | FR-CNN FL | F-LTN | F-LTN $\alpha$ | F-LTN bg | F-LTN bg+$\alpha$ |
|---|---|---|---|---|---|---|
| aeroplane | 66.5 | 56.9 | 87.1 | 85.1 | 87.8 | 85.2 |
| bicycle | 69.9 | 64.1 | 75.6 | 77.3 | 77.8 | 77.4 |
| bird | 70.8 | 68.4 | 84.9 | 87.8 | 87.2 | 87.1 |
| boat | 41.3 | 35.8 | 59.7 | 70.3 | 62.2 | 67.1 |
| bottle | 51.0 | 44.1 | 48.2 | 45.8 | 43.7 | 47.0 |
| bus | 75.8 | 71.3 | 79.1 | 79.0 | 79.8 | 78.6 |
| car | 59.0 | 53.1 | 60.0 | 58.7 | 62.9 | 60.1 |
| cat | 92.4 | 90.0 | 93.5 | 92.4 | 94.1 | 94.8 |
| chair | 32.1 | 32.7 | 53.4 | 42.8 | 53.4 | 42.9 |
| cow | 64.6 | 60.7 | 67.1 | 66.3 | 60.1 | 72.6 |
| diningtable | 57.2 | 51.1 | 74.2 | 77.0 | 71.3 | 77.1 |
| dog | 85.3 | 83.3 | 93.6 | 92.3 | 92.5 | 92.0 |
| horse | 61.1 | 62.3 | 82.2 | 80.4 | 85.4 | 85.0 |
| motorbike | 62.0 | 65.3 | 86.7 | 81.0 | 85.6 | 85.0 |
| person | 70.7 | 68.7 | 72.6 | 49.5 | 74.1 | 53.3 |
| pottedplant | 29.0 | 25.4 | 53.1 | 49.2 | 48.8 | 51.8 |
| sheep | 62.2 | 62.1 | 71.2 | 71.4 | 74.7 | 69.1 |
| sofa | 59.9 | 51.9 | 79.2 | 82.0 | 86.4 | 80.1 |
| train | 73.3 | 73.2 | 75.4 | 77.2 | 79.6 | 81.6 |
| tvmonitor | 68.7 | 63.3 | 78.5 | 76.6 | 77.1 | 76.6 |
| **mAP** | **62.6** | **59.2** | **73.8** | **72.1** | **73.3** | **73.25** |

**Faster-LTN.** The architecture of Faster-LTN was the same as Faster R-CNN, except for the classifier head in which the LTN was embedded.

Each predicate is defined by Eq. 5, with $k = 6$ kernels. Łukasiewicz's t–norm was chosen to encode the literals' disjunction, and the focal log-product, with $\gamma = 2$, was selected as the aggregation function. $\mathcal{T}_{prior}$ included mutual exclusion constraints for PASCAL VOC, and mutual exclusion and mereological constraints for PASCAL PART experiments. In the latter case, the LTN was expanded to include *part-of* predicates, but for the sake of comparison with Faster R-CNN, only the object detection performance was evaluated.

On the PASCAL VOC dataset, different experiments were performed with variations of the focal log-product aggregation function: with and without class weights $\alpha$, and with and without adding an additional predicate *bg* to represent the background class. The experiments are denoted as Faster-LTN, Faster-LTN $\alpha$, Faster-LTN *bg*, and Faster-LTN *bg*+$\alpha$. Experiments on PASCAL-PART were performed with the Faster-LTN *bg* configuration. All networks were trained for

**Table 2.** Comparison of Faster R-CNN and Faster-LTN (including mereological constraints) on the PASCAL PART dataset.

| Dataset | Metric | FR-CNN | F-LTN $\mathcal{T}_{prior}$ |
|---|---|---|---|
| PASCAL PART | mAP | 35.1 | 41.2 |
| PASCAL PART REDUCED | mAP | 28.5 | 32.8 |

150 epochs using the Adam optimizer, with weight decay (decay rate $5 \times 10^{-4}$), random horizontal flip and L2 regularization ($\lambda$ is set to $5 \times 10^{-4}$). The learning rate was set to $10^{-5}$ for the first 60 epochs, and then reduced to $10^{-6}$.

All experiments were performed on the HPC@Polito cluster, equipped with V100 NVIDIA GPU. The performance metric was the mean Average Precision (MAP) implemented as in the PASCAL VOC challenge 2010 [20].

### 4.3   Results

Experiments on Pascal VOC, summarized in Table 1, show that Faster LTN achieved competitive and even superior results compared to the original Faster R-CNN architecture, with the mAP increasing from 62.6 to 73.8. In this version of the LTN, the only axiomatic constraint was the one imposing mutual exclusivity (see Eq. 11). We observed comparable performance when including the background as an additional class (mAP from 73.8 to 73.4); on the other hand, weighting positive and negative samples according to their frequency did not improve results (mAP from 73.8 to 72.1).

Qualitatively, we observed that Faster LTN was able to detect more objects than Faster R-CNN. Given that log-product aggregation is mathematically equivalent to the cross-entropy loss, and the backbone is the same, this difference can be attributed to the different classification setting ($K$ one-vs-all classifiers instead of a single multi-class classifier) or the use of the focal loss [17]. However, when changing the loss of the Faster R-CNN classifier head to the focal loss, performance dropped from 62.6 to 59.2. Hence, we attribute Faster-LTN performance to the greater flexibility offered by a more complex classifier head, with higher number of parameters. In fairness, Faster LTN took a few more epochs to reach convergence.

In the PASCAL PART experiments, shown in Table 2, additional mereological axioms were included in $\mathcal{T}_{prior}$. This allowed to increase performance from 35.1 to 41.2; when reducing the training set size by half, the performance gap was maintained (28.5 to 32.8). The comparable quality of the learned features is further supported by the t-SNE embeddings of the extracted features, which are shown in Fig. 2.

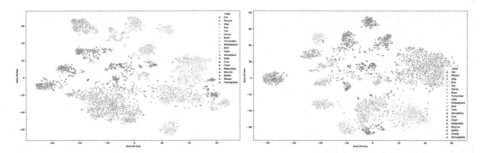

**Fig. 2.** Comparison of the t-SNE embeddings of the features extracted for the *whole* objects classes in the test. Features extracted from Faster R-CNN (left) and Faster-LTN with axiomatic constraints (right).

## 5    Conclusion and Future Works

The availability of large scale, high quality, labelled datasets is one of the major hurdles in the application of deep learning. A tighter integration between perception and reasoning, which is enabled by emerging Neural-Symbolic techniques, allows to complement learning by examples with the integration of axiomatic background knowledge. In this paper, we introduced the Faster-LTN architecture, an end-to-end object detector composed by a convolutional backbone and RPN (based on the Faster R-CNN architecture) and a LTN module. The detector is trained end-to-end by maximizing the satisfiability of a grounded theory combining clauses derived from labelled examples with axiomatic constraints.

Our goal was to establish the feasibility of this approach, and indeed the results, albeit preliminary, prove that Faster-LTN is competitive or can even outperform the baseline Faster R-CNN. However, the scalability of this approach to larger training sets and other object detector (e.g., single-stage detectors) should be further investigated. Through the Faster-LTN model, available at https://gitlab.com/grains2/Faster-LTN, we aim to provide a baseline architecture on which new experiments and applications can be built. Future work will investigate how high-level symbolic constraints can shape the learning process, increasing robustness in the presence of noise and dataset bias.

**Acknolewdgement.** The authors wish to thank Ivan Donadello for the helpful discussions. Computational resources were in part provided by HPC@POLITO, a project of Academic Computing at Politecnico di Torino (http://www.hpc.polito.it).

## References

1. Aditya, S., Yang, Y., Baral, C.: Integrating knowledge and reasoning in image understanding. In: Proceedings of the 28th International Joint Conference on Artificial Intelligence, IJCAI 2019, pp. 6252–6259 (2019)

2. Raedt, L.D., Dumančić, S., Manhaeve, R., Marra, G.: From statistical relational to neuro-symbolic artificial intelligence. In: Proceedings of the Twenty-Ninth International Joint Conference on Artificial Intelligence, IJCAI-20, pp. 4943–4950 (2020)
3. Donadello, I., Serafini, L., Garcez, A.D.: Logic tensor networks for semantic image interpretation. In: Proceedings of the 26th International Joint Conference on Artificial Intelligence, pp. 1596–1602. AAAI Press (2017)
4. Badreddine, S., Garcez, A.d., Serafini, L., Spranger, M.: Logic tensor networks. ArXiv abs/2012.13635 (2020)
5. Donadello, I., Serafini, L.: Compensating supervision incompleteness with prior knowledge in semantic image interpretation. In: 2019 International Joint Conference on Neural Networks (IJCNN), pp. 1–8 (2019)
6. Shanahan, M., Nikiforou, K., Creswell, A., Kaplanis, C., Barrett, D., Garnelo, M.: An explicitly relational neural network architecture. In: Proceedings of the 37th International Conference on Machine Learning, vol. 119, pp. 8593–8603. PMLR (2020)
7. Lamb, L.C., Garcez, A.D., Gori, M., Prates, M.O., Avelar, P.H., Vardi, M.Y.: Graph neural networks meet neural-symbolic computing: a survey and perspective. In: Proceedings of the Twenty-Ninth International Joint Conference on Artificial Intelligence, IJCAI-20, pp. 4877–4884 (2020)
8. Yi, K., Wu, J., Gan, C., Torralba, A., Kohli, P., Tenenbaum, J.B.: Neural-symbolic VQA: disentangling reasoning from vision and language understanding. In: Proceedings of the 32nd International Conference on Neural Information Processing Systems, pp. 1039–1050. Curran Associates Inc. (2018)
9. Besold, T.R., et al.: Neural-symbolic learning and reasoning: a survey and interpretation. ArXiv abs/1711.03902 (2017)
10. Garcez, A., Gori, M., Lamb, L., Serafini, L., Spranger, M., Tran, S.: Neural-symbolic computing: an effective methodology for principled integration of machine learning and reasoning. FLAP **6**, 611–632 (2019)
11. Zhu, Y., Fathi, A., Fei-Fei, L.: Reasoning about object affordances in a knowledge base representation. In: Fleet, D., Pajdla, T., Schiele, B., Tuytelaars, T. (eds.) ECCV 2014. LNCS, vol. 8690, pp. 408–424. Springer, Cham (2014). https://doi.org/10.1007/978-3-319-10605-2_27
12. Lu, C., Krishna, R., Bernstein, M., Fei-Fei, L.: Visual relationship detection with language priors. In: Leibe, B., Matas, J., Sebe, N., Welling, M. (eds.) ECCV 2016. LNCS, vol. 9905, pp. 852–869. Springer, Cham (2016). https://doi.org/10.1007/978-3-319-46448-0_51
13. Marino, K., Salakhutdinov, R., Gupta, A.: The more you know: using knowledge graphs for image classification. In: 2017 IEEE Conference on Computer Vision and Pattern Recognition (CVPR), pp. 20–28 (2017)
14. van Krieken, E., Acar, E., Harmelen, F.V.: Analyzing differentiable fuzzy logic operators. ArXiv abs/2002.06100 (2020)
15. Ren, S., He, K., Girshick, R., Sun, J.: Faster R-CNN: towards real-time object detection with region proposal networks. IEEE Trans. Pattern Anal. Mach. Intell. **39**(6), 1137–1149 (2017)
16. Dutta, S., Basu, S., Chakraborty, M.K.: Many-valued logics, fuzzy logics and graded consequence: a comparative appraisal. In: Logic and its Applications, pp. 197–209 (2013)
17. Lin, T.Y., Goyal, P., Girshick, R., He, K., Dollár, P.: Focal loss for dense object detection. In: 2017 IEEE International Conference on Computer Vision (ICCV), pp. 2999–3007 (2017)

18. Everingham, M., Van Gool, L., Williams, C.K.I., Winn, J., Zisserman, A.: The PASCAL Visual Object Classes Challenge 2010 (VOC2010) Results (2010)
19. Chen, X., Mottaghi, R., Liu, X., Fidler, S., Urtasun, R., Yuille, A.: Detect what you can: Detecting and representing objects using holistic models and body parts. In: Proceedings of the IEEE conference on computer vision and pattern recognition, pp. 1971–1978 (2014)
20. Cartucho, J., Ventura, R., Veloso, M.: Robust object recognition through symbiotic deep learning in mobile robots. In: 2018 IEEE/RSJ International Conference on Intelligent Robots and Systems (IROS), pp. 2336–2341 (2018)

# GC-MRNet: Gated Cascade Multi-stage Regression Network for Crowd Counting

Ying Shi[1,2], Jun Sang[1,2]($\boxtimes$), Jinghan Tan[1,2], Zhongyuan Wu[1,2], Bin Cai[1,2], and Nong Sang[3]

[1] Key Laboratory of Dependable Service Computing in Cyber Physical Society of Ministry of Education, Chongqing University, Chongqing 400044, China
jsang@cqu.edu.cn
[2] School of Big Data and Software Engineering, Chongqing University, Chongqing 401331, China
[3] School of Artificial Intelligence and Automation, Huazhong University of Science and Technology, Wuhan 430074, China

**Abstract.** Crowd counting is a challenging task due to occlusions, continuous scale variation of target and perspective distortion. The existing density-based approaches usually utilize deep convolutional neural network (CNN) to regress a density map from deep level features and obtained the counts. However, the best results may be obtained from the features of lower level instead of deep level. It is mainly due to the overfitting that degrades the adaptability towards the continuous scale variation of target. To address the issue of overfitting, a novel approach, called gated cascade multi-stage regression network (GC-MRNet), was proposed. It aims to maintain the adaptability towards scale variation of target and generate higher accuracy estimated density maps. Firstly, the dense scale network (DSNet) was used as the backbone and multi-stage regression was employed to achieve different density map regressors in different levels. Then, the features derived from the density map were cascaded to assist generating a higher quality density map in next stage. Finally, the gated blocks were designed to achieve the controllable information interaction between cascade and backbone. Extensive experiments were conducted on the ShanghaiTech, UCF-QNRF and UCF-CC-50 datasets. The results demonstrated significant improvements of GC-MRNet, almost over the state-of-the-art on ShanghaiTech Part A.

**Keywords:** Crowd counting · Kernel density estimation · Feature extraction · Cascade stages · Gated block

## 1 Introduction

The performance of crowd counting is limited by occlusions, continuous scale variation of target, background interference (e.g., trees, leaves), non-uniform crowd distortion and other factors. Current approaches tend to design a variety of deep convolutional neural networks (CNNs) to estimate one more accurate

I. Farkaš et al. (Eds.): ICANN 2021, LNCS 12892, pp. 53–66, 2021.
https://doi.org/10.1007/978-3-030-86340-1_5

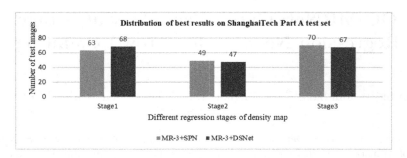

**Fig. 1.** The distribution of the best results on ShangahiTech Part A test set (182 images) after employing multi-stage regression for SPN and DSNet. For MR-3+SPN, the best results were obtained in Stage1 for 63 images (34.62%), 49 images (27.22%) in stage2 and 70 images (38.46%) in the final regression stage (Stage3). For MR-3+DSNet, The best results were obtained in Stage1 for 68 images (37.36%), 47 images (25.82%) in Stage2 and 67 images (36.81%) in Stage3.

density map corresponding to the crowd scene image. It not only can acquire the final counts by integrating the estimated density map, but also can obtain the information of crowd distortion. In addition, both leverage auxiliary tasks and a variety of multi-scale strategies have been proved to be reliable and can obtain promising results.

According to some previous papers [1], it is obvious that, in crowd counting, there exists the phenomenon of overfitting, which leads to the degradation of adaptability towards scale variation of heads. In high-density scenes, the result will be overestimated, while it will be underestimated in low-density scenes. Due to overfitting, to verify the best results could be obtained from the features of lower levels, we employed multi-stage regression (MR, i.e., multi-stage regression of density maps from deep features of different levels) to scale pyramid network, called SPN [2]. And the dense scale network, called DSNet [3], was adopted as backbone. MR-X represents the number of employed regression stage is X. For example, MR-3+SPN and MR-3+DSNet represent employing 3 regression stages to SPN and DSNet. As shown in Fig. 1, we can observe the best results (best result means the obtained estimation count is mostly close to the ground truth count) will show in different regression stages for scenes in ShanghaiTech Part A [4] test set which the overfitting lead to.

We mainly focus on maintaining the adaptability towards scale variation of target and generate more accurate estimated density maps with an approximately ensemble approach. In this way, the proportion of the best results obtained in the final regression stage may be increased and improve the performance of crowd counting.

In this paper, to address the degradation of adaptability towards scale variation of target existing in current approaches, a novel gated cascade multi-stage regression network called GC-MRNet for crowd counting was proposed. Our GC-MRNet was based on DSNet for its suitable structure for employing multi-stage regression and well-performance for crowd counting. In addition to multi-stage regression, the cascade block, referred to some ideas of cascade approaches [5], was adopted. The features derived from the estimated density map obtained in one regressor were cascaded to assist retaining the scale variation information from the former for next regression stage. Also, inspired by the long short-term memory [6], the gate blocks were employed in several stages to achieve the controllable information interaction of cascade features and the features of backbone.

Unlike previous papers, we verified the existence of overfitting and proposed a novel architecture to solve this issue in crowd counting. In summary, the contributions of this paper can be summarized as follows:

– We pointed out the existing degradation of the adaptability to the continuous scale variation of target degrades in the process of layer by layer feature extraction for some scenes when employ multi-stage regression to current deep CNN model (e.g., SPN and DSNet).
– We proposed a novel gated cascade multi-stage regression network inspired by RNNs to maintain the adaptability towards scale variation of target for more accurate crowd counting.
– The proposed approach achieved well-performance on ShanghaiTech (Part A and Part B), UCF-QNRF and UCF CC 50 datasets and almost achieved the state-of-the art on ShanghaiTech Part A.

## 2 Related Work

### 2.1 Detection-Based Approaches

Detection-based approaches tend to predict the number of people by detecting each person in the images and count the number. Early approaches leveraged sliding windows and hand-crafted features, such as haar wavelets [7] and HOG [8] to distinguish people in the images. Limited to the crude detection approach at that time, detection-based approaches obtained the poor performance in congested crowd scene. In (Liu et al. 2019) [9], a new deep detection network with only point supervision required in both dense and sparse scenes was proposed and reached the exciting performance.

### 2.2 Counts Regression-Based Approaches

Counts regression-based approaches tend to learn a mapping between features extracted from local imaged patches and its counts. In the early stage, typical examples include [10,11]. For more early regression-based related works, the survey [12] may be referred to. In (Wang et al. 2015; Fu et al. 2015) [13,14], CNN models were employed to regress the crowd count.

### 2.3 Density Map-Based Approaches

Density map-based approaches mainly tend to regress a density map and integrate it to obtain the final counts. In (Zhang et al. 2016) [4] a multi-column convolutional neural network with different kernel size was proposed to adapt to object scale variance. In (Sam, Surya, and Babu 2017) [15] a switching-based multi-CNN for crowd counting, which selectively inputted the crowd image into the corresponding CNN by classification was proposed. After 2017, many works focused on dealing with scale variance or background interference and obtained promising results. In (Jiang et al. 2018; Liu et al. 2019; Zhao et al. 2019) [9,16,17], auxiliary tasks (e.g., segmentation, classify, depth estimation and counts regression) were adopted to assist distinguishing the background area and foreground to decrease the background interference. In (Li, Zhang, and Chen 2018) [18] and (Chen et al. 2019) [2] dilated kernels were proposed to deliver larger reception fields to adapt to scale variance. In (Varior et al. 2019) [19], multi-scale density map estimation from different layers of the architecture was proposed to guide each density map to specialize on a particular scale. In (Dai et al. 2019) [3], a dense dilated convolution block was leveraged to preserve information from continuously varied scales and residual connections was leveragded to further enlarge the model's generalization capability.

## 3   Our Approach

### 3.1   Architecture of GC-MRNet

As discussed above, we aim to maintain the adaptability towards scale variation of target by an approximately ensemble approach. Therefore, we introduced a new deep net architecture based on DSNet. Figure 2 shows the architecture of our GC-MRNet. In Fig. 2, the blue blocks with the addition symbol represent our backbone network (DSNet) and the yellow block is the gated cascade module, which was designed to reduce the degradation of the adaptability towards scale variation of target in deep level features.

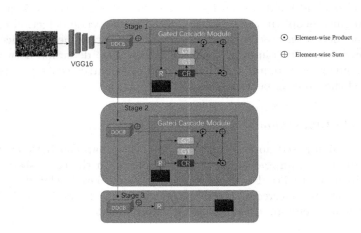

**Fig. 2.** The architecture of our GC-MRNet for crowd counting. DDCB represents the dense dilated convolutional block. R represents the regression block. CR represents the cascade block. G (G1 and G2 are two gates in one stage) represents the gated block. (Color figure online)

## 3.2   Backbone Network

The backbone network follows the setups in DSNet, which contains the first ten convolutional layers of pretrained VGG16 and three dense dilated convolution blocks (DDCB). The addition symbol represents dense residual connections described in (Dai et al. 2019) [3]. Details about the DDCB are shown in Fig. 3. DDCB contains three dilated convolutional layers with increasing dilation rate of 1, 2, 3 and the interior uses concatenation to capture large scale variation. The more details about backbone network (DSNet) may refer to (Dai et al. 2019) [3].

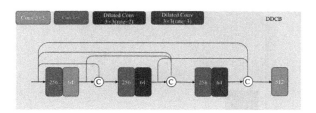

**Fig. 3.** The structure of dense dilated convolution blocks (DDCB).

## 3.3   Gated Cascade Module

Details about the Gated Cascade Module are shown in Fig. 4. The gated cascade module consists of regression block, cascade block and gated block. Regression block (R) is designed to estimated density maps in different regression stages and R contains (Conv-128-3; ReLU; Conv-64-3; ReLU; Conv-1-1; ReLU). Cascade block (CR) is designed to retain appropriate scale information for the next regression stage from the estimated density map in the former stage. CR contains (Conv-512-3; ReLU). Intuitively, during the cascade phase, the information obtained from the backbone network and the estimated density map should be fused selectively. And inspired by recurrent neural network (RNN), gated block (G) is designed to suppress and retain some appropriate scale information selectively in our GC-MRNet. G contains (Conv-512-3; ReLU; Conv-512-3; ReLU Conv-512-3; Tanh).

Given an image of size H × W, the feature of image before regression block in each stage of backbone network is denoted as $f_r$. The feature obtained from the gated cascade module is denoted as $Y_r$, which may be described as:

$$Y_r = f_r \odot g_{2r} + c\,r_r \odot g_{1r} \tag{1}$$

$$c\,r_r = C\,R_r\,(d_r) \tag{2}$$

$$g_{1r} = G_{1r}\,(f_r) \tag{3}$$

$$g_{2r} = G_{2r}\,(c\,r_r) \tag{4}$$

In particular, $d_r$ indicates the estimated density map obtained after regression block (R) in stage r, which is defined as:

$$d_r = R_r\,(f_r) \tag{5}$$

As shown in Fig. 2, three regression blocks with two gated cascade modules are employed in GC-MRNet. As a matter of fact, according to our ablation study on number of regression stages, the best performance for crowd counting may be obtained by only employing 2 regression blocks with one gated cascade module and our comparisons experiments with state-of-the art with follow such setup.

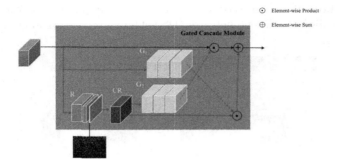

**Fig. 4.** The structure of Gated Cascade Module.

### 3.4   Loss Function

This paper adopted Euclidean loss and Multi-scale density level consistency loss following those in (Dai et al. 2019) [3]. The difference is that we employ these two training losses to each regression stage. The Euclidean loss is defined as follows:

$$L_e = \frac{1}{N} \sum_{i=1}^{N} \| D_i (X_i; \theta) - D_i^{GT} \|_2^2 \tag{6}$$

Where $N$ represents the number of images, $D_i$ represents the estimated density map and $D_i^{GT}$ represents the ground truth density map.

The Multi-scale density level consistency loss is defined as follow:

$$L_c = \frac{1}{N} \frac{1}{M} \sum_{i=1}^{N} \sum_{j=1}^{M} \frac{1}{k_j^2} \left\| P_{ave} (D_i, k_j) - P_{ave} \left( D_i^{GT}, k_j \right) \right\|_1 \tag{7}$$

Where $M$ represents the number of scale levels for consistency checking. Pave represents average pooling operation and $k$ is the specified output size of average pooling. Following DSNet, $M$ was set to be 3, and the output sizes of different scale levels were set to be $1 \times 1$, $2 \times 2$ and $4 \times 4$ respectively. There is one difference from DSNet: for the M-scale level of consistency losses, the average operation was performed instead of the sum operation.

For that, we should regress one density map in each stage. Our final loss function may be defined as follows:

$$L = \sum_{i=1}^{S} L_{e_i} + \lambda\, L_{c_i} \tag{8}$$

Where $\lambda$ is the weight to balance these two loss functions and $S$ represents the number of regression stages.

# 4   Implementation Details

## 4.1   Ground Truth Density Map

Following the approach of generating density map in (Zhang et al. 2016) [4], the geometry-adaptive gaussian kernels were adopted to tackle the highly dense crowd scenes, including UCF-QNRF [20] and UCF CC 50 [21]. The ground truth density map could be obtained by blurring each head annotation using a normalized Gaussian kernel. The geometry-adaptive kernel is defined as follows:

$$F(x) = \sum_{i=1}^{N} \delta(x - x_i) \times G_{\sigma_i}(x), \; with \; \sigma_i = \beta\overline{d_i} \tag{9}$$

Where $x$ represents the position of each pixel and $N$ is the number of head annotations in the image. For each target $x_i$ in the ground truth, using $\overline{d_i}$ to indicate the average distance of its k nearest neighbors. And then convolve $\delta(x - x_i)$ with Gaussian kernel with standard deviation parameter $\sigma$. The configuration in (Zhang et al. 2016) [4] where $\beta = 0.3$ and $k = 3$ were followed in this paper. For ShanghaiTech Part A and Part B, the fixed Gaussian kernels where $\sigma = 4.0$ and $\sigma = 15.0$ respectively, will be more suitable.

## 4.2   Training Details

Similar to DSNet, the first ten convolutional layers were fine-tuned from a well-trained VGG-16 [22]. All new layers were initialized from a Gaussian distribution with zero mean and 0.01 standard deviation. Adam optimizer was applied with fixed learning rate at $5e-6$ and weight decay of $5e-4$. Furthermore, the network was trained with batch size of 1. And We set different value of $\lambda$ for different datasets to balance the Euclidean loss and multi-scale density level consistency loss during training. For ShanghaiTech Part A, UCF-QNRF and UCF CC 50, $\lambda$ was set to be 1000. For ShangahaiTech Part B, $\lambda$ was set to be 10000.

Online data augmentation approach was adopted during the training process. We cropped images patch of 1/4 size of the original images at four quarters of the images without overlapping, and other five patches were randomly cropped from the images. After that, the cropped image patches were horizontally flipped randomly with the probability of 0.5. The color images were randomly change to the grayscale ones with the probability of 0.1. And the contrast was randomly changed by using parameter $c\,(c \in \{1.2, 1.5, 1.8\})$ with the probability of 0.1, which could be described as follows:

$$z_i = \max\,(c \times z_i + 20, 255) \tag{10}$$

Where $z$ represents the images and $z_i$ represents the pixel value in the corresponding position of image.

To mitigate overfitting, we generated some negative samples with positive ground truth by using parameters $b\,(b \in \{0.2, 1.5\})$ with the probability of 0.3 randomly, and it could be described as follows:

$$z_i = \sqrt[b]{\frac{z_i}{\max\,(z)}} \tag{11}$$

### 4.3  Evaluation Metrics

The mean absolute error (MAE) and the root mean square error (RMSE) are usually adopted to evaluate the counting performance. Moreover, the MAE reflects the accuracy of model, while the RMSE reflects the robustness of model. These two metrics could be defined as follows:

**Table 1.** The MAE result of different regression stage and manually selected ideal.

| Approach | Stage1 | Stage2 | Stage3 | Ideal |
|---|---|---|---|---|
| MR-3+SPN | 64.2 | 61.8 | 60.4 | 52.5 |
| C-MR-3+SPN | 63.9 | 60.7 | 60.0 | 52.8 |
| MR-3+DSNet | 60.9 | 60.7 | 60.2 | 55.1 |
| C-MR-3+DSNet | 60.6 | 60.4 | 59.6 | 56.1 |

$$MAE = \frac{1}{N}\sum_{i=1}^{N}\left|C_i - C_i^{GT}\right| \tag{12}$$

$$RMSE = \sqrt{\frac{1}{N}\sum_{i=1}^{N}\left|C_i - C_i^{GT}\right|^2} \tag{13}$$

Where $N$ is the number of images in test datasets, $C_i$ represents the estimated counts, while $C_i^{GT}$ represents the ground truth counts.

# 5  Experiments

## 5.1  Datasets

**ShanghaiTech.** [4] This dataset contains 1198 images with 330,165 annotated heads. It includes two parts: Part A contains 482 images (300 for training, 182 for testing), and Part B contains 716 images(400 for training, 316 for testing).

**UCF-QNRF.** [20] It consists of 1535 images which has a wider variety of scenes containing the most diverse set of viewpoints, lighting variations and densities that counts varies from 49 to 12865. Moreover, the image resolution is also very large leading to the drastic variation of the size of heads. We limited the maximum size 1024p of each image by resize operation before augmentation during training and validation phrase. While the final best result was obtained by testing under the limitation of maximum size 1200p.

**UCF CC 50.** [21] The UCF CC 50 dataset has only 50 images captured from various perspectives. It contains 1280 persons per image ranging from 94 to 4543 on average. For a fairer comparison, 5 times 5-fold cross-validation were conducted to evaluate our proposed approach and the sequence of the test images was shuffled randomly in each time.

## 5.2  Ablation Study on ShanghaiTech Part A

**Cascade Block.** Cascade block is based on multi-stage regression (MR), therefore we employed our cascade block to MR-3+SPN and MR-3+DSNet to evaluate its effectiveness. As shown in Table 1, for both C-MR-3+SPN (Cascade Multi-stage Regression-3+SPN) and C-MR-3+DSNet (Cascade Multi-stage Regression-3+DSNet), better results were obtained comparing with MR-3+SPN and MR-3+DSNet, respectively, which proved the positive effectiveness of our

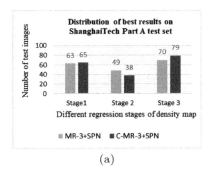

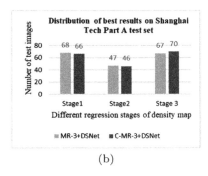

(a)                                    (b)

**Fig. 5.** The distribution of the best results on ShangahiTech Part A test set after employing multi-stage regression and cascade multi-stage regression for SPN (Fig. 5(a)) and DSNet (Fig. 5(b)).

**Table 2.** The result of MAE and root mean square error (RMSE) for the different number of regression stages.

| Approach | MAE | RMSE |
|---|---|---|
| C-MR-2+SPN | 59.7 | 99.5 |
| C-MR-3+SPN | 60.0 | 104.2 |
| C-MR-2+DSNet | 58.9 | 98.0 |
| C-MR-3+DSNet | 59.6 | 101.4 |

cascade block. For manually selecting the ideal result, comparing the experimental results with cascade block (SPN-52.8, DSNet-56.1) and those without cascade block (SPN-52.5, DSNet-55.1), it was found that it got worse with cascade block. We adopted a trade-off approach to maintain the adaptability towards the continuous scale variation of target in different stages at the expense of the overall adaptability, instead of learning distinguishing features to select a best output automatically from different stages. To some extension, the results showed in Table 2 demonstrated that the degradation of the adaptability towards the continuous scale variation of target has been eased with cascade block.

As shown in Fig. 5(a), comparing with MR-3+SPN in stage2, the number of test images with best result in stage2 were down, while it increased in stage3. This trend also exists in Fig. 5(b) which proved the better result can be mostly probably obtained in the last regression stage.

**Number of Stages (Number of Regression Stages).** Since SPN and DSNet are suitable for us to employ multi-stage regression (2 stages or 3 stages), we conducted 2 regression stages and 3 regression stages to explore the best setup. The comparison in Table 2 shows that the best setup was 2 for regression stages (corresponding to the last two regression stages, stage2 and stage3, shown in Fig. 2). It can be inferred that the more regression stages, the harder it is to train.

**Table 3.** The results of MAE and RMSE with gated blocks.

| Approach | MAE | RMSE |
|---|---|---|
| C-MR-2+SPN | 59.7 | 99.5 |
| GC-MR-2+SPN | 59.0 | 102.5 |
| C-MR-2+DSNet | 58.9 | 98.0 |
| GC-MR-2+DSNet (Our GC-MRNet) | 57.8 | 96.8 |

**Gated Block.** The gated blocks were designed to further achieve the controllable information interaction of cascade features and the features of backbone. In this ablation study, gated blocks were added to C-MR-2+SPN and C-MR-2+DSNet. As shown in Table 3, the MAE of GC-MR-2+SPN (C-MR-2+SPN with gated block) reduced by 0.7, though RMSE increased by 3.0. The MAE of GC-MR-2+DSNet (C-MR-2+DSNet with gated block) reduced by 1.1 and RMSE reduced by 1.2. With gated block, better performance was obtained for crowd counting.

From these three ablation studies, it can be concluded that it works best when the number of cascade multi-stage regression is 2 with gated blocks. Therefore, we employed the same setups in the following experiments and we call it GC-MRNet directly.

**Table 4.** The results of MAE and RMSE with gated blocks.

| Approach | PartA | | PartB | | UCF-QNRF | | UCF_CC_50 | |
|---|---|---|---|---|---|---|---|---|
| | MAE | RMSE | MAE | RMSE | MAE | RMSE | MAE | RMSE |
| MCNN [4] | 110.2 | 173.2 | 26.4 | 41.3 | 277.0 | 426.0 | 377.6 | 509.1 |
| SwitchCNN [15] | 90.4 | 135.0 | 21.6 | 33.4 | 228.0 | 445.0 | 318.1 | 439.2 |
| CSRNet [18] | 68.2 | 115.0 | 10.6 | 16.0 | – | – | 226.1 | 397.5 |
| PACNN [23] | 62.4 | 102.0 | 7.6 | 11.8 | – | – | 241.7 | 320.7 |
| SPN [2] | 61.7 | 99.5 | 9.4 | 14.4 | – | – | 259.2 | 335.9 |
| DSNet [3] | 61.7 | 102.6 | **6.7** | **10.5** | 91.4 | 160.4 | **183.3** | **240.6** |
| BL [24] | 62.4 | 101.8 | 7.7 | 12.7 | **88.7** | 154.8 | 229.3 | 308.2 |
| S-DCNet [25] | 58.3 | **95.0** | **6.7** | 10.7 | 104.4 | 176.1 | 204.2 | 301.3 |
| Our GC-MRNet | **57.8** | 96.8 | 7.0 | 11.3 | 90.7 | **153.3** | 210.2 | 294.6 |

**Table 5.** The MAE of different stage and the MAE of ideal result by selecting the best output from different regression stage manually on different datasets.

| Dataset | Satge1 | Stage2 | Stage3 | Ideal |
|---|---|---|---|---|
| PartA | – | 60.6 | 57.8 | 53.2 |
| PartB | – | 7.3 | 7.0 | 6.1 |
| UCF-QNRF | – | 91.1 | 90.7 | 85.1 |

## 5.3   Comparisons with State-of-the-Art

We evaluated our approach on the above mentioned three crowd count-ing datasets and compared the results with our baseline DSNet and other approaches. The whole experimental results were shown in Table 4. For Shang-haiTech Part A, our model achieved the lowest MAE (57.8), which was reduced by 0.5 compared with the state-of-the art approach S-DCNet [25]. Compared with our baseline, the MAE and RMSE were reduced by 3.9 and 5.8 respec-tively. For ShanghaiTech Part B, DSNet achieved the state-of-the art (MAE is

**Fig. 6.** The distribution of the best results on different datasets for testing in different regression stages.


6.7 and RMSE is 10.5), while our model only achieved 7.0 of MAE and 11.3 of RMSE. There may be one reason which led to the results. Actually, for our experiments, the recurrence of DSNet could only reaching 7.8 of MAE and 13.2 of RMSE, while our results exceeded those of recurrence of DSNet. For UCF-QNRF dataset, we achieved the lowest RMSE (153.3) compared with the state-of-the art approach BL [24] and the RMSE was reduced by 1.5. Compared with our baseline, the MAE and RMSE were reduced by 0.7 and 7.1 respectively. For a fairer comparison, we conducted 5-fold cross-validation experiments and computed the average result on UCF CC 50 dataset, which exceeded most approaches except our baseline and S-DCNet. Also, the result analysis of ideal selecting manually had great potential of deep CNN-based multi-stage regression approach which was sufficiently verified by Table 5. Finally, we showed several examples in Fig. 6. It is evident that our approach is well-performance on crowd counting both in sparse and congested crowd scenes. And for some scenes, such as the rows one, the result of the former regression stage (stage2) is better than that of stage3.

## 6   Conclusion

In this paper, we pointed out that existing degradation of the adaptability to the continuous scale variation of target degrades in the process of layer by layer feature extraction of deep level features. Also, we proposed a gated cascade multi-stage regression network (GC-MRNet) for crowd counting to mitigate the occurrence of the degradation, resulting in well-performance counting results on three bench-mark datasets.

**Acknowledgements.** This work was supported by National Natural Science Foundation of China (No. 61971073).

# References

1. Jiang, X., et al.: Attention scaling for crowd counting. In: Proceedings of the IEEE/CVF Conference on Computer Vision and Pattern Recognition, pp. 4706–4715 (2020)
2. Chen, X., Bin, Y., Sang, N., Gao, C.: Scale Pyramid network for crowd counting. In: WACV, pp. 1941–1950. IEEE (2019)
3. Dai, F., Liu, H., Ma, Y., Cao, J., Zhao, Q., Zhang, Y.: Dense scale network for crowd counting. arXiv preprint arXiv:1906.09707 (2019)
4. Zhang, Y., Zhou, D., Chen, S., Gao, S., Yi, M.: Single-image crowd counting via multi-column convolutional neural network. In: CVPR, pp. 589–597 (2016)
5. Cai, Z., Vasconcelos, N.: Cascade R-CNN: delving into high quality object detection. In: CVPR, pp. 6154–6162 (2018)
6. Hochreiter, S., Schmidhuber, J.: Long short-term memory. Neural Comput. **9**(8), 1735–1780 (1997)
7. Viola, P., Jones, M.J.: Robust real-time face detection. In: Proceedings 8th IEEE International Conference on Computer Vision, p. 747. IEEE (2001)
8. Dalal, N., Triggs, B.: Histograms of oriented gradients for human detection. In: CVPR 2005, vol. 1, pp. 886–893. IEEE (2005)
9. Liu, N., Long, Y., Zou, C., Niu, Q., Pan, L., Wu, H.: ADCrowdNet: an attention-injective deformable convolutional network for crowd understanding. In: CVPR, pp. 3225–3234 (2019)
10. Chan, A.B., Vasconcelos, N.: Bayesian Poisson regression for crowd counting. In: ICCV, pp. 545–551. IEEE (2009)
11. Chen, K., Loy, C.C., Gong, S., Xiang, T.: Feature mining for localised crowd counting. In: BMVC, vol. 1, p. 3 (2012)
12. Sindagi, V.A., Patel, V.M.: A survey of recent advances in CNN-based single image crowd counting and density estimation. Pattern Recogn. Lett. **107**, 3–16 (2018)
13. Wang, C., Zhang, H., Yang, L., Liu, S., Cao, X.: Deep people counting in extremely dense crowds. In: Proceedings of the 23rd ACM International Conference on Multimedia, pp. 1299–1302 (2015)
14. Fu, M., Xu, P., Li, X., Liu, Q., Ye, M., Zhu, C.: Fast crowd density estimation with convolutional neural networks. Eng. Appl. Artif. Intell. **43**, 81–88 (2015)
15. Sam, D.B., Surya, S., Babu, R.V.: Switching convolutional neural network for crowd counting. In: CVPR, pp. 4031–4039. IEEE (2017)
16. Zhao, M., Zhang, J., Zhang, C., Zhang, W.: Leveraging heterogeneous auxiliary tasks to assist crowd counting. In: CVPR, pp. 12736–12745 (2019)
17. Jiang, S., Lu, X., Lei, Y., Liu, L.: Mask-aware networks for crowd counting. IEEE Trans. Circ. Syst. Video Technol. **30**, 3119–3129 (2019)
18. Li, Y., Zhang, X., Chen, D.: CSRNet: dilated convolutional neural networks for understanding the highly congested scenes. In: CVPR, pp. 1091–1100 (2018)
19. Varior, R.R., Shuai, B., Tighe, J., Modolo, D.: Multi-scale attention network for crowd counting. arXiv preprint arXiv:1901.06026 (2019)
20. Idrees, H., Tayyab, M., Athrey, K., Zhang, D., Al-Maadeed, S., Rajpoot, N., Shah, M.: Composition loss for counting, density map estimation and localization in dense crowds. In: Ferrari, V., Hebert, M., Sminchisescu, C., Weiss, Y. (eds.) ECCV 2018. LNCS, vol. 11206, pp. 544–559. Springer, Cham (2018). https://doi.org/10.1007/978-3-030-01216-8_33
21. Idrees, H., Saleemi, I., Seibert, C., Shah, M.: Multi-source multi-scale counting in extremely dense crowd images. In: CVPR, pp. 2547–2554 (2013)

22. Simonyan, K., Zisserman, A.: Very deep convolutional networks for large-scale image recognition. arXiv preprint arXiv:1409.1556 (2014)
23. Shi, M., Yang, Z., Xu, C., Chen, Q.: Revisiting perspective information for efficient crowd counting. In: CVPR, pp. 7279–7288 (2019)
24. Shi, M., Yang, Z., Xu, C., Chen, Q.: Bayesian loss for crowd count estimation with point supervision. In: ICCV, pp. 6142–6151 (2019)
25. Xiong, H., Lu, H., Liu, C., Liu, L., Cao, Z., Shen, C.: From open set to closed set: counting objects by spatial divide-and-conquer. In: ICCV, pp. 8362–8371 (2019)

# Latent Feature-Aware and Local Structure-Preserving Network for 3D Completion from a Single Depth View

Caixia Liu⬛, Dehui Kong⬛, Shaofan Wang$^{(\boxtimes)}$⬛, Jinghua Li⬛,
and Baocai Yin⬛

Beijing Key Laboratory of Multimedia and Intelligent Software Technology,
Beijing Institute of Artificial Intelligence, Faculty of Information Technology,
Beijing University of Technology, Beijing 100124, China
lcxxib@emails.bjut.edu.cn, {kdh,wangshaofan}@bjut.edu.cn

**Abstract.** Recovering the geometry of an object from a single depth image is an interesting yet challenging problem. While the recently proposed learning based approaches have demonstrated promising performance, they tend to produce unfaithful and incomplete 3D shape. In this paper, we propose Latent Feature-Aware and Local Structure-Preserving Network (LALP-Net) for completing the full 3D shape from a single depth view of an object, which consists of a generator and a discriminator. In the generator, we introduce Latent Feature-Aware (LFA) to learn a latent representation from the encoded input for a decoder generating the accurate and complete 3D shape. LFA can be taken as a plug-and-play component to upgrade existing networks. In the discriminator, we combine a Local Structure Preservation (LSP) module regarding visible regions and a Global Structure Prediction (GSP) module regarding entire regions for faithful reconstruction. Experimental results on both synthetic and real-world datasets show that our LALP-Net outperforms the state-of-the-art methods by a large margin.

**Keywords:** 3D completion · Depth view · Latent shape representation · Local structure

## 1 Introduction

3D completion aims to recover the geometry of an object and has become one of the current research topics recently. With the increasing availability of consumer depth cameras and geometry acquisition devices, robust reconstruction of complete 3D shapes from noisy, partial geometric data remains a challenging problem. Owing to the recent success of learning techniques, a number of

---

Supported by the National Natural Science Foundation of China (No. 61772049, 61632006, 61876012, U19B2039, 61906011), Beijing Natural Science Foundation (4202003).

I. Farkaš et al. (Eds.): ICANN 2021, LNCS 12892, pp. 67–79, 2021.
https://doi.org/10.1007/978-3-030-86340-1_6

approaches have been proposed to leverage deep networks to capture prior knowledge in a data-driven way and infer occluded/missing regions of objects through the learned knowledge. These approaches use different shape representations, such as point clouds, meshes, implicit surface and voxels. It is noticed that point clouds [7,22] lack the connectivity structure of underlying meshes. Existing mesh representations [5,14] can only handle simple topologies. Implicit surfaces [1,2,8,9,19] focus on 2D feature maps to represent objects. The above approaches cannot maximize the capacity of deep networks learning object. However, voxel representations [12,13,16,20,21] as a regular structure are a straightforward generalization of pixels to the 3D case and can be easily fitted into deep networks. Thus voxels are popular for 3D completion.

For voxel-based 3D completion approaches, they usually adopt Convolutional Neural Network (CNN), Recurrent Neural Network (RNN) and AutoEncoder (AE), which tends to predict many possible 3D shapes for an object. Wang et al. [15] introduced Generative Adversarial Network (GAN) into RNN to inpaint 3D models with semantic plausibility. Smith et al. [12] combined GAN and Variational AE to learn the complex joint data distribution over objects of many categories. Wu et al. [16] integrated trained GAN into CNN to penalize unrealistic shapes and to reduce the ambiguity of objects. Yang et al. [20,21] combined conditional GAN [4] and AE to generate the complete 3D occupancy grid by filling in the occluded regions. However, these methods still have the following two major issues which affect 3D completion application.

Firstly, they mainly use conventional encoder-fc-decoder frameworks, which encode the input as low-resolution 3D feature maps and then utilize fully connected (FC) layers to embed the maps as a latent shape representation for a decoder. However, the full connection tends to ignore the spatial structure of objects, which restricts the improvement of reconstruction performance. In this paper, we design a encoder-LFA-decoder framework and introduce Latent Feature Aware (LFA) to replace fully connected layers. LFA is to learn a latent shape representation from the encoded input for a decoder generating the accurate 3D shape. The latent representation has better ability of describing the potential characteristics of objects by exploring the dependency across local regions and thus provides more available cues for modeling occluded regions than traditional representations. Besides, LFA can be taken as a plug-and-play component to upgrade existing networks with only a few parameters.

Secondly, they have the same weights on both visible and occluded regions for predicted full shapes of objects, which compromises the reconstruction accuracy. As observed in the qualitative results of [18], generating high-quality visible regions is helpful to recover occluded regions via learned knowledge which is some relationships (e.g., symmetry, support) between visible and occluded regions through deep networks during the reconstruction. In this paper, we design a discriminator consisting of Local Structure Preservation (LSP) and Global Structure Prediction (GSP). LSP is to specially refine visible regions after GSP improving entire regions for faithful reconstruction. GSP and LSP are performed adversarial learning in a two-stream manner, which ensures the high-quality recovery of visible parts and thus improves the reconstruction accuracy of occluded parts. The discriminator has better ability of modeling the real shape distribution of objects than traditional methods.

In summary, we propose Latent Feature-Aware and Local Structure-Preserving Network (LALP-Net) for 3D completion from a single depth view. LALP-Net consists of a generator and a discriminator. Different from traditional GAN based 3D completion approaches, LALP-Net enhances the learning ability of spatial features of objects by introducing LFA in the generator and faithful reconstruction ability of entire regions by combining LSP and GSP in the discriminator. Experimental results on both synthetic and real-world datasets show that our proposed LALP-Net improves average IoU by 8.6% (5.2%, resp.), 3.0% (3.4%, resp.) and 7.2% (4.7%, resp.) for per-category, multi-category and cross-category on ModelNet (KinectData, resp.).

## 2    Related Work

### 2.1    Single-View 3D Completion

In earlier works, Wu et al. [17] used deep neural networks to estimate a 3D shape from a single depth view. Sharma et al. [11] designed a full convolutional autoencoder to learn 3D volumetric representation from noisy data. Varley et al. [13] proposed a convolutional neural network to infer a 3D shape from a single depth view. However, these approaches are only able to generate low-resolution shapes and unlikely to capture fine geometric details. Some works [2,15] inferred high-resolution shapes, however, they relied on a shape database, or strong voxel-level annotations. Recent works [16,20,21] used AE to predict a coarse 3D shape from a single depth view, and then adopted adversarial networks to deal with the ambiguity and unnaturalness of predicted shapes. However, these approaches have limited ability for reconstructing occluded regions and produce noise.

### 2.2    3D Shape Representation

Zamorski et al. [22] and Lin et al. [7] designed deep networks for 3D point clouds. However, these point cloud-based approaches require additional nontrivial post-processing steps. Existing mesh-based approaches are only able to generate meshes with simple topologies [3,14], which requires a reference template and cannot guarantee closed surfaces. Dai et al. [2] used a voxel-based Signed Distance Functions (SDF) representation for shape inpainting. Park et al. [9] introduced DeepSDF for shape completion, however, their networks are not feed-forward, which limits the efficiency and capability of the approach. Mescheder et al. [8] iteratively predicted the probability of each active cell in a volumetric grid being occupied or not. However, most of works [13,16,18,20,21] resort to voxel representations, which are a regular structure and can be easily fitted into deep model architectures. Voxel-based approaches enable various deep networks to exert their capacity of learning objects in 3D shape space.

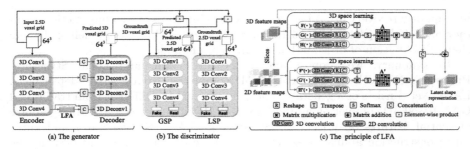

**Fig. 1.** The architecture of LALP-Net. In the generator, we first use a encoder to obtain 3D feature maps from the $64^3$ voxel grid representation of a single depth view of an object, and then introduce Latent Feature-Aware (LFA) to learn a latent shape representation, and finally use a decoder to generate a $64^3$ complete 3D occupancy grid of the object from the representation (see Sect. 3.2). In the discriminator, we first use Global Structure Prediction (GSP) to perform adversarial learning of entire regions of the object, and then introduce Local Structure Preservation (LSP) with the same network structure as GSP, to refine visible regions (see Sect. 3.2).

## 3 Proposed Method

### 3.1 Overview

As shown in Fig. 1, LALP-Net consists of two main networks: a generator and a discriminator. In particular, the generator encodes the voxel grid representation of a single depth view as 3D feature maps, then uses LFA to learn a refined shape representation of objects in the latent space, and finally decodes the representation to reconstruct the complete 3D occupancy grid. The discriminator integrates GSP and LSP to perform adversarial learning in a two-stream manner, aims to distinguish whether predicted occupancy voxels (especially visible voxels) of objects are plausible or not.

**Notations:** Scalars, vectors, matrices, and tensors are denoted by non-bold letters, bold lowercase letters, bold uppercase letters, and calligraphic uppercase letters respectively. Denote $[\mathbf{A}]_{ij}$ to be the $(i, j)$th element of a matrix $\mathbf{A}$, $[\mathcal{A}]_{ijk}$ to be the $(i, j, k)$th element of a tensor $\mathcal{A}$. Denote $(I, J, K)$ to be the size of a voxel grid ($I = J = K = 64$), and $\mathcal{X}, \mathcal{Y} \in \{0,1\}^{I \times J \times K}$, $\mathcal{Y}' \in (0, 1)^{I \times J \times K}$, to be the 2.5D voxel grid of input single depth view, the groundtruth 3D voxel grid, the predicted 3D voxel grid, and $\mathbb{E}$ to be the expectation operator.

### 3.2 Network Architecture

**Generator.** The generator includes an encoder, a LFA module and a decoder. The generator adopts symmetrical skip connections [10] which ensure the preserving and propagation of local structure of a single depth view.

*Encoder.* It is to extract a set of feature maps for LFA learning a shape representation. We design four 3D convolutional layers, each layer of which has a bank of $4^3$ filters of $1^3$ strides, followed by a leaky ReLU function and a max pooling layer which has $2^3$ filters of $2^3$ strides. The number of output channels of these layers starts with 64, doubles at each subsequent layer and ends up with 512. The encoder outputs 3D feature maps of $4^3$ resolutions.

*LFA.* It is to learn a latent shape representation of objects for the decoder. We design a space-aware module to learn the latent shape representation $\mathcal{LR}$ from encoded 3D feature maps $\mathcal{M} \in \mathbb{R}^{512 \times 4 \times 4 \times 4}$. $\mathcal{LR}$ is defined as:

$$\mathcal{LR} = \psi(\mathcal{M}) = \mathrm{CR}\left[\varphi(\mathcal{M}), \varphi'(\mathcal{N})\right] \tag{1}$$

For the function $\psi$, it consists of two parts: 3D space learning $\varphi$ and 2D space learning $\varphi'$ for robust features of objects. $\mathcal{N} \in \mathbb{R}^{2048 \times 4 \times 4}$ is regarded as a 2D slice set of $\mathcal{M}$. CR is a synthesized operator consisting of the concatenation and reshape operations.

We use self-attention to achieve two space learning by two steps. (1) learn attention weights $\mathbf{A}$ and $\mathbf{A}'$ which are used to measure the relevance of each part of input data to the reconstruction task in 3D space and 2D space respectively; (2) learn latent shape features $\varphi$, $\varphi'$ which are obtained by scaling each part with the attention weights in 3D space and 2D space respectively.

$$\varphi(\mathcal{M}) = \mathbf{H}(\mathcal{M})\mathbf{A} \tag{2}$$

$$[\mathbf{A}]_{jk} = \frac{\left[\exp\left(\mathbf{F}(\mathcal{M})^\top \mathbf{G}(\mathcal{M})\right)\right]_{jk}}{\sum_{j=1}^{64}\left[\exp\left(\mathbf{F}(\mathcal{M})^\top \mathbf{G}(\mathcal{M})\right)\right]_{jk}}, \quad k = 1, \ldots, 64 \tag{3}$$

$$\varphi'(\mathcal{N}) = \mathbf{H}'(\mathcal{N})\mathbf{A}' \tag{4}$$

$$[\mathbf{A}']_{j'k'} = \frac{\left[\exp\left(\mathbf{F}'(\mathcal{N})^\top \mathbf{G}'(\mathcal{N})\right)\right]_{j'k'}}{\sum_{j'=1}^{16}\left[\exp\left(\mathbf{F}'(\mathcal{N})^\top \mathbf{G}'(\mathcal{N})\right)\right]_{j'k'}}, \quad k' = 1, \ldots, 16 \tag{5}$$

where $\mathbf{F}(\mathcal{M}) \in \mathbb{R}^{64 \times 64}, \mathbf{G}(\mathcal{M}) \in \mathbb{R}^{64 \times 64}$ and $\mathbf{H}(\mathcal{M}) \in \mathbb{R}^{512 \times 64}$ are obtained by $\mathcal{M}$ mapped into three 3D feature spaces. $\mathbf{F}'(\mathcal{N}) \in \mathbb{R}^{256 \times 16}, \mathbf{G}'(\mathcal{N}) \in \mathbb{R}^{256 \times 16}$ and $\mathbf{H}'(\mathcal{N}) \in \mathbb{R}^{2048 \times 16}$ by $\mathcal{N}$ mapped into three 2D feature spaces. $\mathbf{F}(\cdot)$, $\mathbf{G}(\cdot)$, $\mathbf{H}(\cdot)$, $\mathbf{F}'(\cdot)$, $\mathbf{G}'(\cdot)$, and $\mathbf{H}'(\cdot)$ denote three synthesized operators consisting of convolution, flatten, and concatenation, where the first three are $1^3$ convolution, and the last three are $1^2$ convolution. $\exp(\cdot)$ is the elementwise exponential operator. LFA outputs a refined shape representation $\mathcal{LR} \in \mathbb{R}^{1024 \times 4 \times 4 \times 4}$.

*Decoder.* It is responsible for transforming the refined shape representation $\mathcal{LR}$ into 3D volumes. We design four deconvolutional layers, each layer of which concatenates the feature layers of the encoder accordingly, followed by ReLU activations except for the last layer with sigmoid function. The number of output channels of these layers start with 256 and decreases by half for the subsequent layer and ends up with 1. The decoder outputs a $64^3$ voxel grid.

**Discriminator.** The discriminator uses LSP to preserve visible local structure of objects after using GSP to refine global structure of objects, in order to make the generator predict realistic 3D shapes.

*GSP.* It is to distinguish whether predicted full 3D shapes are reasonable or not. We design GSP as an encoder, which consists of four 3D convolutional layers whose channels start with 64, double at each subsequent layer and end up with 512. Each convolutional layer has a bank of $4^3$ filters of $2^3$ strides, followed by a ReLU function except for the last layer with a sigmoid function. GSP outputs a feature vector of $\mathbb{R}^{32768}$.

*LSP.* It is to distinguish whether predicted visible parts are reasonable or not. Motivated by Li et al. [6] which represent an incomplete data case as a pair of a partially-observed data vector and a corresponding mask for image completion, We represent predicted visible shapes by the element-wise product of predicted 3D voxel grids and corresponding input 2.5D ones. GSP is also concreted as an encoder whose setting is the same as that of GSP and outputs a feature vector of $\mathbb{R}^{32768}$.

### 3.3   Loss Functions

**Generator Loss.** The loss function of the generator is given by a convex combination of the reconstruction loss of AE (which is set as $L_{ae}$) and the generator loss of GAN (which is set as $L_g$). Minimizing $L_{ae}$ tends to learn a complete 3D shape, whilst minimizing $L_g$ tends to estimate more plausible 3D shape conditioned on a single depth view. Thus the 3D generator loss $L_{gen}$ is defined as:

$$L_{gen} = (1 - \gamma)L_{ae} + \gamma L_g \tag{6}$$

$$L_{ae} = -\beta \mathcal{Y} \log (\mathcal{Y}') - (1 - \beta)(1 - \mathcal{Y}) \log(1 - \mathcal{Y}') \tag{7}$$

$$L_g = -\mathbb{E}[D_{gsp}(\mathcal{Y}') - \mathbb{E}[D_{lsp}(\mathcal{Y}' \odot \mathcal{X})], \tag{8}$$

where $D_{gsp}$, $D_{lsp}$ denote the GSP network and the LSP network respectively in the discriminator.

**Discriminator Loss.** GSP optimizes the network by narrowing distance between the real 3D shape and the predicted 3D shape. LSP optimizes the network using distance between the real visible shape and the predicted visible shape. The 3D discriminator loss $L_{dis}$ is defined as:

$$L_{dis} = L_{dis}^{gsp} + L_{dis}^{lsp}, \tag{9}$$

$$L_{dis}^{gsp} = \mathbb{E}[D_{gsp}(\mathcal{Y}')] - \mathbb{E}[D_{gsp}(\mathcal{Y})] + \lambda \mathbb{E}[(||\nabla_{\widehat{\mathcal{Y}}} D_{gsp}(\widehat{\mathcal{Y}})||_2 - 1)^2], \tag{10}$$

$$L_{dis}^{lsp} = \mathbb{E}[D_{lsp}(\mathcal{Y}' \odot \mathcal{X})] - \mathbb{E}[D_{lsp}(\mathcal{Y} \odot \mathcal{X})] + \lambda \mathbb{E}[(||\nabla_{\widehat{\mathcal{X}}} D_{lsp}(\widehat{\mathcal{X}})||_2 - 1)^2], \tag{11}$$

where $\widehat{\mathcal{Y}} = \epsilon \mathcal{Y} + (1 - \epsilon) \mathcal{Y}'$, $\widehat{\mathcal{X}} = \epsilon \mathcal{X} + (1 - \epsilon) (\mathcal{Y}' \odot \mathcal{X})$, $\epsilon \sim \mathbf{Uniform}[0, 1]$, $\lambda$ controls the tradeoff between optimizing the gradient penalty and the original objective. $\mathcal{Y}'$, $\mathcal{Y}$ denote the predicted full shape and the real full shape respectively. $(\mathcal{Y}' \odot \mathcal{X})$, $(\mathcal{Y} \odot \mathcal{X})$ denote the predicted visible shape and the real visible shape respectively.

In the experiments, for each iteration, these loss functions are optimized in the order of $L_{\mathrm{dis}}^{gsp}, L_{\mathrm{dis}}^{lsp}, L_{\mathrm{gen}}$ by Adam algorithm. The learning rates are set to 0.0001, 0.0001, 0.0005 respectively. Besides, the weight $\gamma$ is set to 0.95 and the weight $\beta$ is set to 0.85. The gradient penalty $\lambda$ is set to 10.

Input     3D-CNN [13] 3D-RecAE [21] 3D-RecGAN [21] LALP-Net Groundtruth

**Fig. 2.** The reconstruction results on ModelNet [21]. The first two rows, the middle two rows and others are respectively single-category, multi-category and cross-category results.

## 4    Experimental Results and Analysis

To evaluate the effectiveness of our method, experiments on both synthetic and real-world dataset were performed. The synthetic datasets include ModelNet [21] and ShapeNet [20], which consist of 3 categories and 4 categories respectively. Each category is trained with around 20K pairs, and tested with 2K (4K, resp.) pairs in ModelNet (ShapeNet, resp.). The real-world dataset [20] (also known as KinectData) is mainly collected from real-world environments (offices, homes, outdoor, etc.) by a Microsoft Kinect sensor. KinectData consists of 4 categories and each category is tested with 250 pairs. The target object instances of each depth view are manually segmented from the background, and groundtruth shapes are not 100% accurate. Before training and testing, a pair denoting each single depth view and the corresponding 3D shape are simultaneously transformed to voxel grids by using virtual camera parameters. Each voxel grid is represented as a binary tensor (Fig. 3).

Input ShapeHD [16] 3D-RecAE++ [20] 3D-RecGAN++ [20] LALP-Net Groundtruth

**Fig. 3.** The reconstruction results on ShapeNet [20]. The first two rows, the middle two rows and others are respectively single-category, multi-category and cross-category results.

Input 3D-CNN [13] 3D-RecGAN [21] 3D-RecGAN++ [20] LALP-Net Groundtruth

**Fig. 4.** The reconstruction results on KinectData [20]. The first row, the middle row and others are respectively single-category, multi-category, cross-category results.

### 4.1 Comparisons with Existing Methods

We compare LALP-Net with several state-of-the-art approaches. Particularly, 3D-CNN [13] completed the 3D shape from a single depth view with a convolution neural network. 3D-RecGAN [21] recovered the 3D structure from a single depth view by combining AE and GAN. ShapeHD [16] completed the 3D shape from a single depth and a normal map by integrating deep generative models with adversarially learned shape priors. 3D-RecGAN++ [20] reconstructed the high-resolution 3D shape from a single depth view by adding two deconvolutional layers in the generator of 3D-RecGAN. 3D-RecAE (3D-RecAE++) analyzed the performance of 3D-RecGAN (3D-RecGAN++) without GAN.

**Experiment Results on Synthetic Datasets.** We conducted three types of experiments: per-category, multi-category and cross-category on ModelNet [21] and ShapeNet [20]. The per-category experiments measure the reconstruction quality over each single category of objects, where the training set and testing set are defined as each category. The multi-category experiments and the cross-category experiments measure the domain adaptation capability among different categories of objects, where the latter is more challenging. The results are shown in Table 1 and Fig. 2.

**Table 1.** The reconstruction results on ModelNet [21] and ShapeNet [20]. In group1, group2 and group3, the network is respectively trained on chair, stool and toilet, tested on other two categories. 'FC' denotes fully connected layers. The greater (↑) the IoU is, the better the reconstructed result is.

| Method | Per-category results IoU↑ $(10^{-2})$ | | | Multi-category results IoU↑ $(10^{-2})$ | | Cross-category results IoU↑ $(10^{-2})$ | | | Parameters' num of FC or LFA layers |
|---|---|---|---|---|---|---|---|---|---|
| | chair | stool | toilet | chair/ toilet | chair/stool/ toilet | group1 | group2 | group3 | layers |
| 3D-CNN [13] | 56.4 | 27.3 | 50.3 | 49.3 | 45.3 | 29.4 | 35.5 | 38.1 | $1.42 \times 10^8$ |
| 3D-RecGAN [21] | 66.1 | 50.1 | 56.9 | 55.4 | 51.3 | 41.3 | 51.7 | 48.3 | $3.28 \times 10^8$ |
| Pix2Vox [18] | 68.0 | 43.8 | 50.1 | 66.4 | 48.8 | 50.3 | 49.5 | 40.7 | $3.36 \times 10^7$ |
| Our LALP-Net | **70.3** | **60.7** | **68.0** | **69.1** | **52.1** | **55.7** | **52.8** | **54.5** | $\mathbf{5.57 \times 10^6}$ |
| | airplane | chair | car | airplane/ car | airplane/ chair/car | group1 | group2 | group3 | |
| ShapeHD [16] | 61.9 | 59.5 | 78.8 | 65.9 | 63.2 | 55.8 | 55.2 | 37.3 | $\mathbf{1.03 \times 10^5}$ |
| 3D-RecGAN++ [20] | 70.6 | 64.6 | 89.6 | 75.3 | 73.9 | 58.2 | 60.5 | 53.8 | $1.31 \times 10^8$ |
| Our LALP-Net | **83.1** | **79.2** | **90.8** | **79.0** | **78.0** | **63.3** | **69.7** | **61.7** | $5.57 \times 10^6$ |

**Table 2.** The reconstruction results on KinectData [20]. In group1, group2, group3 and group4, the network is respectively trained on bench, chair, coach and table, tested on other three categories. The greater (↑) the IoU is, the better the reconstructed result is.

| Method | Per-category results IoU $(10^{-2})$ | | | | Multi-category results IoU $(10^{-2})$ | | | | Cross-category results IoU $(10^{-2})$ | | | |
|---|---|---|---|---|---|---|---|---|---|---|---|---|
| | bench | chair | coach | table | bench | chair | coach | table | group1 | group2 | group3 | group4 |
| 3D-CNN [13] | 26.9 | 27.0 | 35.0 | 15.4 | 23.3 | 17.6 | 36.0 | 21.2 | 23.5 | 25.2 | 22.4 | 19.4 |
| 3D-RecGAN [21] | 38.1 | 36.8 | 66.0 | 35.6 | 32.3 | 34.1 | 56.8 | 29.1 | 44.0 | 28.5 | 27.8 | 37.9 |
| 3D-RecGAN++ [20] | 43.3 | 36.5 | 66.9 | 30.7 | 39.6 | 36.3 | 59.8 | 28.5 | 38.7 | 53.6 | 36.0 | 39.1 |
| Pix2Vox [18] | 36.3 | 29.3 | 62.2 | 36.6 | 24.0 | 25.1 | 30.2 | 27.0 | 35.6 | 47.2 | 24.8 | 43.2 |
| Our LALP-Net | **44.1** | **41.0** | **73.3** | **39.8** | **41.1** | **37.4** | **65.0** | **34.2** | **51.2** | **54.1** | **36.1** | **44.7** |

Experiments show that our proposed LALP-Net outperforms other methods. In particular, 3D-CNN only infers a part of occluded regions and generates unrealistic shapes. 3D-RecGAN improves the reconstruction accuracy, however, fail to guarantee the reconstruction quality of visible regions, even produce noise.

3D-RecGAN++ can predict shapes with geometrical details, however, fail to infer strong occlusion in the depth view. ShapeHD can predict shapes with large variance and fine details, however, sometimes get confused by deformable object parts, miss uncommon object parts and have difficulty in recovering very thin structure. Conversely, LALP-Net is able to reconstruct complete and plausible shapes that look good perceptually. From Fig. 2, LALP-Net can not only predict more occluded parts, ensure reconstruction quality of visible parts, but reduce noise when reconstructing parts not present in the input depth view. This is because LALP-Net can learn a refined shape representation in the latent space by LFA, which helps infer occluded voxels from input voxels. Besides, LALP-Net constrains visible regions by LSP, which helps ensure the fidelity of visible parts and reduce noise.

**Experiment Results on Real-World Dataset.** All networks were trained on ShapeNet [20] and tested on KinectData [20]. We also conducted three types of experiments. The results are shown in Table 2 and Fig. 4.

Due to the limitation of sensors (e.g., reflective surfaces, outdoor light), input depth views and corresponding groundtruth shapes are noisy and incomplete. In addition, their transformed voxels are empty rather than solid, and are only occupied on the surface, which leads to low accuracy. However, when the benchmarking algorithms are not robust to noise and unable to generate compelling results, LALP-Net is still able to reconstruct reasonable shapes.

### 4.2    Ablation Study

We conducted multi-category experiments on ShapeNet [20] to analyse the importance of each component from LALP-Net. The results are shown in Table 3 and Fig. 6.

**Table 3.** The ablation results. 'ED' denotes encoder and decoder in the generator of LALP-Net. 'DIS' denotes discriminator. 'LFA$^{3D}$, LFA$^{2D}$' denote 3D space learning and 2D space learning in a LFA module respectively. 'LFA$_i(i = 2,3)$' denote new LFA modules (see Fig. 5). The greater ($\uparrow$) the IoU is, the better the reconstructed result is.

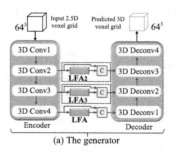

(a) The generator

**Fig. 5.** The generator with multiple LFA modules. C is the concatenation operation.

| | $L_{ae}$ | $L_g$ | $L_{dis}^{gsp}$ | $L_{dis}^{lsp}$ | LFA$^{3D}$ | LFA$^{2D}$ | IoU$\uparrow(10^{-2})$ |
|---|---|---|---|---|---|---|---|
| ED | ✓ | | | | | | 52.0 |
| ED-GSP | ✓ | ✓ | ✓ | | | | 60.7 |
| ED-GSP-LSP | ✓ | ✓ | ✓ | ✓ | | | 67.5 |
| ED-DIS-LFA$^{3D}$ | ✓ | ✓ | ✓ | ✓ | ✓ | | 71.3 |
| ED-DIS-LFA$^{2D}$ | ✓ | ✓ | ✓ | ✓ | | ✓ | 75.5 |
| Our LALP-Net | ✓ | ✓ | ✓ | ✓ | ✓ | ✓ | 78.0 |
| Our LALP-Net+ | ✓ | ✓ | ✓ | ✓ | +LFA$_3$ | | 81.7 |
| Our LALP-Net++ | ✓ | ✓ | ✓ | ✓ | +LFA$_3$+LFA$_2$ | | **83.7** |

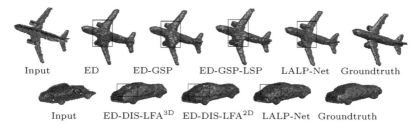

Fig. 6. Ablation study of our approach.

**LFA**. Our full model presents a more detailed and realistic shape than its variants. Starting by $L_{ae}$, the networks produce a basic shape, however, the details such as fuselages of planes are not faithfully predicted. With the help of adversarial training, the results become less blurry. When we construct our full model by adding LFA, the predictions contain more details and look very similar to groundtruth 3D shapes. This benefits from LFA being able to learn an abundant shape representation which helps predict complete and accurate objects. In addition, it is concluded that the combined features from 2D and 3D spaces are more representative than those learned from a single space for recovering 3D shapes.

As is shown in Table 1, Our LFA layer produces fewer parameters than FC layers of other approaches, and this is because LFA shares weights in 2D and 3D convolutions. For a lightweight model, we only use a LFA module in LALP-Net. However, we also provide LALP-Net with multiple LFA modules, that is, connecting features $LFA_2$, $LFA_3$ learned from the outputs of the 2th and 3th convolutional layers to corresponding deconvolution layers of the generator (see Fig. 5). From Table 3, it shows that LFA can be taken as a plug-and-play component to upgrade existing networks.

**LSP**. LALP-Net can predict higher fidelity regions of shapes with $L_{dis}^{lsp}$ in Fig. 6. This means that LSP is useful for uncertain 3D shapes. LSP adds weights to the loss of visible regions in the whole adversarial losses, which helps make the model retain visible information and avoid the influence of noise when predicting occluded regions.

## 5    Conclusion

In this paper, we present a novel framework LALP-Net, that recoveries both global and local 3D structure of the object from a single depth view. By using a Latent Feature-Aware based generator, LALP-Net effectively captures the dependence among local regions of objects, which provides useful cues for recovering a complete 3D shape with fine details and reduces the number of parameters. In addition, by using Local Structure-Preserving based discriminator, LALP-Net enhances the reliability of visible regions and reduces noise when predicting occluded regions. Experiments demonstrates that LALP-Net outperforms the state-of-art approaches on both synthetic data and real-world data for per-category, multi-category and cross-category. In the future, we also plan to apply LFA on other general networks.

# References

1. Chen, Z., Zhang, H.: Learning implicit fields for generative shape modeling. In: CVPR, pp. 5939–5948 (2019)
2. Dai, A., Qi, C.R., Nießner, M.: Shape completion using 3D-encoder-predictor CNNs and shape synthesis. In: CVPR, pp. 6545–6554 (2017)
3. Groueix, T., Fisher, M., Kim, V.G., Russell, B.C., Aubry, M.: A papier-mâché approach to learning 3D surface generation. In: CVPR, pp. 216–224 (2018)
4. Gulrajani, I., Ahmed, F., Arjovsky, M., Dumoulin, V., Courville, A.C.: Improved training of wasserstein GANs. In: NIPS, pp. 5767–5777 (2017)
5. Kanazawa, A., Tulsiani, S., Efros, A.A., Malik, J.: Learning category-specific mesh reconstruction from image collections. In: Ferrari, V., Hebert, M., Sminchisescu, C., Weiss, Y. (eds.) ECCV 2018. LNCS, vol. 11219, pp. 386–402. Springer, Cham (2018). https://doi.org/10.1007/978-3-030-01267-0_23
6. Li, S.C.X., Jiang, B., Marlin, B.M.: MisGAN: learning from incomplete data with generative adversarial networks. In: ICLR, pp. 1–20 (2019)
7. Lin, C.H., Kong, C., Lucey, S.: Learning efficient point cloud generation for dense 3D object reconstruction. In: AAAI, pp. 7114–7121 (2018)
8. Mescheder, L.M., Oechsle, M., Niemeyer, M., Nowozin, S., Geiger, A.: Occupancy networks: learning 3D reconstruction in function space. In: CVPR, pp. 4460–4470 (2019)
9. Park, J.J., Florence, P., Straub, J., Newcombe, R., Lovegrove, S.: DeepSDF: learning continuous signed distance functions for shape representation. In: CVPR, pp. 165–174 (2019)
10. Ronneberger, O., Fischer, P., Brox, T.: U-Net: convolutional networks for biomedical image segmentation. In: Navab, N., Hornegger, J., Wells, W.M., Frangi, A.F. (eds.) MICCAI 2015. LNCS, vol. 9351, pp. 234–241. Springer, Cham (2015). https://doi.org/10.1007/978-3-319-24574-4_28
11. Sharma, A., Grau, O., Fritz, M.: VConv-DAE: deep volumetric shape learning without object labels. In: Hua, G., Jégou, H. (eds.) ECCV 2016. LNCS, vol. 9915, pp. 236–250. Springer, Cham (2016). https://doi.org/10.1007/978-3-319-49409-8_20
12. Smith, E., Meger, D.: Improved adversarial systems for 3D object generation and reconstruction. In: CoRL, pp. 87–96 (2017)
13. Varley, J., DeChant, C., Richardson, A., Ruales, J., Allen, P.K.: Shape completion enabled robotic grasping. In: IROS, pp. 2442–2447 (2017)
14. Wang, N., Zhang, Y., Li, Z., Fu, Y., Liu, W., Jiang, Y.: Pixel2mesh: generating 3D mesh models from single RGB images. ECCV. **11**, 55–71 (2018)
15. Wang, W., Huang, Q., You, S., Yang, C., Neumann, U.: Shape inpainting using 3D generative adversarial network and recurrent convolutional networks. In: ICCV, pp. 2298–2306 (2017)
16. Wu, J., Zhang, C., Zhang, X., Zhang, Z., Freeman, W.T., Tenenbaum, J.B.: Learning shape priors for single-view 3D completion and reconstruction. In: Ferrari, V., Hebert, M., Sminchisescu, C., Weiss, Y. (eds.) ECCV 2018. LNCS, vol. 11215, pp. 673–691. Springer, Cham (2018). https://doi.org/10.1007/978-3-030-01252-6_40

17. Wu, Z., Song, S., Khosla, A., Yu, F., Zhang, L., Tang, X., Xiao, J.: 3D ShapeNets: a deep representation for volumetric shapes. In: CVPR, pp. 1912–1920 (2015)
18. Xie, H., Yao, H., Sun, X., Zhou, S., Zhang, S.: Pix2Vox: context-aware 3D reconstruction from single and multi-view images. In: ICCV, pp. 2690–2698 (2019)
19. Xu, Q., Wang, W., Ceylan, D., Mech, R., Neumann, U.: DISN: deep implicit surface network for high-quality single-view 3D reconstruction. In: NIPS, pp. 490–500 (2019)
20. Yang, B., Rosa, S., Markham, A., Trigoni, N., Wen, H.: 3D object dense reconstruction from a single depth view. TPAMI **41**(12), 2820–2834 (2019)
21. Yang, B., Wen, H., Wang, S., Clark, R., Markham, A., Trigoni, N.: 3D object reconstruction from a single depth view with adversarial learning. In: ICCV Workshop, pp. 679–688 (2017)
22. Zamorski, M., et al.: Adversarial autoencoders for compact representations of 3D point clouds. TVIU **193**, 1–8 (2020)

# Facial Expression Recognition by Expression-Specific Representation Swapping

Jie Lei[1]([✉]), Zhao Liu[2], Zeyu Zou[2], Tong Li[2], Juan Xu[2], Zunlei Feng[3], and Ronghua Liang[1]

[1] Zhejiang University of Technology, Hangzhou 310023, People's Republic of China
{jasonlei,rhliang}@zjut.edu.cn
[2] Ping An Life Insurance Of China, Ltd.,
Shanghai 200120, People's Republic of China
{liuzhao556,zouzeyu313,litong300,xujuan635}@pingan.com.cn
[3] Zhejiang University, Hangzhou 310027, People's Republic of China
zunleifeng@zju.edu.cn

**Abstract.** In the field of facial expression recognition (FER), various FER systems have been explored to encode expression information from facial representations. Although significant progress has been made towards improving the expression classification, challenges due to the large variations of individuals and the lack of consistent annotated samples still remain. In this paper, we propose to disentangle facial representations into expression-specific representations and expression-unrelated representations with a representation swapping procedure, called SwER. First, we adopt a variational auto-encoder (VAE) structure to obtain latent vectors (*i.e.*, facial representations) from face images. Next, the representation swapping procedure is introduced for paired face images to disentangle the expression-specific representations from facial representations. Finally, the expression-specific representations and the expression-unrelated representations are jointly learned for facial expression recognition and face comparison tasks, respectively. In this way, better facial representations are obtained by discarding unrelated factors, and the expression-specific representations are more independent. The proposed method has been evaluated on five databases, CK+, Oulu-CASIA, MMI, RAF-DB, and AffectNet. The experimental results demonstrate the superior performance of the proposed method.

**Keywords:** Facial expression recognition · Representation swapping

## 1 Introduction

Facial expression is an essential factor in conveying human emotional states and intentions. As a consequence, numerous studies have been conducted on facial

J. Lei and Z. Liu–contributed equally.

expression recognition for potential use in sociable robots, medical treatment, driver fatigue surveillance, and many other human-computer interaction systems.

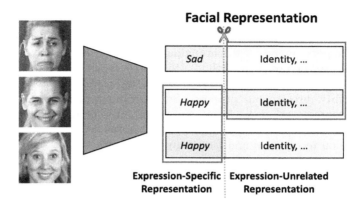

**Fig. 1.** Facial representation can be disentangled into expression-specific representations (the former part) and expression-unrelated representations (the latter part). The first and the second faces are similar in the identity, while the second and the third faces are similar in the expression.

There has been significant progress towards improving the facial expression classification, from handcrafted feature classification, shallow learning, to deep learning [7]. However, the existing well-constructed FER systems still face two challenges: the large variations of individuals and the lack of consistent annotated samples. There are many expression unrelated variations in face images, such as illumination, head pose, age, gender, and background, *i.e.*, facial expressions may appear different for people with different personalities. These disturbances are nonlinearly confounded with facial expressions and address large intra-class variability, making it hard to learn effective expression-specific representations. Meanwhile, as the subjectivity of human annotators and the ambiguous nature of the expression labels, the annotation inconsistency is widespread and consistent annotated samples are limited.

Researches have shown that people are capable of recognizing facial expressions by comparing a subject's expression with a reference expression [16]. In other words, a facial expression can be disentangled in the image representation space. Inspired by this fact, we introduce a swapping procedure in paired face image representations for expression-specific representation learning. We employ a VAE structure to learn latent vectors as facial representations from face images. The facial representations are divided into two parts (Fig. 1), with the former part for facial expression recognition and the latter part for face comparison. During the joint training process, face image pairs are selected as inputs. In this way, we can make full use of limited but consistent annotated samples extracted from face image sequences. For facial expression recognition, we swap the former part of the paired image representations to reconstruct the corresponding face images with expected expressions, thus making the former part more specified for expression. For face comparison, the network is further trained based on the differences of the latter part in the representations to predict whether the two input face images share the same identity. As the expression is irrelevant to the identity, the latter part restrains the expression-specific representation, improving the performance of disentangling for the former part in return.

In contrast to the previous methods [16], which focused on introducing well-designed auxiliary blocks or layers to enhance the expression-related representation capability directly, our proposed SwER framework learns the relatively easier facial representations on facial expression datasets and then disentangles more independent expression-specific representations, with jointly learning of facial expression recognition and face comparison tasks.

The major contributions of this paper are two-fold. Firstly, we introduce a representation swapping procedure for disentangling expression-specific representations from face image representations. Secondly, we propose jointly learning of facial expression recognition and face comparison tasks from paired face images, thus taking full advantage of limited consistent annotated samples and improving the disentanglement performance.

## 2    Related Work

To reduce the impacts of widespread expression-unrelated variations in learning expression-specific representations, several studies have proposed well-designed auxiliary modules to enhance the foundation architecture of deep models. Yao *et al.* [17] proposed HoloNet with three critical considerations in the network design. Li *et al.* [9] proposed an end-to-end trainable Patch-Gated Convolution Neural Network (PG-CNN) that can automatically percept the possible regions of interest on the face. Another area for expression-specific representation learning focuses on facial expression data. Wang *et al.* [15] proposed Self-Cure Network (SCN) to suppress the uncertainties efficiently and prevent deep networks from over-fitting uncertain face images. In [18], the authors proposed an end-to-end trainable LTNet to discover the latent truths with the auxiliary annotations from different datasets. There are other existing works that suggest facial expression recognition could benefit from using a reference image. Yang *et al.* [16] recognized facial expression by learning the residual expressive component in the generative model. Kim *et al.* [5] employed a contrastive representation in the networks to extract the feature level difference between a query face image and a neutral face image. Zhao *et al.* [20] presented a novel peak-piloted deep network (PPDN) that used the peak expression (easy sample) to supervise the non-peak expression (hard sample) of the same type and from the same subject.

The above works focus on directly learning expression-specific representation or expression-specific difference to a reference face image, which is relatively hard for training with a lack of diverse samples for widespread expression unrelated variations. Unlike these works, we propose to learn facial representation at first, which is relatively easy on limited consistent annotated samples. The expression-specific representation is further disentangled from the facial representation. The recent utility of representation disentangling shows success in learning disassembled object representation from images [4]. Lin *et al.* [10] proposed SPACE to factorize object representations of foreground objects and decompose background segments of complex morphology. Comparing with the object, the expression is implicitly and dispersive in the image. We adopt an auxiliary expression-unrelated task of face comparison to suppress the expression-specific representation on the latter part of the facial representation. In return, the former part can concentrate on learning the expression-specific representation.

## 3    Proposed Method

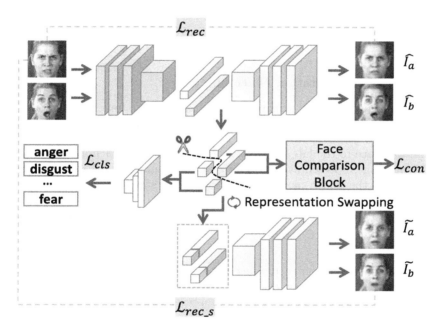

**Fig. 2.** Framework of the proposed SwER method, which is composed with two reconstruction modules, an expression classification module, and an auxiliary face comparison block.

The framework of our proposed method - SwER is illustrated in Fig. 2, where the network takes a pair of face images as inputs. As shown in Fig. 2, SwER contains three learning processes: the first is learning facial representations from face images; the second is learning expression-specific representations (the former part) disentangled from facial representations; the third is learning to suppress the expression-specific representations on the latter part of facial representations. In this section, we illustrate details of these learning processes.

### 3.1   Paired Face Images

We take pairs of face images $\langle I_a, I_b \rangle$ as inputs. Specifically, we consider two types of pairs. One is a pair of face images with the same identity and different expressions, the other is a pair of face images with different identities and the same expression. Here, we use $D(I_a, I_b) = 1$ and $E(I_a, I_b) = 1$ to denote $\langle I_a, I_b \rangle$ sharing the same identity or expression, respectively. In Sect. 3.3, we will demonstrate that the supervision information for reconstructed images after expression-specific representation swapping can naturally derived from the inputs, *i.e.*, $\langle I_a, I_b \rangle$.

In the experiments, we sample face images from image sequences. A face image sequence typically begins with a neutral expression and reaches a peak near the middle before returning to the neutral expression. The expression annotations are relatively consistent as frames in the same sequence can be taken as reference images for each other. However, the number of sequences is relatively smaller in comparison to static images. By adopting pairs of images, we can significantly enlarge the number of training samples.

### 3.2   Facial Representation Learning

A variational auto-encoder structure [14] is exploited to generate a good facial representation from a face image. Without loss of generality, this structure contains an encoder $f_E$ and a decoder $f_D$. The input face images $\langle I_a, I_b \rangle$ are mapped from image space to the latent representation space by $f_E$, denoted as $\langle R_a, R_b \rangle$. The latent image representations $\langle R_a, R_b \rangle$ are then mapped back by decoder $f_D$ to reconstruct the image pair. The objective is to simultaneously optimize $f_E$ and $f_D$ for minimizing the reconstruction error:

$$\mathcal{L}_{rec} = \left\| I_a - \widehat{I_a} \right\|_2^2 + \left\| I_b - \widehat{I_b} \right\|_2^2, \tag{1}$$

where $\widehat{I_a}$ and $\widehat{I_b}$ are reconstructed face images. All the input image pairs $\langle I_a, I_b \rangle$ are pre-processed by face detection and face alignment, so the latent representations $\langle R_a, R_b \rangle$ can be referred as facial representations.

### 3.3   Expression-Specific Representation Swapping

The facial representations $\langle R_a, R_b \rangle$ are divided into two parts: $\left[ R_a^E, R_a^U \right]$ and $\left[ R_b^E, R_b^U \right]$, respectively. The former parts $R_a^E$ and $R_b^E$ are referred as expression-specific representations. The latter parts $R_a^U$ and $R_b^U$ are expression-unrelated facial representations.

We introduce a swapping procedure to disentangle $\langle R_a^E, R_b^E \rangle$ from $\langle R_a, R_b \rangle$. After swapping $R_a^E$ and $R_b^E$, the hybrid latent representations $R_a^{'} = \left[ R_b^E, R_a^U \right]$ and $R_b^{'} = \left[ R_a^E, R_b^U \right]$ are decoded by $f_D$ and reconstructed as hybrid images $\widetilde{I_a}$ and $\widetilde{I_b}$, respectively.

For pairs $\langle I_a, I_b \rangle$ where $D(I_a, I_b) = 1$ and $E(I_a, I_b) = 0$, the desired reconstruction images for $R'_a$ and $R'_b$ should swap the expression for each other. As we encourage the representation of different expressions to be discriminated, we use $\langle I_b, I_a \rangle$ for supervision:

$$\mathcal{L}_{rec\_s} = \left\| I_b - \tilde{I}_a \right\|_2^2 + \left\| I_a - \tilde{I}_b \right\|_2^2. \tag{2}$$

For pairs $\langle I_a, I_b \rangle$ where $D(I_a, I_b) = 0$ and $E(I_a, I_b) = 1$, the desired reconstruction images for $R'_a$ and $R'_b$ should be similar to the inputs. In other words, the expression-specific representation is personality unrelated. We encourage the representation of the same expression to be similar for different people. $\langle I_a, I_b \rangle$ are used for supervision as:

$$\mathcal{L}_{rec\_s} = \left\| I_a - \tilde{I}_a \right\|_2^2 + \left\| I_b - \tilde{I}_b \right\|_2^2. \tag{3}$$

Expression-specific representation swapping aims to model the expression factor that affects the appearance of face images. If the expression-specific representation is well disentangled, the change of expression only causes the change of the face on the expression factor, while the other factors are uninfluenced.

$\langle R_a^E, R_b^E \rangle$ are used for expression classification, the loss function is

$$\mathcal{L}_{cls} = - \sum_{r}^{\{a,b\}} \log(\frac{\exp(p^{(k_r)}(R_r^E))}{\sum_i^K \exp(p^{(i)}(R_r^E))}), \tag{4}$$

where $p^{(i)}(\cdot)$ is the $i$-th expression predicted probability of the classifier, $K$ is the total number of facial expression expression classes, and $k_a$ and $k_b$ are the target expressions for $I_a$ and $I_b$, respectively.

## 3.4   Auxiliary Face Comparison Block

In further, we introduce an auxiliary face comparison block for an expression unrelated task - face comparison, where a change of expression shall not affect the identity. On one hand, better facial representations are obtained by paying more attention to describing the face. On the other hand, as we use $\langle R_a^U, R_b^U \rangle$ for the comparison, the expression-specific representations are suppressed on the latter representations. In return, more expression-specific representations are contained in $\langle R_a^E, R_b^E \rangle$.

Contrastive loss [2] is used for the auxiliary block as:

$$\mathcal{L}_{con} = D(I_a, I_b)d^2 + (1 - D(I_a, I_b)) \max(m - d, 0)^2, \tag{5}$$

where $d = \left\| R_a^U - R_b^U \right\|_2$ is the distance between two face images in the representation space, and $m$ is a threshold for the distance.

### 3.5  Complete Algorithm

In summary, the total loss $\mathcal{L}$ is a combination of the above modules. The inputs are $\langle I_a, I_b \rangle$, the annotated expression labels $\langle k_a, k_b \rangle$, and $D(I_a, I_b)$. $\langle k_a, k_b \rangle$ and $D(I_a, I_b)$ are used in facial expression classification and face comparison, respectively. The facial representation learning and expression-specific representation swapping take $\langle I_a, I_b \rangle$ as supervision information. The total loss is given as follows:

$$\mathcal{L} = \lambda_1 \mathcal{L}_{rec} + \lambda_2 \mathcal{L}_{rec\_s} + \lambda_3 \mathcal{L}_{cls} + \lambda_4 \mathcal{L}_{con}, \tag{6}$$

where $\lambda_1$, $\lambda_2$, $\lambda_3$, and $\lambda_4$ are balanced parameters which are used to control the influence of different learning processes.

## 4  Experiments

### 4.1  Datasets and Setting

The proposed SwER approach is evaluated on five public facial expression datasets, inculuding CK+ [11], MMI [13], Oulu-CASIA [19], RAF-DB [8], and AffectNet [12].

CK+ contains 593 video sequences collected from 123 subjects. Among them, 327 video sequences with 118 subjects are labeled as one of seven expressions, *i.e.*, *anger* (AN), *disgust* (DI), *fear* (FE), *happiness* (HA), *sadness* (SA), *surprise* (SU), and *contempt* (CO). Each sequence starts with a peak expression. We chose the first frame as the neutral face (NE) and the last three frames as the expressive face, resulting in 1307 images with 1047 for training and 260 for testing. MMI has 236 sequences with expressions recorded from 30 subjects, where each sequence starts with a neutral face, shifts to a peak expression, and return to a neutral face in the end. In our experiments, for each sequence, the first two images are selected as neutral faces while the middle one-fifth part are chosen as expressive faces. In total, we have 1103 images for training and 399 images for testing. Oulu-CASIA has 480 sequences captured from 80 objects. We use the cropped face images provided by the author, resulting in 29932 images with 21070 images for training and 8862 images for testing. The annotated labels for MMI and Oulu-CASIA are six basic expressions (except for *contempt*) and neutral.

RAF-DB is divided into training and test sets with a size of 12,271 and 3,068, respectively. AffectNet contains more than 400k annotated images. We select 19,239 images for training and 2,518 images for testing, all of which are labeled with six basic expressions and neutral .

For CK+, MMI, Oulu-CASIA, we separate the training set and the testing set by subjects, *i.e.*, the subjects in the two subsets are mutually exclusive. To generate image pairs, we randomly select pairs from the training set on the condition that each sample will be included for at least once. In total, we obtain 24,994, 67,779 and 147,490 pairs for the three datasets, respectively. Since the identities of subjects are not accessible on RAF-DB and AffectNet, we use CK+ for pre-training and conduct fine-tuning on the expression classification module with their training sets. The face images are pre-processed by face detection and face alignment [3]. The basic variational auto-encoder structure [14] is adopted, with the dimensions for the face representation and expression-specific representation are set as 512 and 64, respectively. We use the Adam optimizer with a learning rate of 0.0001. The parameters $\lambda_{\{1-4\}}$ are empirically chosen from the scales of $\{0.01, 0.1, 0.5, 1, 1.5, 2, 10\}$ and finally set as $\lambda_1 = 1$, $\lambda_2 = 2$, $\lambda_3 = 0.5$, and $\lambda_4 = 0.1$ for the loss function.

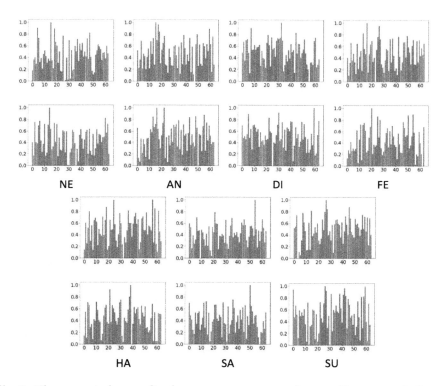

**Fig. 3.** The generated normalized average seven expression-specific representations of two subjects on CK+. The expression-specific components are similar for the same expression and distinguishable among other expressions for different subjects.

### 4.2 Results

In Fig. 3, we demonstrate an example of the generated expression-specific representations of two subjects on CK+. The average representations for *neutral, anger, disgust, fear, happiness, sadness,* and *surprise* are displayed, where each histogram is calculated and normalized from all samples with the same expression for the subject. As we can see, the expression-specific components are similar for the same expression and distinguishable among other expressions for different subjects.

**Table 1.** The average accuracies of expression recognition on CK+, MMI, and Oulu-CASIA, where $\text{SwER}^-_{rec\_s}$ and $\text{SwER}^-_{con}$ are variants of the proposed SwER for ablation studies.

| Dataset | CK+ | MMI | Oulu-CASIA |
|---------|-----|-----|-----------|
| FRAME [6] | 0.9077 | 0.5689 | 0.5971 |
| LTNet [18] | 0.9385 | 0.6065 | 0.5837 |
| FMPN [1] | 0.9731 | 0.4390 | 0.5330 |
| SCN [15] | 0.9769 | 0.6717 | 0.7512 |
| $\text{SwER}^-_{rec\_s}$ | 0.9173 | 0.5514 | 0.5349 |
| $\text{SwER}^-_{con}$ | 0.9474 | 0.6424 | 0.7257 |
| SwER | **0.9846** | **0.6729** | **0.7708** |

**Table 2.** The average accuracies of expression recognition on RAF-DB and AffectNet.

| Dataset | RAF-DB | AffectNet |
|---------|--------|-----------|
| DLP [8] | 0.6874 | 0.4865 |
| LTNet [18] | 0.7864 | 0.5306 |
| FMPN [1] | 0.6610 | 0.4527 |
| SCN [15] | 0.8589 | 0.5786 |
| SwER | **0.8750** | **0.6250** |

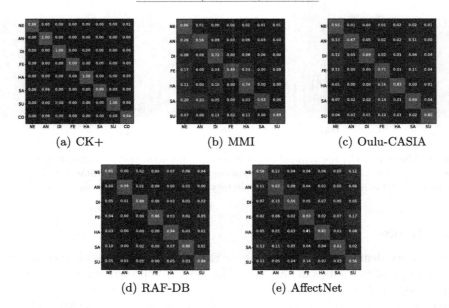

(a) CK+          (b) MMI          (c) Oulu-CASIA

(d) RAF-DB          (e) AffectNet

**Fig. 4.** Confusion Matrixes on CK+, MMI, Oulu-CASIA, RAF-DB, and AffectNet, where the horizontal axis and vertical axis are predicted label and groundtruth label, respectively.

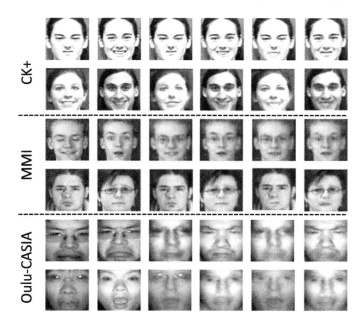

**Fig. 5.** Face image reconstruction on CK+, MMI, and Oulu-CASIA The first and the second columns are original input face images, the third and the fourth columns are reconstructed images, and the fifth and the sixth columns are reconstructed images after expression-specific representation swapping.

Figure 5 illustrates face image reconstruction on CK+, MMI, and Oulu-CASIA, where the first and the second columns are original input face images, the third and the fourth columns are reconstructed images, and the fifth and the sixth columns are reconstructed images after expression-specific representation swapping. As shown in Fig. 5, the reconstructed face images are similar to the inputs, indicating the facial representation could well describe the face. For the first example of each dataset where two face images share the same identity and have different expressions, the expressions of the reconstructed face images after swapping are similar to the expression in the other input face image. For example, the expressions for the input face images are *disgust* and *happiness* in the first row. After expression-specific representation swapping, the *disgust* face is happier and the *happiness* face is getting disgustting. For the second example of each dataset where two face images share the same expression and have different identity, the reconstructed face images after swapping are similar to the inputs. From these examples, we can conclude that the expression-specific representation is disentangled.

The average accuracies on expression recognition are shown in Table 1 and Table 2. The results are reported as the average of 10 runs. Our SwER method achieves the highest accuracy compared to those of state-of-the-art methods, including FRAME [6], LTNet [18], FMPN [1], and SCN [15]. The confusion matrixes are also provided in Fig. 4, where the proposed SwER performs very well in recognizing *neutral, disgust,* and *happiness,* while *sadness* shows the relatively low recognition rate, which is mostly confused with *neutral.*

### 4.3   Ablation Study

In SwER, the total loss function is composed of four items. To verify the necessities of the modules of reconstruction with swapping and auxiliary face comparison, we conduct ablation studies by removing $\mathcal{L}_{rec\_s}$ and $\mathcal{L}_{con}$, respectively, denoted as $SwER_{rec\_s}^{-}$ and $SwER_{con}^{-}$.

The average accuracies on CK+, MMI, and Oulu-CASIA for $SwER_{rec\_s}^{-}$ and $SwER_{con}^{-}$ are included in Table 1. It is noticeable SwER achieves the best classification performance than other variants, which demonstrates that the loss of reconstruction with swapping and face comparison can improve the disentanglement performance of expression-specific representations.

## 5   Conclusion

In this paper, we propose SwER for facial expression recognition by disentangling expression-specific representations from facial representations. SwER is composed with two reconstruction modules, an expression classification module, and an auxiliary face comparison block. The experimental results demonstrate the superior performance of the proposed method over other state-of-the-art methods. Our future work will incorporate the expression-specific representations with temporal information for addressing the issues of AU detection.

**Acknowledgements.** This work was supported in part by the National Key Research and Development Program of China (No. 2020YFB1707700) and the National Natural Science Foundation of China (No. 62036009).

## References

1. Chen, Y., Wang, J., Chen, S., Shi, Z., Cai, J.: Facial motion prior networks for facial expression recognition. In: VCIP (2019)
2. Chopra, S., Hadsell, R., Lecun, Y.: Learning a similarity metric discriminatively, with application to face verification. In: CVPR (2005)
3. Deng, J., Guo, J., Zhou, Y., Yu, J., Kotsia, I., Zafeiriou, S.: RetinaFace: single-stage dense face localisation in the wild. In: arXiv preprint arXiv:1905.00641 (2019)
4. Feng, Z., et al.: One-sample guided object representation disassembling. In: NeurIPS (2020)
5. Kim, Y., Yoo, B., Kwak, Y., Choi, C., Kim, J.: Deep generative-contrastive networks for facial expression recognition. In: CVPR (2017)
6. Kuo, C.M., Lai, S.H., Sarkis, M.: A compact deep learning model for robust facial expression recognition. In: CVPRW (2018)
7. Li, S., Deng, W.: Deep facial expression recognition: a survey. IEEE Trans. Affect. Comput. (99) (2018)

8. Li, S., Deng, W., Du, J.P.: Reliable crowdsourcing and deep locality-preserving learning for expression recognition in the wild. In: CVPR (2017)
9. Li, Y., Zeng, J., Shan, S., Chen, X.: Patch-gated CNN for occlusion-aware facial expression recognition. In: ICPR (2018)
10. Lin, Z., et al.: SPACE: unsupervised object-oriented scene representation via spatial attention and decomposition. In: ICLR (2020)
11. Lucey, P., Cohn, J.F., Kanade, T., Saragih, J., Matthews, I.: The extended Cohn-Kanade Dataset (CK+): a complete dataset for action unit and emotion-specified expression. In: CVPRW (2010)
12. Mollahosseini, A., Hasani, B., Mahoor, M.H.: AffectNet: a database for facial expression, valence, and arousal computing in the wild. In: IEEE Transactions on Affective Computing (2017)
13. Pantic, M.V.: Induced disgust, happiness and surprise: an addition to the mmi facial expression database. In: Proceedings 3rd Intern. Workshop on EMOTION (satellite of LREC): Corpora for Research on Emotion and Affect (2010)
14. Sohn, K., Yan, X., Lee, H., Arbor, A.: Learning structured output representation using deep conditional generative models. In: NeurIPS (2015)
15. Wang, K., Peng, X., Yang, J., Lu, S., Qiao, Y.: Suppressing uncertainties for large-scale facial expression recognition. In: CVPR (2020)
16. Yang, H., Ciftci, U., Yin, L.: Facial expression recognition by de-expression residue learning. In: CVPR (2018)
17. Yao, A., Cai, D., Hu, P., Wang, S., Chen, Y.: HoloNet: towards robust emotion recognition in the wild. In: ICMI (2016)
18. Zeng, J., Shan, S., Chen, X.: Facial expression recognition with inconsistently annotated datasets. In: ECCV (2018)
19. Zhao, G., Huang, X., Taini, M., Li, S.Z., Pietikälnen, M.: Facial expression recognition from near-infrared videos. In: Image and Vision Computing (2011)
20. Zhao, X., Liang, X., Liu, L., Li, T., Yan, S.: Peak-piloted deep network for facial expression recognition. In: ECCV (2016)

# Iterative Error Removal
# for Time-of-Flight Depth Imaging

Zhuolin Zheng[1,2,3], Yinzhang Ding[1,2,3], Xiaotian Tang[1,2,3], Yu Cai[1,2,3], Dongxiao Li[1,2,3(✉)], Ming Zhang[1,2,3], Hongyang Xie[4], and Xuanfu Li[4]

[1] College of Information Science and Electronic Engineering, Zhejiang University, Hangzhou, China
{zhengzhuolin,dingyzh,3160101464,yucaimr,lidx,zhangm}@zju.edu.cn
[2] Zhejiang Provincial Key Laboratory of Information Processing Communication and Networking, Hangzhou, China
[3] State Key Laboratory of CAD and CG, Hangzhou, China
[4] Huawei Technologies Co. Ltd., Shenzhen, China
xiehongyang@hisilicon.com, lixuanfu@huawei.com

**Abstract.** Depth information plays an increasingly important role in computer vision tasks. As one of the most promising depth sensing techniques, Amplitude Modulated Continuous Wave (AMCW)-based indirect Time-of-Flight (ToF) has been widely used in recent years. Unfortunately, the depth acquired by ToF sensors is often corrupted by imaging noise, multi-path interference (MPI), and low intensity. Different methods have been proposed for tackling these issues. Nevertheless, they failed to exploit the characteristics of the ToF depth map to propose a targeted solution, and are unable to achieve various error removal. We present a new iterative method for removing various errors simultaneously through cascaded Convolutional Neural Networks (CNNs). A Synthetic Dataset is created using computer graphics, and a Real-World Dataset is developed via RGBD-based 3D reconstruction, both contain the raw measurement acquired by a certain ToF camera and corresponding dense ground truth depth. Experimental results demonstrate the superior performance of the proposed iterative method in removing various ToF depth errors, compared to state-of-the-art methods, on both the newly developed datasets and existing public datasets.

**Keywords:** Time-of-flight · Convolutional neural networks · Three-dimensional vision · Depth sensor

## 1  Introduction

Depth acquisition is not only the key to most 3D vision tasks but also playing an increasingly important role in traditional RGB-based computer vision tasks such as gesture recognition and semantic segmentation in the past few years. Previous representative depth acquisition approaches including structured light and stereo vision have some critical limitations [20], either cannot be used for

© Springer Nature Switzerland AG 2021
I. Farkaš et al. (Eds.): ICANN 2021, LNCS 12892, pp. 92–105, 2021.
https://doi.org/10.1007/978-3-030-86340-1_8

mid-to-long-distance ranging, or require sufficient texture in the scene. Recently, Time-of-Flight (ToF) [11] based depth camera has attracted more and more attention due to its inexpensiveness, lightweight, fair accuracy, and robustness.

The Time-of-Flight technique obtains depth by measuring the time it takes for a wave or pulse to travel from the emitter to object and back to the receiver. For the particular Amplitude Modulated Continuous Waves (AMCW) implementation of the ToF camera, the depth is acquired indirectly by measuring the cross-correlation between emitted and received wave and calculating the phase delay to represent depth. Modern AMCW-ToF camera usually uses multiple modulation frequencies to enlarge the sensing range of the camera while remaining accuracy.

Various errors may occur during this imaging procedure. There are two main types of errors. The first is the common error in digital imaging system, such as Gaussian imaging noise, temperature drift. The second type of error occurs when the real scenario does not follow the assumption of the working principle of the ToF camera, that the light received at each pixel position consists only of the light firstly reflected from that position. When in a complex scene or there are surfaces with low reflectance or mirror reflection, this principle is often violated. Some pixels may receive light reflected multiple times from elsewhere, thus cause the so-called Multipath Interference (MPI). Some pixels may suffer low intensity that the power of light received there is too low to get sufficient Signal-Noise Ratio (SNR) to calculate precise depth, due to low retroreflectivity on the surface. When in a multi-frequency ToF camera, these errors can then be transmitted and amplified by phase-unwrapping and induce a significant error on the final depth map due to incorrect estimation of rounds.

Earlier ToF depth refinement work [7,10] mostly adopts various sparse simplified assumptions about the response characteristics of the scene (e.g. Lambertian [6], Two-bounce light [17] and Two-path-caused MPI [8]), based on which to model the local light path, and then solve it through probability models [8] or optimization methods [5] to find the optimal solution.

In recent years, many learning-based methods have begun to emerge. Despite few other learning-based methods [12], most of them adopt CNN to their methods. Marco et al. [16] designed a network of encoder-decoder structure and used a two-stage training scheme to correct for MPI. Su et al. [22] proposed to directly use the correlation map obtained by the ToF camera as input, and then designed an end-to-end CNN based on U-Net [19] to replace the traditional pipeline, Generative Adversarial Networks (GAN) is also included in consideration of deep image generation. Guo et al. [9] noticed that multiple sampling of ToF cameras could cause artifacts in dynamic scenes, and proposed an encoder-decoder CNN to deal with the artifacts and eliminating MPI meanwhile. Qiu et al. [18] proposed a network that used RGBD as input, utilizing cross-modal dense optical flow for image alignment, and used the aligned depth map to pass a kernel prediction network (KPN) to get a refined depth map. Agresti et al. [1,2] designed a coarse-fine CNN to capture multi-scale information and later developed this approach by performing unsupervised learning on unlabeled data with GAN.

There are also some work focused on ToF imaging problems under special situations via CNN, such as translucent objects [21] and short exposure [3]. Although CNN based methods have achieved good results, these methods did not exploit characteristics of the ToF depth map.

Instead of a usual end-to-end approach, we designed a multi-stage iterative CNN to tackle this problem for three main reasons. First, the end-to-end CNN cannot realize the discontinuous mapping from multi-frequency raw measurement to depth map in the underlying principles. Second, unlike RGB generation, which has a higher tolerance for pixel-level error due to human visual perception, the results completely output by CNN are not perfectly competent for prediction of ToF depth map in a pixel-level millimeter accuracy. And it will be very likely to degrade when odd input is encountered. Third, for different kinds of error, different ideas and principles are needed to remove, it is difficult to predict the nonlinear coupling of different types of error in a single output. Our iterative method can avoid the above issues by continuous residual prediction of the current depth map and retaining the information for the next refinement.

In order to achieve a robust and effective solution for multiple types of ToF depth map error removal. We present a newly designed CNN specifically for this problem. We devise a CNN module and use it to implement this network architecture. Moreover, we also develop two new large ToF datasets, one is a Synthetic dataset made by computer graphics techniques, and the other is a Real-World dataset generated by 3D reconstruction. Both of them consist of plentiful types of data, and all the critical error mentioned above is considered in the proposed datasets.

Our main contributions are summarized as follows:

- We proposed a targeted, iterative-based CNN method that can significantly remove various types of error by utilizing principles of ToF imaging and avoiding the shortcomings of existing methods.
- We created two large ToF datasets via computer graphics and 3D reconstruction, especially the firstly proposed large real-world dataset. Both cover various error types and provide plenty of types of data access, especially the ToF raw measurement and dense ground truth depth.
- Through qualitative and quantitative experiments, we showed that our proposed method is able to remove most of the error on the ToF depth map and surpass the previous method on our datasets and other public avaliable datasets.

Code and datasets are available from the authors upon reasonable request or with permission of Huawei Technologies Co., Ltd.

## 2    Method

### 2.1    Formulating for ToF Depth Imaging

The working principle of the ToF camera based on AMCW is briefly introduced as follows. When the camera is imaging, the transmitter on camera will emit an amplitude modulated near-infrared (NIR) wave. The receiver at each pixel position will receive the echo and calculates the cross-correlation between the received signal and the reference signal from the transmitter. This inner production process will automatically complete the demodulation and filter out the signal on other frequency bands such as ambient light. Since we only focus on the part that actually carries information in the modulated wave, we use the phasor to express it concisely as Eq. 1.

$$C_i = \mathrm{CC}\,(\boldsymbol{S}, \boldsymbol{S}_{ref,i}) = \frac{<\boldsymbol{S}, \boldsymbol{S}_{ref,i}>}{\|\boldsymbol{S}_{ref,i}\|} = \frac{\int_0^T \boldsymbol{S}(t) \cdot \boldsymbol{S}_{ref,i}(t)dt}{\sqrt{\int_0^T \boldsymbol{S}_{ref,i}(t)^2 dt}} = I \cdot \cos \Delta \varphi_i \quad (1)$$

where $C_i$ represents for the i-th imaging result of ToF raw measurement. CC denotes for the cross-correlation operation. $I$ represents the intensity of this imaging. $\boldsymbol{S}$ is the phasor of the received signal, $\boldsymbol{S}_{ref,i}$ is the reference signal used for every imaging, $i = 0 \ldots n-1$, n denote times of imaging. This imaging will be performed multiple times by shifting the phase of the reference signal (or received signal) to eliminate ambiguity of cosine. Take four times as an example, $\boldsymbol{S}_{ref,0}$ is the reference signal from the transmitter when received returned signal, the other reference signals will be expressed in this way. $j$ is the imaginary unit.

$$\boldsymbol{S}_{ref,i} = \boldsymbol{S}_{ref,i-1} \cdot e^{-\frac{j\pi}{2}} \quad (2)$$

Four imaging will be performed according to Eq. 1. By basic mathematical transformations we can calculate the radius depth and intensity map, which is the typical output of the ToF camera. * represents for depth or intensity directly output by camera.

$$Depth^* = arctan2\,(C_1 - C_3,\ C_0 - C_2) \cdot c/(4\pi f) \quad (3)$$

$$Intensity^* = \sqrt{(C_1 - C_3)^2 + (C_0 - C_2)^2}/2 \quad (4)$$

For a multi-frequency ToF camera, the camera needs to first calculate the phase measured at each frequency separately, and then use the half-wavelength at each modulation frequency as the base to establish a linear congruence equation to solve the real depth via a phase unwrapping algorithm [15] based on Chinese Remainder Theorem.

## 2.2   Input and Output Defining

We first define the input and output of the problem.

For input, most of the previous methods used the direct output of the ToF camera, i.e., the depth map and the intensity map as input. Later other work [9, 22] pointed out that using ToF raw correlation information can lead to a more accurate depth prediction, since it avoids losing the luminosity and geometric information contained in it. However, this approach has a major flaw in the bottom layer: If the ToF camera uses multiple modulation frequencies, the solving of linear congruence equations will be involved. The remainder operation in it make the mapping from correlation maps to the depth map discontinuous and undifferentiable. However, neural networks are not able to fit a discontinuous mapping in principle. Therefore, an end-to-end fashion CNN can only fit some appearance, it is still not able to solve the problem essentially.

For output, previous work [16,22] often adopts the outputs completely generated by CNN as the results, since most visual applications is done by this approach. But there is an important difference between depth map generation and RGB generation, that depth maps are very sensitive to values. A certain number of abnormal pixels may not affect visual perception, but it will surely affect the accuracy of the depth map. Therefore, CNNs based on human vision can generate visually impressive images, but the result is unreliable and unstable in terms of pixel-wise accuracy. On the one hand, it is not capable to achieve high accuracy, on the other hand, it is not robust enough, once odd input is encountered, the output tends to fail.

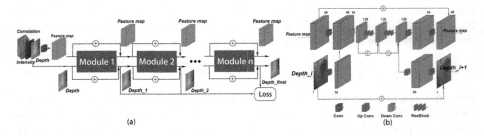

**Fig. 1.** (a) Overview of our iterative CNN for ToF error removal. Each module takes a depth map and a feature map as input, outputs an residual prediction to refine the depth map, and gives deeper features for the next iteration. The initial feature map is obtained from the ToF raw correlation map, intensity map and depth map. (b) The iterative module structure built for our CNN.

To solve these problems, we keep the depth map and intensity map output by the ToF camera and feed them to CNN together with the raw correlation maps. This approach directly provides the solution of the congruence equation, frees the CNN from the complicated remainder problem and enables the network to focus on the information contained in the raw measurement that contributes to the error removal. Also, we turn the task of the network into predicting the errors in the ToF depth map, making the input depth as anchor. This approach makes the network robust and prevents possible performance degradation of CNN.

## 2.3   Proposed Iterative CNN

This problem has the following characteristics. First, the input depth map and the output depth map are signals in the same domain, which means that if a naive method is defined to eliminate the error in the depth map as much as possible, then a better result could be expected by using the output as the input. This inspired us to design an iterative method. Second, the entropy contained in this problem is large, since this is a dense prediction at a relatively high spatial resolution [12]. Besides, with a full range 4 m to 10 m and accuracy in millimeter [11], the SNR required for each pixel in this task reaches 60 dB, which is much higher than that in the image generation task e.g. image super-resolution with state-of-the-art PSNR around 35 dB [23]. Therefore, residual prediction is necessary and enough spatial information should be retained during the whole processing. Third, there are various errors in the ToF depth map, e.g. the imaging noise, MPI and low intensity, the way and level they affect the depth map vary [15,20]. It's difficult for CNN to make a single residual prediction to the highly coupled nonlinear superposition of all different kinds of errors. So based on these features, we proposed our method.

First, we designed a CNN module as shown in Fig. 1(b) The input of this module is feature maps of 48 channels and a depth map of one channel. Depth map passes through a convolution layer and fuse with feature maps in channel dimension, then a down convolution is used to scale down these feature maps, and doubled channel to 128. The feature will pass through two cascaded Res-blocks. Then the resulted feature maps will proceed to two different sets of up convolution and standard convolution, respectively, to obtain feature maps and a residual prediction. Feature maps and residual depth map are of the same size as the input feature maps and depth map, and will be added to them to form the outputs of module.

Proposed CNN is built using this module, as shown in Fig. 1(a). First, the correlation maps at different frequencies as well as depth map and intensity map are pre-fused via atrous and standard convolution to obtain a rough feature map. This feature map will be input in this module together with the ToF depth map. The module architecture will be iterated several times with different parameters while the outputs of previous module serve as the inputs of the next module. The depth map output by each module will be constrained by loss function. And naturally, the depth map from the last module will be the final depth map output.

From overview, the flow of feature maps followed a multi-level residual network fashion; from a detailed perspective of each module, the flow of feature maps and depth maps has followed the spirit of U-Net [19]: Multi-scale information extraction and reusing. The module continuously up and down sampling to extract multi-scale contexts and creating a shortcut from shallow to deep to retain spatial information of the original depth map space.

For loss function, we adopt L1-loss as data term loss for its simplicity.

$$L_{l1} = \sum_i ||Depth_{gt} - Depth_{CNNi}||_1 \tag{5}$$

Here, i represents for the depth map output from the i-th module.

And we utilize second order total variation as regularization term to impose an artificial prior constraint, since depth are mostly first-order smooth within occlusion boundary.

$$L_r = ||f(Depth_{CNN} \circledast LoG)||_1 \qquad (6)$$

$$f(x) = \begin{cases} x, & if \quad x < threshold \\ 0, & else \end{cases} \qquad (7)$$

This term only act on the final output depth. LoG represents for the Laplace of Gaussian filter. $f(x)$ and *threshold* are there to prevent the impact on object edges. The weight ratio of L1-loss to second order total variation loss is $1 * 10^{-4}$.

We built this iterative network based on the module. The input of each module of the network is a depth map and a feature map containing depth information, the task of each module is to make a residual prediction, add it to input depth of the module to obtain a finer depth map, and meanwhile output a feature map with deeper information for the next module to exploit. Depth map and feature maps are both iteratively improved with the cascading of modules. Our network architecture is also efficient, containing only 2.08 million parameters with two Resblocks in each module and five modules cascading to form the CNN.

**Fig. 2.** (a) 3D scene reconstruction result. UpperLeft: Bookstore, UpperRight: Laboratory, LowerLeft: Living-room, LowerRight: PhotoBooth (b) (c) Partial datatype of our Real-World Dataset and Synthetic Dataset respectively. UpperLeft: Four ToF raw correlation maps; UpperRight: ToF Intensity map; LowerLeft: ToF Depth map; LowerRight: Ground Truth Depth map.

## 3    Datasets

Data is crucial for CNN, however, most of the previous work uses only the synthetic dataset with limited error simulation, and lacks real-world dataset for training. We successfully generated a large Synthetic dataset and a large Real-World dataset by computer graphics and 3D reconstruction techniques, respectively. Both contain dense ground truth depth and ToF raw correlation measurements (Fig. 2).

## 3.1   Synthetic Dataset

Our Synthetic dataset contains six main indoor scenes: living room, bedroom, bathroom, dining room, kitchen, and staircase. There are 1379 sets of data contained in total, we split them into a training set of size 1260 and a test set of size 119. We simulated the imaging system of the LUCID Helios camera. Except for the RGB images that LUCID cannot capture, all our simulations use the same internal parameters and resolution as the camera, i.e. 480 * 640. Each set of data includes the raw correlation measurements on 100 MHz and 75 MHz, with each frequency containing two imaging results of phase shift $\pi/2$, the ToF depth map, the intensity map, the ground truth depth, and RGB image of resolution 1440 * 1920. In terms of error simulation, raw measurements in the dataset include imaging noise, MPI, low reflectivity, and specular reflections which are typical errors that may occur in the actual application of ToF cameras, the depth map and intensity map generated by correlation maps will also be introduced to these errors.

The scenes of the dataset are mainly taken from the 3D models shared by the Blender community. The simulation of the correlation map and the ground truth depth is attributed to the work of Jarabo et al. [14] on transient rendering. By rendering the light received by the camera in every time interval, then amplitude modulating the rendering result and integrating them to obtain the correlation maps. Support for ray tracing allows us to simulate MPI. Simulation for low reflectivity, and specular reflection are done by adjusting the material and reflectivity of different objects. Imaging noise is treated as additive Gaussian noise. The surface normal map and RGB map are generated thanks to Blender and its Cycles Renderer.

## 3.2   Real-World Dataset

Our Real-World dataset contains 1060 sets of data in total and is split into a train/test sets of size 964 and 96, which is significantly larger than the Real-World dataset [2, 22] used only for testing. We reconstruct several different indoor scenes, namely bathroom, bedroom, bookstore, cafe, dining room, library, laboratory, kitchen, living room, and read room, to ensure the diversity of the dataset and take common errors of ToF cameras into consideration. Each set of data includes the same data in the same resolution as the Synthetic dataset except for the surface normal map.

Modern portable RGB-Depth sensors are used in this 3D reconstruction. We attached an Azure Kinect camera with a Lucid Helios camera, to form a data acquisition system. The transformation of two camera poses can be estimated by SfM (Struct from Motion) algorithm [13]. Azure Kinect provides RGB-Depth streams for reconstruction while Lucid Helios camera is set to capture ToF raw measurement stream in both 75 MHz and 100 MHz. To the best of our knowledge, BundleFusion [4], with reconstruction error in millimeter level, is the start-of-the-art work to reconstruct a scene from RGB-D stream input. We reconstructed scenes from dense frames, estimated the camera poses of every frame via Bundle-Fusion and projected the reconstructed scene onto the camera pose to get a dense depth map.

## 4  Experiments

We will show that our method achieves the comprehensive correction of various errors in the ToF depth map, and surpasses the state-of-the-art work in quantitative evaluations, in both our datasets and other publicly available datasets. We use five modules to build the CNN used in this work, because this is the minimum number to achieve convergence of performance on iteration.

### 4.1  Error Removal

We first trained our CNN on the Synthetic dataset and tested it on its test set in different scenes. And for the Real-World dataset, we adopted the model trained on the Synthetic dataset and performed a fine-tuning. The model trained for 150 epochs on our Synthetic dataset and fine tuning for 30 epochs on our Real-World dataset. We compared our result to the ToF depth map directly output by camera without additional processing, which serves as the baseline.

**Table 1.** The performance of the depth map output by each module on test sets of Synthetic and RealWorld Dataset, expressed in absolute error and relative error (in the form of **cm/%**).

|  | Module1 | Module2 | Module3 | Module4 | Module5 |
|---|---|---|---|---|---|
| Synthetic | 2.59/1.10 | 1.74/0.78 | 1.58/0.72 | 1.49/0.68 | 1.46/0.67 |
| RealWorld | 2.51/1.56 | 2.10/1.30 | 1.94/1.22 | 1.84/1.15 | 1.79/1.12 |

Figure 3(a) qualitatively demonstrates the effectiveness of our method. There are many typical errors in the original ToF depth map. The first is the common imaging noise that exists in both cases. Secondly, there is a bathtub with high mirror reflectivity and concave shape in case 1, which forms a very typical local MPI; the corner in case 2 has the same but slighter effect. Thirdly, the mirror in case 1 has a very high specular reflectance and a very low retroreflectivity, resulting in most of the echo received in this direction is the signal which from other surfaces, this phenomenon also occurs in other surfaces that have a large angle with imaging plane. The last is low intensity, the black velvet curtain in case 2 with a very low reflectivity absorbed most of the light, lead to missing information in this part of the ToF depth map. All the errors mentioned above are strongly removed by our network architecture, and we could obtain a corrected depth map very close to the ground truth.

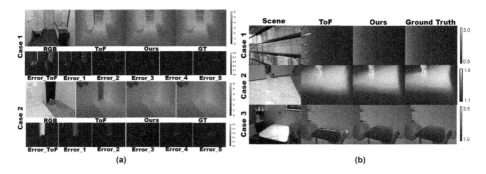

**Fig. 3.** (a) The results of ToF depth map error elimination in different stages, including RGB image (For visualize only, not the input of our method), ToF depth map, Result of our method, Ground Truth depth map, Absolute Error of the ToF depth map, Absolute Error of the depth map from module 1–5. (b) Results of our method on RealWorld dataset.

The six error maps below each case show the process of error removal from the ToF depth map by our proposed CNN. It can be seen from these error maps, that most of the imaging noise has been removed after the ToF depth map passes through the first module, and the relatively simple local MPI occurs in the bathtub and corner is reduced, too; while errors from other sources are still there. When the depth map passes through the second and third modules, various MPI begin to be eliminated. Also, with cascading of the modules, the feature map of each module captures higher and higher levels of information, so the understanding of the scene steadily increases. As a result, low intensity caused noise is gradually recovered, wrong depths are being corrected and missing depths are being filled. The last module refine the depth map from the antecedent module and is tend to convergence. Table 1 shows a quantitative evaluation that with iteration of modules, the performance gradually improves, and reach convergence on last two modules. This is the reason that we use five modules in total.

We selected several ToF depth maps with representative error patterns in different challenging scenes, which are a bookstore, kitchen, and dining room, respectively. From Fig. 3(b), it can be seen that our CNN still shows fine performance under the real-world dataset. In case 1, the depth on the lower reflectivity part of the bookshelf gap is completed. The general local MPI in case 2 makes the depth of the ToF camera notably larger around the corners, and our CNN outputs a result precisely removed the error. In case 3, the depth of the marble tabletop, which is affected by serious MPI due to the high specular reflectivity of the surface, is also corrected.

## 4.2    Compared to State-of-the-Art Methods

**Table 2.** Quantitative testing results of our method and other state-of-the-art methods on our dataset. Results with the best performance are marked in bold.

|  | Synthetic dataset | | RealWorld dataset | |
|---|---|---|---|---|
|  | MAE (cm) | Rela. MAE (%) | MAE (cm) | Rela. MAE (%) |
| ToF | 9.73 | 3.47 | 4.17 | 2.51 |
| Su et al. [22] | 4.23 | 1.78 | 3.32 | 2.21 |
| Agresti et al. [2] | 1.87 | 0.81 | 2.27 | 1.38 |
| Ours | **1.46** | **0.67** | **1.79** | **1.12** |

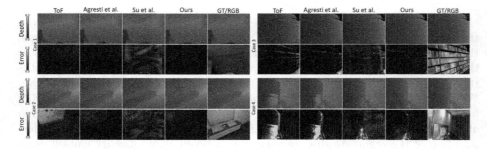

**Fig. 4.** Comparison between our method and other state-of-the-art methods. Each case shows the depth map and error map obtained by different methods, and provides the RGB image of the scene for reference.

**On Our Datasets.** We conducted a comprehensive evaluation to prove that our method is better than the state-of-the-art method. Specifically, we compare our work with Su et al. [22] and Agresti et al. [2], because they are representative and state-of-the-art work that focused on ToF depth error removal. The former takes only the raw correlation measurements at two modulation frequencies as input to predict a depth map in an end-to-end fashion. The latter input the depth map and intensity map at three modulation frequencies and make one residual prediction. We retrained them on our Synthetic and Real-World datasets to work with our data type using the same training procedure. Models are trained on Synthetic Dataset, and are fine tuned on RealWorld Dataset. These training procedures are all convergent to ensure reaching their optimal performance. Table 2 shows that our work surpassed other methods by a large margin, achieving the best performance on both datasets. Figure 4 shows a more intuitive and detailed comparison, with case 1 and case 2 on Synthetic dataset, case 3 and case 4 on our Real-World dataset. Our approach gracefully removed most of the error mentioned above, including local MPI in case 1, imaging noise and mirror reflection in case 2 and case 4, and typical low intensity in case 3, and gave a clean smooth depth map and error map close to zero.

These two methods, one overly relies on the fitting ability of CNN in terms of input and output, leading to artifacts and performance degradation in some area [22]; the other only performs a single error prediction via a rather small-scale network, thus is unable to detect and correct all kinds of error, especially the part that needs the understanding of scenes [2]. This also proves the advanced nature of iterative error correction from the negative side since it avoids these issues.

**Table 3.** Quantitative testing results of our method and other state-of-the-art methods on datasets where they were proposed. Results with the best performance are marked in bold. (*) is the result on its MPI removal network. Median and Interquartile Range (IQR) are calculated on error (not absolute error).

| Dataset | Datatype | Proposed approach on this dataset | Ours |
|---------|----------|-----------------------------------|------|
| Marco et al. [16] | Depth map | First quartile: 4 cm<br>Second quartile: 9 cm<br>Third quartile: 17 cm | **First quartile: 2.24 cm**<br>**Second quartile: 4.89 cm**<br>**Third quartile: 8.68 cm** |
| Su et al. [22] | Correlation maps in 40 MHz and 70 MHz | MAE: 2.9 cm<br>SSIM: 0.9631 | **MAE: 2.28 cm**<br>**SSIM: 0.9906** |
| Agresti et al. [2] | Depth, Amplitude and Intensity map in 20 MHz, 50 MHz and 60 MHz | (Synthetic) MAE: 7.49 cm<br>(RealWorld) MAE: 3.19 cm | **(Synthetic) MAE: 5.80 cm**<br>**(RealWorld) MAE: 2.95 cm** |
| Guo et al. (FLAT) [9] | Correlation maps in 10 MHz, 50 MHz, 75 MHz | **Median: −0.01 cm***<br>IQR: 2.63 cm<br>Percentile 90th: 4.16 cm | Median: −0.07 cm<br>**IQR: 1.75 cm**<br>**Percentile 90th: 2.60 cm** |

**On Other Datasets.** We also compared our approach on the datasets on which previous methods are proposed. We collected, to our best knowledge, all publicly available datasets in the recent years proposed for ToF error correction. We then trained the proposed CNN on these datasets, with the number of modules and Resblocks slightly adjusted. By adjusting the early fusion of our CNN, we enable their data to fit in our network, and compare our method with the native methods on these datasets with the same quantitative evaluation. The results are shown in Table 3, which clearly shows the excellence of our method since our approach outperforms the previous methods proposed on its dataset in most of the indicators. Through testing on different datasets, feeding different inputs, and comparing with different evaluation criteria, we demonstrated the superiority and robustness of our method.

## 5    Conclusion and Future Work

In this paper, we proposed a new method for ToF depth error removal. We have shown that an iteratively error removing CNN can produce a better depth map for ToF imaging, because it conforms to the nature of the ToF depth map and can avoid the inherent defects of CNN, theoretically and experimentally. We achieved this by analyzing ToF error removal principles, designing a CNN framework for this problem, introducing two new large datasets, and experimenting on different datasets. In future work, we plan to perform super-resolution to the depth map of the ToF camera so that it can be aligned with an RGB image.

## References

1. Agresti, G., Schaefer, H., Sartor, P., Zanuttigh, P.: Unsupervised domain adaptation for ToF data denoising with adversarial learning. In: Proceedings of the IEEE Conference on Computer Vision and Pattern Recognition, pp. 5584–5593 (2019)
2. Agresti, G., Zanuttigh, P.: Deep learning for multi-path error removal in ToF sensors. In: Proceedings of the European Conference on Computer Vision (ECCV) (2018)
3. Chen, Y., Ren, J., Cheng, X., Qian, K., Wang, L., Gu, J.: Very power efficient neural time-of-flight. In: The IEEE Winter Conference on Applications of Computer Vision, pp. 2257–2266 (2020)
4. Dai, A., Nießner, M., Zollhöfer, M., Izadi, S., Theobalt, C.: BundleFusion: real-time globally consistent 3D reconstruction using on-the-fly surface reintegration. ACM Trans. Graph. (ToG) **36**(4), 1 (2017)
5. Dorrington, A.A., Godbaz, J.P., Cree, M.J., Payne, A.D., Streeter, L.V.: Separating true range measurements from multi-path and scattering interference in commercial range cameras. In: Three-Dimensional Imaging, Interaction, and Measurement, vol. 7864, p. 786404. International Society for Optics and Photonics (2011)
6. Freedman, D., Smolin, Y., Krupka, E., Leichter, I., Schmidt, M.: SRA: fast removal of general multipath for ToF sensors. In: Fleet, D., Pajdla, T., Schiele, B., Tuytelaars, T. (eds.) ECCV 2014. LNCS, vol. 8689, pp. 234–249. Springer, Cham (2014). https://doi.org/10.1007/978-3-319-10590-1_16
7. Fuchs, S.: Multipath interference compensation in time-of-flight camera images. In: 2010 20th International Conference on Pattern Recognition, pp. 3583–3586. IEEE (2010)
8. Godbaz, J.P., Cree, M.J., Dorrington, A.A.: Closed-form inverses for the mixed pixel/multipath interference problem in AMCW lidar. In: Computational Imaging X, vol. 8296, p. 829618. International Society for Optics and Photonics (2012)
9. Guo, Q., Frosio, I., Gallo, O., Zickler, T., Kautz, J.: Tackling 3D ToF artifacts through learning and the flat dataset. In: Proceedings of the European Conference on Computer Vision (ECCV), pp. 368–383 (2018)
10. Gupta, M., Nayar, S.K., Hullin, M.B., Martin, J.: Phasor imaging: a generalization of correlation-based time-of-flight imaging. ACM Trans. Graph. (ToG) **34**(5), 1–18 (2015)
11. Hansard, M., Lee, S., Choi, O., Horaud, R.P.: Time-of-flight cameras: principles, methods and applications. Springer Science and Business Media (2012). https://doi.org/10.1007/978-1-4471-4658-2

12. He, Y., Liang, B., Zou, Y., He, J., Yang, J.: Depth errors analysis and correction for time-of-flight (ToF) cameras. Sensors **17**(1), 92 (2017)
13. Izadi, S., et al.: KinectFusion: real-time 3D reconstruction and interaction using a moving depth camera. In: Proceedings of the 24th Annual ACM Symposium on User Interface Software and Technology, pp. 559–568 (2011)
14. Jarabo, A., Marco, J., Muñoz, A., Buisan, R., Jarosz, W., Gutierrez, D.: A framework for transient rendering. ACM Trans. Graph. (ToG) **33**(6), 1–10 (2014)
15. Jongenelen, A.P., Bailey, D.G., Payne, A.D., Dorrington, A.A., Carnegie, D.A.: Analysis of errors in ToF range imaging with dual-frequency modulation. IEEE Trans. Instrum. Meas. **60**(5), 1861–1868 (2011)
16. Marco, J., et al.: DeepToF: off-the-shelf real-time correction of multipath interference in time-of-flight imaging. ACM Trans. Graph. (ToG) **36**(6), 1–12 (2017)
17. Naik, N., Kadambi, A., Rhemann, C., Izadi, S., Raskar, R., Bing Kang, S.: A light transport model for mitigating multipath interference in time-of-flight sensors. In: Proceedings of the IEEE Conference on Computer Vision and Pattern Recognition, pp. 73–81 (2015)
18. Qiu, D., Pang, J., Sun, W., Yang, C.: Deep end-to-end alignment and refinement for time-of-flight RGB-D module. In: Proceedings of the IEEE International Conference on Computer Vision, pp. 9994–10003 (2019)
19. Ronneberger, O., Fischer, P., Brox, T.: U-Net: convolutional networks for biomedical image segmentation. In: Navab, N., Hornegger, J., Wells, W.M., Frangi, A.F. (eds.) MICCAI 2015. LNCS, vol. 9351, pp. 234–241. Springer, Cham (2015). https://doi.org/10.1007/978-3-319-24574-4_28
20. Sarbolandi, H., Lefloch, D., Kolb, A.: Kinect range sensing: structured-light versus time-of-flight Kinect. Comput. Vis. Image Underst. **139**, 1–20 (2015)
21. Song, S., Shim, H.: Depth reconstruction of translucent objects from a single time-of-flight camera using deep residual networks. In: Jawahar, C.V., Li, H., Mori, G., Schindler, K. (eds.) ACCV 2018. LNCS, vol. 11365, pp. 641–657. Springer, Cham (2019). https://doi.org/10.1007/978-3-030-20873-8_41
22. Su, S., Heide, F., Wetzstein, G., Heidrich, W.: Deep end-to-end time-of-flight imaging. In: Proceedings of the IEEE Conference on Computer Vision and Pattern Recognition, pp. 6383–6392 (2018)
23. Wang, Z., Chen, J., Hoi, Steven C.H.: Deep learning for image super-resolution: a survey. IEEE Trans. Patt. Anal. Mach. Intell., 1–1 (2020). https://doi.org/10.1109/TPAMI.2020.2982166

# Blurred Image Recognition: A Joint Motion Deblurring and Classification Loss-Aware Approach

Wenjie Zhang[1] and Zhi Wang[1,2(✉)]

[1] Tsinghua Shenzhen International Graduate School, Shenzhen, China
`zhang-wj18@mails.tsinghua.edu.cn`, `wangzhi@sz.tsinghua.edu.cn`
[2] Peng Cheng Laboratory, Shenzhen, China

**Abstract.** Image motion blur can severely affect the performance of the image recognition model. Traditional methods to tackle this problem usually involve image motion deblurring to improve the image quality before its recognition. However, traditional motion deblurring methods try to minimize the pixel-level distance between the deblurred image and the original image, which is not directly designed for improving the image recognition accuracy of the deblurred image. In this paper, we propose a joint motion deblurring and classification loss-aware solution. First, we introduce recognition loss into the motion deblurring model to improve the semantic quality of the deblurred image. Furthermore, we design a motion-blurred image recognition framework that involves both a motion deblurring module and an image recognition module, which enables the joint learning of the two modules. Finally, we propose to enhance the motion deblurring network with parameterized short-cut connections (PSCs) for balancing the importance between low-level and high-level features in the deblurring process. Experiments on our synthesized datasets have shown the effectiveness of our methods, with significant improvement in both SSIM and classification accuracy, as well as the perceptual quality of the deblurred images.

**Keywords:** Image motion deblurring · Image classification · Joint learning · Neural networks · Deep learning

## 1 Introduction

### 1.1 Motivation

Convolutional neural networks (CNNs) have achieved state-of-the-art performance on many image recognition tasks including image classification, object detection and segmentation. However, the recognition performance of CNN models can suffer severely from image degradation, especially motion blur [16].

Traditional methods for solving this problem try to deblur the image before its recognition. However, state-of-the-art image motion deblurring methods are

© Springer Nature Switzerland AG 2021
I. Farkaš et al. (Eds.): ICANN 2021, LNCS 12892, pp. 106–117, 2021.
https://doi.org/10.1007/978-3-030-86340-1_9

aiming at reducing the pixel error of deblurred image, while deblurred image with lower pixel error does not always have better recognition result (see Fig. 1). Therefore, it is necessary to develop a motion deblurring method that is targeted at increasing the recognition performance of deblurred images.

In this paper, we try to improve the learning-based image motion deblurring methods towards generating more recognizable deblurred images in two directions: loss function and model structure. For loss function, we propose to use recognition loss and joint learning strategy in the training of motion deblurring models; for model structure, we propose to introduce parameterized shortcut connections (PSCs) into motion deblurring models that are based on fully convolutional network (FCN) structure. Experiments on our synthesized datasets have shown that our methods can not only improve the classification accuracy on the deblurred image, but also improve the perceptual quality of the deblurred image.

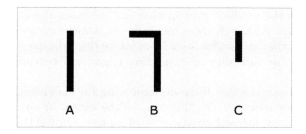

**Fig. 1.** Deblurred image with lower pixel error does not always have better recognition result. Here A represents the sharp image, while B and C are two deblurred versions. B has 4 different pixels with A while C has 5 different pixels with A. Nevertheless, A and C are both recognized as number 1, while B is classified to number 7.

### 1.2   Contributions

The main contributions of our work can be summarized as follows:

1. Firstly, to improve the performance of motion deblurring model with respect to the classification accuracy on deblurred images, we propose to introduce recognition loss into the learning process of the motion deblurring model. This loss function can effectively lead the motion deblurring model towards generating deblurred images that are not only semantically closer to sharp images and more recognizable by the classification model, but also have higher SSIM, which is proved to be close the human perceptual quality.
2. Furthermore, we propose a joint training framework that enables the joint learning of image motion deblurring model and classification model. Through the iterative training of these two models, the classification model can better recognize the deblurred images produced by the deblurring model and the deblurring model can generate deblurred images that are more recognizable by the classification model.

3. Finally, we propose to introduce parameterized shortcut connection (PSC) into the deblurring network, so that the model can be able to learn how to balance the importance between low-level and high-level image features, which are both important for generating desirable deblurred results with both fine details and accurate semantic information.

## 2   Related Works

### 2.1   Image Classification

Image classification is the fundamental task in computer vision. State-of-the-art methods have achieved better performance than traditional methods with CNNs. VGG [18] and GoogleNet [20] have shown that larger network depth can bring significant increase in classification accuracy. ResNet [6] introduces residual learning, which facilitates the gradient propagation and makes it possible to train a very deep network. DenseNet [7] proposes densely connection, which further facilitates the gradient propagation and increases the utilization of previous feature maps. Although these methods can achieve considerable accuracy on sharp images, they can suffer a lot from image degradation like motion blur, probably due to the difficulty of extracting edges and textures from blurred images.

There are some works that focus on improving the classification accuracy on noisy [12] and low-resolution [2]. However, to the extent of our knowledge, few research interests are focused on the case of motion blur. [11] proposes to use the early layers of the pretrained image recovering model to initialize the early layers of the classification model. However, the image features used for recovering and classification might be very different. The former contains many details and localization information, while the latter focuses on the high-level semantic information. Besides, it requires the recovering model and the classification model to have the exactly same architecture in the early layers, which restricts the utilization of state-of-the-art recovering and classification models which has different architectures specifically designed for each task.

### 2.2   Single Image Motion Deblurring

Motion blur is commonly modeled as the convolution between a sharp image and a blur kernel [9,15]: $I_B(x,y) = I_S(x,y) * k(x,y) + n(x,y)$, where $I_B$, $I_S$, $k$ and $n$ represent motion-blurred image, latent sharp image, blur kernel and additional noise, respectively. Single image motion deblurring methods can be roughly divided into two categories: optimization-based and learning-based.

**Optimization-Based Image Motion Deblurring.** Approaches in this literature estimate $k$ and $I_S$ by minimizing the distance between $I_B$ and $I_S * k$. Many natural image priors have been proposed as regularization terms for this optimization goal, including total variation minimization [3], dark channel prior [15], and learned prior [8].

**Learning-Based Image Motion Deblurring.** In recent years, state-of-the-art motion deblurring methods are based on deep learning. DMCNN [14] uses end-to-end multi-scale CNN to predict latent sharp image directly from blurred input and trains the model with MSE loss. SRN [21] proposes to use recurrent structure for deblurring. DeblurGAN [9] uses adversarial loss and perceptual loss for generating more realistic deblurred images. Nevertheless, most loss functions used by these methods are not directly aimed at increasing the semantic correctness and recognition accuracy of the deblurred results. The perceptual loss can also improve the semantic quality of deblurred images. However, it tries to minimize the distance between the feature maps of sharp and deblurred images, while our method tries to minimize the distance between the recognition results and ground-truth labels, which is a stronger constraint for the deblurring model that can lead it towards generating more semantically correct deblurred image.

## 3    Methods

### 3.1    Task Formulation

Our main goal is to improve the recognition accuracy upon deblurred image by improving the semantic quality of deblurred image produced by motion deblurring model. In the following sections, we will denote the classification model as $R$ and the motion deblurring model as $D$. $x, y, z$ are the motion-blurred observation, ground-truth sharp image, and ground-truth classification label, respectively. $\hat{y}$ is the deblurred image, and $\hat{z}$ is the predicted image label:

$$\hat{y} = D(x), \hat{z} = R(\hat{y}) = R(D(x)). \tag{1}$$

### 3.2    Recognition Loss

We propose to introduce recognition loss into image motion deblurring. It is defined as the classification loss of the deblurred images produced by $D$, given $R$ pretrained on sharp images. The recognition loss can be written as below, where $L_{cla}$ is the classification loss of $R$:

$$L_{rec}(x, z) = L_{cla}(R(D(x)), z), \tag{2}$$

During experiments, we have found that when only using recognition loss, the training of motion deblurring model can not converge to a meaningful state. Inspired by many previous motion deblurring methods [14,21] which have used the MSE criterion and achieved good convergence with respect to both faster speed and better local minimum, we combine the recognition loss with the MSE criterion in order to make the training process more stable:

$$L_{mse}(x, y) = \frac{1}{WHC}||y - D(x)||_2^2, \tag{3}$$

where $W, H, C$ represent the width, height, and number of channels of the image, respectively. And the final loss function for the deblurring model is the weighted sum of recognition loss and MSE loss, with a hyperparameter $\lambda$ used for balancing the importance between the two loss functions:

$$L = L_{mse} + \lambda \cdot L_{rec}. \tag{4}$$

### 3.3  Joint Training Framework

The recognition loss can be seen as a supervisor for the $D$ that leads it towards generating more semantically correct and recognizable results. From another perspective, we can also use it as a classifier for the deblurred images, and train it on the deblurred images that are produced by $D$. Specifically, $R$ is originally pretrained on the labelled sharp images subjected to natural sharp image distribution ($x \sim p_{sharp}$), and learns a mapping from $p_{sharp}$ to $p_{label}$. However, when we use it for classifying the deblurred image, the input is the deblurred result $D(x)$, which has a different distribution ($D(x) \sim p_D$) with sharp image. To deal with this distribution shift, we propose to further fine-tune $R$ on the deblurred images produced by $D$, so it can also learn the mapping from $p_D$ to $p_{label}$ and classify the deblurred images better. After the fine-tuning, $R$ now becomes a better supervisor for $D$ which can produce more accurate recognition loss and can supervise the training of $D$ more effectively. Therefore, we propose to train $D$ and $R$ iteratively and let the two models learn from each other in a joint manner.

The joint training framework is illustrated as Fig. 2. $D$ and $R$ are trained iteratively in order to let the two models mutually. Note that when $N_D$ and $N_R$ are both equal to 1, the joint training algorithm is similar to concatenate these two models into a single unified model. However, the converging speed of the two models are quite different. In our experiments, the time cost for training the deblurring model is about 16× longer than the classification model. Therefore, training these two models as a unified network is not the optimal solution. Instead, our joint learning algorithm provides a more flexible mechanism for controlling the training paces of the two models by training them iteratively. The training process can be described as Algorithm 1.

### 3.4  Parameterized Shortcut Connection

Most state-of-the-art learning-based motion deblurring methods [9,21] have adopted the fully convolutional network (FCN) [13] structure. Shortcut connections are used in FCN to facilitate gradient propagation and combine low-level features and high-level features, which are both important in motion deblurring. The former can provide detailed and localization information, while the latter can provide semantic information.

The fusion method of shortcut connection is important for effectively combining low-level and high-level features. In [17], the fusion is implemented by channel-wise concatenation. In [13,21], the fusion is implemented by element-wise addition, which is proved to work well in motion deblurring. However, the importance of low-level features and high-level features might be different in

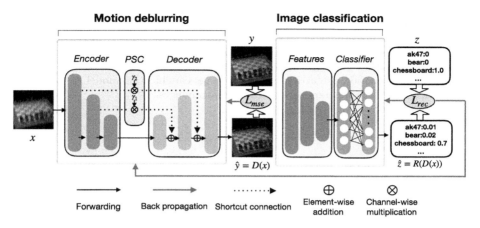

**Fig. 2.** Joint training framework. Here $x$, $y$, $z$ are the input blurred image, ground-truth sharp image and ground-truth classification label, respectively. PSC is short for parameterized shortcut connection. During the training phase, the two modules are trained iteratively. Note that all learning-based motion deblurring and image classification models can be embedded into this framework.

motion deblurring. Inspired by the highway networks [19], which uses carry gate and transform gate to control the proportion of input signals and transformed signals passed to the next layer, we propose to introduce parameterized shortcut connection (PSC) into the motion deblurring model, which can balance the importance of low-level and high-level feature maps. Specifically, each channel of low-level feature map is multiplied with a learnable parameter that controls the importance of low-level feature on this channel before passed through the shortcut connection and added with the high-level feature map. The learnable parameters enable the model to automatically learn to decide the importance of low-level features and high-level features from data (see Fig. 2).

The original shortcut connection based on element-wise addition used by [21] can be described as:

$$a_i = F_i(a_{i-1} + a_j), \qquad (5)$$

where $F_i$ is the non-linear transformation in the i-th layer, $a_i$ is the output of $F_i$, and $a_j$ is the output from an early layer before $a_{i-1}$. Note that this is not the same with the residual connection. Here $a_i$ and $a_j$ can have a large distance in the network, usually representing low-level image features and high-level semantic features, respectively.

In comparison, our PSC has a group of learnable parameters $\gamma$, which is used to control the importance of low-level feature:

$$a_i = F_i(a_{i-1} + \gamma a_j) \qquad (6)$$

where $\gamma$ is a weight vector that has an equal length with $a_j$ in channel dimension. Here the multiplication is channel-wise, and $\gamma_k$ is the weight of the k-th channel in $a_j$.

---

**Algorithm 1.** Joint learning algorithm

---

**Input:** Motion blurred image $x$, latent sharp image $y$, classification label $z$, number of epochs $N$, number of steps for training $D$ ($R$) in each epoch $N_D$ ($N_R$), the learning rate of $D$ ($R$) denoted as $\eta_D$ ($\eta_R$), the weight of recognition loss $\lambda$.

**Output:** Image motion deblurring model $D$, image classification model $R$.

  Initialize $R$ with parameters pretrained on sharp images.

  **for** $i = 1 : N$ **do**

    **for** $j = 1 : N_D$ **do**

      $\theta_D \leftarrow \theta_D - \eta_D \cdot \frac{\Delta L(x,y,z|\theta_R)}{\Delta \theta_D}$

    **end for**

    **for** $k = 1 : N_R$ **do**

      $\theta_R \leftarrow \theta_R - \eta_R \cdot \frac{\Delta L_{cla}(x,z|\theta_D)}{\Delta \theta_R}$

    **end for**

  **end for**

---

## 4    Experiments

### 4.1    Dataset

To evaluate the classification accuracy upon motion-blurred images, we need motion-blurred images paired with their ground-truth classification labels. However, to the extent of our knowledge, there is no such dataset available by now. Therefore, we have to synthesize data for the validation of our methods. There are some motion deblurring datasets that have paired sharp and blurred images. However, labelling these images needs extensive human labor with a relatively high cost. A more cost-effective way for synthesizing our dataset is to generate motion-blurred versions of the sharp images from existing image classification datasets. We use two datasets in our experiments: PASCAL VOC 2012 [4] and Caltech256 [5].

Many methods have been proposed for generating motion-blurred image from single sharp image. In our work, we adopt the method introduced in [1] since it can generate realistic motion-blurred images and has been adopted by many previous works [9,10]. [1] proposed to generate random 2-D camera trajectory with a Markov process and synthesize the blur kernel from the trajectory with bilinear interpolation.

### 4.2    Baselines and Ablation Groups

The recognition loss and joint training strategy can actually be applied to any learning-based motion deblurring and classification method, and the PSC can also be used in any motion deblurring method which uses FCN as the network architecture. To verify the effectiveness of our methods, we choose SRN [21] as the basic deblurring model. And we use DenseNet-121 [7] as the classification model to classify the deblurred images and provide recognition loss for the deblurring model, which is pretrained on ImageNet and fine-tuned on the sharp images from Caltech256/PASCAL VOC.

To the extent of our knowledge, there are currently few researches on improving the classification accuracy of motion-blurred images. One comparable method is DeblurGAN [9], which uses perceptual loss produced by pretrained classification model for improving the semantic quality and recognition accuracy of the deblurred image. We transplant the perceptual loss to the training of SRN. Since the training can not converge when SRN is solely trained on perceptual loss in our experiments, we also combined it with MSE loss. This baseline is denoted as SRN-P. We use two implementations of SRN-P. One of them is the implementation described in [9], which uses the output of the third convolutional layer after the third pooling layer (denoted as $VGG_{3,3}$) of VGG19, denoted as SRN-P (VGG). For VGG19, we also use the parameters pretrained on ImageNet and fine-tune it on the sharp images from Caltech256/PASCAL VOC. Another implementation is using the output of the first dense block in DenseNet-121 (we choose this layer because the number of convolutional layers with stride $>1$ before it is 7, same as $VGG_{3,3}$) for producing perceptual loss, denoted as SRN-P (Dense). Besides, we also conducted ablation studies to evaluate how much improvement can each part of our method brings. Blurred and Blurred-D both use blurred image as the input of the classification model, while other methods perform motion-deblurring on the input beforehand. The methods are listed as below.

- **Blurred**: Input motion-blurred image into DenseNet-121.
- **Blurred-D**: Input motion-blurred image into DenseNet-121 trained on the blurred images.
- **SRN**: The original SRN trained with MSE loss.
- **SRN-P (VGG)**: SRN trained with MSE loss and perceptual loss produced by $VGG_{3,3}$.
- **SRN-P (Dense)**: SRN trained with MSE loss and perceptual loss produced by the first denseblock in DenseNet-121.
- **SRN-PSC**: SRN equipped with PSC trained with MSE loss.
- **SRN-R**: SRN trained with MSE loss and recognition loss produced by DenseNet-121.
- **SRN-RJ**: SRN-R trained using joint learning strategy.
- **SRN-PSC-RJ**: SRN-PSC trained with MSE loss and recognition loss using joint learning strategy.

### 4.3    Implementation

We use PyTorch 1.3.1 for the implementation. The models are trained on a NVIDIA GeForce RTX 2080 Ti GPU with CUDA 10.0. We use parameters pretrained on ImageNet to initialize DenseNet-121, then fine-tuned it on our synthesized datasets. This transfer learning process can alleviate the over-fitting caused by small data size and reduce training time. The optimizers for SRN and DenseNet-121 are Adam and SGD (with momentum = 0.9 and Nesterov momentum enabled), respectively. For $\lambda$, we try several values in the training process of SRN-R on the PASCAL VOC 2012 dataset (note that SRN-R is equal to SRN when $\lambda = 0$) and find that the best result is achieved when $\lambda$ is set to $1e-2$ (see Table 2), so we use this value in all experiments. This value is relatively low because the recognition loss is approximately 1–2 orders of magnitude larger than the MSE loss. At each epoch, SRN is trained for 2000 steps, then DenseNet-121 is trained for 160 steps. The initial learning rate is set to $1e-2$ for $\gamma_1$ and $\gamma_2$ in PSC, and $1e-4$ for other parameters in SRN. The learning rate for DenseNet-121 is set to $1e-4$ initially and drops by 0.5 after every 5 epochs. All models are trained until the loss stops dropping in 3 epochs. For SRN-PSC-RJ, training converges after 20 epochs.

**Table 1.** Experimental results: Image classification

| Methods | PASCAL VOC | Caltech256 | |
| --- | --- | --- | --- |
| | mAP | Accuracy | Top-5 accuracy |
| Blurred | 0.544 | 0.408 | 0.686 |
| Blurred-D | 0.594 | 0.429 | 0.713 |
| SRN | 0.641 | 0.601 | 0.811 |
| SRN-P (VGG) | 0.645 | 0.610 | 0.815 |
| SRN-P (Dense) | 0.648 | 0.614 | 0.817 |
| SRN-PSC | 0.665 | 0.621 | 0.821 |
| SRN-R | 0.652 | 0.620 | 0.826 |
| SRN-RJ | 0.661 | 0.626 | 0.830 |
| SRN-PSC-RJ | **0.687** | **0.631** | **0.837** |

**Table 2.** mAP on PASCAL VOC 2012 under different values of $\lambda$

| $\lambda$ | 0 | $1e-3$ | $1e-2$ | $1e-1$ | 1.0 |
| --- | --- | --- | --- | --- | --- |
| **mAP** | 0.641 | 0.648 | **0.652** | 0.639 | 0.624 |

**Table 3.** Experimental results: Motion deblurring

| lMethods | PASCAL VOC | | Caltech256 | |
|---|---|---|---|---|
| | PSNR | SSIM | PSNR | SSIM |
| SRN | 24.10 | 0.704 | 25.89 | 0.780 |
| SRN-P (VGG) | 24.08 | 0.712 | 25.57 | 0.785 |
| SRN-P (Dense) | 23.57 | 0.716 | 25.47 | 0.792 |
| SRN-PSC | **24.19** | 0.723 | **26.03** | 0.787 |
| SRN-R | 24.03 | 0.726 | 25.59 | 0.801 |
| SRN-RJ | 23.69 | 0.729 | 25.46 | 0.807 |
| SRN-PSC-RJ | 23.73 | **0.733** | 25.71 | **0.815** |

## 4.4 Experimental Results

We will show and discuss the experiment results qualitatively and quantitatively. Some deblurred results produced by our methods are shown in Fig. 3. It can be seen that our (SRN-PSC-RJ) deblurred results have fewer artifacts (the unnatural patterns that are often presented in recovered images) and higher perceptual quality than the original SRN.

From the results on image classification (see Table 1), we can conclude that:

1. Comparing SRN-R and SRN-P, we can see that both perceptual loss and recognition loss can increase the classification accuracy on deblurred images by forcing the deblurring model to generate deblurred images with richer semantic information. Recognition loss brings larger improvement than perceptual loss because rather than reducing the distance between high-level features of sharp image and deblurred image, the recognition loss exerts a stronger force on the deblurring model by reducing the distance between the recognition results on deblurred images with ground-truth labels.
2. Comparing SRN-R and SRN-RJ, we can see that joint training strategy further improves the classification accuracy/mAP on deblurred images. This verifies that $D$ and $R$ can improve mutually through the joint learning process.
3. Comparing SRN and SRN-PSC, we can see that the proposed PSC can improve the classification accuracy upon deblurred image. This is probably because PSC can improve the overall quality of the deblurred image with respect to both PSNR and SSIM (see Table 3).

From the results on motion deblurring (see Table 3 and Fig. 3), we can see that our methods can improve the image quality in terms of SSIM, which is considered to be closer to the human perceptual quality than PSNR. In the meanwhile, PSNR drops because increasing PSNR is equivalent to reducing MSE loss, and adding recognition loss into the loss function will decrease the PSNR.

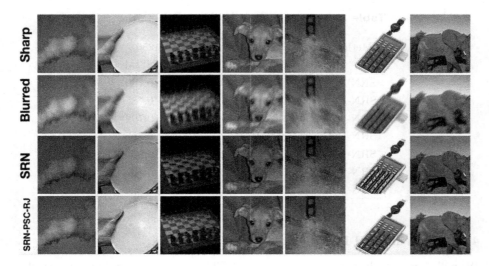

**Fig. 3.** Some deblurred results. It can be seen that our deblurred results have fewer artifacts and higher perceptual quality than the original SRN.

## 5   Conclusion

In this paper, we propose recognition loss in image motion deblurring, aiming at improving the semantic quality and classification accuracy of deblurred images. Furthermore, we propose to train the deblurring model and the classification model in a joint training framework to enable mutual learning of the two models. Experiments on our synthesized datasets have shown that the recognition loss and joint training strategy can improve not only classification accuracy on the deblurred images, but also SSIM and the perceptual quality of the deblurred images. Finally, we introduce parameterized shortcut connection (PSC) into the motion deblurring model, which can improve the quality of the deblurred images in terms of both PSNR and SSIM.

**Acknowledgements.** This work is supported in part by NSFC (Grant No. 61872215), Shenzhen Science and Technology Program (Grant No. RCYX20200714114523079), and Shenzhen Nanshan District Ling-Hang Team Project (Grant No. LHTD20170005).

## References

1. Boracchi, G., Foi, A.: Modeling the performance of image restoration from motion blur. IEEE Trans. Image Process. **21**(8), 3502–3517 (2012)
2. Cai, D., Chen, K., Qian, Y., Kämäräinen, J.K.: Convolutional low-resolution fine-grained classification. Pattern Recogn. Lett. **119**, 166–171 (2019)
3. Chan, T.F., Wong, C.K.: Total variation blind deconvolution. IEEE Trans. Image Process. Publ. IEEE Signal Process. Soc. **7**(3), 370 (1998)

 4. Everingham, M., Van Gool, L., Williams, C.K.I., Winn, J., Zisserman, A.: The PASCAL visual object classes challenge 2012 (VOC2012) results (2012). http://www.pascal-network.org/challenges/VOC/voc2012/workshop/index.html
 5. Griffin, G., Holub, A., Perona, P.: The caltech 256 (technical report). Caltech Computation and Neural Systems (2006)
 6. He, K., Zhang, X., Ren, S., Sun, J.: Deep residual learning for image recognition. IEEE (2016)
 7. Huang, G., Liu, Z., Laurens, V., Weinberger, K.Q.: Densely connected convolutional networks. IEEE Computer Society (2016)
 8. Kai, Z., Zuo, W., Gu, S., Lei, Z.: Learning deep CNN denoiser prior for image restoration. In: 2017 IEEE Conference on Computer Vision and Pattern Recognition (CVPR) (2017)
 9. Kupyn, O., Budzan, V., Mykhailych, M., Mishkin, D., Matas, J.: DeblurGAN: blind motion deblurring using conditional adversarial networks. In: 2018 IEEE/CVF Conference on Computer Vision and Pattern Recognition (CVPR) (2018)
10. Kupyn, O., Martyniuk, T., Wu, J., Wang, Z.: DeblurGAN-v2: deblurring (orders-of-magnitude) faster and better. IEEE (2019)
11. Liu, D., Cheng, B., Wang, Z., Zhang, H., Huang, T.S.: Enhance visual recognition under adverse conditions via deep networks. IEEE Trans. Image Process. **28**(9), 4401–4412 (2017)
12. Liu, D., Wen, B., Liu, X., Wang, Z., Huang, T.S.: When image denoising meets high-level vision tasks: a deep learning approach (2017)
13. Long, J., Shelhamer, E., Darrell, T.: Fully convolutional networks for semantic segmentation. IEEE Trans. Pattern Anal. Mach. Intell. **39**(4), 640–651 (2015)
14. Nah, S., Hyun Kim, T., Mu Lee, K.: Deep multi-scale convolutional neural network for dynamic scene deblurring. In: Proceedings of the IEEE Conference on Computer Vision and Pattern Recognition, pp. 3883–3891 (2017)
15. Pan, J., Sun, D., Pfister, H., Yang, M.H.: Blind image deblurring using dark channel prior. In: 2016 IEEE Conference on Computer Vision and Pattern Recognition (CVPR) (2016)
16. Pei, Y., Huang, Y., Zou, Q., Zang, H., Zhang, X., Wang, S.: Effects of image degradations to CNN-based image classification. arXiv preprint arXiv:1810.05552 (2018)
17. Ronneberger, O., Fischer, P., Brox, T.: U-Net: convolutional networks for biomedical image segmentation. In: Navab, N., Hornegger, J., Wells, W.M., Frangi, A.F. (eds.) MICCAI 2015. LNCS, vol. 9351, pp. 234–241. Springer, Cham (2015). https://doi.org/10.1007/978-3-319-24574-4_28
18. Simonyan, K., Zisserman, A.: Very deep convolutional networks for large-scale image recognition. Computer Science (2014)
19. Srivastava, R.K., Greff, K., Schmidhuber, J.: Highway networks. Computer Science (2015)
20. Szegedy, C., Wei, L., Jia, Y., Sermanet, P., Rabinovich, A.: Going deeper with convolutions. IEEE Computer Society (2014)
21. Tao, X., Gao, H., Wang, Y., Shen, X., Wang, J., Jia, J.: Scale-recurrent network for deep image deblurring. In: 2018 IEEE/CVF Conference on Computer Vision and Pattern Recognition (2018)

# Learning How to Zoom In: Weakly Supervised ROI-Based-DAM for Fine-Grained Visual Classification

Wenjie Chen[1,2(✉)], Shuang Ran[2], Tian Wang[2], and Lihong Cao[1,2,3]

[1] State Key Laboratory of Media Convergence and Communication,
Communication University of China, Beijing, China
`jessiechen@cuc.edu.cn`
[2] Neuroscience and Intelligent Media Institute, Communication University of China,
Beijing, China
`{rans,tian_wang}@cuc.edu.cn`
[3] State Key Laboratory of Mathematical Engineering and Advanced Computing,
Wuxi, China
`lihong.cao@cuc.edu.cn`

**Abstract.** Fine-grained visual classification (FGVC) is challenging due to the difficulty of finding discriminative features and insufficient labeled training data. How to efficiently localize the subtle but discriminative features with limited data is not straightforward. In this paper, we propose a simple yet efficient region of interest based data augmentation method (ROI-based-DAM) to handle the circumstance. The proposed ROI-based-DAM can first localize the most discriminative regions without the need of bounding box or part annotations. Based on these regions, ROI-based-DAM then carries out selective sampling and multi-scale cropping for constructing a series of high-quality ROI-based images. Thanks to its simplicity, our method can be easily implemented in the standard training and inference phases to boost the fined-grained classification accuracy. Our experimental results on extensive FGVC benchmark datasets show that the baseline model such as ResNeXt-50 can achieve competitive state-of-the-art performance by utilizing the proposed ROI-based-DAM, which demonstrate its effectiveness.

**Keywords:** Fine-grained visual classification · Region of interest based data augmentation · Weakly supervision

## 1 Introduction

Fine-Grained Visual Classification (FGVC) has a history of more than 20 years [1], which has always been a frequent subject in the field of computer vision. FGVC is defined to solve the problem of distinguishing subclasses of the same kind, such as species of the bird.

© Springer Nature Switzerland AG 2021
I. Farkaš et al. (Eds.): ICANN 2021, LNCS 12892, pp. 118–130, 2021.
https://doi.org/10.1007/978-3-030-86340-1_10

Compared with general image classification, FGVC is more challenging because it has lower inter-class variances and higher inner-class variances. Moreover, insufficient labeled data for training in FGVC makes it harder to distinguish between different similar objects.

Data augmentation such as center/random cropping is a common technique for data preprocessing and has been proven to play a positive role in improving generalization performance in computer vision tasks. However, adopting them blindly might make the training inefficient as these methods are independent of the image context. See Fig. 1 for some failure cases that center cropping drops out some informative regions of birds.

In this paper, we propose a region of interest based data augmentation method, ROI-based-DAM, to solve the problem of inefficient training caused by data augmentation methods independent of image context. See Fig. 1 for some examples of the proposed ROI-based-DAM. Our method is inspired by the eye movement trajectory when humans try to distinguish two or more similar objects, we assume that it is essential to pay attention to the most discriminative regions as well as the global structure of objects or the complementary feature regions.

**Fig. 1.** Comparison between center image cropping and the proposed ROI-based image cropping. Given the same images, the first row shows the results of center image cropping; the second row shows the results of the proposed ROI-based image cropping (here $K = 2$ for explanation; $K$ is the number of multi-scale ROIs generated by ROI-based-DAM).

ROI-based-DAM is a weakly-supervised data augmentation method which only requires the fine-grained classification labels. The basic idea of ROI-based-DAM is to localize the most discriminative regions or ROI in the first place. Unlike traditional object localization methods such as Faster R-CNN [15], our method requires no bounding box annotation to generate ROI. Specifically, our method is based on Guided-Grad-CAM [16,17], an effective class-discriminative localization technique, to generate template ROI in each image. Then an ROI-based selective sampling method is designed to make template ROI more precise by generating several candidate ROIs in its neighborhood. Furthermore, based on these ROIs, we design a multi-scale image cropping method for constructing a series of high-quality ROI-based images from fine-scale to coarse-scale. The advantages of this method are two-fold. Firstly, it can compensate for the limitations of single-scale ROI cropping. Secondly, if the finest-scale ROI happens to hold the complete target object of which the scale is relatively small in an image, then the ROI-based multi-scale cropping can provide a series of images of the object from coarse-scale to fine-scale, which can be beneficial for convolutional neural network (CNN) to form a scale-invariant representation of the object.

In summary, the advantages of the proposed ROI-based-DAM are as follows:

- It can localize the most discriminative parts (template ROI) in a given image without any bounding box or part annotations;
- It can construct a series of high-quality ROI-based images of different scales at a very low cost;
- It can be easily implemented in the standard training and testing phases as an efficient data preprocessing method to boost the FGVC accuracy; hence can be regarded as an alternative to frequently-used data augmentation methods such as random cropping and center cropping.

## 2    Related Work

### 2.1    Fine-Grained Visual Classification

The past decade has seen the rapid development of deep learning in FGVC. Broadly, these methods can be organized into three main paradigms [20], i.e., fine-grained recognition (1) with localization-classification subnetworks; (2) with end-to-end feature encoding and (3) with external information. Since the idea of proposed ROI-based DAM is similar to the first paradigm to some extent, we will mainly review the previous works belong to this paradigm.

The basic idea of the first paradigm is to firstly capture discriminative parts by a localization network and then construct representations of these parts for the final classification. Spatial transformer [7] proposes a dynamic mechanism that can actively spatially transform an image for more accurate classification. Liu et al. [11] propose Fully Convolutional Attention Networks (FCANs) to glimpse local discriminative regions adaptive to different fine-grained domains under a reinforcement learning framework. Fu et al. [5] propose a recurrent attention convolutional neural network (RA-CNN) to search for the most informative regions from coarse-scale to finer-scale. Zhange et al. [23] propose a multi-attention convolutional neural network (MA-CNN) to do better part learning, where part generation and feature learning can reinforce each other. Yang et al. [22] propose Navigator-Teacher-Scrutinizer Network (NTS-Net) to locate the most informative regions in a self-supervised way. Zheng et al. [24] propose a Trilinear Attention Sampling Network (TASN) to learn important fine-grained features from hundreds of part proposals in an efficient teacher-student manner. Ding et al. [4] propose a Selective Sparse Sampling Networks (S3Ns) to capture fine-grained details as well as preserve the context at the same time. Liu et al. [10] propose a a novel Filtration and Distillation Learning (FDL) model to enhance the region attention of discriminate parts for FGVC.

Different from some of the methods described above, which adopt specific neural networks and elaborate loss functions to locate the most informative parts or regions of objects, the proposed ROI-based DAM method can directly locate the most informative regions by making the best use of Guided-Grad-CAM. Specifically, the proposed ROI-based-DAM only needs a pre-trained model to do localization, which make it simpler than previous methods.

## 2.2    Data Augmentation

To compensate for the inefficiency of random data augmentation, a few methods have been proposed to take data distribution into consideration. Ekin D. Cubuk *et al.* [2] propose AutoAugment to automatically search for improved data augmentation policies. Peng *et al.* [14] propose adversarial data augmentation to jointly optimize the data augmentation and network training phase. Hu *et al.* [6] propose Weakly Supervised Data Augmentation Network (WS-DAN) to explore the potential of data augmentation. The WS-DAN first generates attention maps to represent the object's discriminative parts and augment the image through attention cropping and attention dropping.

Amongst the methods above, our method is similar to WS-DAN at some extent. We both locate the most informative parts of object and zoom them in for learning details. Instead of doing attention dropping for finding other complementary feature regions, we merely do selective sampling and multi-scale cropping. In all, compared with WS-DAN, our ROI-based-DAM can be easier to implement in the standard training and inference phases at a very low cost.

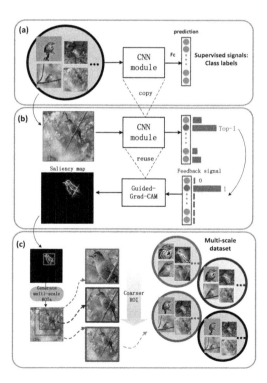

**Fig. 2.** An overview of the proposed ROI-based-DAM for fine-grained image recognition. (a) shows the process of finetuning a CNN module on the target dataset only using the fine-grained classification labels; (b) shows the process of generating a saliency map of an input image based on Guided-Grad-CAM; (c) shows the process of multi-scale ROI-based image cropping for constructing a set of high-quality images for training.

## 3    Methodology

In this section, we will introduce the proposed ROI-based-DAM in detail. See Fig. 2 for an overview of the proposed ROI-based-DAM.

### 3.1    Saliency Map Generation

Saliency map can demonstrate each pixel's unique quality [8] and plays an important role in analyzing image content and locating the region of interest. Before generating the saliency map, we firstly fine-tune a CNN module on the target FGVC dataset using only the fine-grained classification labels, gradually adapting the network to the distribution of target dataset. Then we adopt Guided-Grad-CAM, a class-discriminative localization technique, to generate the saliency map of input image. Specifically, each image $I \in R^{3 \times H \times W}$ (here $H$ and $W$ are the height and width of $I$, respectively) is forward propagated through the CNN module. The top-1 predicted class is regarded as the desired class. A feedback signal, of which the gradients are set to zero for all classes except the desired class, is backpropagated to the input image. We denote acquired Guided-Grad-CAM mask as $M_{ggcm} \in R^{3 \times H \times W}$. Finally, we convert $M_{ggcm}$ to a single-channel saliency map $M_{GSM}$ by summing up the elements in $M_{ggcm}$ along the channel axis and obtain a new single-channel tensor $M_G$ and then normalize each element in $M_G$ by (1):

$$M_{GSM}(i) = \frac{M_G(i) - M_{min}}{M_{max} + M_{min}} \tag{1}$$

where $M_{min} = minM_G$, $M_{max} = maxM_G$ and $1 \leq i \leq (3 \times H \times W)$. See Fig. 2 (b) for an example of a saliency map given an image.

### 3.2    Template ROI Localization

Based on the saliency map $M_{GSM}$ generated in the Sect. 3.1, we utilize the following steps to locate the template ROI of a given image. Firstly, we binarize the saliency map $M_{GSM}$ with the threshold $V_b$ using (2):

$$M_{BGSM}(i) = \begin{cases} 1, & M_{GSM}(i) \geq V_b \\ 0, & M_{GSM}(i) < V_b \end{cases} \tag{2}$$

Then, a standard grid of $N \times N$ is used to divide the $M_{BGSM}(i)$ into $N \times N$ subregions.

To make it clear, we define the pixel-of-interest as the pixel with a value of one in $M_{BGSM}$ and the significant score of each subregion as the proportion of pixels-of-interest inside it, which indicates the probability of a subregion being part of the desired class.

Furthermore, we define the subregion of interest $SR_{interest}$ as the subregion of which the significant score exceeds a pre-defined threshold $thr_s$.

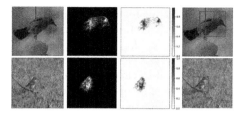

**Fig. 3.** The first column shows the original images. The second to fourth columns show the saliency maps, the significant score matrixes (the size of which are $64 \times 64$ for explanation), and the template ROIs (denoted by red rectangles) of corresponding images, respectively. (Color figure online)

$N_{sr}$ is the number of subregions of interest in a saliency map. For each subregion of interest $SR_{interest}(j)$, where $1 \leq j \leq N_{sr}$, we record the coordinates of its top-left corner and bottom-right corner, which are $(x_{j,min}, y_{j,min})$ and $(x_{j,max}, y_{j,max})$, respectively. The outermost boundary coordinates of these subregions of interest can be calculate by (3):

$$
\begin{aligned}
x_{min} &= \min_{1 \leq j \leq N_{sr}} \{x_{j,min}\} \\
y_{min} &= \min_{1 \leq j \leq N_{sr}} \{y_{j,min}\} \\
x_{max} &= \max_{1 \leq j \leq N_{sr}} \{x_{j,max}\} \\
y_{max} &= \max_{1 \leq j \leq N_{sr}} \{y_{j,max}\}
\end{aligned}
\tag{3}
$$

We then expand this region, of which the coordinates of top-left corner and bottom-right corner are $(x_{min}, y_{min})$ and $(x_{max}, y_{max})$, respectively, to a larger region having the same aspect ratio as input image $I$. This region we obtained from the above process is denoted as template ROI. See Fig. 3 for examples of localization of template ROI.

### 3.3 Selective Sampling

In order to do selective sampling, we firstly calculate the center $(x_c, y_c)$ of template ROI: $x_c = \frac{x_{min}+x_{max}}{2}$, $y_c = \frac{y_{min}+y_{max}}{2}$; and height $H_{roi}$ and width $W_{roi}$ of template ROI: $H_{roi} = y_{max} - y_{min}$ and $W_{roi} = x_{max} - x_{min}$.

Next, we build up the selective sampling functions for generating candidate ROIs in the neighborhood of template ROI. Set $x$ and $y$ are the central coordinates of a candidate ROI. We assume that the probability density function of $x$ follows gaussian distribution with a mean of $x_c$ and a standard deviation of g($W_{roi}$), where g($W_{roi}$) is a linear function of $W_{roi}$. $x$ can be written as: $x \sim N(x_c, g(W_{roi})^2)$. The similar assumption for $y$ is written as: $y \sim N(y_c, g(H_{roi})^2)$. For simplicity, we set $g(v) = \lambda \cdot v$, where $\lambda$ controls the dispersion of the distribution.

To bring more variation, we transform the scale of template ROI by merely multiplying a random variable $r$, which is sampled from a uniform distribution and can be written as $r \sim U(L_{low}, L_{high})$. Hence the height and width of a candidate ROI become $(r \cdot H_{roi})$ and $(r \cdot W_{roi})$, respectively.

We adopt the following method to check whether the most salient regions are inside a candidate ROI. We first sum up all elements inside the template ROI in a saliency map and get a template score denoted as $S_{troi}$. Then the score of a candidate ROI $S_{croi}$ is calculated. We only feed the candidate ROI whose $S_{croi}$ is no lower than $(thre_c \cdot S_{troi})$ to CNN.

To make it clear, we denote both template ROI and candidate ROI as finest-scale ROI. In addition, we only adopt selective sampling during training for alleviating model overfitting.

### 3.4   Multi-scale ROI-based Cropping

Given an image $I$, the coordinates of a finest-scale ROI are $x_{min}$, $y_{min}$, $x_{max}$ and $y_{max}$. $K$ is the number of ROIs needed to be generated and $K \geq 1$. The coordinates of the jth-scale ($1 \leq j \leq K$) ROI can be calculated by using (4):

$$x_{min}^{(j)} = x_{min} - \frac{(j-1) \cdot x_{min}}{K+1}, \; y_{min}^{(j)} = y_{min} - \frac{(j-1) \cdot y_{min}}{K+1}$$
$$x_{max}^{(j)} = x_{max} + \frac{(j-1) \cdot (W - x_{max})}{K+1}, \; y_{max}^{(j)} = y_{max} + \frac{(j-1) \cdot (H - y_{max})}{K+1}$$

$$(4)$$

After multi-scale ROI-based cropping, all these ROIs are resized to a same resolution. See Fig. 2 (c) for an example of the multi-scale ROI-based cropping.

### 3.5   Testing Strategy Based on ROI-Based-DAM

For an image $I$ in the testset, we firstly localize the template ROI based on its saliency map generated by Guided-Grad-CAM. Then, we generate ROIs of $K$ different scales using the method described in Sect. 3.4. All these ROIs are resized to the same resolution and fed to the CNN module. Finally, we do the pointwise summation of all these ROIs' softmax outputs.

## 4   Experiments

### 4.1   Dataset

We conduct experiments on three widely-used fine-grained image datasets: Caltech-UCSD Birds (CUB-200-2011) [19], FGVC-Aircraft [12] and Stanford-Cars [9]. Bounding box or part annotations are not available in all the experiments.

## 4.2    Implementation Details

We adopt ResNeXt-50 [21] as the backbone. For the baseline, ResNeXt-50 is firstly pre-trained on the ImageNet dataset [3] and then fine-tuned on different target datasets. There are four stages in ResNeXt-50 backbone. During training, we fix the parameters in stage one and fine-tune the rest. The model is trained using Stochastic Gradient Descent (SGD) with the momentum of 0.9, epoch number $N_{epoch}$ of 60, weight decay of 0.0001, label smoothing [18] of 0.1, and a mini-batch size of 16. The initial learning rate is set to 0.01 and is decayed to 0.001 in the last 40% epochs. The model is implemented using PyTorch [13] on a TitanXP GPU.

**Data Preprocessing.** In the training phase, each image is first resized to a resolution of (600, 600), from which regions of (448, 448) are randomly cropped. Besides, random horizontal image flipping is used when training. The data pre-processing of each image for inference is the same, except that a center region of (448, 448) is cropped.

**Table 1.** Comparison of our approach to recent results on CUB-200-2011, FGVC-Aircraft and Stanford Cars

| Method | CUB | Aircraft | Cars |
|---|---|---|---|
| FCAN [11] | 84.3 | – | 91.5 |
| RA-CNN [5] | 85.3 | – | 92.5 |
| MA-CNN [23] | 86.5 | 89.9 | 92.8 |
| NTS-NET [22] | 87.5 | 91.4 | 93.9 |
| TASN [24] | 87.9 | – | 93.8 |
| S3N [4] | 88.5 | 92.8 | 94.7 |
| FDL [10] | 88.6 | 93.4 | 94.3 |
| WS-DAN [6] | 89.4 | 93.0 | 94.5 |
| FT baseline | 86.6 | 91.5 | 93.0 |
| ROI-based-DAM (ours) | 88.5 | 92.8 | 94.5 |

**ROI-Based-DAM.** The parameter settings in ROI-based-DAM are as follow: $N = 64$, $V_b = 0.5$, $thr_s = 0.1$, $\lambda = 0.1$, $L_{low} = 0.9$, $L_{high} = 1.3$, $thre_c = 0.95$. All ROIs are resized to the same resolution of (448, 448) before feeding to the CNN. We denote $K_{tr}$ ($K_{tr} \geq 1$) as the number of multi-scale ROIs generated from an image in the training phase, and $K_{te}$ ($K_{te} \geq 1$) as the number of multi-scale ROIs generated from an image in inference. Since the original dataset is expanded ($K_{tr} + 1$) times after utilizing the ROI-based-DAM, we reduce the epoch number by multiplying $\frac{1}{(K_{tr}+1)}$ for fair comparison. For example, if $K_{tr}$ = 3, the epoch number $N_{ROI,epoch}$ is $\frac{N_{epoch}}{K_{tr}+1} = \frac{60}{4} = 15$.

### 4.3 Numerical Results

The classification performance is evaluated by the top-1 classification accuracy (%). Average test accuracy of the ROI-based-DAM under $K_{tr} = 3$ and $K_{te} = 3$ is recorded in our experiments. As shown in Table 1, our model (ROI-based-DAM) significantly outperforms the ResNeXt-50 baseline (FT Baseline) on all three datasets, and can achieve comparable performance with state-of-the-art, which demonstrates the effectiveness of ROI-based-DAM to FGVC.

### 4.4 Ablation Study

In this section, we evaluate the contribution of $K_{tr}$ and $K_{te}$ in CUB-200-2011 and compare the proposed ROI-based-DAM with standard data augmentation method such as multi-scale randomly-zoom-in to test its efficiency.

**Table 2.** Test accuracy under different $K_{tr}$; $Ori$ represents the original dataset and $\Delta$ denotes the improvement.

| Trainset | Max (%) | Min (%) | Avg ± std(%) | $\Delta$ (%) | P-value |
|---|---|---|---|---|---|
| $Ori$ | 86.7 | 86.5 | 86.6 ± 0.1 | 0 | – |
| $Ori$ with $K_{tr} = 1$ | 87.4 | 87.0 | 87.2 ± 0.2 | +0.6 | $2.16 \times 10^{-4}$ |
| $Ori$ with $K_{tr} = 2$ | 88.0 | 87.3 | 87.7 ± 0.2 | +1.1 | $3.07 \times 10^{-5}$ |
| $Ori$ with $K_{tr} = 3$ | 87.9 | 87.4 | 87.6 ± 0.2 | +1.0 | $1.28 \times 10^{-5}$ |

**The Contribution of $K_{tr}$.** In this section, we study the effect of $K_{tr}$ on test accuracy. For a fair comparison, only center crop (CC) is used for inference. Each experiment is run under five random seeds and statistic data of these comparison results are recorded in Table 2. T-tests are used to determine whether these improvements of different $K_{tr}$ are significant to the baseline.

It can be seen from Table 2 that training DNN with larger $K_{tr}$ such as 2 or 3 can bring about a clear and significant improvement of 1% to the test accuracy compared with the baseline, indicating that effectiveness of the proposed ROI-based-DAM in training.

**The Contribution of $K_{te}$.** In this section, we study the effect of $K_{te}$ on test accuracy. In the comparison experiments, we keep $K_{tr}$ fixed and only vary $K_{te}$ to see its influence on test accuracy. Each experiment is run under five random seeds. See Table 3 for the statisitc results.

First of all, we demonstrate that network training's randomness has little influence on the network performances since STDs of these test results, caused by this randomness, are small on the CUB-200-2011. Secondly, it can be seen that even setting $K_{te} = 1$ can bring about a significant improvement to the baseline under the same $K_{tr}$. Furthermore, it seems that the average test accuracy has a clear trend towards increasing if $K_{te}$ increases, indicating that larger $K_{te}$ (the max $K_{te}$ we adopted in the experiments is 3) might bring about more improvements. For example, when $K_{tr}$ is fixed as 1, setting $K_{te}$ to 3 can bring about a significant improvement of 1% to the test accuracy compared with the corresponding baseline. All these results indicate that the more ROIs of different scales are used, the better the inference could be. The reason that multi-scale ROIs works for inference could be that these ROIs' softmax outputs complement each other and further boost the test accuracy after doing pointwise summation. In short, we recommend $K_{tr} = 3$ and $K_{te} = 3$ in experiments.

**Comparison with Random Data Augmentation.** Since ROI-based-DAM knows how to zoom in and crop the input image for training, we want to see whether ROI-based-DAM is more efficient than standard data augmentation such as multi-scale randomly-zoom-in (RZI). As for RZI, we define $K_{Rtr}$ to be the number of multi-scale cropped regions for an image in the training set. For fair comparison, we set $K_{Rtr} = K_{tr} = 3$ in the experiment. In order to implement RZI, we first rescale the image to a resolution of $(448 \times r, 448 \times r)$, here $r$ is randomly sampled from a predefined list $[1.0, 1.2, 1.4, 1.6]$. Then we randomly crop a region of $(448, 448)$ from this rescale image. In addition, we compare the ROI-based-DAM with standard five-crop (four corners and central crop) to see which one is more efficient in inference. See Table 4 for the statistic data of these comparison results.

We can see that, in Table 4, when only center crop is used for inference, the proposed ROI-based-DAM can bring about a significant improvement of 1.0% to the test accuracy on the baseline, while the RZI can only bring about an improvement of 0.3%. Moreover, when five-crop is used for inference, our method can bring about a significant improvement of 1.5% to the baseline, while the RZI has no advantage compared with the baseline. All the comparison results indicate that the proposed ROI-based-DAM is more efficient than standard data

**Table 3.** Test accuracy under different $K_{te}$ and $K_{tr}$. $Ori$ represents the original dataset. $CC$ represents center image cropping. $\Delta$ denotes the improvement

| Trainset | Testset | Max (%) | Min (%) | Avg $\pm$ std (%) | $\Delta$ (%) | P-value |
|---|---|---|---|---|---|---|
| $Ori$ with $K_{tr} = 1$ | $CC$ | 87.4 | 87.0 | $87.2 \pm 0.2$ | 0 | – |
| $Ori$ with $K_{tr} = 1$ | $CC$ with $K_{te} = 1$ | 87.9 | 87.6 | $87.8 \pm 0.1$ | +0.6 | $5.67 \times 10^{-4}$ |
| $Ori$ with $K_{tr} = 1$ | $CC$ with $K_{te} = 2$ | 88.3 | 87.7 | $88.1 \pm 0.2$ | +0.9 | $1.75 \times 10^{-4}$ |
| $Ori$ with $K_{tr} = 1$ | $CC$ with $K_{te} = 3$ | 88.4 | 87.8 | $88.2 \pm 0.2$ | +1.0 | $5.16 \times 10^{-5}$ |
| $Ori$ with $K_{tr} = 2$ | $CC$ | 88.0 | 87.3 | $87.7 \pm 0.2$ | 0 | – |
| $Ori$ with $K_{tr} = 2$ | $CC$ with $K_{te} = 1$ | 88.6 | 88.0 | $88.3 \pm 0.2$ | +0.6 | $7.69 \times 10^{-3}$ |
| $Ori$ with $K_{tr} = 2$ | $CC$ with $K_{te} = 2$ | 88.7 | 88.0 | $88.3 \pm 0.2$ | +0.6 | $6.30 \times 10^{-3}$ |
| $Ori$ with $K_{tr} = 2$ | $CC$ with $K_{te} = 3$ | 88.9 | 88.1 | $88.4 \pm 0.3$ | +0.7 | $5.01 \times 10^{-3}$ |
| $Ori$ with $K_{tr} = 3$ | $CC$ | 87.9 | 87.4 | $87.6 \pm 0.2$ | 0 | – |
| $Ori$ with $K_{tr} = 3$ | $CC$ with $K_{te} = 1$ | 88.6 | 87.8 | $88.1 \pm 0.3$ | +0.5 | $2.22 \times 10^{-2}$ |
| $Ori$ with $K_{tr} = 3$ | $CC$ with $K_{te} = 2$ | 88.6 | 88.1 | $88.4 \pm 0.2$ | +0.8 | $4.56 \times 10^{-4}$ |
| $Ori$ with $K_{tr} = 3$ | $CC$ with $K_{te} = 3$ | 88.7 | 88.3 | $88.5 \pm 0.2$ | +0.9 | $1.03 \times 10^{-4}$ |

**Table 4.** Comparison with RZI in CUB-200-2011 Dataset. *Ori* represents the original dataset. *CC* represents center image cropping. $\Delta$ denotes the improvement

| Method | Trainset | Testset | Max (%) | Min (%) | Avg ± std (%) | $\Delta$ (%) | P-value |
|---|---|---|---|---|---|---|---|
| Baseline | *Ori* | CC | 86.7 | 86.5 | 86.6 ± 0.1 | 0 | – |
| RZI | *Ori* with $K_{Rtr} = 3$ | CC | 87.1 | 86.7 | 86.9 ± 0.1 | +0.3 | $7.98 \times 10^{-3}$ |
| ROI-based-DAM | *Ori* with $K_{tr} = 3$ | CC | 87.9 | 87.4 | 87.6 ± 0.2 | +1.0 | $1.28 \times 10^{-5}$ |
| RZI | *Ori* with $K_{Rtr} = 3$ | Five-crop | 87.1 | 86.4 | 86.6 ± 0.2 | +0 | 0.875 |
| ROI-based-DAM | *Ori* with $K_{tr} = 3$ | Five-crop | 88.3 | 87.9 | 88.1 ± 0.1 | +1.5 | $1.50 \times 10^{-7}$ |

augmentations during training and in inference, suggesting that the ROI-based data augmentation can play an important role in FGVC.

### 4.5 Qualitative Results

To analyze why the ROI-based-DAM works, we draw the multi-scale ROIs generated by the proposed ROI-based-DAM, see Fig. 4. We use red and blue rectangles to denote the regions at $K$ scales generated by ROI-based-DAM, with red rectangle denoting the finest-scale ROI and blue rectangle denoting other coarser-scale ROIs. It can be seen that in Fig. 4 the finest-scale ROIs are indeed informative for fine-grained classification. Moreover, all of these multi-scale ROIs can complement each other and be helpful for final inference.

**Fig. 4.** The multi-scale ROIs proposed by the ROI-based-DAM. The first two rows show K = 3 in CUB-200-2011. The third and fourth rows show K = 3 in Stanford Cars.

## 5   Conclusion

In this paper, we propose a simple yet efficient data augmentation method ROI-based-DAM. The ROI-based-DAM can first locate the most informative regions in an image without any bounding box or part annotations and then generate a set of high-quality multi-scale ROI-based images at a very low cost. Moreover, it can be easily implemented in the standard training and inference phases to boost the test accuracy of FGVC. Extensive experiments on FGVC datasets demonstrate the effectiveness of the proposed ROI-based-DAM.

# References

1. Biederman, I., Subramaniam, S., Bar, M., Kalocsai, P., Fiser, J.: Subordinate-level object classification reexamined. Psychol. Res. **62**(2), 131–153 (1999)
2. Cubuk, E.D., Zoph, B., Mane, D., Vasudevan, V., Le, Q.V.: AutoAugment: learning augmentation policies from data (2019)
3. Deng, J., Dong, W., Socher, R., Li, L.J., Li, K., Fei-Fei, L.: ImageNet: a large-scale hierarchical image database. In: 2009 IEEE Conference on Computer Vision and Pattern Recognition, pp. 248–255. IEEE (2009)
4. Ding, Y., Zhou, Y., Zhu, Y., Ye, Q., Jiao, J.: Selective sparse sampling for fine-grained image recognition. In: Proceedings of the IEEE/CVF International Conference on Computer Vision, pp. 6599–6608 (2019)
5. Fu, J., Zheng, H., Mei, T.: Look closer to see better: recurrent attention convolutional neural network for fine-grained image recognition. In: Proceedings of the IEEE Conference on Computer Vision and Pattern Recognition, pp. 4438–4446 (2017)
6. Hu, T., Qi, H., Huang, Q., Lu, Y.: See better before looking closer: weakly supervised data augmentation network for fine-grained visual classification. arXiv preprint arXiv:1901.09891 (2019)
7. Jaderberg, M., Simonyan, K., Zisserman, A., Kavukcuoglu, K.: Spatial transformer networks. arXiv preprint arXiv:1506.02025 (2015)
8. Kadir, T., Brady, M.: Saliency, scale and image description. Int. J. Comput. Vis. **45**(2), 83–105 (2001)
9. Krause, J., Stark, M., Deng, J., Fei-Fei, L.: 3D object representations for fine-grained categorization. In: 4th International IEEE Workshop on 3D Representation and Recognition (3dRR-13), Sydney, Australia (2013)
10. Liu, C., Xie, H., Zha, Z.J., Ma, L., Yu, L., Zhang, Y.: Filtration and distillation: enhancing region attention for fine-grained visual categorization. In: Proceedings of the AAAI Conference on Artificial Intelligence, vol. 34, pp. 11555–11562 (2020)
11. Liu, X., Xia, T., Wang, J., Yang, Y., Zhou, F., Lin, Y.: Fully convolutional attention networks for fine-grained recognition. arXiv preprint arXiv:1603.06765 (2016)
12. Maji, S., Kannala, J., Rahtu, E., Blaschko, M., Vedaldi, A.: Fine-grained visual classification of aircraft. Technical report (2013)
13. Paszke, A., et al.: PyTorch: an imperative style, high-performance deep learning library. arXiv preprint arXiv:1912.01703 (2019)
14. Peng, X., Tang, Z., Yang, F., Feris, R.S., Metaxas, D.: Jointly optimize data augmentation and network training: adversarial data augmentation in human pose estimation. In: Proceedings of the IEEE Conference on Computer Vision and Pattern Recognition, pp. 2226–2234 (2018)
15. Ren, S., He, K., Girshick, R., Sun, J.: Faster R-CNN: towards real-time object detection with region proposal networks. arXiv preprint arXiv:1506.01497 (2015)

16. Selvaraju, R.R., Cogswell, M., Das, A., Vedantam, R., Parikh, D., Batra, D.: Grad-CAM: visual explanations from deep networks via gradient-based localization. In: Proceedings of the IEEE International Conference on Computer Vision, pp. 618–626 (2017)
17. Springenberg, J.T., Dosovitskiy, A., Brox, T., Riedmiller, M.: Striving for simplicity: the all convolutional net. arXiv preprint arXiv:1412.6806 (2014)
18. Szegedy, C., Vanhoucke, V., Ioffe, S., Shlens, J., Wojna, Z.: Rethinking the inception architecture for computer vision. In: Proceedings of the IEEE Conference on Computer Vision and Pattern Recognition, pp. 2818–2826 (2016)
19. Wah, C., Branson, S., Welinder, P., Perona, P., Belongie, S.: The Caltech-UCSD Birds-200-2011 dataset (2011)
20. Wei, X.S., Wu, J., Cui, Q.: Deep learning for fine-grained image analysis: a survey. arXiv preprint arXiv:1907.03069 (2019)
21. Xie, S., Girshick, R., Dollár, P., Tu, Z., He, K.: Aggregated residual transformations for deep neural networks. In: Proceedings of the IEEE Conference on Computer Vision and Pattern Recognition, pp. 1492–1500 (2017)
22. Yang, Z., Luo, T., Wang, D., et al.: Learning to navigate for fine-grained classification. In: Proceedings of the European Conference on Computer Vision (ECCV), pp. 420–435 (2018)
23. Zheng, H., Fu, J., Mei, T., Luo, J.: Learning multi-attention convolutional neural network for fine-grained image recognition. In: Proceedings of the IEEE International Conference on Computer Vision, pp. 5209–5217 (2017)
24. Zheng, H., Fu, J., Zha, Z.J., Luo, J.: Looking for the devil in the details: learning trilinear attention sampling network for fine-grained image recognition. In: Proceedings of the IEEE/CVF Conference on Computer Vision and Pattern Recognition, pp. 5012–5021 (2019)

# Convolutional Neural Networks
# and Kernel Methods

# (Input) Size Matters for CNN Classifiers

Mats L. Richter[1]([✉]), Wolf Byttner[2], Ulf Krumnack[1], Anna Wiedenroth[1],
Ludwig Schallner[1], and Justin Shenk[3]

[1] Department of Cognitive Science, Universität Osnabrück,
49069 Osnabrück, Germany
matrichter@uni-osnabrueck.de
[2] Rapid Health, London, UK
[3] VisioLab, Berlin, Germany

**Abstract.** Fully convolutional neural networks (CNNs) can process
input of arbitrary size by applying a combination of downsampling and
pooling. However, we find that fully convolutional image classifiers are
not agnostic to the input size but rather show significant differences in
performance: presenting the same image at different scales can result in
different outcomes. A closer look reveals that there is no simple relationship between input size and model performance (no 'bigger is better'),
but that each network has a preferred input size, for which it shows
best results. We investigate this phenomenon by applying different methods, including spectral analysis of layer activations and probe classifiers,
showing that there are characteristic features depending on the network
architecture. From this we find that the size of discriminatory features
is critically influencing how the inference process is distributed among
the layers. Based on these findings we are able to derive basic design
guidelines for optimizing neural architectures on specific datasets.

**Keywords:** Convolutional neural networks · Input size · Resolution ·
Scale

## 1 Introduction

The superior performance of convolutional neural networks in computer vision
can be attributed to the way they extract information from image data. The
information processing follows a bottom-up approach, where smaller, less complex features, extracted by earlier layers, are successively combined to larger
and more complex features in later layers. The receptive field of a convolutional
layer can be seen as an upper bound of the size of features it can extract.[1] This
property results in deeper layers being able to detect larger patterns than earlier
layers, since they are able to "see" an increasingly wider area on the input image.
This also means that the size of the input image controls to some degree how

---

[1] In this work we refer to the height and width measured in pixels (absolute size) as
"size".

© Springer Nature Switzerland AG 2021
I. Farkaš et al. (Eds.): ICANN 2021, LNCS 12892, pp. 133–144, 2021.
https://doi.org/10.1007/978-3-030-86340-1_11

the inference process is distributed inside the network's structure [9]. In classification tasks the images fed into the network is by convention resized to a fixed sized square (often 224 × 224 pixels), which means that there is also an upper limit to the usefulness of increasingly larger receptive field sizes. The relevance of this is demonstrated by Tan and Le [12], who show that a network needs to be scaled together with the input resolution to achieve good efficiency.

In this work, we further investigate this relationship between input size and model architecture by answering the following questions:

- Has the size of the input image an effect on the predictive performance of CNN classifiers? Answer: yes, altering the resolution and adding details improves performance independent of each other (Sect. 3.1).
- Does the size of the input image influence how the information is processed in the network? Answer: yes, we can show that processing significantly differs depending on input size (Sect. 3.2) and the size of the depicted objects (Sect. 3.3).
- Can we know in advance which layers will contribute to the quality of the prediction based on the input size? Answer: For strictly sequential architectures the receptive field size allows identifying unproductive layers (Sect. 3.4).
- Do residual connections influence the observed behavior? Yes, residual connections can help to involve more layers in the inference process (Sect. 3.5).
- Are there implications for neural architecture design? Answer: Yes; we propose methods to optimize architectures before and after training (Sect. 4).

## 2   Background

### 2.1   Fully Convolutional Networks

This work focuses on fully convolutional neural network classifiers; the current de facto standard for CNN classifier architectures [3,5,12]. The key difference is the use of a global average pooling layer (GAP), that replaces the flattening operation in older architectures like AlexNet [7]. After a global pooling layer, every dense layer is functionally a 1 × 1 convolution. Since convolutions are agnostic towards the height and width of the input, the model can now process images of arbitrary size. Being able to change the size of the input image without altering the architecture of the CNN is important for avoiding potential artifacts induced by architectural changes. For this reason, we also modify non-fully convolutional architectures such as the VGG-family of networks by [11] to be fully convolutional. This is done by making the final pooling layer global [8].

### 2.2   Probe Classifiers, Saturation and Tail Patterns

For the analysis of trained models, we use probe classifiers. Probe classifiers are a tool for analyzing how the solution quality progresses while the data is propagated through neural networks [1]. In order to do this, logistic regression "probes" are trained on the same task as the model, using the output of individual

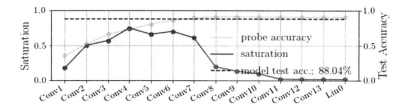

**Fig. 1.** VGG16 exhibits a tail pattern starting from Conv8. In the tail, saturation is low, and probe accuracy is stagnating at the same level as the model output.

layers from the trained model as input. Since the softmax layer and the probes effectively solve the same task, the probes can be used to judge the quality of the intermediate solutions. Typically, probe performance increases layer by layer approaching the model's performance (Fig. 1 demonstrates).

We previously proposed saturation as another one-dimensional metric quantitatively describing a neural network layer [9]. Saturation is the percentage of eigendirections on the layer's output required to explain 99% of the variance. Intuitively saturation measures a percentage of how much the output space of a layer is "filled" or "saturated" with the data. A sequence of low-saturated layers (<50% of the average saturation of all other layers) is referred to a "tail pattern" and indicates that these layers are not contributing qualitatively to the prediction (see Fig. 1). Probe performance typically stagnates, or even falls, in tail layers [9].

### 2.3  Receptive Field Size

The receptive field is the area on an image that influences the output of a convolution operation. For this work, the size of the receptive field (described as a scalar[2]) is important, since it reflects a spatial upper bound of visual patterns detectable by the respective layer.

For sequential convolutional neural networks (no multiple pathways during the forward pass) the receptive field size can be computed analytically. We refer to the receptive field $r$ of the $l$th layer of sequential network structure as $r_l$ (with $r_0 = 1$, which is the "receptive field" of the input). For all layers $l > 0$ in the convolutional part of a sequential network, the receptive field can be computed with

$$r_l = r_{l-1} + ((k_l - 2) \prod_{i=0}^{l-1} s_i) \tag{1}$$

where $r_{l-1}$ is the receptive field of the previous layer, $k_l$ refers to the kernel size of the layer $l$ (with potential dilation already accounted for) and $s_i$ to the stride size of the layer $i$. The receptive field increases with every convolutional

---

[2] Technically a 2-tuple, however since square kernels are the norm we can make this simplification.

layer with a stride or kernel size greater 1. Strides also multiplicatively effect the growth rate of consecutive layers $r_{l+n}$, since the feature map is downsampled.

For the purpose of this work, we ignore skip connection for this computation, since we are only interested in the receptive field size as a spatial upper bound. This allows us to compute the receptive field sizes in ResNet-models.

### 2.4   Methodology

**Choice of Models.** The experiments are primarily conducted on VGG and ResNet-style architectures [3,11]. VGG-style architectures serve as a baseline, since they are simple sequential CNN architectures.

For more complex architectures we choose the ResNet family - primarily ResNet18. There are two reasons for this. First, ResNet networks utilize many ideas of modern neural architectures, like the building block design and residual connections, while being rather simple in their structure [5,12]. Second, the ResNet family[3] (ResNet18 in particular) is easy to visualize, while many more complex derivative architectures feature a more non-sequential structure and large numbers of consecutive layers, making experimental results harder to interpret.

**Training Setup.** The training data was augmented by random cropping, horizontal flipping and channel-wise normalization of the data points, using the means and standard deviations of every color channel in ImageNet. Except where noted, the network's input resolution was the native resolution of the dataset. Images that were resized were re-sampled by bilinear interpolation after the data preprocessing and augmentation. All experiments used a batch size of 64.

Throughout our experiments, we used Stochastic Gradient Descent to train the network. The initial learning rate was 0.1. This decreased to 0.01 after one third of the epochs and 0.001 after two thirds. Models (except ResNet50) were trained for 30 epochs. ResNet50 was trained for 60 epochs, due to its slower rate of convergence. Hyperparameters were not fine-tuned, since state-of-the-art performance was not the goal of this study. We found that different learning rates, optimizers, batch sizes, data augmentations and number of epochs trained did not noticeably affect any model that successfully converged.

**Datasets.** For the experiment in Sect. 3.1 we used the iNaturalist and ImageNet benchmarks [4,10]. In other sections we used CIFAR10 [6], which allowed for a more in-depth analysis due to its limited size [6]. Experiments were reproduced on MNIST and TinyImageNet. Our code is publically available[4].

---

[3] For the sake of consistency and comparability, when we talk about to ResNet models we specifically refer to the ImageNet versions of these architectures, unless specified.

[4] https://github.com/delve-team/phd-lab.

# 3   Experiments

We first demonstrate that input size affects the predictive performance of models even though no information is added when upsampling an image. We investigate this behavior further by analyzing networks trained on CIFAR10. Based on these results, we investigate the role of locality of discriminatory features in the image. Finally, we discuss the role of the receptive field in these observations and analyze the influence of residual connections.

## 3.1   Image Size Affects Model Performance Even with No Additional Detail

Tan and Le [12] explained that classifiers perform better on larger images because they feature additional detail. From this statement we derived our working hypothesis - *additional detail is the only reason larger images are classified more accurately.* By increasing the image size - with or without adding detail - we were able to investigate this working hypothesis.

We trained models on ImageNet and iNaturalist in three different settings that we refer to as A, B and C. Models of set A were trained on images with a size of $224 \times 224$ pixels, providing the performance baseline. Set B models were trained on the images in set A downsampled to $32 \times 32$ pixels. Based on our hypothesis, we expected a drop in performance relative to set A. Set C was trained on the images used in set B up-sampled to $224 \times 224$ pixels, increasing the image size but not adding any detail. According to the working hypothesis, model performance should not be higher than in set B.

**Table 1.** Relative top1-accuracy: the models are trained twice, first on downscaled data with $32 \times 32$ resolution. The second training scales the images up to $224 \times 224$ again. The accuracy is relative to a baseline model of the same architecture trained on regular $224 \times 224$ pixels images.

|  | Dataset | VGG16 | ResNe18 | ResNet50 | EfficientNet-B0 |
|---|---|---|---|---|---|
| Downscaled ($32 \times 32$) | ImageNet | 15.35% | 66.08% | 28.21% | 19.32% |
| Upscaled ($224 \times 224$) | ImageNet | 45.74% | 67.39% | 71.8% | 64.45% |
| Downscaled ($32 \times 32$) | iNaturalist | 36.83% | 30.4% | 33.87% | 15.34% |
| Upscaled ($224 \times 224$) | iNaturalist | 45.74% | 52.68% | 54.38% | 63.79% |

In the results in Table 1 we see that decreasing the resolution had a negative effect on performance. Upsampling Set B images partially regained the lost performance. This contradicts our working hypothesis - the size of the input image is an additional factor affecting model accuracy. Models do not perform better on larger images solely because they have more information to work with.

## 3.2 Input Size Affects the Inference Process of the CNN

To understand why upsampling images improves performance, we investigated how the input resolution affects inference in the trained model. We trained ResNet18 on three CIFAR10 resolutions; 32×32 pixels, upsampled to ResNet18's default input 224 × 224 pixels and intentionally oversized to 1024 × 1024 pixels.

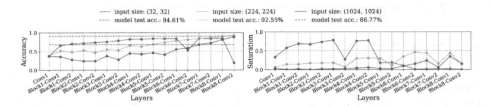

**Fig. 2.** Changing the input size changes how the inference is distributed among the layers, affecting performance in the process.

The results in Fig. 2 show that the image size redistributes the network's inference process. At 224 × 224 pixels the inference is distributed most evenly. This is also where the network performs the best, at 92.79% accuracy. At 32 × 32 pixels performance drops to 84.64%. We also observe that layer saturation decreases sharply after two-thirds of the network in a clear tail pattern,[5] while probe performance flat-lines at this point.

Shrinking the input size shifts much of the inference process to earlier layers of the network. Similarly, a drastically increased resolution of 1024 × 1024 pixels shifts the inference process closer to the final layer. Oversizing the input image also reduces the network's predictive performance to 86.77%.

## 3.3 The Role of the Size of Discriminatory Features in the Relation of Model and Input Resolution

From object detection research, we know that learned patterns in CNNs are often not scale-invariant [2]. This indicates that processing objects of different size is handled by different parts of the network. Based on our previous observations, we hypothesized that the uneven distribution of the inference is caused by the size of features on the images used for classification.

To verify this experimentally, we trained models on a modified version of the CIFAR10 dataset. In this version, the CIFAR10 images are randomly embedded in a black canvas of 160×160 pixels. This restricted all potentially discriminatory features to a 32 × 32 pixel region. If the absolute size of the object influences which parts of the network process the information, the resulting tail pattern and evolution of the probe performances should be similar to the same model trained on CIFAR10 on its native resolution.

---

[5] Sudden drops of probe performance are caused by ResNet skipping layers [1,9].

The results in Fig. 3 show that this is the case. The tail pattern starts at the Conv8 layer in both scenarios. Upscaling the images to $160 \times 160$ results in different saturation and probe patterns (see Fig. 3).

This is convincing evidence that the relevance of the input size when training classifiers comes from the absolute size of the discriminatory features (measured in pixels) detected by the model.

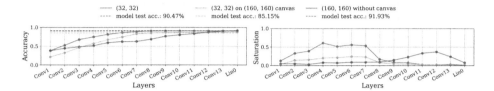

**Fig. 3.** Similar object size results in similar distribution of the inference process, as indicated by the probe performances (left) and the position of the tail (right).

### 3.4  The Role of the Receptive Field in Relation to the Object Size

Our experiments thus far hint that features of different sizes are recognized by different layers in the model. In this section, we will investigate the causes of this phenomenon from an architectural point of view. From the perspective of the architecture, the receptive field of a layer can be considered an *upper bound* for the size of recognizable features. Since the receptive field expands with every layer that has stride and/or kernel size >1, increasingly large features can be recognized. We hypothesize that for simple, sequential architectures like the VGG-family of networks[6] the receptive field is the dominating factor influencing whether unproductive layers are present, and where they are in the network.

We studied this property of the receptive field by training the VGG-style networks on CIFAR10 and adding the receptive field as an additional information to our analysis. In Fig. 4 we indicate the first layer that processes input from a layer with a receptive field size greater than the input size with a black border. We will refer to this layer as the *border layer*. For both architectures, this border separates layers contributing to the inference process from layers that do not contribute to the quality of the inference significantly. This suggests that a layer in a simple, sequential architecture can only substantially improve the performance when novel information is integrated into positions on its feature map.

---

[6] We define a simple architecture as a sequential architecture consisting only of convolutional, pooling and fully connected layers.

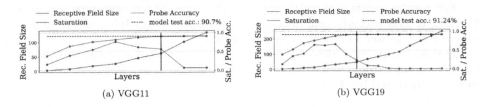

(a) VGG11                              (b) VGG19

**Fig. 4.** The border layer (black vertical bar) separates the "solving" part from the "compressing" part of the model, as indicated by the probes and saturation.

We investigated this observation further by testing architectures that alter the receptive field size differently than VGG-style networks. We tested the effect of dilated convolutions by training a modified VGG19 with a dilation rate of 2 in all convolutional layers. This modification effectively increases the kernel sizes of all layers, which in turn increases the receptive field size without changing the number of parameters. We also turned ResNet18 into a sequential model by removing the residual connections. This ResNet-variant differs from VGG-style models in multiple ways. It uses mostly convolutions with $stride = 2$ for downsampling and a more aggressive downsampling strategy, by using 2 additional downsampling layers right after the input, resulting in a much larger receptive field. From the results in Fig. 5 we can see that the behavior of both models is consistent with previous observations.

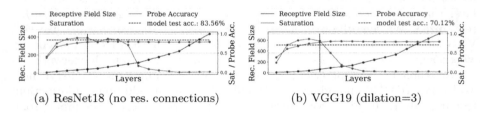

(a) ResNet18 (no res. connections)          (b) VGG19 (dilation=3)

**Fig. 5.** ResNet18 exhibits the same patterns observed in Fig. 4, when the skip-connections are removed (a). Increasing the receptive field by dilating convolutions (b) for VGG19 produces results consistent with Fig. 4.

Finally, we investigated how the solution develops inside the feature maps of different parts of the network. We modified our logistic regression probes [1] method by applying a single probe to every position of every layer's feature map. We then computed the relative performance of the probes by dividing the probe accuracy with the network's accuracy (both evaluated on the test set). By doing so, we can visualize the quality of the partial solutions contained in every position of the feature map based on their position. We observe in Fig. 6 that in early layers the central positions on the feature map generally perform best, while outer positions perform increasingly worse, with the corner positions generally being the worst. We suspect that the receptive field is at least partially responsible for this, since outer positions on the feature map will receive more black padding and thus less information with the receptive field expansion as a center pixel.

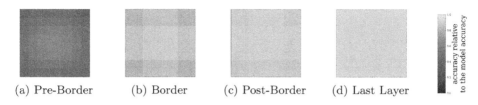

(a) Pre-Border          (b) Border          (c) Post-Border          (d) Last Layer

**Fig. 6.** The heatmaps display the performance of probes relative to the model performance. Each probe is trained on a single position of the feature map.

Another interesting observation in Fig. 6 is, that the centermost positions on the feature map contain partial solutions roughly equivalent to the performance of the entire model. As the saturation drops and layers become part of the low-saturated tail, the partial solution quality becomes increasingly homogeneous across feature map positions. In the last layer, each vector on the feature map is as linearly separable regarding the classification task as the average pooled solution. We conclude based on these measurements that this homogenization of partial solution quality is also responsible for the drop in saturation.

Based on these observations, we conclude that simple, sequential neural networks may develop two stages of inference when the image is smaller than the receptive field size of the model: The first being the solving stage, where the data is processed incrementally to achieve loss minimization. The second stage, starting from the border layer, is the compressing stage. This stage compresses the latent space by homogenization of the partial solutions for every position in the feature map.

### 3.5   The Role of Residual Connections

Residual connections are often used in neural network architectures [3,5,12]. Networks with residual connections can add "deltas" to the existing representation of the data rather than transforming it entirely [3]. The residual connection itself does not expand or change the receptive field. Features based on lower receptive field sizes might then "skip" layers, to be processed later in the network. As a consequence, information based on multiple receptive field sizes may be present after a residual connection. Thus, inference can be distributed across more layers.

We would therefore expect that models utilizing residual connections use layers after the border layer to improve the prediction. As was previously defined, the border layer is the first layer to receive an input produced by a layer with a receptive field size larger than the image. In sequential architectures, it is also the layer separating the solving and compressing stage of the model.

In Fig. 7 we observe such a *post-border layer* improvement. Both networks improve the probe performances and stay highly saturated long after the border layer has processed the data. Since we tested ResNet18 without residual connections in the previous section (see Fig. 5), we can attribute this behavior to the residual connections.

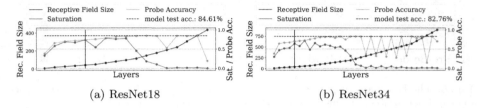

(a) ResNet18                          (b) ResNet34

**Fig. 7.** Residual connections allow networks to utilize layers past the border layer (marked with the vertical bar). Drops in probe performance are an artifact of ResNet skipping layers [1, 9]

While residual connections have a positive effect on the predictive performance of ResNet18 (84.61% accuracy with and 79.05% accuracy without residual connections), the performance still remains worse than VGG-style models. We attribute this to the lower overall receptive field size of VGG19, which is only 252 pixels. ResNet models downsample more aggressively in the beginning, resulting in receptive field sizes of 413 (ResNet18) and over 800 pixels (Resnet34) respectively. This suggests, that matching the receptive field size with the input size remains important when using residual connections in the architecture.

Therefore, it should be possible to improve the performance of the (ImageNet optimized) ResNet18 and 34 by reducing the size of the receptive field. This was implicitly done by [3], who proposed a CIFAR10-optimized ResNet variant. This architecture has no max-pooling layer and the first layer has its stride size and kernel size halved, reducing the receptive field from 413 to 109 pixels. The effect of these reductions can be seen in Fig. 8: the proportion of low-saturated layers is drastically reduced for both models and the inference process is now more evenly distributed. This explains the performance increases relative to ImageNet-optimized models. By redistributing the inference we increased performance from 84.61% to 91.95% for ResNet18 and from 82.76% to 92.21% for ResNet34, demonstrating how the receptive field is an important architectural consideration.

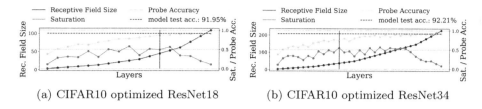

(a) CIFAR10 optimized ResNet18          (b) CIFAR10 optimized ResNet34

**Fig. 8.** Removing the Stem from ResNet18 and 34 quarters receptive field size, resulting in better distributed inference and accuracy.

## 4  Implications on Neural Architecture Design

**During Architecture Selection.** From the observations made in this work, we can derive some basic guidelines regarding the design of neural architectures. We show in Sect. 3.4 that sequential models stop improving the intermediate solution qualitatively at the border layer - the first layer to receive input from a layer with a receptive field size greater than the input size. Since the receptive field size is known beforehand, we can adjust the architecture before training, such that the receptive field matches the input resolution, avoiding the unproductive layers at the design stage.

**Post-training.** We also show in Sect. 3.3 that the size of discriminatory features is the underlying reason for the observed behavior. The size of the largest feature is bounded by the image size. When the entire image is classified, like in ImageNet, MNIST or CIFAR10, the largest feature is likely almost as large as the image itself. However, for general image datasets the largest feature might well be significantly smaller than the image. When training, this would show up as a saturation tail pattern, indicating that layers in the tail do not contribute significantly to inference. When such a tail is detected, the architecture can be adjusted accordingly (see examples in Fig. 8). Alternatively, unproductive tail pattern layers can be replaced with a global pooling layer followed by the fully connected end layer(s).

Another advantage of post-training saturation-based optimization is that it also applies to networks with residual connections, since they too produce tail patterns when the receptive field is too large (see Fig. 2).

## 5  Conclusion

For a long time deep learning has been about developing bigger, deeper and more complex models to improve performance. Our work provides a counterpoint, showing that neural networks can have too big receptive fields, leading to some layers not contributing to the solution. This leads both to wasted computations and sub-optimal performance. We further showed that residual connections counteract too-large receptive fields to a certain degree by allowing more layers to contribute to the inference process. This has long been suspected, but there has been little direct evidence.

Finally, we demonstrated that probe classifiers and layer saturation are useful tools to analyze the relationship between dataset and model architecture. These tools let practitioners quantitatively evaluate their models with orders-of-magnitude less data and give insight into the inference process inside the model. It shines some light into the black box that is a neural network, and lets us study networks more rigorously.

# References

1. Alain, G., Bengio, Y.: Understanding intermediate layers using linear classifier probes. In: ICLR 2017 Workshop (2016)
2. Han, D., Kim, J., Kim, J.: Deep pyramidal residual networks. In: IEEE Conference on Computer Vision and Pattern Recognition (CVPR), pp. 6307–6315 (2017). https://doi.org/10.1109/CVPR.2017.668
3. He, K., Zhang, X., Ren, S., Sun, J.: Deep residual learning for image recognition. In: 2016 IEEE Conference on Computer Vision and Pattern Recognition (CVPR), pp. 770–778 (2016). https://doi.org/10.1109/CVPR.2016.90
4. Horn, G.V., et al.: The iNaturalist challenge 2017 dataset. arXiv preprint arXiv:1704.06642 (2017)
5. Iandola, F.N., Moskewicz, M.W., Karayev, S., Girshick, R.B., Darrell, T., Keutzer, K.: DenseNet: implementing efficient convnet descriptor pyramids. arXiv preprint arXiv:1404.1869 (2014)
6. Krizhevsky, A., Hinton, G.: Learning multiple layers of features from tiny images. Master's thesis, Department of Computer Science, University of Toronto (2009)
7. Krizhevsky, A., Sutskever, I., Hinton, G.E.: ImageNet classification with deep convolutional neural networks. In: Pereira, F., Burges, C.J.C., Bottou, L., Weinberger, K.Q. (eds.) Advances in Neural Information Processing Systems 25, pp. 1097–1105. Curran Associates, Inc. (2012)
8. Lin, M., Chen, Q., Yan, S.: Network in network. arXiv preprint arXiv:1312.4400 (2013)
9. Richter, M.L., Shenk, J., Byttner, W., Arpteg, A., Huss, M.: Feature space saturation during training. arXiv preprint arXiv:2006.08679 (2020)
10. Russakovsky, O., et al.: ImageNet large scale visual recognition challenge. Int. J. Comput. Vis. **115**(3), 211–252 (2015). https://doi.org/10.1007/s11263-015-0816-y
11. Simonyan, K., Zisserman, A.: Very deep convolutional networks for large-scale image recognition. In: Bengio, Y., LeCun, Y. (eds.) 3rd International Conference on Learning Representations (ICLR) (2015)
12. Tan, M., Le, Q.: EfficientNet: rethinking model scaling for convolutional neural networks. In: Chaudhuri, K., Salakhutdinov, R. (eds.) Proceedings of the 36th International Conference on Machine Learning. Proceedings of Machine Learning Research, vol. 97, pp. 6105–6114. PMLR (09–15 June 2019)

# Accelerating Depthwise Separable Convolutions with Vector Processor

Yuekai Zhao$^{(\boxtimes)}$ ⓘ, Jianzhuang Lu, and Xiaowen Chen

College of Computer, National University of Defense Technology, Changsha, China
{zhaoyuekai,xwchen}@nudt.edu.cn

**Abstract.** Depthwise separable convolution has demonstrated its advantages in reducing the number of parameters and neural network calculations. Convolution-oriented hardware accelerators are outstanding in terms of saving resources and energy. However, lightweight networks designed for small processors do not perform efficiently on these accelerators. Moreover, there are too many models to design an application-specific circuit for each model. In this work, we propose a method of mapping depthwise separable convolution on a general-purpose vector processor. This method achieves high computational performance by increasing data reuse and parallel execution. First of all, we propose a multi-vector parallel convolution method to reduce the number of data reads and increase data utilization in depthwise convolution. Then, we divide the data of pointwise convolution into coarse-grained blocks and compute matrix multiplication in parallel on a multi-core processor, achieving high computational efficiency. Furthermore, we use a double buffer mechanism to optimize data transfer and shorten execution time. Overall, using MobileNet to evaluate depthwise separable convolution, multi-vector parallel convolution method on M-DSP reduces the number of reads and writes by up to 4 times. We achieve 1518 FPS and 1.783 TFLOPS at a batch size of 1, which is 1.87× faster than ZU9 MPSoc and 3.89× more calculation-efficient than 2080Ti GPU.

**Keywords:** Depthwise separable convolution · Multi-vector parallel convolution · Matrix multiplication

## 1 Introduction

Convolutional neural networks (CNNs) are widely used in image recognition, target detection and instance segmentation for their great success. CNNs are formed by a stack of different layers including convolution, activation, pooling and fully connected layers. The new models increase the number of convolution layers to enhance the feature extraction capability, but this also leads to the high latency of network inference. To reduce the neural network's hardware threshold and increase the calculation speed, new neural network reduces the use of

Supported by organization the Hunan Provincial Science and Technology Plan Project. The specific grant number is 2018XK2102.

layers with low computational efficiency (such as the pooling layer). This design idea can make full use of the processor's computing power and increase the program's running speed. Besides, new calculation methods, like depthwise separable convolution (DSC), are proposed to replace standard convolutions, which reduce computation size and the number of parameters. A standard convolution is broken down into two steps, a depthwise convolution (DWC) for filtering and a pointwise convolution (PWC) for combining. These methods are hardware-oriented and suitable for the temporal and spatial locality of the program. Compared with previous neural networks, the networks using these methods reduce calculation, training time, and inference time.

In recent years, many hardware accelerators have been proposed to deal with deep neural networks. Dadiannao [2] is designed for general neural network reasoning. In [6], FPGA is used to implement neural networks with high energy efficiency. The limited hardware resources on FPGA lead to poor computational performance, and a single acceleration circuit cannot support multiple convolution calculations simultaneously. On the other hand, TensorRT is a software development kit designed by NVIDIA for high-performance deep learning inference on Graphics Processing Unit (GPU). However, the calculation speed of a single computing unit is weaker than that of a single-core processor, making a single data need a longer running time in the GPU. GPU has too many parallel computing units for DSC, resulting in a waste of computational performance. How to effectively process small batch tasks on a parallel structure has become a problem faced by these processors.

Since the image can be converted into a matrix, the convolution of the image and the filter can be converted into a matrix multiplication. Several accelerators are specially optimized for matrix multiplication to accelerate convolution. [9] designs an architecture called SIGMA, which has a good effect on matrix multiplication. SIGMA includes a novel reduction tree microarchitecture named forwarding adder network, which offers high utilization of all its processing elements. Although PWC can be calculated by matrix multiplication, DWC must convert the image to a matrix, generating much overhead.

Considering that digital signal processor (DSP) performs fast Fourier transform (FFT) efficiently, [7] calculates convolution through time domain and frequency domain transform. However, FFT produces complex numbers in its implementation, which takes up much space and increases real number calculations. Experiments show that using FFT for convolution kernels larger than 5×5 has a good effect, but FFT is not suitable for small convolution kernels, especially for DSC. Texas Instruments DSP (TI DSP) supports users in using Code Composer Studio (CCS) to develop convolutional neural network applications quickly. However, due to the lack of library functions and optimization of image processing applications, TI DSP has poor convolutional network acceleration performance. [10] designed DSP-oriented vectorization method of matrix multiplication. It is an effective method, which is suitable for general-purpose DSP processors to process matrix multiplication. However, under normal circumstances, the calculation amount of the depthwise separable convolution is much smaller than that of the standard convolution, resulting in many idle cycles of the processor.

In this work, we propose an algorithm for mapping depthwise separable convolutions on a high-performance DSP chip called M-DSP. Firstly, we propose multi-vector parallel convolution (MVPC) for depthwise convolution, which realizes the reuse of input data, output data, and kernel data. MVPC is suitable for small convolution kernels, and we utilize the vector registers in the DSP cores effectively to reduce data reads and writes. We use multiple multiply and add operators to achieve parallel computing and use numerous computing elements to achieve data vectorization. Secondly, we treat pointwise convolution as matrix multiplication and decompose it into multiple blocks. We execute General Matrix Multiplication (GEMM) distributedly on multi-core processors to accelerate pointwise convolution and minimize its execution time. Finally, we use a double buffering mechanism to establish a coarse-grained pipeline, reducing the internal and external data transfer time of DSCs.

## 2  Related Work

Compared with software, hardware has a significant advantage in accelerating programs and reducing energy consumption. Many works map algorithms on application-specific circuits to improve the computational efficiency of CNNs. [4] design a CNN accelerator called WAX that pushes the boundaries of near-data execution and short-wire data movement, improving energy consumption by a minimum of 2.6 times compared with Eyeriss. [5] design the hardware-oriented ERNets for the adopted block-based inference flow, construct the coarse-grained FBISA to achieve highly parallel convolution. These accelerators have high computational efficiency for mapping neural networks. However, due to the limitation of hardware resources, the computational performance is poor. And it is cost-effective to increase computing performance by increasing FPGA hardware resources or manufacturing hardware circuits.

Many works aim to reduce the complexity of convolution. [6] supports efficient indexing and storage of matrices through a combination of software and hardware. RAMMER [8] improves the computational performance of a deep neural network from the compiler's perspective. Standard accelerators treat data flow graphs as library functions without processing, resulting in greater scheduling overhead and hardware load. RAMMER generates an efficient static spatio-temporal schedule for a DNN at compile-time to minimize overhead and maximize hardware utilization. We introduce this idea into the programming of vector processors to realize coarse-grained parallelism on multi-core DSP. In addition, we optimize the flow of convolution, standardization, and activation functions, reducing data reading and writing from the perspective of compilation.

Memory-efficient convolution (MEC) [3] algorithm reduces memory overhead substantially and accelerates the convolution process. MEC lowers the input matrix in a simple yet efficient way and then executes multiple small matrix multiplications in parallel to get convolution completed. The method adjusts the order of the data to reduce the number of accesses to the memory. We port this method to a vector processor and increased the parallelism through vectorization.

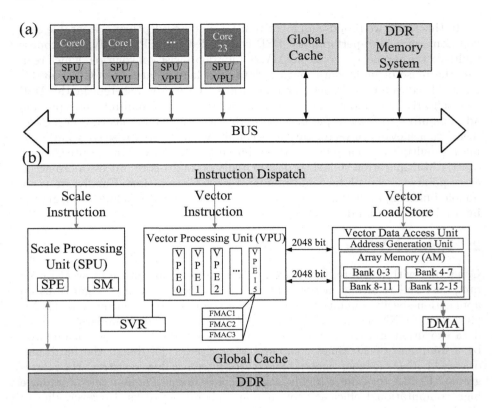

**Fig. 1.** (a) Interconnect structure of M-DSP. (b) Hardware architecture of a single M-DSP core.

## 3    Algorithm Mapping

### 3.1    Architecture of Vector Processor

We conduct experiments on a 24-core vector accelerator called M-DSP. It is designed by the national university of defense technology for high-performance floating-point operations. It has a peak performance of 4.608 tera floating-point operations per second (TFLOPS), and its highest read-write bandwidth is 307 GB/s.

Figure 1(a) describes the interconnect structure of M-DSP. The cores exchange data through the global cache (GC), which has a size of the global cache is 6 MB. Storage units at all levels have direct memory access (DMA) units, which can carry out data transmission independent of calculations. Transmission methods include point-to-point, segmentation, and broadcast. Finally, the vector processor communicates with the master device through the bus and double data rate SDRAM (DDR). M-DSP supports up to 128 GB of memory.

The hardware architecture of a single DSP core is shown in Fig. 1(b). M-DSP uses a tight coupling mechanism to combine scalar processing units (SPU)

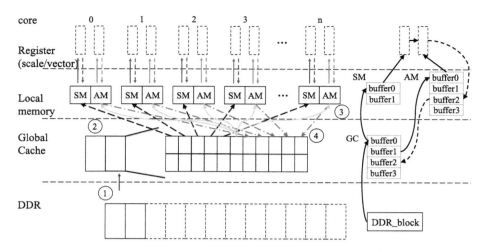

**Fig. 2.** Multilevel storage architecture and double buffering mechanism of M-DSP

and vector processing units (VPU) in each core. The scalar processing elements (SPE) in SPU are used for scalar calculation and process control. VPU has sixteen vector processing elements (VPE) for vector calculations, in which there are three floating-point multiply-and-add operators. In M-DSP, a single core's internal vector storage space (AM) is 768 KB, and the scalar storage space (SM) is 64 KB. The bandwidth between AM and VPU is 2048 bits. AM is divided into sixteen banks and four partitions to increase data access speed. The scalar in SM can be copied and expanded into a vector by the scalar-to-vector register (SVR). There are scalar and vector registers and local storage space inside the core. The on-chip global cache exchanges data with SM and AM through the bus. Sixteen 64-bit VPEs in a VPU can implement 32-dimensional single-precision floating-point vector operations or 64-dimensional half-precision floating-point vector operations.

### 3.2 Data Distribution and Optimization on Multi-core DSP

In order to reduce the time of program execution, we use all the cores of M-DSP for calculation, which makes data transmission a performance bottleneck. Figure 2 shows the multi-level storage structure of the vector processor. According to the double buffering mechanism, SM is divided into two areas, AM and GC are divided into four partitions. Mark ① refers to the process of transferring data from DDR to GC. The black dotted line indicated by mark ② describes the realization of segmented transmission. The orange line indicated by mark ③ describes how to implement broadcasting. Mark ④ introduces the process of on-chip cache passing calculation results to GC through point-to-point transmission. All processors use fences to realize synchronization. Algorithm 1 presents the data distribution scheme when M-DSP runs depthwise convolution, and algorithm 2 describes the steps of calculating pointwise convolution.

---

**Algorithm 1.** Calculation process of depthwise convolution

---

**Input:** height, input channel

1: Determine the calculation amount of DWC for each core according to the number of cores, and transfer the source data to AM_buffer0 in the manner of segmented transmission (Follow arrow ②);

2: Organize the data of different channels at the same position into vectors, and read 32-dimensional data at a time according to the capacity of the vector register;

3: Broadcast the weight data of DWC to AM_buffer1 of each core (Follow arrow ③). Organize the data of different channels at the same position into vectors, and read 32-dimensional data at a time according to the capacity of the vector register;

4: Calculate DWC according to section 3.2;

5: Each core transmits the calculation result to AM_buffer2 in a point-to-point manner (Follow arrow ④).

---

**Algorithm 2.** Calculation process of pointwise convolution

---

**Input:** height, input channel, output channel

1: Divide the input data of PWC evenly according to the number of cores, and transfer the source data to SM_buffer0 in the manner of segmented transmission;

2: Broadcast the weight data of PWC to AM_buffer0 of each core. Assuming that the number of input channels of 1*1 convolution is m and the number of output channels is n, the convolution kernel can be regarded as a matrix of size $[m, n]$. We divide the matrix into m parts, each of which is an n-dimensional vector;

3: Transmit a scalar data from SM to AM each time according to section 3.3. Copy and expand it into an n-dimensional vector;

4: Calculate PWC according to section 3.3;

5: Each core transmits the calculation result to AM_buffer2 in a point-to-point manner.

---

Unlike depthwise convolution, there is no overlapping data between data blocks transmitted by pointwise convolution. Depthwise convolution uses a 3×3 kernel, and data needs to be reused when the filter larger than 1×1. Pointwise convolution uses a 1×1 filter with a step size of 1, so the input data is divided evenly. Each core processes pointwise convolution independently and transmits the GC results according to the core number and data block size.

We design a mapping algorithm to improve the general-purpose vector processor's computational efficiency to run convolution, thereby converting the hardware's computing power into the algorithm's performance. Optimization mainly includes two aspects, computing optimization, and storage optimization.

In terms of calculation optimization, due to the poor efficiency of executing jump structures on the Very Long Instruction Word (VLIW) structure, we minimize the occurrence of judging jump statements and loop statements during execution. According to the timeline, we expand the CNN algorithm's instructions and schedule them to achieve maximum parallel execution. We use instruction delay slots to increase hardware utilization. Finally, we use scalar calculations for essential data preparation and instruction scheduling.

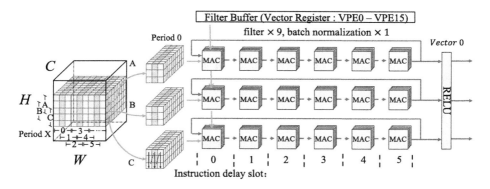

**Fig. 3.** Introduction to multi-vector parallel convolution method.

In terms of storage optimization, we use a multi-level storage structure and use a double buffer mechanism to reduce data read and write overhead. Since the DMA component's operation does not require a processor, data transmission and calculation can be performed simultaneously. For example, while calculating DWC, the weight of PWC is transmitted to AM. The measure of hiding the data transmission time in the calculation time improves the calculation efficiency.

### 3.3   Depthwise Convolution Mapping on Single-Core DSP

In the previous subsection, we introduced how to distribute depthwise convolution data on a multi-core vector processor. Next, we will illustrate the characteristics of DWC and introduce its mapping method on a single-core DSP.

As the name suggests, depthwise convolution uses the different kernels to convolve on different channels. Therefore, we can achieve n-fold parallelism by using n-dimensional vectors. Inspired by the MEC algorithm, we proposed a multi-vector parallel convolution (MVPC) method to achieve data reuse and parallelism. Figure 3 shows the implementation method of MVPC. We assumed that there are three multiply-and-accumulate units (MAC), and the step size is 1, so we can process three convolutional blocks at the same time. To achieve data multiplexing, we move the convolution filter in the horizontal direction and process the data in parallel from the vertical direction. In this way, we get a data block of size $[5, 3, C]$ and store it in 15 $C$-dimensional vectors. They can be combined into three logical data blocks of size $[3, 3, C]$. In each cycle, the data block selection frame is shifted right by step 1, and only five $C$-dimensional vectors need to be updated. We store data in registers so that the number of reading data dropped nine to two.

Each logical data block is connected to a vector multiply-add operator according to Fig. 3, and each position represents a vector composed of sixteen VPEs. Vertically, a vector of the filter data is transferred to each MAC. For the same picture, the convolution kernel data is unchanged. Horizontally, the figure shows the five command delay slots in the concept of time because multiply-add operation takes six cycles. The result needs to be fed back ten times, nine of which are used to calculate the filter, and one is used for data normalization. Finally, in the ReLU module, the activation function is realized by comparing it with the zero vector.

### 3.4   Pointwise Convolution Mapping on Single-Core DSP

Pointwise convolution uses a convolution kernel of $1 \times 1$, and the calculation result is the same as the matrix multiplication. Therefore, we use the general matrix multiplication (GEMM) function to implement pointwise convolution on the vector processor.

Equation (1) shows the method of calculating matrix multiplication by column ($C_{m \times n} = A_{m \times k} * B_{k \times n}$). We divide matrix $C$ into n column vectors and matrix $A$ into $k$ column vectors. If matrix $B$ is stored as a row vector, we can use (1) to get a row of matrix $C$ at the same time. In (1), $O_i$ and $I_j$ are m-dimensional column vectors, and $W_{(i,j)}$ is a scalar.

$$
\begin{aligned}
\begin{bmatrix} O_1\ O_2\ O_3 \cdots O_n \end{bmatrix} = & I_1 \ \times \begin{bmatrix} W_{(1,1)}\ W_{(1,2)}\ W_{(1,3)} \cdots W_{(1,n)} \end{bmatrix} + \\
& I_2 \ \times \begin{bmatrix} W_{(2,1)}\ W_{(2,2)}\ W_{(2,3)} \cdots W_{(2,n)} \end{bmatrix} + \\
& \cdots \qquad\qquad\qquad\qquad\qquad\qquad + \\
& I_k \ \times \begin{bmatrix} W_{(k,1)}\ W_{(k,2)}\ W_{(k,3)} \cdots W_{(k,n)} \end{bmatrix}
\end{aligned}
\tag{1}
$$

Here are the steps of calculating PWC: First, copy and expand the data in the first column of $A$ matrix into matrix $D$ of size $[m,\ n]$; then multiply each row of $D$ with the first row of matrix $B$. After that, take the second column of matrix $A$ and the second row of the $B$ matrix. Repeat the above process, and finally, we will get the row vectorized result of the matrix multiplication.

## 4   Experiments and Evaluation

In this section, we evaluate the performance of depthwise separable convolutions with MobileNet and analyze the influence of convolution kernel size on computational efficiency.

### 4.1   Performance Analysis of Depthwise Convolution

First, we give the calculation method of calculation efficiency.

$$
Efficiency = \frac{calculation}{time \times peak\ performance}
\tag{2}
$$

**Table 1.** Computational performance of depthwise separable convolutions.

| | Height/width (step) | Input channel | Output channel | DWC's runtime $(10^{-6})$ | DWC's computational efficiency | PWC's runtime $(10^{-6})$ | PWC's computa-tional efficiency |
|---|---|---|---|---|---|---|---|
| DSC1 | 112(1) | 32 | 64 | 17.91 | 9.72% | 14.96 | 78.02% |
| DSC2 | 112(2) | 64 | 128 | 19.62 | 17.75% | 12.74 | 89.57% |
| DSC3 | 56(1) | 128 | 128 | 5.82 | 29.89% | 38.38 | 58.79% |
| DSC4 | 56(2) | 128 | 256 | 5.89 | 29.55% | 13.65 | 82.64% |
| DSC5 | 28(1) | 256 | 256 | 3.87 | 22.46% | 27.35 | 82.01% |
| DSC6 | 28(2) | 256 | 512 | 3.82 | 22.76% | 22.39 | 50.10% |
| DSC7 | 14(1) | 512 | 512 | 2.88 | 15.09% | 44.74 | 49.99% |
| DSC8 | 14(1) | 512 | 512 | 2.92 | 14.89% | 44.85 | 49.87% |
| DSC9 | 14(1) | 512 | 512 | 2.97 | 14.62% | 44.71 | 50.03% |
| DSC10 | 14(1) | 512 | 512 | 2.98 | 14.60% | 44.81 | 49.91% |
| DSC11 | 14(2) | 512 | 512 | 2.95 | 14.71% | 44.74 | 50.00% |
| DSC12 | 7(1) | 512 | 1024 | 2.95 | 3.68% | 43.96 | 25.44% |
| DSC13 | 7(1) | 1024 | 1024 | 1.36 | 15.98% | 87.81 | 25.43% |

Table 1 shows the size and computational efficiency of all depthwise convolutions and pointwise convolutions in MobileNet. The calculation efficiency of DWC is no more than 30%. We can see that as the height decreases, the computational efficiency shows a decreasing trend.

From a computing point of view, the size of the image becomes smaller, and the amount of calculation cannot meet the computing power of the M-DSP, resulting in many idle cycles. From the perspective of data transmission, DWC starts by transmitting input data and filtering data. Next, calculate the DWC and transfer the result to the GC. We found that preparing data takes a lot of time, which keeps the computational efficiency of DWC at a low level. Moreover, as the image size decreases, the situation becomes worse. Generally, the larger the amount of data, the longer the transmission time. However, in the hardware environment, if fragmented data is frequently transmitted, the transmission component's activation will also cause loss. Therefore, we can find that in Table 1, except for the performance jitter caused by program optimization, the smaller the calculation amount, the lower the calculation efficiency.

However, from the perspective of time consumption, we can draw an opposite conclusion. As the amount of calculation decreases, the calculation time of DWC becomes shorter. Simultaneously, as the parameters decrease, the amount of data transmission in each layer becomes smaller. These two reasons make DWC less time-consuming.

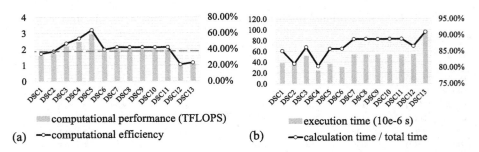

**Fig. 4.** (a) Compare the computational efficiency of each layer of DSC with the entire network. (b) Execution time of DSC.

### 4.2   Performance Analysis of Pointwise Convolution

Table 1 shows the size and computational efficiency of all pointwise convolutions in MobileNet. We found that the computational efficiency of PWC is higher than that of DWC in the same layer.

Although the calculation efficiency of PWC is also showing a downward trend, most of the calculation efficiency of PWC exceeds 50%. That is because matrix multiplication is a computationally intensive operation. The calculation time occupies the majority of the runtime. In a single cycle, we fill the entire VPU with row vectors. Inside instruction delay slots, we use software pipelining and compilation optimization to increase the use of VPUs. Therefore we achieve high computational efficiency. However, the filter becomes larger, which increases the transmission time. As a result, the calculation efficiency of DSC12 and DSC13 is lower than 50%.

### 4.3   Overall Performance Evaluation

Figure 4(a) shows the overall computational efficiency of the depthwise separable convolution of each layer in the network. We can see that as the amount of pointwise convolution calculation increases, its proportion in the entire DSC gradually increases. Especially for the last two layers, the computational efficiency of pointwise convolution is approximately equal to the overall computational efficiency.

The horizontal dashed line represents the computational efficiency of the entire MobileNet. It can be found that the calculation efficiency of eight layers is close to the overall calculation efficiency. For the whole network, the performance reached 1.7 TFLOPS. As the amount of data decreases in the first five layers, computational efficiency is on the rise. The data volume of the last eight layers is greater than the buffer capacity in AM, so the weight data of pointwise convolution needs to be divided into AM multiple times, which leads to an increase in transmission time. The weight data of the last two layers of PWC is the most in the entire network, so these two layers' calculation efficiency is the lowest.

Figure 4(b) shows the consumption time of each layer and the proportion of calculation time to the total time. Though three parts of the data transmission time cannot be hidden (transferring DWC data, writing back the result of DWC, and writing back the result of pointwise convolution), the proportion of computationally intensive PWC becomes larger, which increases the calculation time of DSC.

**Table 2.** Comparison of different accelerators

| Accelarator (batch size) | peak performance (TFLOPS) | Speed (FPS) | Computational efficiency |
|---|---|---|---|
| 2080TI (1) [1] | 13.4 | 1132 | 9.88% |
| 2080TI (8) [1] | 13.4 | 2950 | 25.75% |
| *M-DSP (1) | 4.608 | 1518 | 38.53% |
| StratixV (1) [12] | 0.78 | 232 | 34.79% |
| ZU9 MPSoC (1) [11] | 1.678 | 809 | 29.73% |

The proportion depends on the amount of calculation. It can be seen that the greater the amount of calculation, the greater the proportion of calculation time to the total time, and the smaller the impact of data transmission on execution time.

Table 2 compares the computational performance of different accelerators running MobileNet. We found that using the TensorRT acceleration library, the GPU achieves high computational performance, but the computational efficiency is low. Increasing the batch size improves the computational efficiency and performance of GPU significantly. Therefore, we use one as the size to test the effectiveness of the method. In actual use, the size can also be increased according to the number of VPEs. FPGAs, such as ZU9 and Stratixv, are computationally efficient. Compared with Stratixv, ZU9 has richer hardware resources and achieves higher computational performance. Our accelerators have high resource utilization and achieve the highest computing efficiency among all accelerators. The computational efficiency on M-DSP is 38.5% while processing 1518 frames per second (FPS).

## 5   Conclusion

This paper designs a mapping method to map depthwise separable convolutions on a general-purpose vector processor. We propose a multi-vector parallel convolution (MVPC) method to calculate depthwise convolution. The method realizes the reuse of input, filter, and output data. We use general matrix multiplication to solve pointwise convolution and fully connected layers. To minimize execution time, we optimize each layer individually on a multi-core DSP and reduce data transmission time. To a certain extent, it achieves a trade-off between power consumption, performance, and price, which is its advantage over existing accelerators. Compared to ASIC implementation, vector processors have higher performance and the flexibility to support multiple networks. Compared with GPUs, vector processors have higher computational efficiency and lower power consumption. Overall, using the same batch size, M-DSP runs MobileNet at a speed of 1518 FPS, which is 1.87 times faster than ZU9 and 1.34 times faster than 2080Ti. The calculation efficiency is 38.5%, which is 1.29× that of ZU9 and 3.89× that of 2080Ti.

# References

1. Machine learning benchmark. https://www.eembc.org/mlmark/scores. Accessed 23 Mar 2021
2. Chen, Y., et al.: Dadiannao: a machine-learning supercomputer. In: 2014 47th Annual IEEE/ACM International Symposium on Microarchitecture, pp. 609–622. IEEE (2014)
3. Cho, M., Brand, D.: Mec: memory-efficient convolution for deep neural network. In: International Conference on Machine Learning, pp. 815–824. PMLR (2017)
4. Gudaparthi, S., Narayanan, S., Balasubramonian, R., Giacomin, E., Kambalasub-ramanyam, H., Gaillardon, P.E.: Wire-aware architecture and dataflow for cnn accelerators. In: Proceedings of the 52nd Annual IEEE/ACM International Symposium on Microarchitecture, pp. 1–13 (2019)
5. Huang, C.T., et al.: ecnn: a block-based and highly-parallel cnn accelerator for edge inference. In: Proceedings of the 52nd Annual IEEE/ACM International Symposium on Microarchitecture, pp. 182–195 (2019)
6. Kanellopoulos, K., et al.: Smash: Co-designing software compression and hardware-accelerated indexing for efficient sparse matrix operations. In: Proceedings of the 52nd Annual IEEE/ACM International Symposium on Microarchitecture, pp. 600–614 (2019)
7. Lee, Y.C., Chi, T.S., Yang, C.H.: A 2.17 mw acoustic dsp processor with cnn-fft accelerators for intelligent hearing aided devices. In: 2019 IEEE International Conference on Artificial Intelligence Circuits and Systems (AICAS), pp. 97–101. IEEE (2019)
8. Ma, L., Xie, Z., Yang, Z., Xue, J., Miao, Y., Cui, W., Hu, W., Yang, F., Zhang, L., Zhou, L.: Rammer: Enabling holistic deep learning compiler optimizations with rtasks. In: 14th {USENIX} Symposium on Operating Systems Design and Implementation ({OSDI} 20), pp. 881–897 (2020)
9. Qin, E., et al.: Sigma: a sparse and irregular gemm accelerator with flexible interconnects for dnn training. In: 2020 IEEE International Symposium on High Performance Computer Architecture (HPCA), pp. 58–70. IEEE (2020)
10. Sohl, J., Wang, J., Liu, D.: Large matrix multiplication on a novel heterogeneous parallel dsp architecture. In: International Workshop on Advanced Parallel Processing Technologies, pp. 408–419. Springer (2009)
11. Wu, D., et al.: A high-performance cnn processor based on fpga for mobilenets. In: 2019 29th International Conference on Field Programmable Logic and Applications (FPL), pp. 136–143. IEEE (2019)
12. Zhao, R., Niu, X., Luk, W.: Automatic optimising cnn with depthwise separable convolution on fpga: (abstact only). In: Proceedings of the 2018 ACM/SIGDA International Symposium on Field-Programmable Gate Arrays, pp. 285–285 (2018)

# KCNet: Kernel-Based Canonicalization Network for Entities in Recruitment Domain

Nidhi Goyal[1]([✉]), Niharika Sachdeva[2], Anmol Goel[3], Jushaan Singh Kalra[4], and Ponnurangam Kumaraguru[5]

[1] Indraprastha Institute of Information Technology, New Delhi, India
nidhig@iiitd.ac.in
[2] InfoEdge India Limited, Noida, India
niharika.sachdeva@infoedge.com
[3] Guru Gobind Singh Indraprastha University, Delhi, India
[4] Delhi Technological University, Delhi, India
[5] International Institute of Information Technology, Hyderabad, India
pk.guru@iiit.ac.in

**Abstract.** Online recruitment platforms have abundant user-generated content in the form of job postings, candidate, and company profiles. This content when ingested into Knowledge bases causes redundant, ambiguous, and noisy entities. These multiple (non-standardized) representation of the entities deteriorates the performance of downstream tasks such as job recommender systems, search systems, and question answering. Therefore, making it imperative to canonicalize the entities to improve the performance of such tasks. Recent research discusses either statistical similarity measures or deep learning methods like word-embedding or siamese network-based representations for canonicalization. In this paper, we propose a Kernel-based Canonicalization Network (KCNet) that outperforms all the known statistical and deep learning methods. We also show that the use of side information such as industry type, url of websites, etc. further enhances the performance of the proposed method. Our experiments on 351,600 entities (companies, institutes, skills, and designations) from a popular online recruitment platform demonstrate that the proposed method improves the overall F1-score by 23% compared to the previous baselines, which results in coherent clusters of unique entities.

**Keywords:** Entity canonicalization · Recruitment domain · Entity normalization

## 1 Introduction

Recruitment platforms such as LinkedIn, Indeed.com ingest an enormous amount of user-generated content in form of job postings, CVs, and company profiles.

---

P. Kumaraguru—Major part of this work was done while Ponnurangam Kumaraguru was a faculty at IIIT-Delhi.

I. Farkaš et al. (Eds.): ICANN 2021, LNCS 12892, pp. 157–169, 2021.
https://doi.org/10.1007/978-3-030-86340-1_13

This content includes diverse set of recruitment domain entities (company names, institute names, skills, designations) that become part of Knowledge base. As the content is user-generated, multiple variations (e.g., *'economictimes.com'; 'eco. times'; 'the economic times'; 'economic times'; 'ET'*) of each entity name also come up into the KBs. Employing these noisy, redundant, and ambiguous variations directly into downstream applications such as semantic search, question answering, and recommender systems results in poor system performance. Therefore, canonicalization of the entities i.e., mapping various references of a unique entity into a representative cluster, is imperative for recruitment platforms.

Canonicalizing named entities involves various challenges including spelling mistakes and variations (*java developer* & *java deveoper*), overlapping but different entities (*Emerald Bikes pvt limited* & *Emerald Jewellery Retail Limited*), hierarchical variations (*Oracle Financial Services Software* & *Oracle Corporation*), domain-specific concepts (*SOAP* & *REST*), short forms (*umbc* & *University of Maryland, Baltimore*), and semantically similar variations (*Accel Frontline* & *Inspirisys*).

Previous approaches focus on statistical methods [5] for entity canonicalization. However, these methods use handcrafted features that are unable to scale well for advanced (semantic, domain-specific) variations of entities. Fatma et al. [4] employ a deep learning method that overcomes challenges of statistical methods by eliminating the need for explicit feature engineering and using character-based word-embeddings for unknown and emerging entities. Recent literature [9] shows that deep learning methods are often very good at minimizing the training errors but fail to generalize. Literature [9] suggests the introduction of learnable kernels in deep neural networks often improves generalizability.

Therefore, we study a kernel-based neural network designed for entity canonicalization in the recruitment domain. Our proposed method outperforms all the known statistical and deep learning methods on canonicalization tasks. We further enhance the performance of the kernel-based network using side-information which is underexplored in the literature. This literature suggests the use of external side information (morphological, IDF token overlap, PPDB [17]) which is rudimentary [21] and has limited utility in domain-specific settings. We leverage more prosperous meta and semantic side information from external sources (Wikipedia, Google KG) [10,22] to improve the entity canonicalization.

In this paper, we propose a novel multi-tier framework using a learnable kernel network [7,9] which implicitly maps the data into high-dimensional feature space. Our framework captures the non-linear mapping between contextual, meta, and semantic representations through learning objective to output the pairwise similarity between recruitment domain entities. Furthermore, we generate the canonicalized clusters for each entity. We demonstrate and validate the efficacy of our approach on proprietary as well as open source datasets including DBpedia and ESCO [1,3] for generalizability of our solution. We summarize the main contributions of *this* paper as follows:

– We propose a Kernel-based Canonicalization Network (KCNet), which induces a non-linear mapping between the contextual vector representations

while capturing fine-granular and high-dimensional relationships among vectors. To the best of our knowledge, this is the first approach towards exploring kernel features for canonicalizing Knowledge Base entities in the recruitment domain.
- KCNet efficiently models more prosperous semantic and meta side information from external knowledge sources to canonicalize domain-specific entities.
- We perform extensive experiments on real-world proprietary and publicly available datasets in the recruitment domain to show the effectiveness of our proposed approach as compared to baselines.

The organization of the rest of the paper is as follows: Sect. 2 contains related works; Sect. 3 elaborates our proposed framework KCNet; Sect. 4 reports the datasets. Section 5 describes the experimental setup, Sect. 6 has results and discussion followed by conclusion in Sect. 7.

## 2   Related Works

This section briefly describes some of the related works on KB Canonicalization, domain-specific methods, kernel methods, and clustering.

**KB Canonicalization.** Existing work [5] use manually defined feature spaces to perform the canonicalization task. This approach encodes limited similarity between different semantic representations. Hence, it results in degradation of performance for real-time applications. Vashishth et al. [21] jointly handle noun and relation phrases using knowledge graph embedding models [16] by optimizing its objective function along with using information from external sources called *'side information'*. However, these state-of-the-art knowledge graph embedding methods [2] achieve below par performance for real-world recruitment domain datasets due to noisy, sparseness [6], and context-sensitive information present in triples. Additionally, the side information methods used in literature [21] is rudimentary and lack domain-specific information. Considering these limitations, we leverage external knowledge sources such as Wikipedia Infobox and Google search API which provides additional knowledge for noisy entities.

**Domain-Specific Methods.** Despite the importance of named-entity canonicalization in the recruitment domain, only a few recent studies have explored the problem with respect to unique domain challenges [12,13]. Yan et al. [24] propose a company name normalization system that employs LinkedIn social graphs and a binary classification approach. In this work, the authors use complete profile information as the context. However, this information will be hard to get for new and emerging entities. Lin et al. [11] uses side information and learns domain knowledge from the source text based on the type of entities. Popular state-of-the-art entity linking tools [14] are probabilistic and requires sufficient contextual information to connect to candidate entity and perform well when standard surface forms are available. For example, recruitment domain-specific documents may contain *'Python'* or *'Python Programming'* while, the former is linked to a different type of entity with a high confidence score using these tools. Similarly, Fatma et al. [4] utilizes word and character-based representations based similarity model along with the attention mechanism to cluster similar entities. However, these works fail to generalize and have limited understanding for more complex and emerging entities.

***Kernel-Based Architectures.*** Kernel methods have proven effective in exploring larger feature space implicitly in deep learning architectures [23]. Customized kernel [8] based deep learning architectures enhance the performance of the model and map data to an optimized high-level feature space where data may have desirable features toward the application. Recent works utilize deep embedding kernel architectures for identity detection, transfer learning, classification and other tasks [9]. We use kernel infused neural networks to capture the latent semantic relationships and non-linearity between different pair of entities in KBs. These kernel methods are robust for collaboration with neural networks and less expensive than training deep learning architectures.

***Clustering Methods.*** Research works have used various clustering techniques for the canonicalization task. Among these methods, Hierarchical Agglomerative Clustering (HAC) is the most extensively used in the literature [5, 21].

Our research is uniquely placed at the intersection of the vast literature on kernel-based neural network learning, and clustering approaches for the canonicalization of domain-specific KBs.

## 3   Kernel-Based Canonicalization Network (KCNet)

In this section, we introduce the proposed KCNet approach. We elaborate on the problem definition and each component of our network architecture in detail.

### 3.1   Problem Definition

Consider $\mathcal{E}$ be the set of entities extracted from job postings, CVs, and company profiles. For each entity $x_i$, we consider its side information $s_i \in \mathcal{S} \ \forall x_i \in \mathcal{E}$ acquired from heterogeneous sources (elaborated in detail in Sect. 4.2). Given a pair of entities $x_1$ and $x_2$ and their corresponding side information $s_1$ and $s_2$ where $x_1, x_2 \in \mathcal{E}$ and $s_1, s_2 \in \mathcal{S}$, the main objective is to find a function $f(x_1, s_1, x_2, s_2) \rightarrow sim(x_1, x_2)$. A pairwise similarity matrix $(\mathcal{M}_{sim})$ is formed by applying $f$ over the set of all entity pairs and then a clustering algorithm is used to form unique canonical clusters of similar entities.

### 3.2   Network Architecture

We propose a multi-tier novel architecture consisting of three modules: Entity embedding generation, Side Information embedding generation, and Kernel network. We apply clustering technique after obtaining output on our proposed architecture. Fig. 1 shows the overall architecture of our proposed approach (KCNet).

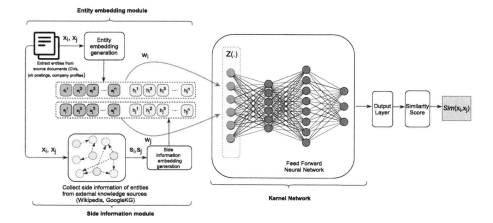

**Fig. 1.** Kernel-based Canonicalization Network for entities in recruitment domain. We first extract entities and combine it with side information. The combination (concat) is passed through the Kernel network. The output is a pairwise similarity matrix.

- **Entity embedding generation.** We obtain an $m$-dimensional ($m = 768$) vector for each entity pair $(x_i, x_j)$ producing $(e_i, e_j)$ in the space $C \in \mathcal{R}^m$. We use a pre-trained distilled version (fewer parameters, less space and time complexity) of S-BERT [19] to generate initial contextual[†][1] embeddings for all entities.
- **Side Information embedding generation.** We represent $(h_i, h_j)$ as $n$-dimensional vector ($n = 768$) for the side information acquired for each entity pair $(x_i, x_j)$ in the space $H \in \mathcal{R}^n$. The formation of side information vector is described in Sect. 4.2. These representations $h_i$ and $h_j$ are concatenated with the corresponding entity representations $e_i$ and $e_j$ to obtain infused vector representations $w_i$ and $w_j$ for the input pair $(x_i, x_j)$. Here, $w_i = e_i \odot h_i$ and $w_j = e_j \odot h_j$, Note that, $\odot$ is the concatenation function of two vectors producing $(w_i, w_j)$ in the space $W \in \mathcal{R}^{m+n}$. The $(m+n)$-dimensional vector representation is fed into the kernel network to learn the similarity function, $sim(x_i, x_j)$.
- **Kernel Network.** We introduce a kernel network to learn the similarity function $f$ to model complex relationships between the data representations of input pairs in an optimized space. The input to this network is denoted as $Z$, formed by the combined representation $w$ in the Eq. (1).

$$Z = (w_i \circ w_j) \odot |w_i - w_j| \tag{1}$$

Here, $\circ$ is a Hadamard (element-wise) product which exploits interactions between two vectors at each dimension. We also determine the $\mathcal{L}_1$ distance

---

[1] † specifies that an entity name such as '*University of Maryland, Baltimore*' contains the location specific context i.e. '*Baltimore*'. The representation of the entire entity is termed as contextual embedding.

for each dimension $w_i$ and $w_j$ and concatenate the interactions of both the components as shown in Eq. (2).

$$Z = \left\{ w_i^1 * w_j^1, \ldots, w_i^{m+n} * w_j^{m+n}, |w_i^1 - w_j^1|, \ldots, |w_i^{m+n} - w_j^{m+n}| \right\} \qquad (2)$$

where $w_i^k$ represents the $k^{th}$ dimension of $w_i$. The dimensionality of $Z$ is $2 * (m + n)$. Kernel function takes in account both element-wise product (design of polynomial kernel) and differences (design of RBF kernel) over each dimension of original entity. This configuration of inputs allows the network to learn a non-linear relationship between the input pairs and symmetric representations at a fine granular level over each input dimension. Therefore, the learned kernel can map a more robust similarity function over the input space in comparison to traditional methods such as RBF and polynomial [8]. Similar observations for the customized kernel have been made in [9]. The newly obtained vector $Z$ captures the latent semantic relationships between the two input entities. This vector is fed into a multi-layer feed-forward neural network with *sigmoid* output, facilitating the learning of a highly non-linear mapping $f$ to predict similarity over entity pairs. The size of hidden layers (number of neurons) in the kernel network is chosen using a hyperparameter $k$. We define $k = \alpha * d$ where $d$ is the dimensionality of $Z$ and typically, $\alpha = \{1, 2, 3\}$, say, $f(x_i, x_j) = f(x_j, x_i) > 0$. The kernel network outputs the probability that input pair $(x_i, x_j)$ belong to the same cluster. Therefore,

$$f(x_i, x_j) = P(y^i = y^j | x_i, x_j) \qquad (3)$$

- *Clustering using pairwise similarity scores.* We compute the pairwise similarity matrix $\mathcal{M}_{sim}$ for all the entity pairs $(x_i, x_j)$ using probability obtained from previous step and apply Hierarchical Agglomerative Clustering (HAC) to form a unique cluster of entities. HAC is popular technique used in literature [5,21] for canonicalization tasks. Each entity is finally mapped to a unique cluster. We choose the number of clusters $k$ using the silhouette index [20]. We repeat the same process for all the datasets (skills, designations, institutes, companies).

## 4    Datasets

In this section, we describe our datasets and side information collection process in detail.

### 4.1    Dataset Description

*Proprietary Datasets.* We use real-world datasets from one of the largest recruitment platforms in India. The dataset i.e., Recruitment Domain Entities (RDE) consists of 25,602 company clusters (RDE (C)), 23,690 institute clusters (RDE (I)), 607 skill clusters (RDE (S)), and 3,894 designation clusters (RDE (D)). The ground truth clusters are manually annotated by domain experts with a kappa agreement of 0.83. Next, we generate the variation pairs- positive and negative samples. Each name variation of entity $e_x \in \mathcal{E}$ is defined as $\{e_x^1, e_x^2, e_x^3, \ldots e_x^n\}$, which belong to same annotated cluster. We remove Non-ASCII characters to form a set of all unique name variations of $e_x$. For each entity pair, $(e_x^i, e_y^j)$, training data is prepared using the mapping function $g$, such that, $g(e_x^i, e_y^j) = 1, \forall(x, y)$ where $i \neq j$ and $x = y$ belongs to same annotated cluster (positive pairs). Similarly, $g(e_x^i, e_y^j) = 0$ where $x \neq y$ belongs to different clusters (negative pairs) using a random sampling approach [15].

**Open Datasets.** We test the effectiveness of our framework (KCNet) using open-source datasets i.e., DBpedia(C) and ESCO. DBpedia(C) [4] dataset is prepared by querying DBpedia for company names to extract *dbo:Company* which contains 2,944 entity clusters and 22,829 variation pairs. ESCO [3] i.e., ESCO(S) and ESCO(D) are open-source recruitment domain datasets for ESCO-skills and ESCO-designations. ESCO(S) has 35,554 variation pairs and 2,644 clusters of ESCO-skills. ESCO(D) has 62,969 variation pairs and 2,903 clusters. Authors [4] prepared and released these datasets for research community.

## 4.2  Side Information Collection

We leverage two sources for side information extraction, *Wikipedia infoboxes* and *Google KG*.

**Wikipedia Infobox.** We query Wikipedia using its advanced search options[2] and extracted knowledge from Wikipedia infoboxes for different datasets such as {*'title_wikis'*, *'websites'*, *'types'*} for RDE(S); {*'Names'*, *'websites'*, *'title_wikis'*} for RDE(D); {*'Names'*, *'websites'*, *'affiliation'*} for RDE(I); {*'Names'*, *'websites'*, *'title_wikis'*, *'types'*} for ESCO(S); {*'Names'*, *'websites'*, *'title_wikis'*} for ESCO(D); {*'types'*, *'industries'*, *'websites'*, *'native names'*, *'title_wikis'*} for DBpedia(C).

**Google KG.** For some entities with short forms, noisy variations, etc. we are unable to fetch knowledge using Wikipedia search; therefore, we leverage Google KG Search API [3] to extract rich semantic textual descriptions of entities to supplement the model with semantic knowledge. Other attributes such as {*location, type, established*} are extracted that form a part of meta knowledge. Finally, we combine the side information extracted from Google KG and Wikipedia infoboxes. For example, an entity *'vb script'* and its combined side information is defined as *'descriptions'*: 'VBScript is an Active Scripting language ... advanced programming constructs'; *'title_wikis'*:'VBScript'; *'websites'* docs.microsoft.com/en-us/previous-versions/t0aew7h6}. We create side information embeddings $s_i$, a concatenated sequence of side information vector representations $\{s_i^1, s_i^2, \ldots s_i^p\}$, where $p$ is the number of attributes obtained from external

---

[2] https://www.mediawiki.org/wiki/MediaWiki.
[3] https://serpapi.com/.

sources. We generate the side information embeddings using a pre-trained distilled version of S-BERT [19] model. We follow the same process across all the entity types.

## 5    Experimental Setup

In this section, we describe our baselines, model configurations, and evaluation metrics.

***Baselines.*** We compare our approach against the following methods:

*Galarraga-IDF.* Authors [5] uses AMIE algorithm and handcrafted features to find the similarity between entity $e_x$ and entity $e_y$. We utilize the weighted word overlap approach as a baseline method.

*Entity Embeddings (Distilled S-BERT(\*)) +cosine.* We generate our entity embeddings (see Sect. 3.2) to obtain the vector representation for the entity pair $(x_i, x_j)$. Instead of using the next module, i.e. Kernel Network, we apply cosine similarity measure to get a pairwise similarity matrix.

*Entity and Side Information Embeddings (Distilled S-BERT(\*\*)) +cosine.* We obtain entity embedding of $(x_i, x_j)$ and side information embedding of $(s_i, s_j)$ to get $(w_i, w_j)$ (see Sect. 3.2). The pairwise similarity matrix is generated using cosine similarity.

*Char-BiLSTM+A.* Fatma et al. [4] describe the architecture which utilize a siamese network that takes characters as input and passes it through the pair of BiLSTM layers enhanced by the attention layer.

*Word-BiLSTM+A.* This baseline modifies the previous method (Char-BiLSTM+A) [4] by replacing character-based representations with word-based representations followed by attention layer.

*Char-BiLSTM+A+Word+A.* Authors [4] combine Char-BiLSTM+A and Word-BiLSTM+A architectures combining word and character representations followed by attention mechanism.

***Model Configurations.*** We learn pairwise similarity models using the proposed architecture for different datasets (companies, institutes, designations, skills). The training and testing dataset split is taken as *(80, 20)*. The optimal value of hyperparameters (*size of hidden layer, α*) for companies, designations, and skills is (*1536, 2*) whereas for institutes, (*768, 2*). Batch-size is *512* and the number of fully connected layers are *3*. Rectified linear units (*ReLU*) is used as activation function and dropout rate is 0.3. *Binary cross-entropy loss* and *Adam* as an optimizer is used to train the kernel network and learn the pairwise similarity matrix ($\mathcal{M}_{sim}$).

***Evaluation Metrics.*** For pairwise similarity results (Table 1), we use *Precision* (P), *Recall* (R) and *F1-score* (F) [18]. We evaluate clusters (see Table 2) using *Micro Precision, Macro Precision, Micro Recall,* and *Macro Recall* used in the literature [21].

# 6   Results and Discussion

***Pairwise Similarity.*** Table 1 summarizes the test results of the pairwise similarity of KCNet along with other baseline approaches. We observe that *Galarraga IDF* (a weighted word overlap similarity measure) and the entity embeddings generated using *Distilled S-BERT(\*)+cosine* results in low pairwise similarity for non-overlapping variations and different surface forms of entities. For e.g. (*'mdx'*, *'MultiDimensional eXpressions'*) has similarity of 0.73 using Distilled S-BERT(\*)+cosine. *KCNet* gives the similarity of 0.84 as it learns the structure and non-linear mapping in latent space, even in the absence of side information. With side information, *KCNet* learns the latent semantic relationships between these two entities and returns a high similarity score of 0.99. Another example is overlapping variations (*uplholstery fillings, upholstery paddings*); *Distilled S-BERT(\*)+cosine* returns a pairwise similarity score of 0.86 for these same entities, whereas *KCNet* learns a better representation and gives a pairwise similarity score of 0.99. *KCNet* generalizes well across all entity types, it gives higher P and F even for all open datasets where it outperforms with 21% F1-score as compared to best baseline.

**Table 1.** Test Results of pairwise similarity using our proposed model in comparison with different baselines. Here S, D, I, C refers to Skills, Designations, Institutes, and Companies datasets respectively. Results of † are taken from [4]. P and F refers to Precision and F1-scores. Distilled S-BERT (\*, \*\*) refers to (entity, entity ⊙ side information) embedding using distilled S-BERT model.

| Model | Performance | | | | | | | | | | | | | |
|---|---|---|---|---|---|---|---|---|---|---|---|---|---|---|
| | Proprietary | | | | | | | | Open | | | | | |
| | S | | D | | I | | C | | ESCO(S) | | ESCO(D) | | DBpedia(C) | |
| | P | F | P | F | P | F | P | F | P | F | P | F | P | F |
| Galarraga-IDF† | 33.2 | 12.5 | 63.0 | 60.3 | 64.3 | 66.5 | 75.8 | 71.2 | 50.8 | 32.8 | 61.7 | 38.9 | 22.6 | 23.6 |
| Distilled S-BERT(\*)+cosine | 47.8 | 47.5 | 49.7 | 48.8 | 49.7 | 49.1 | 49.2 | 49.1 | 49.3 | 44.4 | 49.3 | 39.0 | 49.6 | 45.3 |
| Distilled S-BERT(\*\*)+cosine | 47.5 | 48.8 | 49.8 | 49.9 | 34.6 | 41.5 | 56.2 | 48.4 | 49.5 | 50.0 | 49.4 | 49.7 | 50.0 | 49.8 |
| CharBiLSTM+A† | 81.8 | 86.9 | 72.6 | 77.2 | 84.5 | 84.8 | 99.3 | 98.9 | 85.9 | 86.9 | 76.3 | 75.1 | 72.1 | 59.7 |
| WordBiLSTM+A† | 80.1 | 86.5 | 90.5 | 94.8 | 80.6 | 83.3 | 95.3 | 95.6 | 85.6 | 89.6 | 83.1 | 83.7 | 77.6 | 70.7 |
| CharBiLSTM+A+Word+A† | 82.7 | 88.5 | 94.4 | 96.3 | 86.7 | 86.7 | 99.5 | 99.2 | 87.3 | 90.7 | 84.2 | 85.4 | 78.0 | 71.3 |
| KCNet (without sideinfo) | **96.7** | **90.6** | **99.6** | 90.9 | **92.4** | **89.3** | 99.4 | 98.8 | **99.0** | **95.1** | **98.8** | **86.9** | **99.0** | **92.5** |
| KCNet (with sideinfo) | **99.5** | **99.4** | **99.7** | **99.6** | **99.5** | **99.5** | **99.5** | **99.3** | **99.2** | **98.3** | **98.8** | **89.4** | **99.1** | **97.0** |

***Clustering results.*** Test results after applying the clustering approach is reported in Table 2. Overall, *KCNet* significantly outperforms the best baseline [4] by an improved micro F1-score by 23% and macro F1-score by 25%. A one-way repeated measures ANOVA test was conducted to determine significance for all evaluation metrics ($p < 0.00003$).

***Side Information for KCNet.*** We evaluate the performances of different versions of *KCNet* (with and without side info). From Table 1, we observe that

**Table 2.** Test Results over HAC using pairwise similarity. Here, $\beta$: baseline (*Char-BiLSTM+A+Word+A*) and $\gamma$: proposed model (*KCNet*) with sideinfo.

| Dataset | Model | Metrics | | | | | |
|---------|-------|---------|---------|------|---------|---------|------|
| | | Micro | | | Macro | | |
| | | P | R | F | P | R | F |
| S | $\beta$ | 0.71 | 0.64 | 0.67 | 0.94 | 0.31 | 0.47 |
| | $\gamma$ | **0.99** | **0.97** | **0.98** | **0.96** | **0.97** | **0.96** |
| D | $\beta$ | 0.95 | 0.53 | 0.67 | 0.83 | 0.15 | 0.24 |
| | $\gamma$ | 0.86 | **0.78** | **0.82** | **0.85** | **0.54** | **0.66** |
| I | $\beta$ | 0.84 | 0.75 | 0.79 | 0.96 | 0.48 | 0.64 |
| | $\gamma$ | 0.83 | **0.85** | **0.84** | 0.74 | **0.71** | **0.72** |
| C | $\beta$ | 0.98 | 0.99 | 0.98 | 0.97 | 0.96 | 0.96 |
| | $\gamma$ | 0.98 | 0.97 | **0.98** | **0.98** | **0.97** | **0.98** |
| ESCO(S) | $\beta$ | 0.84 | 0.82 | 0.83 | 0.65 | 0.49 | 0.55 |
| | $\gamma$ | **0.93** | **0.92** | **0.92** | **0.89** | **0.75** | **0.81** |
| ESCO(D) | $\beta$ | 0.49 | 0.79 | 0.61 | 0.21 | 0.32 | 0.25 |
| | $\gamma$ | **0.91** | 0.61 | **0.73** | **0.81** | 0.22 | **0.34** |
| DBpedia(C) | $\beta$ | 0.88 | 0.52 | 0.65 | 0.92 | 0.25 | 0.39 |
| | $\gamma$ | **0.93** | **0.75** | **0.83** | 0.86 | **0.60** | **0.70** |

P and F performance benefits from increased performance in the presence of side information. *Char-BiLSTM+A+Word+A* captures limited patterns and unable to model similar semantic variations (*mycology, fungi studies*) for which *KCNet* gives a pairwise similarity score of 0.98. This shows that *KCNet* is able to model these variations well when supplemented with side-information. Even though side information might be unavailable for a some entities, the proposed framework results in overall better entity canonicalization.

***Error Analysis:*** Although KCNet gives promising results across all datasets, it wrongly clusters some entities; for example, some skills such as *bees wax* and *natural wax* signify same concept but occur in the different cluster. One possible reason could be that the representation of words *bees* and *natural* are far apart in the contextual vector representation space, so the model assigns a lower similarity score and hence, incorrectly classifies it. Similarly, *'packager'* is incorrectly placed in cluster of [*'dozer driver'*, *'dozer/crawler driver'*, *'packager'*]. The possible reason could be the complete absence of side information for three entities confuses KCNet with closer contextual vector representations. Despite this, KCNet addresses the challenge of handling abbreviations, short forms, and non-overlapping entities by learning vector representations of these entities in the kernel space.

# 7    Conclusion

Our research focused upon canonicalizing real-world entities from the recruitment domain such as companies, designations, institutes, and skills by designing a novel multi-tier framework Kernel-based Canonicalization Network (KCNet). KCNet induces a non-linear mapping between the contextual vector representations while capturing fine-granular and high-dimensional relationships among vectors. KCNet efficiently models more prosperous semantic and meta side information from external knowledge towards exploring kernel features for canonicalizing entities in the recruitment domain. Furthermore, we applied Hierarchical Agglomerative Clustering (HAC) using the pairwise similarity matrix $\mathcal{M}_{sim}$ to create unique clusters of entities. Experiments revealed that the Kernel-based neural network approach achieves significantly higher performance on both proprietary and open datasets. We demonstrate that our proposed methods are also generalizable to domain-specific entities in similar scenarios.

**Acknowledgements.** We would like to acknowledge the support from SERB, InfoEdge India Limited, and FICCI. We are grateful to PreCog Research Group and Dr. Siddartha Asthana for critically reviewing the manuscript and stimulating discussions.

# References

1. Auer, S., Bizer, C., Kobilarov, G., Lehmann, J., Cyganiak, R., Ives, Z.: DBpedia: A Nucleus for a Web of Open Data. In: Aberer, K., Choi, K.-S., Noy, N., Allemang, D., Lee, K.-I., Nixon, L., Golbeck, J., Mika, P., Maynard, D., Mizoguchi, R., Schreiber, G., Cudré-Mauroux, P. (eds.) ASWC/ISWC -2007. LNCS, vol. 4825, pp. 722–735. Springer, Heidelberg (2007). https://doi.org/10.1007/978-3-540-76298-0_52
2. Bordes, A., Usunier, N., Garcia-Duran, A., Weston, J., Yakhnenko, O.: Translating embeddings for modeling multi-relational data. In: Advances in Neural Information Processing Systems (2013)
3. European Commission: ESCO handbook. EU publications (2019)
4. Fatma, N., Choudhary, V., Sachdeva, N., Rajput, N.: Canonicalizing knowledge bases for recruitment domain. In: Lauw, H.W., Wong, R.C.-W., Ntoulas, A., Lim, E.-P., Ng, S.-K., Pan, S.J. (eds.) PAKDD 2020. LNCS (LNAI), vol. 12085, pp. 500–513. Springer, Cham (2020). https://doi.org/10.1007/978-3-030-47436-2_38
5. Galárraga, L., Heitz, G., Murphy, K., Suchanek, F.M.: Canonicalizing open knowledge bases. In: Proceedings of the 23rd ACM International Conference on Conference on Information and Knowledge Management, pp. 1679–1688 (2014)
6. Gupta, S., Kenkre, S., Talukdar, P.: Care: Open knowledge graph embeddings. In: Proceedings of the 2019 Conference on Empirical Methods in Natural Language Processing and the 9th International Joint Conference on Natural Language Processing (EMNLP-IJCNLP), pp. 378–388 (2019)
7. Hofmann, T., Schölkopf, B., Smola, A.J.: Kernel methods in machine learning. The Annals of Statistics, pp. 1171–1220 (2008)
8. Kuo, B.C., Ho, H.H., Li, C.H., Hung, C.C., Taur, J.S.: A kernel-based feature selection method for SVM with RBF kernel for hyperspectral image classification. IEEE J. Selected Top. Appl. Earth Observations Remote Sensing **7**(1), 317–326 (2013)

9. Le, L., Xie, Y.: Deep embedding kernel. Neurocomputing **339**, 292–302 (2019)
10. Lehmann, J., Isele, R., Jakob, M., Jentzsch, A., Kontokostas, D., Mendes, P.N., Hellmann, S., Morsey, M., Van Kleef, P., Auer, S., et al.: Dbpedia-a large-scale, multilingual knowledge base extracted from wikipedia. Semantic Web **6**(2), 167–195 (2015)
11. Lin, X., Chen, L.: Canonicalization of open knowledge bases with side information from the source text. In: 2019 IEEE 35th International Conference on Data Engineering (ICDE), pp. 950–961. IEEE (2019)
12. Liu, Q., Javed, F., Dave, V.S., Joshi, A.: Supporting employer name normalization at both entity and cluster level. In: Proceedings of the 23rd ACM SIGKDD International Conference on Knowledge Discovery and Data Mining, pp. 1883–1892 (2017)
13. Liu, Q., Javed, F., Mcnair, M.: Companydepot: Employer name normalization in the online recruitment industry. In: Proceedings of the 22nd ACM SIGKDD International Conference on Knowledge Discovery and Data Mining, pp. 521–530 (2016)
14. Mendes, P.N., Jakob, M., García-Silva, A., Bizer, C.: Dbpedia spotlight: shedding light on the web of documents. In: Proceedings of the 7th International Conference on Semantic Systems, pp. 1–8 (2011)
15. Neculoiu, P., Versteegh, M., Rotaru, M.: Learning text similarity with siamese recurrent networks. In: Proceedings of the 1st Workshop on Representation Learning for NLP, pp. 148–157 (2016)
16. Nickel, M., Rosasco, L., Poggio, T.A., et al.: Holographic embeddings of knowledge graphs. AAAI. **2**, 3–2 (2016)
17. Pavlick, E., Rastogi, P., Ganitkevitch, J., Van Durme, B., Callison-Burch, C.: Ppdb 2.0: Better paraphrase ranking, fine-grained entailment relations, word embeddings, and style classification. In: Proceedings of the 53rd Annual Meeting of the Association for Computational Linguistics and the 7th International Joint Conference on Natural Language Processing (Volume 2: Short Papers), pp. 425–430 (2015)
18. Raghavan, V., Bollmann, P., Jung, G.S.: A critical investigation of recall and precision as measures of retrieval system performance. ACM Trans. Inf. Syst. (TOIS) **7**(3), 205–229 (1989)
19. Reimers, N., Gurevych, I.: Sentence-BERT: sentence embeddings using Siamese BERT-networks. In: Proceedings of the 2019 Conference on Empirical Methods in Natural Language Processing and the 9th International Joint Conference on Natural Language Processing (EMNLP-IJCNLP), pp. 3982–3992. Association for Computational Linguistics, Hong Kong, China, November 2019
20. Starczewski, A., Krzyżak, A.: Performance evaluation of the silhouette index. In: Rutkowski, L., Korytkowski, M., Scherer, R., Tadeusiewicz, R., Zadeh, L.A., Zurada, J.M. (eds.) ICAISC 2015. LNCS (LNAI), vol. 9120, pp. 49–58. Springer, Cham (2015). https://doi.org/10.1007/978-3-319-19369-4_5
21. Vashishth, S., Jain, P., Talukdar, P.: CESI: canonicalizing open knowledge bases using embeddings and side information. In: Proceedings of the 2018 World Wide Web Conference, WWW 2018, International World Wide Web Conferences Steering Committee, Republic and Canton of Geneva, Switzerland, pp. 1317–1327 (2018)
22. Vrandečić, D., Krötzsch, M.: Wikidata: a free collaborative knowledgebase. Commun. ACM **57**(10), 78–85 (2014)

23. Weston, J., Ratle, F., Mobahi, H., Collobert, R.: Deep learning via semi-supervised embedding. In: Montavon, G., Orr, G.B., Müller, K.-R. (eds.) Neural Networks: Tricks of the Trade. LNCS, vol. 7700, pp. 639–655. Springer, Heidelberg (2012). https://doi.org/10.1007/978-3-642-35289-8_34

24. Yan, B., Bajaj, L., Bhasin, A.: Entity resolution using social graphs for business applications. In: 2011 International Conference on Advances in Social Networks Analysis and Mining, pp. 220–227. IEEE (2011)

# Deep Unitary Convolutional Neural Networks

Hao-Yuan Chang$^{(\boxtimes)}$ ⓘ and Kang L. Wang ⓘ

University of California, Los Angeles, Los Angeles, CA 90095, USA
{h.chang,klwang}@ucla.edu

**Abstract.** Deep neural networks can suffer from the exploding and vanishing activation problem, in which the networks fail to train properly because the neural signals either amplify or attenuate across the layers and become saturated. While other normalization methods aim to fix the stated problem, most of them have inference speed penalties in those applications that require running averages of the neural activations. Here we extend the unitary framework based on Lie algebra to neural networks of any dimensionalities, overcoming the major constraints of the prior arts that limit synaptic weights to be square matrices. Our proposed unitary convolutional neural networks deliver up to 32% faster inference speeds and up to 50% reduction in permanent hard disk space while maintaining competitive prediction accuracy.

**Keywords:** Neural network · Lie algebra · Image recognition

## 1 Introduction

### 1.1 Problem Statement

Recent advancements in semiconductor technology [1] have enabled neural networks to grow significantly deeper. This abundant computing power enabled computer scientists to drastically increase the depths of neural networks from the 7-layer LeNet network [2] to the 152-layer contest-wining ResNet architecture [3]. More layers usually lead to higher recognition accuracy because neural networks make decisions by drawing decision boundaries in the high dimensional space [4]. A decision boundary is a demarcation in the feature space that separates the different output classes. The more layers the network has, the more precise these boundaries can be in the high dimensional feature space; thus, they can achieve higher recognition rates [5]. However, deep networks often fail to train properly due to poor convergence.

There are many reasons why a deep network fails to train [6], and the problem that our proposal fixes is the instability of the forward pass, in which neural activations either saturate to infinity or diminish to zero. More precisely, depending on the eigenvalues of the synaptic weight matrices [7], neural signals may grow or attenuate as they travel across neural layers when unbounded activation functions such as the rectified linear units (Relu) are used [8]. The Relu is the most popular nonlinearity due to its computational efficiency. Suppose the activation is extremely large or small; in this case, the weight

© Springer Nature Switzerland AG 2021
I. Farkaš et al. (Eds.): ICANN 2021, LNCS 12892, pp. 170–181, 2021.
https://doi.org/10.1007/978-3-030-86340-1_14

update will scale proportionally during training, resulting in either a massive or a tiny step.

In short, vanishing and exploding activations occur when the neural signals are not normalized, and the backpropagated gradients either saturate or die out during network training [9]. Although other schemes such as batch normalization [10], learning rate tuning [11], and gradient highways [3] can mitigate the issue, none of these methods eliminate the core problem—the weight matrices have eigenvalues that are larger or smaller than one. Furthermore, most normalization methods have inference time penalties. In this work, we aim to devise a way to fundamentally fix the exploding and vanishing activation problem without slowing down the inference speed.

## 1.2 Proposed Solution

Our proposed solution (Fig. 1) is to eliminate the need to normalize the neural signals after each layer by constraining the weight matrices, $W$, to be unitary. Unitary matrices represent rotations in the n-dimensional space[1]; hence, they preserve the norm (i.e., the amplitude) of the input vector. With this unique property, unitary networks can maintain the neural signal strengths without explicit normalization. This technique allows the designers to eliminate the networks' normalization blocks and make inference faster.

We aim to engineer a way to constrain the weights to be *unitary*. To achieve this, we leverage the previously reported framework for constructing orthogonal matrices in recurrent neural networks using Lie algebra [12], which we will explain briefly in Sect. 2.1. Unlike other approximation methods, this framework guarantees strictly unitary matrices; however, it is currently limited to square matrices. *Our main contribution is that we found a way (Sect. 2.2) to extend the unitary framework based on Lie algebra to weight matrices of any shapes.* By doing so, we expand the applicability of this framework from recurrent neural networks with square weight matrices to any neural network structures, drastically increasing its usefulness in state-of-the-art network architectures.

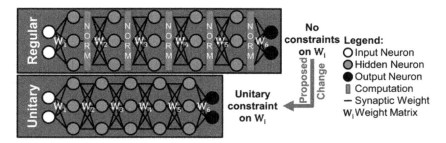

**Fig. 1.** Unitary network for mitigating exploding and vanishing activations.

---

[1] Unitary matrices can have complex values. When the matrices only contain real components, they are called orthogonal matrices, which is a subset of unitary matrices, and our proposal works in both cases. The eigenvalues of a unitary matrix have modulus 1.

### 1.3 Literature Review

Lie algebra is not the only way to construct unitary matrices. Researchers have explored many options to construct unitary weights for RNNs, including eigendecomposition [13], Cayley transform [14], square decomposition [15], Householder reflection [16], and optimization over Stiefel manifolds [17]. These methods decompose the unitary matrix into smaller parameter spaces with mathematical processes that guarantee unitarity; however, the weight matrices in these approaches must be square. For convolutional neural nets with rectangular weights, there are approximation techniques based on least square fitting [18], singular value decomposition [19], and soft regularization [20] due to the additional complexity of rectangular filters. These techniques find the best approximates to the unitary weights, but they do not guarantee the weight matrices to be strictly unitary. *On the contrary, our approach combines the best of the two schools—it is both strictly unitary and applicable to non-square matrices.* Our work is the first report of applying the unitary weights based on the Lie algebra framework for a deep convolutional neural network with a comprehensive performance study, aiming to make the unitary network an attractive alternative to conventional normalization methods in inference-time-critical applications.

## 2  Unitary Neural Networks with Lie Algebra

### 2.1  Square Unitary Weight Matrices

In this section, we explain the mathematical framework [12] for representing the unitary group with orthogonal matrices, collectively known as the Lie group [21]. Linearization of the Lie group about its identity generates a new set of operators; these new operators form a Lie algebra. Lie algebra is parameterized by the Lie parameters, which we arrange as a traceless lower triangular matrix, $L$. We name it Lie parameters because it contains independent trainable parameters for the neural networks. The representable algebra through this parameterization is only a subspace of unitary groups, and it is sufficient for guaranteeing signal stability in deep neural networks.

The Lie parameters ($L$) are related to the Lie algebra ($A$) by the following equation:

$$A = L - L^T,\tag{1}$$

where $T$ corresponds to taking the matrix transpose. An essential feature of matrix $A$ is that it is a skew-symmetric matrix, i.e., $A^T = -A$, because any compact metric-preserving group, including the orthogonal group, has anti-symmetric Lie algebra [22]. Furthermore, the following equation proves that the chosen representation for the Lie parameters will produce an anti-symmetric Lie algebra:

$$A^T + A = \left(L - L^T\right)^T + L - L^T = 0.\tag{2}$$

Additionally, in the last step of our pipeline to construct unitary matrices, we exponentiate the Lie algebra, $A$, to obtain the group representation, which will be a unitary matrix ($U$):

$$U = EXP(A) = \sum_{N=0}^{\infty} \frac{A^N}{N}!.\tag{3}$$

We approximate this matrix exponentiation with an 18-term Taylor series in our implementation. Besides eliminating any term beyond the $18^{th}$ order in Eq. (3), we efficiently group the computation to avoid redundant multiplications, a standard approach used in many matrix computation software to save time [23, 24].

Suppose the neural network has square weight matrices. In that case, we can use the unitary matrices ($U$) to replace the original weights, forcing the neural signals to maintain their norms without explicit normalization. We can train the Lie parameters using backpropagation and automatic differentiation because all steps in the pipeline above are algebraic functions [25, 26]. As mentioned previously, researchers have only applied the unitary pipeline to a small recurrent neural network (RNN), which has a single *square* weight matrix repeatedly applied in time [12]. Nevertheless, the requirement for the weights to be square severely limits the usefulness of the presented framework. Using the Lie algebra formalism to construct unitary weights is an elegant method to regulate signals, and we wish to find a way to bring this concept to deep convolutional neural nets with any non-square weight matrices.

## 2.2   Unitary Weight Matrices of Any Shapes and Dimensions

In the above section, the weight matrices must be square, forcing the number of neurons for both the input and output of a particular layer to be identical. This requirement cannot be satisfied in most convolutional neural nets. Convolutional layers have weight matrices commonly referred to as "filters." These filters will convolute with the input image as the following [5]:

$$O(i,j) = (I * F)(i,j) = \sum_m \sum_n I(i + m, j + n)F(m, n), \qquad (4)$$

where $O$ is the output activation map of this layer, $I$ is the input image, and $F$ is the convolutional filer. An example of convolution is illustrated in Fig. 2(a).

Moreover, we can succinctly represent the convolution as a single dot product through the Toeplitz matrix arrangement [27, 28]. Suppose we arrange the input image as a Toeplitz matrix and flatten out the filters to a 2-dimensional weight matrix. In that case, the convolution simplifies to a dot product between the Toeplitz matrix of the image and the flattened filter weights. Effectively, we convert the convolution between high-dimensional tensors to *multiplications* between 2-dimensional matrices. These flattened filters are usually rectangular $m \times k$ matrices, where $m \neq k$. If $m$ matches $k$, the weight matrix is square, allowing us to apply the unitary pipeline to ensure each row of the Toeplitz matrix will maintain its norm. On the other hand, when dealing with rectangular weights, we need to handle them with special care to achieve the desired effect of norm preservation.

Our innovation is that we discard the excess columns in the unitary matrix when $m \neq k$ (i.e., when the weight matrix has unequal width vs. height); for now, we will assume $m > k$ because the other cases only require a few slight adjustments. Even though there is no way around the fact the unitary matrices must be square, *we discovered that it is unnecessary to use the whole unitary matrix: we can just take the first few columns that we need*. We will construct the unitary matrix as a $m$ x $m$ matrix (i.e., in the larger of the two dimensions). This way, we can reuse the existing pipeline in Sect. 2.1. Our proposed pipeline is as follows. We only keep the first $k$ columns of the Lie parameters, setting everything else to zero. Likewise, we only take the first $k$ columns of the resulting unitary matrix ($U$), discarding the rest (Fig. 2(b)). Because the rectangular matrix now has the correct dimensions, we multiply the input image (in the Toeplitz form) with the unitary weight matrix. Below is a summary of our process to construct the unitary rectangular weights in the mathematical form:

$$\overline{y} = W \, \overline{x}, \tag{5}$$

where

$$W = \left[ \overline{u_1} \, \overline{u_2} \ldots \overline{u_k} \right] \in R^{m \times k}. \tag{6}$$

$\overline{u_1} \ldots \overline{u_k}$ are the first $k$ column vectors from the unitary matrix $U$ (Note that when $m \leq k$, we still construct the unitary matrix $U$ in the larger dimension, but $W$ will be transposed to obtain the desired dimensionality for the matrix multiplication). Lastly, the output vector is explicitly normalized using the Euclidean metric when $m > k$; this step is not required for $m \leq k$:

$$\overline{y_{final}} = \begin{cases} \overline{y}/\|\overline{y}\|_2 \, for \, m > k \\ \overline{y} \, for \, m \leq k \end{cases}, \tag{7}$$

where $\|\cdot\|_2$ denotes the Euclidean norm (a.k.a., Euclidean metric or the L2 norm), a distance measure calculated by squaring all the coordinates, summing the results, and taking the square root.

In theory, it is possible to avoid the explicit normalization Eq. (7) completely by one of the following two ways: by partitioning the tall rectangular weight matrix into a vertical stack of smaller matrices that are either square or wide. Or, by exploring alternative mappings from the various dimensions of $W$ to $m$ and $k$ to ensure $m \leq k$. Nevertheless, we took the direct normalization approach in this work for conceptual clarity, and it is only required in a small portion of the network. Moreover, even though it is not ideal to add normalization back to portions of our network, the unitary weights offer other benefits over conventional normalization. Researchers have found orthogonal weights lead to more efficient filters with fewer redundancies [20]. Our normalization process does not add additional training parameters to keep track of the activations' mean and variance.

Discarding columns of unitary matrices has important geometrical meanings. A unitary matrix represents a rotation in the n-dimensional space when $m = k$; additionally, its columns form a complete set of orthonormal bases in the rotated coordinate system. We have utilized the latter to paint a geometric understanding of our procedure—each of the $k$ columns is an orthonormal basis in the m-dimensional space. For $m > k$, the unitary weight ($W$) is projecting an input row vector $\overline{x}$ to a lower-dimensional manifold spanned by the unitary matrix's first $k$ columns, a subset of orthonormal bases. When we multiply the Toeplitz matrix with this unitary weight matrix, we perform a dot product between the row vectors against each orthonormal basis, measuring how much the input vector aligns with a specific basis. According to the Pythagorean theorem, this projection will produce a shorter vector than the original one because we dispose of those vector components associated with the unitary matrix's discarded columns. As a result, we need to normalize the output to recuperate the signals lost in missing dimensions.

On the contrary, for $m < k$, each row of the weight matrix is an orthonormal basis. In that case, we are mixing the orthonormal bases according to the ratio prescribed by the input row vector $\bar{x}$, resulting in a higher-dimensional output vector $\bar{y}$. This dimensionality expansion happens when we multiply the weight matrix with a row vector $(\bar{x})$ of the Toeplitz matrix that encodes the input image. Effectively, we are projecting a vector to the larger dimensions through the wide unitary weight $(W)$, and this operation preserves the Euclidean norm of the input vector $\bar{x}$. To prove this property mathematically, we simply compare the norm of $\bar{x}$ against the norm of $\bar{y}$. When we use the orthonormal bases defined by the unitary matrix $(U)$ to describe vector locations, the first p coordinates of $\bar{y}$ match $\bar{x}$, and the rest of the coordinates are zeros. Hence, $\|\bar{y}\|_2$ is the same as $\|\bar{x}\|_2$ because the Euclidean norm is defined as the square root of the sum of the squared coordinates.

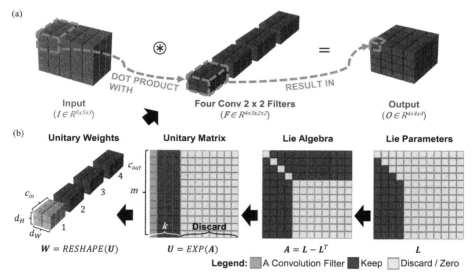

**Fig. 2.** Pipeline to construct unitary weights for a convolutional neural network. (a) convolution between an example input image and filters. (b) our proposed way of constructing unitary weights of any dimensions. From the right, Lie parameters contain all the trainable parameters, and we only need the first $k$ columns. Similarly, we keep the first $k$ columns of the resulting unitary matrix and reshape them to match the desired dimensionality for the convolutional filters. In this example, $k = c_{out}$ and $m = c_{in} \times d_H \times d_W$. This mapping will depend on the target applications.

## 3 Experiments

### 3.1 Network Architecture

We applied the proposed unitary weight matrices to the residual neural network (ResNet) for image recognition; our architecture is a narrower and shorter variant of the popular

ResNet-50 [3]. We picked a smaller model to prevent overfitting to the training data because ResNet-50 was designed for the more complex ImageNet dataset. Our network (uResNet-44) has only 43 convolutional layers with a fully connected layer at the end for projecting the high-dimensional neural signals to ten output classes. We documented the sizes and number of convolutional filters in Fig. 3 for reproducibility. Also, we studied the scalability in terms of depth with the 92 and 143-layer networks (uResNet-92 and uResNet-143). See our source code for details[2].

### 3.2  Dataset

We used the CIFAR-10 image recognition dataset created by the Canadian Institute for Advanced Research, and it contains 60,000 32 × 32 color images with ten labeled classes. The recognition task is to predict the correct class of each image in the dataset. CIFAR-10 is freely available for download [29]. We split the dataset into 50,000 training and 10,000 test images with the same data argumentation scheme as the original ResNet paper [3]. We also tested our unitary neural network's susceptibility to overfitting with the CIFAR-100 dataset [29].

### 3.3  Training Details

We modified the source code found in this reference [30] for comparison against conventional normalization techniques, sharing the same learning rate (0.1), learning schedule (divide by 10 at 100, 150, and 200 epochs), batch size (128), and training epochs (250). The only modification we made for the unitary neural net is that we added the unitary pipeline using the method described previously in Sect. 2.2 for the convolutional layers. We also removed all the normalization blocks in the unitary version. We trained the regular and the unitary networks with the stochastic gradient descent optimizer in PyTorch with a momentum setting of 0.9 and weight decay of 2e−4. We measured the neural networks' speed and memory usage by simulating each neural architecture one at a time on a single NVIDIA RTX3090 graphics card with 24 GB total video memory.

### 3.4  Caching of the Unitary Weights

During training, the entire neural pathway is enabled, including the block that contains the Lie parameters, Lie algebra, and Lie group (Fig. 3). Gradients are backpropagated from the output to update the Lie parameters. After training is complete, the best unitary weights are cached; thus, we do not need to recompute the unitary weights during inference.

---

[2] https://github.com/h-chang/uResNet.

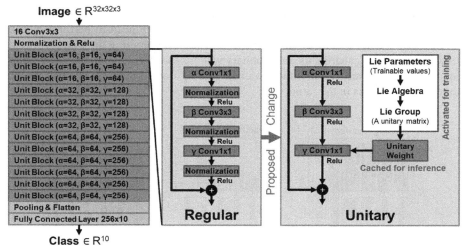

**Fig. 3.** The unitary convolutional neural network (CNN) architecture. There are two main differences between the regular and the unitary CNN. Firstly, in unitary CNNs, we permanently remove the normalization blocks to speed up computation because the unitary weights already preserve the signal strengths across layers. Secondly, unitary CNNs have an additional Lie block labeled "Activated for training" on the right. The Lie block is active only during the training mode to learn the Lie parameters. At the end of the training mode, a set of unitary weights is constructed from the Lie parameters and cached. The convolutional filters will use these pre-recorded unitary weights during inference. The removal of normalization significantly improves inference speed. We enlarge one of the unit blocks to illustrate its content; each unit block contains three convolutional layers. Unit blocks are cascaded to create a feed-forward convolutional neural network. The only difference between the unit blocks is the number of convolutional filters, which we label as $\alpha$, $\beta$, and $\gamma$ in the figure. $\alpha$ Conv1 $\times$ 1 for a layer with $\alpha = 16$ means that there are 16 convolutional filters with size $3 \times 3$ in that layer. The rectified linear unit (Relu) is used as nonlinearity at locations depicted in the figure.

## 4   Results and Discussion

With our proposed unitary convolutional neural network from Sect. 3, we compare the performance of our proposal against popular normalization methods and summarize the main results of our experiment in Fig. 4 below. By removing the network's unitary pipeline (the block with Lie parameters, Lie algebra, and Lie group in Fig. 3) during test time, we achieved a much faster inference speed than other normalization methods, including the batch norm [10], group norm [31], layer norm [32], and instance norm [33]. Each of these methods addresses a specific problem; therefore, the designer might favor one over the other depending on the application. *With our unitary convolution, we offer the community another tool in the toolbox that is lightning fast—32% faster than the instance norm in inference.* We compute the speedup by dividing the inference time of the unitary norm with the instance norm's in Fig. 4(e). Our method shares many characteristics with the instance norm; however, instead of normalizing based on the neural signals' statistics, we devise a set of unitary weights to ensure signals maintain their norm per Toeplitz matrix row. Compared to the instance norm's training time, our training time for the unitary network is also long due to the need to perform matrix exponentiation. Still, it is possible to further expedite it by limiting the frequency that we exponentiate (i.e., sharing the same unitary weights for several iterations). The result shown in Fig. 4 is measured without weight sharing during training; we will report further improvements in the future.

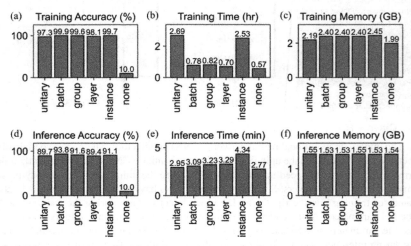

**Fig. 4.** Performance comparison between our proposed unitary convolutional network and other normalization methods. Other methods include the batch norm [10], group norm [31], layer norm [32], and instance norm [33]. We also included the case without any normalization for comparison. All metrics are average measurements over four simulation runs. We used the residual network (ResNet) architecture with 43 convolutional layers to measure the accuracy, the time, and the memory benchmarks when the networks perform image recognition tasks on the CIFAR-10 dataset, which has ten unique classes of objects. The accuracy reports the percentage of time the network determines the image class correctly with one try. (a, d for training, inference accuracies, respectively). The training time is the time to train the network with 12.5 million images, while the inference time reports the time to recognize 2.5 million images (b, e). Because we trained these networks on graphics processors, memory benchmarks measure the maximum video memory a network consumed during each operation mode (c, f).

In our experiment, both unitary network and batch normalization do not calculate running statistics (i.e., means and variances) during inference while group, layer, and instance norms track running statistics in the test set. Batch normalization is the second fastest and can potentially match the speed of the unitary network if the batch normalization layer is absorbed into the previous convolutional filters. However, batch normalization will not perform well in applications that require small batch sizes or normalization per data sample such as making adjustments to the contrast of individual images [33]. Group, layer, and instance normalizations work on a per-image basis; the difference between them is the number of channels that they average over. In our experiment, we picked a group size of eight; hence, the group normalization needs to keep track of eight means and variances per image. Contrary to layer norm that only requires one mean and one variance per image, instance norm track as many means and variances as the number of channels, which is up to 256 in our architecture. Our unitary network maintains the L2 norm of each row in the Toeplitz matrix representation per image, delivering similar effects as the instance norm but without the inference speed penalty. The mapping between the filters and the unitary matrix determines which dimension of the activation map that the unitary network is effectively normalizing. For this reason, practitioners should assign $c_{out}$, $c_{in}$, $d_H$, and $d_W$ to $m$ and $k$ in Fig. 2 differently based on the target applications.

The unitary network also uses less temporary memory (dynamic random-access memory or DRAM) required to backpropagate neural signals through the normalization layers during training; more specifically, 8% less than all other normalization methods. Despite our advantages in inference speed and training memory, unitary networks' accuracy is slightly lower in general. Unitary weights constrain the signals to be on the n-sphere (or k-sphere since we have $k$ dimensions) by design and are less expressive than free weights. Nevertheless, our accuracy is comparable to other normalizations and even surpasses the inference accuracy of layer norm. An additional advantage for the unitary network is apparent when we save the model parameters to hard disks: as we demonstrated in Fig. 2, the matrices encoding the Lie parameters have many zeros, which lead to better compression of the parameter files. An approximation for model size saving is roughly a 15% to 50% reduction in disk space when working with unitary convolutional architectures. We compute the 50% reduction by leveraging the fact that we only need to record half of the values in a triangular Lie parameter matrix, assuming that the weight matrix is square.

Our unitary neural networks are less susceptible to overfitting. Using the CIFAR-100 dataset and the same network structure (uResNet-44), we discovered that unitary networks have a smaller gap between the training loss (1.44) and the testing loss (1.62). While Regular neural networks with batch normalization have a larger gap between the training loss (0.0699) and the testing loss (1.56). Furthermore, our unitary networks can be deepened to 100 + layers without the costly normalization blocks: the 92-layer version (uResNet-92) achieves 99.6% and 90.4% in training and testing accuracies, respectively, on CIFAR-10. Similarly, the 143-layer version (uResNet-143) delivers 99.7% and 90.7% in training and testing accuracies.

## 5    Conclusion

We report here the first instance of using unitary matrices constructed according to the Lie algebra for rectangular convolutional filters, which eliminates the exploding and vanishing activations in deep convolutional neural networks. With clear geometrical interpretations, our theory is a breakthrough based on rigorous, exact construction of the unitary weights applicable to all types of neural networks including but not limited to convolution. The key innovation is that we found a way to ensure signal unitarity with unitary weight matrices of any shapes and dimensions such that the neural signals will propagate across the network without amplification or degradation. Moreover, unlike traditional normalization, our approach has the least impact on inference time, achieving a

32% speedup in recognizing color images when compared to instance normalization. The effective normalization dimension is adjustable in our framework through the mapping between the convolutional filters and the unitary matrices. Our proposal also reduces hard disk storage by up to 50% depending on the neural architectures. The presented framework establishes unitary matrices as a design principle for building fundamentally stable neural systems.

# References

1. Mollick, E.: Establishing Moore's law. IEEE Ann. Hist. Comput. **28**, 62–75 (2006). https://doi.org/10.1109/MAHC.2006.45
2. LeCun, Y., et al.: Backpropagation applied to handwritten zip code recognition. Neural Comput. **1**, 541–551 (1989). https://doi.org/10.1162/neco.1989.1.4.541
3. He, K., Zhang, X., Ren, S., Sun, J.: Deep residual learning for image recognition. In: Proceedings of the IEEE Conference on Computer Vision and Pattern Recognition, pp. 770–778 (2015)
4. Montufar, G.F., Pascanu, R., Cho, K., Bengio, Y.: On the number of linear regions of deep neural networks. Adv. Neural Inf. Process. Syst. **27** (2014)
5. Goodfellow, I.: Deep Learning. MIT Press (2016)
6. Pascanu, R., Mikolov, T., Bengio, Y.: On the difficulty of training recurrent neural networks. arXiv:1211.5063 [cs]. (2013)
7. Haber, E., Ruthotto, L.: Stable architectures for deep neural networks. Inverse Prob. **34**, 014004 (2017). https://doi.org/10.1088/1361-6420/aa9a90
8. Nair, V., Hinton, G.E.: Rectified linear units improve restricted Boltzmann machines. In: Proceedings of the 27th International Conference on International Conference on Machine Learning, pp. 807–814. Omnipress, Madison (2010)
9. Bengio, Y., Simard, P., Frasconi, P.: Learning long-term dependencies with gradient descent is difficult. IEEE Trans. Neural Netw. **5**, 157–166 (1994)
10. Ioffe, S., Szegedy, C.: Batch normalization: accelerating deep network training by reducing internal covariate shift. In: Proceedings of the 32nd International Conference on Machine Learning, pp. 448–456. PMLR (2015)
11. Wei, J.: Forget the Learning rate, decay loss. IJMLC. **9**, 267–272 (2019)
12. Lezcano-Casado, M., Martínez-Rubio, D.: Cheap orthogonal constraints in neural networks: a simple parametrization of the orthogonal and unitary group. In: Proceedings of the 36th International Conference on Machine Learning, pp. 3794–3803. PMLR (2019)
13. Arjovsky, M., Shah, A., Bengio, Y.: Unitary evolution recurrent neural networks. In: International Conference on Machine Learning, pp. 1120–1128. PMLR (2016)
14. Helfrich, K., Willmott, D., Ye, Q.: Orthogonal recurrent neural networks with scaled cayley transform. In: International Conference on Machine Learning, pp. 1969–1978. PMLR (2018)
15. Jing, L., et al.: Tunable efficient unitary neural networks (EUNN) and their application to RNNs. In: International Conference on Machine Learning, pp. 1733–1741. PMLR (2017)
16. Mhammedi, Z., Hellicar, A., Rahman, A., Bailey, J.: Efficient orthogonal parametrisation of recurrent neural networks using householder reflections. In: International Conference on Machine Learning, pp. 2401–2409. PMLR (2017)
17. Wisdom, S., Powers, T., Hershey, J., Le Roux, J., Atlas, L.: Full-capacity unitary recurrent neural networks. In: Lee, D.D., Sugiyama, M., Luxburg, U.V., Guyon, I., Garnett, R. (eds.) Advances in Neural Information Processing Systems, vol. 29, pp. 4880–4888. Curran Associates, Inc. (2016)

18. Huang, L., Liu, X., Lang, B., Yu, A.W., Wang, Y., Li, B.: Orthogonal weight normalization: solution to optimization over multiple dependent stiefel manifolds in deep neural networks. Presented at the 32nd AAAI Conference on Artificial Intelligence (2018)
19. Vorontsov, E., Trabelsi, C., Kadoury, S., Pal, C.: On orthogonality and learning recurrent networks with long term dependencies. In: International Conference on Machine Learning, pp. 3570–3578. PMLR (2017)
20. Wang, J., Chen, Y., Chakraborty, R., Yu, S.X.: Orthogonal convolutional neural networks. In: 2020 IEEE/CVF Conference on Computer Vision and Pattern Recognition (CVPR), pp. 11502–11512. IEEE, Seattle (2020)
21. Gilmore, R., Hermann, R.: Lie Groups, Lie Algebras, and Some of Their Applications. John Wiley & Sons, New York (1974)
22. Gilmore, R.: Lie Groups, Physics, and Geometry: An Introduction for Physicists, Engineers and Chemists. Cambridge University Press, New York (2008)
23. Bader, P., Blanes, S., Casas, F.: Computing the matrix exponential with an optimized taylor polynomial approximation. Mathematics 7, 1174 (2019)
24. Torch Contributors: torch.matrix_exp — PyTorch 1.7.0 documentation. https://pytorch.org/docs/stable/generated/torch.matrix_exp.html
25. LeCun, Y., Bengio, Y., Hinton, G.: Deep learning. Nature **521**, 436–444 (2015)
26. Paszke, A., et al.: Automatic differentiation in PyTorch. NIPS 2017 Workshop Autodiff Submission (2017). https://openreview.net/pdf?id=BJJsrmfCZ
27. Chen, Y., Xie, Y., Song, L., Chen, F., Tang, T.: A survey of accelerator architectures for deep neural networks. Engineering **6**, 264–274 (2020)
28. Araujo, A., Negrevergne, B., Chevaleyre, Y., Atif, J.: On Lipschitz regularization of convolutional layers using toeplitz matrix theory. In: 35th AAAI Conference on Artificial Intelligence, Vancouver, Canada (2021)
29. Krizhevsky, A.: Learning Multiple Layers of Features from Tiny Images. University of Toronto (2009)
30. Chiley, V., et al.: Online Normalization for training neural networks. In: Advances in Neural Information Processing Systems, vol. 32, pp. 8433–8443. Curran Associates, Inc. (2019)
31. Wu, Y., He, K.: Group normalization. Int. J. Comput. Vis. **128**, 742–755 (2020)
32. Ba, J.L., Kiros, J.R., Hinton, G.E.: Layer normalization. arXiv:1607.06450 [cs, stat]. (2016)
33. Ulyanov, D., Vedaldi, A., Lempitsky, V.: Instance normalization: the missing ingredient for fast stylization. arXiv:1607.08022 [cs] (2017)

# Deep Learning and Optimization I

# DPWTE: A Deep Learning Approach to Survival Analysis Using a Parsimonious Mixture of Weibull Distributions

Achraf Bennis[(⊠)], Sandrine Mouysset[(⊠)], and Mathieu Serrurier[(⊠)]

I.R.I.T - Université Toulouse III Paul Sabatier, Toulouse, France
{achraf.bennis,sandrine.mouysset,mathieu.serrurier}@irit.fr

**Abstract.** Survival analysis is widely used in medicine, engineering, finance, and many other areas. The fundamental problem considered in this branch of statistics is to capture the relationship between the covariates and the event time distribution. In this paper, we propose a novel network-based approach to survival analysis, called DPWTE, that uses a neural network to learn the distribution of the event times. DPWTE makes an assumption that (individual) event time distribution follows a finite mixture of Weibull distribution whose parameters are functions of the covariates. In addition, given a fixed upper bound of the mixture size, the model finds the optimal combination of Weibull distributions to model the underlying distribution. For this purpose, we introduce the *Sparse Weibull Mixture* layer, in the network, that selects through its weights, the Weibull distributions composing the mixture, whose mixing parameters are significant. To stimulate this selection, we apply a sparse regularization on this layer by adding a penalty term to the loss function that takes into account both observed and censored events, i.e. events that are not observed before the end of the period study. We conduct experiments on real-world datasets showing that the proposed model provides a performance improvement over the state-of-the-art models.

**Keywords:** Survival analysis · Deep learning · Weibull distribution

## 1 Introduction

Survival analysis, also known as time-to-event analysis, concerns the prediction of when a future event will occur. Applications of survival analysis can be found in many areas such as prediction of cardiovascular death and failure times of power grids. Survival analysis has primarily focused on interpretability at the expense of predictive accuracy. This is eventually the reason why machine-learning-based classifiers are commonly used in real-world applications while it would be more useful to apply survival methods. Certainly, some classifiers may have the best accuracy. However, these binary models can only provide predictions for a predetermined point in time. One loses the interpretability and flexibility which are guaranteed by the modeling of the event densities as a function of time. Moreover, in survival data, it is common that a part of a population

© Springer Nature Switzerland AG 2021
I. Farkaš et al. (Eds.): ICANN 2021, LNCS 12892, pp. 185–196, 2021.
https://doi.org/10.1007/978-3-030-86340-1_15

in which the event is not observed within the relevant time period, and could potentially occur after this recorded time or removed from the study, producing so-called *censored* data. In this case, the individuals of this sub-population provided us with censored times rather than event times. While this type of data is not taken into consideration by standard classifiers, survival analysis bridges this gap. In this work, we propose a novel approach to survival analysis: the event time distribution is assumed to follow a finite mixture of Weibull distributions, whose parameters depend on an individual's covariates. No particular assumption about the nature of the relationship between the parameters and the features is made. The main idea behind the proposed model called DPWTE, that stands for *Deep Parsimonious Weibull Time-to-Event*, is to estimate the optimal combination of Weibull distributions that models the underlying distribution using a neural network. This paper makes the following contributions:

- The event times are assumed to be drawn from a random variable following a finite mixture of Weibull distributions.
- DPWTE extends the idea behind DeepWeiSurv [3]. In fact, the latter considers the size of the combination $p$, as a parameter of the model whose different values are to be tested. While DPWTE, starting with an upper bound of the mixture size, learns the optimal combination of Weibull distributions (among the initial mixture) that can model the underlying distribution. For this purpose, we introduce a layer which we call the Sparse Weibull Mixture (SWM) layer on which we apply a sparse regularization. By doing this, we enforce the selection of the Weibull distributions that have a significant contribution to the time-to-event modeling.
- The censored observations are considered in the conception of the model.

This paper is organized as follows: In Sect. 2, we summarize the previous related works. In Sect. 3, we review some basic definitions in survival analysis and Weibull distributions. In Sect. 4, we describe the proposed model with a special focus on the role of the SWM layer. Section 5 is dedicated to the experiments conducted on real-world datasets.

## 2    Related Work

Kaplan-Meier estimator is the most widely used in survival analysis which has the advantage of being able to learn very flexible survival curves, but it doesn't incorporate individual covariates. However, the semi-parametric Cox Proportional Hazards [4] (CPH) model incorporates the covariates but assumes that the risk effect is linear with respect to the covariates, which may be too simplistic since, in the real-world data, the covariate effects are often non-monotonic. The ability of neural networks to learn nonlinear functions has encouraged many researchers to model the relationship between the covariates and the survival data. An extension of CPH with neural networks was first proposed by Faraggi and Simon [6] who replaced the linear risk of the Cox regression model, with one hidden layer multi-layer perceptron but without performance improvement.

Katzman et al. [10] revisited the Cox model in the framework of deep learning, which removes the proportionality constraint and showed that it outperforms CPH in terms of concordance index [8]. Most of the previous works benchmark their methods against the random survival forests (RSF) [9] which computes a random forest using the log-rank test as the splitting criterion, and is considered as a flexible continuous-time method that is not constrained by the proportionality assumption. Other previous works proposed network-based methods based on Cox regression such as SurvivalNet [14] and Zhu et al. [15,16] who proposed a convolutional network model that replaces multi-layer perceptron architecture of DeepSurv [10] and applied this methodology to pathological images. An alternative approach to survival analysis is to discretize the duration and compute the survival function on this predetermined time grid. Lee et al. [12] proposed a network used in competing risks setting, called DeepHit, that estimates the probability distribution and combines the log-likelihood with a ranking loss. Fotso [7] proposed N-MTLR which, using a multi-task regression, calculates the survival probabilities on the points of the time grid. Unlike discrete-time models, DeepWeiSurv [3] models a continuous survival function that allows estimating the survival probability at any survival time horizon.

## 3    Background

In this section, we briefly review some basics in survival analysis and Weibull distributions.

### 3.1    Survival Analysis

Let $X = \{x_i, y_i = (t_i, \delta_i)\}_{i=1}^N$ a survival data, of covariates $x_i \in \mathbb{R}^d$ and event pairs $(t_i, \delta_i)$, where $(t_i)_{1 \leq i \leq N}$ is the times recorded represented by the random variable $T$, and $(\delta_i)_{1 \leq i \leq N} \in \{0, 1\}^d$ is the event indicator. Typically, $\delta_i = 1$ if the event associated to the $i^{th}$ individual is observed, otherwise, $\delta_i = 0$ which indicates censoring. The survival function is defined by the following equation:

$$S_T(t_h) = P(T > t_h) = 1 - F_T(t_h) \tag{1}$$

Survival models characterize $S_T$, defined as the complementary of the cumulative density function $F_T$, and thus the fraction of the population that survives up to a time horizon $t_h$ given a covariate $\mathbf{x}$. Therefore the aim of these models is to estimate the probability of the occurrence of the event after or at $t_h$.

### 3.2    Mixture Weibull Distributions Estimation

We suppose that $T$ follows a finite mixture of two-parameter Weibull distributions conditionally to the baseline data features. In this context, it is easy to calculate $F_T$ at any time $t$. As this latter totally depends on the mixture parameters, we only need to estimate each couple of parameters of Weibull distributions that compose this mixture as well as its weighting coefficients. Let

$T$ follows $\mathcal{W}_p$ a mixture of $p$ Weibull distributions denoted by $W(\beta_i, \eta_i)$ with $\alpha_i, \beta_i$ and $\eta_i$ are respectively the weighting coefficient, shape and scale of the $i^{th}$ Weibull distribution of density $f_{W(\beta_i,\eta_i)}$ and survival function $S_{W(\beta_i,\eta_i)}$. Then the density and survival function of $\mathcal{W}_p$ can be written as follows:

$$f_{\mathcal{W}_p} = \sum_k \alpha_k f_{W(\beta_k,\eta_k)} \qquad S_{\mathcal{W}_p} = \sum_k \alpha_k S_{W(\beta_k,\eta_k)} \qquad (2)$$

The log-likelihood of $\mathcal{W}_p$, considering the censored data, is defined as follows:

$$\mathcal{LL}(\beta, \eta, \alpha|y) = \overbrace{\sum_{i=1}^n \delta_i log\ f_{\mathcal{W}_p}(t_i)}^{\mathcal{LL}_{\delta=1}} + \overbrace{\sum_{i=1}^n (1-\delta_i) log\ S_{\mathcal{W}_p}(t_i)}^{\mathcal{LL}_{\delta=0}} \qquad (3)$$

Thus, we estimate $\mathcal{W}_p$ parameters $(\alpha, \beta, \eta)$ by solving the *Maximum Likelihood Estimation* problem defined by the following equation:

$$(\hat{\beta}, \hat{\eta}, \hat{\alpha}) = \arg\min_{\substack{\beta,\eta,\alpha \\ \beta \geq 1}} \{-\mathcal{LL}(\beta, \eta, \alpha|y)\} \qquad (4)$$

As we notice in Eq. (4), we set a constraint linked to the shape parameter. In fact, by definition, $\beta$ and $\eta$ are strictly positive. However, to assure the convexity of the $\mathcal{LL}$, we need to consider that $\beta$ is at least equal to 1. Let $\mu_i$ be the mean lifetime of the $i^{th}$ individual. Given that the mean of a mixture $\mu$ is a weighted combination of the means of the distributions that compose this mixture and knowing the single Weibull's mean [2], we have:

$$\mu_i = \sum_k \alpha_k \eta_{ik} \Gamma(1 + \frac{1}{\beta_{ik}}) \qquad (5)$$

where $\beta_{ik}$ and $\eta_{ik}$ are the $i^{th}$ components of $\beta_k$ and $\eta_k$ respectively. $\mu_i$ can be used as an estimate of the survival time of the individual $i$.

## 4  Deep Parsimonious Weibull Time-to-Event Model

In this section, we first describe the architecture of DPWTE (Sect. 4.1). Then, we explain the role of the Sparse Weibull Mixture layer (Sect. 4.2). After that, we describe the post-training steps (Sect. 4.3). Finally, we present the loss function used to train DPWTE (Sect. 4.4).

### 4.1  Description

As for DeepWeiSurv [3], we consider the relationship between the features and $\mathcal{W}_p$ parameters. Estimation of the mixture parameters is therefore equivalent to model this dependence. In fact, DPWTE learns the following function:

$$\begin{aligned} f_p : \mathbb{R}^d &\to \mathbb{R}^{p \times 3} \\ x_i &\mapsto (\alpha, \beta, \eta) \end{aligned} \qquad (6)$$

The aim is therefore to train the network in order to learn the above function and thus the estimate of the triplet $(\alpha, \beta, \eta)$ that minimizes the log-likelihood of the distribution. DPWTE consists of a common sub-network which takes the observations $X$ as an input and outputs a latent vector Z, this latter serves in turn as an input to both the *classifier* and *regression* sub-networks whose tasks are learning $\alpha$ and $(\beta, \eta)$ respectively. Figure 1 represents the global architecture of DPWTE. For the regression sub-network, we use ELU[1] (by setting its constant to 1) as the activation function for both output layers. As the codomain of ELU in this case is $[-1, +\infty[$, to respect the optimization problem constraints as seen in Eq. (4), the network will learn $\beta + 2$ and $\eta + 1 + \varepsilon$, $\varepsilon > 0$. As for the classifier sub-network, we use the softmax activation function and interleave the SWM layer, which is described in Sect. 4.2, between the softmax and the output layer of this network. At the architecture level, the only difference between DPWTE and DeepWeiSurv is the so-called SWM layer through which the proposed model implicitly selects the significant contribution distribution.

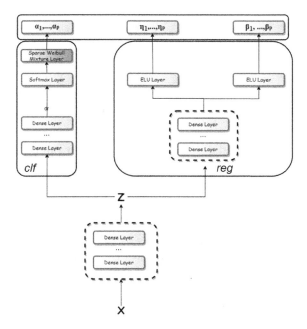

**Fig. 1.** The global architecture of DPWTE: clf and reg denotes the classifier and regression sub-networks respectively.

---

[1] We choose ELU because it becomes smooth slowly, whereas ReLU sharply smoothes. That means that with ELU we have enough gradient to learn the parameters.

## 4.2   Sparse Weibull Mixture Layer

It should be recalled that we seek to learn the optimal mixture of Weibull distributions that models $\mathcal{D}$, which leads us to estimate the optimal size $p$ that we denote by $\tilde{p}$. We initially set $p$ to an upper bound $p_{max}$. For this purpose, we introduce the SWM layer just before the output layer of the classifier sub-network. This layer performs an element-wise multiplication of its weights by the softmax layer output. As we see in Fig. 2, we put $\alpha_k = \omega_k \odot q_k$. In order to get an idea of the importance of each Weibull distribution, through its associated probability, we need to have the following constraints: $(\omega_k, \alpha_k) \in [0,1]^2, k = 1, .., p$ and $\sum_{k=1}^{p} \alpha_k = 1$. However, we cannot guarantee the constraint on $\omega_k$ even if we initialize them manually and thus the constraint on $\alpha_k$ either. To ensure implicitly these constraints, we apply the following transformations: $\forall k \in [|1, p|]$,

$$(T1) \quad \omega_k \leftarrow \frac{|\omega_k|}{\sum_{j=1}^{p} |\omega_j|} q_k \in [0,1], \forall k \in [|1,p|] \qquad (T2) \quad \alpha_k \leftarrow \frac{\alpha_k}{\sum_{k=1}^{p} \alpha_k}$$

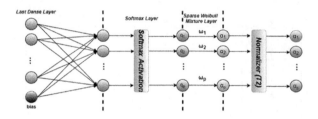

**Fig. 2.** Softmax and SWM layers of the classifier sub-network.

## 4.3   Post-Training Steps: Selection of Weibull Distributions to Combine for Time-to-Event Modeling

So far, we have not yet estimated the value of $\tilde{p}$. The training phase is the same as for DeepWeiSurv regardless of the loss function (described in Sect. 4.4). However, after the network is trained, we select the triplets $(\alpha_k, \beta_k, \eta_k)$ such as $\alpha_k$ is greater or equal to certain threshold denoted by $\omega_{th}$ that we fix beforehand. As the distribution of $\alpha$ changes after this selection while the probability constraint must be maintained, we apply T2 to the new $\alpha$. Thus, if $A = \{(\alpha_k, \beta_k, \eta_k) | \alpha_k \geq \alpha_{th}\}$ is the set of selected triplets for modeling, then:

1. $\tilde{p} = Card(A)$
2. $\alpha = (\alpha_k, \alpha_k \geq \alpha_{th}) \xrightarrow[T_2]{} \alpha'$
3. $\beta = (\beta_k, \alpha_k \geq \alpha_{th}) \xrightarrow[offset(+2)]{} \beta'$
4. $\eta = (\eta_k, \alpha_k \geq \alpha_{th}) \xrightarrow[offset(+1+\epsilon)]{} \eta'$
5. the event times distribution can be modeled by $\sum\limits_{(\alpha_k, \beta_k, \eta_k) \in A} \alpha'_k W(\beta'_k, \eta'_k)$

This post-processing is described by the Fig. 3.

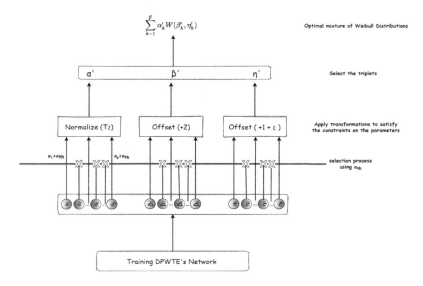

**Fig. 3.** Post-training steps to compose the optimal mixture of Weibull distributions.

### 4.4 Loss Function

As discussed above, DPWTE learns the optimal combination of Weibull distributions. To do so, we use the following loss function:

$$loss = -\mathcal{LL}(\beta, \eta, \alpha | (t_i, \delta_i)_i) + \lambda ||\omega||_{\frac{1}{2}}, \qquad (7)$$

where $\lambda$ is the regularization parameter and $||\omega||_{\frac{1}{2}} = \sum_{k=1}^{p} \sqrt{|w_k|}$. The first element of the loss is the negative log-likelihood which is used as a loss function for DeepWeiSurv [3]. To stimulate the triplet selection process discussed in the previous section, we apply a *sparse* regularization on $\omega = (\omega_k)_{1 \geq k \geq p}$ by adding a penalty term (second operand) to the loss function, hence the name of SWM layer and the word 'Parsimonious' in the name of the model. The purpose behind the sparse regularization is to encourage sparsity in the vector $\omega$ or at least some $\omega_k$ to become almost zero, and then apply the threshold $\omega_{th}$. Xu et al. [13] proposed $L_{0.5}$ as the new regularizer which is more sparse than the $L_1$ regularizer while it is still easier to be solved than the $L_0$ regularizer (because it is non-differentiable). The sparsity property of $L_{0.5}$ was demonstrated by Fan et al. [5].

## 5 Experiments on Real-World Datasets

In this section, we evaluate our proposed model on real data sets and compare its predictive performance with state-of-the-art methods. Table 1 gives an overview of descriptive statistics of these datasets. All the models are evaluated in the same experimental protocol.

**Table 1.** Descriptive statistics of real-world datasets

| Datasets | No. uncensored | No. censored | No. features | Censoring time | | | Event time | | |
|---|---|---|---|---|---|---|---|---|---|
| | | | | Min | Max | Mean | Min | Max | Mean |
| SEER BC | 9152(42.8%) | 12221 (57.2%) | 34 | 1 | 227 | 181.5 | 1 | 226 | 63.7 |
| SEER HD | 12014 (49.6%) | 12221 (50.4%) | | | | | 1 | 224 | 76.7 |
| SUPPORT | 5844 (68.1%) | 2735 (31.9%) | 36 | 344 | 2029 | 1060.2 | 3 | 1944 | 206.0 |
| METABRIC | 888 (44.8%) | 1093 (55.2%) | 21 | 1 | 308 | 116.0 | 1 | 299 | 77.8 |

### 5.1   Description of the Real-World Datasets

In this experiment, we use three real-worlds datasets:

- SEER[2]: a program that provides cancer incidence data from population-based cancer registries covering approximately 34.6% of the U.S. population. We focused on the patients recorded between 1998 and 2002 with Breast Cancer (BC) or Heart Disease (HD) or who have survived to the end of this period. We generated from this database two single-event datasets (BC and HD) keeping survivors in both of them.
- SUPPORT [11]: this dataset is good for learning how to fit nonlinear predictor effects. We studied 9105 patients, of which almost 32% are survivors, with their 36 attributes including age, sex, urine output creatinine, etc.
- METABRIC [3]: contains gene expressions and clinical features including age, tumor size, PR Status, etc.

### 5.2   Experimental Setting

For evaluation, we applied 5-fold cross validation: the data is randomly splitted into training and validation set (80-20 split). For each iteration, the models are fitted by the corresponding training set (4 folds) and evaluated on the validation set (1 fold) by calculating $C^{td}$. Once all iterations are executed, we obtain for each method and for each dataset, a vector (of size 5) containing $C^{td}$ scores for each iteration. This experimental protocol is applied on the following models:

- Cox Proportional Hazards CPH [4] with a penalty term in the order of $10^{-1}$.
- Random Survival Forest RSF [9] with 100 trees.
- DeepSurv [10] with 2 layers of 32 nodes.
- DeepHit [12] with a dropout probability of 0.6 between all the hidden layers.
- DeepWeiSurv [3] with $p = 10$.
- The proposed model DPWTE with $p_{max} = 10$ and $\lambda = 10^{-4}$.

All the methods are trained via Adam optimizer with a learning rate of $10^{-4}$. DPWTE has the shared sub-network which is 2 fully connected layers (the batch normalization is applied before the second layer). The regression sub-network

---

[2] https://seer.cancer.gov.
[3] https://ega-archive.org/studies/EGAS00000000083.

consists of 1 fully connected layer with batch normalization and two ELU layers as output layers, while the classifier sub-network is composed of 2 fully connected layers and a softmax layer followed by an SWM layer. Hidden layers are activated by ReLU. The network is trained via SGD optimizer and learning rate of $10^{-4}$.

As evaluation metric, we use *concordance index* $C^{td}$ [1] which calculates, among all the comparable pairs of observations $(i, j)$ $(\delta_i = \delta_j = 1)$, the number of concordant ones:

$$C^{td} = \frac{\sum_{i,j} \mathbb{1}_{t_i > t_j} \cdot \mathbb{1}_{\hat{t}_i > \hat{t}_j} \cdot \delta_j}{\sum_{i,j} \mathbb{1}_{t_i > t_j} \cdot \delta_j}, \tag{8}$$

$C^{td}$ estimates the probability of the event $\{\hat{t}_i > \hat{t}_j | t_i > t_j\}$ which compares the rankings of two independent and comparable pairs (non censored) of survival times $(t_i, t_j)$ and the times predicted $(\hat{t}_i, \hat{t}_j)$.

## 5.3    Results

The results are summarized in Table 2 where we calculated the confidence interval and the average of the concordance index scores over the 5-fold cross-validation folds. In METABRIC, DeepHit and our proposed models provided a significant improvement in terms of concordance scores when compared to other competing methods, especially DPWTE, using one ($\tilde{p} = 1$) Weibull distribution, provides a mean concordance index slightly greater than that of Deep-Hit and DeepWeiSurv, but with wider interval confidence. We can say that for METABRIC, DeepHit and DPWTE have practically the same ordering performance, when we take into account the trade-off between the mean and the variance of $C^{td}$. For the SUPPORT dataset, DeepHit outperforms, on average, the other models in terms of times ordering, but DeepSurv and DPWTE, using in average $\tilde{p} = 3$ Weibull distributions, minimized the difference between their respective concordances and that of DeepHit compared to RSF, CPH. In the SEER dataset, for Breast Cancer and Heart Disease populations alike, we can notice that DeepWeiSurv and DPWTE (using in average $\tilde{p} = 2$ for both datasets) have shown a large significant outperformance over the competing methods, with a slight improvement from DeepWeiSurv with $p = 2$ to DPWTE. We can also remark that the standard deviation of $C^{td}$ for METABRIC is relatively greater than that of SEER and SUPPORT. We suspect this comes from the small size of METABRIC regarding the other datasets. Furthermore, another thing to point out is that for all the datasets, except METABRIC, the respective confidence intervals of DPWTE and DeepWeiSurv are narrower than those of the competing methods, which means that our proposed method produced a more stable estimation. DPWTE has clearly the best overall predictive performance.

**Table 2.** $C^{td}$ calculated over 5-fold cross validation for each model and dataset (mean ± standard deviation) as well as the mean estimate $\tilde{p}$.

| Models | Datasets | | | |
|---|---|---|---|---|
| | SEER BC | SEER HD | SUPPORT | METABRIC |
| CPH | 0.831±7.5e–3 | 0.785±3.5e–3 | 0.805±7e–3 | 0.661±2.6e–2 |
| DeepSurv | 0.841±5.5e–3 | 0.786±7.5e–3 | 0.826±1.5e–3 | 0.662±1.8e–2 |
| RSF | 0.838±9.5e–3 | 0.755±1e–2 | 0.783±4.5e–3 | 0.667±3.1e–2 |
| DeepHit | 0.875±8e–3 | 0.846±4.5e–3 | **0.835±1.3e–2** | 0.821±1.1e–2 |
| DeepWeiSurv | 0.908±1.5e–3 | 0.863±1.1e–2 | 0.815±1.5e–2 | 0.819±1.3e–2 |
| DPWTE | **0.912±1.5e–3** | **0.871±3.5e–3** | 0.831±9.5e–3 | **0.829±1.08e–2** |
| $\tilde{p}$ | 2 | 2 | 3 | 1 |

### 5.4  Censoring Threshold Sensitivity Experiment

The main objective of this experiment is to measure the performance of DPWTE with respect to the censoring rate, that is, the ratio of censored events against the observed ones. Because of lack of space, we choose to run the experiment only on METABRIC (as the smallest dataset and thus more challenging) and SEER BC (as the dataset with the highest score). The main results are similar for SEER HD and SUPPORT. In this experiment, we apply the same experimental protocol as the previous one on different censoring thresholds. These thresholds, expressed in quantiles of the recorded times vector, are selected such as each quantile $t_c$ adds a significant portion of censored data against the previous one and thus, change significantly the time distribution. Table 3 gives the distribution of data of each configuration. For METABRIC and SEER, we choose the following thresholds: $Q_1 = (q_{0.5}, q_{0.45}, q_{0.35}, q_{0.25})$ and $Q_2 = (q_{0.85}, q_{0.65}, q_{0.5}, q_{0.4}, q_{0.25})$ respectively. The *Added portion* column represents the percentage of data that became censored out of the initial set of censored data. For each value $t_c \in Q_i$, we apply 5-fold cross validation and then calculate the predictions for all time horizons $t_h \in Q_i$[4]. Then, we measure the quality of these predictions using $C^{td}$. Figure 4 shows the $C^{td}$ scores calculated over the cross validation as well as the estimate $\tilde{p}$ for each scenario in both datasets. Firstly, we should note that the model performs well for SEER BC (higher average scores and narrower standard deviation as seen in the previous experiment). Furthermore, we can remark that in general, the further the censoring rate (for training) and the time horizon $t_h$ (for predictions) is pushed back, the lower is the score. This result was expected because of the fact that the more we have non-censored data the easier it is to model the survival times distribution of the population. We also suspect the decreasing of $\tilde{p}$ comes from the fact that the more we increase the censoring rate the more the network ignores a part of the underlying distribution and

---

[4] $t_{METABRIC}$ is not a censoring threshold but represents the initial survival time vector as used in the previous experiment (see statistics in Table 1).

**Table 3.** Distribution of METABRIC (left) and SEER BC (right) for each selected censoring threshold.

| $t_c$ | No. censored | No. non-censored | Added portion |
|---|---|---|---|
| $t_{METABRIC}$ | 1093 | 888 | – |
| $q_{0.5}$ | 1285 | 696 | 17.6% |
| $q_{0.45}$ | 1411 | 570 | 29% |
| $q_{0.35}$ | 1559 | 422 | 42.6% |
| $q_{0.25}$ | 1670 | 311 | 52.8% |

| $t_c$ | No. censored | No. non-censored | Added portion |
|---|---|---|---|
| $q_{0.85}$ | 13270 | 8103 | 8.6% |
| $q_{0.65}$ | 15207 | 6166 | 24.4% |
| $q_{0.5}$ | 16568 | 4805 | 35.5% |
| $q_{0.4}$ | 17503 | 3870 | 43.2% |
| $q_{0.25}$ | 18912 | 2461 | 54.75% |

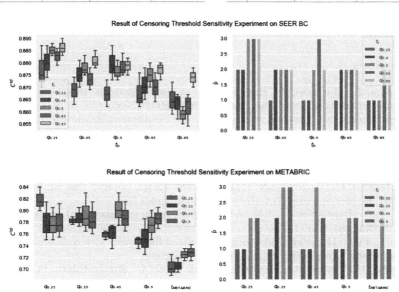

**Fig. 4.** Box plots (left) of $C^{td}$ as well as the mean values of the estimate $\tilde{p}$ (right) calculated over the 5-fold cross validation for each censoring threshold $t_c$ in both SEER BC (top) and METABRIC (bottom).

thus model the latter with an insufficient combination of Weibull distributions. However, DPWTE still performing well even in the highly censored setting.

# 6   Conclusion

In this paper, we proposed a novel approach for survival analysis. A network-based model, assuming a Weibull mixture character of the survival time, was presented to address this problem. We could, by parametrizing the mixture with neural networks, model rich relationships between the covariates and event times. DPWTE leverages Weibull advantages, namely the fact that these distributions are known to be a good representation for survival time distribution and it also allows to consider any time horizon. This is because DPWTE learns a continuous probability density function and through the *Sparse Weibull Mixture* layer selects the optimal combination of Weibull distribution to model the underlying event-time distribution. We conducted experiments on real-world datasets where DPWTE has clearly outperformed the alternative approaches. Furthermore, we assessed the censoring sensitivity of our model with a real-data experiment which demonstrates its ability to generally handle highly censored settings and consider any survival time horizon. Interesting expansions include extending our methodology to models that handle competing events, time-dependent covariates. In addition, it would be interesting to explore other data types and sources that require some advanced network structures notably convolutions neural networks or generative adversarial models.

# References

1. Antolini, L., Boracchi, P., Biganzoli, E.: A time-dependent discrimination index for survival data. Statist. Med. **24**(24), 3927–3944 (2005)
2. Balakrishnan, N., Johnson, N.L., Kotz, S.: Continuous univariate distributions (1994)
3. Bennis, A., Mouysset, S., Serrurier, M.: Estimation of conditional mixture Weibull distribution with right censored data using neural network for time-to-event analysis. In: Lauw, H.W., Wong, R.C.-W., Ntoulas, A., Lim, E.-P., Ng, S.-K., Pan, S.J. (eds.) PAKDD 2020. LNCS (LNAI), vol. 12084, pp. 687–698. Springer, Cham (2020). https://doi.org/10.1007/978-3-030-47426-3_53
4. Cox, D.R.: Regression models and life tables (with discussion). J. R. Statist. Soc. Ser. B. **34**, 187–220 (1972)
5. Fan, J., Peng, H., et al.: Nonconcave penalized likelihood with a diverging number of parameters. Ann. Statist. **32**(3), 928–961 (2004)
6. Faraggi, D., Simon, R.: A neural network model for survival data. Statist. Med. **14**(1), 73–82 (1995)
7. Fotso, S.: Deep neural networks for survival analysis based on a multi-task framework. arXiv preprint arXiv:1801.05512 (2018)
8. Harrell, F.E., Califf, R.M., Pryor, D.B., Lee, K.L., Rosati, R.A.: Evaluating the yield of medical tests. Jama **247**(18), 2543–2546 (1982)
9. Ishwaran, H., Kogalur, U.B., Blackstone, E.H., Lauer, M.S., et al.: Random survival forests. Ann. Appl. Statist. **2**(3), 841–860 (2008)
10. Katzman, J.L., Shaham, U., Cloninger, A., Bates, J., Jiang, T., Kluger, Y.: Deep survival: a deep cox proportional hazards network. stat **1050**, 2 (2016)
11. Knaus, W.A., et al.: The support prognostic model: objective estimates of survival for seriously ill hospitalized adults. Ann. Intern. Med. **122**(3), 191–203 (1995)
12. Lee, C., Zame, W.R., Yoon, J., van der Schaar, M.: Deephit: a deep learning approach to survival analysis with competing risks. In: Thirty-Second AAAI Conference on Artificial Intelligence (2018)
13. Xu, Z., Zhang, H., Wang, Y., Chang, X., Liang, Y.: L 1/2 regularization. Sci. China Inf. Sci. **53**(6), 1159–1169 (2010)
14. Yousefi, S., et al.: Predicting clinical outcomes from large scale cancer genomic profiles with deep survival models. Sci. Rep. **7**(1), 1–11 (2017)
15. Zhu, X., Yao, J., Huang, J.: Deep convolutional neural network for survival analysis with pathological images. In: 2016 IEEE International Conference on Bioinformatics and Biomedicine (BIBM), pp. 544–547. IEEE (2016)
16. Zhu, X., Yao, J., Zhu, F., Huang, J.: Wsisa: making survival prediction from whole slide histopathological images. In: Proceedings of the IEEE Conference on Computer Vision and Pattern Recognition, pp. 7234–7242 (2017)

# First-Order and Second-Order Variants of the Gradient Descent in a Unified Framework

Thomas Pierrot[1,2], Nicolas Perrin-Gilbert[1(✉)], and Olivier Sigaud[1]

[1] Sorbonne Université, CNRS, Institut des Systèmes Intelligents et
de Robotique, ISIR, 75005 Paris, France
`{nicolas.perrin,olivier.sigaud}@sorbonne-universite.fr`
[2] InstaDeep, Paris, France
`t.pierrot@instadeep.com`

**Abstract.** In this paper, we provide an overview of first-order and second-order variants of the gradient descent method that are commonly used in machine learning. We propose a general framework in which 6 of these variants can be interpreted as different instances of the same approach. They are the vanilla gradient descent, the classical and generalized Gauss-Newton methods, the natural gradient descent method, the gradient covariance matrix approach, and Newton's method. Besides interpreting these methods within a single framework, we explain their specificities and show under which conditions some of them coincide.

**Keywords:** Machine learning · Gradient descent

## 1 Introduction

Machine learning in general, and deep learning (LeCun 2015) in particular often amount to solving an optimization problem where a loss function has to be minimized. For complex problems (due to nonlinearity, non-convexity, etc.), the best recourse seems often to rely on iterative schemes that exploit first-order or second-order derivatives of the loss function to get successive improvements and converge towards a local minimum. This explains why variants of gradient descent are becoming increasingly ubiquitous in machine learning and have been made widely available in the main deep learning libraries, being the tool of choice to optimize deep neural networks. Among these methods, vanilla gradient descent strongly benefits from its computational efficiency as it simply computes partial derivatives at each step of an iterative process. Though it is widely used, it is limited for two main reasons: it depends on arbitrary parameterizations and may diverge or converge slowly if the step size is not properly tuned. To address these issues, several lines of improvement exist. Here, we focus on two of them. On the one hand, first-order methods such as the natural gradient introduce

---

T. Pierrot and N. Perrin-Gilbert—Equal contribution.

© Springer Nature Switzerland AG 2021
I. Farkaš et al. (Eds.): ICANN 2021, LNCS 12892, pp. 197–208, 2021.
https://doi.org/10.1007/978-3-030-86340-1_16

particular metrics to restrict gradient steps and make them independent from parametrization choices (Amari 1998). On the other hand, second-order methods use the Hessian matrix of the loss or its approximations to take into account its local curvature.

Both types of approaches enhance the vanilla gradient descent update, multiplying it by the inverse of a large matrix (of size $d^2$, where $d$ is the dimensionality of the parameter space). The contribution of this paper is to study connections between 6 popular first-order and second-order improvements of the gradient descent seen as different variants of a unique simple framework. This general framework uses a first-order approximation of the loss and constrains the step with a quadratic norm. Therefore, each modification $\delta\boldsymbol{\theta}$ of the vector of parameters $\boldsymbol{\theta}$ is computed via an optimization problem of the following form:

$$\begin{cases} \min_{\delta\theta} \nabla_\theta L(\boldsymbol{\theta})^T \delta\boldsymbol{\theta} \\ \delta\boldsymbol{\theta}^T M(\boldsymbol{\theta})\delta\boldsymbol{\theta} \leq \epsilon^2, \end{cases} \tag{1}$$

where $\nabla_\theta L(\boldsymbol{\theta})$ is the gradient of the loss $L(\boldsymbol{\theta})$, and $M(\boldsymbol{\theta})$ a symmetric positive-definite (SPD) matrix. The 6 methods differ by the matrix $M(\boldsymbol{\theta})$, which has an effect not only on the size of the steps, but also on the direction of the steps, as illustrated in Fig. 1.

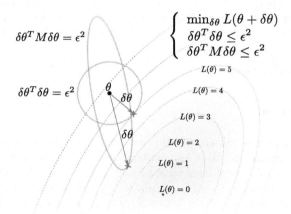

**Fig. 1.** Different metrics affect both the gradient step size and direction. Here, a different $\delta\boldsymbol{\theta}$ is obtained with $M = I$ or $M$ an arbitrary SPD matrix.

The solution of the minimization problem (1) has the following form:

$$\delta\boldsymbol{\theta} = -\alpha M(\boldsymbol{\theta})^{-1}\nabla_\theta L(\boldsymbol{\theta}).$$

Section 2 mainly defines notations, and the rest of the paper is organized as follows. In Sect. 3, we show how the vanilla gradient descent, the classical Gauss-Newton method and the natural gradient descent method fit into the proposed framework, with constraints that are independent from the loss function. In Sect. 4, we consider approaches that depend on the loss, namely the gradient covariance matrix approach, Newton's method, and the generalized Gauss-Newton method, and show that they also fit into the framework. Table 1 summarizes the values of $M(\boldsymbol{\theta})$ for all 6 approaches.

**Table 1.** The matrices $M(\boldsymbol{\theta})$ associated to 6 popular variants of the gradient descent, when interpreted as instances of the optimization problem (1). See Sect. 2 for the definitions of the notations.

| $M(\boldsymbol{\theta})$ | Corresponding approach |
|---|---|
| $I$ | Vanilla gradient descent |
| $\mathbb{E}_s\left[J_x(\boldsymbol{\theta})^T J_x(\boldsymbol{\theta})\right] + \lambda I$ | Classical Gauss-Newton |
| $\mathbb{E}_s\left[\nabla_\theta \log(p_\theta(\boldsymbol{y}|\boldsymbol{x}))\nabla_\theta \log(p_\theta(\boldsymbol{y}|\boldsymbol{x}))^T\right] + \lambda I$ | Natural gradient (empirical Fisher matrix) |
| $\mathbb{E}_s\left[\nabla_\theta l_\theta(s)\nabla_\theta l_\theta(s)^T\right] + \lambda I$ | Gradient covariance matrix |
| $H(\boldsymbol{\theta}) + \lambda I$ | Newton's method |
| $\mathbb{E}_s\left[J_x(\boldsymbol{\theta})^T \mathcal{H}_y(h_\theta(\boldsymbol{x}))J_x(\boldsymbol{\theta})\right] + \lambda I$ | Generalized Gauss-Newton |

Providing a unifying view of several first-order and second-order variants of the gradient descent, the framework presented in this paper makes the connections between different approaches more obvious, and can hopefully give insights on these connections and help clarifying some of the literature.

## 2    Problem Statement and Notations

| Notation | Description |
|---|---|
| $J_x(\boldsymbol{\theta})$ | Jacobian of the function $\boldsymbol{\theta} \mapsto h_\theta(\boldsymbol{x})$ |
| $\mathbb{E}_{a \sim p_\theta(\cdot|x)}[f(a)]$ | Expected value of $f(a)$, when $a$ follows the distribution $p_\theta(\cdot|\boldsymbol{x})$ |
| $H(\boldsymbol{\theta})$ | Hessian of the loss $L$, defined by $[H(\boldsymbol{\theta})]_{i,j} = \frac{\partial^2 L}{\partial \theta_i \partial \theta_j}(\boldsymbol{\theta})$ |
| $\mathcal{H}_y(h_\theta(\boldsymbol{x}))$ | Hessian of the function $\boldsymbol{h} \mapsto l(\boldsymbol{y}, \boldsymbol{h})$ at $\boldsymbol{h} = h_\theta(\boldsymbol{x})$ |

We consider a context of regression analysis[1] in which, based on samples $\boldsymbol{s} = (\boldsymbol{x}, \boldsymbol{y})$, the objective is to estimate the conditional distribution of $\boldsymbol{y}$ given $\boldsymbol{x}$. More formally, this distribution is estimated by a parametrized probability density function (p.d.f.) $p_\theta(\boldsymbol{y}|\boldsymbol{x})$, and the goal of the learning is to progressively optimize the vector $\boldsymbol{\theta}$ to improve the accuracy of this estimation. We furthermore assume that the p.d.f. $p_\theta(\cdot|\boldsymbol{x})$ can be represented by a finite-dimensional vector

---

[1] This context helps to simplify notations, and give examples, but the results obtained are not specific to this setting.

$h_\theta(x)$. For instance, in many applications, $p_\theta(\cdot|x)$ is a multivariate Gaussian distribution, and in this case the vector $h_\theta(x)$ would typically contain the mean and covariance matrix components.

The accuracy of $p_\theta(\cdot|x)$ is measured via a loss function $L$ estimated over a dataset of samples $s$. $L$ depends only on $\theta$ and we assume that it is expressed as the expected value (over the sample distribution) of an atomic loss, a loss *per sample* $l_\theta(s)$:

$$L(\theta) = \mathbb{E}_s[l_\theta(s)].$$

In the remainder of the paper, for simplicity we keep $L$ expressed as an expected value over the samples, but in practice it is replaced by an empirical mean over a batch, which makes its gradient expressible from the gradient of the atomic loss (w.r.t. $\theta$). The dependency of the atomic loss to $\theta$ is via $p_\theta(\cdot|x)$, so we can also express it as a function of the finite-dimensional representation $h_\theta(x)$:

$$l_\theta(s) = l(y, h_\theta(x)).$$

## 3    Vanilla, Classical Gauss-Newton and Natural Gradient Descent

### 3.1    Vanilla Gradient Descent

The core objective of gradient descent algorithms is to determine the direction and magnitude of $\delta\theta$, a small modification of $\theta$ computed iteratively to decrease the value of $L$. The so-called "vanilla" gradient descent is a first-order method that relies on a first-order Taylor approximation of the loss function $L$:

$$L(\theta + \delta\theta) \simeq L(\theta) + \nabla_\theta L(\theta)^T \delta\theta. \tag{2}$$

At each iteration, the objective is the minimization of $\nabla_\theta L(\theta)^T \delta\theta$ with the variable $\delta\theta$. If the gradient is non-zero, the value of this term is unbounded below: it suffices for instance to set $\delta\theta = -\alpha\nabla_\theta L(\theta)$ with $\alpha$ arbitrarily large. As a result, constraints are needed to avoid making excessively large steps. In vanilla approaches, the Euclidean norm $\|\delta\theta\| = \sqrt{\delta\theta^T \delta\theta}$ is used to bound the increments $\delta\theta$. The optimization problem solved at every step of the scheme is:

$$\begin{cases} \min_{\delta\theta} \nabla_\theta L(\theta)^T \delta\theta \\ \delta\theta^T \delta\theta \le \epsilon^2, \end{cases} \tag{3}$$

where $\epsilon$ is a user-defined upper bound. It is the most trivial instance of the general framework (1), and the solution of this problem is $\delta\theta = -\alpha\nabla_\theta L(\theta)$, with $\alpha = \frac{\epsilon}{\|\nabla_\theta L(\theta)\|}$. To set the size of the step, instead of tuning $\epsilon$, the most common approach is to use the expression $-\alpha\nabla_\theta L(\theta)$ and directly tune $\alpha$, which is called the *learning rate*. An interesting property with this approach is that, as $\theta$ gets closer to an optimum, the norm of the gradient $\|\nabla_\theta L(\theta)\|$ decreases, so the $\epsilon$ corresponding to the fixed $\alpha$ decreases as well. This means that steps tend to become smaller and smaller, which is a necessary property to make asymptotic convergence possible.

## 3.2   Classical Gauss-Newton

As mentioned in Sect. 2, the atomic loss function $l_\theta(s) = l(y, h_\theta(x))$ depends indirectly on the parameters $\theta$ via the vector $h_\theta(x)$, which is a finite-dimensional representation of the p.d.f. $p_\theta(\cdot|x)$. So it may be more meaningful to measure the modifications arising from an update $\delta\theta$ by looking at the change on $h_\theta(x)$, not simply on $\delta\theta$ as with the vanilla gradient descent approach. The constraint $\delta\theta^T\delta\theta \le \epsilon^2$ acts as if all components of $\delta\theta$ had the same importance, which is not necessarily the case. Some components of $\theta$ might have much smaller effects on $h_\theta(x)$ than others, and this will not be taken into account with the vanilla gradient descent method, which typically performs badly with unbalanced parametrizations. Measuring and bounding the change on the vector $h_\theta(x)$ makes the updates independent from the way $h_\theta$ is parametrized. To do this, a natural choice is to bound the expected squared Euclidean distance between $h_\theta(x)$ and $h_{\theta+\delta\theta}(x)$:

$$\mathbb{E}_s\left[\|h_{\theta+\delta\theta}(x) - h_\theta(x)\|^2\right] \le \epsilon^2.$$

Using again a first-order approximation, we have $h_{\theta+\delta\theta}(x) - h_\theta(x) \simeq J_x(\theta)\delta\theta$, where $J_x(\theta)$ is the Jacobian of the function $\theta \mapsto h_\theta(x)$. The constraint can be rewritten:

$$\mathbb{E}_s\left[\|J_x(\theta)\delta\theta\|^2\right] = \delta\theta^T\mathbb{E}_s\left[J_x(\theta)^TJ_x(\theta)\right]\delta\theta \le \epsilon^2,$$

resulting in the optimization problem:

$$\begin{cases} \min_{\delta\theta} \nabla_\theta L(\theta)^T\delta\theta \\ \delta\theta^T\mathbb{E}_s\left[J_x(\theta)^TJ_x(\theta)\right]\delta\theta \le \epsilon^2, \end{cases} \tag{4}$$

which fits into the general framework (1) $M_{CGN}(\theta) = \mathbb{E}_s\left[J_x(\theta)^TJ_x(\theta)\right]$ is SPD.

*Damping.* The structure of the matrix $M_{CGN}(\theta)$ makes it symmetric and positive semi-definite, but not necessarily definite-positive. To ensure the definite-positiveness, a regularization or damping term $\lambda I$ can be added, resulting in the constraint $\delta\theta^T\left(M_{CGN}(\theta) + \lambda I\right)\delta\theta \le \epsilon^2$, which can be rewritten:

$$\delta\theta^T M_{CGN}(\theta)\delta\theta + \lambda\delta\theta^T\delta\theta \le \epsilon^2.$$

This damping, often called Tikhonov damping (Martens and Sutskever 2012), regularizes the constraint with a term proportional to the squared Euclidean norm of $\delta\theta$, and it must be noted that with it the constraint is not independent to the parametrization in $\theta$ anymore.

*Classical Gauss-Newton as a Second Order Approximation.* Let us assume that the atomic loss $l_\theta(s)$ is defined as follows: $l_\theta(s) = \frac{1}{2}\|\Delta_\theta(s)\|^2$, where $\Delta_\theta(s)$ is a vector-valued function. Functions of the form $\Delta_\theta(s) = y - f_\theta(x)$ are typical examples in the context of regression. Denoting by $\mathcal{J}_s^\Delta(\theta)$ the Jacobian of $\theta \mapsto \Delta_\theta(s)$, it can be shown that the following expression is a second-order Taylor expansion of the loss in which the terms involving second derivatives of $\Delta_\theta$ with respect to $\theta$ have been dropped (Bottou et al. 2018):

$$L(\theta + \delta\theta) = L(\theta) + \nabla_\theta L(\theta)^T \delta\theta + \frac{1}{2}\delta\theta^T \mathbb{E}_s\left[J_s^\Delta(\theta)^T J_s^\Delta(\theta)\right]\delta\theta + O(\delta\theta^3).$$

Assuming that $\mathbb{E}_s\left[J_s^\Delta(\theta)^T J_s^\Delta(\theta)\right]$ is positive-definite, the minimum is reached with

$$\delta\theta = -\mathbb{E}_s\left[J_s^\Delta(\theta)^T J_s^\Delta(\theta)\right]^{-1}\nabla_\theta L(\theta).$$

As in the update obtained with the optimization problem (4), the matrix with a structure of type Jacobian transpose-times-Jacobian is characteristic of the classical Gauss-Newton approach. To ensure positive-definiteness, damping can be added in the exact same way. The derivation that lead to (4) shows that this kind of update does not only make sense with a squared error-type of loss, so in some sense it is a generalization of the context in which a classical Gauss-Newton approach may be useful. If the dependency of the loss to $\theta$ is naturally expressed via a finite-dimensional vector $v(\theta)$ (e.g. $h_\theta(x)$ or $\Delta_\theta(s)$ in the above cases), then measuring the quantity $\|v(\theta + \delta\theta) - v(\theta)\|$ to evaluate the magnitude of the modifications induced by $\delta\theta$ is likely to be more meaningful than using the vanilla approach (i.e. simply measuring $\|(\theta + \delta\theta) - \theta\| = \|\delta\theta\|$).

*Learning Rate.* The solution $\delta\theta = -\alpha M(\theta)^{-1}\nabla_\theta L(\theta)$ to the general framework (1) is such that $\alpha = \frac{\epsilon}{\sqrt{\nabla_\theta L(\theta)^T M(\theta)^{-1}\nabla_\theta L(\theta)}}$. The classical Gauss-Newton approach corresponds to $M(\theta) = M_{CGN}(\theta) + \lambda I$, or $M(\theta) = M_{CGN}(\theta)$ if we ignore the damping. With the approach based on the second-order approximation of the loss expressed as a squared error, the resulting update has the form $\delta\theta = -M(\theta)^{-1}\nabla_\theta L(\theta)$, which is similar to the above expression except that $\alpha = 1$. However, this theoretical difference in $\alpha$ (referred to as the learning rate in Sect. 3.1) is not significant in practice since its value is usually redefined separately, for various reasons. In particular, when $M(\theta)$ is a very large matrix, $M(\theta)^{-1}$ is often estimated via drastic approximations. In that case, it can be preferable to only compute the update direction, and then perform a line search to find a value of $\alpha$ for which it is verified that the corresponding step size is reasonable. This line search is an important component of the popular reinforcement learning (RL) algorithm TRPO (Schulman et al. 2015).

### 3.3  Natural Gradient

To further improve the independence to parametrization, it is possible to directly measure the change from $p_\theta(\cdot|x)$ to $p_{\theta+\delta\theta}(\cdot|x)$ with a metric on probability density functions. This way, the updates do not even depend on the choice of finite-dimensional representation via $h_\theta$. Amari (1997; 1998) proposed and popularized the notion of natural gradient, which is based on a matrix called the Fisher information matrix, defined for the p.d.f $p_\theta(\cdot|x)$ by:

$$\mathcal{I}_x(\theta) = \mathbb{E}_{a \sim p_\theta(\cdot|x)}\left[\nabla_\theta \log(p_\theta(a|x))\nabla_\theta \log(p_\theta(a|x))^T\right].$$

It can be used to measure a "distance" $d\ell$ between two infinitesimally close probability distributions $p_{\theta}(\cdot|\boldsymbol{x})$ and $p_{\theta+\delta\theta}(\cdot|\boldsymbol{x})$ as follows:

$$d\ell^2(p_{\theta}(\cdot|\boldsymbol{x}), p_{\theta+\delta\theta}(\cdot|\boldsymbol{x})) = \delta\boldsymbol{\theta}^T \mathcal{I}_{\boldsymbol{x}}(\boldsymbol{\theta})\delta\boldsymbol{\theta}.$$

Averaging over the samples, we extrapolate a measure of distance between $\boldsymbol{\theta}$ and $\boldsymbol{\theta} + \delta\boldsymbol{\theta}$:

$$DL^2(\boldsymbol{\theta}, \boldsymbol{\theta} + \delta\boldsymbol{\theta}) = \delta\boldsymbol{\theta}^T \mathbb{E}_s\left[\mathcal{I}_{\boldsymbol{x}}(\boldsymbol{\theta})\right]\delta\boldsymbol{\theta},$$

where $\mathbb{E}_s\left[\mathcal{I}_{\boldsymbol{x}}(\boldsymbol{\theta})\right] = \mathbb{E}_s\left[\mathbb{E}_{a\sim p_{\theta}(\cdot|x)}\left[\nabla_{\theta}\log\left(p_{\theta}(a|\boldsymbol{x})\right)\nabla_{\theta}\log\left(p_{\theta}(a|\boldsymbol{x})\right)^T\right]\right]$ is the averaged Fisher information matrix. It is common to approximate $\mathbb{E}_s\left[\mathbb{E}_{a\sim p_{\theta}(\cdot|x)}[\cdot]\right]$ with the empirical mean over the samples, which reduces the above expression to

$$DL^2(\boldsymbol{\theta}, \boldsymbol{\theta} + \delta\boldsymbol{\theta}) \approx \delta\boldsymbol{\theta}^T \mathbb{E}_s\left[\nabla_{\theta}\log\left(p_{\theta}(\boldsymbol{y}|\boldsymbol{x})\right)\nabla_{\theta}\log\left(p_{\theta}(\boldsymbol{y}|\boldsymbol{x})\right)^T\right]\delta\boldsymbol{\theta}.$$

$\mathbb{E}_s\left[\nabla_{\theta}\log\left(p_{\theta}(\boldsymbol{y}|\boldsymbol{x})\right)\nabla_{\theta}\log\left(p_{\theta}(\boldsymbol{y}|\boldsymbol{x})\right)^T\right]$ is usually called the *empirical* Fisher matrix (Martens 2014). We denote it by $F(\boldsymbol{\theta})$. Putting an upper bound on $\delta\boldsymbol{\theta}^T F(\boldsymbol{\theta})\delta\boldsymbol{\theta}$ results in the following optimization problem:

$$\begin{cases} \min_{\delta\theta} \nabla_{\theta}L(\boldsymbol{\theta})^T\delta\boldsymbol{\theta} \\ \delta\boldsymbol{\theta}^T F(\boldsymbol{\theta})\delta\boldsymbol{\theta} \leq \epsilon^2, \end{cases} \tag{5}$$

which yields *natural* gradient steps of the form

$$\delta\boldsymbol{\theta} = -\alpha F(\boldsymbol{\theta})^{-1}\nabla_{\theta}L(\boldsymbol{\theta}),$$

provided that $F(\boldsymbol{\theta})$ is invertible. $F(\boldsymbol{\theta})$ is always positive semi-definite. Therefore, as in Sect. 3.2 with the classical Gauss-Newton approach, a damping term can be added to ensure invertibility (but again, by doing so the independence to the parametrization is lost). The Fisher information matrix is in some sense uniquely defined by the property of invariance to reparametrization of the metric it induces (Čencov 1982), and can be obtained from many different derivations. But a particularly interesting fact is that $d\ell^2(p_{\theta}(\cdot|\boldsymbol{x}), p_{\theta+\delta\theta}(\cdot|\boldsymbol{x}))$ corresponds to the second-order approximation of the Kullback-Leibler (KL) divergence $KL(p_{\theta}(\cdot|\boldsymbol{x}), p_{\theta+\delta\theta}(\cdot|\boldsymbol{x}))$ (Kullback 1997; Akimoto and Ollivier 2013). Hence, the terms $\delta\boldsymbol{\theta}^T \mathcal{I}_{\boldsymbol{x}}(\boldsymbol{\theta})\delta\boldsymbol{\theta}$ and $\delta\boldsymbol{\theta}^T F(\boldsymbol{\theta})\delta\boldsymbol{\theta}$ share some of the properties of the KL divergence. For instance, when the variance of the probability distribution $p_{\theta}(\cdot|\boldsymbol{x})$ decreases, the same parameter modification $\delta\boldsymbol{\theta}$ tends to result in increasingly large measures $\delta\boldsymbol{\theta}^T \mathcal{I}_{\boldsymbol{x}}(\boldsymbol{\theta})\delta\boldsymbol{\theta}$ (see Fig. 2).

Consequently, if the bound $\epsilon^2$ of Eq. (5) is kept constant, possible modifications of $\boldsymbol{\theta}$ become smaller when the variance of the parametrized distribution decreases. Thus natural gradient iterations slow down when the variance becomes small, which is a desirable property when keeping some variability matters. Typically, in RL, this variability can be related to exploration, and should not vanish early, which is one of the reasons why some RL algorithms benefit from natural gradient steps (Peters and Schaal 2008; Schulman et al. 2015; Wu et al. 2017).

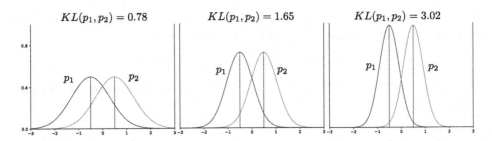

**Fig. 2.** The same parameter change (here, a constant shift of the mean to the right) yields a larger KL divergence when the variance is small.

*Relation Between Natural Gradient and Classical Gauss-Newton.* Let us consider a very simple case where $p_\theta(\cdot|x)$ is a multivariate normal distribution with fixed covariance matrix $\Sigma = \beta^2 I$. The only variable parameter on which the distribution $p_\theta(\cdot|x)$ depends is its mean $\mu_\theta$, so we can use it as a representation of the distribution itself and write

$$h_\theta(x) = \mu_\theta.$$

It can be shown that the KL divergence between two normal distributions of equal variance is proportional to the squared Euclidean distance between the means. More precisely, the KL divergence between $p_\theta(\cdot|x)$ and $p_{\theta+\delta\theta}(\cdot|x)$ is equal to $\frac{1}{2\beta^2}\|h_{\theta+\delta\theta}(x) - h_\theta(x)\|^2$. For small values of $\delta\theta$, it is approximately equal to the measure obtained with the true Fisher information matrix:

$$\frac{1}{2\beta^2}\|h_{\theta+\delta\theta}(x) - h_\theta(x)\|^2 \approx \delta\theta^T \mathcal{I}_x(\theta)\delta\theta.$$

Bounding the average over the samples of the right term is the motivation of the natural gradient descent method. Besides, we have seen in Sect. 3.2 that the classical Gauss-Newton method can be considered as a way to bound $\mathbb{E}_s[\|h_{\theta+\delta\theta}(s) - h_\theta(x)\|^2]$, which is equal to the average of the left term over the samples, up to a multiplicative constant. Hence, even though both methods introduce slightly different approximations, in this context the classical Gauss-Newton and natural gradient descent methods are very similar. This property is used in Pascanu and Bengio (2013) to perform a natural gradient descent on deterministic neural networks, by interpreting their outputs as the mean of a conditional Gaussian distribution with fixed variance.

## 4    Gradient Covariance Matrix, Newton's Method and Generalized Gauss-Newton

The previous approaches fit into the general framework (1) with matrices $M(\theta)$ that do not depend on the loss function, while the 3 approaches presented in this section fit into the same framework but with matrices $M(\theta)$ that do depend on the loss.

## 4.1   Gradient Covariance Matrix

The simplest way to exploit the loss to measure magnitude of changes is to consider the expected squared difference between $l_\theta(s)$ and $l_{\theta+\delta\theta}(s)$:

$$\mathbb{E}_s\left[\left(l_{\theta+\delta\theta}(s) - l_\theta(s)\right)^2\right].$$

For a single sample $s$, changing slightly $\theta$ does not necessarily modify the atomic loss $l_\theta(s)$, but in many cases it can be assumed that this loss becomes different for at least some of the samples, yielding a positive value for $\mathbb{E}_s\left[\left(l_{\theta+\delta\theta}(s) - l_\theta(s)\right)^2\right]$ which quantifies in some sense the amount of change introduced by $\delta\theta$ with respect to the objective. It can be a meaningful measure as it usually depends on the most relevant features for the task to achieve. Let us replace $l_{\theta+\delta\theta}(s)$ by a first-order approximation: $l_{\theta+\delta\theta}(s) \simeq l_\theta(s)+\nabla_\theta l_\theta(s)^T\delta\theta$. The above expectation simplifies to

$$\mathbb{E}_s\left[\left(\nabla_\theta l_\theta(s)^T\delta\theta\right)^2\right] = \delta\theta^T\mathbb{E}_s\left[\nabla_\theta l_\theta(s)\nabla_\theta l_\theta(s)^T\right]\delta\theta.$$

$\mathbb{E}_s\left[\nabla_\theta l_\theta(s)\nabla_\theta l_\theta(s)^T\right]$ is called the outer product metric (Ollivier 2015) or the gradient covariance matrix (Bottou and Bousquet 2008). Putting a bound on the term $\delta\theta^T\mathbb{E}_s\left[\nabla_\theta l_\theta(s)\nabla_\theta l_\theta(s)^T\right]\delta\theta$, the iterated optimization becomes:

$$\begin{cases} \min_{\delta\theta} \nabla_\theta L(\theta)^T\delta\theta \\ \delta\theta^T\mathbb{E}_s\left[\nabla_\theta l_\theta(s)\nabla_\theta l_\theta(s)^T\right]\delta\theta \le \epsilon^2. \end{cases} \quad (6)$$

It results in updates of the form:

$$\delta\theta = -\alpha\mathbb{E}_s\left[\nabla_\theta l_\theta(s)\nabla_\theta l_\theta(s)^T\right]^{-1}\nabla_\theta L(\theta).$$

Again, a regularization term may be added to ensure the invertibility of the matrix.

*Link with the Natural Gradient.* Let us assume that the atomic loss on a sample $s = (x, y)$ is the negative log-likelihood (a common case): $l_\theta(s) = -\log(p_\theta(y|x))$. It follows that the empirical Fisher matrix, as defined in Sect. 3.3, is equal to $\mathbb{E}_s\left[\nabla_\theta l_\theta(s)\nabla_\theta l_\theta(s)^T\right]$, which is exactly the definition of the gradient covariance matrix. Thus, in this case, the two approaches are identical. Several algorithms use this identity for the natural gradient computation, e.g. George et al. (2018).

## 4.2   Newton's Method

Let us consider now a second-order approximation of the loss:

$$L(\theta + \delta\theta) \approx L(\theta) + \nabla_\theta L(\theta)^T\delta\theta + \frac{1}{2}\delta\theta^T H(\theta)\delta\theta,$$

where $H(\boldsymbol{\theta})$ is the Hessian matrix: $[H(\boldsymbol{\theta})]_{i,j} = \frac{\partial^2 L}{\partial \theta_i \partial \theta_j}(\boldsymbol{\theta})$. Although there are obvious counterexamples, one can argue that the first-order approximation, i.e. $L(\boldsymbol{\theta}+\delta\boldsymbol{\theta}) \approx L(\boldsymbol{\theta})+\nabla_\theta L(\boldsymbol{\theta})^T\delta\boldsymbol{\theta}$ (which is used as minimization objective for gradient descents), is most likely good as long as the second-order term $\frac{1}{2}\delta\boldsymbol{\theta}^T H(\boldsymbol{\theta})\delta\boldsymbol{\theta}$ remains small. Therefore, it makes sense to directly put an upper bound on this quantity to restrict $\delta\boldsymbol{\theta}$, as follows:

$$\delta\boldsymbol{\theta}^T H(\boldsymbol{\theta})\delta\boldsymbol{\theta} \leq \epsilon^2.$$

If $H(\boldsymbol{\theta})$ is SPD, this constraint defines a trust region, i.e. a neighborhood of $\boldsymbol{\theta}$ in which the first-order approximation of $L(\boldsymbol{\theta} + \delta\boldsymbol{\theta})$ is supposed to be reasonably accurate. However, $H(\boldsymbol{\theta})$ is symmetric but not even necessarily positive semi-definite, unlike the matrices obtained with the previous approaches. Therefore the damping required to make it definite-positive may be larger than with other methods. It leads to the following optimization problem solved at every iteration:

$$\begin{cases} \min_{\delta\theta} \nabla_\theta L(\boldsymbol{\theta})^T\delta\boldsymbol{\theta} \\ \delta\boldsymbol{\theta}^T(H(\boldsymbol{\theta}) + \lambda I)\delta\boldsymbol{\theta} \leq \epsilon^2, \end{cases} \tag{7}$$

and to updates of the form: $\delta\boldsymbol{\theta} = -\alpha(H(\boldsymbol{\theta}) + \lambda I)^{-1}\nabla_\theta L(\boldsymbol{\theta})$.

*Newton's Method as a Second-Order Approximation.* The same update direction is obtained by directly minimizing the damped second-order approximation:

$$L(\boldsymbol{\theta}) + \nabla_\theta L(\boldsymbol{\theta})^T\delta\boldsymbol{\theta} + \frac{1}{2}\delta\boldsymbol{\theta}^T(H(\boldsymbol{\theta}) + \lambda I)\delta\boldsymbol{\theta}.$$

When $(H(\boldsymbol{\theta}) + \lambda I)$ is SPD, the minimum of this expression is obtained for $\delta\boldsymbol{\theta} = -(H(\boldsymbol{\theta}) + \lambda I)^{-1}\nabla_\theta L(\boldsymbol{\theta})$.

## 4.3   Generalized Gauss-Newton

$L(\boldsymbol{\theta})$ is equal to $\mathbb{E}_s[l(\boldsymbol{y}, \boldsymbol{h}_\theta(\boldsymbol{x}))]$: it does not depend directly on $\boldsymbol{\theta}$ but on the outputs of $\boldsymbol{h}_\theta$, which are vectors of finite dimension. Posing $\delta\boldsymbol{h} = \boldsymbol{h}_{\theta+\delta\theta}(\boldsymbol{x}) - \boldsymbol{h}_\theta(\boldsymbol{x})$, a second-order Taylor expansion of $l(\boldsymbol{y}, \boldsymbol{h}_{\theta+\delta\theta}(\boldsymbol{x}))$ can be written:

$$l(\boldsymbol{y}, \boldsymbol{h}_{\theta+\delta\theta}(\boldsymbol{x})) = l(\boldsymbol{y}, \boldsymbol{h}_\theta(\boldsymbol{x})) + \frac{\partial l(\boldsymbol{y}, \boldsymbol{h}_\theta(\boldsymbol{x}))}{\partial \boldsymbol{h}}^T \delta\boldsymbol{h} + \frac{1}{2}\delta\boldsymbol{h}^T \mathcal{H}_y(\boldsymbol{h}_\theta(\boldsymbol{x}))\delta\boldsymbol{h} + O(\delta\boldsymbol{h}^3),$$

where $\mathcal{H}_y(\boldsymbol{h}_\theta(\boldsymbol{x}))$ is the Hessian matrix of the atomic loss $l(\boldsymbol{y}, \boldsymbol{h}_\theta(\boldsymbol{x}))$ with respect to variations of $\boldsymbol{h}_\theta(\boldsymbol{x})$, and $\frac{\partial l(\boldsymbol{y}, \boldsymbol{h}_\theta(\boldsymbol{x}))}{\partial \boldsymbol{h}}$ is the gradient of $l(\boldsymbol{y}, \boldsymbol{h}_\theta(\boldsymbol{x}))$ w.r.t. variations of $\boldsymbol{h}_\theta(\boldsymbol{x})$. Using the equality $\delta\boldsymbol{h} = J_x(\boldsymbol{\theta})\delta\boldsymbol{\theta} + O(\delta\boldsymbol{\theta}^2)$ (with $J_x(\boldsymbol{\theta})$ the Jacobian of the function $\boldsymbol{\theta} \mapsto \boldsymbol{h}_\theta(\boldsymbol{x})$):

$$l(\boldsymbol{y}, \boldsymbol{h}_{\theta+\delta\theta}(\boldsymbol{x})) = l(\boldsymbol{y}, \boldsymbol{h}_\theta(\boldsymbol{x})) + \frac{\partial l(\boldsymbol{y}, \boldsymbol{h}_\theta(\boldsymbol{x}))}{\partial \boldsymbol{h}}^T J_x(\boldsymbol{\theta})\delta\boldsymbol{\theta} + \frac{\partial l(\boldsymbol{y}, \boldsymbol{h}_\theta(\boldsymbol{x}))}{\partial \boldsymbol{h}}^T O(\delta\boldsymbol{\theta}^2)$$

$$+ \frac{1}{2}\delta\boldsymbol{\theta}^T J_x(\boldsymbol{\theta})^T \mathcal{H}_y(\boldsymbol{h}_\theta(\boldsymbol{x})) J_x(\boldsymbol{\theta})\delta\boldsymbol{\theta} + O(\delta\boldsymbol{\theta}^3).$$

The generalized Gauss-Newton approach is an approximation that consists in dropping the term $\frac{\partial l(y, h_\theta(x))}{\partial h}^T O(\delta\theta^2)$. Averaging over the samples yields the following approximation of $L(\theta + \delta\theta)$:

$$L(\theta) + \mathbb{E}_s \left[ \frac{\partial l(y, h_\theta(x))}{\partial h}^T J_x(\theta) \right]^T \delta\theta + \frac{1}{2}\delta\theta^T \mathbb{E}_s \left[ J_x(\theta)^T \mathcal{H}_y(h_\theta(x)) J_x(\theta) \right] \delta\theta.$$

Noticing that $\mathbb{E}_s \left[ \frac{\partial l(y, h_\theta(x))}{\partial h}^T J_x(\theta) \right] = \nabla_\theta L(\theta)$, it can be rewritten:

$$L(\theta + \delta\theta) \approx L(\theta) + \nabla_\theta L(\theta)^T \delta\theta + \frac{1}{2}\delta\theta^T \mathbb{E}_s \left[ J_x(\theta)^T \mathcal{H}_y(h_\theta(x)) J_x(\theta) \right] \delta\theta.$$

As for Newton's method, the usual way to derive the generalized Gauss-Newton method is to directly minimize this expression (see Martens (2014)), but we can also put a bound on the quantity $\delta\theta^T \mathbb{E}_s \left[ J_x(\theta)^T \mathcal{H}_y(h_\theta(x)) J_x(\theta) \right] \delta\theta$ to define a trust region for the validity of the first-order approximation (as in Sect. 4.2), provided that $\mathbb{E}_s \left[ J_x(\theta)^T \mathcal{H}_y(h_\theta(x)) J_x(\theta) \right]$ is SPD. If the loss $l(y, h_\theta(x))$ is convex in $h_\theta(x)$ (which is often true), the matrix is at least positive semi-definite, so a small damping term suffices to make it positive-definite. If a non-negligible portion of the matrices $J_x(\theta)$ are full rank, the damping term may be added to $\mathcal{H}_y(h_\theta(x))$ rather than to the full matrix. See Martens and Sutskever (2012) for an extensive discussion on different options for the damping and their benefits and drawbacks. With the damping on the full matrix, the optimization problem to solve at every iteration becomes:

$$\begin{cases} \min_{\delta\theta} \nabla_\theta L(\theta)^T \delta\theta \\ \delta\theta^T \left( \mathbb{E}_s \left[ J_x(\theta)^T \mathcal{H}_y(h_\theta(x)) J_x(\theta) \right] + \lambda I \right) \delta\theta \le \epsilon^2, \end{cases} \quad (8)$$

with updates $\delta\theta = -\alpha \left( \mathbb{E}_s \left[ J_x(\theta)^T \mathcal{H}_y(h_\theta(x)) J_x(\theta) \right] + \lambda I \right)^{-1} \nabla_\theta L(\theta).$

## 5   Summary and Conclusion

In Sects. 3 and 4 we motivated and derived 6 different ways to compute parameter updates, that can all be interpreted as solving an optimization problem of this type:

$$\begin{cases} \min_{\delta\theta} \nabla_\theta L(\theta)^T \delta\theta \\ \delta\theta^T M(\theta)\delta\theta \le \epsilon^2, \end{cases}$$

resulting in updates of the form $\delta\theta = -\alpha M(\theta)^{-1}\nabla_\theta L(\theta)$, with $M(\theta)$ SPD.

The quadratic term of the inequality corresponds to a specific metric defined by $M(\theta)$ used to measure the magnitude of the modification induced by $\delta\theta$. To evaluate this magnitude, the focus can be simply on the norm of $\delta\theta$, or on the effect of $\delta\theta$ on the loss, or on the effect of $\delta\theta$ on $h_\theta(x)$ or on $p_\theta(\cdot|x)$, resulting in various approaches, with various definitions of $M(\theta)$. In a context of probabilistic regression, we gave 6 examples that correspond to popular variants of the gradient descent, summarized in Table 1. All methods except the natural gradient can be declined to deterministic cases. Unifying several first-order or second-order variants of the gradient descent method reveals links between these different approaches, and contexts in which some of them are equivalent. The proposed framework gives a compact overview of common variants of the gradient descent, and can hopefully help choosing adequately between them depending on the problem to solve.

**Acknowledgements.** This research was partially supported by the French National Research Agency (ANR), Project ANR-18-CE33-0005 HUSKI.

# References

Akimoto, Y., Ollivier, Y.: Objective improvement in information-geometric optimization. In: Proceedings of the 12th Workshop on Foundations of Genetic Algorithms XII, pp. 1–10. ACM (2013)

Amari, S.: Neural learning in structured parameter spaces-natural Riemannian gradient. In: Advances in Neural Information Processing Systems, pp. 127–133 (1997)

Amari, S.: Natural gradient works efficiently in learning. Neural Comput. **10**(2), 251–276 (1998)

Bottou, L., Bousquet, O.: The tradeoffs of large scale learning. In: Advances in Neural Information Processing Systems, pp. 161–168 (2008)

Bottou, L., Curtis, F.E., Nocedal., J.: Optimization methods for large-scale machine learning. SIAM Rev. **60**(2), 223–311 (2018)

Čencov, N.N.: Statistical Decision Rules and Optimal Inference. Translations of Mathematical Monographs, vol. 53. American Mathematical Society, Providence (1982). ISBN 0-8218-4502-0

George, T., Laurent, C., Bouthillier, X., Ballas, N., Vincent, P.: Fast approximate natural gradient descent in a Kronecker-factored eigenbasis. arXiv preprint arXiv:1806.03884 (2018)

LeCun, Y., Bengio, Y., Hinton, G.: Deep learning. Nature **521**, 436–444 (2015)

Kullback, S.: Information Theory and Statistics. Dover Publications Inc., Mineola (1997). ISBN 0-486-69684-7

Martens, J.: New insights and perspectives on the natural gradient method. arXiv preprint arXiv:1412.1193 (2014)

Martens, J., Sutskever, I.: Training deep and recurrent networks with hessian-free optimization. In: Montavon, G., Orr, G.B., Müller, K.-R. (eds.) Neural Networks: Tricks of the Trade. LNCS, vol. 7700, pp. 479–535. Springer, Heidelberg (2012). https://doi.org/10.1007/978-3-642-35289-8_27

Ollivier, Y.: Riemannian metrics for neural networks I: feedforward networks. Inf. Infer. **4**(2), 108–153 (2015)

Pascanu, R., Bengio, Y.: Revisiting natural gradient for deep networks. arXiv preprint arXiv:1301.3584 (2013)

Peters, J., Schaal, S.: Natural actor-critic. Neurocomputing **71**(7), 1180–1190 (2008)

Schulman, J., Levine, S., Moritz, P., Jordan, M.I., Abbeel, P.: Trust region policy optimization. CoRR, abs/1502.05477 (2015)

Wu, Y., Mansimov, E., Grosse, R.B., Liao, S., Ba, J.: Scalable trust-region method for deep reinforcement learning using Kronecker-factored approximation. In: Advances in Neural Information Processing Systems, pp. 5279–5288 (2017)

# Bayesian Optimization for Backpropagation in Monte-Carlo Tree Search

Nengli Lim[(✉)] and Yueqin Li

Singapore University of Technology and Design, Singapore, Singapore

**Abstract.** In large domains, Monte-Carlo tree search (MCTS) is required to estimate the values of the states as efficiently and accurately as possible. However, the standard update rule in backpropagation assumes a stationary distribution for the returns, and particularly in min-max trees, convergence to the true value can be slow because of averaging. We present two methods, Softmax MCTS and Monotone MCTS, which generalize previous attempts to improve upon the backpropagation strategy. We demonstrate that both methods reduce to finding optimal monotone functions, which we do so by performing Bayesian optimization with a Gaussian process (GP) prior. We conduct experiments on computer Go, where the returns are given by a deep value neural network, and show that our proposed framework outperforms previous methods.

**Keywords:** Monte-carlo tree search · Bayesian optimization · Gaussian processes · Computer Go · Deep neural networks

## 1 Introduction

Monte-Carlo tree search (MCTS) [3,6], or more specifically its most common variant UCT (Upper Confidence Trees; see Sect. 2) [10], has seen great successes recently and has propelled, especially in combination with deep neural networks, the performance of computer Go past professional levels [15,16]. The robust nature of MCTS, versus a traditional approach like depth-first search in alpha-beta pruning, has not only enabled a leap-frog in performance in computer Go, but has also led to its utilization in other games where it is difficult to evaluate states, as well as in other domains [3].

However, MCTS is known to suffer from slow convergence in certain situations [5], in particular when the precise calculation of a narrow tactical sequence is critical for success. For example in boardgames, [11] defines a level-$k$ search trap for player $p$ after a move $m$ as a state of the game where the opponent of $p$ has a guaranteed $k$-move winning strategy. More relevantly, they show through a series of experiments that MCTS performs poorly even in shallow traps, in contrast to regular minimax search; see also [12,13].

ⓒ Springer Nature Switzerland AG 2021
I. Farkaš et al. (Eds.): ICANN 2021, LNCS 12892, pp. 209–221, 2021.
https://doi.org/10.1007/978-3-030-86340-1_17

To better understand this phenomenon, we take a closer look at the update rule

$$Q_n \leftarrow Q_{n-1} + \frac{R_{n-1} - Q_{n-1}}{n} \tag{1}$$

which is performed during the backpropagation phase of MCTS. Here, the current estimate of the value of a state is taken to be the simple average of all previous returns accrued upon visiting that state. Proceeding, we discuss various methods which seek to improve backpropagation by challenging the basic assumptions implied by (1):

(i) Value estimation by averaging returns:
Instead of updating a parent node's value with that of its MAX (MIN) child as in minimax search, backpropagation in MCTS averages all returns to obtain a good signal in noisy environments (this is equivalent to setting the value of the parent node to be the weighted average (by visits) of its children's values).

(ii) Stationarity:
The returns are assumed to follow a stationary distribution.

With regard to the first point, one of the first published works on MCTS [6] posits that taking the value of the best child leads to an overestimation (cf. [2]) of the value of a MAX node, whereas taking the weighted average (by number of visits) of the children's values leads to an underestimation. The paper proposes using an interpolated value, with weights dependent on the current number of visits of the best child:

$$Q_{parent} = \left( \frac{N_{best}}{N_{best} + M} \right) Q_{best} + \left( 1 - \frac{N_{best}}{N_{best} + M} \right) Q_{mean}. \tag{2}$$

Here, $N_{best}$ and $Q_{best}$ respectively denote the number of visits and backed-up value of the best child, and $M$ is a variable which slowly increases after some fixed threshold to dampen the increasing weight.

Similarly in [9], a backup strategy MaxMCTS ($\lambda$) is proposed where an eligibility parameter $\lambda$ can be adjusted to strike a balance between taking the weighted average of the children's values ($\lambda = 1$) and taking the value of the best child ($\lambda = 0$). In addition, they show that the optimal value for $\lambda$ depends on the context; e.g. in Grid World experiments, it is demonstrated that the more obstacles that are present in the grid, the more $\lambda$ has to be lowered in order to maintain good performance. This corresponds with the findings in [11–13], in that standard MCTS may perform well in environments, for example in the opening stages of Go, where global strategy is more important, but its performance tends to degrade in highly tactical situations; see also [1].

Moving on to the second premise, while stationarity may be a viable assumption in multi-armed bandit problems, and although MCTS can be viewed as a sequential multi-armed bandit problem, it is evident that the later simulations explore a larger tree than the earlier simulations. This implies that the sequence of rewards follows a non-stationary distribution, where the returns from later simulations are more informative than the earlier ones, and hence it would be natural to weight them more heavily.

One way of doing this is to simply employ the exponential recency-weighted average update (ERWA) [18] where (1) is replaced by

$$Q_n \leftarrow Q_{n-1} + \alpha \left( R_{n-1} - Q_{n-1} \right), \qquad \alpha \in (0, 1]; \tag{3}$$

see also [8] where they employ a similar backup strategy.

A more sophisticated method called feedback adjustment policy is explored in [21], where here they test four different weight profiles of varying shapes. The following figure provides an illustration.

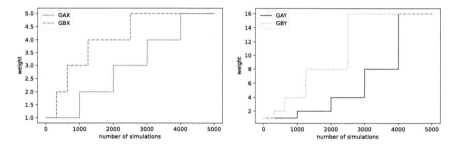

**Fig. 1.** Graph depicting the weight increase of four profiles in feedback adjustment policy; $GAX$: linear increase on a uniform partition; $GAY$: exponential increase on a uniform partition; $GBX$: linear increase on a partition with exponentially increasing widths; $GBY$: exponential increase on a partition with exponentially increasing widths.

Experiments on $9 \times 9$ Go show that $GBY$ gives the highest winning rate over original MCTS, but more importantly, they show that in spite of the fact that the functions all monotonically weight the later simulations more heavily, differences in their particular shapes lead to varying performance gains [21].

Despite differences in these various methods, we can summarize the overarching principles they have in common as follows:

(i) the best child should be weighted more heavily as the number of simulations increase;
(ii) later simulations should be weighted more strongly than earlier ones.

Taking this into account, in this paper we propose Monotone MCTS and Softmax MCTS, two backpropagation strategies which aim to generalize and improve upon the previous methods. We first represent the weights as a function of the number of visits of the node in question, and naturally constrain it to be a monotone function. We then propose to use black-box Bayesian optimization to find these optimal monotone functions.

The rest of the paper is structured as follows. In Sect. 2, we give a brief review of MCTS and Bayesian optimization using a Gaussian process prior. In Sect. 3, we go into the details of Monontone MCTS and Softmax MCTS. We show the effectiveness of our approach in experiments on $9 \times 9$ and $19 \times 19$ Go in Sect. 4. Finally, we conclude in the last section with some direction on future work.

## 2    Preliminaries

### 2.1    Monte-Carlo Tree Search

In comparison to depth-first search in alpha-beta pruning, MCTS uses best-first search to gather information for planning the next action. This is important particularly in computer Go where the branching factor is large, and the tree is best explored asymmetrically to strike a balance between searching deep sequences in tactical situations and searching wide options in factoring in strategic considerations. This also allows it to be an anytime algorithm, in that terminating the search prematurely can still yield acceptable results.

MCTS consists of the following four steps:

(i) Selection: Starting from the root node, the search process descends down the tree by successively selecting child nodes according to the *tree policy*. The most common example is Upper Confidence Bound 1 (UCB1) [10]

$$\underset{a}{\arg\max} \quad Q_a + c \sqrt{\frac{\ln N_{parent}}{N_a + 1}}, \tag{4}$$

and another example is the following variant of PUCB (Predictor + UCB) [14, 15]

$$\underset{a}{\arg\max} \quad Q_a + c \, P_a \frac{\sqrt{N_{parent}}}{N_a + 1}. \tag{5}$$

Here, $P_a$, $Q_a$ and $N_a$ denote the policy weight, mean and visits respectively of node $a$, and $c$ is a constant that can be tuned to balance exploration versus exploitation.

(ii) Expansion: When the simulation phase reaches a leaf node, children of the leaf node are added to the tree, and one of them is selected by the tree policy.

(iii) Simulation: One (or multiple) random playout(s) is performed until a terminal node is reached. More recently, simulation can be augmented or even replaced by a suitable evaluation function such as a deep neural network.

(iv) Backpropagation: The result of the playout is computed and (1) is used to update each node visited in the selection phase.

Averaging the results in each node is essential in noisy environments and when it is critical not to back up values in a manner such that outliers affect the algorithm adversely. However, it can be slow to converge to the optimal value in min-max trees, particularly in nodes where the siblings of an optimal child node are all lower in value [7].

## 2.2   Bayesian Optimization with a Gaussian Process Prior

Given an index set $T$, $\{X_t; t \in T\}$ is a Gaussian process if for any finite set of indices $\{t_1, ..., t_n\}$ of $T$, $(X_{t_1}, ..., X_{t_n})$ is a multivariate normal random variable. By specifying a mean function $\mu : \mathbb{R}^d \to \mathbb{R}$ and a symmetric, positive semi-definite kernel function $k : \mathbb{R}^d \times \mathbb{R}^d \to \mathbb{R}$, one can uniquely define a Gaussian process by setting

$$(X_{t_1}, ..., X_{t_n}) \sim \mathcal{N}([\mu(x_1), \dots, \mu(x_n)]^T, K)$$

for any finite subset $\{t_1, ..., t_n\}$ of $T$. Here, the covariance function $K$ refers to

$$K = \begin{bmatrix} k(x_1, x_1) & \cdots & k(x_1, x_n) \\ \vdots & \ddots & \vdots \\ k(x_n, x_1) & \cdots & k(x_n, x_n) \end{bmatrix}.$$

In addition, we assume that the model $f$ is perturbed with noise,

$$y = f(x) + \epsilon,$$

where $\epsilon \sim \mathcal{N}(0, \tau^2)$, and is assumed to be independent between samples.

In many machine learning problems, the objective function $f$ to optimize is a black-box function which does not have an analytic expression, or may have one that is too costly to compute. Hence, a Gaussian processes are used as surrogate models to approximate the true function as they yield closed-form solutions. For example, if we stipulate that $f(\cdot) \sim \mathcal{N}(0, k)$, then given a history of input-observation pairs $\left(x^{(1)}, t^{(1)}\right), \dots, \left(x^{(n)}, t^{(n)}\right)$, and a new input point $x^{(n+1)}$, we can predict $y^{(n+1)}$ by computing the posterior distribution

$$p\left(y^{(n+1)} \,\middle|\, y^{(1)} = t^{(1)}, \dots, y^{(n)} = t^{(n)}\right),$$

which is Gaussian with mean $\mu$ and variance $\sigma^2$ given by the formulas

$$\mu = r^T (K^n)^{-1} t_n, \tag{6}$$

$$\sigma^2 = c - r^T (K^n)^{-1} r. \tag{7}$$

Here, we denote

$$r = \left[k\left(x^{(1)}, x^{(n+1)}\right), \dots, k\left(x^{(n)}, x^{(n+1)}\right)\right]^T,$$

$$c = k\left(x^{(n+1)}, x^{(n+1)}\right) + \tau^2,$$

$$t_n = \left[t^{(1)}, \dots, t^{(n)}\right]^T,$$

and $K^n$ is the covariance matrix corresponding to the first $n$ inputs. For more information on Gaussian processes for machine learning, we refer the reader to [20].

Another reason for Bayesian optimization becomes apparent when finding the optimal value of $f$ is costly, for example in high-dimensional problems where performing a grid search to find the optimal value is prohibitive, e.g. hyper-parameter tuning in deep learning models.

In such cases, an *acquisition function* is selected to guide sampling to areas where one will have an increased probability of finding the optimum. Two common examples are Expected Improvement (EI)

$$A(x, f^*) = \mathbb{E}\left[max\left\{f_x - f^*, 0\right\}\right]$$
$$= \sigma_x \left[\gamma_x \Phi(\gamma_x) + \phi(\gamma_x)\right],$$
$$\gamma_x = \frac{\mu_x - f^*}{\sigma_X}, \quad f_x \sim \mathcal{N}(\mu_x, \sigma_x^2),$$

where $f^*$ denotes the maximum value of $f$ found so far, and Upper Confidence Bound (UCB)

$$A(x) = \mu_x + \kappa \sigma_x.$$

In both examples, $\mu_x$ and $\sigma_x$ are obtained from (6), and there is a trade-off between exploration and exploitation in the selection of the next point.

For greater efficiency, we use Spearmint [17], which allows the optimization procedure to be run in parallel on multiple cores. Spearmint adopts the Matérn $\frac{5}{2}$ kernel

$$K(x, y) = c\left(1 + \sqrt{5\|x - y\|^2} + \frac{5}{3}\|x - y\|^2\right)e^{-\sqrt{5\|x-y\|^2}}$$

for the Gaussian process prior, and chooses the next point based on the expected acquisition function under all possible outcomes of the pending evaluations. It was shown to be effective for many algorithms including latent Dirichlet allocation and hyper-parameter tuning in convolutional neural networks [17].

In the context of computer Go, Bayesian optimization with a Gaussian process prior has also previously been used in [4]. With regard to MCTS, they perform optimization over the UCT exploration constant and the mixing ratio between fast rollouts and neural network evaluations.

## 3    Methods

To find optimal backpropagation strategies, we first parameterize a family of smooth monotone functions, then perform Bayesian optimization with a Gaussian process prior as reviewed in the previous section. To fully prescribe this family of functions, we invoke the following lemma.

**Lemma 1.** $w : [a, b] \to \mathbb{R}$ *is continuously differentiable and strictly monotonic if and only if there exists a continuous function* $p : [a, b] \to \mathbb{R}$ *such that*

$$w(t) = w(a) + \int_a^t e^{p(s)} \, \mathrm{d}s. \tag{8}$$

The proof of this lemma follows from the mean-value theorem, which gives $w'(t) > 0$ for all $t \in (a, b)$. Thus we can write

$$w(t) = w(a) + \int_a^t w'(s)\, \mathrm{d}s = w(a) + \int_a^t e^{\log w'(s)}\, \mathrm{d}s.$$

Finding the optimal monotone function, even when restricted to continuously differentiable ones, is a functional Bayesian optimization [19] problem as the optimization is taking place over an infinite dimensional Hilbert space of functions. However, for practical reasons, we instead restrict the class of functions we are optimizing over to be

$$\mathcal{W} = \left\{ w \;\middle|\; w(t) = w(0) + \int_0^t e^{p(s)}\, \mathrm{d}s,\; p \in \mathcal{P} \right\},$$

where

$$\mathcal{P} = \left\{ p \;\middle|\; p(s) = \sum_{i=0}^{m-1} \mathbb{1}_{[i\Delta,(i+1)\Delta)}(s)\tilde{p}_i(s) \right\},$$

$$\tilde{p}_i(s) := p(i\Delta) + \left(\frac{s}{\Delta} - i\right)\left(p((i+1)\Delta) - p(i\Delta)\right),$$

is the $m$-dimensional space of functions obtained from linearly interpolating between $m$ points $(p(0), p(\Delta), \ldots, p(N))$ which are uniformly separated by an interval $\Delta$ (in our context, we take $\Delta$ to be $\frac{N}{m-1}$, where $N$ denotes the number of simulations).

Another possibility for the finite-dimensional space $\mathcal{P}$ would be the space spanned by the first few terms of a Hilbert basis, such as the trigonometric polynomials or some other set of orthogonal polynomials. We briefly considered this approach but ultimately settled on the current choice for ease of implementation, and will defer an investigation of the other options to future work.

### 3.1  Monotone MCTS

The first backpropagation strategy we propose is Monotone MCTS. We first run the optimization procedure, with respect to win-rate, over $m$ parameters $\{p(0), p(\Delta), \ldots, p(N)\}$. Each set of parameters yields a continuous function $p \in \mathcal{P}$ by interpolation and a monotone weight function $w$ using (8) with $w(0)$ set to 1. Upon choosing the optimal set of parameters, the update rule is then modified to be

$$Q_n \leftarrow \frac{w(0)}{S(n)}r(0) + \frac{w(1)}{S(n)}r(1) + \cdots + \frac{w(n)}{S(n)}r(n), \tag{9}$$

where we denote $S(n) := \sum_{t=0}^n w(t)$.

Despite being a subset of all possible monotone functions, we consider $\mathcal{W}$ to be sufficiently rich as it contains all increasing linear functions (starting at 1)

$$(c, c, \ldots, c) \implies w(t) = 1 + e^c t,$$

all exponential functions

$$(\log(ra), \log(ra) + r\Delta, \log(ra) + 2r\Delta, \ldots)$$
$$\implies w(t) = (1 - a) + ae^{rt},$$

as well as their linear combinations and other monotone functions such as those in [21]. As an example, the following simple Proposition shows how to convert between ERWA with parameter $\alpha$ and our formulation.

**Proposition 1.** *ERWA with parameter $\alpha < 1$ is equivalent to Monotone MCTS where we set $p(s) = (\log \lambda)s + \log(\alpha \log \lambda)$, with $\lambda := \frac{1}{1-\alpha}$.*

*Proof.* We can expand (3) to obtain

$$Q_n = (1 - \alpha)^n r(0) + \alpha(1 - \alpha)^{n-1} r(1) + \cdots + \alpha r(n).$$

To obtain the weights $w$, we now simply compare coefficients with (9) to derive

$$w(t) = \alpha(1 - \alpha)^{-t}$$
$$= \alpha + \int_0^t e^{(\log \lambda)s + \log(\alpha \log \lambda)} \, ds.$$

## 3.2   Softmax MCTS

For our second backpropagation strategy, we draw inspiration from the softmax distribution

$$p(x_1, \ldots, x_d)_i = \frac{e^{wx_i}}{\sum_{j=1}^d e^{wx_j}},$$

which converges as $w \to \infty$ to $e_k = (0, \ldots, 1, \ldots 0)$, with 1 in the $k^{th}$ position, when $x_k$ is the maximum of $\{x_i\}$. We develop a new robust method, Softmax MCTS, which strikes a balance between the theoretical minimax value of the node and the original averaged value in standard MCTS as follows.

Let $Q_j$ and $N_j$ respectively denote the mean and number of visits of the $j^{th}$ child. In Softmax MCTS, we define the backpropagation update after every simulation for every parent node as

$$Q_{parent} \leftarrow \frac{\sum_{j=1}^d \alpha_j Q_j}{\sum_{j=1}^d \alpha_j},$$

where

$$\alpha_j = N_j \, e^{Q_j w(N_{parent})}.$$

Here, $w$ is a monotonically increasing function of the number of visits of the parent node, which will be optimized in the same manner as given in the previous subsection, with the difference that now $w(0)$ is set to 0. In early stages when $w$ is close to 0, $w_j$ is approximately $N_j$, which means that

$$Q_{parent} \approx \frac{\sum_{j=1}^{d} N_j Q_j}{\sum_{j=1}^{d} N_j}.$$

This is equivalent to the weighted-average update rule in standard MCTS. As $w$ increases with the number of visits, the weights will gradually favour the child with the maximum mean (minimum if the parent is a MIN node).

We believe that this is more robust than the method given in [6] as at any given time the interpolation is taken between the soft maximum and the averaged value, rather than between the averaged value and the hard maximum which is volatile to outliers in the returns.

## 4  Experiments

We use $9 \times 9$ and $19 \times 19$ Go as a testbed for our experiments, and first establish a baseline by running previous methods in the literature against standard MCTS (Table 1).

**Table 1.** Win-rates (%) for the previous methods (left column) versus standard MCTS.

|  | $9 \times 9$ Go | $19 \times 19$ Go |
|---|---|---|
| Coulom (2, 16) | 44.9 | 53.3 |
| Coulom (4, 32) | 45.8 | 51.2 |
| Coulom (8, 64) | 48.3 | 50.2 |
| $GAY$ | 50.2 | 56.1 |
| $GBY$ | 51.8 | 54.5 |
| ERWA, $\alpha = 0.00001$ | 51.2 | 53.9 |
| ERWA, $\alpha = 0.0001$ | 50.3 | 56.9 |
| ERWA, $\alpha = 0.001$ | 52.9 | 55.1 |

In the table above, Coulom $(x, y)$ refers to the method in [6], where $x$ is proportional to the parameter $M$ in (2) and $y$ controls when it begins increasing. $GAY$ and $GBY$ refer to the best performing policies in [21] (see Fig. 1).

For these baselines, we report the range over which they give the best results. Indeed, further decreasing $\alpha$ in ERWA or increasing the parameters in Coulom's method makes them indistinguishable from standard MCTS, whereas we find that going in the converse direction leads to a rapid deterioration in performance.

We use 5000 moves per simulation for $9 \times 9$ Go, and 1600 moves per simulation for $19 \times 19$ Go, and the win-rates are computed based on 1000 games.

We follow the architecture in [16] for the neural nets. This consists of an input convolutional layer, followed by several layers of residual blocks with batch normalization (4 layers for $9 \times 9$, 10 layers for $19 \times 19$), followed by two "heads", one which outputs the policy vector and the other the value of the position. Both heads start with a convolutional layer, and is followed by a fully-connected layer before the output. The input layer has 10 (18 for $19 \times 19$) channels encoding the current position and the previous 4 (8 for $19 \times 19$) positions. In each residual block, we used 64 filters for $19 \times 19$ in the convolutional layers and 32 filters for $9 \times 9$.

The neural net for $9 \times 9$ was trained tabula rasa using reinforcement learning [16] over 600,000 training steps, with each step processing a minibatch of 16 inputs. We trained the $19 \times 19$ neural net by supervised learning over the GoGod database of approximately 15 million datapoints from 80,000 games. In all tests, we use PUCB (5) with the exploration constant set to 0.5, and weight the exploration term by the distribution given by the policy vector output of the neural networks [15, 16].

## 4.1   Monotone MCTS and Softmax MCTS

To find the optimal backpropagation parameters, we set up Spearmint to search over $m = 6$ parameters. For every set of parameters, 400 games are run to determine the win-rate, which is then used to update Spearmint at the end of the round to obtain the next set of parameters. This procedure is repeated for a total of 40 rounds, after which we select the best set of parameters (Table 2).

**Table 2.** Win-rates (%) for Monotone MCTS versus various methods (left column).

| | 1st set of parameters (−10.0,−10.0,−4.0,−4.0,− 4.0,−10.0) | 2nd set of parameters (−4.0,−4.0,−4.0,−10.0,− 4.0,−4.0) |
|---|---|---|
| $(9 \times 9)$ Standard MCTS | 53.1 | **54.5** |
| $(19 \times 19)$ Standard MCTS | **56.0** | 54.3 |
| $(9 \times 9)$ ERWA, $\alpha = 0.00001$ | 50.3 | 52.3 |
| $(9 \times 9)$ ERWA, $\alpha = 0.0001$ | 52.8 | 50.5 |
| $(9 \times 9)$ ERWA, $\alpha = 0.001$ | 52.8 | 53.1 |
| $(9 \times 9)$ $GAY$ | 51.5 | 52.3 |
| $(9 \times 9)$ $GBY$ | 51.0 | 51.1 |

The table above records the results of Monotone MCTS versus standard MCTS, ERWA and the feedback adjustment policies in [21], whereas the table below records the results of Softmax MCTS versus standard MCTS and the Coulom method [6]. In both cases, we report the results for the best two sets of parameters found (Table 3).

**Table 3.** Win-rates (%) for Softmax MCTS versus various methods (left column).

|  | 1st set of parameters (−4.0,−10.0,−4.0,−4.0,−10.0,−4.0) | 2nd set of parameters (−4.0,−10.0,−7.9,−10.0,−10.0,−7.8) |
|---|---|---|
| $(9 \times 9)$ Standard MCTS | 56.3 | 57.8 |
| $(19 \times 19)$ Standard MCTS | 53.2 | 55.9 |
| $(9 \times 9)$ Coulom (2,16) | **59.3** | 57.6 |
| $(9 \times 9)$ Coulom (4, 32) | 55.5 | **59.5** |
| $(9 \times 9)$ Coulom (8, 64) | 55.1 | 51.9 |

The figure below depicts the weight profiles of both Monotone MCTS and Softmax MCTS (Fig. 2).

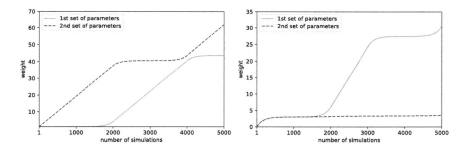

**Fig. 2.** Weight profiles of Monotone MCTS (left) and Softmax MCTS (right)

## 5    Discussion and Future Work

In this paper, we present a unifying framework for backpropagation strategies in MCTS for min-max trees. Our proposed method allows one to perform optimization in two orthogonal directions. The first algorithm Softmax MCTS allows one to find the optimal schedule that weights the best child more gradually as the tree grows, and the second method Monotone MCTS generalizes previous work in adapting the update rule to get the most accurate estimate of a node's value in a non-stationary setting.

Doing so requires optimization over the space of monotone functions, a high-dimensional problem we overcome efficiently by using parallelized Bayesian optimization over a Gaussian process prior. This is done by first simplifying the search for an optimal backpropagation operator by considering a finite-dimensional subspace of the monotone functions (the space $\mathcal{W}$ in Sect. 3), thus reducing a functional Bayesian optimization problem to a regular Bayesian optimization problem.

Once the parameters that define the optimal monotone function are found, they can be incorporated into the backpropagation phase of MCTS with essentially zero overhead. Our experiments show that Softmax MCTS posts stronger gains than Monotone MCTS, in particular when compared to Coulom's method. Most importantly, the experiments show that both strategies are superior to previous methods in the recent context of MCTS augmented by deep neural networks, and across a range of parameter settings.

To conclude, we would like to note that it is possible to perform the optimization in conjunction with the exploration constant in the selection phase, but we have decided in this paper to focus solely on the backpropagation phase and to elucidate the effects of different monotone weight profiles on the win-rate. Combining these optimal backup strategies with other phases of MCTS will be the topic of future work.

# References

1. Baier, H., Winnands, M.H.M.: MCTS-minimax hybrids with state evaluations. J. Artif. Intell. Res. **62**, 193–231 (2018)
2. Blumenthal, S., Cohen, A.: Estimation of the larger of two normal means. J. Am. Statist. Assoc. **63**(323), 861–876 (1968)
3. Browne, C.B., et al.: A survey of Monte-Carlo tree search methods. IEEE Trans. Comput. Intell. AI Games **4**(1), 1–43 (2012)
4. Chen, Y., et al.: Bayesian optimization in AlphaGo. arXiv preprint https://arxiv.org/abs/1812.06855 (2018)
5. Coquelin, P.A., Munos, R.: Bandit algorithms for tree search. In: Proceedings of the Twenty-Third Conference on Uncertainty in Artificial Intelligence, pp. 67–74 (2007)
6. Coulom, R.: Efficient selectivity and backup operators in Monte-Carlo tree search. In: International Conference on Computers and Games, pp. 72–83 (2006)
7. Fu, M.: Monte-Carlo tree search and minimax combination, MSc thesis, University of Maryland at College Park (2017)
8. Hashimoto, J., Kishimoto, A., Yoshizoe, K., Ikeda, K.: Accelerated UCT and its application to two-player games. In: van den Herik, H.J., Plaat, A. (eds.) ACG 2011. LNCS, vol. 7168, pp. 1–12. Springer, Heidelberg (2012). https://doi.org/10.1007/978-3-642-31866-5_1
9. Khandelwal, P., Liebman, E., Niekum, S., Stone, P.: On the analysis of complex backup strategies in Monte-Carlo tree search. In: International Conference on Machine Learning, pp. 1319–1328 (2016)
10. Kocsis, L., Svepesvári, C.: Bandit based Monte-Carlo planning. In: Proceedings of the 17th European Conference on Machine Learning, pp. 282–293 (2006)
11. Ramanujan, R., Sabharwal, A., Selman, B.: On adversarial search spaces and sampling-based planning. In: Proceedings of the International Conference on Automated Planning and Scheduling, vol. 20, no. 1 (2010)
12. Ramanujan, R., Sabharwal, A., Selman, B.: On the behavior of UCT in synthetic search spaces. In: Proceedings of the International Conference on Automated Planning and Scheduling, vol. 21, no. 1 (2011)
13. Ramanujan, R., Selman, B.: Trade-offs in sampling-based adversarial planning. In: Proceedings of the International Conference on Automated Planning and Scheduling, vol. 21, no. 1 (2011)

14. Rosin, C.: Multi-armed bandits with episode context. Ann. Math. Artif. Intell. **61**(3), 203–230 (2011)
15. Silver, D., et al.: Mastering the game of Go with deep neural networks and tree search. Nature **529**, 484–489 (2016)
16. Silver, D., et al.: Mastering the game of Go without human knowledge. Nature **550**, 354–359 (2017)
17. Snoek, J., Larochelle, H., Adams, R.P.: Practical Bayesian optimization of machine learning algorithms. In: Advances in Neural Information Processing Systems, pp. 2951–2959 (2012)
18. Sutton, R.S., Barto, A.G.: Reinforcement Learning: An Introduction. MIT press (2018)
19. Vien, N.A., Zimmermann, H., Toussaint, M.: Bayesian functional optimization. In: Thirty-Second AAAI Conference on Artificial Intelligence (2018)
20. Williams, C.K., Rasmussen, C.E.: Gaussian processes for machine learning, vol. 2. MIT press, Cambridge (2006)
21. Xie, F., Liu, Z.: Backpropagation modification in Monte-Carlo game tree search. In: Third International Symposium on Intelligent Information Technology Application, vol. 2, pp. 125–128 (2009)

# Growing Neural Networks Achieve Flatter Minima

Paul Caillon[✉] and Christophe Cerisara[✉]

Université de Lorraine, CNRS, LORIA, 54500 Vandoeuvre-les-Nancy, France
{paul.caillon,cerisara}@loria.fr

**Abstract.** Deep neural networks of sizes commonly encountered in practice are proven to converge towards a global minimum. The flatness of the surface of the loss function in a neighborhood of such minima is often linked with better generalization performances. In this paper, we present a new model of growing neural network in which we incrementally add neurons throughout the learning phase. We study the characteristics of the minima found by such a network compared to those obtained with standard feedforward neural networks. The results of this analysis show that a neural network grown with our procedure converges towards a flatter minimum than a standard neural network with the same number of parameters learned from scratch. Furthermore, our results confirm the link between flatter minima and better generalization performances as the grown models tend to outperform the standard ones. We validate this approach both with small neural networks and with large deep learning models that are state-of-the-art in Natural Language Processing tasks.

## 1  Introduction

Over the last few years, deep learning [19] has had empirical successes in multiple research domains, such as computer vision, speech recognition, and machine translation [11,27,34]. Along with its practical success, the theoretical properties of deep learning have been a subject of active investigation, from the expressivity [1,20] and the generalization properties to the trainability [3,15] of a network.

Some empirical works observe that generalization and flatness of the minima found during training are related [2,32]. However, [7] questions this assumption, by showing that for deep neural networks with rectifier units, most Hessian-based measures of the flatness of the loss minimum are sensible to rescaling, making it possible to build equivalent models corresponding to arbitrarily sharper minima. To address this issue, a recent work [31] introduced a particular measure invariant to rescaling to show that flatter minima obtain better generalization performances than sharper ones. Sharper minima are thus believed to be suboptimal and should be avoided during learning. A recent work, [16] theoretically proves a related result, which is that adding one special neuron by output unit eliminates all suboptimal local minima of any neural network.

In Natural Language Processing, the models used in practice consist in millions of parameters. For example, BERT [6] is a well-known contextual word

© Springer Nature Switzerland AG 2021
I. Farkaš et al. (Eds.): ICANN 2021, LNCS 12892, pp. 222–234, 2021.
https://doi.org/10.1007/978-3-030-86340-1_18

embeddings model that is pre-trained with a Denoising Autoencoding objective and is at the basis of most state-of-the-art results in many Natural Language Processing (NLP) tasks. We study in this work, in the context of NLP and pattern recognition tasks, whether adding neurons incrementally instead of learning them all from the beginning could achieve a flatter minimum for the neural network. In the following, we propose to experimentally investigate this hypothesis by comparing an incrementally growing network with one with a fixed architecture learned from scratch, with both small and competitive models. The results we present tend to confirm our hypothesis as flatter minima are indeed achieved by growing networks, which also often leads to better generalization performances.

## 2   Related Work

**Trainability of a Neural Network.** Training neural networks can be seen as a non convex optimization problem. However because of the absence of poor local minima, the trainability of a Deep Neural Network is proven to be possible [15]. Recent results theoretically prove that gradient descent can find a global minimum for nonlinear deep neural networks of sizes commonly encountered in practice [16]. In fact a linear increase of the number of trainable parameters as the size of the dataset increases is sufficient to find a global minimum. Such a network generalizes well on unseen test samples.

**Growing Neural Networks.** The properties of growing networks, notably with regard to training convergence, are more and more investigated. The authors of [16] for example add a special neuron by output unit in order to eliminate all suboptimal local minima of any deep neural network. This idea of a network adapting its architecture to the dataset it is trained on is also found in automated Neural Architecture Search (NAS, see [8]). Typical works in this field are [4] and [5], where the authors use a grow-and-prune training paradigm to iteratively add and remove units in order to achieve more compact networks with state of the art performances.

The idea of progressive growing of models has also been explored in the context of Generative Adversarial Networks (GAN) [10] to increasingly add new details as the training progresses. In [14], the authors start with low-resolution images, and then progressively increase the resolution by adding layers to the networks. This allows the model to learn increasingly finer scale detail, instead of having to learn all scales simultaneously.

This kind of growing approach can be used in continual learning [29], where the goal is to train models that must be capable of progressively learning knowledge over long time spans. One of the main challenges in continual learning is catastrophic forgetting, i.e., the fact that new information interferes with previously learned knowledge [25]. Recent works in this field showed that growing a small network both wider and deeper allows to learn accurate and relatively small networks that can prevent catastrophic forgetting, achieving state-of-the-art performances with methods such as Learn-to-Grow [22], Compact-Pick-Grow [13] or recently Firefly Neural Architecture Descent [38]. However the question as to why those growing neural networks reach state of the art performance while being smaller than most of the other competitive models (comparable test accuracy as the full model with only 4% of the full model's size in [38]) is still to be investigated, one idea being that when a network grows, the parameter space becomes larger and what was previously a local minima can become a saddle point and hence can be escaped, which yields a monotonic decrease of the loss [35].

**Smooth and Sharp Minima.** On top of these considerations, the abilities to generalize to unseen data is often linked to the flatness of the minima found during training in empirical works [2,32] sharp minima leading to poorer generalization. In a recent work, [37] notably shows that smoothing out and eliminating sharp minima by perturbing multiple copies of the DNN by noise injection and then averaging these copies lead to an improvement of the generalization properties. Another equivalent idea is explored in [33], which proposes to smooth activations instead of using noise or progressively adding units during training. A very interesting idea recently developed to enhance the performances of deep neural networks is to track the sharpness of the loss model and to jointly optimize the loss and its sharpness [9]. In particular, this procedure, called Sharpness-Aware Minimization (SAM), seeks parameters that lie in neighborhoods having uniformly low loss and present empirical results showing model generalization improvement across a variety of benchmark datasets.

In order to correctly evaluate the flatness of minima, measures invariant to the rescaling issue pointed out in [7] now exist [30,31] and can be used to evaluate the difference of flatness in minima between models of the same size. The goal of our work is to investigate whether growing a feedforward neural network (FNN) from scratch throughout the learning phase yields better loss surface properties at minima than learning a standard FNN, both having ultimately the same number of parameters, using the measure developed in [31].

## 3    Model Description

### 3.1    Notations

The following notations are inspired by [17]. We consider the general case of neural networks of any depth for $k$-class classification that can be topologically considered as a directed acyclic graph (DAG) with non-linearity functions such as ReLU, tanh or sigmoid. This includes any structure of feedforward neural network with or without fully connected layers and with potentially skip-connections.

Let $N = \{1, \ldots, n\}$ be the set of neurons in a network. For two neurons $(i, j) \in N^2$, we note :

- $w_{j,i}$ the weight of the connection from $j$ to $i$. If there is no connection, then $w_{j,i} = 0$. Note that the sparse $n \times n$ matrix $W = [w_{j,i}]_{1 \leq j, i \leq n}$ is constrained to define an acyclic graph;

- $\sigma_i$ the activation function at the output of neuron $i$;
- $\pi(i)$ the set of parents of neuron $i$: $\pi(i) = \{j | w_{j,i} \neq 0\}_{1 \leq j \leq n}$
- $d(i)$ the depth of neuron $i$: it is the longest path to reach $i$ from any input.

Every DAG has at least one topological ordering, which can be used to create a layered structure with possible skip connections as shown for example in [12] and [28]. There is thus an equivalence between the representation of a neural network either with depths or with layers, as the layer $l$ is composed of all the neurons at depth $l$. Given an input vector $x$, we define the pre-activation of a neuron $i$ at depth $l$ recursively as

$$z_i(x, W) = \sum_{j \in \pi(i)} \sigma_j \left( z_j(x, W) \right) w_{j,i}.$$

## 3.2   Model Presentation

Recent works [23] and [16] propose to insert neurons in order to avoid bad minima. We investigate next the impact on the loss surface when inserting neurons into the model progressively throughout the learning process.

More precisely, our work's main focus is to explore whether growing approaches intrinsically leads to flatter minima. We do not seek an increase in the model performances per se. We rather try to understand why the growing approaches lead to better results than the standard ones in the recent works. To the extent of our knowledge, no similar work on the sharpness of the loss surface of growing networks exist. That is also why our model does not rely on complex heuristics to decide how and when the model's size should be increased. We rather choose a simple approach, based on random picks as it has been shown in previous works [21, 26] that advanced NAS techniques are often only marginally superior to simple random search.

In our model, the neurons are inserted incrementally at a regular pace (i.e., with a constant time interval) during the learning phase, starting with a minimum number of parameters (just the input and output layers) in order to increase the number of learnable parameters with the number of epochs. Intuitively, our growing procedure is a naive insertion process: first, an existing neuron is randomly chosen and splitted to create a new child neuron, which inherits most of its children. The new neuron also gets new parent connections with existing neurons randomly chosen in the previous layers. More formally, we have initially:

- The set of neurons is $N = \{1, \ldots, n_I, n_{I+1}, \ldots, n\}$: the first $n_I$ neurons are the input neurons, while the last $n - n_I$ neurons are the output neurons;
- The weight matrix $W$ is symmetrical and is initially strictly equivalent to a feedforward neural network with no hidden layer, with non-null transitions that are initialized randomly, e.g., with Glorot or uniform initialization;
- The depth of the input neurons is 0, and the depth of the output neurons is 1.

Then, we randomly choose a neuron from the current network, called the *primary parent*, as well as $I-1$ other neurons on lower depths, which are just called the *parents*. The primary parent is randomly sampled among all existing neurons, as previous works [21,26] found that advanced NAS techniques are often only marginally superior to simple random search. With each neuron insertion, the total number of parameters of the model is increased by $I$, as each link created between the new neuron and its parents adds a parameter. This process is iterated until we reach the desired number of parameters. Intuitively, insertion proceeds by splitting the primary parent, i.e., inserting a new neuron after the primary parent that inherits its children, as detailed in Algorithm 1.

The connection between the primary parent and the neuron inserted is stored in $\pi^0$ which is the set containing all of the pairs *(primary parent, neuron inserted)*. We initialize $\pi^0$ as the set containing all the connections between input and output neurons, considering that all input neurons are "primary parents" of all of the output neurons : $\pi^0 = \{(1, n_{I+1}), \ldots, (1, n), \ldots, (n_I, n_{I+1}), \ldots, (n_I, n)\}$. In this way, we are able to track the multiple insertions and to grow the hidden layers of the network both deeper and wider. The insertion process is illustrated in Fig. 1.

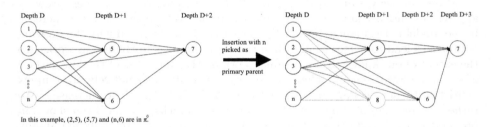

In this example, (2,5), (5,7) and (n,6) are in $\pi^0$.

**Fig. 1.** Example of parents/children inheritance before and after insertion; the new weights are: $\forall i \in [1, n], w'_{i,8} \sim \mathcal{U}(-0.5, 0.5), w'_{8,6} = w_{n,6}$.

*Remark 1.* Steps 1 and 8 of the algorithm ensure that all the output units and only them are at maximum depth as when we insert a neuron n+1 on the maximal depth, n+1 is a primary parent to every output unit which means the maximal depth is updated :

if $d(n + 1) = D, \forall i \in \{n_{I+1}, \ldots, n\}, (n + 1, i) \in \pi^0$

*Remark 2.* In Step 4 we sample the primary parents $j|d(j) < D$. The output neurons are thus the only neurons to have multiple primary parents as they are considered as the only neurons that cannot be primary parents themselves

*Remark 3.* Step 6 of the algorithm ensures that $d(n + 1) = d(j) + 1$ as $\forall i \in \pi(n + 1), d(i) \leq d(j)$.

---

**Algorithm 1:** Insertion Algorithm

---

**Input:** Weight matrix $W \in \mathbb{R}^{n \times n}$
**Output:** Weight matrix $W' \in \mathbb{R}^{(n+1) \times (n+1)}$

1  Save the initial set of primary parents $\pi^0$
2  Create a new neuron $n + 1$
3  Create $W'$ by copying all weights from $W$ and initializing the new dimension with null weights.
4  Sample the primary parent: $j \sim \mathcal{U}(\{j | d(j) < D\}_{1 \leq j \leq n})$ where $\mathcal{U}$ is the uniform distribution, and $D = \max_{1 \leq i \leq n} d(i)$ is the depth of the network.
5  Save the new primary parent: $\pi^0 \leftarrow \pi^0 \cup \{(j, n+1)\}$
6  Insert $n + 1$ by setting $w'_{j,n+1} \sim \mathcal{U}(-0.5, 0.5)$
7  Connect children of $j$ as children of $n + 1$:
8  **for** $i \in \{1, \ldots, n\}$ *so that* $w_{j,i} \neq 0$ **do**

   – if $d(i) > d(n+1)$:
     • Set $w'_{n+1,i} = w_{j,i}$
     • Set $w'_{j,i} = 0$
   – if $d(i) = d(n+1)$ and $(j, i) \in \pi^0$:
     • Set $w'_{n+1,i} = w_{j,i}$
     • Set $w'_{j,i} = 0$
     • $\pi^0 \leftarrow (\pi^0 - \{(j,i)\}) \cup \{(n+1,i)\}$

9  Add new parents for $n + 1$:
10 **for** *I-1 times* **do**

   – Sample a node $k \sim \mathcal{U}(\{i | w'_{i,n+1} = 0)$ and $d(i) \leq d(j)\}_{1 \leq i \leq n})$.
   – Add $k$ as a parent of $n + 1$: $w'_{k,n+1} \sim \mathcal{U}(-0.5, 0.5)$
   – Iterate

---

*Remark 4.* The concept of primary parents in Step 8 allows us to balance between the depth and width of the architecture of the network. When there are still only a small number of units in the network, a primary parent can be picked multiple times. If this is the case, Step 8 allows the network to grow deeper and not only wider.

## 4 Experimental Results

### 4.1 Experiments with Small Models

We implement our model in PyTorch and evaluate it on AGNews and MNIST [18].

**AGNews:** AG News (AG's News Corpus) is a sub-dataset of A. Gulli's corpus of news articles constructed by assembling titles and description fields of articles from the 4 largest classes ("World", "Sports", "Business", "Sci/Tech") of AG's Corpus. The AG News contains 30,000 training and 1,900 test samples per class.

**MNIST:** The handwritten digit benchmark MNIST is a large collection of handwritten digits. It has a training set of 60,000 examples, and a test set of 10,000 examples.

We compare our model with a fully connected network with the same number of parameters as the final number of parameters of our model (after insertions). Our objective is to study the properties of the final loss surface when adding neurons one by one, all other hyper-parameters being equal (number of parameters, activation functions, weight initialization, accuracy, batch size, SGD algorithm, ...).

In order to study the loss surface, we use the metric proposed in [31], and more precisely the scale invariant measure to compare the flatness of the minima found by our different models. This Hessian-based measure for flatness is invariant to rescaling as the authors use a metric on a quotient manifold structure that captures the rescaling that is natural to the space of parameters of neural networks with positively homogeneous activations.

As done in [31], we train each network architecture and dataset up to 100% of training accuracy with stochastic gradient descent (SGD). We test two different batch sizes of 10 and 100 samples for MNIST, and 1 and 16 samples for AGNews. No pre-trained word embeddings are used for AGNews. For both datasets we use the categorical cross entropy loss. On AGNews, the learning rate is initially $10^{-4}$ and $10^{-3}$ on MNIST.

We further test two final model sizes, respectively with 10 and 500 hidden neurons for MNIST, and 10 and 100 hidden neurons for AGNews. On both the AGNews and MNIST corpora, we train the growing models for 100 epochs, reaching 100% of training accuracy. We let the model learn the new inserted parameters for a few epochs before inserting new neurons again. We used the following insertion scheme:

- (MNIST, 10 final hidden neurons) 1 new unit every 10 epochs from epoch 5
- (AGNews, 10 final hidden neurons) 1 new unit every 10 epochs from epoch 5
- (MNIST, 500 final hidden neurons) 50 new units every 10 epochs from epoch 10 to 60
- (AGNews, 100 final hidden neurons) 10 new units every 10 epochs from epoch 5

The initialization scheme for all the models follows a uniform distribution between $-0.5$ and $0.5$. The inserted neurons are thus initialized in the same way as those in the standard feedforward neural networks we compare our network with. In this way, the insertion process is the only difference between the two training methods, every hyper-parameter being equal otherwise.

Furthermore, we train different feedforward neural network architectures with a various number of hidden layers:

- (MNIST, 10 final hidden neurons):
  - 1 hidden layer of 10 neurons
- (AGNews, 10 final hidden neurons)
  - 1 hidden layer of 10 neurons

- (MNIST, 500 final hidden neurons)
  - **architecture a**: 1 hidden layer of 500 neurons
  - **architecture b**: 2 hidden layers of 400 then 100 neurons
  - **architecture c**: 3 hidden layers of 300 then 150 then 50 neurons
- (AGNews, 100 final hidden neurons)
  - **architecture a**: 1 hidden layer of 100 neurons
  - **architecture b**: 2 hidden layers of 80 then 20 neurons
  - **architecture c**: 3 hidden layers of 60 then 30 then 10 neurons

Testing multiple architectures with the same number of neurons allows us to verify whether the results presented in Table 1 are due to the insertion process or are influenced by the possible difference in terms of depth between the standard feedforward networks and the layered structure obtained through our growing process.

### 4.2    Growing RoBERTa's Classification Head

BERT [6] is a well-known and reference contextual word embeddings model that is pre-trained with a Denoising Autoencoding objective and is at the basis of most state of the art results in many Natural Language Processing (NLP) tasks. RoBERTa [24] builds on BERT's language masking strategy, but fine-tunes the original BERT model with a different choice of tasks and conditions.

As most of today's state of the art NLP models, RoBERTa is a complex and large neural network, which thus faces the issue of over-parametrization. It is composed of 355 million parameters stored in 24 layers of self-attention, with a classification head on top to output the desired number of classes. In our experiments, we strictly keep the same number of parameters, without adding more complexity to the model. The classification head is classically composed of a two-layers feed-forward network with 1024 hidden neurons. We thus propose next to replace this classification head with a bare one-layer feed-forward network, and to grow it until it reaches the same number of parameters as the reference classification layer. The rest of the pre-trained Roberta large model, i.e., the self-attention layers, stays the same. We use the standard CoLA benchmark [36] to train and evaluate our growing model against RoBERTa. The CoLA dataset is composed of 9594 training and 1063 test sentences. The objective is to classify each sentence into two classes: grammatically correct and incorrect English sentences.

In order to study the impact of growing the network, we insert neurons progressively throughout the whole learning process, which consists in 10 epochs in the original RoBERTa experiment. To do so, a total of 1024 hidden neurons are inserted through three different phases: after the second, fifth and seventh epoch. We also compute the sharpness of both the original RoBERTA model and of our grown model, and compare the models performances and loss characteristics. The batch size used is 16. The results are compiled in Table 2.

**Table 1.** Test Accuracy and Spectral Norm of Hessian at Minima for different trained networks.

| Corpus : MNIST | | | |
|---|---|---|---|
| Model | Batch size | Test accuracy | Spectral norm |
| 10 hidden neurons | | | |
| Growing | 10 | 84% | **2.23** |
| | 100 | 77.91% | **24.29** |
| Fully connected | 10 | 84.03% | 38.01 |
| | 100 | 77.74% | 68.39 |
| 500 hidden neurons | | | |
| Growing | 10 | **96.98%** | **4.45** |
| | 100 | **94.84%** | **179.01** |
| Fully Connected a | 10 | 87.27% | 1030.07 |
| | 100 | 66.86% | 12111.28 |
| Fully Connected b | 10 | 84.57% | 820.54 |
| | 100 | 64.17% | 21517.66 |
| Fully Connected c | 10 | 84.26% | 1253.72 |
| | 100 | 74.01% | 12893.59 |

(a) Results on MNIST corpus

| Corpus : AGNews | | | |
|---|---|---|---|
| Model | Batch Size | Test Accuracy | Spectral Norm |
| 10 hidden neurons | | | |
| Growing | 1 | 90.2% | $\mathbf{9.83 \cdot 10^{-5}}$ |
| | 16 | 88.2% | **3.22** |
| Fully Connected | 1 | 90.1% | $7.91 \cdot 10^{-4}$ |
| | 16 | 88.3% | 20.83 |
| 100 hidden neurons | | | |
| Growing | 1 | 90.7% | **0.57** |
| | 16 | 89.2% | **31.31** |
| Fully Connected a | 1 | 90.5% | 3.43 |
| | 16 | 89.0% | 69.53 |
| Fully Connected b | 1 | 90.4% | 7.02 |
| | 16 | 89.0% | 60.89 |
| Fully Connected c | 1 | 90.5% | 3.25 |
| | 16 | 88.9% | 73.28 |

(b) Results on AGNews

**Table 2.** Test Accuracy and Spectral Norm of Hessian at Minima on COLA

| Model | Test Accuracy | Spectral Norm |
|---|---|---|
| Growing | 68.2% | $\mathbf{1.8945 \cdot 10^5}$ |
| Fully connected | 68% | $6.7778 \cdot 10^5$ |

## 5    Discussion

The results obtained with our small models experiments first confirm what was shown in [31], i.e., that by increasing the batch size, we increase the sharpness of the minima. But these experiments further show that inserting neurons during the training phase of the model allows to decrease the sharpness of the minima. These results are obtained with shallow networks and standard but relatively simple classification tasks.

Another interesting observation is that our method not only decreases the spectral norm and thus improves the flatness of the minima of a shallow network, but we can also observe in Table 1, that a lower spectral norm seems to correlate with higher generalization performances, as the test accuracies are better for the growing networks when the number of parameters is larger.

Another interesting conclusion that can be drawn from Table 2 is that these good results translate to complex and state-of-the-art neural networks. Indeed, we can observe that growing the final classification head of such a model leads to an optimum solution that is flatter by an order of magnitude, according to the flatness metric, without any negative impact in terms of accuracy. We note that the classification head represents approximately only 0.6% of the total number of parameters of the model, which may explain why the models performances in terms of accuracy are similar. Despite the fact that only a small proportion of the total number of parameters is grown, it is interesting to note that the growing process leads to spectral norm of the optimum that is much lower, which means that we reach a flatter minimum.

Our results tend to show that the growing paradigm, more and more used in the Neural Architecture Search field, is an important asset to reach flatter minima. However, there is no theoretical guarantee for now that a flatter minimum will systematically translate into better generalization performances, although several related works results tend to exhibit such a correlation.

With regard to this question, we can observe in our experiments that with very small neural networks (the case with only 10 hidden neurons in Table 1), the performances are similar although the growing method achieves a minimum that is at least 2.5 (up to more than 10) times flatter than the standard method. We believe that this is due to the small capacity of the neural network, which can not learn more because of its limited size.

Second, when inserting a greater amount of neurons, we can observe two different behaviors. On the one hand, when comparing on MNIST, the growing method leads to flatter minima and better Test Accuracy, as it was also shown in [31]. On the other hand, the flatter minima given by the growing approach do not correlate with better performances on AG News: models with 10 and 100 hidden neurons have roughly the same performances. Similarly, when trained on CoLA with a complex structure, the growing method still leads to a flatter minimum but no significant improvement in accuracy is observed. Our hypothesis is that, in these two cases, the number of parameters of the growing model is too small when compared to the total number of parameters of the model to have a real impact on accuracy, as most of the information is learned in the embeddings.

## 6    Conclusion and Future Work

Our main contribution is the proposal of a growing neural network approach, which we experimentally validate in several conditions on three tasks and with small and large deep learning models. The results show that the resulting loss function has flatter minima than with the traditional training procedure on the full network. We further show that such flatter minima improves the generalization capability of the trained models when they do not rely on complex embeddings. These results tend to show that the paradigm of growing neural networks during the learning phase intrisically leads to flatter minima, which is an interesting observation, although these results have to be confirmed on different datasets, potentially with transfer learning experiments in order to better assess the generalization performances across related tasks. Furthermore, in the case of Natural Language Processing tasks, a potentially interesting extension could be to adapt the approach to further grow the embeddings in order to have a greater impact on both the loss surface characteristics and model's performances. As this work focuses on feedforward neural networks, an extension to more complex structures, such as convolutions and recurrent networks is also envisaged.

## References

1. Barron, A.R.: Approximation and estimation bounds for artificial neural networks. Mach. Learn. **14**(1), 115–133 (1994)
2. Chaudhari, P., et al.: Entropy-SGD: biasing gradient descent into wide valleys. arXiv e-prints arXiv:1611.01838, November 2016
3. Choromanska, A., Henaff, M., Mathieu, M., Arous, G.B., LeCun, Y.: The loss surfaces of multilayer networks. arXiv e-prints arXiv:1412.0233, November 2014
4. Dai, X., Yin, H., Jha, N.K.: NeST: a neural network synthesis tool based on a grow-and-prune paradigm. arXiv e-prints arXiv:1711.02017, November 2017
5. Dai, X., Yin, H., Jha, N.K.: Grow and prune compact, fast, and accurate LSTMs. arXiv e-prints, page arXiv:1805.11797, May 2018
6. Devlin, J., Chang, M.-W., Lee, K., Toutanova, K.: BERT: pre-training of deep bidirectional transformers for language understanding. arXiv e-prints arXiv:1810.04805, October 2018

7. Dinh, L., Pascanu, R., Bengio, S., Bengio, Y.: Sharp minima can generalize for deep nets. arXiv e-prints arXiv:1703.04933, March 2017
8. Elsken, T., Metzen, J.H., Hutter, F.: Neural architecture search: a survey. arXiv e-prints arXiv:1808.05377, August 2018
9. Foret, P., Kleiner, A., Mobahi, H., Neyshabur, B.: Sharpness-aware minimization for efficiently improving generalization. arXiv e-prints arXiv:2010.01412, October 2020
10. Goodfellow, I.J., et al.: Generative adversarial networks. arXiv e-prints arXiv:1406.2661, June 2014
11. Graves, A., Mohamed, A.-R., Hinton, G.: Speech recognition with deep recurrent neural networks. arXiv e-prints arXiv:1303.5778, March 2013
12. Healy, P., Nikolov, N.S.: How to layer a directed acyclic graph. In: Graph Drawing (2001)
13. Hung, S.C.Y., Tu, C.-H., Wu, C.-E., Chen, C.-H., Chan, Y.-M., Chen, C.-S.: Compacting, picking and growing for unforgetting continual learning. arXiv e-prints arXiv:1910.06562, October 2019
14. Karras, T., Aila, T., Laine, S., Lehtinen, J.: Progressive growing of GANs for improved quality, stability, and variation. arXiv e-prints arXiv:1710.10196, October 2017
15. Kawaguchi, K.: Deep learning without poor local minima. arXiv e-prints arXiv:1605.07110, May 2016
16. Kawaguchi, K., Pack Kaelbling, L.: Elimination of all bad local minima in deep learning. arXiv e-prints arXiv:1901.00279, January 2019
17. Kawaguchi, K., Kaelbling, L.P., Bengio, Y.: Generalization in deep learning. arXiv e-prints arXiv:1710.05468, October 2017
18. Lecun, Y., Bottou, L., Bengio, Y., Haffner, P.: Gradient-based learning applied to document recognition. Proc. IEEE **86**(11), 2278–2324 (1998)
19. Lecun, Y., Bengio, Y., Hinton, G.: Deep learning. Nature Cell Biol. **521**(7553), 436–444 (2015)
20. Leshno, M., Lin, V.Y., Pinkus, A., Schocken, S.: Multilayer feedforward networks with a nonpolynomial activation function can approximate any function (1993)
21. Li, L., Talwalkar, A.: Random search and reproducibility for neural architecture search. arXiv e-prints arXiv:1902.07638, February 2019
22. Li, X., Zhou, Y., Wu, T., Socher, R., Xiong, C.: Learn to grow: a continual structure learning framework for overcoming catastrophic forgetting. arXiv e-prints arXiv:1904.00310, March 2019
23. Liang, S., Sun, R., Lee, J.D., Srikant, R.: Adding one neuron can eliminate all bad local minima. arXiv e-prints arXiv:1805.08671, May 2018
24. Liu, Y., et al.: RoBERTa: a robustly optimized BERT pretraining approach. arXiv e-prints arXiv:1907.11692, July 2019
25. McCloskey, M., Cohen, N.J.: Catastrophic interference in connectionist networks: the sequential learning problem. Psychol. Learn. Motiv. Adv. Res. Theo. **24**(C), 109–165, January 1989. Funding Information: The research reported in this chapter was supported by NIH grant NS21047 to Michael McCloskey, and by a grant from the Sloan Foundation to Neal Cohen. We thank Sean Purcell and Andrew Olson for assistance in generating the figures, and Alfonso Caramazza, Walter Harley, Paul Macaruso, Jay McClelland, Andrew Olson, Brenda Rapp, Roger Rat-cliff, David Rumelhart, and Terry Sejnowski for helpful discussions
26. Negrinho, R., Patil, D., Le, N., Ferreira, D., Gormley, M., Gordon, G.: Towards modular and programmable architecture search. arXiv e-prints arXiv:1909.13404, September 2019

27. Netzer, Y., Wang, T., Coates, A., Bissacco, A., Wu, B., Ng, A.Y.: Reading digits in natural images with unsupervised feature learning. In: NIPS Workshop on Deep Learning and Unsupervised Feature Learning 2011 (2011)
28. Neyshabur, B., Tomioka, R., Srebro, N.: Norm-based capacity control in neural networks. arXiv e-prints arXiv:1503.00036, February 2015
29. Parisi, G.I., Kemker, R., Part, J.L., Kanan, C., Wermter, S.: Continual lifelong learning with neural networks: a review. arXiv e-prints arXiv:1802.07569, February 2018
30. Petzka, H., Adilova, L., Kamp, M., Sminchisescu, C.: A reparameterization-invariant flatness measure for deep neural networks. arXiv e-prints arXiv:1912.00058, November 2019
31. Rangamani, A., Nguyen, N.H., Kumar, A., Phan, D., Chin, S.H., Tran, T.D.: A scale invariant flatness measure for deep network minima. arXiv e-prints arXiv:1902.02434, February 2019
32. Keskar, N.S., Mudigere, D., Nocedal, J., Smelyanskiy, M., Tang, P.T.P.: On large-batch training for deep learning: generalization gap and sharp minima. arXiv e-prints arXiv:1609.04836, September 2016
33. Sinha, S., Garg, A., Larochelle, H.: Curriculum by smoothing. arXiv e-prints arXiv:2003.01367, March 2020
34. Sutskever, I., Vinyals, O., Le, Q.V.: Sequence to sequence learning with neural networks. arXiv e-prints, page arXiv:1409.3215, September 2014
35. Wang, D., Li, M., Wu, L., Chandra, V., Liu, Q.: Energy-aware neural architecture optimization with fast splitting steepest descent. arXiv e-prints arXiv:1910.03103, October 2019
36. Warstadt, A., Singh, A., Bowman, S.R.: Neural network acceptability judgments. arXiv e-prints arXiv:1805.12471, May 2018
37. Wen, W, et al.: SmoothOut: smoothing out sharp minima to improve generalization in deep learning. arXiv e-prints arXiv:1805.07898, May 2018
38. Wu, L., Liu, B., Stone, P., Liu, Q.: Firefly neural architecture descent: a general approach for growing neural networks. arXiv e-prints, page arXiv:2102.08574, February 2021

# Dynamic Neural Diversification: Path to Computationally Sustainable Neural Networks

Alexander Kovalenko[ID], Pavel Kordík[ID], and Magda Friedjungová[✉][ID]

Faculty of Information Technology, Czech Technical University in Prague, Prague, Czech Republic
{kovalale,pavel.kordik,magda.friedjungova}@fit.cvut.cz

**Abstract.** Small neural networks with a constrained number of trainable parameters, can be suitable resource-efficient candidates for many simple tasks, where now excessively large models are used. However, such models face several problems during the learning process, mainly due to the redundancy of the individual neurons, which results in sub-optimal accuracy or the need for additional training steps. Here, we explore the diversity of the neurons within the hidden layer during the learning process, and analyze how the diversity of the neurons affects predictions of the model. As following, we introduce several techniques to dynamically reinforce diversity between neurons during the training. These decorrelation techniques improve learning at early stages and occasionally help to overcome local minima faster. Additionally, we describe novel weight initialization method to obtain decorrelated, yet stochastic weight initialization for a fast and efficient neural network training. Decorrelated weight initialization in our case shows about 40% relative increase in test accuracy during the first 5 epochs.

**Keywords:** Diversification · Negative correlation · Weight initialization · Computational sustainability · Neural networks

## 1   Introduction

Over the last decade, machine learning algorithms have achieved vast progress in various fields. Namely, general approach called deep neural networks (DNN) with multiple hidden layers [16], has enabled machine learning algorithms to perform at an acceptable level in the many areas, in some cases outperforming human accuracy [7]. Such progress, in no small measure, has become available due to modern hardware computational capabilities, enabling the training of large DNN on an immense amount of data.

On the other hand, even though large models perform very well on complex tasks, we cannot endlessly rely on an infinite increase in computational resources and size of datasets. Training large neural networks is energy, time and memory demanding task. Recently, researchers started questioning energy consumption

© Springer Nature Switzerland AG 2021
I. Farkaš et al. (Eds.): ICANN 2021, LNCS 12892, pp. 235–247, 2021.
https://doi.org/10.1007/978-3-030-86340-1_19

of machine learning algorithms and their carbon footprint [24]. Thus it will not be superfluous to develop a strategy for the models that have a constrained number of parameters, sufficient enough for the certain task, and can be trained fast, rather than chasing higher accuracy by enlarging the number of parameters and using more complex hardware.

Universal approximation theorem [8] claims that a feed-forward artificial neural network with a single hidden layer can approximate any continuous well-behaved function of arbitrary number of variables with any accuracy. The conditions are: a sufficient number of neurons in the hidden layer, and a correct weight selection. Above mentioned theorem for an arbitrary width case was originally proved by Cybenko [8] and Hornik [19] and later extended to an arbitrary depth case (DNN) in [27].

In this paper we get a deeper insight on the practical application of Cybenko's theorem, in order to train a neural network, where all hidden neurons will be used efficiently. Therefore, we have to pay attention to two following aspects: number of neurons and correct weight selection.

*Number of neurons* in a hidden layer is a quite straightforward parameter that became trendy with availability of multi-threaded parallel computing on GPU [30]. Models of a vast number of trainable parameters are not devoid of logic, as they generalize better and can be so-called 'universal learners'. For example, GPT-3 having 175 billion parameters, is a perfect example of a universal learner [5]. Thus, the community has been experimenting with model architectures increasing width [27] or depth [36] of neural networks. Issues, such as vanishing gradient [17,18] was resolved by applying methods, including second-order Hessian-free optimization [29], training schedules by using greedy layer-wise training [15,34,39], sparse rectifier activation function, widely known as ReLU [11], layer-size-dependent initialization, such as Xavier [10] and Kaiming [14] and skip connections [13]. Even though, we can make arbitrarily large models make good predictions, to achieve computational sustainability by expanding the number of trainable parameters up to infinity, would not be the best option for the tasks of lower complexity. The community has been already trying to address this problem, thus several solutions dealing with this issue have occurred. For example, widely used ReLU activation function, saturated only in one dimension, which helps with vanishing gradient problem, on the other hand results in so-called 'dying neurons' [26], modified activation functions such as Leaky ReLU [41], adaptive convolutional ReLU [9], Swish [32], Antirectifier [28] and many other were addressed to solve the problem of 'neural graveyard'. Resource efficient solutions, such as pooling operations [33], LightLayers [21] depth-wise separable convolutions [6] were developed to reduce the complexity of the models.

*Correct weight selection*, at first sight, depends on training parameters, such as loss function, number of epochs, learning rate etc. However, to train the neural network competently these weights have to be initialized stochastically. There are several ways to initialize weight, mainly aimed to avoid vanishing gradients. Nevertheless, stochastic weight initialization can result in neuron redundancy, when different neurons are trained in a similar manner. This is not crucial if the neural network is excessively large, however, in computationally sustainable models, neuron redundancy and 'neural graveyards' are undesirable. Moreover, there are numerous application when memory efficient model is required (e.g. autonomous devices such as sensors, detectors, mobile or portable devices). Such devices require memory and performance efficient solutions to learn spontaneously and improve from experience. In this case adding excessive parameters to the model can be rather questionable for the model application.

Therefore, once we consider each neuron of the model as an individual learner, the neural network can be seen as an ensemble. It is known that for ensembles diversity of learners is desirable to some extent [4]. Thus, we can assume that diversity between neurons or reinforced diversification during the training can be beneficial for the model.

In this paper we foremost explore how the diversity between neurons evolves during the training and as a following step suggest methods for diversification of the neurons during the model training. This is especially relevant in resource constrained models, where neuron redundancy means reducing the number of predictors. Additionally, we show how weight pre-initialization can affect neural network training at the early steps.

## 2   Our Approach

Let us start with a term *negative correlation* (NC) learning [4], which is a simple, yet elegant technique to diversify individual base-models in the ensemble and reduce their correlations. Ambiguity decomposition [12] of the loss function raises the possibility of controlling the trade-off between bias, variance, and covariance [38] using the strength parameter, to reduce covariance. In its order the concept of an NC learning is originated from bias-variance decomposition [3,20] of ensemble learning. In this case, bias is the output shift from the true value, and variance is the measure of ensemble ambiguity, which simply means dispersion around the mean output value.

As it was first demonstrated by Krogh and Vedelsby [23] quadratic error of ensemble prediction is always less that the quadratic error of each individual estimator of the ensemble:

$$(f_{\text{ens}} - d)^2 = \sum_i w_i \left(f_i - d\right)^2 - \sum_i w_i \left(f_i - f_{\text{ens}}\right)^2 \tag{1}$$

Later Brown [4] demonstrated decomposition of ensemble error into three components - bias, variance and covariance, and shown, the connection between ambiguity and covariance:

$$E\left\{ \tfrac{1}{M} \sum_i \left(f_i - d\right)^2 - \tfrac{1}{M} \sum_i \left(f_i - \bar{f}\right)^2 \right\} =$$

$$\overline{bias}^2 + \tfrac{1}{M}\overline{var} + \left(1 - \tfrac{1}{M}\right)\overline{\text{covar}} \tag{2}$$

The ensemble ambiguity is nothing less than the variance of the weighted ensemble around the weighted mean. Therefore, higher ambiguity, i.e. decorrelation between the ensemble output is desirable up to some measure.

Our *first trial* was to decorrelate neurons in the hidden layer by penalizing the difference between mean weight of the neurons $\bar{w}$ and each neuron $w_i$:

$$NC = \frac{1}{n}\gamma \sum_i (\bar{w} - w_i) \qquad (3)$$

where $\gamma$ is the regularization strength parameter, and $n$ is the number of neurons in a layer.

However, it is likely more profitable to compare not only single weights, but weight matrices or e.g. kernels in convolutional neural networks (CNN), as trainable kernels represent. Thus, the *second* way to define diversity is comparing neurons by cosine similarity:

$$\frac{1}{D} = \frac{1}{n}\gamma \sum_i \sum_j w_i \cdot w_j \qquad (4)$$

where $\mathbf{w}$ are weights of individual neurons and $D$ is the diversity measure.

In this technique we compare each weight in the layers and define a diversity measure $D$. However, it has quadratic complexity of such expression, which would oppose the idea of the current work, as our indent is fast and efficient training of resource constrained neural networks.

Therefore, combining the first two approaches we introduce and explore *another method* to define diversity in the neural networks:

$$\frac{1}{D} = \frac{1}{n}\gamma \sum_i \bar{w} \cdot w_i \qquad (5)$$

After observing the training process and evolution of diversity measure in the models, we explored the possibility of weight pre-optimization using diversification. In this case, we used Kaiming weight initialization, with further optimization to enlarge the diversity between the weights, and at the same time keep weight mean and standard deviation of the weight matrix close to initial:

$$L = \left(\left|\bar{W} - \bar{w}_k\right| + \left|\sigma_W - \sigma_{w_i}\right|\right) \sum_i \sum_j w_i \cdot w_j \qquad (6)$$

where $L$ is loss, $\bar{W}$ is the initial weight mean, $\bar{w}_k$ is the weight mean at $k$ training step, $\sigma_W$ is standard deviation of the initial weights array, and $\sigma_{w_i}$ is standard deviation of the weights array at $k$ training step.

## 3   Experiments

We perform some initial experiments using DNN in order to study diversity evolution during the model training and demonstrate the effectiveness of proposed diversification mechanisms.

The experiments were performed on publicly available benchmark dataset Fashion MNIST [40]. This dataset was chosen as it is suitable for DNN training and has higher variance than traditional hand-written digits dataset MNIST [25]. We implemented one-hidden-layer neural network with 16, 32, 64, 128, and 256 neurons in the hidden layer (see Table 1), using PyTorch [31] library. Otherwise, we used standard parameters for the training, including Adam optimizer [22] with a learning rate of 0.01, cross entropy loss function with penalization terms (Eq. 3–5):

$$H(T, p) = -\sum_{i=1}^{N} \frac{1}{N} \log_2 q(x_i) + \frac{1}{D} \tag{7}$$

where $T$ presents training set, $p$ is true distribution, $q$ is predicted distribution, $N$ is standard deviation of the weights array at $k$ training step, $q(x)$ is the probability of event $x$ estimated from the training set, and $D$ is the diversity measure, obtained using Eq. 3, 4, or 5.

# 4    Results and Discussion

## 4.1    Evolving Diversity and Symmetry Breaking

During the model training, one can notice sub-optimal accuracy stagnation for a several epochs, this can be associated with the existence of local minima on a loss function surface [2,35]. This can be associated with a symmetry in the neural network layer, which is shown to be a critical point especially for small neural networks [1,37]. We found out that naturally the model tends to decrease the correlation between the neurons, however when the model converges to a local minimum with a sub-optimal accuracy, the similarity between the neurons rises up until the moment when the optimization process surpasses the local minimum and the accuracy increases. (see Fig. 1) This correlates with an existence of symmetry in the weights, once weights are symmetrical (correlated) and the number of neurons is constrained, the overall output of the model will likely to be inefficient.

## 4.2    Negative Correlation Learning

The experiment above inspired us to study certain ways to decorrelate neurons in the hidden layer, thus brake the symmetry that can appear during the learning process. As we discussed earlier, we consider the output of neural network as an output of an ensemble. Thus, first, we did simple NC learning, applied to the individual neurons, rather than ensemble of classifiers. The logic behind this experiment was rather comprehensible. Once the model has constrained number of parameters to generalize the data, higher variance would help to eliminate redundant neurons and overall prediction has to be more accurate. As it can be seen from the Fig. 2. Decorrelation mechanism helps to avoid local minima at the

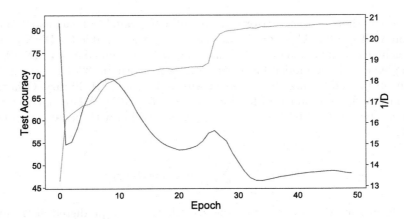

**Fig. 1.** Training curve and Diversity measure (Eq. 4) for the first 50 epochs on Fashion MNIST dataset. DNN with 1 hidden layer of 32 neurons.

**Table 1.** First 10 epochs average of the neural network training for various number of neurons, hidden layer diversified according to the Eq. 5.

| $\gamma$ | Number of neurons & Test accuracy, % | | | | |
|---|---|---|---|---|---|
| | 16 | 32 | 64 | 128 | 256 |
| 0.0 | 54.19 | 58.25 | 62.46 | 69.62 | 72.10 |
| $1 \cdot 10^{-5}$ | 55.17 | 60.17 | 62.45 | 68.64 | 70.65 |
| $1 \cdot 10^{-4}$ | **56.41** | **61.25** | 64.13 | 70.32 | 72.27 |
| $1 \cdot 10^{-3}$ | 54.48 | 60.81 | **65.04** | **70.45** | **72.83** |
| $1 \cdot 10^{-2}$ | 53.54 | 60.04 | 63.19 | 70.26 | 72.36 |
| $1 \cdot 10^{-1}$ | 54.22 | 59.46 | 62.23 | 70.20 | 71.64 |
| 1.0 | 50.09 | 57.49 | 60.53 | 69.84 | 71.65 |

early stage on the model learning. Nevertheless, decorrelation using NC learning generally did not result in the higher accuracy overall. We associate it to several factors, such as Kaiming weight initialization that help to avoid vanishing gradient, and Adam optimizer which is a replacement optimization algorithm that can handle sparse gradients on noisy data, and thus is able to efficiently overcome local minima due to adaptive learning rated for each parameter. Eventhough, these widely used techniques are dealing with the above mentioned problem of the neuron redundancy, our proposed model can help at the early stages of a model training.

Moreover, with an increasing number of neurons the influence of decorrelation diminishes, this can be explained, that excessively large NN performs good at the low variance data as well as not every neuron is needed for a good prediction. However, in the present work we consider computationally sustainable DNN, where all the neuron are forced to contribute the prediction and on the other

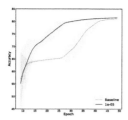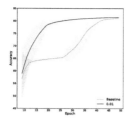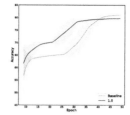

**Fig. 2.** Validation accuracy training curves of the model with various $\gamma$ values.

hand, for complex data larger amount of neurons would be needed to generalize the dataset. Therefore, for more sophisticated problems neuron diversification may be efficient for a larger number of neurons. However, in the present case we performed further experiments on the model with 64 neurons in the hidden layer, which we consider sufficient for a given dataset. All the models were trained for 10 times to calculate mean and standard deviation. In Table 2 the average testing accuracy of the first 10 epoch for the DNN with 64 neurons in the hidden layer trained using negative correlation learning (Eq. 3) is shown.

**Table 2.** First 10 epochs average of the neural network training, hidden layer diversified according to the Eq. 3.

| $\gamma$ | Train Acc., % | Test Acc., %, | Test Acc. STD |
|---|---|---|---|
| 0.0 | 61.46 | 62.46 | 2.34 |
| $1 \cdot 10^{-5}$ | 62.26 | 62.45 | 2.34 |
| $1 \cdot 10^{-4}$ | 63.65 | 64.13 | 1.59 |
| $1 \cdot 10^{-3}$ | 63.12 | **65.04** | 1.76 |
| $1 \cdot 10^{-2}$ | 62.54 | 63.19 | 1.03 |
| $1 \cdot 10^{-1}$ | **64.23** | 62.23 | 0.95 |
| 1.0 | 59.56 | 60.53 | 1.57 |

### 4.3    Pairwise Cosine Similarity Diversification

It has to be noted that, unlike in [4], where universal diversification strength parameter was found for the ensembles of all sizes, in our case $\gamma$ value depends on the size of the hidden layer and has to be rather considered as $\gamma$ *per neuron*. However, on the other hand it is loss-dependent, which means that, ideally, it has to be same or one order of magnitude smaller than the output of the loss function during the training, otherwise, rather than the model loss (e.g. cross entropy), reciprocal diversity measure $\frac{1}{D}$ will be optimized. Thus, the reader has to consider optimizing $\gamma$ value for each certain neural network and loss function. Thus optimal $\gamma$ approximately can be estimated as:

$$\gamma = \frac{0.5 \cdot 10^{b_{loss}}}{n} \tag{8}$$

where n is the number of neurons in the hidden layer and $b_{loss}$ is the loss function order of magnitude.

In addition to NC learning, we introduced diversity measure based on cosine similarity between the neurons (Eq. 4). Such technique, seems to be promising due to several reasons: first, we, rather that mean values, compare patterns, which can be useful for more complex models, such as CNNs or transformers, moreover here, each neuron is compared with each, thus such model is intended to be more robust. Nevertheless, at least for DNN, results we comparable with NC learning (see Table 3), additionally, such method has quadratic complexity, which opposes our initial aim to train small models faster and more efficient.

**Table 3.** First 10 epochs average of the neural network training, hidden layer diversified according to the Eq. 4.

| $\gamma$ | Train Acc., % | Test Acc., %, | Test Acc. STD |
|---|---|---|---|
| 0.0 | 55.94 | 62.83 | 1.18 |
| $5 \cdot 10^{-8}$ | 56.52 | 64.20 | 1.11 |
| $5 \cdot 10^{-7}$ | **57.98** | **65.76** | 0.92 |
| $5 \cdot 10^{-6}$ | 55.48 | 59.96 | 0.71 |
| $5 \cdot 10^{-5}$ | 56.47 | 49.20 | 1.52 |
| $5 \cdot 10^{-4}$ | 56.47 | 44.60 | 1.06 |
| $5 \cdot 10^{-3}$ | 42.66 | 38.61 | 1.10 |

### 4.4    Reaching Linear Complexity

To enable our diversification method to compare patterns, however avoid quadratic complexity, we combined the fist concept of NC learning with the second one, and implemented diversity measure based on penalization of the cosine similarity of each neuron in the hidden and layer's neurons mean (Eq. 5). The algorithm (see Table 4) overhead is comparable with $L$ regularization. Moreover, it has shown the highest accuracy gain among three.

### 4.5    Iterative Diversified Weight Initialization

However, it can be noticed, that occasionally, during the training, the model do not behave exactly as expected, creating an outlying learning curves. This is most likely associated with stochastic weight initialization. In this case Kaiming initalization is used [13]. Kaiming initialization is widely used for the neural networks with ReLU activation functions and related to the nonlinearities of

**Table 4.** First 10 epochs average of the neural network training, hidden layer diversified according to the Eq. 5.

| $\gamma$ | Train Acc., % | Test Acc., %, | Test Acc. STD |
|---|---|---|---|
| 0.0 | 61.54 | 63.15 | 2.08 |
| $5 \cdot 10^{-7}$ | 62.37 | 63.3 | 1.63 |
| $5 \cdot 10^{-6}$ | 63.60 | 64.54 | 1.25 |
| $5 \cdot 10^{-5}$ | **64.87** | **64.95** | 1.66 |
| $5 \cdot 10^{-4}$ | 60.36 | 62.14 | 1.66 |
| $5 \cdot 10^{-3}$ | 52.54 | 55.86 | 0.45 |
| $5 \cdot 10^{-2}$ | 41.26 | 42.71 | 1.32 |

the ReLU activation function, which make it non-differentiable at $x = 0$. The weights, in this case are initialized stochastically with the variance that depends on the number of neurons $N$:

$$v^2 = 2/N \tag{9}$$

It is fair to suggest, that correlation between the initialized weights can play significant role in the model learning process. Indeed, in the Fig. 1. It is clearly seen, the model gained the most of its accuracy while reducing the correlation between neurons during the first few epochs. However, the aim of weight initialization is to prevent layer activation outputs from exploding or vanishing during the course of a forward pass through a deep neural network. Usually weight are initialized stochastically with a small number to avoid vanishing gradients especially if *tanh* or *sigmoid* activation functions are used. Thus, to obtain stochastically initialized, yet decorrelated, weights we introduced iteratively diversified Weight initialization, using custom loss function based on Eq. 6. The logic behind such initialization is to reduce the diversity measure between the weights and at the same time keep weights mean $\bar{w}$ and weights standard deviation $\sigma_w$ close to the originally initialized using Kaiming initialization (Table 5).

**Table 5.** First 5 epochs average of the neural network training initialized with decorrelated weights according to the Eq. 6 pre-optimized for 5 epochs.

| $\gamma$ | Train Acc., % | Test Acc., %, | Test Acc. STD |
|---|---|---|---|
| 0.0 | 29.54 | 34.23 | 2.04 |
| $1 \cdot 10^{-4}$ | 42.43 | 43.43 | 1.81 |
| $1 \cdot 10^{-3}$ | 43.92 | 45.65 | 1.53 |
| $1 \cdot 10^{-2}$ | **44.65** | **47.01** | 1.24 |
| $1 \cdot 10^{-1}$ | 38.32 | 39.83 | 1.06 |
| 1.0 | 36.64 | 38.94 | 1.37 |
| 10.0 | 32.5 | 37.57 | 1.41 |

# 5    Conclusion

In this paper we show how to explore and tame the diversity of neurons in the hidden layer. We studied how the correlation between the neurons evolves during the training and what is the effect on prediction accuracy. In appears, that once the model is converged to the local minimum on the loss landscape, correlation between the neurons increases up to the point when the optimization process overcome the local minimum. Thus, we introduced three methods how to dynamically reinforce diversification and thus decorrelate neural network layer. The concept of negative correlation suggested by Brown [4] was reviewed and expanded. Instead of decorrelation individual neural networks in the ensemble we diversified neurons in the hidden layer, using three techniques: *negative correlation learning, cosine pairwise similarity, cosine similarity around the mean.*

First technique is originated from the neural networks ensembles and shows a decent performance in our example using DNN, however for more sophisticated models, such as CNNs and transformers, second and third technique is likely to be more advantageous as far as it can compare patterns. Additionally to reach correct weight selection, we introduced weight iterative optimization using weight diversification. It was shown that such techniques are suitable for the fast training of small models and notably affect their accuracy at the early stage. Which is a small, yet important step towards the development of a strategy towards energy-efficient training of neural networks.

Our future plans for using neural network diversification primarily consists in using above described diversification techniques in more sophisticated models in order to explore the possibility to improve training speed and reduce the number of training parameters. Popular architectures, such as transformers can benefit from the individual head diversification in multi-head attention block, as far as multiple heads are intended to learn various representation. Furthermore, we are planning to explore more pattern-oriented techniques for defining diversity between neurons to enable efficient diversification application in CNNs.

**Acknowledgment.** This research is supported by the Czech Ministry of Education, Youth and Sports from the Czech Operational ProgrammeResearch, Development, and Education, under grant agreement No. CZ.02.1.01/0.0/0.0/15003/0000421 and the Czech Science Foundation (GAČR 18-18080S).

# References

1. Arjevani, Y., Field, M.: Symmetry & critical points for a model shallow neural network (2020)
2. Atakulreka, A., Sutivong, D.: Avoiding local minima in feedforward neural networks by simultaneous learning. In: Orgun, M.A., Thornton, J. (eds.) AI 2007: Advances in Artificial Intelligence, pp. 100–109. Springer, Heidelberg (2007). https://doi.org/10.1007/978-3-540-76928-6_12
3. Bian, Y., Chen, H.: When does diversity help generalization in classification ensembles? (2021)
4. Brown, G.: Diversity in neural network ensembles. Tech. rep. (2004)
5. Brown, T.B., et al.: Language models are few-shot learners (2020)
6. Chollet, F.: Xception: deep learning with depthwise separable convolutions (2017)
7. Ciresan, D.C., Meier, U., Masci, J., Gambardella, L.M., Schmidhuber, J.: Flexible, high performance convolutional neural networks for image classification. In: Twenty-Second International Joint Conference on Artificial Intelligence (2011)
8. Cybenko, G.: Approximation by superpositions of a sigmoidal function. Math. Control Signals Syst. **2**(4), 303–314 (1989)
9. Gao, H., Cai, L., Ji, S.: Adaptive convolutional relus. In: Proceedings of the AAAI Conference on Artificial Intelligence, vol. 34, pp. 3914–3921 (2020)
10. Glorot, X., Bengio, Y.: Understanding the difficulty of training deep feedforward neural networks. In: Proceedings of the Thirteenth International Conference on Artificial Intelligence and Statistics, pp. 249–256. JMLR Workshop and Conference Proceedings (2010)
11. Glorot, X., Bordes, A., Bengio, Y.: Deep sparse rectifier neural networks. In: Proceedings of the Fourteenth International Conference on Artificial Intelligence and Statistics, pp. 315–323. JMLR Workshop and Conference Proceedings (2011)
12. Hansen, L.K., Salamon, P.: Neural network ensembles. IEEE Trans. Pattern Anal. Mach. Intell. **12**(10), 993–1001 (1990)
13. He, K., Zhang, X., Ren, S., Sun, J.: Deep residual learning for image recognition (2015)
14. He, K., Zhang, X., Ren, S., Sun, J.: Delving deep into rectifiers: surpassing human-level performance on ImageNet classification. In: Proceedings of the IEEE International Conference on Computer Vision, pp. 1026–1034 (2015)
15. Hinton, G.E., Osindero, S., Teh, Y.W.: A fast learning algorithm for deep belief nets. Neural Comput. **18**(7), 1527–1554 (2006)
16. Hinton, G.E., Salakhutdinov, R.R.: Reducing the dimensionality of data with neural networks. Science **313**(5786), 504–507 (2006)
17. Hochreiter, S., Bengio, Y., Frasconi, P., Schmidhuber, J.: Gradient flow in recurrent nets: the difficulty of learning long-term dependencies. In: Kremer, S.C., Kolen, J.F. (eds.) A Field Guide to Dynamical Recurrent Neural Networks. IEEE Press (2001)
18. Hochreiter, S.: The vanishing gradient problem during learning recurrent neural nets and problem solutions. Int. J. Uncertainty Fuzziness Knowl. Based Syst. **6**(02), 107–116 (1998)

19. Hornik, K.: Approximation capabilities of multilayer feedforward networks. Neural Netw. **4**(2), 251–257 (1991)
20. Izmailov, P., Podoprikhin, D., Garipov, T., Vetrov, D., Wilson, A.G.: Averaging weights leads to wider optima and better generalization (2019)
21. Jha, D., Yazidi, A., Riegler, M.A., Johansen, D., Johansen, H.D., Halvorsen, P.: LightLayers: parameter efficient dense and convolutional layers for image classification (2021)
22. Kingma, D.P., Ba, J.: Adam: a method for stochastic optimization (2017)
23. Krogh, A., Vedelsby, J.: Validation, and active learning. In: Advances in Neural Information Processing Systems, vol. 7, no. 7, p. 231 (1995)
24. Lacoste, A., Luccioni, A., Schmidt, V., Dandres, T.: Quantifying the carbon emissions of machine learning. arXiv preprint arXiv:1910.09700 (2019)
25. LeCun, Y., Cortes, C.: MNIST handwritten digit database (2010). http://yann.lecun.com/exdb/mnist/
26. Lu, L.: Dying relu and initialization: theory and numerical examples. Commun. Comput. Phys. **28**(5), 1671–1706 (2020). https://doi.org/10.4208/cicp.oa-2020-0165. http://dx.doi.org/10.4208/cicp.OA-2020-0165
27. Lu, Z., Pu, H., Wang, F., Hu, Z., Wang, L.: The expressive power of neural networks: a view from the width (2017)
28. Luijten, B., et al.: Deep learning for fast adaptive beamforming. In: ICASSP 2019–2019 IEEE International Conference on Acoustics, Speech and Signal Processing (ICASSP), pp. 1333–1337. IEEE (2019)
29. Martens, J., Sutskever, I.: Learning recurrent neural networks with hessian-free optimization. In: ICML (2011)
30. Marziale, L., Richard, G.G., Roussev, V.: Massive threading: using GPUs to increase the performance of digital forensics tools. Digital Invest. **4**, 73 – 81 (2007). https://doi.org/10.1016/j.diin.2007.06.014. http://www.sciencedirect.com/science/article/pii/S1742287607000436
31. Paszke, A., et al.: Pytorch: an imperative style, high-performance deep learning library. In: Advances in Neural Information Processing Systems, vol. 32, pp. 8024–8035. Curran Associates, Inc. (2019). http://papers.neurips.cc/paper/9015-pytorch-an-imperative-style-high-performance-deep-learning-library.pdf
32. Ramachandran, P., Zoph, B., Le, Q.V.: Searching for activation functions. arXiv preprint arXiv:1710.05941 (2017)
33. Scherer, D., Müller, A., Behnke, S.: Evaluation of pooling operations in convolutional architectures for object recognition. In: Diamantaras, K., Duch, W., Iliadis, L.S. (eds.) ICANN 2010. LNCS, vol. 6354, pp. 92–101. Springer, Heidelberg (2010). https://doi.org/10.1007/978-3-642-15825-4_10
34. Schmidhuber, J.: Learning to control fast-weight memories: an alternative to dynamic recurrent networks. Neural Comput. **4**(1), 131–139 (1992)
35. Swirszcz, G., Czarnecki, W.M., Pascanu, R.: Local minima in training of neural networks (2017)
36. Szegedy, C., et al.: Going deeper with convolutions (2014)
37. Tayal, K., Lai, C.H., Kumar, V., Sun, J.: Inverse problems, deep learning, and symmetry breaking (2020)
38. Ueda, N., Nakano, R.: Generalization error of ensemble estimators. In: Proceedings of International Conference on Neural Networks (ICNN 1996), vol. 1, pp. 90–95. IEEE (1996)
39. Vincent, P., Larochelle, H., Bengio, Y., Manzagol, P.A.: Extracting and composing robust features with denoising autoencoders. In: Proceedings of the 25th International Conference on Machine Learning, pp. 1096–1103 (2008)

40. Xiao, H., Rasul, K., Vollgraf, R.: Fashion-MNIST: a novel image dataset for bench-marking machine learning algorithms. arXiv preprint arXiv:1708.07747 (2017)
41. Xu, B., Wang, N., Chen, T., Li, M.: Empirical evaluation of rectified activations in convolutional network. arXiv preprint arXiv:1505.00853 (2015)

# Curved SDE-Net Leads to Better Generalization for Uncertainty Estimates of DNNs

YongGuang Wang[1] ![ORCID], HuoBin Tan[2]([✉]) ![ORCID], and ShuZhen Yao[1] ![ORCID]

[1] School of Computer Science and Engineering, Beihang University, Beijing 100191, China
{wangyongguang,szyao}@buaa.edu.cn
[2] School of Software, China, Beihang University, Beijing 100191, China
thbin@buaa.edu.cn

**Abstract.** Reliable uncertainty estimates of Deep Neural Networks (DNNs) are significant for safety-critical domains. Existing Neural Stochastic Differential Equation model (SDE-Net) can quantify epistemic uncertainties of DNNs from the perspective of a dynamical system. The SDE-Net is dominated by its drift net with In-Distribution (ID) data to obtain good predictive accuracy, or dominated by its diffusion net with Out-Of-Distribution (OOD) data to generate high diffusion for characterizing model uncertainty. However, the SDE-Net does not consider the local optimal problem caused by the high-dimensional parameter spaces of DNNs, which still leads to unstable prediction results. Therefore, we propose a curved SDE-Net (cSDE-Net) model which is implemented with a quadratic Bezier curve to discover high-accuracy and nearly constant loss paths between pretrained SDE-Net models. In the cSDE-Net, the optimization goal is transformed from the weights of DNNs to the parameters of Bezier curve. Experimental results show that, the proposed cSDE-Net model can not only provide more stable and reliable prediction results than ensembling of independent trained SDE-Net (iSDE-Net), but also be more effective for general situation, where aleatoric uncertainty is caused by ID data with noise or missing rate.

**Keywords:** Neural Stochastic Differential Equation · Deep Neural Networks · Uncertainty estimates · Bezier curve

## 1 Introduction

Deep learning model has achieved great success in various fields, such as image classification [1], computer vision [2], machine translation [3] and reinforcement learning [4] and so on. However, uncertainty estimates of deep learning are critical for decision making to avoid dangerous accidents in safety-critical areas, such as in medical diagnoses or autonomous vehicles. Existing studies have shown that Deep Neural Networks (DNNs) models are usually overconfident in prediction results, which can result in misleading decisions, so it is very significant to add credible uncertainty estimates to the prediction results [5].

© Springer Nature Switzerland AG 2021
I. Farkaš et al. (Eds.): ICANN 2021, LNCS 12892, pp. 248–259, 2021.
https://doi.org/10.1007/978-3-030-86340-1_20

Bayesian Neural Networks (BNNs) method was once regarded as a gold standard for uncertainty estimates in machine learning field [6, 7]. Unfortunately, Bayesian approach is inefficient to perform Bayesian inference in high-dimensional parameter space of DNNs. Existing studies apply Principal Components Analysis (PCA) or non-linear Incremental Kernel PCA (InKPCA) method to construct parameter subspace of DNNs for Bayesian inference [8, 9].

Non-Bayesian methods are also studied for uncertainty estimates of DNNs models. For example, ensemble learning approach can train several DNNs models with diverse initialization seeds and apply predicted values for uncertainty estimates [10]. Meanwhile, if DNNs are trained with a Stochastic Gradient Descent (SGD), the training procedure can average multiple points along the trajectory of SGD to construct a Stochastic Weight Averaging (SWA), which can generate much broader optima than SGD method [11]. And due to the loss functions of DNNs are complex and high-dimensional in parameters space, the previous study [12] finds that the optima of these complex loss functions can be connected by simple curves, which can build a rich subspace containing diverse high performing models with nearly constant accuracy.

Meanwhile, the process of forward passes in DNNs can be regarded as state transformations of a dynamical system, which can be defined by a neural network parameterized Ordinary Differential Equation (ODE) [13]. However, ODE method is a deterministic expression so that epistemic uncertainty message of DNNs cannot be obtained.

Recently, an original SDE-Net model for uncertainty estimates of DNNs has been proposed to capture epistemic uncertainty with Brownian motion [14, 15], which is widely used to model uncertainty or randomness in mathematics, physics and economics [16, 17]. The SDE-Net uses two separate neural networks (NNs): the drift net and diffusion net. The drift net $f$ is designed to control the system to obtain good predictive accuracy and describe the aleatoric uncertainty for ID data. The diffusion net $g$ is used to master the variance of the Brownian motion based on the regions of In-Distribution (ID) or Out-Of-Distribution (OOD) dataset, that is, when training ID dataset the diffusion should be small and training OOD dataset the diffusion should be large. The components of SDE-Net are described in Fig. 1(a).

However, most uncertainty estimates models mentioned above mainly consider the predictive uncertainty, which comes from models and their training processes, and this situation is called epistemic uncertainty. Meanwhile, the other predictive uncertainty derives from natural randomness such as data noise, class overlap, data missing and so on, we call this situation aleatoric uncertainty, which is inherent in the task. Another important source of uncertainty is the local optimal of DNNs, which is caused by the high-dimensional parameter space of DNNs and leads to different prediction results after each training. The problems of SDE-Net that need to be improved are described in Fig. 1(b).

Therefore, we propose a curved SDE-Net (cSDE-Net), which is implemented with a quadratic Bezier curve to discover high-accuracy and nearly constant loss paths for stably achieving train and test results.

Experimental results show that, the proposed cSDE-Net model can not only provide more stable and reliable prediction results than ensembling of independent trained SDE-Net (iSDE-Net), and be more effective for general situation, such as encountering noisy

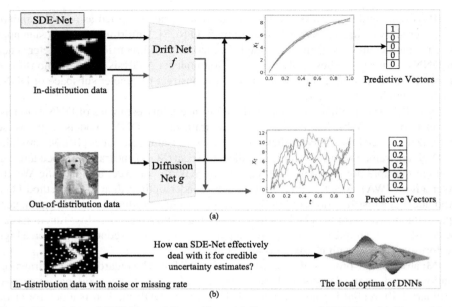

**Fig. 1.** Illustration of SDE-Net and its problem. (a) Components of SDE-Net; (b) The problem of SDE-Net should be improved.

ID dataset or ID dataset with missing rate, which can generate aleatoric uncertainty in predictions. Benchmark datasets MNIST and CIFAR10 are used for experiments. The major contributions of our work are summarized as follows.

1. We propose the curved SDE-Net model, which serves to discover high-accuracy and nearly constant loss paths between pretrained models.
2. When dealing with ID and OOD data, the cSDE-Net can produce more stable and accurate results.
3. We extend cSDE-Net to the field of aleatoric uncertainty and find it still useful.

This paper is organized as follows: Sect. 2 describes the materials. Sect. 3 presents the objective function and implementation algorithm of the proposed cSDE-Net for image classification tasks. Sect. 4 presents the experimental results. Finally, Sect. 5 gives the conclusions and future work.

## 2   Describing Ensembled SDE-Net by Bezier Curve

### 2.1   Connection Curves: Bezier Curve

Assume $\hat{w}_1$ and $\hat{w}_2$ be two sets of weights corresponding to two trained neural networks, which are independently trained by minimizing loss function $L(w)$. Let $n$ represents for the number of weights of the DNNs, and $\phi_\theta : [0, 1] \to \mathbb{R}^n$ is a continuous piecewise smooth curve with parameters $\theta$, where $\hat{w}_1 = \phi_\theta(0)$ and $\hat{w}_2 = \phi_\theta(1)$.

Suppose there exists a curve path $\phi_\theta(T)$ and $T \in [0, 1]$, which has a high accuracy between $\hat{w}_1$ and $\hat{w}_2$, so the loss function of DNNs can be described as follows [12]:

$$\ell(\theta) = \int_0^1 L(\phi_\theta(T))dT = \mathbb{E}_{T \sim U(0,1)} L(\phi_\theta(T)) \tag{1}$$

At each iteration, we sample $t$ from the uniform distribution $U(0, 1)$ and then perform gradient descent for optimizing the parameter $\theta$ with respect to the loss $L(\phi_\theta(T))$. Then we can obtain unbiased estimates of the gradients of loss $\ell(\theta)$:

$$\nabla_\theta L(\phi_\theta(t)) \approx \mathbb{E}_{T \sim U(0,1)} \nabla_\theta L(\phi_\theta(T)) = \nabla_\theta \mathbb{E}_{T \sim U(0,1)} L(\phi_\theta(T)) = \nabla_\theta \ell(\theta) \tag{2}$$

To be specific, a quadratic Bezier curve $\phi_\theta(T)$ is adopted to provide a smooth path with given endpoints $\hat{w}_1$ and $\hat{w}_2$, so $\phi_\theta(T)$ can be expressed as follows:

$$\phi_\theta(t) = (1 - t)^2 \hat{w}_1 + 2t(1 - t)\theta + t^2 \hat{w}_2, t \in [0, 1] \tag{3}$$

Where the Bezier curve $\phi_\theta(T)$ can be generalize by $n$ bends, that is $\theta = \{w_1, w_2, \ldots, w_n\}$.

## 2.2 Definition of SDE-Net

**Neural ordinary differential equation (ODE-Net)** [13]. Existing neural nets such as residual networks (ResNet) [18], normalizing flows [19], and recurrent neural network decoders [20] can map an input $x$ to an output $y$ through a sequence of hidden layers, the hidden representations can be viewed as the states of a dynamical system:

$$x_{t+1} = x_t + f(x_t, t) \tag{4}$$

Where $t \in \{0 \cdots T\}$ is the index of the layer, $x_t \in \mathbb{R}^D$ is the hidden state at neural network layer t. The equation can be reorganized as $\frac{x_{t+\Delta t} - x_t}{\Delta t} = f(x_t, t)$, where $\Delta t = 1$. If we assuming $\Delta t \to 0$, then we can obtain the parameterized continuous dynamics of hidden units, which can apply an ODE specified by NNs:

$$\lim_{\Delta t \to 0} \frac{x_{t+\Delta t} - x_t}{\Delta t} = \frac{dx_t}{dt} = f(x_t, t, \theta) \tag{5}$$

The solution of ODE-Net can be computed by a black-box differential equation solver to evaluate the hidden unit state wherever necessary. However, ODE-Net is a deterministic model for predictions and it cannot model epistemic uncertainty. To overcome the disadvantage, the novel SDE-Net model can characterize a stochastic dynamical system and capture epistemic uncertainty with Brownian motion, which is widely used to model the randomness of the motion of atoms or molecules in Physics [16].

**SDE-Net** [14]. A standard Brownian motion term is added into (4) to form a neural SDE dynamical system. The continuous-time dynamical system is expressed as follows:

$$dx_t = f(x_t, t)dt + g(x_t, t)dW_t \tag{6}$$

Where $g(x_t, t)$ indicates the variance of the Brownian motion and represents the epistemic uncertainty for the dynamical system. However, a standard Brownian motion $W_t$ is a stochastic process, which follows the three nproperties:

1)  $W_0 = 0$;
2)  $\nabla W = W_t - W_s$ should follow normal distribution $N(0, t - s)$ for all $t \geq s \geq 0$;
3)  For any two different time intervals, the increments $\nabla W_1$ and $\nabla W_2$ are independent random variables.

More importantly, $f(x_t, t)$ and $g(x_t, t)$ in (6) can be represented by neural networks to construct SDE-Net. Where $f(x_t, t)$ is used as drift net to control the system to achieve good predictive accuracy and aleatoric uncertainty, and $g(x_t, t)$ is utilized as diffusion net to represent the epistemic uncertainty of dynamical system.

**Theorem 1.** When there exists $C > 0$ such that [14]:

$$\|f(x, t; \theta_f) - f(y, t; \theta_f)\| + \|g(x; \theta_g) - g(y; \theta_g)\| \leq C\|x - y\|, \forall x, y \in \mathbb{R}^n, t \geq 0$$

Then for every $x_0 \in \mathbb{R}^n$, there exists a unique continuous and adapted process $\left(x_t^{x_0}\right)_{t \geq 0}$ such that for $t \geq 0$:

$$x_t^{x_0} = x_0 + \int_0^t f\left(x_s^{x_0}, t; \theta_f\right)ds + \int_0^t g\left(x_0; \theta_g\right)dW_s$$

Moreover, for every $T \geq 0$, $\mathrm{E}\left(\sup_{1 \leq s \leq T}|x_s|^2\right) < +\infty$.

Where $f(x, t; \theta_f)$ and $g(x_0; \theta_g)$ are uniformly Lipschitz continuous to use Lipschitz nonlinear activations in the NNs, such as ReLU, sigmoid and Tanh.

## 3   Methods

The overview of our algorithm is illustrated in Fig. 2, including two main parts: cSDE-Net model can give reliable and accurate uncertainty estimates of DNNs, and the parameter generation module produces parameters from two pretrained vanilla SDE-Net by Bezier curve. Then the curved parameters of NNs and the location information of fix points are assigned to cSDE-Net model, $\theta$ is the parameter needed to be trained.

### 3.1   The Objective Function of CSDE-Net

Since we use Bezier curve $\phi_\theta(T)$ to reconstruct the SDE-Net parameter space based on two pretrained vanilla SDE-Net models, the training target becomes the parameter $\theta$ of Bezier curve. However, vanilla SDE-Net contains drift net $f$ and diffusion net $g$ and has more than 200K parameters in total, so to train parameter $\theta$ of Bezier curve has the similar complexity to vanilla SDE-Net. Assume $\theta$ has the parameters $\theta_{c-f}$ and $\theta_{c-g}$ corresponding to net $f$ and $g$.

Assume the bends of Bezier curve is 1, *fix-points* = [*True, False, True*], which means the two pretrained $\hat{w}_1$ and $\hat{w}_2$ are fixed at the endpoints of Bezier curve, and the middle point corresponding to Bezier curve value $\phi_\theta(t)$ in defined Eq. (4) needs to be trained, and each training iteration sample $t \in [0, 1]$ to train $\theta$.

The objective function for training cSDE-Net model can be described as follows:

$$\min_{\theta_{c-f}} E_{x_0 \sim P_{\mathrm{ID}}} E\big(f\left(x_T,\ t;\theta_{c-f}\ ;fix-points\right),\ L(x_T)\big)+$$

$$\min_{\theta_{c-g}} E_{x_0 \sim P_{\mathrm{ID}}}\ g\left(x_0;\theta_{c-g};fix-points\right)+\ \max_{\theta_{c-g}} E_{\tilde{x}_0 \sim P_{\mathrm{OOD}}}\ g\left(\tilde{x}_0;\theta_{c-g};fix-points\right) \quad (7)$$

$$s.t.\ dx_t = \underbrace{f\left(x_t,t;\theta_{c-f};fix-points\right)}_{\text{drift neural net}} dt + \underbrace{g\left(x_0;\theta_{c-g};fix-points\right)}_{\text{diffusion neural net}} dW_t$$

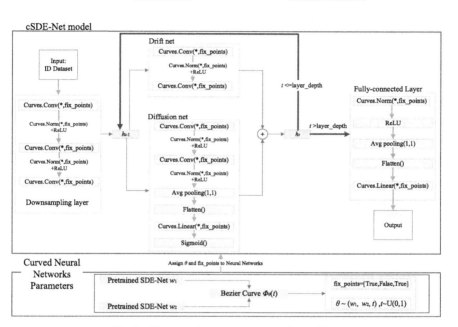

**Fig. 2.** The overview of the proposed algorithm

Where the first item of Eq. (7) represents for the training parameters and loss function $L$ of drift net $f$, $T$ is the terminal time of the stochastic processes, and $P_{\mathrm{ID}}$ represents for the distribution of ID dataset.

The second item of (7) stands for the training parameters of diffusion net $g$ with ID dataset. The last item of (7) indicates the net $g$ is trained with OOD dataset, where $P_{\mathrm{OOD}}$ stands for the distribution of OOD dataset, which can be obtained by adding additive Gaussian noise to the inputs $x_0$, such as $\tilde{x}_0 = x_0 + \epsilon$ and $\epsilon \sim N(0, 1)$.

Finally, Eq. (7) should subject to Eq. (6) to construct a cSDE-Net.

### 3.2 Algorithm of CSDE-Net Model

The algorithm 1 of cSDE-Net is used for training classification tasks, and the benchmark datasets MNIST and CIFAR10 are adopted for this algorithm. Because cSDE-Net contains different net architectures for different goals, the training processes are designed respectively.

For training MNIST and CIFAR10 datasets, the vanilla SDE-Net has $n_{mnist} = 283723$ and $n_{cifar10} = 322507$ parameters respectively. For training the parameter $\theta$ of Bezier curve in cSDE-Net, we need to pretrain vanilla SDE-Net twice for two fix points $\hat{w}_1$ and $\hat{w}_2$, and training the parameter $\theta$ has the similar complexity to vanilla SDE-Net. So cSDE-Net has the time cost $O(3n_{mnist})$ and $O(3n_{cifar10})$ of MNIST and CIFAR10 respectively, however, cSDE-Net and vanilla SDE-Net have similar computational cost.

For training drift net $f$ of cSDE-Net model, first of all, ID dataset passes through a downsampling net to generate latent variable $X_0^m$, and then $X_0^m$ is iteratively processed by a vanilla SDE-Net to produce a latent state $X_k^m$ according to Eq. (6). Finally, the latent state $X_k^m$ passes through a fully-connected layer. $L_1$ represents for cross entropy loss function.

For training diffusion net $g$ of cSDE-Net model, $L_2$ represents for binary cross entropy loss function. The dataset from ID or OOD is respectively marked with label 0 and 1, so the process of training diffusion net $g$ in line 14 of algorithm1 is to minimize the loss function $L_2$ for ID dataset and maximize $L_2$ for OOD dataset.

---

**Algorithm 1** Implementation of cSDE-Net model

**Inputs**: $p_{ID}(x,y)$ represents for ID dataset; $h_1$ is the downsampling net ; $h_2$ is the fully connected net; drift net $f$ and diffusion net $g$; $t$ is the layer depth; pretrained $w_1$ of vanilla SDE-Net$_1$ and $w_2$ of vanilla SDE-Net$_2$; $L_1, L_2$ are the loss function; bend = 1; Bezier curve $\phi_\theta(T)$.

**Outputs**: *Means* and *Vars*

    **for** #training iterations **do**

1. Sample minibatch of $m$ data: $(X^m, Y^m) \sim p_{ID}(x, y)$
2. Sample $t \in [0, 1]$
3. $\phi_\theta(t) = (1 - t)^2 w_1 + 2t(1 - t)\theta + t^2 w_2, t \in [0, 1]$
4. Assign Bezier curve $\phi_\theta(t)$ values to vanilla SDE-Net to construct cSDE-Net model with parameter $\theta$
5. Forward through the downsampling net $h_1$ of cSDE-Net: $X_0^m = h_1(X^m, Y^m, fix\text{-}points)$
6.     **for** $k = 0$ to $t$-1 **do**
7.       Sample $Z_k^m \sim \mathcal{N}(0,1)$
    $X_{k+1}^m = X_k^m + f(X_k^m, t, fix\text{-}points)\Delta t + g(X_0^m, fix\text{-}points)\sqrt{\Delta t}Z_k$
8.     **end for**
9. Forward through the fully-connected layer $h_2$ of cSDE-Net: $Y_f^m = h_2(X_k^m, fix\text{-}points)$
10. Update $h_1, h_2$ and $f$ by $\nabla_\theta \frac{1}{m}L_1(Y_f^m, Y^m)$
11. Sample minibatch of $m$ data from ID: $(X^m, 0) \sim p_{ID}(x, y)$
12. Sample minibatch of $m$ data from OOD: $(\tilde{X}^m, 1) \sim p_{OOD}(x, y)$
13. Forward through the downsampling net of cSDE-Net: $X_0^m, \tilde{X}_0^m = h_1(X^m, fix\text{-}points), h_1(\tilde{X}^m, fix\text{-}points)$
14. Update $g$ by $\nabla_\theta \frac{1}{m}L_2(g(X_0^m), 0) - \nabla_\theta L_2(g(\tilde{X}_0^m), 1)$
    **end for**

# 4   Experiments

## 4.1   Datasets

We perform experiments on cSDE-Net and iSDE-Net model with two benchmark ID datasets MNIST and CIFAR10. The MNIST dataset consists of 70,000 28×28 monochrome images in handwritten digits from 0 to 9, including 60,000 training images and 10,000 test images. And the CIFAR-10 dataset consists of 60,000 32 × 32 color images in 10 classes, each class has 6,000 images, including 50,000 training images and 10,000 test images. SVHN is used as an OOD dataset in our experiments, SVHN is a real-world MNIST-like 32 × 32 image dataset from house numbers in Google Street View images, and it has 73257 digits for training and 26032 digits for testing.

## 4.2   Parameter Setting

**Model Setting and Parameter.** For iSDE-Net model with MNIST dataset, we follow the settings of paper [14]. That is for the downsampling layers of iSDE-Net, which contain three 2-dimensional convolution (*Conv2d*) layers, and the Conv2d can be traditionally described as $[in\_channel, out\_channel, kernel\_size, stride, padding]$, so the architecture of the downsampling layer is {[1, 64, 3, 1, 0],[64, 64, 4, 2, 1],[64, 64, 4, 2, 1]}. The drift net of iSDE-Net contains two *Conv2d* layers with {[65, 64, 3, 1, 1],[65, 64, 3, 1, 1]} architecture. The diffusion net has the same convolutional layers as drift net, but has an extra linear connection described as [*inputs*, *outputs*], which is [64, 1] in the last layer of diffusion net. The fully-connected layer of iSDE-Net is [64, 10]. To independently train vanilla SDE-Net, the model parameter defined as follows: the layer depth is 6 and training epochs are 100, batch size is 128, SGD is used as the optimizer, the learning rate for diffusion net is 0.01 and for the other nets is 0.1, the momentum and weight decay are 0.9 and 5e-4 respectively. For iSDE-Net model with CIFAR10 dataset, the *in_channel* of the first *Conv2d* in downsampling layer is 3, and the other settings and parameters are the same as MNIST dataset.

For cSDE-Net model with MNSIT and CIFAR10 dataset, the bend of Beizer curve is one, so the *fix_points* = [*True*, *False*, *True*], which means that we fix two pretrained vanilla SDE-Nets' parameters as endpoints, and the parameter $\theta$ of Bezier curve between the two fixed endpoints needs to be trained. Importantly, *Conv2d* and *GroupNorm* are reconstructed according to *fix_points*.The settings of other parameters are the same as iSDE-Net model. All experiments are performed on NVIDIA GeForce RTX 3090 and based on PyTorch.

## 4.3   Quantitative Analysis of ID Dataset

As is shown in Fig. 3, the cSDE-Net is trained for 60 epochs with two pretrained vanilla SDE-Net, and iSDE-Net is ensembled by the two vanilla SDE-Net. We mainly compare the accuracy of test sets, which are showed in red and blue dashed lines.

In Fig. 3(a), we find that red dashed line reaches the peak of accuracy faster, and the test accuracy results of cSDE-Net are relatively more stable than the blue dashed line of iSDE-Net.

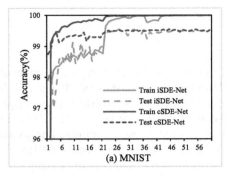 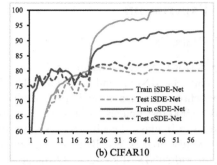

(a) MNIST          (b) CIFAR10

**Fig. 3.** The train and test accuracy of cSDE-Net and iSDE-Net for MNIST and CIFAR10 datasets.

Figure 3(b) and Fig. 3(a) show the similar results. Besides, we also find that the accuracy of iSDE-Net described with blue dashed line has degraded after the 22nd epoch in Fig. 3(b), this phenomenon presents that ensemble learning method does not guarantee a more optimal and stable performance. Meanwhile, the accuracy of cSDE-Net is about 2% higher than that of iSDE-Net for color image dataset CIFAR10.

### 4.4 Bezier Curve Finding Experiment

To construct cSDE-Net and iSDE-Net model, we train two vanilla SDE-Net model with different initializations to generate two models. For iSDE-Net model, we just average the results of two vanilla SDE-Net. For cSDE-Net model, we use the proposed algorithm 1 to find a path connecting the two pretrained models, which have the weight parameter space with a quadratic Bezier curve.

Figure 4 shows the results of the proposed model connecting procedure for cSDE-Net and iSDE-Net on benchmark datasets MNIST and CIFAR10. Experimental results show that Bezier curve $\phi(t)$ found by cSDE-Net can produce nearly constant train loss of cross-entropy and test error of accuracy. However, the line segment $\phi(t) = (1 - t) * \phi(0) + t * \phi(1)$ connects the two models' parameters $\phi(0)$ and $\phi(1)$ for iSDE-Net, when $\phi(t)$ is far away from two endpoints $\phi(0)$ and $\phi(1)$, segment iSDE-Net generates higher train loss and test error than cSDE-Net in Fig. 4.

Finally, we believe there may be many other curves, which can connect the two models to form a better generalization performance of DNNs, and these curves can be further studied in the future.

### 4.5 Quantitative Analysis of ID Dataset with Missing Rate

Although vanilla SDE-Net can effectively capture the epistemic uncertainty of DNNs model, duo to the high-dimensional parameter space of DNNs, the local optimal problem still leads to unstable results of DNNs. The introduction of the Bezier curve into SDE-Net can generate more stable and reliable model performance than ensemble learning method, this is very important for the study of uncertainty estimates in deep learning.

We have tested the performance of cSDE-Net model between ID and OOD dataset, however, for aleatoric uncertainty caused by the noisy dataset, we still want to know

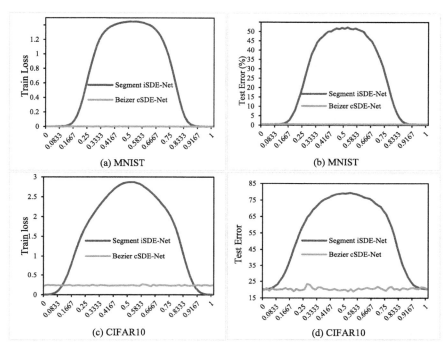

**Fig. 4.** The cross-entropy train loss (a), (c) and test error (b), (d) as a function of Bezier curve $\phi(t)$ found by cSDE-Net or line segment $\phi(t)$ found by iSDE-Net on the point $t$, and $t$ is the value of the interval [0,1] divided equally into 61 points. Endpoints $\phi(0)$ and $\phi(1)$ represent for the parameters of two pretrained vanilla SDE-Net,$\phi(t) = (1 - t) * \phi(0) + t * \phi(1)$ is the line segment.

the performance of cSDE-Net in general situation for ID dataset with noise and missing rate.

To evaluate the performance of iSDE-Net and cSDE-Net models for ID dataset $I$ with missing rate in classification tasks MNIST and CIFAR10.We assume missing rate (MR) takes values from [0.0,0.1,0.3,0.5,0.7,0.9], so the *mask* = Bernoulli (1-MR) and the masked ID dataset can be obtained by *mask\*I*. Then we can evaluate the average performance and standard deviation with 5 independently running the two models with masked data.

Table 1 shows that as the MR increases, the advantages of cSDE model over iSDE-Net are becoming more and more obvious in classification accuracy. Especially for color image dataset CIFAR10, when missing rate is 0.1, the performance of iSDE-Net has a great degradation from accuracy 79.87 to 23.23. From these experiments, we find that cSDE-Net can still achieve better performance than iSDE-Net, even when it encounters the general situation with noisy ID dataset.

**Table 1.** Detection results of cSDE-Net and iSDE-Net model on ID dataset with missing rate = [0.0, 0.1, 0.3, 0.5, 0.7, 0.9] and OOD dataset is SVHN.

| MR | Model | MNIST | CIFAR10 |
|---|---|---|---|
| MR = 0.0 | cSDE-Net | **99.43** ± 0.06 | **81.54** ± 0.02 |
|  | iSDE-Net | 99.40 ± 0.10 | 79.87 ± 0.06 |
| MR = 0.1 | cSDE-Net | **98.87** ± 0.03 | **51.33** ± 0.04 |
|  | iSDE-Net | **98.87** ± 0.06 | 23.23 ± 0.25 |
| MR = 0.3 | cSDE-Net | **94.99** ± 0.02 | **33.31** ± 0.04 |
|  | iSDE-Net | 94.98 ± 0.19 | 13.11 ± 2.89 |
| MR = 0.5 | cSDE-Net | **80.96** ± 0.03 | **25.40** ± 0.03 |
|  | iSDE-Net | 80.54 ± 0.36 | 10.33 ± 0.06 |
| MR = 0.7 | cSDE-Net | **55.61** ± 0.33 | **19.13** ± 0.02 |
|  | iSDE-Net | 49.25 ± 0.11 | 10.10 ± 0.08 |
| MR = 0.9 | cSDE-Net | **22.78** ± 0.58 | **14.10** ± 0.03 |
|  | iSDE-Net | 14.56 ± 0.34 | 10.18 ± 0.06 |

## 5    Discussion and Further Work

In this paper, we propose a cSDE-Net model, which can connect two different pretrained models and produce more stable and consistent predictions along with the Bezier curve than ensembled iSDE-Net model. Experimental results show that cSDE-Net not only can produce more stable results, but also it is effective for aleatoric uncertainty derived from the noisy ID dataset. cSDE-Net and vanilla SDE-Net has the smilar computational cost, but cSDE-Net takes about three times as much time cost as vanilla SDE-Net.

There are two promising directions for future research. On the one hand, neural processes (NPs) family, including conditional NPs, attentive NPs and convolutional conditional NPs, which have the permutation invariance property or translation equivariance and can be incorporated into SDE-Net to improve the performance in dealing with the noisy ID dataset. On the other hand, advanced ResNets such as VGGs, ResNet-18/34/152 and DenseNets can be applied to replace the ordinary drift and diffusion nets in SDE-Net, for improving the performance when dealing with big datasets such as CIFAR10/100, COCO and ImageNet.

**Acknowledgment.** This work was supported by the National Key Research and Development Program of China under Grant 2018YFB1402600.

## References

1. Krizhevsky, A., Sutskever, I., Hinton, G. E.: Imagenet classification with deep convolutional neural networks. In: 26th Advances in Neural Information Processing Systems, pp. 1097–1105 (2012)

2. He, K., Zhang, X., Ren, S., Sun, J.: Deep residual learning for image recognition. In: IEEE Conference on Computer Vision and Pattern Recognition, pp.770–778 (2016)
3. Singh, S.P., Kumar, A., Darbari, H., Singh, L., Jain, S.: Machine translation using deep learning: an overview. In: 2017 International Conference on Computer, Communications and Electronics, pp.162–167 (2017)
4. Mousavi, S.S., Schukat, M., Howley, E.: Deep reinforcement learning: an overview. In: Bi, Y., Kapoor, S., Bhatia, R. (eds.) IntelliSys 2016. LNNS, vol. 16, pp. 426–440. Springer, Cham (2018). https://doi.org/10.1007/978-3-319-56991-8_32
5. Guo, C., Pleiss, G., Sun, Y., Weinberger, K.Q.: On calibration of modern neural networks. In: Proceedings of the 34th International Conference on Machine Learning, pp.1321–1330 (2017)
6. Blundell, C., Cornebise, J., Kavukcuoglu, K., Wierstra, D.: Weight uncertainty in Neural Network. In: Proceedings of the 32nd International Conference on Machine Learning, pp.1613–1622 (2015)
7. Kingma, D.P., Salimans, T., Welling, M.: Variational dropout and the local reparameterization trick. In: Proceedings of the 28th International Conference on Neural Information Processing Systems, pp. 2575–2583 (2015)
8. Izmailov, P., Maddox, W.J., Kirichenko, P., Garipov, T., Vetrov, D.P., Wilson, A G.: Subspace Inference for Bayesian deep learning. In: 35th Conference on Uncertainty in Artificial Intelligence, pp. 1169–1179 (2019)
9. Wang, Y., Yao, S., Xu, T.: Incremental Kernel principal components subspace inference with nyström approximation for Bayesian deep learning. IEEE Access 9, 36241–36251 (2021)
10. Lakshminarayanan, B., Pritzel, A., Blundell, C.: Simple and scalable predictive uncertainty estimation using deep ensembles. In: Advances in Neural Information Processing Systems, pp. 6402–6413 (2017)
11. Izmailov, P., Podoprikhin, D., Garipov, T., Vetrov, D.P., Wilson, A.G.: Averaging weights leads to wider optima and better generalization. In: 34th Conference on Uncertainty in Artificial Intelligence, pp. 876–885 (2018)
12. Garipov, T., Izmailov, P., Podoprikhin, D., Vetrov, D.P., Wilson, A.G.: Loss surfaces, mode connectivity, and fast ensembling of DNNs. In: 32nd Conference on Neural Information Processing Systems, pp. 8789–8798 (2018)
13. Chen, R.T.Q., Rubanova, Y., Bettencourt, J., Duvenaud, D.: Neural ordinary differential equations. In: Proceedings of the 32nd International Conference on Neural Information Processing Systems, pp. 6572–6583 (2018)
14. Kong, L., Sun, J., Zhang, C.: SDE-Net: equipping deep neural networks with uncertainty estimates. In: 37th International Conference on Machine Learning, pp. 5405–5415 (2020)
15. Øksendal, B.: Stochastic differential equations. In: Stochastic differential equations, Springer, p. 11 (2003)
16. Bass, R.F.: Stochastic processes. In: Cambridge Series in Statistical and Probabilistic Mathematics. Cambridge University Press, 40 W.20 St. (2011)
17. Jeanblanc, M., Yor, M., Chesney, M.: Continuous-path random processes: mathematical prerequisites. In: Avellaneda, M., Barone-Adesi, G. (eds.) Mathematical Methods for Financial Markets, Springer Dordrecht Heidelberg, London New York (2009). https://doi.org/10.1007/978-1-84628-737-4_1
18. He, K., Zhang, X., Ren, S., Sun, J.: Identity mappings in deep residual networks. In: Leibe, B., Matas, J., Sebe, N., Welling, M. (eds.) ECCV 2016. LNCS, vol. 9908, pp. 630–645. Springer, Cham (2016). https://doi.org/10.1007/978-3-319-46493-0_38
19. Rezende, D., Mohamed, S.: Variational inference with normalizing flows. In: Proceedings of the 32nd International Conference on Machine Learning, pp.1530–1538 (2015)
20. Raissi, M., Karniadakis, G.E.: Hidden physics models: machine learning of nonlinear partial differential equations. J. Comput. Phys. 357, 125–141 (2018)

# EIS - Efficient and Trainable Activation Functions for Better Accuracy and Performance

Koushik Biswas[1]([📧])[iD], Sandeep Kumar[1,3][iD], Shilpak Banerjee[2][iD], and Ashish Kumar Pandey[2]

[1] Department of Computer Science, IIIT Delhi, New Delhi, India
{koushikb,sandeepk}@iiitd.ac.in
[2] Department of Mathematics, IIIT Delhi, New Delhi, India
{shilpak,ashish.pandey}@iiitd.ac.in
[3] Department of Mathematics, Shaheed Bhagat Singh College, University of Delhi, New Delhi, India
sandeep_kumar@sbs.du.ac.in

**Abstract.** Activation functions play a pivotal role in function learning using neural networks. The non-linearity in a neural network is achieved by repeated use of the activation function. Over the years, numerous activation functions have been proposed to improve neural network performance in several deep learning tasks. Basic functions like ReLU, Sigmoid, Tanh, or Softplus have been favorites among the deep learning community because of their simplicity. In recent years, several novel activation functions arising from these basic functions have been proposed, which have improved accuracy in some challenging datasets. We propose three activation functions with trainable parameters, namely EIS-1, EIS-2, and EIS-3. We show these three activation functions outperform widely used activation functions on some well-known datasets and models. For example, EIS-1, EIS-2, and EIS-3 beats ReLU by 5.55%, 5.32%, and 5.60% on ResNet V2 34, 5.27%, 5.24%, and 5.76% on VGG 16, 2.02%, 1.93%, and 2.01% on Wide-Res-Net 28-10, 2.30%, 2.11%, and 2.50% on Shufflenet V2 in CIFAR100 dataset while 1.40%, 1.27%, and 1.45% on ResNet V2 34, 1.21%, 1.09%, and 1.17% on VGG 16, 1.10%, 1.04%, and 1.16% on Wide-Res-Net 28-10, 1.85%, 1.60%, and 1.67% on Shufflenet V2 in CIFAR10 dataset respectively. The proposed functions also perform better than traditional activation functions like ReLU, Leaky ReLU, Swish, etc. in Object detection, Semantic segmentation, and Machine Translation problems.

**Keywords:** Deep learning · Neural networks · Trainable activation function

## 1 Introduction

Multi-layered neural networks are widely used to learn nonlinear functions from complex data. An activation function is an integral part of neural networks that

© Springer Nature Switzerland AG 2021
I. Farkaš et al. (Eds.): ICANN 2021, LNCS 12892, pp. 260–272, 2021.
https://doi.org/10.1007/978-3-030-86340-1_21

provides essential non-linearity. A universal activation function may not be suitable for all datasets, and it is important to select an appropriate activation function for the task at hand. Nevertheless, a piecewise activation function, Rectified Linear Unit (ReLU) [16], defined as $\max(x, 0)$, is widely used due to its simplicity, convergence speed, and lesser training time.

Despite its simplicity and better convergence rate than Sigmoid and Tanh, ReLU has drawbacks like non-zero mean, negative missing, unbounded output, dying ReLU, to name a few (see[40]). Various activation functions have been proposed to overcome the drawbacks of ReLU and improve performance over it. Some of the variants of ReLU are Leaky ReLU [25], Randomized Leaky Rectified Linear Units (RReLU) [38], Exponential Linear Unit (ELU) [5], Inverse Square Root Linear Units (ISRLUs) [3], and Parametric Rectified Linear Unit (PReLU) [13]. But none of the above-mentioned activation functions has come close to ReLU in terms of popularity. Most recently, Swish [30] has managed to gain attention from the deep learning community. Swish is a one-parameter family of activation functions defined as $x\,\mathrm{sigmoid}(\beta x)$. Worth noting that what is popularly recognized by the machine learning community now as the Swish function was first indicated in 2016 as an approximation to the GELU [15] function, and again in 2017 was introduced as the SiLU [7] function, and again for a third time in 2017 as the Swish [30] function. Though for the time being, we have stuck to the name Swish. Some other hyper-parametrized families of activation functions include Soft-Root-Sign [40] and TanhSoft [2]. In fact, many functions from the TanhSoft family have managed to outperform ReLU and Swish as well.

The most prominent drawback of ReLU is the dying ReLU that is providing zero output for negative input. Many novel activation functions are built to overcome this problem. It was resolved by many activation functions by simply defining a piecewise function that resembles ReLU for positive input and takes non-zero values for negative input. Swish is different from such piecewise activation functions in the sense that it is a product of two smooth functions and manages to remain close to ReLU for positive input and takes small negative values for the negative input. Recently, a four hyper-parameters family of activation functions, TanhSoft [2], have been proposed and showed that many functions from TanhSoft have a similar closeness to ReLU as Swish and perform better when compared to ReLU and Swish.

In the next sections, we have proposed three parametric activation functions and shown that they outperform widely used activation functions, including ReLU and Swish. To validate the performance of these activations, we have performed a wide range of experiments, and the results are reported in the experiment section.

## 2   Related Works

Several activation functions have been proposed as a substitute to ReLU that can overcome its drawbacks. Because of the dying ReLU problem, it has been observed that a large fraction of neurons become inactive due to zero outcome.

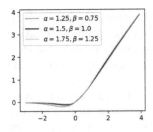
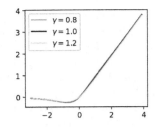
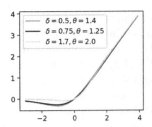

**Fig. 1.** Graph of $\mathcal{F}_1(x; \alpha, \beta)$ for different values of $\alpha, \beta$.

**Fig. 2.** Graph of $\mathcal{F}_2(x; \gamma)$ for different values of $\gamma$.

**Fig. 3.** Graph of $\mathcal{F}_3(x; \delta, \theta)$ for different values of $\delta, \theta$.

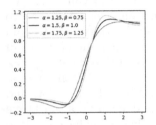
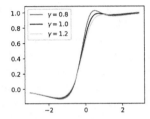
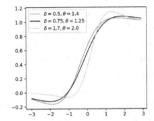

**Fig. 4.** Graph of first derivative of $\mathcal{F}_1(x; \alpha, \beta)$ for different values of $\alpha, \beta$.

**Fig. 5.** Graph of first derivative of $\mathcal{F}_2(x; \gamma)$ for different values of $\gamma$.

**Fig. 6.** Graph of first derivative of $\mathcal{F}_3(x; \delta, \theta)$ for different values of $\delta, \theta$.

Another issue which activation functions face is that during the flow of gradient in the network, the gradient can become zero or diverge to infinity, which is commonly known as vanishing and exploding gradient problems. Leaky Relu [25] has been introduced with a small negative linear component to solve the dying ReLU problem and has shown improvement over ReLU. A hyper-parametric component is incorporated in PReLU [13] to find the best value in the negative linear component. Many other improvements have been proposed over the years - Randomized Leaky Rectified Linear Units (RReLU) [38], Exponential Linear Unit (ELU) [5], and Inverse Square Root Linear Units (ISRLUs) [3] to name a few. Swish [30] is proposed by a team of researchers from Google Brain by an exhaustive search [27] and reinforcement learning techniques [1].

## 3    EIS-1, EIS-2, and EIS-3

We have proposed three families of activation functions with learnable parameters. We call them EIS-1 ($\mathcal{F}_1(x; \alpha, \beta)$), EIS-2 ($\mathcal{F}_2(x; \gamma)$), and EIS-3 ($\mathcal{F}_3(x; \delta, \theta)$). They are defined as follows:-

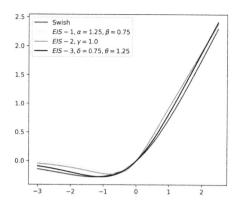 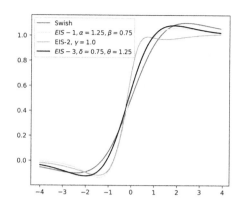

**Fig. 7.** Graph of Swish, $\mathcal{F}_1(x; \alpha, \beta)$, $\mathcal{F}_2(x; \gamma)$ and $\mathcal{F}_3(x; \delta, \theta)$

**Fig. 8.** Graph of first order derivatives of Swish, $\mathcal{F}_1(x; \alpha, \beta)$, $\mathcal{F}_2(x; \gamma)$, and $\mathcal{F}_3(x; \delta, \theta)$

$$\mathcal{F}_1(x; \alpha, \beta) = \frac{x \ln(1 + e^x)}{x + \alpha e^{-\beta x}}, \tag{1}$$

$$\mathcal{F}_2(x; \gamma) = \frac{x \ln(1 + e^x)}{\sqrt{\gamma + x^2}}, \tag{2}$$

$$\mathcal{F}_3(x; \delta, \theta) = \frac{x}{1 + \delta e^{-\theta x}}. \tag{3}$$

The derivative of the above activations are:-

$$\frac{d}{dx}\mathcal{F}_1(x; \alpha, \beta) = \frac{\ln(1 + e^x)}{x + \alpha e^{-\beta x}} + \frac{x}{x + \alpha e^{-\beta x}} \frac{e^x}{1 + e^x} - \frac{(1 - \alpha \beta e^{-\beta x})(x \ln(1 + e^x))}{(x + \alpha e^{-\beta x})^2} \tag{4}$$

$$\frac{d}{dx}\mathcal{F}_2(x; \gamma) = \frac{\ln(1 + e^x)}{\sqrt{\gamma + x^2}} + \frac{x}{\sqrt{\gamma + x^2}} \frac{e^x}{1 + e^x} - \frac{x^2 \ln(1 + e^x)}{(\gamma + x^2)^{\frac{3}{2}}}, \tag{5}$$

$$\frac{d}{dx}\mathcal{F}_3(x; \delta, \theta) = \frac{1}{1 + \delta e^{-\theta x}} + \frac{\delta \theta x e^{-\theta x}}{(1 + \delta e^{-\theta x})^2}. \tag{6}$$

The hyper-parameters $\alpha, \beta$ for EIS-1, $\gamma$ for EIS-2, and $\delta, \theta$ for EIS-3 controls the slope of the functions in both negative and positive axes as evident from Fig. 1, 2, and 3. For square root function, we have considered only the positive branch. Note that $\mathcal{F}_1(x; 0, \beta)$ and $\mathcal{F}_2(x; 0)$ recovers the Softplus function while $\mathcal{F}_3(x; 0, \theta)$ recovers the identity function $x$. Moreover,

$$\lim_{\delta \to \infty} \mathcal{F}_3(x; \delta, \theta) = 0 \quad \forall x \in \mathbb{R}. \tag{7}$$

Graph of some functions from these three families are given in Figs. 1, 2, and 3. The first-order derivatives of these functions are shown in Figs. 4, 5, and 6. Moreover, one function from each of these three families and their derivatives are compared with Swish in Figs. 7 and 8. As evident from graphs, chosen functions of these three subfamilies have bounded negative domain, smooth derivative and, non-monotonic curve like Swish.

## 4    Experiments with EIS-1, EIS-2, and EIS-3

In all the experiments, the learnable parameters in EIS-1, EIS-2, and EIS-3 are first initialized and then updated using the back propagation [22] algorithm (see [13]). For a single layer, the gradient of a hyper-parameter $\eta$ is:

$$\frac{\partial E}{\partial \eta} = \sum_x \frac{\partial E}{\partial F(x)} \frac{\partial F(x)}{\partial \eta} \tag{8}$$

where E is the objective function, $\eta \in \{\alpha, \beta, \gamma, \delta, \theta\}$ and $F(x) \in \{\mathcal{F}_1(x; \alpha, \beta), \mathcal{F}_2(x; \gamma), \mathcal{F}_3(x; \delta, \theta)\}$. Table 1 provides a detailed comparison of EIS-1, EIS-2, and EIS-3 with seven baseline activation functions, ReLU [16], Leaky Relu [25], ELU [5], Softplus [10], Swish [30], Mish [26], and GELU [15]. We have given detailed experimental setup and results for different deep learning problems like image classification, object detection, semantic segmentation, and Machine translation in the next section. We have initialized the learnable parameters at $\alpha = 1.25$, $\beta = 0.75$ for EIS-1, $\gamma = 1.0$ for EIS-2, and $\delta = 0.75$, $\theta = 1.25$ for EIS-3 throughout all the experiments and they are updated in network models during back-propagation.

**Table 1.** Baseline table for EIS-1, EIS-2, and EIS-3. The integers represents the total number of models in which EIS-1, EIS-2, and EIS-3 outperforms, equal or underperforms when compared to baseline activations

| Baselines | ReLU | Leaky ReLU | ELU | Swish | Softplus | Mish | GELU |
|---|---|---|---|---|---|---|---|
| EIS-1 > Baseline | 29 | 29 | 29 | 28 | 29 | 26 | 29 |
| EIS-1 = Baseline | 0 | 0 | 0 | 0 | 0 | 0 | 0 |
| EIS-1 < Baseline | 0 | 0 | 0 | 1 | 0 | 3 | 0 |
| EIS-2 > Baseline | 29 | 29 | 29 | 28 | 29 | 26 | 29 |
| EIS-2 = Baseline | 0 | 0 | 0 | 0 | 0 | 0 | 0 |
| EIS-2 < Baseline | 0 | 0 | 0 | 1 | 0 | 3 | 0 |
| EIS-3 > Baseline | 29 | 29 | 29 | 28 | 29 | 26 | 29 |
| EIS-3 = Baseline | 0 | 0 | 0 | 0 | 0 | 0 | 0 |
| EIS-3 < Baseline | 0 | 0 | 0 | 1 | 0 | 3 | 0 |

It is evident from the baseline Table 1 that EIS-1, EIS-2, and EIS-3 outperform when compared to baseline activations in most cases and perform equally or underperform occasionally. The forward pass is implemented in both Pytorch [29] & Tensorflow-Keras [4] API and automatic differentiation updates the parameters. All the experiments are conducted on an NVIDIA tesla V-100 GPU with 16 GB RAM.

## 4.1   Image Classification:

We have reported results for image classification with six benchmarking databases like MNIST, Fashion MNIST, Street View House Numbers (SVHN), CIFAR10, CIFAR100, and Tiny Imagenet. A brief description of the databases and experimental setup is as follows.

**MNIST:** MNIST [23] is a well established standard databases consisting of 28 × 28 pixels grey-scale images of handwritten digits from 0 to 9. The dataset consists of 60k training images and 10k testing 28 × 28 grey-scale images. We consider a custom 8-layer homogeneous convolutional neural network (CNN) architecture to carried out experiments on MNIST. Channel depths of size 128 (twice), 64 (thrice), 32 (twice), a dense layer of size 128, Max-pooling layer(thrice), batch-normalization [19] and dropout [34] is being used on the CNN architecture. No data augmentation is used. The results are reported in Table 2.

**Fashion-MNIST:** :- Fashion-MNIST [37] is a database consisting of 28 × 28 pixels grey-scale images of Zalando's ten fashion items class like T-shirt, Trouser, Coat, Bag, etc. It's consists of 60k training examples and 10k testing examples. No data augmentation is used. The same CNN model architecture used in the MNIST dataset is also used for this database as well for training and testing purpose and, the results are given in Table 2.

**Table 2.** Results on MNIST, Fashion-MNIST and SVHN Datasets.

| Activation function | 5-fold mean accuracy on MNIST data | 5-fold mean accuracy on Fashion MNIST data | 5-fold mean accuracy on SVHN data |
|---|---|---|---|
| EIS-1 | **99.39** | **93.32** | **95.46** |
| EIS-2 | **99.38** | **93.29** | **95.45** |
| EIS-3 | **99.44** | **93.30** | **95.43** |
| ReLU | 99.17 | 92.95 | 95.20 |
| Swish | 99.21 | 92.92 | 95.21 |
| Leaky ReLU | 99.18 | 92.99 | 95.18 |
| ELU | 99.15 | 92.83 | 95.10 |
| Softplus | 99.02 | 92.51 | 95.01 |
| GELU | 99.20 | 93.08 | 95.23 |
| Mish | 99.26 | 93.16 | 95.29 |

**Street View House Numbers (SVHN) Database:** SVHN [28] is a popular computer vision database consists of real-world house numbers with $32 \times 32$ RGB images. The database has 73257 training images and 26032 testing images. The database has a total of 10 classes. We have used the data augmentation method in this database. The same CNN model architecture used in the MNIST dataset is also used for this database as well for training and testing purpose and, the results are given in Table 2.

**CIFAR:** The CIFAR [21], is another standard well established computer-vision dataset that is generally used to establish the efficacy of deep learning models. It contains 60k color images of size $32 \times 32$, out of which 50k are training images, and 10k are testing images. It has two versions CIFAR 10 and CIFAR100, which contains 10 and 100 target classes, respectively. Top-1 accuracy for mean of 9 different runs is reported on CIFAR10 and CIFAR100 datasets in Table 3 and Table 4 respectively on ResNet-50 (RN 50) [12], ResNet V2 34 (RN-V2 34) [14], VGG-16 (with Batch-normalization) [33], Densenet-121 (DN 121) [17], DenseNet-169 (DN 169) [17], InceptionNet V3 (IN V3) [35], SimpleNet (SN) [11], MobileNet V2 (MN V2) [32], WideResNet 28-10 (WRN 28-10) [39], ShuffleNet V2 (SF Net) [24] and SqueezeNet (SQ Net) [18] models. The networks have been trained with batch size 128, Adam optimizer [20] with 0.001 learning rate and up-to 100 epochs for all the models mentioned above except SimpleNet and VGG-16 which is trained till 200 epochs. Data augmentation is used for both datasets. Accuracy and loss graphs on WRN 28-10 model with CIFAR100 dataset for ReLU, Swish, EIS-1, EIS-2, and EIS-3 are given in Figs. 9 and 10.

**Table 3.** Comparison between baseline activation functions and EIS-1, EIS-2, & EIS-3 on image classification problem on CIFAR10 dataset based on top-1 test accuracy. Top-1 accuracy(in %) for mean of 9 different runs have been reported.

| AF | VGG 16 | WRN 28-10 | RN 50 | RN-V2 34 | DN 121 | DN 169 | IN V3 | MN V2 | SN | SQ Net | SF Net |
|---|---|---|---|---|---|---|---|---|---|---|---|
| EIS-1 | **90.83** | **92.75** | **91.37** | **91.92** | 91.29 | 91.17 | **92.11** | **91.22** | **92.45** | **87.09** | **90.17** |
| EIS-2 | **90.71** | **92.69** | **91.35** | **91.79** | 91.17 | 91.33 | **92.02** | **91.11** | **92.37** | 86.99 | 90.02 |
| EIS-3 | **90.79** | **92.81** | **91.30** | **91.97** | 91.29 | 91.31 | **92.15** | **91.32** | **92.47** | **87.22** | 90.09 |
| ReLU | 89.62 | 91.65 | 90.35 | 90.52 | 90.31 | 90.47 | 91.25 | 89.77 | 91.01 | 86.72 | 88.42 |
| Leaky ReLU | 89.64 | 91.77 | 90.53 | 90.62 | 90.69 | 90.52 | 91.52 | 89.71 | 91.15 | 86.22 | 88.40 |
| ELU | 89.01 | 91.22 | 90.22 | 90.27 | 90.23 | 90.27 | 91.02 | 89.09 | 90.89 | 86.31 | 88.31 |
| Swish | 89.86 | 92.01 | 90.77 | 90.87 | 90.71 | **91.34** | 91.32 | 90.12 | 91.41 | 86.41 | 89.01 |
| Softplus | 89.22 | 91.36 | 89.67 | 89.98 | 90.12 | 90.17 | 91.11 | 88.99 | 91.23 | 85.61 | 88.01 |
| Mish | 90.01 | 92.23 | 90.99 | 90.87 | **91.45** | 90.77 | 91.52 | 90.42 | 91.99 | 86.71 | 89.00 |
| GELU | 89.72 | 92.11 | 90.78 | 90.91 | 90.42 | 90.73 | 91.77 | 90.01 | 91.52 | 86.80 | 89.19 |

**Table 4.** Comparison between baseline activation functions and EIS-1, EIS-2, & EIS-3 on image classification problem on CIFAR100 dataset based on top-1 test accuracy. Top-1 accuracy(in %) for mean of 9 different runs have been reported.

| AF | VGG 16 | WRN 28-10 | RN 50 | RN-V2 34 | DN 121 | DN 169 | IN V3 | MN V2 | SN | SQ Net | SF Net |
|---|---|---|---|---|---|---|---|---|---|---|---|
| EIS-1 | **62.52** | **69.22** | **65.62** | **65.44** | 67.05 | 64.92 | **69.29** | **65.87** | **65.11** | **61.42** | **63.42** |
| EIS-2 | **62.49** | **69.11** | **65.52** | **65.21** | 67.01 | 64.94 | **69.27** | **65.71** | **64.99** | **61.23** | **63.23** |
| EIS-3 | **63.01** | **69.21** | **65.61** | **65.49** | 67.11 | 65.19 | **69.52** | **65.90** | **65.40** | **61.50** | **63.62** |
| ReLU | 57.25 | 67.20 | 64.45 | 59.89 | 66.11 | 64.01 | 68.11 | 63.24 | 63.12 | 60.12 | 61.12 |
| Leaky ReLU | 57.29 | 67.86 | 64.15 | 60.22 | 66.82 | 64.49 | 68.01 | 63.27 | 63.64 | 60.01 | 61.03 |
| ELU | 56.12 | 67.58 | 64.11 | 59.87 | 66.11 | 64.02 | 67.99 | 63.02 | 63.45 | 60.00 | 61.07 |
| Swish | 60.25 | 68.22 | 65.01 | 60.89 | 66.92 | 64.52 | 68.42 | 64.11 | 64.74 | 60.45 | 61.15 |
| SoftPlus | 54.13 | 67.01 | 62.20 | 59.11 | 66.20 | 64.54 | 68.02 | 62.98 | 62.81 | 59.79 | 60.89 |
| Mish | 60.02 | 68.99 | 65.11 | 62.33 | **67.42** | **65.20** | 68.51 | 64.82 | 64.68 | 60.12 | 61.48 |
| GELU | 59.89 | 68.71 | 64.92 | 62.45 | 66.52 | 64.54 | 68.40 | 64.10 | 64.49 | 60.03 | 61.55 |

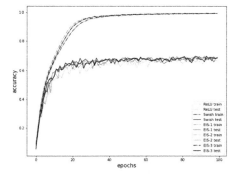

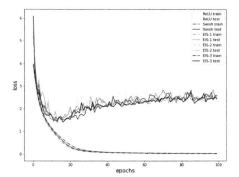

**Fig. 9.** Graph for train and test accuracy on CIFAR100 dataset on WideResNet 28-10 model

**Fig. 10.** Graph for train and test loss on CIFAR100 dataset on WideResNet 28-10 model

**Tiny Imagenet.** The ImageNet Large Scale Visual Recognition Challenge (ILS-VRC) is the standard and most popular benchmark for image classification problems. The database contains images of size $64 \times 64$ with 200 image classes with a training dataset of 100,000 images, a validation dataset of 10,000 images, and a test dataset of 10,000 images. Top-1 accuracy for mean of 5 runs for different activation functions are reported in Table 5 on WideResNet 28-10 (WRN 28-10) [39] model. The model is trained with a batch size of 32, He Normal initializer [13], 0.2 dropout rate [34], adam optimizer, initial learning rate(lr rate) 0.01, and reduce lr rate by a factor of 10 after every 50 epochs up-to 250 epochs. Data augmentation is used.

## 4.2   Object Detection

Object Detection is one of the most important problems in computer vision. We have shown our experimental results on the Pascal VOC dataset [8]. Results are reported on Single Shot MultiBox Detector(SSD) 300 model. VGG-16(with batch-normalization) is used as the base network. No pre-trained weight is used in the network. The network is trained on Pascal VOC 07+12 training data and tested model performance on Pascal VOC 2007 test data. The model is trained with a batch size of 8, 0.001 learning rate, SGD optimizer with 0.9 momentum, $5e^{-4}$ weight decay for 120000 iterations. A mean of 5 different runs for the mean average precision(mAP) is reported in Table 6.

**Table 5.** Comparison between baseline activation functions and EIS-1, EIS-2, & EIS-3 on Tiny ImageNet dataset on WRN 28-10 model. Results are reported for mean of 5 different runs.

| Activation function | Wide ResNet 28-10 model |
|---|---|
| EIS-1 | **61.85** |
| EIS-2 | **61.70** |
| EIS-3 | **61.95** |
| ReLU | 60.11 |
| Leaky ReLU | 60.05 |
| Swish | 60.45 |
| ELU | 59.87 |
| Softplus | 59.55 |
| Mish | 60.61 |
| GELU | 60.59 |

**Table 6.** Comparison between baseline activation functions and EIS-1, EIS-2, & EIS-3 on Object Detection problem on SSD 300 model on Pascal-VOC dataset. Results are reported for mean of 5 different runs.

| Activation function | mAP |
|---|---|
| EIS-1 | **77.7** |
| EIS-2 | **77.6** |
| EIS-3 | **77.7** |
| ReLU | 77.2 |
| Swish | 77.3 |
| Leaky ReLU | 77.2 |
| ELU | 75.1 |
| Softplus | 74.2 |
| Mish | 77.4 |
| GELU | 77.3 |

## 4.3   Semantic Segmentation

We carry out our experiment for semantic segmentation task on the CityScapes dataset [6]. We use U-net [31] as the base network and train till 250 epochs, with adam optimizer [20], learning rate $5e^{-3}$, batch size 32 and Xavier Uniform initializer [9]. Mean of 5 different runs for Pixel Accuracy and mean Intersection-Over-Union (mIOU) on test data is reported on Table 7.

## 4.4   Machine Translation

In this section, we report results for the machine translation problem. For this problem, we use WMT 2014 English→German dataset, which has 4.5 million training sentences, and evaluate model performance on the newstest2014 dataset using BLEU score metric. We use an Attention-based multi-head transformer model [36]. 8-head attention model is used with Adam optimizer, 0.1 dropout, and trained for 100000 steps. We try to kept other hyper-parameters similar as mentioned in the original paper [36]. Table 8 shows the results on the test dataset(newstest2014). A mean of 5 different runs is reported on Table 8.

**Table 7.** Comparison between baseline activation functions and EIS-1, EIS-2, & EIS-3 on semantic segmentation problem on U-NET model on CityScape dataset. Results are reported for mean of 5 different runs.

| Activation function | Pixel accuracy | mIOU |
|---|---|---|
| EIS-1 | **80.55** | **70.34** |
| EIS-2 | **80.61** | **70.29** |
| EIS-3 | **80.51** | **70.27** |
| ReLU | 79.64 | 69.45 |
| Swish | 79.94 | 69.73 |
| Leaky ReLU | 79.71 | 69.65 |
| ELU | 79.05 | 68.07 |
| Softplus | 78.98 | 68.02 |
| Mish | 80.03 | 69.55 |
| GELU | 79.77 | 69.67 |

**Table 8.** Comparison between baseline activation functions and EIS-1, EIS-2, & EIS-3 on Machine translation problem on multi-head transformer model on WMT-2014 dataset. Results are reported for mean of 5 different runs.

| Activation function | BLEU Score on the newstest2014 dataset |
|---|---|
| EIS-1 | **26.6** |
| EIS-2 | **26.5** |
| EIS-3 | **26.6** |
| ReLU | 26.2 |
| Swish | 26.4 |
| Leaky ReLU | 26.3 |
| ELU | 25.1 |
| Softplus | 23.6 |
| Mish | 26.3 |
| GELU | 26.2 |

## 4.5   Computational Time Comparison

In this section, computational time comparison are reported for baseline activation functions and EIS-1, EIS-2, & EIS-3 for both forward and backward pass for a 32 × 32 RGB image on the VGG-16 model. All the runs are performed on an NVIDIA Tesla V100 GPU with 16 GB ram, and results are reported in Table 9 for the mean of 100 runs.

**Table 9.** Runtime comparison between baseline activation functions and EIS-1, EIS-2, & EIS-3 for the forward and backward passes for a 32 × 32 RGB image. Results are reported for mean of 100 runs.

| Activation function | Forward pass (STD) | Backward pass (STD) |
|---|---|---|
| EIS-1 | 6.52 (±0.99) μs | 7.11 (±0.96) μs |
| EIS-2 | 6.34 (±1.17) μs | 7.81 (±1.74) μs |
| EIS-3 | 6.99 (±1.01) μs | 6.96 (±1.34) $\mu s$ |
| ReLU | 5.10 (±1.02) μs | 4.95 (±0.81) μs |
| Swish | 5.52 (±1.11) μs | 5.70 (±1.05) μs |
| Leaky ReLU | 5.11 (±0.59) μs | 4.99 (±1.01) μs |
| ELU | 5.15 (±0.70) μs | 5.01 (±0.45) μs |
| Softplus | 5.12 (±1.01) μs | 5.07 (±0.99) μs |
| Mish | 6.29 (±1.16) μs | 5.52 (±0.79) μs |
| GELU | 7.59 (±1.04) μs | 7.89 (±1.11) μs |

## 5    Conclusion

In this paper, we proposed three parametric activation functions, which we call EIS-1, EIS-2, and EIS-3, and exhibit that they consistently outperform well-known activation functions such as ReLU and Swish, as evident from the baseline table on several well-known datasets and models.

We also advocate through this article that it is time to move away from simple activation functions and adopt comprehensive search schemes on parametric functions to build models. This allows for building more accurate and dependable models. Another scope of future research is to develop a mathematical understanding of reasons leading to improved accuracy.

## References

1. Baker, B., Gupta, O., Naik, N., Raskar, R.: Designing neural network architectures using reinforcement learning (2016)
2. Biswas, K., Kumar, S., Banerjee, S., Pandey, A.K.: TanhSoft - a family of activation functions combining Tanh and Softplus (2020)
3. Carlile, B., Delamarter, G., Kinney, P., Marti, A., Whitney, B.: Improving deep learning by inverse square root linear units (ISRLUs) (2017)
4. Chollet, F.: Keras (2015). https://github.com/fchollet/keras
5. Clevert, D.A., Unterthiner, T., Hochreiter, S.: Fast and accurate deep network learning by exponential linear units (ELUs) (2015)
6. Cordts, M., et al.: The cityscapes dataset for semantic urban scene understanding (2016)
7. Elfwing, S., Uchibe, E., Doya, K.: Sigmoid-weighted linear units for neural network function approximation in reinforcement learning (2017)
8. Everingham, M., Gool, L., Williams, C.K., Winn, J., Zisserman, A.: The pascal visual object classes (VOC) challenge. Int. J. Comput. Vis. **88**(2), 303–338 (2010)

9. Glorot, X., Bengio, Y.: Understanding the difficulty of training deep feedforward neural networks. In: Teh, Y.W., Titterington, M. (eds.) Proceedings of the Thirteenth International Conference on Artificial Intelligence and Statistics. JMLR Workshop and Conference Proceedings, Chia Laguna Resort, Sardinia, Italy, 13–15 May 2010. Proceedings of Machine Learning Research, vol. 9, pp. 249–256 (2010) http://proceedings.mlr.press/v9/glorot10a.html

10. Zheng, H., Yang, Z., Liu, W., Liang, J., Li, Y.: Improving deep neural networks using Softplus units. In: 2015 International Joint Conference on Neural Networks (IJCNN), pp. 1–4 (2015)

11. Hasanpour, S.H., Rouhani, M., Fayyaz, M., Sabokrou, M.: Lets keep it simple, using simple architectures to outperform deeper and more complex architectures (2016)

12. He, K., Zhang, X., Ren, S., Sun, J.: Deep residual learning for image recognition (2015)

13. He, K., Zhang, X., Ren, S., Sun, J.: Delving deep into rectifiers: surpassing human-level performance on ImageNet classification (2015)

14. He, K., Zhang, X., Ren, S., Sun, J.: Identity mappings in deep residual networks. In: Leibe, B., Matas, J., Sebe, N., Welling, M. (eds.) ECCV 2016. LNCS, vol. 9908, pp. 630–645. Springer, Cham (2016). https://doi.org/10.1007/978-3-319-46493-0_38

15. Hendrycks, D., Gimpel, K.: Gaussian error linear units (GELUs) (2020)

16. Hinton, G.E.: Rectified linear units improve restricted Boltzmann machines Vinod Nair (2010)

17. Huang, G., Liu, Z., van der Maaten, L., Weinberger, K.Q.: Densely connected convolutional networks (2016)

18. Iandola, F.N., Han, S., Moskewicz, M.W., Ashraf, K., Dally, W.J., Keutzer, K.: SqueezeNet: AlexNet-level accuracy with 50x fewer parameters and <0.5MB model size (2016)

19. Ioffe, S., Szegedy, C.: Batch normalization: accelerating deep network training by reducing internal covariate shift (2015)

20. Kingma, D.P., Ba, J.: Adam: a method for stochastic optimization (2017)

21. Krizhevsky, A.: Learning multiple layers of features from tiny images. Technical report (2009)

22. LeCun, Y., et al.: Backpropagation applied to handwritten zip code recognition. Neural Comput. $\mathbf{1}$(4), 541–551 (1989). https://doi.org/10.1162/neco.1989.1.4.541

23. LeCun, Y., Cortes, C., Burges, C.: Mnist handwritten digit database, February 2010. ATT Labs http://yann.lecun.com/exdb/mnist

24. Ma, N., Zhang, X., Zheng, H.-T., Sun, J.: ShuffleNet V2: practical guidelines for efficient CNN architecture design. In: Ferrari, V., Hebert, M., Sminchisescu, C., Weiss, Y. (eds.) Computer Vision – ECCV 2018. LNCS, vol. 11218, pp. 122–138. Springer, Cham (2018). https://doi.org/10.1007/978-3-030-01264-9_8

25. Maas, A.L., Hannun, A.Y., Ng, A.Y.: Rectifier nonlinearities improve neural network acoustic models. In: ICML Workshop on Deep Learning for Audio, Speech and Language Processing (2013)

26. Misra, D.: Mish: a self regularized non-monotonic activation function (2020)

27. Negrinho, R., Gordon, G.: Deeparchitect: automatically designing and training deep architectures (2017)

28. Netzer, Y., Wang, T., Coates, A., Bissacco, A., Wu, B., Ng, A.Y.: Reading digits in natural images with unsupervised feature learning (2011)

29. Paszke, A., et al.: PyTorch: an imperative style, high-performance deep learning library (2019)

30. Ramachandran, P., Zoph, B., Le, Q.V.: Searching for activation functions (2017)
31. Ronneberger, O., Fischer, P., Brox, T.: U-Net: convolutional networks for biomedical image segmentation. In: Navab, N., Hornegger, J., Wells, W.M., Frangi, A.F. (eds.) MICCAI 2015. LNCS, vol. 9351, pp. 234–241. Springer, Cham (2015). https://doi.org/10.1007/978-3-319-24574-4_28
32. Sandler, M., Howard, A., Zhu, M., Zhmoginov, A., Chen, L.C.: MobileNetV2: inverted residuals and linear bottlenecks (2019)
33. Simonyan, K., Zisserman, A.: Very deep convolutional networks for large-scale image recognition (2015)
34. Srivastava, N., Hinton, G., Krizhevsky, A., Sutskever, I., Salakhutdinov, R.: Dropout: a simple way to prevent neural networks from overfitting. J. Mach. Learn. Res. **15**(1), 1929–1958 (2014)
35. Szegedy, C., Vanhoucke, V., Ioffe, S., Shlens, J., Wojna, Z.: Rethinking the inception architecture for computer vision (2015)
36. Vaswani, A., et al.: Attention is all you need (2017)
37. Xiao, H., Rasul, K., Vollgraf, R.: Fashion-MNIST: a novel image dataset for benchmarking machine learning algorithms. arXiv preprint arXiv:1708.07747 (2017)
38. Xu, B., Wang, N., Chen, T., Li, M.: Empirical evaluation of rectified activations in convolutional network (2015)
39. Zagoruyko, S., Komodakis, N.: Wide residual networks (2016)
40. Zhou, Y., Li, D., Huo, S., Kung, S.Y.: Soft-root-sign activation function (2020)

# Deep Learning and Optimization II

# Why Mixup Improves the Model Performance

Masanari Kimura$^{(\boxtimes)}$ 🆔

Ridge-i Inc., Tokyo, Japan
mkimura@ridge-i.com

**Abstract.** Machine learning techniques are used in a wide range of domains. However, machine learning models often suffer from the problem of over-fitting. Many data augmentation methods have been proposed to tackle such a problem, and one of them is called mixup. Mixup is a recently proposed regularization procedure, which linearly interpolates a random pair of training examples. This regularization method works very well experimentally, but its theoretical guarantee is not adequately discussed. In this study, we aim to discover why mixup works well from the aspect of the statistical learning theory.

**Keywords:** Machine learning · Data augmentation · Generalization bounds

## 1 Introduction

Machine learning has achieved remarkable results in recent years. However, despite such excellent performance, machine learning models often suffer from the problem of over-fitting [5]. In recent years, a concept called mixup [12] has attracted attention as one of the powerful regularization methods for machine learning models. The main idea of these regularization methods is to prepare

$$(\tilde{\boldsymbol{x}}_{ij}, \tilde{y}_{ij}) = (\lambda \boldsymbol{x}_i + (1 - \lambda)\boldsymbol{x}_j, \lambda y_i + (1 - \lambda)y_j) \tag{1}$$

mixed with random pairs $(\boldsymbol{x}_i, \boldsymbol{x}_j)$ of input vectors and their corresponding labels $(y_i, y_j)$ and use them as training data. This regularization method is very powerful and has been applied in various fields such as image recognition [9] or speech recognition [6]. Despite these strong experimental results, there is not enough discussion about why this method works well.

In this paper, we give theoretical guarantees for regularization by mixup and reveal how regularization changes in each setting. To summarize our results, mixup regularization leads to the following effects:

- For linear classifiers, the effect of regularization is higher when the sample size is small, and the sample standard deviation is large.
- For neural networks, the effect of regularization is higher when the number of samples is small, and the training dataset contains outliers.

I. Farkaš et al. (Eds.): ICANN 2021, LNCS 12892, pp. 275–286, 2021.
https://doi.org/10.1007/978-3-030-86340-1_22

- When the parameter $\lambda$ is close to 0 or 1, mixup can reduce the variance of the estimator, but this will be affected by bias.
- When the parameter $\lambda$ has near the optimal value, mixup can reduce both the bias and variance of the estimator.
- Geometrically, mixup reduces the second-order derivative of the convex function that characterizes the Bregman divergence.

## 2     Related Works

### 2.1     Mixup Variants

Mixup is originally proposed by [11]. The main idea of these regularization methods is to prepare

$$(\tilde{\boldsymbol{x}}_{ij}, \tilde{y}_{ij}) = (\lambda \boldsymbol{x}_i + (1 - \lambda)\boldsymbol{x}_j, \lambda y_i + (1 - \lambda)y_j)$$

mixed with random pairs $(\boldsymbol{x}_i, \boldsymbol{x}_j)$ of input vectors and their corresponding labels $(y_i, y_j)$ and use them as training data, where $\lambda \sim Beta(\alpha, \alpha)$, for $\alpha \in (0, \infty)$.

Because of its power and ease of implementation, several variants have been studied [3, 10]. However, most of them are heuristic methods and have insufficient theoretical explanations.

## 3     Notations and Preliminaries

We consider a binary classification problem in this paper. However, our analysis can easily be applied to a multi-class case.

Let $\mathcal{X}$ be the input space, $\mathcal{Y} = \{-1, +1\}$ be the output space, and $\mathcal{C}$ be a set of concepts we may wish to learn, called concept class. We assume that each input vector $\boldsymbol{x} \in \mathbb{R}^d$ is of dimension $d$. We also assume that examples are independently and identically distributed (i.i.d) according to some fixed but unknown distribution $D$.

We consider a fixed set of possible concepts $H$, called hypothesis set. We receive a sample $B = (\boldsymbol{x}_1, \ldots, \boldsymbol{x}_n)$ drawn i.i.d. according to $D$ as well as the labels $(c(\boldsymbol{x}_1), \ldots, c(\boldsymbol{x}_n))$, which are based on a specific target concept $c \in \mathcal{C} : \mathcal{X} \mapsto \mathcal{Y}$. Our task is to use the labeled sample $B$ to find a hypothesis $h_B \in H$ that has a small generalization error with respect to the concept $c$. The generalization error $\mathcal{R}(h)$ is defined as follows.

**Definition 1** *(Generalization error).* *Given a hypothesis $h \in H$, a target concept $c \in \mathcal{C}$, and unknown distribution $D$, the generalization error of $h$ is defined by*

$$\mathcal{R}(h) = \mathbb{E}_{x \sim D}\left[\mathbb{1}_{h(\boldsymbol{x}) \neq c(\boldsymbol{x})}\right], \tag{2}$$

*where $\mathbb{1}_\omega$ is the indicator function of the event $\omega$.*

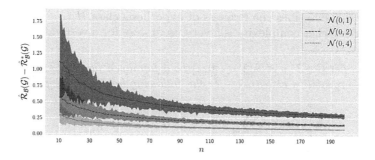

**Fig. 1.** The relationship between $\hat{\mathfrak{R}}_B(H_\ell) - \hat{\mathfrak{R}}_B^*(H_\ell)$ and the number of samples $n$ and variance $\sigma^2$ when mixup is applied. Each data point was sampled from the normal distribution $\mathcal{N}(0, \sigma^2)$ and the constant part was set to 1.

The generalization error of a hypothesis $h$ is not directly accessible since both the underlying distribution $D$ and the target concept $c$ are unknown Then, we have to measure the empirical error of hypothesis $h$ on the observable labeled sample $B$.

**Definition 2** *(Empirical error). Given a hypothesis $h \in H$, a target concept $c \in C$, and a sample $B = (x_1, \ldots, x_n)$, the empirical error of $h$ is defined by*

$$\hat{\mathcal{R}}(h) = \frac{1}{n} \sum_{i=1}^{n} \mathbb{1}_{h(x_i) \neq c(x_i)}. \tag{3}$$

In learning problems, we are interested in how much difference there is between empirical and generalization errors. Therefore, in general, we consider the relative generalization error $\hat{\mathcal{R}}(h) - \mathcal{R}(h)$.

**Definition 3** *(Empirical Rademacher complexity). Given a hypothesis set $H$ and a sample $B = (x_1, \ldots, x_n)$, the empirical Rademacher complexity of $H$ is defined as:*

$$\hat{\mathfrak{R}}_B(H) = \mathbb{E}_\sigma \left[ \sup_{h \in H} \frac{1}{n} \sum_{i=1}^{n} \sigma_i h(x_i) \right], \tag{4}$$

*where $\sigma = (\sigma_1, \ldots, \sigma_n)^T$ with Rademacher variables $\sigma_i \in \{-1, +1\}$ which are independent uniform random variables.*

**Definition 4** *(Rademacher complexity). Let $D$ denote the distribution according to which samples are drawn. For any sample size $n \geq 1$, the Rademacher complexity of $H$ is the expectation of the empirical Rademacher complexity over all samples of size $n$ drawn according to $D$:*

$$\mathfrak{R}_n(H) = \mathbb{E}_{B \sim D^n} \left[ \hat{\mathfrak{R}}_B(H) \right]. \tag{5}$$

Intuitively, this describes the richness of hypothesis class $H$.

The Rademacher complexity is a very useful tool for investigating hypothesis class $H$.

**Lemma 1.** *Let $\mathcal{G} : \mathcal{Z} = \mathcal{X} \times \mathcal{Y} \mapsto [0,1]$ be a family of functions. Then, for any $\delta > 0$, with probability at least $1 - \delta$, the following holds for all $g \in \mathcal{G}$:*

$$\mathbb{E}\left[g(z) \leq \frac{1}{n}\sum_{i=1}^{n} g(z_i) + 2\Re_n(G) + \sqrt{\frac{\log\frac{1}{\delta}}{2m}}\right] \tag{6}$$

$$\mathbb{E}\left[g(z) \leq \frac{1}{n}\sum_{i=1}^{n} g(z_i) + 2\Re_B(G) + 3\sqrt{\frac{\log\frac{2}{\delta}}{2m}}\right]. \tag{7}$$

*Proof.* For any sample $B = (z_1, \ldots, z_n)$ and for any $g \in \mathcal{G}$, we denote by $\hat{\mathbb{E}}_B[g]$ the empirical average of $g$ over $B$ : $\hat{\mathbb{E}}_B[g] = \frac{1}{n}\sum_{i=1}^{n} g(z_i)$. We define the function $\Phi(\cdot)$ for any sample $B$ as follows:

$$\Phi(B) = \sup_{g \in \mathcal{G}} \mathbb{E}[g] - \hat{\mathbb{E}}_B[g]. \tag{8}$$

Let $B$ and $B'$ be two samples differing by exactly one point, which mean $z_n \in B \wedge z_n \notin B'$ and $z_n' \in B' \wedge z_n' \notin B$. Then, we have

$$\Phi(B') - \Phi(B) \leq \sup_{g \in \mathcal{G}} \hat{\mathbb{E}}_B[g] - \hat{\mathbb{E}}_{B'}[g] = \sup_{g \in \mathcal{G}} \frac{g(z_n) - g(z_n')}{n} \leq \frac{1}{n} \tag{9}$$

$$\Phi(B) - \Phi(B') \leq \sup_{g \in \mathcal{G}} \hat{\mathbb{E}}_{B'}[g] - \hat{\mathbb{E}}_B[g] = \sup_{g \in \mathcal{G}} \frac{g(z_n') - g(z_n)}{n} \leq \frac{1}{n}. \tag{10}$$

Then, by McDiarmid's inequality, for any $\delta > 0$, with probability at least $1 - \frac{\delta}{2}$, the following holds:

$$\Phi(B) \leq \mathbb{E}_B[\Phi(B)] + \sqrt{\frac{\log\frac{2}{\delta}}{2n}} \tag{11}$$

$$\mathbb{E}_B[\Phi(B)] \leq \mathbb{E}_{\sigma,B,B'}\left[\sup_{g \in \mathcal{G}} \frac{1}{n}\sum_{i=1}^{n} \sigma_i(g(z_i') - g(z_i))\right] = 2\mathbb{E}_{\sigma,B}\left[\sup_{g \in \mathcal{G}} \frac{1}{n}\sum_{i=1}^{n} \sigma_i g(z_i)\right]$$

Then, using MacDiarmid's inequality, with probability $1 - \frac{\delta}{2}$, $\Re_n(\mathcal{G}) \leq \hat{\mathcal{R}}_B(\mathcal{G}) + \sqrt{\frac{\log\frac{2}{\delta}}{2n}}$. Finally, we use the union bound and we can have the result of this lemma.

**Lemma 2.** *Let $H$ be a family of functions taking values in $\{-1, +1\}$ and let $\mathcal{G}$ be the family of loss functions associated to $H$: $\mathcal{G} = \{(x, y) \mapsto \mathbb{1}_{h(x) \neq y} : h \in H\}$. For any samples $B = ((x_1, y_1), \ldots, (x_n, y_n))$, let $\mathcal{S}_{\mathcal{X}}$ denote the its projection over $\mathcal{X}$ : $\mathcal{S}_{\mathcal{X}} = (x_1, \ldots, x_n)$. Then, the following relation holds between the empirical Rademacher complexities of $\mathcal{G}$ and $H$:*

$$\hat{\Re}_B(\mathcal{G}) = \frac{1}{2}\hat{\Re}_{\mathcal{S}_{\mathcal{X}}}(H). \tag{12}$$

*Proof.* For any sample $B = ((\boldsymbol{x}_1, y_1), \ldots, (\boldsymbol{x}_2, y_2))$ of elements in $\mathcal{X} \times \mathcal{Y}$, the empirical Rademacher complexity of $\mathcal{G}$ can be written as:

$$\hat{\mathfrak{R}}_B(\mathcal{G}) = \mathbb{E}_\sigma \left[ \sup_{h \in H} \frac{1}{n} \sum_{i=1}^n \sigma_i \mathbb{1}_{h(\boldsymbol{x}_i) \neq y_i} \right] = \frac{1}{2} \mathbb{E}_\sigma \left[ \sup_{h \in H} \frac{1}{n} \sum_{i=1}^n \sigma_i h(\boldsymbol{x}_i) \right]. \tag{13}$$

**Theorem 1.** *Given a hypothesis $h \in H$ and the distribution $D$ over the input space $\mathcal{X}$, we assume that $\hat{\mathfrak{R}}_B(H)$ is the empirical Rademacher complexity of the hypothesis class $H$. Then, for any $\delta > 0$, with probability at least $1 - \delta$ over a sample $B$ of size $n$ drawn according to $D$, each of the following holds over $H$ uniformly:*

$$\mathcal{R}(h) - \hat{\mathcal{R}}(h) \leq \hat{\mathfrak{R}}_n(H) + \sqrt{\frac{\log \frac{1}{\delta}}{2m}}, \tag{14}$$

$$\mathcal{R}(h) - \hat{\mathcal{R}}(h) \leq \hat{\mathfrak{R}}_B(H) + 3\sqrt{\frac{\log \frac{2}{\delta}}{2m}}. \tag{15}$$

*Proof.* From Lemma 1 and Lemma 2, we can have the result of Theorem 1 immediately.

From the above discussion, we can see that if we can quantify the change of empirical Rademacher complexity before and after mixup, we can evaluate the relative generalization error of the hypothesis class $H$. Our main idea is to clarify the effects of the mixup regularization by examining how these Rademacher complexity changes before and after regularization. Note that we are not interested in the tightness of the bound, but only in the difference in the bound.

## 4   Complexity Reduction of Linear Classifiers with Mixup

In this section, we assume that $H_\ell$ is a class of linear functions:

$$h(\boldsymbol{x}) \in H_\ell = \left\{ \boldsymbol{x} \mapsto \boldsymbol{w}^T \boldsymbol{x} \mid \boldsymbol{w} \in \mathbb{R}^d, \ \|\boldsymbol{w}\|_2 \leq \Lambda \right\}, \tag{16}$$

where $\boldsymbol{w}$ is the weight vector and $\Lambda$ is a constant that regularizes the L2 norm of the weight vector.

**Theorem 2.** *Given a hypothesis set $H_\ell$ and a sample $B = (\boldsymbol{x}_1, \ldots, \boldsymbol{x}_n)$, we assume that $\hat{\mathfrak{R}}_B(H_\ell)$ is the empirical Rademacher complexity of the hypothesis class $H_\ell$ and $\hat{\mathfrak{R}}_B^*(H_\ell)$ is the empirical Rademacher complexity of $H_\ell$ when mixup is applied. The difference between the two Rademacher complexity $\hat{\mathfrak{R}}_B(H_\ell) - \hat{\mathfrak{R}}_B^*(H_\ell)$ is less than or equal to a constant multiple of the sample variance of the norm of the input vectors:*

$$\hat{\mathfrak{R}}_B(H_\ell) - \hat{\mathfrak{R}}_B^*(H_\ell) \leq \frac{C_\lambda^\Lambda}{\sqrt{n}} \sqrt{s^2 \|\boldsymbol{x}\|_2}, \tag{17}$$

*where $C_\lambda^\Lambda$ is a constant that depends on the parameter $\lambda$ of mixup and $s^2$ is the sample variance computed from the sample set.*

*Proof.* By the Definition 3, empirical Rademacher complexity of $h(\boldsymbol{x}) = \boldsymbol{w}^T \boldsymbol{x}$ is as follows:

$$\hat{\mathfrak{R}}_B(H) = \mathbb{E}_\sigma \left[ \frac{1}{n} \sup_{\|\boldsymbol{w}\|_2 \leq \Lambda} \sum_{i=1}^n \sigma_i \boldsymbol{w}^T \boldsymbol{x}_i \right] = \mathbb{E}_\sigma \left[ \frac{1}{n} \sup_{\|\boldsymbol{w}\|_2 \leq \Lambda} \boldsymbol{w}^T \sum_{i=1}^n \sigma_i \boldsymbol{x}_i \right]$$

$$= \frac{1}{n} \mathbb{E}_\sigma \left[ \sup_{\|\boldsymbol{w}\|_2 \leq \Lambda} \boldsymbol{w}^T \sum_{i=1}^n \sigma_i \boldsymbol{x}_i \right] = \frac{1}{n} \mathbb{E}_\sigma \left[ \Lambda \left\| \sum_{i=1}^n \sigma_i \boldsymbol{x}_i \right\|_2 \right]$$

$$\leq \frac{\Lambda}{n} \left( \mathbb{E}_\sigma \left[ \left\| \sum_{i=1}^n \sigma_i \boldsymbol{x}_i \right\|_2^2 \right] \right)^{\frac{1}{2}} = \frac{\Lambda}{n} \left( \sum_{i=1}^n \|\boldsymbol{x}_i\|_2^2 \right)^{\frac{1}{2}}. \tag{18}$$

Let $\tilde{\boldsymbol{x}}_i = \mathbb{E}_{\boldsymbol{x}_j}[\lambda \boldsymbol{x}_i + (1-\lambda)\boldsymbol{x}_j]$ be the expectation of the linear combination of input vectors by mixup, where $\lambda$ is a parameter in mixup and is responsible for adjusting the weights of the two vectors. Then, we have

$$\hat{\mathfrak{R}}_B^*(H) \leq \frac{\Lambda}{n} \left( \sum_{i=1}^n \|\tilde{\boldsymbol{x}}_i\|_2^2 \right)^{\frac{1}{2}} = \frac{\Lambda}{n} \left( \sum_{i=1}^n \left\| \mathbb{E}_{\boldsymbol{x}_j} \left[ \lambda \boldsymbol{x}_i + (1-\lambda)\boldsymbol{x}_j \right] \right\|_2^2 \right)^{\frac{1}{2}}$$

$$= \frac{\Lambda}{n} \left( \sum_{i=1}^n \left\| \lambda \boldsymbol{x}_i + (1-\lambda)\mathbb{E}_{\boldsymbol{x}_j}[\boldsymbol{x}_j] \right\|_2^2 \right)^{\frac{1}{2}}$$

$$\leq \frac{\Lambda}{n} \left( \sum_{i=1}^n \left( \|\lambda \boldsymbol{x}_i\|_2^2 + \left\| (1-\lambda)\mathbb{E}_{\boldsymbol{x}_j}[\boldsymbol{x}_j] \right\|_2^2 \right) \right)^{\frac{1}{2}}$$

$$= \frac{\Lambda}{n} \left( \lambda^2 \sum_{i=1}^n \|\boldsymbol{x}_i\|_2^2 + (1-\lambda)^2 \sum_{i=1}^n \left\| \mathbb{E}_{\boldsymbol{x}_j}[\boldsymbol{x}_j] \right\|_2^2 \right)^{\frac{1}{2}}. \tag{19}$$

From (18) and (19), we can have

$$\hat{\mathfrak{R}}_B(H) - \hat{\mathfrak{R}}_B^*(H) \leq \frac{\Lambda|1-\lambda|}{n} \left( \sum_{i=1}^n \|\boldsymbol{x}_i\|_2^2 - \sum_{i=1}^n \left\| \mathbb{E}_{\boldsymbol{x}_j}[\boldsymbol{x}_j] \right\|_2^2 \right)^{\frac{1}{2}}$$

$$= \frac{\Lambda|1-\lambda|}{\sqrt{n}} \left( \frac{1}{n} \sum_{i=1}^n \|\boldsymbol{x}_i\|_2^2 - \frac{1}{n} \sum_{i=1}^n \|\bar{\boldsymbol{x}}\|_2^2 \right)^{\frac{1}{2}}$$

$$= \frac{\Lambda|1-\lambda|}{\sqrt{n}} \left( s^2(\|\boldsymbol{x}\|_2) + \|\bar{\boldsymbol{x}}\|_2^2 - \|\bar{\boldsymbol{x}}\|_2^2 \right)^{\frac{1}{2}}$$

$$= \frac{\Lambda|1-\lambda|}{\sqrt{n}} \sqrt{s^2(\|\boldsymbol{x}\|_2)} \geq 0. \tag{20}$$

The above results are in line with our intuition and illustrate well how mixup depends on the shape of the data distribution. As can be seen from the (17), the complexity relaxation by mixup decreases as the number of samples $n$ increases (see Fig. 1).

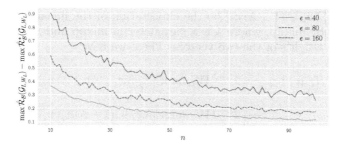

**Fig. 2.** The relationship between $\max \hat{\mathfrak{R}}_B(H_{L,\boldsymbol{W}_L}) - \max \hat{\mathfrak{R}}_B^*(H_{L,\boldsymbol{W}_L})$ and the number of samples $n$ and the noise of the outliers $\epsilon$.

## 5    Complexity Reduction of Neural Networks with Mixup

Let $H_{L,\boldsymbol{W}_L}$ be the function class of a neural network:

$$h(\boldsymbol{x}) \in H_{L,\boldsymbol{W}_L} = \Big\{ h : \|\boldsymbol{v}\|_2 = 1, \prod_{i=1}^{L} \|\boldsymbol{W}_i\|_F \leq \boldsymbol{W}_L \Big\}, \tag{21}$$

where $L$ is the number of layers, $\boldsymbol{W}_i$ is the weight matrix, $\boldsymbol{v} \in \mathbb{R}^{M_L}$ represents the normalized linear classifier operating on the output of the neural networks with input vector $\boldsymbol{x}$ and $\|\boldsymbol{A}\|_F$ is the Frobenius norm of the matrix $\boldsymbol{A} = (a_{ij})$.

**Theorem 3.** *Given a hypothesis set $H_{L,\boldsymbol{W}_L}$ and a sample $B = (\boldsymbol{x}_1, \ldots, \boldsymbol{x}_n)$, we assume that $\hat{\mathfrak{R}}_B(H_{L,\boldsymbol{W}_L})$ is the empirical Rademacher complexity of the hypothesis class $H_{L,\boldsymbol{W}_L}$ and $\hat{\mathfrak{R}}_B^*(H_{L,\boldsymbol{W}_L})$ is the empirical Rademacher complexity of $H_{L,\boldsymbol{W}_L}$ when mixup is applied. In addition, we assume that each sample $\boldsymbol{x}_i$ occurs with the population mean $\boldsymbol{\mu}_{\boldsymbol{x}}$ plus the some noise $\epsilon_i$. In other words, we assume that $\boldsymbol{x}_i = \boldsymbol{\mu}_{\boldsymbol{x}} + \epsilon_i$. The difference between the maximum of two Rademacher complexity $\hat{\mathfrak{R}}_B(H_{L,\boldsymbol{W}_L}) - \hat{\mathfrak{R}}_B^*(H_{L,\boldsymbol{W}_L})$ is less than or equal to a constant multiple of the maximum value of noise in a sample of training data when the number of samples $n$ is sufficiently large:*

$$\max \hat{\mathfrak{R}}_B(H_{L,\boldsymbol{W}_L}) - \max \hat{\mathfrak{R}}_B^*(H_{L,\boldsymbol{W}_L}) \leq \frac{C_\lambda^L}{\sqrt{n}} \max_i \|\epsilon_i\|, \tag{22}$$

*where $C_\lambda^L$ is a constant that depends on the parameter $\lambda$ of mixup and the number of layers $L$ of neural networks.*

*Proof.* By the upper bound of [8], empirical Rademacher complexity of $h(x) \in H_{L,\boldsymbol{W}_L}$ is as follows:

$$\hat{\mathfrak{R}}_B(H_{L,\boldsymbol{W}_L}) \leq \frac{1}{\sqrt{n}} 2^{L+\frac{1}{2}} \boldsymbol{W}_L \max_i \|\boldsymbol{x}_i\|. \tag{23}$$

Let $\tilde{x}_i = \mathbb{E}_{x_j}[\lambda x_i + (1 - \lambda)x_j]$ be the expectation of the linear combination of input vectors by mixup, where $\lambda$ is a parameter in mixup and is responsible for adjusting the weights of the two vectors. Then, we have

$$\hat{\mathfrak{R}}_B^*(H_{L,W_L}) \leq \frac{1}{\sqrt{n}} 2^{L+\frac{1}{2}} W_L \max_i \|\mathbb{E}_j[\lambda x_i + (1 - \lambda)x_j]\|$$

$$= \frac{1}{\sqrt{n}} 2^{L+\frac{1}{2}} W_L \max_i \|\lambda x_i + (1 - \lambda)\mathbb{E}_j[x_j]\|$$

$$\leq \frac{1}{\sqrt{n}} 2^{L+\frac{1}{2}} W_L \max_i \left\{ \lambda\|x_i\| + (1 - \lambda)\|\mathbb{E}_j[x_j]\| \right\}. \qquad (24)$$

Now we consider to bound the difference between the maximum values of each quantity,

$$\max \hat{\mathfrak{R}}_B(H_{L,W_L}) = \frac{1}{\sqrt{n}} 2^{L+\frac{1}{2}} W_L \max_i \|x_i\|,$$

$$\max \hat{\mathfrak{R}}_B^*(H_{L,W_L}) = \frac{1}{\sqrt{n}} 2^{L+\frac{1}{2}} W_L \max_i \left\{ \lambda\|x_i\| + (1 - \lambda)\|\mathbb{E}_j[x_j]\| \right\},$$

and then, from (23) and (24), and let $\mathcal{J}(H_{L,W_L}, B) = \max \hat{\mathfrak{R}}_B(H_{L,W_L}) - \max \hat{\mathfrak{R}}_B^*(H_{L,W_L})$ we can have

$$\mathcal{J}(H_{L,W_L}, B) \leq \frac{1-\lambda}{\sqrt{n}} 2^{L+\frac{1}{2}} W_L \max_i \left| \|x_i\|_2 - \|\bar{x}\|_2 \right|$$

$$= \frac{1-\lambda}{\sqrt{n}} 2^{L+\frac{1}{2}} W_L \max_i \left| \|\mu_x + \epsilon_i\|_2 - \|\bar{x}\|_2 \right|$$

$$\leq \frac{1-\lambda}{\sqrt{n}} 2^{L+\frac{1}{2}} W_L \max_i \left| \|\mu_x\|_2 + \|\epsilon_i\|_2 - \|\bar{x}\|_2 \right|$$

$$= \frac{1-\lambda}{\sqrt{n}} 2^{L+\frac{1}{2}} W_L \max_i \|\epsilon_i\|_2 \geq 0 \quad (\because 1 - \lambda \geq 0, \|\epsilon_i\|_2 \geq 0),$$

According to the above theorem, mixup allows the neural networks robust learning for outliers with accidentally large noise $\epsilon$ in the training sample $B$ (see Fig. 2).

## 6    The Optimal Parameters of Mixup

Here, we let the parameter $\lambda \in (0,1)$. From (17) and (22), we can see that a large $1 - \lambda$ has a good regularization effect. By swapping $i$ and $j$, we can see that $\lambda$ should be close to 0 or 1.

In the original mixup paper [12], the parameter $\lambda$ is sampled from the Beta distribution $Beta(\alpha, \alpha)$, where $\alpha$ is another parameter. We can see that when $\alpha < 1$, $\lambda$ is sampled such that one of the input vectors has a high weight (in other words, $\lambda$ is close to 0 or 1). We treated $\lambda$ as a constant in the above discussion, but if we treat it as a random variable $\lambda \sim Beta(\alpha, \alpha)$, we can obtain

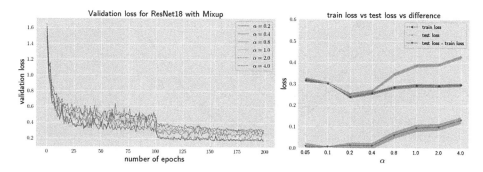

**Fig. 3.** Experimental results for CIFAR-10 dataset.We use ResNet-18 as a classifier and apply mixup with each parameter $\alpha$ for $\lambda \sim Beta(\alpha, \alpha)$. Left: Learning curve of ResNet-18 with mixup.

$\mathbb{E}[\lambda] = \frac{\alpha}{\alpha+\alpha} = \frac{1}{2}$ and $Var(\lambda) = \frac{\alpha^2}{(\alpha+\alpha)^2(\alpha+\alpha+1)} = \frac{\alpha^2}{4\alpha^2(2\alpha+1)} = \frac{1}{4(2\alpha+1)}$, where $\alpha > 0$. Since the $\mathbb{E}[\lambda]$ is a constant, we can see that when the weight parameter $\lambda$ is close to 0 or 1, $\alpha$ is expected to be close to 0.

Figure 3 shows the experimental results for CIFAR-10 [4]. We use ResNet-18 [2] as a classifier with $lr = 0.1$, $epochs = 200$ and apply mixup with each parameter $\alpha$ for $\lambda \sim Beta(\alpha, \alpha)$. In addition, we performed 10 trials with different random seeds and reported the mean values of the trials. This shows that the generalization performance is higher when the parameter $\alpha$ is a small value. The right side of Fig. 3 shows a plot of the training loss and test loss of the classifier and their differences for each $\alpha$. We can see that when the value of parameter $\alpha$ is small, the difference between train loss and test loss is small. Table 1 shows the effect of the parameter $\alpha$ on the generalization gap between train and test loss for each dataset.

**Table 1.** Effect of the parameter $\alpha$ on the generalization gap between train and test loss for each dataset.

| Dataset | $\alpha = 0.1$ | $\alpha = 0.2$ | $\alpha = 0.4$ | $\alpha = 0.8$ | $\alpha = 1.0$ | $\alpha = 2.0$ | $\alpha = 4.0$ |
|---|---|---|---|---|---|---|---|
| CIFAR10 [4] | **0.006** | 0.012 | 0.010 | 0.061 | 0.093 | 0.098 | 0.130 |
| CIFAR100 [4] | **0.182** | 0.259 | 0.277 | 0.292 | 0.348 | 0.596 | 0.695 |
| STL10 [1] | **0.013** | 0.0215 | 0.029 | 0.090 | 0.121 | 0.120 | 0.169 |
| SVHN [7] | **0.049** | 0.050 | 0.057 | 0.062 | 0.087 | 0.133 | 0.182 |

# 7 Geometric Perspective of Mixup Training: Parameter Space Smoothing

**Definition 5** *(Bregman divergence). For some convex function $\varphi(\cdot)$ and d-dimensional parameter vector $\boldsymbol{\xi} \in \mathbb{R}^d$, the Bregman divergence from $\boldsymbol{\xi}$ to $\boldsymbol{\xi}'$*

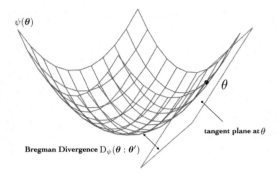

**Fig. 4.** Bregman divergence from $\boldsymbol{\theta}'$ to $\boldsymbol{\theta}$. This divergence derived from the convex function $\psi(\boldsymbol{\theta})$ and its supporting hyperplane with normal vector $\nabla\psi(\boldsymbol{\theta}_0)$.

*is defined as follows:*

$$D_\varphi[\xi : \xi'] = \varphi(\xi) - \varphi(\xi') - \nabla\varphi(\xi') \cdot (\xi - \xi'). \tag{25}$$

**Theorem 4.** *Let $p(\boldsymbol{x};\boldsymbol{\theta})$ be the exponential distribution family that depends on the unknown parameter vector $\boldsymbol{\theta}$. When mixup is applied, the second-order derivative $\nabla\nabla\psi_\lambda(\boldsymbol{\theta})$ of $\psi_\lambda(\boldsymbol{\theta})$ that characterizes the Bregman divergence between the parameter $\theta$ and $\theta + d\theta$, which is a slight change of the parameter, satisfies the following:*

$$\nabla\nabla\psi_\lambda(\boldsymbol{\theta}) = \lambda^2(\nabla\nabla\psi(\boldsymbol{\theta})), \tag{26}$$

*where $\psi(\boldsymbol{\theta})$ is a convex function of the original data distribution and $\lambda \in (0,1)$ is a parameter of the mixup (Fig. 4).*

*Proof.* An exponential family of probability distributions is written as

$$p(\boldsymbol{x};\boldsymbol{\theta}) = \exp\left\{\sum \theta_i x_i + k(\boldsymbol{x}) - \psi(\boldsymbol{\theta})\right\}, \tag{27}$$

where $p(\boldsymbol{x};\boldsymbol{\theta})$ is the probability density function of random variable vector $\boldsymbol{x}$ specified by parameter vector $\boldsymbol{\theta}$ and $k(\boldsymbol{x})$ is a function of $\boldsymbol{x}$. Since $\int p(\boldsymbol{x};\boldsymbol{\theta}) = 1$, the normalization term $\psi(\boldsymbol{\theta})$ can be written as:

$$\psi(\boldsymbol{\theta}) = \log\int \exp\left\{\sum_i \theta_i\, x_i + k(\boldsymbol{x})\right\} d\boldsymbol{x} \tag{28}$$

which is known as the cumulant generating function in statistics. By differentiating (28), we can confirm that the Hessian becomes a positive definite matrix, which means that $\psi(\boldsymbol{\theta})$ is a convex function. Here, the Bregman divergence from $\xi$ to $\xi'$ is defined by using the convex function $\varphi(\xi)$:

$$D_\varphi[\xi : \xi'] = \varphi(\xi) - \varphi(\xi') - \nabla\varphi(\xi') \cdot (\xi - \xi') \tag{29}$$

Let $\psi(\cdot) = \varphi(\cdot)$ and $\boldsymbol{\theta} = \boldsymbol{\xi}$, then we can naturally define the Bregman divergence for $\psi(\cdot)$ and $\boldsymbol{\theta}$. Differentiating (27), we can obtain

$$
0 = \frac{\partial}{\partial \theta_i} \int \exp\left\{ \sum_i \theta_i x_i + k(\boldsymbol{x}) - \psi(\boldsymbol{\theta}) \right\} d\boldsymbol{x}
$$

$$
= \int \left\{ x_i - \frac{\partial}{\partial \theta_i} \psi(\boldsymbol{\theta}) \right\} p(\boldsymbol{x}; \boldsymbol{\theta}) d\boldsymbol{x} = \int x_i p(\boldsymbol{x}; \boldsymbol{\theta}) d\boldsymbol{x} - \frac{\partial}{\partial \theta_i} \psi(\boldsymbol{\theta})
$$

$$
\therefore \frac{\partial}{\partial \theta_i} \psi(\boldsymbol{\theta}) = \int x_i p(\boldsymbol{x}; \boldsymbol{\theta}) d\boldsymbol{x} = \mathbb{E}[x_i]
$$

$$
\nabla \psi(\boldsymbol{x}) = \mathbb{E}[\boldsymbol{x}]. \tag{30}
$$

Differentiating it again,

$$
0 = \int \frac{\partial}{\partial \theta_j} \left\{ x_i - \frac{\partial}{\partial \theta_i} \psi(\boldsymbol{\theta}) \right\} p(\boldsymbol{x}; \boldsymbol{\theta}) + \left\{ x_i - \frac{\partial}{\partial \theta_i} \psi(\boldsymbol{\theta}) \right\} \frac{\partial}{\partial \theta_j} p(\boldsymbol{x}; \boldsymbol{\theta}) d\boldsymbol{x}
$$

$$
= \int -\frac{\partial^2}{\partial \theta_i \partial \theta_j} \psi(\boldsymbol{\theta}) d\boldsymbol{x} + \int \left\{ x_i - \frac{\partial}{\partial \theta_i} \psi(\boldsymbol{\theta}) \right\} \left\{ x_j - \frac{\partial}{\partial \theta_j} \psi(\boldsymbol{\theta}) \right\} p(\boldsymbol{x}; \boldsymbol{\theta}) d\boldsymbol{x}
$$

$$
= -\frac{\partial^2}{\partial \theta_i \partial \theta_j} \psi(\boldsymbol{\theta}) + \int (x_i - \mathbb{E}[x_i])(x_j - \mathbb{E}[x_j]) p(\boldsymbol{x}; \boldsymbol{\theta}) d\boldsymbol{x}
$$

$$
= -\frac{\partial^2}{\partial \theta_i \partial \theta_j} \psi(\boldsymbol{\theta}) + \mathbb{E}[(x_i - \mathbb{E}[x_i])(x_j - \mathbb{E}[x_j])]
$$

$$
\therefore \nabla\nabla \psi(\boldsymbol{\theta}) = Var(\boldsymbol{x}). \tag{31}
$$

Here, if we adopt the linear combination $\tilde{\boldsymbol{x}} = \lambda \boldsymbol{x} + (1-\lambda)\boldsymbol{x}_j$ to find the parameter $\boldsymbol{\theta}$, we can obtain

$$
\nabla \psi_\lambda(\boldsymbol{\theta}) = \mathbb{E}[\tilde{\boldsymbol{x}}] = \mathbb{E}[\lambda \boldsymbol{x} + (1-\lambda)\mathbb{E}[\boldsymbol{x}]] = \mathbb{E}[\boldsymbol{x}], \tag{32}
$$

$$
\nabla\nabla \psi_\lambda(\boldsymbol{\theta}) = Var(\lambda \boldsymbol{x} + (1-\lambda)\mathbb{E}[\boldsymbol{x}])
$$

$$
= \lambda^2 Var(\boldsymbol{x}) + (1-\lambda)^2 Var(\mathbb{E}[\boldsymbol{x}]) = \lambda^2 Var(\boldsymbol{x}) = \lambda^2 \psi(\boldsymbol{\theta}) \tag{33}
$$

where $\psi_\lambda(\cdot)$ is defined by

$$
p(\tilde{\boldsymbol{x}}; \boldsymbol{\theta}) = \exp\left\{ \sum_i \theta_i \tilde{x}_i + k(\tilde{\boldsymbol{x}}) - \psi_\lambda(\boldsymbol{\theta}) \right\}. \tag{34}
$$

From Bayes theorem, we would be computing the probability of a parameter given the likelihood of some data: $p(\tilde{\boldsymbol{x}}; \boldsymbol{\theta}) = \frac{p(\tilde{\boldsymbol{x}}; \boldsymbol{\theta}) p(\boldsymbol{\theta})}{\sum_{\theta} p(\tilde{\boldsymbol{x}}; \boldsymbol{\theta}') p(\boldsymbol{\theta}')}$, and applying mixup means $p(\boldsymbol{x}; \boldsymbol{\theta}) \to p(\tilde{\boldsymbol{x}}; \boldsymbol{\theta})$. And then, we can obtain (26).

Bregman divergence is a generalization of KL-divergence, which is frequently used in probability distribution spaces. The above theorem means that the magnitude of the gradient of the convex function characterizing the Bregman divergence can be smoothed by using the mixup.

# 8    Conclusion and Discussion

In this paper, we provided a theoretical analysis of mixup regularization for linear classifiers and neural networks with ReLU activation functions. Our results show that a theoretical clarification of the effect of the mixup training.

# References

1. Coates, A., Ng, A., Lee, H.: An analysis of single-layer networks in unsupervised feature learning. In: Proceedings of the Fourteenth International Conference on Artificial Intelligence and Statistics, pp. 215–223 (2011)
2. He, K., Zhang, X., Ren, S., Sun, J.: Deep residual learning for image recognition. In: Proceedings of the IEEE Conference on Computer Vision and Pattern Recognition, pp. 770–778 (2016)
3. Kim, J.H., Choo, W., Song, H.O.: Puzzle mix: exploiting saliency and local statistics for optimal mixup. In: International Conference on Machine Learning (ICML) (2020)
4. Krizhevsky, A., Hinton, G., et al.: Learning multiple layers of features from tiny images (2009)
5. Lawrence, S., Giles, C.L.: Overfitting and neural networks: conjugate gradient and backpropagation. In: Proceedings of the IEEE-INNS-ENNS International Joint Conference on Neural Networks. IJCNN 2000. Neural Computing: New Challenges and Perspectives for the New Millennium, vol. 1, pp. 114–119. IEEE (2000)
6. Medennikov, I., et al.: An investigation of mixup training strategies for acoustic models in ASR. In: Interspeech, pp. 2903–2907 (2018)
7. Netzer, Y., Wang, T., Coates, A., Bissacco, A., Wu, B., Ng, A.Y.: Reading digits in natural images with unsupervised feature learning (2011)
8. Neyshabur, B., Tomioka, R., Srebro, N.: Norm-based capacity control in neural networks. In: Conference on Learning Theory, pp. 1376–1401 (2015)
9. Tokozume, Y., Ushiku, Y., Harada, T.: Between-class learning for image classification. In: Proceedings of the IEEE Conference on Computer Vision and Pattern Recognition, pp. 5486–5494 (2018)
10. Verma, V., et al.: Manifold mixup: better representations by interpolating hidden states. In: Chaudhuri, K., Salakhutdinov, R. (eds.) Proceedings of the 36th International Conference on Machine Learning. Proceedings of Machine Learning Research, vol. 97, pp. 6438–6447. PMLR, Long Beach, California, USA (2019). http://proceedings.mlr.press/v97/verma19a.html
11. Xu, K., et al.: Mixup-based acoustic scene classification using multi-channel convolutional neural network. In: Hong, R., Cheng, W.-H., Yamasaki, T., Wang, M., Ngo, C.-W. (eds.) PCM 2018. LNCS, vol. 11166, pp. 14–23. Springer, Cham (2018). https://doi.org/10.1007/978-3-030-00764-5_2
12. Zhang, H., Cisse, M., Dauphin, Y.N., Lopez-Paz, D.: mixup: Beyond empirical risk minimization. In: International Conference on Learning Representations (2018). https://openreview.net/forum?id=r1Ddp1-Rb

# Mixup Gamblers: Learning to Abstain with Auto-Calibrated Reward for Mixed Samples

Takumi Yamaguchi[1,2]([envelope])[iD] and Masahiro Murakawa[1,2][iD]

[1] University of Tsukuba, Tsukuba, Japan
[2] National Institute of Advanced Industrial Science and Technology (AIST),
Tsukuba, Japan
{yamaguchi.t,m.murakawa}@aist.go.jp

**Abstract.** Deep learning models have recently been used in a wide range of fields. However, one of the problems with deep learning is the reliability of the inference results. Models that can evaluate the reliability of their inference results are important, and therefore methods such as selective classification have been proposed. Selective classification is classification with a reject option, which reduces false inferences by allowing an inference to be rejected. Inspired by portfolio theory, L. Ziyin et al. proposed a deep gamblers method that learns to reject. Taking this approach a step further, we propose a learning method for selective classification, *mixup gamblers*, to improve rejection ability. This method exploits data augmentation parameters for rejection learning. The proposed method outperforms existing state-of-the-art methods on a selective classification benchmark.

**Keywords:** Classification with a reject option · Selective classification · Data augmentation · Loss adjustment

## 1 Introduction

In recent years, deep learning has been applied in various fields [2–4,10] because of its ability to perform highly accurate inference using convolutional neural networks (CNNs) [7,8,15]. However, there are some issues regarding the reliability of a model's inference results, such as susceptibility to adversarial examples [12] and tendency to memorize the training data [1]. These problems can lead to an incorrect inference by a model and consequently to the failure of embedded systems based on deep learning models. Therefore, models that can evaluate the reliability of their own inference results are required.

One approach to evaluate prediction results is selective classification [5]. Selective classification refers to classification with a reject option, which enables an inference to be rejected. This method does not make any inferences for samples that are likely to be misclassified. The inference is therefore performed

© Springer Nature Switzerland AG 2021
I. Farkaš et al. (Eds.): ICANN 2021, LNCS 12892, pp. 287–294, 2021.
https://doi.org/10.1007/978-3-030-86340-1_23

only on the samples that are not rejected, thereby improving classification accuracy. Y. Geifman et al. proposed softmax response [6], which adopts the most straightforward policy of using the maximum value after softmax activation as the confidence, and L. Ziyin et al. proposed deep gamblers [17], which learns rejection by adding the $(m + 1)$-th rejection class to an $m$-class classifier.

Deep gamblers is a practically useful model because it can be trained in an end-to-end manner and does not require significant changes in the model structure or complex resampling during inference. In this approach, the rejection class is trained with a rejection reward, which is a hyperparameter. Thus, the value of the rejection reward must be adjusted using validation data. This is a problem because the quality of the validation data determines the performance of the model. It is therefore necessary to conduct a large number of trials to determine the optimal rejection reward. Another problem is that the rejection reward is constant for all samples. Essentially, every sample has a different level of inference difficulty. Therefore, the rejection reward should also vary.

To tackle the aforementioned problems, we propose a learning method that adjusts the rejection reward for each sample. We need to determine the rejection reward for each sample to use this method for model training. Thus, we must increase the rejection reward so that difficult samples are rejected and also decrease the rejection reward so that easy samples are not rejected. However, humans cannot determine the rejection reward for each sample because the difficulty of inferring a sample is not the same for deep learning models and humans. To solve this problem, we propose an auto-calibration of the rejection reward using mixup data augmentation. In mixup data augmentation [16], new data are generated by linearly combining two training samples weighted by the mixup ratio $\lambda$. We assume that the mixup ratio is correlated with the difficulty of inference. On the basis of this assumption, we propose using the mixup ratio to tune the rejection reward during training. The rejection reward is the highest when the mixup ratio is 0.5 because this generated sample can be the most difficult to infer, and it decreases as the mixup ratio deviates from 0.5. Thus, we exploit the mixup ratio to adjust the rejection reward automatically for each sample. The proposed method outperforms existing state-of-the-art methods on a selective classification task on the CIFAR-10 dataset [11], achieving an error rate of less than 1% with 85% test coverage.

The remainder of this paper is structured as follows. We introduce the related studies in Sect. 2, then propose our method in Sect. 3. The proposed method's effectiveness is evaluated in Sect. 4. A summary of this study is given in Sect. 5.

## 2    Related Work

### 2.1    Selective Classification

Selective classification generally has a trade-off between classifier accuracy and predictive coverage, which is the fraction of samples in a dataset that can be inferred. A model with a low error rate at a high level of coverage is ideal. However, the coverage will be lower if only samples that can be inferred with high confidence are inferred to increase the classification accuracy. In contrast, the coverage will be higher if the classification accuracy is sacrificed by inferring samples that can only be inferred with low confidence. In selective classification, the trade-off between coverage and accuracy is used to control the error rate by adjusting the coverage.

Let $X$ be the input space and $Y$ be the label space. A prediction model $f : X \rightarrow Y$ and a selection function $g : X \rightarrow \mathbb{R}$ are defined. The selective prediction model $(f, g)$ makes inferences on $D$-dimensional input feature $\boldsymbol{x} \in \mathbb{R}^D$ only when the predicted value of $g(\boldsymbol{x})$ exceeds the threshold $h$, and it rejects inferences in other cases as follows.

$$(f, g)(\boldsymbol{x}) = \begin{cases} f(\boldsymbol{x}), & g(\boldsymbol{x}) \geq h \\ \text{ABSTAIN}, & \text{otherwise} \end{cases} \tag{1}$$

## 2.2    Softmax Response

Softmax response is a baseline method for selective classification. It adopts the most straightforward policy of using the maximum value after softmax activation as the confidence level. Because it does not explicitly learn to reject results, there is no change in the learning process. The selection function, $g_{sr}$, is defined as follows

$$\hat{\boldsymbol{p}} = f(\boldsymbol{x}) \tag{2}$$

$$g_{sr}(\boldsymbol{x}) = \max_j \hat{\boldsymbol{p}}_j \tag{3}$$

where $\hat{\boldsymbol{p}} \in [0, 1]^m$ is the $m$-class classification model's prediction that satisfies $\sum_{i=1}^m \hat{\boldsymbol{p}}_i = 1$.

## 2.3    Deep Gamblers

Deep gamblers extends the $m$-class classification to $(m + 1)$-class classification and designates the $(m + 1)$-th class as an "abstain" class. It uses a loss function based on the doubling rate of gambling, inspired by portfolio theory [13]. In this method, the reward for rejection is given as a hyperparameter, and the rejection class is learned accordingly; that is, the value of the rejection reward must be adjusted using validation data.

Let $\hat{\boldsymbol{p}} \in [0, 1]^{(m+1)}$ be the model's prediction and rejection score $(\hat{\boldsymbol{p}}_{m+1})$ that satisfies $\sum_{i=1}^{(m+1)} \hat{\boldsymbol{p}}_i = 1$ and $\boldsymbol{p} \in [0, 1]^m$ be the target vector. The selection function $g_{dg}$ and loss function $L_{dg}$ are expressed as follows.

$$g_{dg}(\boldsymbol{x}) = 1 - \hat{\boldsymbol{p}}_{m+1} \tag{4}$$

$$L_{dg}(\hat{\boldsymbol{p}}|\boldsymbol{p}) = -\sum_{i=1}^m \boldsymbol{p}_i \log \left( \hat{\boldsymbol{p}}_i + \frac{1}{o}\hat{\boldsymbol{p}}_{m+1} \right) \tag{5}$$

The hyperparameter $o \in [1, m]$ is the rejection reward through training, and it needs to be tuned to the dataset.

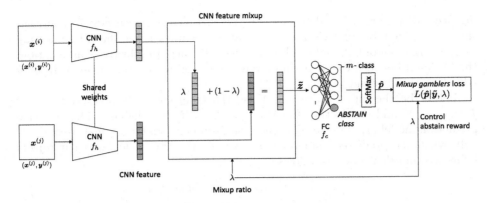

**Fig. 1.** Overview of proposed *mixup gamblers*

The problem with this approach is that the rejection reward is constant for all samples. Because humans cannot determine the rejection reward for each sample, the only way to learn rejection is to use the predictor's output as a cue under a constant rejection reward. However, keeping the rejection reward constant throughout training means that both difficult and easy samples are used for training with the same rejection reward, which does not reflect reality.

### 2.4  Mixup Augmentation

Mixup augmentation is a recent data augmentation technique. It creates a new training sample using a linear combination of two data points. A training sample is created by adding two samples weighted by the mixup ratio $\lambda \in [0, 1]$. The generalization and robustness of CNNs are improved by learning the linearly interpolated training samples. The mixup data augmentation is done by

$$\tilde{x} = \lambda x^{(i)} + (1 - \lambda)x^{(j)} \tag{6}$$

$$\tilde{y} = \lambda y^{(i)} + (1 - \lambda)y^{(j)} \tag{7}$$

where $x^{(i)} \in \mathbb{R}^D$ and $y^{(i)} \in [0, 1]^m$ denote input feature and target vector at $i$-th sample. $(x^{(i)}, y^{(i)})$ and $(x^{(j)}, y^{(j)})$ $(i \neq j)$ are two input-target pairs from training samples.

## 3  Proposed Method

Our aim is to improve the rejection performance by learning while adjusting the rejection reward for each sample. In this study, we introduce two key components for determining the rejection reward: 1) mixup augmentation of the samples and 2) mixup at the CNN feature level. An overview of the proposed method is shown in Fig. 1. The learning algorithm is given in Algorithm 1.

**Algorithm 1.** Training procedure of *mixup gamblers*

---

**Input:** Sample batch $X$, Target batch $Y$, Batch size $b$, CNN feature extractor $f_h$ with parameters $\theta_h$, Fully Connected layer $f_c$ with parameters $\theta_c$, learning rate $\eta$, a range of $\lambda$ from $\lambda_{min} > 0$ to $\lambda_{max} < 1$ steps by $\lambda_s$, *mixup gamblers* loss function $L(\hat{p}|\tilde{y}, \lambda)$

**Output:** Model parameters $\theta_h$, $\theta_c$

1:  $X', Y' \leftarrow \text{RandomShuffle}(X, Y)$                     ▷ Shuffle batch for mixup pairs
2:  $\mathcal{L} \leftarrow 0$
3:  **for** $\lambda = \lambda_{min}$ **to** $\lambda_{max}$ **steps by** $\lambda_s$ **do**
4:      **for** $i = 1$ **to** $b$ **do**
5:          $\boldsymbol{x} \leftarrow X[i], \boldsymbol{x}' \leftarrow X'[i]$            ▷ $D$-dimensional input feature $\boldsymbol{x} \in \mathbb{R}^D$
6:          $\boldsymbol{y} \leftarrow Y[i], \boldsymbol{y}' \leftarrow Y'[i]$               ▷ $m$-class target vector $\boldsymbol{y} \in [0, 1]^m$
7:          $\tilde{z} \leftarrow \lambda f_h(\boldsymbol{x}) + (1 - \lambda) f_h(\boldsymbol{x}')$         ▷ Mixup in CNN feature
8:          $\tilde{\boldsymbol{y}} \leftarrow \lambda \boldsymbol{y} + (1 - \lambda) \boldsymbol{y}'$             ▷ New target for mixed feature
9:          $\hat{\boldsymbol{p}} \leftarrow f_c(\tilde{z})$                      ▷ Classify on mixed feature
10:         $\mathcal{L} \leftarrow \mathcal{L} + L(\hat{\boldsymbol{p}}|\tilde{\boldsymbol{y}}, \lambda)/b$           ▷ Summarize the loss
11:     **end for**
12: **end for**
13: $\theta_h \leftarrow \theta_h - \eta \nabla_{\theta_h} \mathcal{L}$
14: $\theta_c \leftarrow \theta_c - \eta \nabla_{\theta_c} \mathcal{L}$

### 3.1 Calibrating the Rejection Reward Utilizing Mixup Augmentation

We use mixup data augmentation to control the difficulty of the generated samples. When mixing ratio $\lambda = 0.5$, the difficulty of classification is the highest, and as the value of $\lambda$ deviates from 0.5, the difficulty decreases. Thus, the value of $\lambda$ is correlated with the difficulty of classification. Therefore, we propose *mixup gamblers*, a mechanism for learning to abstain in a supervised manner by using mixup to generate samples with controlled difficulty. Let the binary entropy function $H(\lambda)$ be the rejection reward for a mixup ratio $\lambda$. In other words, when the mixup ratio is close to 0.5, the rejection reward increases, and as the mixing ratio deviates from 0.5, the rejection reward decreases. The rejection performance should improve because the model learns by adjusting the rejection reward for each sample. In addition, mixup data augmentation encourages the learning of the linear interpolation of two data points, which should improve the classifier accuracy.

### 3.2 CNN Feature Mixup

For *mixup gamblers* to work, the intermediate feature of the CNN should be mixed up instead of the pixel feature. In our proposed learning method, augmenting in an abstract feature space is essential.

Let $Z$ be the hidden feature space extracted by CNNs. The prediction function $f : X \rightarrow Y$ can be divided into two functions, the CNN feature extractor $f_h : X \rightarrow Z$ and the classifier $f_c : Z \rightarrow Y$. Thus, our proposed CNN feature mixup is represented as follows

**Table 1.** Selective classification error rate (%) on the CIFAR-10 dataset at various test coverage levels. CF: CNN feature mixup, P: Pixel feature mixup, mixup+SR: softmax response with pixel feature mixup training without gamblers loss, SA: Self-Adaptive Training, DG: deep gamblers, SR: softmax response.

| Coverage (%) | Ours (CF) | Ours (P) | mixup+SR | SA | DG | SR |
|---|---|---|---|---|---|---|
| 100 | 5.28 ± 0.10 | **4.75 ± 0.17** | 5.48 ± 0.14 | 6.05 ± 0.20 | 6.12 ± 0.09 | 6.79 ± 0.03 |
| 95 | **3.20 ± 0.15** | 4.33 ± 0.19 | **3.18 ± 0.18** | 3.37 ± 0.05 | 3.49 ± 0.15 | 4.55 ± 0.07 |
| 90 | **1.69 ± 0.10** | 4.26 ± 0.29 | **1.64 ± 0.11** | 1.93 ± 0.09 | 2.19 ± 0.12 | 2.89 ± 0.03 |
| 85 | **0.86 ± 0.07** | 4.24 ± 0.28 | 1.02 ± 0.13 | 1.15 ± 0.18 | 1.09 ± 0.15 | 1.78 ± 0.09 |
| 80 | **0.51 ± 0.06** | 4.30 ± 0.31 | 0.94 ± 0.10 | 0.67 ± 0.10 | 0.66 ± 0.11 | 1.05 ± 0.07 |
| 75 | **0.42 ± 0.11** | 4.38 ± 0.35 | 0.92 ± 0.06 | **0.44 ± 0.03** | 0.52 ± 0.03 | 0.63 ± 0.04 |
| 70 | **0.39 ± 0.14** | 4.41 ± 0.39 | 0.89 ± 0.10 | **0.34 ± 0.06** | 0.43 ± 0.07 | 0.42 ± 0.06 |

$$\tilde{z} = \lambda f_h(x^{(i)}) + (1 - \lambda) f_h(x^{(j)}) \tag{8}$$

$$\hat{p} = f_c(\tilde{z}) \tag{9}$$

where $\hat{p} \in [0, 1]^{(m+1)}$ denotes the output prediction of the model in $m$-class classification and rejection that satisfies $\sum_{i=1}^{(m+1)} \hat{p}_i = 1$.

Finally, we propose the *mixup gamblers* loss function.

$$L(\hat{p}|\tilde{y}, \lambda) = -\sum_{i=1}^{m} \tilde{y}_i \log \left( \hat{p}_i + \frac{1}{1 + H(\lambda)(m - 1)} \hat{p}_{m+1} \right) \tag{10}$$

$$H(\lambda) = -\lambda \log_2 \lambda - (1 - \lambda) \log_2(1 - \lambda) \tag{11}$$

Here, $\tilde{y} \in [0, 1]^m$ denotes the target vector generated by mixup that satisfies $\sum_{i=1}^{m} \tilde{y}_i = 1$. In addition, we sum up losses with several mixup ratio $\lambda \in [0, 1]$ and optimize a model to minimize the total loss.

## 4    Experiments

In this section, we demonstrate the effectiveness of the proposed method through comparative experiments on the selective classification task. For a fair comparison, the experiments were conducted under the same conditions used in previous studies. We used an open-source script[1] by [17] and modified the loss function in the training phase. We used a VGG16 [15] with batch normalization and dropout for training and evaluation. We optimized the model using stochastic gradient descent with an initial learning rate of 0.1, momentum of 0.9, weight decay of 0.0005, batch size of 128, and a total of 300 training epochs. Furthermore, the learning rate decayed by a factor of 0.5 every 25 epochs. We report the mean and standard deviation of each model's performance over three trials on the CIFAR-10 and SVHN [14] datasets for each level of coverage. In both experiments, we trained the model on classification for 100 epochs before training with

---

[1] https://github.com/Z-T-WANG/NIPS2019DeepGamblers.

**Table 2.** Selective classification error rate (%) on the SVHN dataset at various test coverage levels.

| Coverage (%) | Ours (CF) | DG | SR |
|---|---|---|---|
| 100 | **2.75 ± 0.08** | 3.24 ± 0.09 | 3.21 |
| 95 | **1.26 ± 0.06** | 1.36 ± 0.02 | 1.39 |
| 90 | 1.02 ± 0.01 | **0.76 ± 0.05** | 0.89 |
| 85 | 0.91 ± 0.09 | **0.57 ± 0.07** | 0.70 |
| 80 | 0.86 ± 0.10 | **0.51 ± 0.05** | 0.61 |

the proposed method. We set the mixup ratio $\lambda$ to a range of $\lambda_{min} = 0.05$ to $\lambda_{max} = 0.5$ steps by $\lambda_s = 0.05$.

The results of the experiment are shown in Table 1 and Table 2, and the results of prior methods are cited from the original papers [6,9,17]. The proposed method with CNN features outperforms state-of-the-art methods for most levels of test coverage. In particular, we achieved an error rate of less than 1% at 85% test coverage in CIFAR-10. However, the rejection class was not learned properly when pixel feature mixup was used. This implies that an abstract mixup at the CNN feature level is essential component in the proposed method.

## 5    Conclusion

We studied a learning method to output a confidence for the reliability of the self-evaluation of inference results. We proposed *mixup gamblers*, which learns to reject inference results from data augmentation parameters. The key concept of *mixup gamblers* is that the mixing ratio of the mixup data augmentation is assumed to indicate the inference difficulty of a generated sample. In the proposed method, when to reject a result is learned by adjusting the rejection reward based on the mixup ratio. Additionally, we proposed using a CNN's intermediate features instead of pixel feature for the mixup data augmentation in the *mixup gamblers* method. Using the proposed method, we achieved state-of-the-art performance in the selective classification task.

Another possible application of the proposed method is to detect unknown classes. In the proposed method, mixup is performed with features abstracted into a class-like feature space; therefore, it can be regarded as learning to reject unknown classes that are not included in the training class. We expect to contribute to the efficiency of human-in-the-loop systems, which involve humans in the machine learning cycle, by improving the detection of unknown classes.

**Acknowledgments.** This paper is partly based on results obtained from a project, JPNP20006, commissioned by the New Energy and Industrial Technology Development Organization (NEDO).

# References

1. Arpit, D., et al.: A closer look at memorization in deep networks. In: International Conference on Machine Learning, pp. 233–242. PMLR (2017)
2. Bojarski, M., et al.: End to end learning for self-driving cars. arXiv preprint arXiv:1604.07316 (2016)
3. Cireşan, D.C., Giusti, A., Gambardella, L.M., Schmidhuber, J.: Mitosis detection in breast cancer histology images with deep neural networks. In: Mori, K., Sakuma, I., Sato, Y., Barillot, C., Navab, N. (eds.) MICCAI 2013. LNCS, vol. 8150, pp. 411–418. Springer, Heidelberg (2013). https://doi.org/10.1007/978-3-642-40763-5_51
4. Clanuwat, T., Bober-Irizar, M., Kitamoto, A., Lamb, A., Yamamoto, K., Ha, D.: Deep learning for classical Japanese literature. arXiv preprint arXiv:1812.01718 (2018)
5. El-Yaniv, R., et al.: On the foundations of noise-free selective classification. J. Mach. Learn. Res. 11(5), 1605–1641 (2010)
6. Geifman, Y., El-Yaniv, R.: Selective classification for deep neural networks. In: Advances in Neural Information Processing Systems, vol. 30, pp. 4878–4887 (2017)
7. He, K., Zhang, X., Ren, S., Sun, J.: Deep residual learning for image recognition. In: Proceedings of the IEEE Conference on Computer Vision and Pattern Recognition (CVPR), June 2016
8. Huang, G., Liu, Z., Van Der Maaten, L., Weinberger, K.Q.: Densely connected convolutional networks. In: Proceedings of the IEEE Conference on Computer Vision and Pattern Recognition, pp. 4700–4708 (2017)
9. Huang, L., Zhang, C., Zhang, H.: Self-adaptive training: beyond empirical risk minimization. In: Advances in Neural Information Processing Systems, vol. 33 (2020)
10. Karpathy, A., Toderici, G., Shetty, S., Leung, T., Sukthankar, R., Fei-Fei, L.: Large-scale video classification with convolutional neural networks. In: Proceedings of the IEEE Conference on Computer Vision and Pattern Recognition, pp. 1725–1732 (2014)
11. Krizhevsky, A.: Learning multiple layers of features from tiny images (2009)
12. Kurakin, A., Goodfellow, I., Bengio, S., et al.: Adversarial examples in the physical world (2016)
13. Markowitz, H.: Portfolio selection (1959)
14. Netzer, Y., Wang, T., Coates, A., Bissacco, A., Wu, B., Ng, A.Y.: Reading digits in natural images with unsupervised feature learning (2011)
15. Simonyan, K., Zisserman, A.: Very deep convolutional networks for large-scale image recognition. arXiv preprint arXiv:1409.1556 (2014)
16. Zhang, H., Cisse, M., Dauphin, Y.N., Lopez-Paz, D.: mixup: Beyond empirical risk minimization. arXiv preprint arXiv:1710.09412 (2017)
17. Ziyin, L., Wang, Z., Liang, P., Salakhutdinov, R., Morency, L., Ueda, M.: Deep gamblers: learning to abstain with portfolio theory. In: Proceedings of the Neural Information Processing Systems Conference (2019)

# Non-iterative Phase Retrieval with Cascaded Neural Networks

Tobias Uelwer$^{(\boxtimes)}$, Tobias Hoffmann, and Stefan Harmeling

Department of Computer Science, Heinrich Heine University, Düsseldorf, Germany
{tobias.uelwer,tobias.hoffmann,stefan.harmeling}@hhu.de

**Abstract.** Fourier phase retrieval is the problem of recovering an image given only the magnitude of its Fourier transformation. Optimization-based approaches, like the well-established Gerchberg-Saxton or the hybrid input output algorithm, struggle at reconstructing images from magnitudes that are not oversampled. This motivates the application of learned methods, which allow reconstruction from non-oversampled magnitude measurements after a learning phase. In this paper, we want to push the limits of these learned methods by means of a deep neural network cascade that reconstructs the image successively on different resolutions from its non-oversampled Fourier magnitude. We evaluate our method on four different datasets (MNIST, EMNIST, Fashion-MNIST, and KMNIST) and demonstrate that it yields improved performance over other non-iterative methods and optimization-based methods.

**Keywords:** Phase retrieval · Neural network cascade · Deep learning

## 1 Introduction

The two-dimensional discrete Fourier transform $\mathcal{F}(x)$ of an image $x \in \mathbb{R}^{n \times n}$ can be represented by the magnitude $\omega$ and the phase $\varphi$, more precisely

$$\omega = |\mathcal{F}(x)| \in \mathbb{R}^{n \times n}, \tag{1}$$

$$\varphi = \arg \mathcal{F}(x) \in [-\pi, \pi]^{n \times n}, \tag{2}$$

where arg denotes the argument of a complex number (that is applied element-wise). Fourier phase retrieval is the problem of reconstructing the original image only from its magnitude $\omega$.

While zero-padding is often assumed, it is a strong assumption on the support of $x$ which facilitates the phase retrieval problem. Concretely, it assumes that we are reconstructing an $m \times m$ image

$$x_{\text{padded}} = \begin{bmatrix} x & 0_{n,m-n} \\ 0_{m-n,n} & 0_{m-n,m-n} \end{bmatrix} \in \mathbb{R}^{m \times m}, \tag{3}$$

where the $0_{a,b}$ denotes the $a \times b$ matrix with zeros. The oversampled magnitude can then be written as

$$\omega_{\text{oversampled}} = |\mathcal{F}(x_{\text{padded}})| \in \mathbb{R}^{m \times m}. \tag{4}$$

© Springer Nature Switzerland AG 2021
I. Farkaš et al. (Eds.): ICANN 2021, LNCS 12892, pp. 295–306, 2021.
https://doi.org/10.1007/978-3-030-86340-1_24

For example, given $m = 2n$, the magnitude is oversampled by a factor of four when considering the two-dimensional case. There exist algorithms, e.g., the Gerchberg-Saxton algorithm [6] or Fienup's hybrid input-output algorithm [5], that are able to reconstruct the image from the magnitude that is oversampled by a factor of four. However, in practice the true images to be recovered are not zero-padded and the magnitude is almost never oversampled. So the assumption of zero-padding does not hold in general, as many applications measure the non-oversampled magnitude (i.e., $m = n$) posing a great challenge for existing phase retrievals methods. In this paper, we try to solve the more difficult problem, where we reconstruct the image from the non-oversampled magnitude $\omega$.

### 1.1    The Phase Contains the Relevant Information

It is well known, that the phase contains most of the information of the image. This can be observed by comparing an image with a random phase to an image with a random magnitude. To create these images we exchange (i) the phase of an image by a random phase $\tilde{\varphi}$ which has entries that were uniformly sampled from $[-\pi, \pi]$ while respecting the symmetries of the phase (to ensure a real-valued image), and (ii) the magnitude with a random magnitude $\tilde{\omega}$ that has been sampled from a truncated normal distribution with appropriate parameters. To create an image given the random phase $\tilde{\varphi}$ and the correct magnitude $\omega$, we apply the relationship

$$x_{\tilde{\varphi}} = \mathcal{F}^{-1}\left(\omega \odot \exp(i\tilde{\varphi})\right), \tag{5}$$

where $\mathcal{F}^{-1}$ is the inverse Fourier transform, $i = \sqrt{-1}$ is the imaginary unit and $\odot$ is the elementwise multiplication. Analogously, we construct the image with the original phase $\varphi$ and a random magnitude $\tilde{\omega}$ as

$$x_{\tilde{\omega}} = \mathcal{F}^{-1}\left(\tilde{\omega} \odot \exp(i\varphi)\right). \tag{6}$$

Figure 1 shows that the image with the random phase is completely destroyed whereas the image with the random magnitude only exhibits some cloud-like artifacts.

### 1.2    Non-iterative Phase Retrieval

To tackle the non-oversampled phase retrieval problem we formulate phase retrieval as a learning problem. Concretely, non-iterative phase retrieval directly recovers the image from the magnitude only using a mapping that has been learned to solve the problem in a particular problem domain. The mapping is parameterized by a neural network $G$ that is trained to invert the measurement process, i.e.,

$$\hat{x} \approx G(\omega). \tag{7}$$

Since the measurement process is known, training pairs can be generated on-the-fly from sample images of a given dataset. The weights of $G$ can then be learned using stochastic gradient descent by minimizing a loss function. The benefit

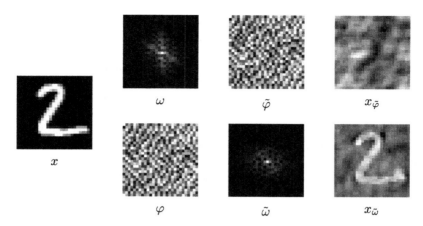

**Fig. 1.** Most information about the image is contained in the phase, which can be demonstrated by exchanging the phase with a random phase. For comparison we also exchange the magnitude with a random magnitude. Original image $x$, original magnitude $\omega$, random phase $\tilde{\varphi}$, image obtained by combining the original magnitude and the random phase $x_{\tilde{\varphi}}$, original phase $\varphi$, random magnitude $\tilde{\omega}$, image obtained by combining the original phase and the random magnitude $x_{\tilde{\omega}}$.

of non-iterative methods is the fast computation of the reconstruction because only a single forward-pass through the neural network is used to calculate the reconstruction.

### 1.3 Contributions

This paper addresses the challenge of improving the performance of non-iterative phase retrieval methods based on neural networks. We show that a multi-scale approach based on cascading neural networks is able to improve previous non-iterative phase retrieval methods.

### 1.4 Related Work

Cascades of neural networks have been proposed previously by Schlemper et al. [19] but in the context of compressed sensing which is a related but different problem than phase retrieval. Phase retrieval has applications in many areas of research, e.g., in X-ray crystallography [15], astronomical imaging [5] or microscopy [25]. We distinguish between three classes of methods for phase retrieval:

1. Iterative methods without a learned component: Gerchberg and Saxton [6] proposed a simple algorithm that is based on alternating reflections. The idea behind this algorithm is to iteratively enforce the constraints in the Fourier space and the image space. Later Fienup modified the Gerchberg-Saxton algorithm in different ways which led to the input-output, the output-output

and the hybrid-input-output (HIO) algorithm [4], where the HIO algorithm is most commonly used for phase retrieval. Luke [12] analyzed the relaxed averaged alternating reflection (RAAR) algorithm. In general, these iterative methods without a learning component work well when the signal is oversampled.

2. Iterative methods with a learned component: For non-oversampled phase retrieval Işıl et al. [9] extend the HIO algorithm by a neural network that removes artifacts. Metzler et al. [14] and Wu et al. [23] use the regularization-by-denoising framework [18] to solve oversampled phase retrieval problems. Another class of learned methods rely on the optimization of a latent variable of a learned generative model [7,21] and produce high quality results. However, these methods require a training phase and an optimization phase during application and are therefore very costly.

3. Non-iterative methods with a learned component: Non-iterative phase retrieval with a deep convolutional neural network that is trained end-to-end is proposed by Nishizaki et al. [16]. Recently, Tayal et al. [13] use symmetry breaking to solve the oversampled phase retrieval problem with neural networks. The benefit of non-iterative learned methods is the highly efficient reconstruction of images using only a single forward-pass through the model while also producing good results in the non-oversampled case.

## 2    Proposed Method

In this paper, we propose to use a cascaded neural network architecture for Fourier phase retrieval. Throughout the paper we refer to it as cascaded phase retrieval (CPR) network. The CPR network consists of multiple sub-networks $G^{(1)}, \ldots, G^{(q)}$ which are updated successively to reconstruct the different down-sampled instances of the original image, where $G^{(2)}, \ldots, G^{(q)}$ are fed with the intermediate reconstruction produced by the previous network. In that way, each of these sub-networks can iteratively refine the reconstruction. In addition to that, each of the sub-networks is provided with the measurement $\omega$ as an input. The first few sub-networks are trained to reconstruct a down-sampled version of the image, where we denote the resolutions by $n_p \times n_p$ for $p = 1, \ldots, q$. The last sub-networks predict the image at full-resolution $n_q \times n_q$. The nearest-neighbor interpolation scheme is used for down-sampling the training images. Figure 2 shows an overview of the CPR network architecture.

### 2.1    Loss Functions

A common choice for reconstruction tasks is the mean squared error (MSE) which can be defined for a batch $X = (x_1, \ldots, x_b)$ of original images and a corresponding batch of reconstructions $\hat{X} = (\hat{x}_1, \ldots, \hat{x}_b)$ as

$$\mathcal{L}_{\mathrm{MSE}}^{(p)}(X, \hat{X}) = \frac{1}{b} \frac{1}{n_p^2} \sum_{k=1}^{b} \sum_{u=1}^{n_p} \sum_{v=1}^{n_p} (x_k[u,v] - \hat{x}_k[u,v])^2. \tag{8}$$

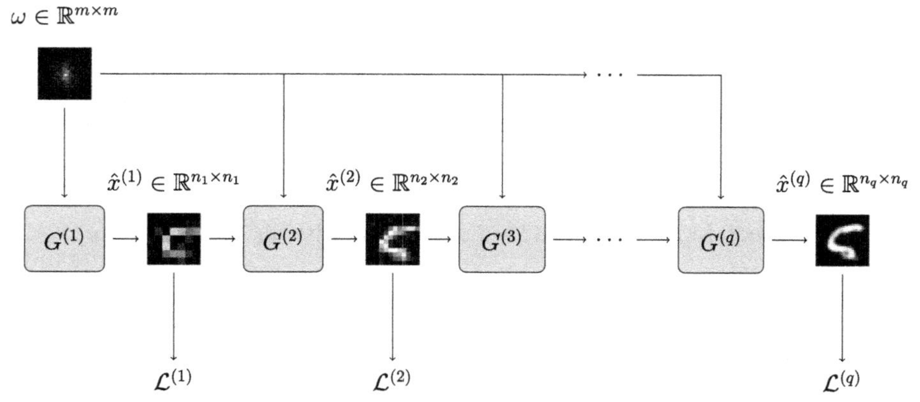

$\omega \in \mathbb{R}^{m \times m}$

**Fig. 2.** An overview of the network architecture of the CPR approach. The magnitude image is fed to each of the networks. The sub-networks are updated stage-wise, i.e., we use $\mathcal{L}_1$ to update $G^{(1)}$, then the output of $G^{(1)}$ is passed as additional input to $G^{(2)}$ and so on. The first few networks focus on reconstructing a sub-sampled instance of the image, whereas the last sub-network predict the image at full-resolution.

Although, it seems to work well in practice and provides good gradients for training, the reconstructions tend to be blurry. This phenomenon has been discussed in [17]. Hence, we also implement the mean absolute error (MAE), i.e.,

$$\mathcal{L}_{\text{MAE}}^{(p)}(X, \hat{X}) = \frac{1}{b} \frac{1}{n_p^2} \sum_{k=1}^{b} \sum_{u=1}^{n_p} \sum_{v=1}^{n_p} |x_k[u, v] - \hat{x}_k[u, v]| \tag{9}$$

for measuring the reconstruction error.

## 2.2 Training

During training, each sub-network $G^{(p)}$ is trained using an individual loss $\mathcal{L}^{(p)}$. Each sub-network is updated one after another, where the loss $\mathcal{L}^{(p)}$ influences only $G^{(p)}$ and does not impact the parameters of the previous sub-networks. Alternatively, the CPR network could be trained in an end-to-end fashion, however, since the intermediate reconstructions have different resolutions, we would need to carefully choose weights to balance the influence of each loss function $\mathcal{L}^{(1)}, \ldots, \mathcal{L}^{(q)}$. The training procedure is shown in more detail in Algorithm 1.

---

**Algorithm 1:** Training algorithm for CPR network

**Input**: Dataset $X$, downsampling functions $g_2, \ldots, g_q$, networks $G_1, \ldots, G_q$, loss functions $\mathcal{L}^{(1)}, \ldots, \mathcal{L}^{(q)}$

1  **for** $e = 1, \ldots, N$ **do**
2    **for** batch $(x_1, \ldots, x_b)$ in $X$ **do**
3       Calculate magnitudes $\Omega = (\omega_1, \ldots, \omega_b)$ with $\omega_k = |\mathcal{F}(x_k)|$, for $k = 1, \ldots, b$
4       **for** $p = 1, \ldots, q$ **do**
5          Calculate $\tilde{X}^{(p)} = (\tilde{x}_1, \tilde{x}_2, \ldots, \tilde{x}_b)$, where $\tilde{x}_k = g_p(x_k)$ for $k = 1, \ldots, b$
6          **if** $p == 1$ **then**
7             $\hat{X}^{(p)} = G_p(\Omega)$
8          **else**
9             $\hat{X}^{(p)} = G_p(\Omega, \hat{X}^{(p-1)})$
10         Update network parameters using $\nabla\mathcal{L}^{(p)}\left(\hat{X}^{(p)}, \tilde{X}^{(p)}\right)$
11       **end**
12    **end**
13 **end**

---

## 3 Experimental Evaluation

In this section, we empirically evaluate the performance of our model. In order to do this, we report the results of the fully-convolutional residual network (ResNet) employed by Nishizaki et al. [16], the multi-layer-perceptron (MLP) used in [21] and the PRCGAN [21]. In addition to these learned networks we include the results of the well-established HIO algorithm [4] and the RAAR algorithm [12] as a baseline.

### 3.1 Datasets

For the experimental evaluation we use the MNIST [11], the EMNIST [3], the Fashion-MNIST [24] and the KMNIST [2] datasets. All datasets consist of $28 \times 28$ grayscale images, i.e., $n = 28$. MNIST contains images of digits, EMNIST contains images of letters and digits, Fashion-MNIST contains images of clothing and KMNIST contains images of cursive Japanese characters. Although these datasets are considered to be toy datasets when it comes to classification tasks, they provide quite challenging data for two-dimensional Fourier phase retrieval. For the EMNIST dataset we use the balanced version of the dataset.

## 3.2   Experimental Setup

We compare our CPR approach with the MLP and the ResNet that are trained to minimize $\mathcal{L}_{\mathrm{MSE}}$ for the MNIST, the EMNIST and the KMNIST dataset. The $\mathcal{L}_{\mathrm{MAE}}$ is used for the Fashion-MNIST dataset. Furthermore, we report the results of an MLP trained with an adversarial loss in combination with $\mathcal{L}_{\mathrm{MAE}}$ (PRCGAN) as proposed in [21]. For our proposed CPR network we consider a cascade of five MLPs with three hidden layers where we increased the scales of the (intermediate) reconstructions according to Table 1. The number of hidden units for each sub-network is also shown in Table 1. Furthermore, we compare the results with a CPR network that produces intermediate reconstructions at full scale. We refer to this variant as CPR-FS. All sub-networks are trained using dropout [20], batch-normalization [8] and ReLU activation functions. For the last layer we use a Sigmoid function to ensure that the predicted pixels are in $[0, 1]$. To optimize the weights we used Adam [10] with learning rate $10^{-4}$. We train all versions of the CPR network for 100 epochs with the $\mathcal{L}_{\mathrm{MSE}}$, except for the Fashion-MNIST dataset where we use $\mathcal{L}_{\mathrm{MAE}}$ for the final layer. These choices gave the best results on the validation dataset.

We ran the HIO algorithm and the RAAR algorithm for 1000 steps each and allowed three random restarts, where we selected the reconstruction $\hat{x}$ with the lowest magnitude error $|||\mathcal{F}(\hat{x})| - \omega||_{\mathrm{Fro}}$. For HIO we set $\beta = 0.8$ and for RAAR we set $\beta = 0.87$.

**Table 1.** Scales used for the (intermediate) reconstructions and number of hidden units used for each network of the cascade.

|  |  | $G^{(1)}$ | $G^{(2)}$ | $G^{(3)}$ | $G^{(4)}$ | $G^{(5)}$ |
|---|---|---|---|---|---|---|
| Scale | CPR | $7 \times 7$ | $12 \times 12$ | $17 \times 17$ | $22 \times 22$ | $28 \times 28$ |
|  | CPR-FS | $28 \times 28$ | $28 \times 28$ | $28 \times 28$ | $28 \times 28$ | $28 \times 28$ |
| Hidden layer size | CPR | 1136 | 1336 | 1536 | 1736 | 1936 |
|  | CPR-FS | 1936 | 1936 | 1936 | 1936 | 1936 |

## 3.3   Metrics

For a quantitative evaluation we compare the MSE and the MAE as defined in Eq. 8 and Eq. 9. Moreover, we report the structural similarity index (SSIM) that was introduced by Wang et al. [22]. The SSIM measures perceived quality of an reconstruction on various windows of an image and takes values between 0 (worst quality) and 1 (perfect reconstruction).

Because translating signals by a constant shift or rotating them by $180°$ does not change their Fourier magnitude, we considered these reconstructions equally correct. Thus, we register the predictions (and their rotated variants) using cross-correlation as described by Brown [1] before calculating the evaluation metrics.

## 3.4 Results

Figure 3 compares six reconstructions by the different methods on the MNIST and the Fashion-MNIST test dataset. We observe that the HIO algorithm and the RAAR algorithm fail to recover the image in most of the cases. From all learned methods, the Resnet produced the worst reconstructions. The estimated images are very blurry and in some cases the reconstruction exhibit deformations (e.g., the last two images from the Fashion-MNIST dataset that are shown in Fig. 3). The PRCGAN produces reconstructions that are sharp and overall the visual quality is similar to the reconstructions of the MLP. Most of the learned methods struggle to recover the first image of the MNIST dataset (depicting the "5"). We suppose that this sample is very different from the samples that were used to train the networks. Only, the CPR and the CPR-FS network are capable of recovering this image.

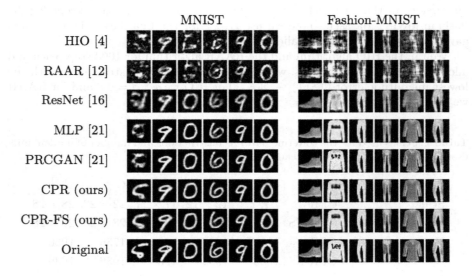

**Fig. 3.** Reconstructions from the Fourier magnitudes of samples from the MNIST and the Fashion-MNIST test dataset.

Table 2 shows the MSE, the MAE and the SSIM of the reconstructions and Fig. 4 visualizes the MSE for the five different learned methods. Overall, the learned methods outperform RAAR and HIO by a large margin. For MNIST, EMNIST and KMNIST we see that the CPR network greatly improves the reconstruction quality compared to the other learned methods. We hypothesize that our proposed CPR network yields better results when the signals of interest have a small support (e.g., MNIST, EMNIST, KMNIST). However, for signals with a large support (e.g., Fashion MNIST) we only observe a small improvement compared to the other learned methods.

**Table 2.** Quantitative comparison of the reconstructions produced by the different methods. We report MSE, MAE and SSIM between the reconstructions and the original images of the test dataset. MSE, MAE: lower is better. SSIM: larger is better. The best result is printed **bold**.

|  | MNIST | | | EMNIST | | |
|---|---|---|---|---|---|---|
|  | MSE | MAE | SSIM | MSE | MAE | SSIM |
| HIO [4] | 0.0441 | 0.1016 | 0.5708 | 0.0653 | 0.1379 | 0.5241 |
| RAAR [12] | 0.0489 | 0.1150 | 0.5232 | 0.0686 | 0.1456 | 0.4973 |
| ResNet [16] | 0.0269 | 0.0794 | 0.6937 | 0.0418 | 0.1170 | 0.5741 |
| MLP [21] | 0.0183 | 0.0411 | 0.8345 | 0.0229 | 0.0657 | 0.7849 |
| PRCGAN [21] | 0.0168 | 0.0399 | 0.8449 | 0.0239 | 0.0601 | 0.8082 |
| CPR (ours) | **0.0123** | **0.0370** | **0.8756** | 0.0153 | 0.0525 | 0.8590 |
| CPR-FS (ours) | 0.0126 | 0.0373 | 0.8729 | **0.0144** | **0.0501** | **0.8700** |
|  | Fashion-MNIST | | | KMNIST | | |
|  | MSE | MAE | SSIM | MSE | MAE | SSIM |
| HIO [4] | 0.0646 | 0.1604 | 0.4404 | 0.0835 | 0.1533 | 0.3414 |
| RAAR [12] | 0.0669 | 0.1673 | 0.4314 | 0.0856 | 0.1559 | 0.3208 |
| ResNet [16] | 0.0233 | 0.0820 | 0.6634 | 0.0715 | 0.1711 | 0.3783 |
| MLP [21] | 0.0128 | 0.0526 | 0.7940 | 0.0496 | 0.1168 | 0.5991 |
| PRCGAN [21] | 0.0151 | 0.0572 | 0.7749 | 0.0651 | 0.1166 | 0.5711 |
| CPR (ours) | 0.0115 | 0.0503 | 0.8077 | 0.0447 | 0.1068 | 0.6488 |
| CPR-FS (ours) | **0.0113** | **0.0497** | **0.8092** | **0.0433** | **0.1034** | **0.6626** |

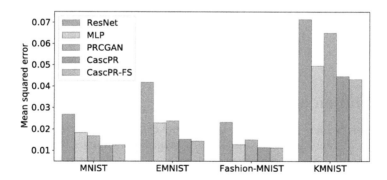

**Fig. 4.** Comparison of the MSE for the results of the learned methods.

## 3.5 Intermediate Prediction at Full-Scale

We briefly study the effect of predicting down-sampled versions of the image. Therefore, we evaluate the CPR-FS network which produces full-scale intermediate reconstructions. Table 2 also shows that the CPR-FS network performs similarly in terms of the overall reconstruction quality. For the EMNIST, the Fashion-MNIST and the KMNIST dataset the full-scale variant is slightly better. However, due to the larger input, the sub-networks need to have more parameters and thus training is more expensive.

### 3.6 Ablation Study

In this section, we demonstrate that increasing the number of sub-networks has a beneficial effect on the overall reconstruction quality. To do so, we train five network cascades exemplarily on the EMNIST dataset where we increase the number of sub-networks from one to five. We report the MSE on the test dataset after 50 epochs. Figure 5 shows that the MSE for the EMNIST dataset decreases with an increasing number of sub-networks used for the CPR-FS approach. Furthermore the gain in terms of MSE saturates after $q = 5$, such that additional sub-networks do not bring any further improvements. We expect the same relative behavior on the other datasets when increasing $q$.

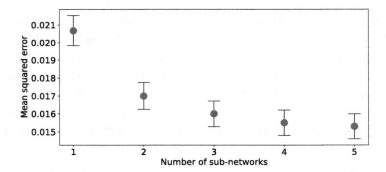

**Fig. 5.** Test MSE on the EMNIST test dataset for different number of sub-networks. Error bars indicate the 95% confidence interval.

## 4    Conclusion and Future Work

In this paper, we use a cascade of neural networks for non-oversampled Fourier phase retrieval. Our approach successively reconstructs images from their Fourier magnitudes and outperforms other existing non-iterative networks noticeably in terms of the reconstruction quality. However, non-iterative methods do not yet reach the reconstruction quality of iterative methods with a learning component which require high computational cost at test time.

Future work could also evaluate different strategies for training the neural network cascade. For example, greedy sub-network-wise training could be implemented and compared with our training procedure. Moreover, the CPR network architecture can easily be adapted to solve inverse problems other than Fourier phase retrieval.

# References

1. Brown, L.G.: A survey of image registration techniques. ACM Comput. Surv. (CSUR) **24**(4), 325–376 (1992)
2. Clanuwat, T., Bober-Irizar, M., Kitamoto, A., Lamb, A., Yamamoto, K., Ha, D.: Deep learning for classical Japanese literature. arXiv preprint arXiv:1812.01718 (2018)
3. Cohen, G., Afshar, S., Tapson, J., Van Schaik, A.: EMNIST: extending MNIST to handwritten letters. In: 2017 International Joint Conference on Neural Networks (IJCNN), pp. 2921–2926. IEEE (2017)
4. Fienup, J.R.: Phase retrieval algorithms: a comparison. Appl. Opt. **21**(15), 2758–2769 (1982)
5. Fienup, J.R., Dainty, J.C.: Phase retrieval and image reconstruction for astronomy. Image Recovery Theory Appl. **231**, 275 (1987)
6. Gerchberg, R.W.: A practical algorithm for the determination of phase from image and diffraction plane pictures. Optik **35**, 237–246 (1972)
7. Hand, P., Leong, O., Voroninski, V.: Phase retrieval under a generative prior. In: Advances in Neural Information Processing Systems, pp. 9136–9146 (2018)
8. Ioffe, S., Szegedy, C.: Batch normalization: accelerating deep network training by reducing internal covariate shift. arXiv preprint arXiv:1502.03167 (2015)
9. Işıl, Ç., Oktem, F.S., Koç, A.: Deep iterative reconstruction for phase retrieval. Appl. Opt. **58**(20), 5422–5431 (2019)
10. Kingma, D.P., Ba, J.: Adam: a method for stochastic optimization. arXiv preprint arXiv:1412.6980 (2014)
11. LeCun, Y., Bottou, L., Bengio, Y., Haffner, P., et al.: Gradient-based learning applied to document recognition. Proc. IEEE **86**(11), 2278–2324 (1998)
12. Luke, D.R.: Relaxed averaged alternating reflections for diffraction imaging. Inverse Probl. **21**(1), 37 (2004)
13. Manekar, R., Tayal, K., Kumar, V., Sun, J.: End-to-end learning for phase retrieval (2020)
14. Metzler, C., Schniter, P., Veeraraghavan, A., Baraniuk, R.G.: prDeep: robust phase retrieval with a flexible deep network. In: International Conference on Machine Learning, pp. 3501–3510 (2018)
15. Millane, R.P.: Phase retrieval in crystallography and optics. JOSA A **7**(3), 394–411 (1990)
16. Nishizaki, Y., Horisaki, R., Kitaguchi, K., Saito, M., Tanida, J.: Analysis of non-iterative phase retrieval based on machine learning. Opt. Rev. **27**(1), 136–141 (2020). https://doi.org/10.1007/s10043-019-00574-8
17. Pathak, D., Krahenbuhl, P., Donahue, J., Darrell, T., Efros, A.A.: Context encoders: feature learning by inpainting. In: Proceedings of the IEEE Conference on Computer Vision and Pattern Recognition, pp. 2536–2544 (2016)
18. Romano, Y., Elad, M., Milanfar, P.: The little engine that could: regularization by denoising (RED). SIAM J. Imaging Sci. **10**(4), 1804–1844 (2017)
19. Schlemper, J., Caballero, J., Hajnal, J.V., Price, A.N., Rueckert, D.: A deep cascade of convolutional neural networks for dynamic MR image reconstruction. IEEE Trans. Med. Imaging **37**(2), 491–503 (2017)
20. Srivastava, N., Hinton, G., Krizhevsky, A., Sutskever, I., Salakhutdinov, R.: Dropout: a simple way to prevent neural networks from overfitting. J. Mach. Learn. Res. **15**(1), 1929–1958 (2014)

21. Uelwer, T., Oberstraß, A., Harmeling, S.: Phase retrieval using conditional generative adversarial networks. In: 2020 25th International Conference on Pattern Recognition (ICPR), pp. 731–738. IEEE (2021)
22. Wang, Z., Bovik, A.C., Sheikh, H.R., Simoncelli, E.P.: Image quality assessment: from error visibility to structural similarity. IEEE Trans. Image Process. **13**(4), 600–612 (2004)
23. Wu, Z., Sun, Y., Liu, J., Kamilov, U.: Online regularization by denoising with applications to phase retrieval. In: 2019 IEEE/CVF International Conference on Computer Vision Workshop (ICCVW), pp. 3887–3895 (2019)
24. Xiao, H., Rasul, K., Vollgraf, R.: Fashion-MNIST: a novel image dataset for benchmarking machine learning algorithms. arXiv preprint arXiv:1708.07747 (2017)
25. Zheng, G., Horstmeyer, R., Yang, C.: Wide-field, high-resolution Fourier ptychographic microscopy. Nat. Photonics **7**(9), 739 (2013)

# Incorporating Discrete Wavelet Transformation Decomposition Convolution into Deep Network to Achieve Light Training

Guihua Tao, Wentao Rong, Wanlin Weng, Tingting Dan, Bin Zhang, and Hongmin Cai[✉]

School of Computer Science and Engineering, South China University of Technology, Guangzhou, China
{csghtao,cswwl,201810102902}@mail.scut.edu.cn, hmcai@scut.edu.cn

**Abstract.** The deep neural network achieves superior performance in various tasks. However, it is notoriously known that its training needs a considerable time cost to refine a large number of parameters. We proposed a deep wavelet network to tackle the issue. The proposed network is built by processing blocks with various decomposition levels which named Discrete Wavelet Transformation Decomposition Convolution (DWTDC). The DWTDC aims to fulfill the task of feature map discrete wavelet transformation decomposition and subbands differential fusion. We employ the DWTDC block to act as the convolution layer so that the parameters are estimated within the frequency domain space. Because of the merits of economic representation in the wavelet domain, the training parameters are greatly reduced, only requiring 33% of the parameters of the popular networks. Extensive experiments by comparing with benchmark models show that the proposed DWTDC dramatically reduced the number of parameters and achieved light training without sacrificing the classification performance.

**Keywords:** Light training · Discrete wavelet transformation decomposition convolution · Feature map decomposition · Subbands differential fusion · Frequency domain

## 1 Introduction

Deep learning has achieved great success in computer vision areas [11]. However, due to the numerous parameters of the deep neural network, the calculation cost of training a deep neural network is very large, which limits the application of these models to a great extent. In case of dealing with challenging computationally intensive applications, such as mobile health, real-time automatic driving, intensive virtual enhancement, which relies on a platform with limited computing power [17], The current deep models are seriously limited by the bottleneck

© Springer Nature Switzerland AG 2021
I. Farkaš et al. (Eds.): ICANN 2021, LNCS 12892, pp. 307–318, 2021.
https://doi.org/10.1007/978-3-030-86340-1_25

of computing ability from the graphics processing unit. Optimizing the neural network to reduce network scale and computing consumption is the key to break through the current limitation.

Intensive efforts have been invested in tackling the issue. For example, [9] regarded filters in a layer as a tensor and utilized Tucker tensor decomposition to speed up CNNs. Gong et al. [8] employed k-means to obtain the cluster centers of weights of convolution filters and then approximately represented convolution filters using their corresponding clustering centers. Wen et al. [20] excavated redundancy by pruning weights in different aspects resulting in a sparse and compact CNN for speeding up.

Wavelet analysis has achieved great successes in engineering [19] due to its elegant mathematical formulation and economic representation. The wavelet transform, evolved from the classical Fourier transform, is a local transformation on space and frequency. It is shown to be powerful to extract information from signals effectively [6]. The applications of wavelet analysis in image recognition, signal analysis, data compression, computer vision, and other fields have achieved scientific significance and application values.

To enjoy the merits of strong feature extraction capability by neural network and economic representation of wavelet decomposition, this paper aims to incorporate the powerful wavelet decomposition within the benchmark deep network. 1) We proposed to fuse the wavelet decomposition and convolution operation jointly to form an independent module, named **DWTDC** block. The module can be freely embedded in most of the popular neural networks. This block contains two sub-operations, including the feature map discrete wavelet transformation decomposition (FM-DWTD) module and the subbands differential fusion (SDF) module. With the DWTDC block, the neural network can be trained within the frequency domain. The entire network is shown to be still trained end-to-end by stochastic gradient descent with backpropagation. It can be easily implemented using the common libraries, e.g., Tensorflow, without modifying the solvers. 2) We conducted extensive experiments by incorporating the proposed DWTDC block into five benchmark networks to evaluate its power in reducing computational consumption. 3) Experiments of performing classification tasks on five popular computer vision datasets and diagnostic tasks on three medical image datasets were conducted. The experimental results show that DWTDC can greatly reduce the volume of network parameters, and achieve comparable performances with benchmark models.

## 2   Related Work

Recently, there are a variety of related works have been proposed to reduce the storage and complexity of CNNs [17,21]. Most of the works attempted to compress the over-parameterized weights to reduce their redundancy [2]. Denton et al. [7] used singular value decomposition technique to discover a low-rank approximation on the weight matrix [1]. Kim et al. [9] used Tucker tensor decomposition in each layer to speed up CNNs. Wen et al. [20] excavated redundancy by pruning weights in different aspects resulting in sparse and compact

CNNs for speeding up. Most of the such works attempted to prune the huge volume of weighting parameters in the spatial domain, which is performed until the training phase is successfully accomplished. Therefore, the training and testing of the networks are typically decoupled.

From the perspective of network structure, MobileNet [17] and Xception [3] explore the separable convolution to maintain accuracy, reduce the number of the parameters. Binarization also can be used to reduce the model size and lower the computation overheads. BinaryNet [5] and XNORNet [16] are typical examples of this way. Such neural networks reduce memory size and access with binary weights and activations at run-time. It is convenient to computation on both forward propagation and backward propagation.

It is important to explore new spaces in which to learn. Recently, Cotter et al. [4] are committed to exploring the new space for the learning of filters. They have proposed a preliminary idea of learning filters by taking activations into the wavelet domain, learning mixing coefficients, and returning to the pixel space by taking the inverse wavelet transform. However, in experiments, they briefly go into the wavelet domain and coming back to the spatial domain to do ReLU nonlinearities. Instead, we try to reduce the parameters of the neural network by exploring the merits of strong feature extraction capability by neural network and economic representation of wavelet decomposition. We go into the wavelet domain and perform feature map discrete wavelet transformation decomposition and subbands differential fusion.

## 3    Preliminaries

The 2D discrete wavelet transformation is the direct generalization of the 1D discrete wavelet transformation. A single level 2D DWT can be separated into two times operations of 1D DWT. Thus, a 1D DWT of a signal $x$ is calculated by passing it through a series of filters, i.e. the samples are passed through a low pass filter with impulse response $g$ resulting in a convolution of the two,

$$y[n] = (x * g)[n] = \sum_{k=-\infty}^{\infty} x[k]g[n-k] \qquad (1)$$

To perform a 1D discrete wavelet transformation, a signal $x[n] \in \mathbb{R}^N$ is firstly passed through a half band high-pass filter $G_H[n]$ and a low-pass filter $G_L[n]$. For example, the classical Haar wavelet [13] are defined by,

$$G_H[n] = \begin{cases} 1, & n = 0 \\ -1, & n = 1 \\ 0, & \text{otherwise} \end{cases}, G_L[n] = \begin{cases} 1, n = 0, 1 \\ 0, & \text{otherwise} \end{cases} \qquad (2)$$

A digital image $x$ can be viewed as a 2D signal with $n$ row and $m$ column. Therefore, the 2D DWT of $x$ can be treated as 1D DWT along rows and columns of $x$. After DWT, although the decomposition has halved the time resolution, the frequency resolution has been doubled. The frequency resolution can be further increased by decomposing the approximation coefficients. After $n$-level DWT, there are about $3n+1$ subbands are obtained.

The 2D-DWT are defined as follows:

$$
\begin{aligned}
x_{\mathrm{LL}}^{J}\left(n_{1}, n_{2}\right) = \sum_{i_{1}=0}^{K-1} \sum_{i_{2}=0}^{K-1} g\left(i_{1}\right) \cdot g\left(i_{2}\right) \\
\cdot x_{\mathrm{LL}}^{J-1}\left(2 n_{1}-i_{1}\right)\left(2 n_{2}-i_{2}\right)
\end{aligned}
\tag{3}
$$

where $J$ is decompostition level, $K$ is filter length, $g(n)$ is the impulse response of the low-pass filter $G(z)$, $h(n)$ is the impulse response of the high-pass filter $H(z)$, $x_{\mathrm{LL}}^{0}\left(n_{1}, n_{2}\right)$ is input image. Detailed wavelet decomposition introduction can be found in [13].

The 2D-DWT converts the raw image into four sub-bands: average (LL), vertical (HL), horizontal (LH), and diagonal (HH) information, corresponding to each wavelet sub-band coefficient. Note that after 2D-DWT decomposition, the combination of four sub-bands always has the same dimensions as the original input images [13]. After decomposing the raw image by DWT, four subbands are obtained. When we examine the frequency distribution of the obtained coefficients in each subband, one will find that most of the values being nearly zero, shown in the second row of Fig. 1. This decomposition provides a nice condition for reducing the network parameters.

## 4    Discrete Wavelet Transformation Decomposition Convolution

This paper proposed a method that combines discrete wavelet transformation and convolution to reduce the spatial size of the parameters used in the deep network. The proposed decomposition and differential fusion method, named by discrete wavelet transformation decomposition convolution, guides the network work on the frequency domain and efficiently differential fuse the subband coefficients after feature map decomposition.

Specifically, in the neural network, discrete wavelet transformation decomposes the image details in four subbands (1-level) or $3N+1$ subbands ($N$-level). In 1-level DWT, note that each subband's spatial size is a quarter of the original input image. Then, the processing in the original image can be transformed into the one in the subbands with a smaller spatial scale and more sparse information. Due to the above fact as well as the convolutional neural network's powerful feature extraction ability and representation ability, we proposed to combine the wavelet transformation with convolution operation and also proposed differential fusion method to combinate high frequency subbands with low frequency subbands.

The entire architecture of the DWTDC block is illustrated in Fig. 2. It can be separated into the decomposition part, the fused part, and further level DWTDC, which are detailed in the following subsections.

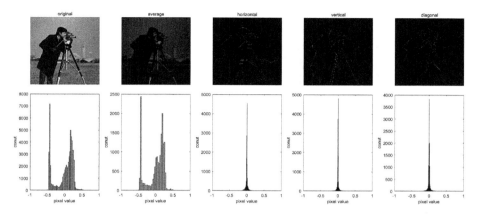

**Fig. 1.** An example of 1-level 2d-DWT with Haar kernel. Most of the resulted coefficients along different directions are nearly to be zero and thus the representation of the image could be economic.

### 4.1 Feature Map DWT Decomposition

To embed DWT in the neural network, we extend 2D discrete wavelet transform to tensor discrete wavelet transform, named by feature map DWT decomposition (FW-DWTD). FM-DWTD can be freely embedded in the neural network. It receives the previous layer's output as its input and generates four sub-bands: average (A), vertical(V), horizontal(H), and diagonal(D) feature map when carrying on 1-level FW-DWTD. Further, the scale of the feature map can be reduced to $\frac{1}{4^N}$ of the original scale after $N$-level FM-DWTD. Obviously, the scale of the feature map is greatly reduced. It means that the subsequent network layer will receive smaller scale feature vectors, which brings many benefits. On the one hand, it can reasonably reduce the depth of the neural network and maintain the same receptive field. On the other hand, it can reduce the neurons of the full connectivity layer, which is notoriously known for its huge parameters. In a word, thank the economic expression of wavelet decomposition, the scale of the feature map is reduced in a reasonable way, which provides conditions for the reduction of parameters and calculation amount of the neural network.

The FM-DWTD is in light-blue background in Fig. 2. As a discrete signal, feature map is inputted into network, and filtered through low-pass filter and high-pass filter to get the low-frequency part and the high-frequency part, respectively. And then the high-frequency part and the low-frequency part can be further filtered to get four subbands, which are average subband, horizontal subband, vertical subband, and radial subband.

### 4.2 Subbands Differential Fusion

By benefiting from the FM-DWTD processing block, the neural network obtains several small scale subbands. The naive method is concatenated all the subbands together and convolute on the concatenated subband. However, in such

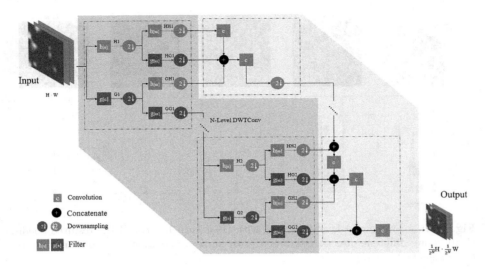

**Fig. 2.** The proposed DWTDC consists of two parts: the feature map DWT decomposition and the subbands differential fusion. The light-blue area represents the DWT decomposition, the light-gray area represents the subbands differential fusion. After N-level DWTDC, DWT decomposition generates $3N + 1$ subbands, SDF fuses all subbands. (Color figure online)

a method, all the subbands will be treated equally. Thus, the solution is not optimal. We proposed a differential fusion scheme, named by SDF, to utilize the subbands with complementary information. This strategy can make rational use of computing resources, reduce parameters, and avoid wasting too many resources on task-irrelevant feature computation.

In the light gray background of Fig. 2, it is subbands differential fusion. $N$ level decomposition generates $3N + 1$ subbands. Different subbands contain different frequencies. The low-frequency part contains coarse content of image while the high-frequency part contains detailed content of image, such as edge boundary details and most of the noises. According to the fact that generalized features are from the low-level layer and task-specific features are from high-level, we proposed a method for preferentially convolution on high frequency. Instead of equally treating convolution, high frequency information is given high priority to convolution to obtain deeper features. Then we concatenate the low frequency part and the convoluted high frequency part to prepare the next SDF operation. Most notably, the convolution performed at low frequency is an adjunct to the high frequency. It results in that relatively few convolution operations are carried out for low frequency information which acts as complementary information. This means that it reduced the computation of task-weak-correlated information reasonably. To sum up, the more important the feature, the higher the priority, the earlier it enters the differential fusion block. The result of the current convolution and the feature maps of the next priority will be taken as the next input.

Differential fusion block continually convolutes, and the attained feature map continually is added by priority, until all feature maps are input into the block.

# 5    Experiments

To evaluate the effectiveness of our proposed method, we compared the performance of PlainNet and DWTNet on eight datasets. The details of datasets and experiment setting, PlainNet, and DWTNet are in Sect. 5.1, Sect. 5.2, and Sect. 5.3, respectively. Finally, the experimental results are in Sect. 5.4.

## 5.1    Datasets and Experiment Setting

We first verify the effectiveness of the proposed method on five computer vision benchmark datasets using five classical neural networks and then experiment to verify the proposed method also achieves light training on medical image datasets. Specifically, the models were trained and evaluated on the various datasets including COVID-19 CT dataset [23], wide-angle retinal images dataset [22], childhood medulloblastoma microscopic images dataset [12], MNIST dataset, cifar10 [10] dataset, cifar100 dataset, Coil20 dataset [14], Coil100 dataset [15]. In experiments, we compared DWTNets with corresponding PlainNets. We compared the number of parameters, the memory occupied by the model, and the classification accuracy of DWTNet with those of plaint net to validate the effectiveness of our block.

## 5.2    PlainNet

Network without DWRDC block, we call it PlainNet, such as LeNet, VGGNet, AlexNet, GoogLeNet, ResNet and so on [18]. As shown in Fig. 3 (a), the PlainNet is the hierarchical model, which is mainly composed of non-linear convolutional layers, pooling layers, and fully connected layers. Five classic PlainNets were trained on five benchmark datasets to record the classification accuracy, loss, memory occupied by the model, and the number of parameters.

## 5.3    DWTNet

Based on the PlainNet, we replaced some convolution layers with the DWTDC block proposed in this paper to get a corresponding new network, which is called DWTNet. As shown in Fig. 3 (b), the DWTNet is the hierarchical model, which is also mainly composed of non-linear convolution layers, pooling layers, and fully connected layers. While different, it also contains DWT convolution layers. Meanwhile, it has shallower architecture than the PlainNet, because the DWT convolution layer has the ability to compress the representation space of the feature map.

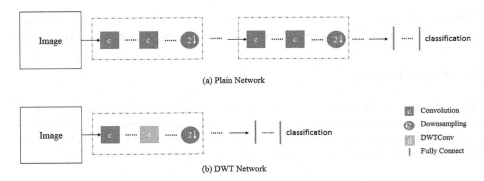

(a) Plain Network

(b) DWT Network

**Fig. 3.** DWTDC for PlainNet. (a): A PlainNet which contains plain operation, such as convolution, downsampling and fully connection. (b): Proposed block as in Fig. 2 for plain net.

## 5.4 Experimental Results

The results in Table 1 show that training DWTNet equipped with DWTDC instead of plain convolution can considerably reduce the parameters scale. Experimental results on five benchmark datasets show its effectiveness and feasibility compared with the plain network's results. Lenet, Vgg16, Alexnet, ResNet, and Inception networks equipped with DWTDC module reduce the model parameters to 57.00%, 15.57%, 48.87%, 19.01% and 36.83%, respectively, while resulting in equivalent or even better performance compared with the original models. Compared with the original network, the parameter amounts of DWTNetworks have greatly decreased by 64.54% on average. Meanwhile, DWTNetworks need less memory consumption. Lenet, Vgg16, Alexnet, ResNet, and Inception networks equipped with DWTDC module reduce the memory consumption to 57.76%, 15.57%, 48.88%, 33.13% and 36.83%, respectively.

In detail, Fig. 4 shows the comparisons of the convergence process of PlainNet and DWTNet trained on Coil datasets. With the number of iterations increasing, the DWTNet converges faster than the PlainNet, and the classification accuracies of the two networks reach the same level. Specifically, the accuracy of the model gradually converges with the increasing of iterations. The DWTNet quickly converges around in the 13th epoch on the coil20 dataset, while the PlainNet model converges around in the 25th epoch. Both methods achieve comparable performance. The parameters used in both two DWTNet neural network models are 75.47% and 74.48% lower than those in the PlainNet models, respectively.

It is worth noting that the deeper and more complex the network is equipped with, the more obviously the parameters drop. In this experiment, the parameters of the five-layer network (LeNet) decreased by 43.00%, and those of the deep, complex network, such as Vgg16, AlexNet, ResNet, and Inception network, decreased by 84.43%, 51.13%, 80.99% and 63.17%, respectively. This is due to DWTDC's powerful ability to spatial scale compression. 1-level DWTDC can reduce the spatial scale size of feature map to a quarter of the original size. This

**Table 1.** Experiments on five benchmark datasets by incorporating the proposed DWTDC block into five benchmark networks.

| | | Datasets | | | | | | | | | |
| | | MNIST | | Cifar10 | | Cifar100 | | Coil20 | | Coil100 | |
| | Measurements | PlainNet | DWTNet | PlainNet | DWTNet | PlainNet | DWTNet | PlainNet | DWTNet | PlainNet | DWTNet |
|---|---|---|---|---|---|---|---|---|---|---|---|
| LeNet | # of Parameters (M) | 0.044 | **0.039** | 0.062 | **0.044** | 0.070 | **0.052** | 1.629 | **0.413** | 1.636 | **0.421** |
| | Memory Cost (MB) | 0.197 | **0.173** | 0.266 | **0.195** | 0.296 | **0.225** | 6.240 | **1.600** | 6.27 | **1.63** |
| | Loss_train | 0.0084 | 0.0199 | 0.968 | 1.0015 | 2.5488 | 2.5035 | 0.0016 | 0.0019 | 0.0023 | 0.0027 |
| | Accuracy_train | 0.9985 | 0.9939 | 0.6606 | 0.6418 | 0.3576 | 0.3604 | 1.0000 | 1.0000 | 1.0000 | 1.0000 |
| | Testing Loss | 0.0359 | 0.0547 | 1.1127 | 1.1723 | 2.9039 | 2.8843 | 0.025 | 0.0145 | 0.0102 | 0.0073 |
| | Testing Accuracy | 0.9888 | 0.9842 | 0.61 | 0.588 | 0.288 | 0.2944 | 0.9931 | 0.9977 | 0.9991 | 1.0000 |
| Vgg16 | # of Parameters (M) | 134.276 | **20.772** | 134.277 | **20.772** | 134.646 | **21.141** | 134.317 | **20.813** | 134.646 | **21.141** |
| | Memory cost (MB) | 512.28 | **79.27** | 512.29 | **79.27** | 513.69 | **80.68** | 512.44 | **79.43** | 513.69 | **80.68** |
| | Loss_train | 0.0101 | 0.02 | 0.5912 | 0.5153 | 1.2354 | 1.2699 | 5.97E−05 | 9.83E−05 | | 4.10E−04 |
| | Accuracy_train | 0.9966 | 0.9934 | 0.792 | 0.8191 | 0.6471 | 0.6344 | 1.0000 | 1.0000 | 0.9996 | 0.9998 |
| | Loss_test | 0.0172 | 0.0183 | 0.8193 | 0.7384 | 2.2308 | 2 | 1.54E−07 | 4.29E−06 | 0.0054 | 7.87E−07 |
| | Accuracy_test | 0.9444 | 0.9944 | 0.721 | 0.7561 | 0.4869 | | 1.0000 | 1.0000 | 1.0000 | 1.0000 |
| Alexnet | # of Parameters (M) | 50.832 | **24.813** | 50.855 | **24.836** | 50.946 | **24.926** | 50.842 | **24.823** | 50.946 | **24.926** |
| | Memory cost (MB) | 193.96 | **94.70** | 194.05 | **94.79** | 194.39 | **95.13** | 193.99 | **94.74** | 194.39 | **95.13** |
| | Loss_train | 0.0101 | 0.0149 | 0.5611 | 0.777 | 1.1693 | 1.6039 | 0.0029 | 0.001 | 7.52E−04 | 0.0028 |
| | Accuracy_train | 0.9968 | 0.9955 | 0.8036 | 0.7281 | 0.652 | 0.5456 | 0.999 | 1.0000 | 0.9996 | 0.9992 |
| | Loss_test | 0.0135 | 0.0209 | 0.7002 | 0.9575 | 1.9222 | 2.3511 | 7.19E−06 | 6.27E−06 | 7.08E−07 | 1.56E−05 |
| | Accuracy_test | 0.9952 | 0.9938 | 0.7673 | 0.6693 | 0.506 | 0.4226 | 1.0000 | 1.0000 | 1.0000 | 1.0000 |
| ResNet | # of Parameters (M) | 0.078 | **0.023** | 0.079 | **0.023** | 0.085 | **0.025** | 0.079 | **0.024** | 0.085 | **0.025** |
| | Memory cost (MB) | 0.376 | **0.126** | 0.378 | **0.125** | 0.401 | **0.132** | 0.379 | **0.126** | 0.401 | **0.132** |
| | Loss_train | 0.0212 | 0.0147 | 0.6338 | 0.7292 | 1.7068 | 2.4425 | 0.0785 | 0.0116 | 0.0749 | 0.0125 |
| | Accuracy_train | 0.9999 | 0.9970 | 0.7994 | 0.7455 | 0.5476 | 0.3572 | 1.0000 | 1.0000 | 0.9994 | 0.9992 |
| | Loss_test | 0.0409 | 0.0365 | 0.8546 | 0.9113 | 2.3088 | 2.7331 | 0.0776 | 0.0210 | 0.0718 | 0.0110 |
| | Accuracy_test | 0.9932 | 0.9908 | 0.7220 | 0.6916 | 0.4240 | 0.3090 | 1.0000 | 0.9954 | 0.9995 | 1.0000 |
| Inception | # of Parameters (M) | 36.661 | **13.472** | 36.661 | **13.473** | 36.800 | **13.611** | 36.677 | **13.488** | 36.900 | **13.612** |
| | Memory cost (MB) | 140.86 | **51.76** | 140.87 | **51.76** | 141.39 | **52.28** | 140.92 | **51.81** | 141.39 | **52.28** |
| | Loss_train | 0.0357 | 0.004 | 0.2578 | 0.4956 | 1.5493 | 2.0172 | 0.0023 | 0.0017 | 0.0011 | 7.98E−04 |
| | Accuracy_train | 0.9906 | 0.9988 | 0.9133 | 0.8303 | 0.5658 | 0.4663 | 1.0000 | 1.0000 | 1.0000 | 1.0000 |
| | Loss_test | 0.0136 | 0.0133 | 0.5075 | 0.7838 | 1.921 | 2.0544 | 1.67E−07 | 6.86E−07 | 2.00E−07 | 8.64E−07 |
| | Accuracy_test | 0.9954 | 0.9957 | 0.8406 | 0.7517 | 0.5224 | 0.4617 | 1.0000 | 1.0000 | 1.0000 | 1.0000 |

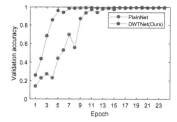 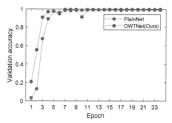

(a) Validation accuracy on dataset coil20.  (b) Validation accuracy on dataset coil100.

**Fig. 4.** Comparisons of convergence process of PlainNet and DWTNet on dataset coil20 and coil100 dataset.

is an exponential powerful compression. As shown in Fig. 2, the feature map of size H · W is transformed into $\frac{1}{2^N}$H · $\frac{1}{2^N}$W through DWTDC.

DWTDC reduces the number of weight parameters and the consumption of memory, with minor (or no) accuracy loss. LeNet, Vgg16, Alexnet, ResNet and Inception network drop by +0.2960%, −1.584%, +6.9220%, +3.0380%, and +2.9860%, respectively. Summarily, the accuracy was reduced by an average of

2.3316%. Compared with the test results, the decline of the parameters does not have a great negative impact on the accuracy and loss of the PlainNet.

The proposed method maintains the same performance on medical images. We take the diagnosis-task experiments on three difficult datasets, there are diagnoses of COVID-19, screening of Retinopathy of prematurity (ROP), and childhood medulloblastoma (CMB) diagnosis respectively. As shown in Table 2, Vgg16 equipped with DWTDC module reduces the PlainNet parameters from 134.244M to 20.739M. And the memory is reduced from 537.039 to 82.995 MB. Besides, the experiment results of COVID-19, ROP, and CMB show that DWT-Nets achieve more stability than original PlainNets. DWTNet's loss is consistently less than the loss of PlainNet. On COVID-19 diagnosis task, training loss, validation loss, and testing loss are reduced from 0.477, 0.712, 0.799 to 0.429, 0.659, 0.692 respectively. On the CMB diagnosis task, training loss, validation loss, and testing loss are reduced from 0.361, 0.309, 0.242 to 0.179, 0.133, 0.146 respectively. Meanwhile, the accuracy of the experiments on COVID-19, ROP, and CMB are improved by −0.005, +0.037 and +0.082 respectively. It means that DWTNets have a scale of only 15.45% of the original model but also can achieve or even surpass the performance of the original model.

Experiments by comparing with benchmark models on cifar10 show that the method equipped with the proposed DWTDC dramatically reduced the number of parameters and achieved light training. It maintains considerable superiority in classification performance. As shown in Table 3, our method, a ResNet-like network equipped with our proposed DWTDC block, achieves better performance than other methods on all the metrics. Specifically, the parameter amount, memory occupy, and classification accuracy of our proposed method is 0.024, 0.126, and 0.9014, which are better than by the BinaryNet (0.171, 0.716, 0.8257), XNORNet (0.171, 0.719, 0.8685), Xception (20.882, 79.960, 0.8768) and Mobilenetv2 (2.271, 9.027, 0.8990).

**Table 2.** Experiment on three diagnosis tasks

| Dataset | Method | # of Parameters(M) | Memory Cost(MB) | Loss | | | Accuracy | | |
|---|---|---|---|---|---|---|---|---|---|
| | | | | train | val | test | train | val | test |
| COVID-19 CT | PlainNet | 134.244 | 537.039 | 0.477 | 0.712 | 0.799 | 0.771 | 0.686 | 0.696 |
| | **DWTNet (Ours)** | **20.739** | **82.995** | **0.429** | **0.659** | **0.692** | **0.799** | **0.720** | 0.691 |
| Wide-angle retina | PlainNet | 134.244 | 537.039 | 0.144 | 0.245 | 0.897 | 0.945 | 0.920 | 0.734 |
| | **DWTNet (Ours)** | **20.739** | **82.995** | 0.209 | **0.245** | **0.579** | 0.916 | 0.909 | **0.771** |
| Medulloblastoma microscopic | PlainNet | 134.244 | 537.039 | 0.361 | 0.309 | 0.242 | 0.792 | 0.821 | 0.871 |
| | DWTNet (Ours) | **20.739** | **82.995** | **0.179** | **0.133** | **0.146** | **0.938** | **0.964** | **0.953** |

**Table 3.** Computation resources costed by the tested models

| Method | # of Parameters (M) | Memory (MB) | Accuracy |
|---|---|---|---|
| BinaryNet [5] | 0.171 | 0.716 | 0.8257 |
| XNORNet [16] | 0.171 | 0.719 | 0.8685 |
| Xception [3] | 20.882 | 79.960 | 0.8768 |
| Mobilenetv2 [17] | 2.271 | 9.027 | 0.8990 |
| **Ours** | **0.024** | **0.126** | **0.9014** |

## 6  Conclusion

Our work presents a deep wavelet convolution technique that reduces a mass of parameters in the neural network with minor (or no) accuracy loss and guides the network to work in the frequency domain whose representation space is sparse and of small spatial size. Moreover, we effectively incorporate the proposed method in the neural network without breaking the end-to-end architecture of the network. In addition, thanks to the wavelets, we are able to guide the network to pay more attention to detailed information. Furthermore, by fusing all the subbands, we reduce the spatial size of the representation to reduce the number of parameters and computation in the network.

**Acknowledgment.** This work was partially supported by the National Natural Science Foundation of China (61771007), Key-Area Research and Development of Guangdong Province (2020B010166002, 2020B111119001), Science and Technology Planning Project of Guangdong Province (2017B020226004), and the Health & Medical Collaborative Innovation Project of Guangzhou City (202002020049).

## References

1. Candès, E.J., Recht, B.: Exact matrix completion via convex optimization. Found. Comput. Math. **9**(6), 717 (2009)
2. Chen, W., Wilson, J., Tyree, S., Weinberger, K., Chen, Y.: Compressing neural networks with the hashing trick. In: International Conference on Machine Learning, pp. 2285–2294 (2015)
3. Chollet, F.: Xception: deep learning with depthwise separable convolutions. In: Proceedings of the IEEE Conference on Computer Vision and Pattern Recognition, pp. 1251–1258 (2017)
4. Cotter, F., Kingsbury, N.: Deep learning in the wavelet domain. arXiv preprint arXiv:1811.06115 (2018)
5. Courbariaux, M., Hubara, I., Soudry, D., El-Yaniv, R., Bengio, Y.: Binarized neural networks: training deep neural networks with weights and activations constrained to +1 or −1. arXiv preprint arXiv:1602.02830 (2016)
6. Daubechies, I.: The wavelet transform, time-frequency localization and signal analysis. IEEE Trans. Inform. Theory **36**(5), 961–1005 (1990)

7. Denton, E.L., Zaremba, W., Bruna, J., LeCun, Y., Fergus, R.: Exploiting linear structure within convolutional networks for efficient evaluation. In: Advances in Neural Information Processing Systems, pp. 1269–1277 (2014)

8. Gong, Y., Liu, L., Yang, M., Bourdev, L.: Compressing deep convolutional networks using vector quantization. arXiv preprint arXiv:1412.6115 (2014)

9. Kim, Y.D., Park, E., Yoo, S., Choi, T., Yang, L., Shin, D.: Compression of deep convolutional neural networks for fast and low power mobile applications. arXiv preprint arXiv:1511.06530 (2015)

10. Krizhevsky, A., Hinton, G., et al.: Learning multiple layers of features from tiny images. Tech. rep. Citeseer (2009)

11. LeCun, Y., Bengio, Y., Hinton, G.: Deep learning. Nature **521**(7553), 436–444 (2015)

12. Mahanta, D.D.D.L.B.: Childhood medulloblastoma microscopic images (IEEE Dataport (2020). https://dxdoi.org/1021227/w0m0-mw21. https://doi.org/10.21227/w0m0-mw21

13. Mallat, S.: A Wavelet Tour of Signal Processing. Elsevier (1999)

14. Nene, S.A., Nayar, S.K., Murase, H.: Columbia object image library (coil-20. Tech. rep. (1996)

15. Nene, S.A., Nayar, S.K., Murase, H.: object image library (coil-100). Tech. rep. (1996)

16. Rastegari, M., Ordonez, V., Redmon, J., Farhadi, A.: XNOR-Net: ImageNet classification using binary convolutional neural networks. In: Leibe, B., Matas, J., Sebe, N., Welling, M. (eds.) ECCV 2016. LNCS, vol. 9908, pp. 525–542. Springer, Cham (2016). https://doi.org/10.1007/978-3-319-46493-0_32

17. Sandler, M., Howard, A., Zhu, M., Zhmoginov, A., Chen, L.C.: Mobilenetv 2: inverted residuals and linear bottlenecks. In: Proceedings of the IEEE Conference on Computer Vision and Pattern Recognition, pp. 4510–4520 (2018)

18. Shrestha, A., Mahmood, A.: Review of deep learning algorithms and architectures. IEEE Access **7**, 53040–53065 (2019)

19. Subhashini, A., Victor, S.: A new approach on denoising for 1D, 2D and 3D images based on discrete wavelet transformation and thresholding. Int. J. Adv. Res. Comp. Sci. **9**(1), 708–710 (2018)

20. Wen, W., Wu, C., Wang, Y., Chen, Y., Li, H.: Learning structured sparsity in deep neural networks. arXiv preprint arXiv:1608.03665 (2016)

21. Yang, L., Yang, P., Ni, R., Zhao, Y.: Xception-based general forensic method on small-size images. In: Pan, J.-S., Li, J., Tsai, P.-W., Jain, L.C. (eds.) Advances in Intelligent Information Hiding and Multimedia Signal Processing. SIST, vol. 157, pp. 361–369. Springer, Singapore (2020). https://doi.org/10.1007/978-981-13-9710-3_38

22. Zhang, Y.: DNN classifier of wide-angle retinal images in computer-aided screening for ROP (IEEE Dataport 2018). https://dxdoi.org/1021227/q5jw-t682. https://doi.org/10.21227/q5jw-t682

23. Zhao, J., Zhang, Y., He, X., Xie, P.: COVID-CT-dataset: a CT scan dataset about COVID-19. arXiv preprint arXiv:2003.13865 (2020)

# MMF: A Loss Extension for Feature Learning in Open Set Recognition

Jingyun Jia[✉][iD] and Philip K. Chan[iD]

Florida Institute of Technology, Melbourne, FL 32901, USA
jiaj2018@my.fit.edu, pkc@fit.edu

**Abstract.** The objective of open set recognition (OSR) is to classify the known classes as well as the unknown classes when the collected samples cannot exhaust all the classes. This paper proposes a loss extension that emphasizes features with larger and smaller magnitudes to find representations that can more effectively separate the known from the unknown classes. Our contributions include: First, we introduce an extension that can be incorporated into different loss functions to find more discriminative representations. Second, we show that the proposed extension can significantly improve the performances of two different types of loss functions on datasets from two different domains. Third, we show that with the proposed extension, one loss function outperforms the others in training time and model accuracy.

**Keywords:** Open set recognition · Feature learning · Loss extensions

## 1 Introduction

The OSR problem aims to classify the multiple known classes for a multinomial classification problem while identifying the unknown classes. The OSR problem defines a more realistic scenario and has drawn significant attention in application areas such as face recognition [12], malware classification [5] and medical diagnoses [15].

In this paper, we introduce a loss extension to help the existing loss functions better handle the open set scenario. The proposed extension is inspired by Extreme Value Signatures (EVS) in [17]. Borrowing from a pre-trained neural network for regular classification, EVS uses only the top $K$ activations (i.e., largest in magnitude) at one layer for calculating the distance between an instance and a class. The EVS distance function can help identify the unknown class. Instead of using a pre-trained network and the top $K$ activations, we directly emphasize features with the largest, as well as smallest, magnitudes during network training. We name our approach Min Max Feature (MMF). Although the MMF extension is not a standalone loss function, it can be incorporated into different loss functions. Our contribution in this paper is threefold:

Partially supported by grants from Amazon and Rockwell Collins to Philip Chan.

I. Farkaš et al. (Eds.): ICANN 2021, LNCS 12892, pp. 319–331, 2021.
https://doi.org/10.1007/978-3-030-86340-1_26

First, we propose MMF as an extension to different types of loss functions for the OSR problem. Second, we show that MMF achieves statistically significant AUC ROC improvement when applied to two types of loss functions (classification and representation loss functions) on four datasets from two different domains (images and malware). Third, our results indicate that the combination of MMF and the ii loss function [5] outperforms the other combinations in both training time and overall F1 score.

We organize the paper as follows. In Sect. 2, we give an overview of related work. Section 3 presents the MMF loss extension. Finally, Sect. 4 shows that the MMF extension can improve different types of loss functions significantly.

## 2   Related Work

The OSR problem is related to PU (Positive and Unlabeled) learning [10], which can be regarded as a binary classification problem with the absence of negative samples. The OSR problem extends the binary classification problem to a multi-class classification problem, with some classes missing from the training set, and will be recognized as an unknown class during testing. We can divide OSR techniques into three categories based on the training set compositions. The first category includes the techniques that borrow additional data in the training set. Dhamija et al. [2] utilize the differences of feature magnitudes between known and borrowed unknown samples as part of the objective function. Hendrycks et al. [6] propose Outlier Exposure(OE) to distinguish between anomalous (unknown) and in-distribution (known) examples. In general, although borrowing and annotating additional data turns OSR into a common classification problem, the retrieval and selection of additional datasets remain an issue.

The research works that generate additional training data fall in the second category of open set recognition techniques. Most data generation methods are based on GANs. Neal et al. [11] add another encoder network to traditional GANs to map from images to a latent space. Lee et al. [9] generate "boundary" samples in the low-density area of in-distribution acting as unknown samples. While generating unknown samples for the OSR problem has achieved great performance, it requires more complex network architectures.

The third category of open set recognition does not require additional data. Most of the research works require outlier detection for the unknown class. Pidhorskyi et al. [13] propose manifold learning based on training an Adversarial Autoencoder (AAE) to capture the underlying structure of the distributions of known classes. Hassen and Chan [5] propose ii loss for open set recognition. It first finds the representations for the known classes during training and then recognizes an instance as unknown if it does not belong to any known classes. In EVS, Schultheiss et al. [17] investigate class-specific representations for novelty detection tasks. The research work shows that each class's mean representation can capture discriminative information of both known and unknown classes. EVS focuses on the top $K$ activations via binarizing the activations; however,

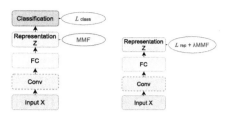

(a) With classifica- (b) With represen-
tion loss                tation loss

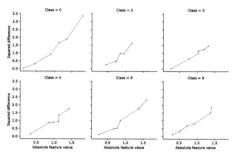

**Fig. 1.** An overview of the network architectures of different types of loss functions. The convolutional layers are optional. The MMF module in red is our proposed loss extension. (Color figure online)

**Fig. 2.** Squared differences of MAV values between the known and unknown classes in Fig. 3a. The x-axis is the absolute feature values in six features, and the y-axis is their corresponding squared differences to the unknown class.

choosing an appropriate $K$ can be challenging. Also, EVS assumes that all the activation values are positive and only looks at the larger ones. We address both limitations in our proposed approach.

While our approach can be incorporated into different loss functions, we focus on two types of loss functions in this paper: the classification loss functions and the representation loss functions. The objective of classification loss, such as cross-entropy loss, is to lower the classification error of the training data. The representation loss functions are normally applied to the representation layers, such as triplet loss in [16] and ii loss in [5]. Triplet loss intends to find an embedding space where the distance between an anchor instance and another instance from the same class is smaller by a user-specified margin than the distance between the anchor instance and another instance from a different class. Ii loss aims to maximize the distance between different classes (inter-class separation) and minimize the distance of an instance from its class mean (intra-class spread).

## 3    Approach

We propose the MMF extension to learn more discriminative representations through known classes, thus better separating known and unknown classes. The proposed MMF extension does not borrow or generate additional data for the unknown class, and it can be incorporated into different loss functions. We focus on classification loss functions such as cross-entropy loss and representation loss functions, such as triplet loss and ii loss (Sect. 2).

A typical classification neural network consists of an input layer, hidden layers, and classification layer. We can consider the hidden layers as different levels of representations of the input. We call the values of the last hidden layer

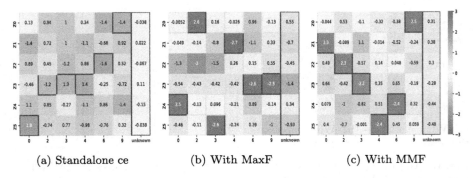

(a) Standalone ce          (b) With MaxF          (c) With MMF

**Fig. 3.** The heatmap of MAVs (columns) of the MNIST classes using cross-entropy loss without and with different extensions. Each row is a learned feature. The largest/smallest magnitude magnitude of a feature in each MAV is in a red/yellow box. MAV of the unknown class is in a green column/box. (Color figure online)

activation vector (AV), and each activation is a learned feature. The mean activation vectors (MAV) of a class is the average of the activation vectors of the class. For example, the network in Fig. 1a contains one convolutional layer, one fully connected layer, one representation layer (representation layer Z), and one classification layer (softmax layer). In some scenarios, a neural network only consists of the input layer and hidden layers as in Fig. 1b, where we use learned representations instead of a classification layer for classification tasks. Figure 3a shows the learned MAV values from the representation layer using standalone cross-entropy loss.

To improve the accuracy of detecting open set samples from unknown classes, we can increase the distances (we use Euclidean distance here) between the learned features of known and unknown samples, summarized by the MAVs of the known and unknown classes. Squared differences are the components of Euclidean distance. Thus we can increase the distance by increasing squared differences. Figure 2 depicts the relationship between squared differences with the absolute feature values (feature magnitudes) of the six known classes. We consider a feature with a larger magnitude is more significant than that with a smaller magnitude. We observe that a more significant feature leads to a higher squared difference to the unknown class. The reason is that the MAV of the unknown class has a relatively small magnitude (green column), as we observe in Fig. 3a. The small magnitude is due to the unknown class being absent from training, and hence its features are not learned. More importantly, the squared difference increases faster with more significant features, which indicates a slight improvement in a more significant feature will increase squared difference more. Thus, we want the features with larger magnitudes to become even more significant to increase the distance between the unknown and known classes.

However, based on the preliminary experiments, we found that after enlarging the magnitudes of the most significant features for the known classes, the unknown class's MAV became further away from the origin, which reduces the increase in the distance between the known and unknown classes. As shown in Fig. 3b, the MAV of the unknown class (green column) has significantly increased compared to the one only using standalone cross-entropy loss in Fig. 3a. To further improve accuracy and increase the magnitudes of the most significant feature, we also decrease the magnitudes of the least significant features to mitigate the increase of the MAV of the unknown class. Comparing Fig. 3c and Fig. 3a, we can see that after reducing the magnitude of the least significant features, the feature values of unknown classes indeed get smaller. Consequently, the distance between the MAV of a known class and the MAV of the unknown class has increased, and the classes are more separated. For example, the Euclidean distance between class "9" and the unknown class learned from standalone cross-entropy loss in Fig. 3a is 2.32. After adding "MMF" in Fig. 3c enlarges the distance to 2.62, making the two classes more separable.

Therefore, our MMF extension has two properties. Property A maximizes the most significant feature, i.e., the feature with the largest magnitude, for all the known classes. Property B minimizes the least significant feature, i.e., the feature with the smallest magnitude, for all the known classes. As a result, the learned representations for known classes should be more discriminative, while the unknown classes should be less affected.

### 3.1   Learning Objectives

Let $x \in \mathbf{X}$ be an instance and $y \in Y$ be its label. The hidden layers in a neural network can be considered as different levels of representations of input $x$. Suppose that there are $C$ known classes in training data, and $C+1$ classes in test data with the additional class as unknown class. We denote the MAV of class $i$ as $\mu_i$, and $\mu_{ij}$ represents the $j^{th}$ feature of the MAV of class $i$. Assume the AVs and MAVs have $F$ dimensions, representing $F$ features, we stack the MAVs for all the classes to form a representation matrix $\mathbb{U}^{C \times F}$. To satisfy Property A, we first select the most significant features for each class to form the "max_feature" vector. The $i^{th}$ element in "max_feature" is for class $i$:

$$max\_feature_i = \max_{1 \leq j \leq F} |\mu_{ij}|, \tag{1}$$

In the example of Fig. 3a, the "max_feature" would be (1.8, 1.2, 1.3, 1.4, 1.6, 1.4) (the absolute values of the red boxes). Likewise, for Property B, we measure the vector of the "min_feature" as the least significant feature for each class. The $i^{th}$ element is for class $i$:

$$min\_feature_i = \min_{1 \leq j \leq F} |\mu_{ij}| \tag{2}$$

The "min_feature" in the example of Fig. 3a would be (0.13, 0.45, 0.27, 0.34, 0.25, 0.32) (the absolute values of the yellow boxes). Then, to maximize all the values in the "max_feature", we maximize the lower boundary (i.e., the smallest value) in "max_feature" directly. Thus the most significant features for all the known classes would be maximized as Property A. Meanwhile, we minimize the largest value in the "min_feature" to implicitly minimize all the values in the "min_feature". The least significant features for all the known classes would be minimized as Property B. As a result, the proposed MMF extension satisfies both properties:

$$MMF = \max_{1 \leq i \leq C}(min\_feature_i) - \min_{1 \leq i \leq C}(max\_feature_i) \tag{3}$$

In the example of Fig. 3a, we would like to maximize the "1.2" in the "max_feature" and minimize the "0.45" in the "min_feature". There are alternative methods to generate the "max_feature" and "min_feature", for example, instead of selecting the highest absolute values for "max_feature", we experimented with the highest values ($max\_feature_{1i} = \max_{1 \leq j \leq F}(\mu_{ij})$) and the lowest values ($max\_feature_{2i} = \max_{1 \leq j \leq F}(-\mu_{ij})$) to form two "max_feature" vectors and later to be maximized at the same time. However, our experiments indicate that using the single "max_feauture" vector can achieve better performances. There are also other methods to implicitly maximize the most significant features and minimize the least significant values for all the classes, such as maximizing the average value of the "max_feature", or minimizing the average value of the "min_feature", i.e. $\sum_{i=1}^{C} \frac{1}{C}(min\_feature_i - max\_feature_i)$. However, the results of using average value are weaker than using the extreme values across all classes, hence we choose to use the extreme values in our extension function and in our experiments.

### 3.2   Training with MMF and Open Set Recognition

In addition to Properties A and B, the MMF extension can be incorporated into different loss functions. We focus on two types of loss functions: a) loss functions designed for decision layers such as cross-entropy loss; b) loss functions designed for representation layers such as triplet loss and ii loss. Notably, we combine the MMF extension with these two types of loss functions differently, as Fig. 1.

We use the network architecture in Fig. 1a to simultaneously train the network with classification loss functions and the MMF extension. During each iteration, first, we extract AVs and generate the representation matrix; second, we construct the MMF extension function from the "max_feature" vector and "min_feature" vector; third, the weights of each layer of the network are first updated to minimize the MMF extension then updated to minimize classification loss functions using stochastic gradient descent.

The MMF extension can also be incorporated into representation loss functions such as triplet loss and ii loss. As both representation loss functions and the MMF extension should be applied to the layer learning representations, their combination gives us:

$$\mathcal{L} = \mathcal{L}_{rep} + \lambda MMF, \tag{4}$$

$\mathcal{L}_{rep}$ is a representation loss function, and $\lambda$ is a hyperparameter that strikes a balance between the representation loss function and the MMF extension.

Figure 1b shows the network architecture using a representation loss function with an MMF extension. The combination serves on the Z-layer of the network. Moreover, the network weights get updated using stochastic gradient descent during each iteration.

After the training process, we obtain the representation centroids for each class. Then during the inference, we use the same strategy as used in ii loss [5]. First, we calculate the outlier score as the distance of learned representation to the nearest representation centroid. Then we sort the outlier score of the training data in descending order and pick the 99 percentile outlier score value as the outlier threshold. If the outlier score of a test sample exceeds the threshold, it will be recognized as the unknown class. Otherwise, it will be classified as the known class with the nearest representation centroid.

# 4 Experimental Evaluation

We evaluate the MMF extension with simulated open-set datasets from the following four datasets.

**MNIST** [14] contains 70,000 handwritten digits from 0 to 9, which is 10 classes in total. To simulate an open-set dataset, we randomly pick six digits as the known classes participant in the training, while the rest are treated as the unknown class only existing in the test set.

**CIFAR-10** [7] contains 60,000 $32 \times 32$ color images in 10 classes, with 6,000 images per class. There are 50,000 training images and 10,000 test images. We first convert the color images to grayscale and randomly pick six classes out of the ten classes as the known classes, while the remaining classes are treated as the known class only existing in the test set.

**Microsoft Challenge (MC)** [8] contains disassembled malware samples from 9 families. We use 10260 samples that can be correctly parsed then extract their function call graphs (FCG) as in [4] for the experiment. The dimensionality of the FCG is $63 \times 63$. Again, to simulate an open-set dataset, we randomly pick six classes as the known classes, while the rest are considered unknowns.

**Android Genome (AG)** [18] consists of malicious android apps from many families in different sizes. We use nine families (986 samples) with a relatively larger size for the experiment to be fairly split into the training set, the test set, and the validation set. We first use [3] to extract the function instructions and then extract 1453 raw FCG features as in [4]. Like the MNIST and the MC dataset, we randomly pick six classes as the known classes in the training set and consider the rest as the unknown class, which are only used in the test phase.

## 4.1 Network Architectures and Evaluation Criteria

We evaluate the MMF extension associated with two types of loss functions: classification loss functions and representation loss functions. Specifically, we use the cross-entropy loss as the example of classification loss functions, and use ii loss [5] and triplet loss [16] as the examples of representation loss functions. Moreover, we compare these pairs with OpenMax [1].

For the MNIST dataset, the padded input layer is of size (32, 32), followed by two non-linear convolutional layers with 32 and 64 nodes. We also use the max-pooling layers with kernel size (3, 3) and strides (2, 2) after each convolutional layer. We use two fully connected non-linear layers with 256 and 128 hidden units after the convolutional component. Furthermore, the linear layer Z, where we extract the representation matrix, is six dimensions in our experiment. We use the Relu activation function for all the non-linear layers and set the Dropout's keep probability as 0.2 for the fully connected layers. We use Adam optimizer with a learning rate of 0.001. The network architecture of the CIFAR-10 experiment is similar to the MNIST dataset, except the padded input layer is of size (36, 36). The experiment for the MS Challenge dataset also implements two convolutional layers. The padded input layer is of size (67, 67). However, we only use one fully connected layer instead of two after the convolutional layers. Also, we make the keep probability of Dropout as 0.9. The Android Genome dataset does not use the convolutional component. We use a network with one fully connected layer of 64 units before the linear layer Z. We also used Dropout with a keep probability of 0.9 for the fully connected layers. We set the learning rate of Adam optimizer as 0.1. Besides, we use batch normalization in all the layers to prevent features from getting excessively large. And as mentioned in Sect. 3.2, we use contamination ratio of 0.01 for the threshold selection.

As we discussed in Eq. 4, we use a hyperparameter $\lambda$ combine the MMF extension with the representation loss functions (i.e. ii loss and triplet loss in the experiments) as: $\mathcal{L} = \mathcal{L}_{rep} + \lambda MMF$. While the range of $\lambda$ is (0, 1], we set $\lambda$ as 0.2 and 0.5 for ii loss and triplet loss for the MNIST and CIFAR-10 datasets. For the MC dataset, we set $\lambda$ as 0.5 and 0.3 for ii loss and triplet loss. We set $\lambda$ as 0.4 for both ii loss and triplet loss in the AG dataset's experiments.

We simulate three different groups of open sets for each dataset then repeat each group 10 runs, so each dataset has 30 runs in total. When measuring the model performance, we use the average AUC scores under 10% and 100% FPR (False Positive Rate) for recognizing the unknown class, as lower FPR is desirable in the real world for cases like malware detection. Furthermore, we measure the F1 scores for known and unknown classes ($C+1$ classes) separately as one of the OSR tasks is to classify the known classes. Moreover, we perform t-tests with 95% confidence in both the AUC scores and F1 scores to see if the proposed MMF extension can significantly improve different loss functions.

## 4.2   Experimental Results

We compare the model performances of OpenMax as well as three loss function quadruples: cross-entropy loss, ii loss, and triplet loss. Table 1 shows the AUC scores of the models in the four datasets; mainly, we focus on comparing the "Standalone" with the corresponding "+MMF" subcolumns. We observe that the quadruples, in general, achieve better AUC scores than OpenMax. Moreover, with the MMF extension, the AUC scores of the loss functions have achieved

**Table 1.** The average AUC scores of 30 runs at 100% and 10% FPR of OpenMax and three loss functions quadruples. The underlined values are statistical significant better than the standalone loss functions via t-test with 95% confidence. The values in bold are the highest values in each quadruple. The values in brackets are the highest values in each row.

| | FPR | OpenMax | ce Standalone | +MMF | +MaxF | +MinF | ii Standalone | +MMF | +MaxF | +MinF | triplet Standalone | +MMF | +MaxF | +MinF |
|---|---|---|---|---|---|---|---|---|---|---|---|---|---|---|
| MNIST | 100% | 0.9138 | 0.9255 | 0.9479 | **0.9515** | 0.9393 | 0.9578 | [0.9649] | 0.9579 | 0.9607 | 0.9496 | **0.9585** | 0.9480 | 0.9404 |
| | 10% | 0.0590 | **0.0765** | 0.0744 | 0.0761 | 0.0751 | 0.0821 | [0.0842] | 0.0826 | 0.0830 | 0.0750 | **0.0796** | 0.0777 | 0.0739 |
| CIFAR-10 | 100% | [0.6757] | 0.5803 | 0.5982 | **0.6103** | 0.5807 | 0.6392 | 0.6419 | 0.6437 | **0.6439** | 0.6106 | **0.6248** | 0.6131 | 0.6127 |
| | 10% | 0.0065 | 0.0070 | 0.0089 | **0.0090** | 0.0077 | [0.0103] | 0.0096 | 0.0100 | 0.0100 | 0.0089 | **0.0102** | 0.0092 | 0.0093 |
| MC | 100% | 0.8739 | 0.9148 | [0.9500] | 0.9387 | 0.9352 | 0.9385 | **0.9461** | 0.9407 | 0.9397 | 0.9240 | **0.9430** | 0.9317 | 0.9178 |
| | 10% | 0.0530 | 0.0530 | 0.0635 | 0.0600 | 0.0588 | 0.0627 | [0.0656] | 0.0629 | 0.0619 | 0.0565 | **0.0622** | 0.0563 | 0.0546 |
| AG | 100% | 0.4150 | 0.7506 | **0.8205** | 0.8152 | 0.7501 | 0.8427 | 0.8694 | 0.8763 | [0.8831] | 0.8271 | **0.8379** | 0.8203 | 0.8256 |
| | 10% | 0.0010 | 0.0058 | 0.0148 | **0.0163** | 0.0036 | 0.0285 | 0.0305 | 0.0366 | [0.0368] | 0.0229 | **0.0275** | 0.0260 | 0.0235 |

**Table 2.** The average F1 scores of 30 runs of OpenMax and three loss functions pairs. The underlined values show statistically significant improvements (t-test with 95% confidence) comparing with the standalone loss functions. The values in bold are the highest values in each column.

| OpenMax | | MNIST Known | Unknown | Overall | CIFAR-10 Known | Unknown | Overall | MC Known | Unknown | Overall | AG Known | Unknown | Overall |
|---|---|---|---|---|---|---|---|---|---|---|---|---|---|
| | | 0.8964 | **0.7910** | 0.8814 | **0.6456** | **0.5407** | **0.6306** | 0.8903 | 0.7329 | 0.8679 | 0.2273 | **0.7761** | 0.3057 |
| ce | Standalone | 0.7596 | 0.7561 | 0.7591 | 0.5672 | 0.3697 | 0.5390 | 0.8881 | 0.6643 | 0.8562 | 0.5346 | 0.0033 | 0.4587 |
| | +MMF | 0.8504 | 0.7902 | 0.8809 | 0.5994 | 0.3271 | 0.5605 | 0.9090 | **0.7963** | 0.8929 | 0.5555 | 0.1142 | 0.4925 |
| ii | Standalone | 0.9320 | 0.8833 | 0.9250 | 0.6206 | 0.3570 | 0.5829 | 0.9128 | 0.7257 | 0.886 | 0.6349 | 0.6677 | 0.6396 |
| | +MMF | **0.9373** | 0.8916 | **0.9308** | 0.6205 | 0.3660 | 0.5842 | 0.9210 | 0.7680 | **0.8991** | 0.6407 | 0.7251 | **0.6528** |
| triplet | Standalone | 0.9103 | 0.8302 | 0.8989 | 0.5798 | 0.4515 | 0.5614 | 0.8998 | 0.7018 | 0.8715 | 0.5929 | 0.6323 | 0.5986 |
| | +MMF | 0.9239 | 0.8625 | 0.9152 | 0.5943 | 0.4790 | 0.5778 | 0.9064 | 0.7213 | 0.8800 | 0.6005 | 0.6895 | 0.6132 |

statistically significant improvements in 16 out of 24 cases (3 loss functions × 4 datasets × 2 FPR values).

Table 2 shows the average F1 scores for the four datasets. We first calculate the F1 scores for each of the $C$ known classes and the unknown class, then average the $C + 1$ classes as the Overall F1 scores. We can see that the loss functions with the MMF extension have better results than their corresponding standalone versions for both the known and the unknown classes. We observe that ii loss with the MMF extension is more accurate than the other five methods in six out of twelve F1 scores. Particularly, it achieves the highest Overall F1 scores for three out of four datasets.

Table 3 shows the comparison of the average training time of the 30 runs for the MNIST dataset with 5000 iterations via NVIDIA Tesla K80 GPU on AWS. We find that adding the MMF extension almost doubles the training time of using standalone cross-entropy. While for ii loss and triplet loss, adding the extension increases the training time by around 1%. The reason is that the MMF extension needs to create the representation matrix from scratch for the network with ce loss, which needs an extra backpropagation step, both of which take more time. We also observe that ii loss has the fastest training time among three loss functions with our MMF extension. Overall F1 scores and training time indicate that "ii+MMF" is the most accurate and efficient combination.

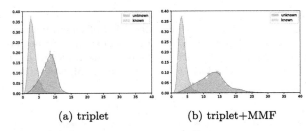

(a) triplet                  (b) triplet+MMF

**Table 3.** The comparison of training time for the MNIST dataset.

|         | Regular | +MMF   | delta   |
|---------|---------|--------|---------|
| ce      | 119.33  | 230.43 | +111.1  |
| ii      | 122.17  | 123.30 | +1.14   |
| triplet | 223.27  | 225.70 | +2.43   |

**Fig. 4.** The distributions of outlier scores in MNIST.

## 4.3   Analysis

Figure 3c shows the heatmap of MAV values of the simulated open MNIST dataset trained by cross-entropy loss with the MMF extension. We take digits "0", "2", "3", "4", "6", "9" as the known classes and the remaining digits as the unknown class. Comparing with the MAV values from the network with standalone cross-entropy loss (Fig. 3a), we can find that the MAVs of the known classes become more discriminative from each other, and each of the known classes has its representative feature. (e.g. Z1 for class "0", Z2 for class "2"). Whereas the MMF extension has less effect on the unknown class, its MAV values are relatively evenly distributed.

Since we recognize the unknown class based on the outlier score described in Sect. 3.3, we analyze both the test samples' outlier scores from the known classes and the unknown class from the MNIST experiment. Figure 4 shows the histogram of the distributions of the outlier scores in triplet loss experiments and triplet loss with the MMF extension. Compared with standalone triplet loss, adding an MMF extension increases the outlier scores of the unknown class, which pushes the score distributions further away from those of the known classes and results in fewer overlaps between the known classes the unknown class. It is the reduced overlaps that make the known classes and the unknown classes more separable than before. Figure 5 shows the t-SNE (perplexity: 50) plots of the Z-layer representations of the MNIST dataset from the same experiments. With the MMF extension, the known classes and the unknown class are more separate from each other, and the known classes become more disparate than before.

We also perform an ablation analysis for the MMF loss extension to understand the importance of the MMF extension's two properties. As shown in Table 1, our baselines include (1) standalone loss functions; (2) loss functions with an extension that maximize the most significant feature as Property A (MaxF); (3) loss functions with an extension that minimizes the least significant feature as Property B (MinF). In general, the MMF extension with both properties outperforms the baselines. This result is consistent with our motivation for the two properties at the beginning of Sect. 3. Moreover, we find that MaxF and MinF extensions can also achieve better performance than standalone loss functions. While both properties improve AUC scores, Property A (MaxF) has

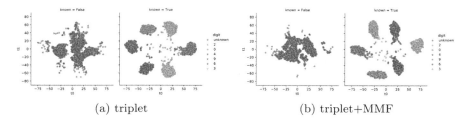

(a) triplet                                    (b) triplet+MMF

**Fig. 5.** The t-SNE plots of the MNIST dataset in the experiments of triplet vs. triplet+MMF. The left subplots of (a) and (b) are the representations of the unknown class (a mixture of digits "1", "5", "7" and "8"), and the right plots are the representations of the known classes.

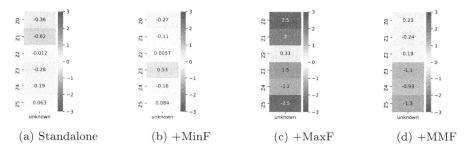

(a) Standalone        (b) +MinF        (c) +MaxF        (d) +MMF

**Fig. 6.** The heatmap of the unknown class's MAV in the experiment of cross entropy loss (ce) on the Microsoft Challenge dataset (MC).

a more significant improvement. Hence, Property A plays a more critical role in AUC improvement than Property B.

To investigate why MinF also helps improve AUC performance, we show the heatmap of the MAV for the unknown class in the experiment of ce on the MC dataset in Fig. 6. Comparing Fig. 6a and Fig. 6b, we observe that MinF reduced the feature magnitudes for the unknown class, thus increased the distance between the known and unknown classes. Similarly, from Fig. 6c and Fig. 6d, we observe that the feature magnitudes of the unknown class in MMF (MaxF+MinF) are much smaller than the ones in MaxF. The second observation is consistent with the earlier discussion on adding MinF to help MaxF in MMF at the beginning of Sect. 3. In addition, we observed similar behaviors from other datasets.

## 5   Conclusion

We introduced a loss function extension for the OSR problem. The extension maximizes the feature with the largest magnitude meanwhile minimizes the one with the smallest magnitude for all the known classes during training so that the learned representations are more discriminative from each other. We have shown that while the known classes are more discriminative from each other, the feature values of unknown classes are less affected by the extension, hence simplifying the open set recognition. We incorporated the proposed extension into classification and representation loss functions and evaluated them in images and malware samples. The results show that the proposed approach has achieved statistically significant improvements for different loss functions.

# References

1. Bendale, A., Boult, T.E.: Towards open set deep networks. In: Proceedings of the IEEE Conference on Computer Vision and Pattern Recognition, pp. 1563–1572 (2016)
2. Dhamija, A.R., Günther, M., Boult, T.E.: Reducing network agnostophobia. In: Advances in Neural Information Processing Systems, vol. 31, pp. 9175–9186 (2018)
3. Gascon, H., Yamaguchi, F., Arp, D., Rieck, K.: Structural detection of android malware using embedded call graphs. In: AISec 2013, pp. 45–54 (2013)
4. Hassen, M., Chan, P.K.: Scalable function call graph-based malware classification. In: Proceedings ACM Conference on Data and Application Security and Privacy, pp. 239–248 (2017)
5. Hassen, M., Chan, P.K.: Learning a neural-network-based representation for open set recognition. In: Proceedings SIAM International Conference Data Mining, pp. 154–162 (2020)
6. Hendrycks, D., Mazeika, M., Dietterich, T.G.: Deep anomaly detection with outlier exposure. In: 7th International Conference on Learning Representations (2019)
7. Krizhevsky, A., Hinton, G., et al.: Learning multiple layers of features from tiny images (2009)
8. LeCun, Y., Cortes, C., Burges, C.J.: The MNIST database (1999). http://yann.lecun.com/exdb/mnist/
9. Lee, K., Lee, H., Lee, K., Shin, J.: Training confidence-calibrated classifiers for detecting out-of-distribution samples. In: International Conference Learning Representations (2018)
10. Li, X.-L., Liu, B.: Learning from positive and unlabeled examples with different data distributions. In: Gama, J., Camacho, R., Brazdil, P.B., Jorge, A.M., Torgo, L. (eds.) ECML 2005. LNCS (LNAI), vol. 3720, pp. 218–229. Springer, Heidelberg (2005). https://doi.org/10.1007/11564096_24
11. Neal, L., Olson, M., Fern, X., Wong, W.-K., Li, F.: Open set learning with counterfactual images. In: Ferrari, V., Hebert, M., Sminchisescu, C., Weiss, Y. (eds.) ECCV 2018. LNCS, vol. 11210, pp. 620–635. Springer, Cham (2018). https://doi.org/10.1007/978-3-030-01231-1_38
12. Ortiz, E.G., Becker, B.C.: Face recognition for web-scale datasets. Comput. Vis. Image Underst. 118, 153–170 (2014)
13. Pidhorskyi, S., Almohsen, R., Doretto, G.: Generative probabilistic novelty detection with adversarial autoencoders. In: NeurIPS, vol. 31, pp. 6823–6834 (2018)
14. Ronen, R., Radu, M., Feuerstein, C., Yom-Tov, E., Ahmadi, M.: Microsoft malware classification challenge. CoRR arXiv:1802.10135 (2018)
15. Schlegl, T., Seeböck, P., Waldstein, S.M., Schmidt-Erfurth, U., Langs, G.: Unsupervised anomaly detection with generative adversarial networks to guide marker discovery. In: Information Processing in Medical Imaging, pp. 146–157 (2017)
16. Schroff, F., Kalenichenko, D., Philbin, J.: FaceNet: a unified embedding for face recognition and clustering. In: Conference on CVPR, pp. 815–823 (2015)

17. Schultheiss, A., Käding, C., Freytag, A., Denzler, J.: Finding the unknown: novelty detection with extreme value signatures of deep neural activations. In: Pattern Recognition - 39th German Conference, pp. 226–238 (2017)
18. Zhou, Y., Jiang, X.: Android malware genome project (2015). http://www. malgenomeproject.org/

# On the Selection of Loss Functions Under Known Weak Label Models

Daniel Bacaicoa-Barber[1]([⊠])[iD], Miquel Perello-Nieto[2][iD],
Raúl Santos-Rodríguez[2][iD], and Jesús Cid-Sueiro[1][iD]

[1] University Carlos III of Madrid, 28670 Leganés, Madrid, Spain
{dbacaico,jcid}@ing.uc3m.es
[2] University of Bristol, Bristol, UK
{miquel.perellonieto,enrsr}@bristol.ac.uk

**Abstract.** This paper considers the problem of constructing proper loss functions for learning from weak labels by means of linear transformations of proper losses based on true labels. Recent works have shown that linear transformations defined by a left inverse of the transition matrix of the weak labelling process, transforms a true-label proper loss into a weak-label proper loss. In this paper, we show that the choice of both the true-label loss and the left inverse has a major influence on the performance of the learning algorithm, and we propose a novel method to optimize the loss selection. Some simulation results demonstrate the advantages of the proposed method.

**Keywords:** Weak labels · Proper loss · Convexity

## 1 Introduction

Supervised learning algorithms rest on the assumption that a reliable set of labeled data is available. However, data labeling is frequently a costly process that can be affected by different sources of errors. In some applications, data samples with labels from the target class are rare, but large datasets with partial information about the class of the data, in the form of weak labels, may be available. Since standard algorithms require a large dataset with true labels for supervised learning, the design of efficient algorithms for learning with imperfect supervision are of great practical importance.

In this work, a weak label is interpreted as an element from a finite set of classes that is statistically related to the target class. This is the denomination used by Cid-Sueiro et al. (2014) or Yoshida et al. (2021), although corrupted labels (Van Rooyen and Williamson 2017) has been used with the same meaning.

This work was supported by FEDER/ Ministerio de Ciencia, Innovación y Universidades – Agencia Estatal de Investigación, grant TEC2017-83838-R; and the SPHERE Next Steps Project funded by the UK Engineering and Physical Sciences Research Council (EPSRC) [grant EP/R005273/1]. RSR is funded by the UKRI Turing AI Fellowship EP/V024817/1.

I. Farkaš et al. (Eds.): ICANN 2021, LNCS 12892, pp. 332–343, 2021.
https://doi.org/10.1007/978-3-030-86340-1_27

The problem of learning from weak labels encompasses several problems that can be taken as particular cases: noisy labels (Biggio et al. 2011), partial labels (Grandvalet 2002; Nguyen and Caruana 2008; Cour et al. 2011) (also named ambiguous (Hüllermeier and Beringer 2006), or candidate labels (Jin and Ghahramani 2002), or complementary labels (Ishida et al. 2017). Also some problems in semi-supervised learning and learning from multiple annotators (Raykar et al. 2010) can be integrated into this framework.

We will focus situations where a statistical model relating the weak labels and the true classes is available, or can be estimated from data. Although in these situations, classification models can be adjusted by maximum likelihood applying and expectation-maximization algorithm (see, for instance Jin and Ghahramani (2002) or Perello-Nieto et al. (2020)), the construction of weak-label losses as a linear transformation of true-label losses is an interesting alternative for several reasons (Cid-Sueiro et al. 2014): (1) the adaptation of code for true labels to weak labels is straightforward, (2) the transformations are robust to some situation of partial knowledge about the true-to-weak transition probabilities, and (3) these adaptations can be applied not only on the proper loss setting but also to construct classification or ranking calibrated losses. The idea was used in Natarajan et al. (2013) for noisy labels, and proposed for general weak label models in Cid-Sueiro (2012), showing that these losses can be robust even in situations where the knowledge of the model relating weak labels and true classes is incomplete. Van Rooyen and Williamson (2017) have shown how to select the transformation in order to preserve convexity.

More recently, Yoshida et al. (2021) has shown that the convexification proposed by Van Rooyen and Williamson (2017) can transform the cross entropy into a convex loss that is not lower-bounded, which undermines the efficiency of learning from a finite set of samples. To solve this issue, a correction method has been proposed to obtain a modified cross entropy which is lower-bounded.

In this paper we provide theoretical an experimental evidence that not only the choice of the true-label loss but also the choice of the linear transformation have a strong influence of the performance of weak label learning algorithms based on transformations. We show that the selection of the loss can be optimized by taking into account the prior distribution of the weak labels. Several experiments will serve to illustrate the advantages of our method.

## 2   Formulation

### 2.1   Notation

Vectors are written in boldface, matrices in boldface capital and sets in calligraphic letters (e.g. $\mathbf{v}$, $\mathbf{M}$, and $\mathcal{S}$ respectively). For any integer $n$, $\mathbf{e}_i^n$ is a $n$-dimensional unit vector with all zero components apart from the $i$-th component which is equal to one, and $\mathbb{1}_n$ is an $n$-dimensional all-ones vector.

Superindex $^\top$ denotes transposition. $\Psi()$ denotes a weak-label loss, and $\tilde{\Psi}$ a true-label loss. The number of classes is $c$, and the number of possible weak label vectors is $d$. $|\mathbf{v}|$ is the number of nonzero elements in vector $\mathbf{v}$. The $n$-dimensional probability simplex is $\mathcal{P}_n = \{\mathbf{p} \in [0,1]^n : \mathbf{p}^\top \mathbb{1}_n = 1\}$.

## 2.2 Learning from Weak Labels

Let $\mathcal{X}$ be a sample space, $\mathcal{Y}$ a finite set of $c$ *target* classes, and $\mathcal{W}$ a finite set of $d \geq c$ *weak* classes. Sample $(\mathbf{x}, \boldsymbol{\omega}) \in \mathcal{X} \times \mathcal{W}$ is drawn from an unknown distribution $P$.

We will assume that the target classes are encoded in one-hot vectors, so that $\mathcal{Y} = \{\mathbf{e}_j^c, j = 0, 1, \ldots, c-1\}$. The goal of learning from weak labels consists on training a predictor of the target class $\mathbf{y} \in \mathcal{Y}$ given sample $\mathbf{x}$, using a dataset $\mathcal{S} = \{(\mathbf{x}_k, \boldsymbol{\omega}_k), k = 0, \ldots, K-1\}$ whose labels correspond to weak classes in $\mathcal{W}$

In general, the meaning of the classes represented in $\mathcal{Y}$ and $\mathcal{W}$ will be specific of each application. Our general formulation is useful to encompass very different scenarios with different forms of partial supervision but, in common situations, the classes in $\mathcal{W}$ represent subsets of the classes in $\mathcal{Y}$. The following are some examples:

- **Supervised learning**: In this case, $\mathcal{W} = \mathcal{Y}$ and $\boldsymbol{\omega} = \mathbf{y}$ with probability 1.
- **Noisy labels** Raykar et al. (2010): $\mathcal{W} = \mathcal{Y}$ but $P\{\boldsymbol{\omega} \neq \mathbf{y}\} > 0$.
- **Semisupervised learning**: $\mathcal{W} = \mathcal{Y} \cup \{\mathbf{0}\}$, where $\boldsymbol{\omega} = \mathbf{0}$ when the true target class is not observed.
- **Partial labels** Jin and Ghahramani (2002), Cour et al. (2011), Grandvalet and Bengio (2004), Ambroise et al. (2001): each label is a set of *candidate* target classes, only one of them being true. In this case, each element in $\mathcal{W}$ is a non empty subset of $\mathcal{Y}$.

When the weak labels represent a subset of classes, we will represent them as binary vectors indicating which of the target classes are observed, e.g. $\boldsymbol{\omega} = (1, 0, 0, 1, 1)$ means that the weak label contains target classes 0, 3 and 4, but not 1 and 2.

For mathematical convenience, we will often represent the weak classes as one-hot vectors. For any ordered set $\mathcal{W} = \{\boldsymbol{\omega}_0, \ldots, \boldsymbol{\omega}_{d-1}\}$ unit vector $\mathbf{e}_i^d$ will be used as the one-hot representation of $\boldsymbol{\omega}_i$, and the set $\mathcal{Z} = \{\mathbf{e}_i^d, i = 0, 1, \ldots, d-1\}$ will be referred as the one-hot representation of $\mathcal{W}$. Also, we will use $\mathbf{z} \in \mathcal{Z}$ to represent the weak class of sample $\mathbf{x}$. Thus, $\mathbf{z} = \mathbf{e}_i^d$ is equivalent to $\boldsymbol{\omega} = \boldsymbol{\omega}_i$.

Using the one-hot representation, the learning goal consists on training a predictor of the target class $\mathbf{y} \in \mathcal{Y}$ given sample $\mathbf{x}$, using a weakly labelled dataset $\mathcal{S} = \{(\mathbf{x}_k, \mathbf{z}_k), k = 0, \ldots, K-1\}$ whose labels are weak classes from $\mathcal{Z}$.

Without loss of generality, we assume that $\mathcal{Z}$ contains only weak classes with nonzero probability (i.e. $P(\mathbf{z}) > 0$ for any $\mathbf{z} \in \mathcal{Z}$).

The dependency between $\mathbf{z}$ and $\mathbf{y}$ is modelled through a $d \times c$ transition probability matrix $\mathbf{M} \in \mathcal{M}$ with components

$$m_{ij} = P\{z_i = 1 | y_j = 1, \mathbf{x}\} \tag{1}$$

We will assume that the transition matrix is independent of $\mathbf{x}$, which is a common assumption in this setting (Raykar et al. 2010; Jin and Ghahramani 2002; Ambroise et al. 2001; Grandvalet and Bengio 2004; Yoshida et al. 2021). Defining posterior probability vectors $\mathbf{p}(\mathbf{x})$ and $\boldsymbol{\eta}(\mathbf{x})$ with components $p_i = P\{z_i = 1|\mathbf{x}\}$ and $\eta_j = P\{y_j = 1|\mathbf{x}\}$, we can write $\mathbf{p}(\mathbf{x}) = \mathbf{M}\boldsymbol{\eta}(\mathbf{x})$. In general, the dependency with $\mathbf{x}$ in posterior probabilities will be omitted and we will write, for instance,

$$\mathbf{p} = \mathbf{M}\boldsymbol{\eta}. \tag{2}$$

### 2.3 Proper Losses

For every input $\mathbf{x}$ the classifier computes a score $\mathbf{f} \in \mathbb{R}^c$ and a prediction $\text{pred}(\mathbf{x}) \in \text{argmax}_i\{f_i(\mathbf{x})\}$. A weak-label loss is any lower bounded function $\Psi(\mathbf{z}, \mathbf{f}) \in \mathbb{R}$. We are interested in losses that are minimized when the score vector is an estimate of the posterior class probabilities:

**Definition 1 (Properness).** *Weak loss $\Psi(\mathbf{z}, \mathbf{f})$ is proper to predict $\mathbf{y}$ from $\mathbf{f}$ if*

$$\boldsymbol{\eta} \in \arg\min_{\mathbf{f}} \mathbb{E}_{\mathbf{z} \sim \mathbf{M}\boldsymbol{\eta}}\{\Psi(\mathbf{z}, \mathbf{f})\}, \tag{3}$$

*where $\boldsymbol{\eta}$ is the probability vector with components $\eta_j = P\{y_j = 1\}$. The loss is strictly proper if $\boldsymbol{\eta}$ is the unique minimizer.*

A vector representation of losses will be useful: we define

$$\boldsymbol{\Psi}(\mathbf{f}) = (\Psi(\mathbf{e}_0^d, \mathbf{f}), \dots \Psi(\mathbf{e}_{d-1}^d, \mathbf{f})) \tag{4}$$
$$\tilde{\boldsymbol{\Psi}}(\mathbf{f}) = (\tilde{\Psi}(\mathbf{e}_0^c, \mathbf{f}), \dots, \tilde{\Psi}(\mathbf{e}_{c-1}^c, \mathbf{f})) \tag{5}$$

as the vector representations of the weak-label loss $\Psi(\mathbf{z}, \mathbf{f})$ and true-label loss $\tilde{\Psi}(\mathbf{y}, \mathbf{f})$, respectively, so that $\Psi(\mathbf{z}, \mathbf{f}) = \mathbf{z}^\intercal \boldsymbol{\Psi}(\mathbf{f})$ and $\tilde{\Psi}(\mathbf{y}, \mathbf{f}) = \mathbf{y}^\intercal \tilde{\boldsymbol{\Psi}}(\mathbf{f})$. Also, the expected los in (3) can be written as

$$\mathbb{E}_{\mathbf{z} \sim \mathbf{M}\boldsymbol{\eta}}\{\Psi(\mathbf{z}, \mathbf{f})\} = \boldsymbol{\eta}^\intercal \mathbf{M}^\intercal \boldsymbol{\Psi}(\mathbf{f}) \tag{6}$$

which shows that, in general, the properness of a given weak-label loss depends on the transition matrix. To make this dependency explicit, we will say that $\boldsymbol{\Psi}$ is $\mathbf{M}$-proper if it is proper for a transition matrix $\mathbf{M}$.

Note, also, that defining the *equivalent* true-label loss

$$\tilde{\boldsymbol{\Psi}}(\mathbf{f}) = \mathbf{M}^\intercal \boldsymbol{\Psi}(\mathbf{f}), \tag{7}$$

it is straightforward to show that weak-loss $\boldsymbol{\Psi}(\mathbf{f})$ is (strictly) $\mathbf{M}$-proper iff true-label loss $\tilde{\boldsymbol{\Psi}}(\mathbf{f})$ is (strictly) proper (Cid-Sueiro et al. 2014; Van Rooyen and Williamson 2017; Yoshida et al. 2021).

Equation (7) can be used to check if a given loss is $\mathbf{M}$-proper. However, since $\mathbf{M}^\intercal$ is $d \times c$, it has no left inverse (in general), and we cannot take $\mathbf{M}^\intercal$ out from the left side of (7) to compute $\Psi$ from $\tilde{\Psi}$. For any given $\mathbf{M}$ and any given true-label loss $\tilde{\boldsymbol{\Psi}}(\mathbf{f})$, there is an uncountable number of losses $\boldsymbol{\Psi}(\mathbf{f})$ satisfying (7).

# 3   Linear Transformations of Losses

The linear relation in (7) suggests to compute a weak-label loss as a linear transformation of a given true-label loss $\tilde{\boldsymbol{\Psi}}$

$$\boldsymbol{\Psi} = \tilde{\mathbf{Y}}^{\mathsf{T}} \tilde{\boldsymbol{\Psi}} \tag{8}$$

Noting that $\Psi(\mathbf{z}, \boldsymbol{\eta}) = (\mathbf{z}^{\mathsf{T}} \tilde{\mathbf{Y}}^{\mathsf{T}}) \tilde{\boldsymbol{\Psi}}(\boldsymbol{\eta})$ and, by analogy with the relation $\tilde{\boldsymbol{\Psi}}(\mathbf{y}, \boldsymbol{\eta}) = \mathbf{y}^{\mathsf{T}} \tilde{\boldsymbol{\Psi}}(\boldsymbol{\eta})$ we can compute weak loss $\boldsymbol{\Psi}$ by replacing in $\tilde{\boldsymbol{\Psi}}$ the target label $\mathbf{y}$ by a *virtual label* $\tilde{\mathbf{y}} = \tilde{\mathbf{Y}}\mathbf{z}$ (which is a column of $\tilde{\mathbf{Y}}$). Following Y). Following (Van Rooyen and Williamson 2017), we will call $\tilde{\mathbf{Y}}$ a *reconstruction* matrix.

Note that, according to (7), if $\tilde{\mathbf{Y}}$ is a left-inverse of $\mathbf{M}$, $\tilde{\boldsymbol{\Psi}}$ in (8) is the equivalent loss of $\boldsymbol{\Psi}$. This can be summarized on the following

**Theorem 1.** *(Cid-Sueiro et al. 2014)   Given a transition matrix* $\mathbf{M}$ *and a bounded and strictly proper loss* $\tilde{\boldsymbol{\Psi}}(\mathbf{f})$, *weak loss* $\boldsymbol{\Psi}(\mathbf{f}) = \tilde{\mathbf{Y}}^{\mathsf{T}} \tilde{\boldsymbol{\Psi}}(\mathbf{f})$ *is strictly* $\mathbf{M}$-*proper if and only if* $\tilde{\mathbf{Y}}\mathbf{M} = \lambda \mathbf{I}$, *for some* $\lambda > 0$.

## 3.1   Characterization of Convex Weak Losses

Since the left inverse of a non-negative matrix $\mathbf{M}$ has, in general, negative components, the convexity of true-label loss $\tilde{\boldsymbol{\Psi}}$ does not imply the convexity of $\boldsymbol{\Psi} = \tilde{\mathbf{Y}}\tilde{\boldsymbol{\Psi}}$. However, taking ideas from the theory of composite losses (Williamson et al. 2016) and the dual representation of losses (Blondel et al. 2020); Van Rooyen and Williamson (2017) have shown that convexity can be preserved with the appropriate choice of the reconstruction matrix and using a *canonical* loss. More specifically, they show that, if the prediction is computed through an inverse link function, $\mathbf{f} = \kappa(\mathbf{v})$, where $\mathbf{v}$ is a linear map in the form

$$\mathbf{v} = \mathbf{W}^{\mathsf{T}}\mathbf{x} - \frac{1}{c}\left(\mathbb{1}_c^{\mathsf{T}}\mathbf{W}^{\mathsf{T}}\mathbf{x}\right)\mathbb{1}_c \tag{9}$$

in such a way that the composite loss $\tilde{\boldsymbol{\Psi}}(\kappa(\mathbf{v}))$ has the form

$$\tilde{\boldsymbol{\Psi}}(\kappa(\mathbf{v})) = -\mathbf{v} + \phi(\mathbf{v})\mathbb{1}_{\mathbf{c}} \tag{10}$$

for some convex function $\phi$, and, in addition, the reconstruction matrix satisfies

$$\tilde{\mathbf{Y}}^{\mathsf{T}}\mathbb{1}_c \succ \mathbf{0} \tag{11}$$

then the transformed loss (8) is a convex function of the weights $\mathbf{W}$. Note that we could make $\mathbf{v}$ in (9) nonlinear by replacing $\mathbf{x}$ with a nonlinear function of the observations.

*Example 1 (Logistic regression).* Taking $\kappa(\mathbf{v})$ as the softmax activation function and $\phi(\mathbf{v}) = \log(\sum_{i=1}^{c} \exp(v_i))$, the true-label loss in (10) is $\tilde{\boldsymbol{\Psi}}(\mathbf{f}) = -\log(\mathbf{f})$, which is the standard cross entropy.

## 3.2   Lower-Bounded Losses

The previous analysis shows that we can construct convex proper weak-label losses from a bounded convex proper true-label loss using a reconstruction matrix that, according to Theorem 1, must be (proportional to) a left-inverse of the transition matrix and satisfy (11). We can be tempted to construct **M**-proper losses based on the cross entropy from this approach. However, as noted by (Yoshida et al. 2021), the resulting loss may be not lower bounded. As an alternative, they propose to use a modified cross entropy given by (10) with

$$\phi(\mathbf{v}) = \log \left( \sum_{i=1}^{c} \exp(v_i) \right) + \frac{k}{2} \sum_{i=1}^{c} |v_i|^\alpha \tag{12}$$

which includes a regularization term with hyperparameters $k > 0$ and $\alpha > 1$.

# 4   Optimizing the Selection of the Weak Loss

Our contribution in this paper is twofold: (1) we will show, experimentally, that both the selection of the loss function (e.g. the value of hyperparameters $k$ and $\alpha$ in (12)) and the reconstruction matrix have a major influence on the performance of the classifiers, measured both in terms of the quality of the probability estimates and also the accuracy of class predictions, and (2) we provide theoretical evidence on the influence of the reconstruction matrix, and propose a method for its optimization. The latter is the goal of this section.

## 4.1   Optimizing Virtual Labels

Even though any virtual label matrix satisfying $\tilde{\mathbf{Y}}\mathbf{M} = \lambda\mathbf{I}$ provides an **M**-proper loss, the choice of the virtual matrix is relevant when $\eta$ is estimated from a finite sample set. A simple way to demonstrate the influence of $\tilde{\mathbf{Y}}$ is to consider a scenario of posterior probability estimation based on a dataset of i.i.d. weak labels (in one hot form), $\mathcal{S} = \{\mathbf{z}_0, \ldots, \mathbf{z}_{K-1}\}$ that have been generated independently from the distribution given by $\mathbf{M}\eta$. We can estimate $\eta$ from $\mathcal{S}$ by minimizing the empirical risk

$$\hat{R}(\Psi) = \sum_{k=0}^{K-1} \Psi(\mathbf{z}_k, \mathbf{f}) = \sum_{k=0}^{K-1} \mathbf{z}_k^\mathsf{T} \tilde{\mathbf{Y}}^\mathsf{T} \tilde{\Psi}(\mathbf{f}) = \left( \sum_{k=0}^{K-1} \tilde{\mathbf{y}}_k^\mathsf{T} \right) \tilde{\Psi}(\mathbf{f}) \tag{13}$$

where $\tilde{\mathbf{y}}_k = \tilde{\mathbf{Y}}\mathbf{z}_k$ is the *virtual label* corresponding to weak label $\mathbf{z}_k$. If $\tilde{\Psi}$ is proper, the empirical risk is minimized for

$$\mathbf{f}^* = \frac{1}{K} \sum_{k=0}^{K-1} \tilde{\mathbf{y}}_k \tag{14}$$

That is, the virtual labels are unbiased estimates of the posterior class probabilities, and the minimizer of the empirical risk (irrespective on the choice of the proper loss) is the average of the virtual labels associated to $\mathcal{S}$. The quality of the estimate can be evaluated as the variance of $\mathbf{f}^*$ over random generations of the sample set,

$$\text{var}\{\mathbf{f}^*\} = \mathbb{E}_{\mathcal{S}}\{\|\mathbf{f}^* - \boldsymbol{\eta}\|^2\} = \frac{1}{K}\mathbb{E}_{\tilde{\mathbf{y}}}\{\|\tilde{\mathbf{y}}^* - \boldsymbol{\eta}\|^2\} \tag{15}$$

The above example suggests that we can select the virtual labels in order to minimize the mean square error

$$\begin{aligned}
\mathbb{E}\{\|\tilde{\mathbf{y}} - \boldsymbol{\eta}\|^2\} &= \sum_{i=0}^{d-1}(\tilde{\mathbf{y}}_i - \boldsymbol{\eta})^{\mathsf{T}}(\tilde{\mathbf{y}}_i - \boldsymbol{\eta})\left((\mathbf{e}_i^d)^{\mathsf{T}}\mathbf{M}\boldsymbol{\eta}\right) \\
&= \text{diag}\left(\left(\tilde{\mathbf{Y}} - \boldsymbol{\eta}\mathbb{1}_d^{\mathsf{T}}\right)^{\mathsf{T}}\left(\tilde{\mathbf{Y}} - \boldsymbol{\eta}\mathbb{1}_d^{\mathsf{T}}\right)\right)^{\mathsf{T}}\mathbf{M}\boldsymbol{\eta} \\
&= \text{diag}\left(\tilde{\mathbf{Y}}^{\mathsf{T}}\tilde{\mathbf{Y}}\right)^{\mathsf{T}}\mathbf{M}\boldsymbol{\eta} - 2\,\boldsymbol{\eta}^{\mathsf{T}}\tilde{\mathbf{Y}}\mathbf{M}\boldsymbol{\eta} + \boldsymbol{\eta}^{\mathsf{T}}\boldsymbol{\eta}
\end{aligned} \tag{16}$$

Assuming $\tilde{\mathbf{Y}}\mathbf{M} = \mathbf{I}$ and using (2),

$$\mathbb{E}\{\|\tilde{\mathbf{y}} - \boldsymbol{\eta}\|^2\} = \text{diag}(\tilde{\mathbf{Y}}^{\mathsf{T}}\tilde{\mathbf{Y}})^{\mathsf{T}}\mathbf{p} - \boldsymbol{\eta}^{\mathsf{T}}\boldsymbol{\eta} \tag{17}$$

where $\mathbf{p} = \mathbf{M}\boldsymbol{\eta}$ are the weak class probabilities. Note that if $\boldsymbol{\eta}$ and $\mathbf{p}$ depend on $\mathbf{x}$, a similar expression is obtained by taking expectations over $\mathbf{x}$:

$$\mathbb{E}_{\mathbf{x}}\{\|\tilde{\mathbf{y}} - \boldsymbol{\eta}\|^2\} = \text{diag}(\tilde{\mathbf{Y}}^{\mathsf{T}}\tilde{\mathbf{Y}})^{\mathsf{T}}\overline{\mathbf{p}} - \mathbb{E}_{\mathbf{x}}\{\boldsymbol{\eta}^{\mathsf{T}}\boldsymbol{\eta}\} \tag{18}$$

where $\overline{\mathbf{p}} = \mathbb{E}_{\mathbf{x}}\{\mathbf{p}\}$ In general, the above expression cannot be computed because neither $\mathbb{E}_{\mathbf{x}}\{\boldsymbol{\eta}^{\mathsf{T}}\boldsymbol{\eta}\}$ nor $\mathbb{E}_{\mathbf{x}}\{\mathbf{p}\}$ are known. However, the former is not relevant for the optimization, and the latter can be estimated from the training set.

Therefore, we can select the virtual labels by solving the quadratic program

$$\min_{\tilde{\mathbf{Y}}}\left\{\text{diag}(\tilde{\mathbf{Y}}^{\mathsf{T}}\tilde{\mathbf{Y}})^{\mathsf{T}}\overline{\mathbf{p}}\right\}, \qquad \text{subject to } \tilde{\mathbf{Y}}\mathbf{M} = \mathbf{I}. \tag{19}$$

whose solution has the closed-form

$$\tilde{\mathbf{Y}} = (\mathbf{M}^{\mathsf{T}}\text{diag}(\overline{\mathbf{p}})^{-1}\mathbf{M})^{-1}\mathbf{M}^{\mathsf{T}}\text{diag}(\overline{\mathbf{p}})^{-1} \tag{20}$$

We can illustrate the influence of the choice of the virtual label matrix on the variance of the estimation with the following example:

*Example 2 (Partial labels).* Consider the scenario given by $\mathcal{W} = \{(1,0,0),(0,1,0),$ $(0,0,1),(0,1,1),(1,0,1),(1,1,0)\}$ transition matrix $\mathbf{M} = (0.2\,\mathbf{I}\mid 0.4(\mathbb{1}_c\mathbb{1}_c^{\mathsf{T}} - \mathbf{I}))^{\mathsf{T}}$, where $\mathbf{I}$ is the identity matrix, and a true class probability vector $\boldsymbol{\eta} = (0.05, 0.6, 0.35)^{\mathsf{T}}$. This corresponds to a scenario of partial labels (Cour et al. 2011), where the weak label contains the true class and possibly another false class taken at random from the other target classes. It is easy to see that virtual matrices $\tilde{\mathbf{Y}}_u = (9\mathbf{I}\mid\mathbf{0})$ and $\tilde{\mathbf{Y}}_d = (\mathbf{0}\mid 1.125\mathbb{1}_3\mathbb{1}_3^{\mathsf{T}} - 2.25\mathbf{I})$ satisfy the condition $\tilde{\mathbf{Y}}\mathbf{M} = \lambda\mathbf{I}$ and, thus, losses

$\boldsymbol{\Psi}_u(\mathbf{f}) = \tilde{\mathbf{Y}}_u\tilde{\boldsymbol{\Psi}}(\mathbf{f})$ and $\boldsymbol{\Psi}_d(\mathbf{f}) = \tilde{\mathbf{Y}}_d\tilde{\boldsymbol{\Psi}}(\mathbf{f})$ are proper. Moreover, any convex combination of the virtual label matrices $\tilde{\mathbf{Y}}_u = (w\tilde{\mathbf{Y}}_u + (1-w)\tilde{\mathbf{Y}}_d)\tilde{\boldsymbol{\Psi}}(\mathbf{f})$ with $0 \le w \le 1$, defines an $\mathbf{M}$-proper loss.

Figure 1 shows the expected MSE in (16) for any mixed loss $\boldsymbol{\Psi}_w(\mathbf{f})$ as a function of $w$, for a set of 1000 samples. We can observe that the MSE depends quadratically on $w$. The horizontal lines represent the MSE for the Moore-Penrose pseudoinverse, and the MSE of the optimal reconstruction in (20), using the true value of the weak probabilities in $\mathbf{p}$ and also an empirical estimate based on 1000 samples.

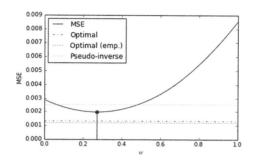

**Fig. 1.** MSE in (16) for loss $\boldsymbol{\Psi}_w(\mathbf{f})$ as a function of $w$, for a set of 1000 samples. The horizontal lines represent the MSE for the Moore-Penrose pseudoinverse, and the MSE of the optimal reconstruction (20), using the true value of the weak probabilities in $\mathbf{p}$ and also an empirical estimate based on 1000 samples.

**Estimating Weak Label Priors.** The prior weak label probabilities in $\overline{\mathbf{p}}$ are, in general, unknown, but they can be estimated from data. Assuming that the number of weak labels from each weak class, $\mathbf{n} = (n_0, \ldots, n_{d-1})$ follows a multinomial distribution

$$f(\mathbf{n}; K, \overline{\mathbf{p}}) = \frac{K!\overline{p}_0^{n_0} \cdots \overline{p}_{d-1}^{n_{d-1}}}{n_0! \cdots n_{d-1}!} \tag{21}$$

for $\sum_{i=0}^{d-1} n_i = K$, the ML estimate of the weak label priors is given by the solution to the optimization problem given by

$$\max_{\mathbf{p} \in \mathcal{P}_d} \mathbf{n}^\mathsf{T} \log \mathbf{p}, \qquad \text{subject to } \mathbf{p} = \mathbf{M}\boldsymbol{\eta}, \ \boldsymbol{\eta} \in \mathcal{P}_c \tag{22}$$

which is equivalent to take $\hat{\mathbf{p}}_{\mathrm{ML}} = \mathbf{M}\boldsymbol{\eta}_{\mathrm{ML}}$ with

$$\boldsymbol{\eta}_{\mathrm{ML}} = \operatorname*{argmax}_{\boldsymbol{\eta} \in \mathcal{P}_c} \mathbf{n}^\mathsf{T} \log (\mathbf{M}\boldsymbol{\eta}). \tag{23}$$

## 4.2   Optimizing Convexity-Preserving Virtual Labels

The weak-label loss given by reconstruction (20) is optimal in the MSE, but may be non convex. In order to obtain a convex loss, we should add in (19) the convexity condition (11), to obtain the quadratic program

$$\min_{\tilde{\mathbf{Y}}} \left\{ \sum_{i=0}^{d-1} \overline{p_i}\, \tilde{\mathbf{y}}_i^{\mathsf{T}} \tilde{\mathbf{y}}_i \right\}, \qquad \text{subject to } \tilde{\mathbf{Y}}\mathbf{M} = \mathbf{I},\ \tilde{\mathbf{Y}}^{\mathsf{T}}\mathbb{1}_c = \mathbb{1}_d \qquad (24)$$

There is no simple closed form solution for this minimization problem, but it can be found using standard optimization methods.

# 5   Experiments

We have conducted two types of experiments in the present study. First, we analyze the impact of the hyperparameters $k$ and $\alpha$ in Eq. (12). Second, we show the advantages of the optimal reconstruction matrices proposed in this paper.

**Datasets.** We have used 2 synthetic datasets based on a given posterior probability model. The marginal input distribution is uniform in one of them (`uniform`), and Gaussian mixture on the other (`blobs`). Synthetic datasets are usefull to analyze the behavior of the algorithm on the realizable case (where the classifier model can fit the posterior map), and to evaluate the quality of the posterior probability estimates.

In addition, we have also tested our models in 3 real world classification datasets from `openml.org`. For illustrating purposes, we chose datasets with a small amount of samples, with number of classes between 3 and 5 and no missing values: `balance-scale` (625 samples, 4 features, 3 classes) `car` (1728 samples, 21 features, 4 classes) and `wine` (178 samples, 13 features, 3 classes).

Before training, all the categorical features were transformed into binary features using a one-hot encoding. Finally, every feature was standardised with mean zero and standard deviation one.

As all datasets have only one true label per sample, we generated synthetic weak labels using transition matrix $\mathbf{M} \in (\mathbf{0}, \mathbf{1})^{\mathbf{2^c} \times \mathbf{c}}$ generated at random, in which the true label appears with probability $(1 - \alpha)$, i.e., $P(z_i = 1|y_j = 1, \mathbf{x}) = (1 - \alpha)$ if $i = 2^j$; while other labels may appear with probability $P(\mathbf{z}|y_j = 1, \mathbf{x})$ modelled as a Dirichlet distribution.

**Implementation.** For each dataset we trained a Logistic Regression (LR) with the BFGS optimization algorithm and 500 epochs. We used the regularized loss function (12) derived from the cross-entropy loss. For each reconstruction, we carried out one hundred repetitions of the algorithm each one with different weak labels generated at random by the same mixture matrix $\mathbf{M}$. All implementations are publicly available[1].

---

[1] https://github.com/DaniBacaicoa/ICANN2021_WeakLabels/.

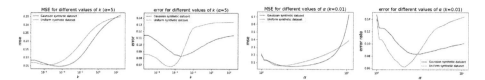

**Fig. 2.** Dependency of the hyperparameters on the dataset agains MSE and error rate.

**Metrics.** We have used two performance metrics: (1) the average square errors $\|\boldsymbol{\eta} - \mathbf{f}\|^2$, to evaluate the quality of the posterior probability estimates; and (2) the classification error rate, to evaluate the efficiency of class predictions. For the synthetic datasets $\boldsymbol{\eta}$ is the exact posterior, while it is an estimate of the prior probabilities in the case of real data. We have evaluated the metrics discussed above on a test set that we have extracted from samples for which we have access to the true labels.

**Models.** We evaluate several reconstruction matrices: (M-pinv) the Moore-Penrose pseudo inverse, equivalent to (20) but using the identity matrix instead of $diag(\overline{\mathbf{p}})$, (M-conv) the pseudo inverse with the convexity condition in (11), (M-opt) the optimal reconstruction proposed in (20), and (M-opt-conv) the solution of (24) that provides the optimal reconstruction with convexity constraints. As a gold standard we include the results of supervised learning using both the loss function with the correction term (SLBL) and the one trained with the standard cross entropy (SCe).

**Results.** Figure 2 shows the dependency of the parameters $\alpha$ and $k$ in (12). The results confirm the observation in Yoshida et al. (2021) that the choice of the hyperparameters has a major influence on the performance metrics. In addition, we have observed that the optimal values of $\alpha$ and $k$ may depend on the dataset. Therefore, for optimal performance, these parameters should be selected using some form of cross-validation (which is non-trivial, since no true test labels will be available in practice).

Figure 3 shows that the reconstruction presented in this study leads to a better estimation of the posterior probabilities than the Moore-penrose reconstruction matrix. This is a key fact as we are dealing with proper losses but we have a finite sample to estimate the posterior probabilities. We also show how, although the difference seems less marked, that the choice of an optimized reconstruction overall results in a better accuracy performance. Note that as $\eta$ is not known in the real datasets, we have replaced it by the prior distribution of the clean labels in order to get a discrepancy measure. We show the mean squared error and the accuracy for the synthetic uniform dataset in Figs. 3a and 3f; for the synthetic uniform dataset in Figs. 3b and 3g; for the Balance-Scale dataset in Figs. 3c and 3h; for the Car dataset in Figs. 3d and 3i and for the Wine dataset in Figs. 3e and 3j.

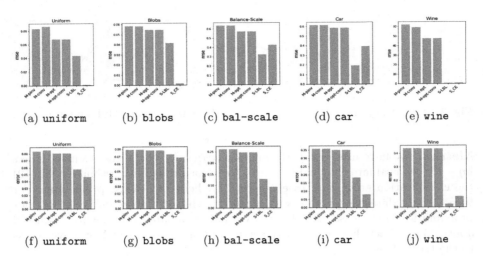

**Fig. 3.** Performance measures for the considered datasets under each reconstruction. First row shows average square errors and second row classification error rate.

As expected optimizing, the virtual label matrix leads to better approximations in average of the true posterior distribution of the clean labels when learning from finite weak datasets.

## 6    Conclusions

This paper analyzes the behavior of weak-label proper losses based on linear transformations of true-label proper losses. We have provided theoretical and experimental evidence that the choice of both the transformation (i.e. the reconstruction matrix) and the true-label proper loss have a major influence of the classification performance under different metrics. We provide a method to compute the optimal reconstruction matrix that only requires an estimate of the weak label prior probabilities, which can be estimated from data.

## References

Ambroise, C., Denoeux, T., Govaert, G., Smets, P.: Learning from an imprecise teacher: probabilistic and evidential approaches. Appl. Stoch. Models Data Anal. **1**, 100–105 (2001)

Biggio, B., Nelson, B., Laskov, P.: Support vector machines under adversarial label noise. In: Asian Conference on Machine Learning, pp. 97–112 (2011)

Blondel, M., Martins, A.F.T., Niculae, V.: Learning with fenchel-young losses. J. Mach. Learn. Res. **21**(35), 1–69 (2020)

Cid-Sueiro, J.: Proper losses for learning from partial labels. In: Advances in Neural Information Processing Systems 25, pp. 1574–1582 (2012)

Cid-Sueiro, J., García-García, D., Santos-Rodríguez, R.: Consistency of losses for learning from weak labels. In: Calders, T., Esposito, F., Hüllermeier, E., Meo, R. (eds.) ECML PKDD 2014. LNCS (LNAI), vol. 8724, pp. 197–210. Springer, Heidelberg (2014). https://doi.org/10.1007/978-3-662-44848-9_13

Cour, T., Sapp, B., Taskar, B.: Learning from partial labels. J. Mach. Learn. Res. **12**, 1225–1261 (2011)

Grandvalet, Y.: Logistic regression for partial labels. In: 9th Information Processing and Management of Uncertainty in Knowledge-Based System, pp. 1935–1941 (2002)

Grandvalet, Y., Bengio, Y.: Learning from partial labels with minimum entropy (2004)

Hüllermeier, E., Beringer, J.: Learning from ambiguously labeled examples. Intell. Data Anal. **10**(5), 419–439 (2006). ISSN 1088-467X

Ishida, T., Niu, G., Hu, W., Sugiyama, M.: Learning from complementary labels. In: Advances in Neural Information Processing Systems, pp. 5639–5649 (2017)

Jin, R., Ghahramani, Z.: Learning with multiple labels. In: Advances in Neural Information Processing Systems 15, pp. 897–904 (2002)

Natarajan, N., Dhillon, I.S., Ravikumar, P.K., Tewari, A.: Learning with noisy labels. In: Advances in Neural Information Processing Systems, pp. 1196–1204 (2013)

Nguyen, N., Caruana, R.: Classification with partial labels. In: Proceedings of the 14th ACM SIGKDD International Conference on Knowledge Discovery and Data Mining, pp. 551–559. ACM, New York (2008). ISBN 978-1-60558-193-4

Perello-Nieto, M., Santos-Rodriguez, R., Garcia-Garcia, D., Cid-Sueiro, J.: Recycling weak labels for multiclass classification. Neurocomputing **400**, 206–215 (2020)

Raykar, V.C., et al.: Learning from crowds. J. Mach. Learn. Res. **99**, 1297–1322 (2010). ISSN 1532-4435

Van Rooyen, B., Williamson, R.C.: A theory of learning with corrupted labels. J. Mach. Learn. Res. **18**(1), 8501–8550 (2017)

Williamson, R.C., Vernet, E., Reid, M.D.: Composite multiclass losses. J. Mach. Learn. Res. **17**, 1–52 (2016)

Yoshida, S.M., Takenouchi, T., Sugiyama, M.: Lower-bounded proper losses for weakly supervised classification. arXiv e-prints, p. arXiv-2103 (2021)

# Distributed and Continual Learning

# Bilevel Online Deep Learning in Non-stationary Environment

Ya-nan Han, Jian-wei Liu$^{(\boxtimes)}$, Bing-biao Xiao, Xin-Tan Wang, and Xiong-lin Luo

Department of Automation, College of Information Science and Engineering, China University of Petroleum, Beijing Campus (CUP), Beijing, China
liujw@cup.edu.cn

**Abstract.** Recent years have witnessed enormous progress of online learning. However, a major challenge on the road to artificial agents is concept drift, that is, the data probability distribution would change where the data instance arrives sequentially in a stream fashion, which would lead to catastrophic forgetting and degrade the performance of the model. In this paper, we proposed a new Bilevel Online Deep Learning (BODL) framework, which combine bilevel optimization strategy and online ensemble classifier. In BODL algorithm, we use an ensemble classifier, which use the output of different hidden layers in deep neural network to build multiple base classifiers, the important weights of the base classifiers are updated according to exponential gradient descent method in an online manner. Besides, we apply the similar constraint to overcome the convergence problem of online ensemble framework. Then an effective concept drift detection mechanism utilizing the error rate of classifier is designed to monitor the change of the data probability distribution. When the concept drift is detected, our BODL algorithm can adaptively update the model parameters via bilevel optimization and then circumvent the large drift and encourage positive transfer. Finally, the extensive experiments and ablation studies are conducted on various datasets and the competitive numerical results illustrate that our BODL algorithm is a promising approach.

**Keywords:** Online Deep Learning · Bilevel optimization · Concept drift

## 1 Introduction

Deep learning techniques have achieved enormous success in a wide range of artificial intelligence (AI) and machine learning applications in recent years [1, 2]. However, most of these existing deep learning approaches suppose that the models often work in a batch learning setting or offline learning fashion, where the entire training dataset must be available to train a model by some learning techniques. Such learning approaches are poorly scalable for many real-word tasks, where the data instances arrive in a sequential manner. Thus, making deep learning available for the streaming data is a desideratum in the field of machine learning.

Unlike traditional batch learning, online learning represents a significant family of learning algorithms that are designed to optimize and learn models incrementally over

© Springer Nature Switzerland AG 2021
I. Farkaš et al. (Eds.): ICANN 2021, LNCS 12892, pp. 347–358, 2021.
https://doi.org/10.1007/978-3-030-86340-1_28

streaming data sequentially [3]. Online learning shows the tremendous advantages that the models can be updated efficiently in an online manner compared with traditional offline learning fashion when the new data instance comes. Similar to batch learning algorithms, online learning can also be applied for various real-word tasks, such as supervised classification task [4], unsupervised learning task [5], and so on.

However, in general, online learning algorithms cannot be directly employed to deep neural network. They have to cope with the intractable convergence problems, such as vanishing gradient. Besides, the traditional shallow or fixed neural network structure is poorly scalable for the most real-world applications where the data instances arrive in a sequential order and the probability distribution of data is non-stationary. Therefore, a promising online deep learning framework should be developed that can effectively and rapidly learn knowledge in non-stationary.

It should also be noted that the probability distribution obeyed by streaming data could occur the concept drift, in other words, the data probability distribution changes. In this circumstance, the leaning algorithms must take some actions to prevent the large drift and encourage positive transfer, in other words, the learner should make a trade-off between both the new and old knowledge and alleviate the catastrophic forgetting. The classical algorithms for catastrophic forgetting are Elastic Weight Consolidation (EWC) [6] and their variants [7], but this kind of algorithms attempt to address catastrophic forgetting by augmenting objective function and then control the whole network, that is, let the learning model's weights balance between these two factors, rather than directly take actions to cope with catastrophic forgetting. Based on the above fact, therefore this reminds us of the importance to enhance the different-depth latent representations and the ability to rapidly adapt to dynamic changing situations.

To achieve this, in this work, we devise a novel Bilevel Online Deep Learning (BODL) framework, which consists of three major components: online ensemble classifier, concept drift detection and bilevel online deep learning. Our BODL framework can effectively utilize the different abstract level latent feature representations to build classifiers via the online ensemble framework, where the important weights of the base classifiers would be updated by online exponential gradient descent strategy. consider the convergence problem of online ensemble framework, we apply the similar constraint to generate the favorable latent representation. Besides, a concept drift detected mechanism is devised according to the error rate of base classifiers. When the concept drift is detected, our BODL model can adaptively update the model parameters via bilevel optimization and then prevent the large drift and encourage positive transfer.

In a summary, our main contributions in this paper are listed below:

1) We design an effective bilevel learning strategy. Specifically, if the concept drift is detected, the model would adaptively adjust the parameters $\theta_n^t$ for all base classifiers and $W_n^t$ of the different-depth feature representation mentioned in Sect. 2 using bilevel optimization, where this process is achieved based on a tiny episodic memory. After that, the model can circumvent the large drift and encourage positive transfer in non-stationary environment.

2) In this work, consider the convergence problem of online ensemble framework, we impose the similar constraint between the shallower and the deeper layer's feature, which would be beneficial to generate the favorable feature representations.

3) The comparative experiments are devised to verify the effectiveness of the proposed BODL algorithm, and we analysis the experimental results of a variety of algorithms from different perspectives in terms of accuracy, precision, recall-score and F-1 score, and then we can see that our BODL algorithm can exploit the different-depth feature representations and adapt to rapidly changing environment.

The remainder of this paper is organized as follows. In Sect. 2, we introduce our BODL algorithm in details, which consists of three parts: online ensemble classifier, concept drift detection mechanism, bilevel learning for concept drift. In Sect. 3 we empirically compare BODL algorithm with several state-of-the-art online learning algorithms. In Sect. 4 we elaborate related works. In Sect. 5 we summarize the whole work and the interested directions in the future.

## 2   Bilevel Online Deep Learning (BODL)

In this work, we present bilevel online deep learning, a conceptually novel framework for online learning based on bilevel optimization [8] and online ensemble framework. Our BODL architecture can be divided into three main parts: online ensemble classifier, concept drift detection mechanism, bilevel learning for concept drift. The online deep ensemble classifier can make a trade-off among the different-level base classifiers and improve the performance of classification; Concept drift detection mechanism is used to monitor the change in non-stationary environment; When the concept drift is detected, bilevel learning is designed to adaptively adjust the parameters $\theta_n^t$ and $W_n^t$, then the model can adapt to the change in non-stationary environment.

### 2.1   Online Ensemble Classifier

We illustrate the online deep ensemble classifier in Fig. 1, where $\omega^t = \left[\omega_1^t, \ldots, \omega_N^t\right]$ represents the importance of the N base classifiers. The online deep ensemble classifier can make a trade-off among the different-level base classifiers via Exponential Gradient Descent (EGD) algorithm in an online manner [4].

More specifically, we character a Deep Neural Network (DNN) with $N+1$ hidden layers, and the final ensemble classifier can be achieved by dynamically updating the weight parameters of the base classifiers for each hidden layer based on their classification loss. The specific ensemble prediction function can be written as Eq. (1).

$$
\begin{aligned}
\mathbf{F}(\mathbf{x}) &= \sum_{n=0}^{N} \omega_n f_n \\
f_n &= soft\max(h_n \theta_n), \ \forall n = 0, \ldots, N \\
h_n &= \sigma(W_n h_{n-1}), \ \forall n = 1, \ldots, N
\end{aligned}
\tag{1}
$$

Compared to the traditional network, in which the feature representation constructed by outputs of the final hidden layer is used as input of the classifier, here we can make a favorable classifier by an online ensemble framework, which can benefit from the different depth feature representation and improve the prediction performance of the whole model. It is noted that the parameters $\omega_n^t$, $\theta_n^t$ and $W_n^t$ in Eq. (1) can be learned in an online flavor.

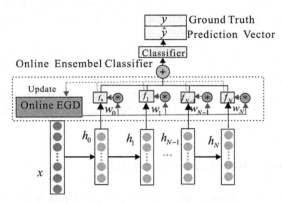

**Fig. 1.** Online deep ensemble classifier.

**Update the Parameters $\omega_n$.** We update the weights $\omega_n$ for base classifiers using exponential gradient descent[11]. Firstly, the weights $\omega$ are initialized using a uniform distribution: $\omega_n = \frac{1}{N+1}$, $n = 0, \ldots, N$, i.e., each base classifier has equal probability to be picked. At each iteration, the prediction loss of the n-th base classifier $f_n$ can be written as $\mathcal{L}(\hat{y}_n^t, y_n^t)$, where $\hat{y}_n^t$ and $y_n^t$ represent the base classifier prediction and the target variable respectively. Then, the weight of each base classifier can be learned according to the loss suffered and the update rule is given by follow:

$$\omega_n^{t+1} \leftarrow \omega_n^t e^{-\eta\mathcal{L}(\hat{y}_n^t, y_n^t)} \tag{2}$$

where $\eta \in (0, +\infty)$ and $\eta$ is set to 0.01 in our work. After that, the trained base classifier's important weight is discounted by an exponential weight $e^{-\eta\mathcal{L}(\hat{y}_n^t, y_n^t)}$.

**Update the Parameters $\theta_n^t$.** The parameters $\theta_n^t$ for all base classifiers are updated using Stochastic Online Gradient Descent (SOGD), and this process is analogical to the traditional feedforward networks.

**Update the Parameters $W_n^t$.** The update rule about the parameters $W_n^t$ of the different-depth feature representation is different from the traditional backpropagation framework. The objective function includes two parts: the adaptive loss function and similar constraint, which are defined as follow:

$$\mathcal{L}(\mathbf{F}(\mathbf{x}), y) = \sum_{n=0}^{N} \omega_n \mathcal{L}_{pre}(f_n(x), y) + \lambda\mathcal{L}_{sim}(h_{sh}, h_{de}) \tag{3}$$

where, the first part in loss function represents the adaptive prediction loss. Note that, the parameters of shallower layer tend to converge faster than the ones of deeper layer, which can lead to deeper base classifiers learn slowly [2]. Thus, we incorporate the similar constraint between the shallower and deeper layer's features, which can be beneficial to generate the favorable feature representations and improve the convergence rate and the prediction performance of the deeper layer. In this work, $\lambda$ is a tradeoff parameter and is set to 0.1. Note that, the similarity can be modelled in multiple manners and we choose the squared distance metric in this paper.

## 2.2  Bilevel Online Deep Learning

As the streaming data comes gradually and the data probability distribution could change. We monitor the change of the data probability distribution utilizing the error rate of classifier. This concept drift detection mechanism is similar to the drift detection method in [10] but the warning phase is not arranged in this paper in order to avoid the use of slide window methods. In this section, we describe our adaptive online deep learning based on bilevel optimization in detail. Figure 2 shows a flowchart of the bilevel online deep learning framework.

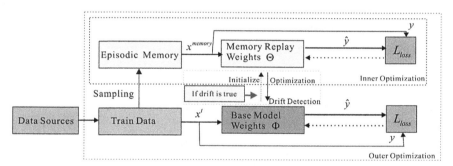

**Fig. 2.** The bilevel online deep learning framework. BODL utilizes the memory replay weights $\Theta$ and the episodic memory to optimize the base classifiers' weights $\Phi$ in the non-stationary environment, where the episodic memory is obtained by reservoir sampling.

### 2.2.1  Bilevel Learning

For each arriving instance in online learning scenario, we detect the concept drift utilizing the error rate of classifier. If the concept drift is observed, the learning algorithm obviously needs to takes some actions to prevent large drift and achieve online incremental learning. Specifically, when the concept drift occurs, BODL initializes a memory weight $\Theta$ to replay the knowledge in the memory. Then we apply the trained memory weight $\Theta^*$ to update $\Phi$ such that it can prevent large drift and weight the new and old knowledge in a non-stationary environment as shown in the Fig. 2.

Bearing this in mind, the objective function can be defined as the following bilevel optimization problem:

$$\min_{\Phi} \mathcal{L}^{outer}\left(\Theta^*(\Phi), \mathcal{B}^t_{train}; \Phi\right)$$
$$s.t.\ \Theta^* = \arg\min_{\Theta} \mathcal{L}^{inner}\left(\Theta^*, \mathcal{M}^{memory}\right) \tag{4}$$

where $\mathcal{B}^t_{train}$ denotes the current training data that exists concept drift. We parameterize each $\Phi$ as an inner optimization problem $\mathcal{L}^{memory}_{\Phi}$, which the learner optimizes the corresponding $\Theta$. During the bilevel learning, firstly the agent learns the memory weight $\Theta^*$ about the inner problem. After that, the agent learns the outer problem with respect to $\Phi$. In this process, we apply the cross-entropy loss as objective function for the inner and outer problems respectively.

### 2.2.2 First Order Approximation

Generally, the data comes gradually in non-stationary environment and the concept drift mechanism will monitor the change in online manner. When the concept drift occurs, the learner can adaptively adjust the model parameters and weight the new and old knowledge in a non-stationary environment via bilevel learning.

Specifically, assume that for an incoming training data $\mathcal{B}^t_{train}$ reported as concept drift, the inner problem is settled by:

$$\Theta_i \leftarrow \Theta_i - \mu \nabla_{\Theta_i} \mathcal{L}\left(\Theta_i, \mathcal{B}^t_{train}; \Phi\right) \text{ where } \Theta_0 \leftarrow \Phi \tag{5}$$

After receiving $\Theta^*$ via Eq. (5), the outer learning for the parameters $\Phi$ can be solved by the chain rule.

$$\Phi_t \leftarrow \Phi_t - \gamma \nabla_{\Phi} \mathcal{L}\left(\Theta^*, \mathcal{M}^{memory}\right)$$
$$\leftarrow \Phi_t - \gamma \frac{\partial \Theta^*}{\partial \Phi} \cdot \frac{\partial}{\partial \Theta^*} \mathcal{L}\left(\Theta^*, \mathcal{M}^{memory}\right) \tag{6}$$

Note that solving the Eq. (6) is a cumbersome problem in real word scenario because of the Hessian vector product in the second term [11]. In order to improve the efficiency of the computation, we apply first-order approximation to simplify the Eq. (6) in this work [12, 13]. Thus, the outer learning is given by interpolating only in the parameter space:

$$\Phi_t = \Phi_t + \gamma\left(\Theta' - \Phi_t\right)$$
$$\text{where } \Theta' = \Theta^* - \mu \nabla_{\Theta^*} \mathcal{L}\left(\Theta^*, \mathcal{M}^{memory}\right) \tag{7}$$

We apply Eq. (7) to obtain a one-step look-ahead parameter $\Theta'$ from $\Theta^*$. After that, we can adjust $\Phi$ by linearly interpolate between the current parameters $\Phi$ and $\Theta'$. It is noted that we only maintain the parameters of the main model $\Phi$, i.e., once the parameters $\Phi$ is obtained and then we discard it after every outer update. In this process, the inner optimization should be carried out via tiny experience memory [14].

### 2.2.3  Bilevel Online Deep Learning Algorithm

In this section, we show that our BODL algorithm can effectively learn in non-stationary environment by an online manner.

Our proposed BODL algorithm is shown in **Algorithm** 1.

---
**Algorithm1:** Bilevel Online Deep Learning algorithm(BODL)

**Inputs:** Discounting coefficient $\eta \in (0, \infty)$; Learning Rates: $\mu$, $\gamma$

**Require:** Memory management strategy for $\mathcal{M}^{memory}$

**Initialize:** $\mathbf{F}(\mathbf{x}) = DNN$ with $N+1$ hidden layers; $\omega_n^t = \frac{1}{N+1}, \forall n=0, K, N$; $\Phi$;

$\mathcal{M}^{memory} \leftarrow \phi$

**For** $t \leftarrow 1$ **to** $T$ **do,**

    Receive instance: $x_t$

    Predict $\hat{y}_t = \mathbf{F}(\mathbf{x}) = \sum_{n=0}^{N} \omega_n f_n$ as Eq.(1)

    Reveal ground truth $y_t$ and Update $\omega_n^{t+1}$ according to Eq.(2)

    Concept Drift Detection

    **If** concept drift is True,

        Update network via bilevel optimization

    **Else**

        Update network via single backpropagation

    Update $\mathcal{M}^{memory}$ via Reservoir Sample

**End**

---

In BODL algorithm, firstly we present an online ensemble framework that attempts to dynamically weight the different depth classifiers and the base classifier's weights for each hidden layer are update based on the exponential gradient descent algorithm in an online manner. In particular, we impose the similar constraint between the shallower and the deeper layer's features, which would be beneficial to generate the favorable feature representations and improve the performance of the convergence.

In addition, consider that the data probability distribution would change in real-world scenarios. Thus, a concept drift detection mechanism is used to monitor the data changes according to the error rate of classifier. Once the drift is detected, the learner would update the model parameters via bilevel optimization. Thus, the learner would effectively prevent the large drift and alleviate the catastrophic forgetting.

## 3  Experiments

In this section, we evaluate the baselines and our proposed BODL algorithm on various stationary and non-stationary datasets. We report and analysis the experimental results in detail.

### 3.1  1Experiment Setup

We use the neural network architecture with 15 hidden layers of 30 units with ReLU nonlinearities. In all experiments, the entire network parameters are updated by Adam optimizer with a learning rate of 0.01. When the drift is detected, the model would adaptively learn the parameters via the tiny memory budge and this process is achieved using the bilevel optimization strategy. It is well worth note that we apply a test-then-train strategy for evaluating the learning algorithms to cast this as a classification task.

We compare against with several state-of-the-art baselines: Perceptron, the Relaxed Online Maximum Margin (ROMMA) [15], OGD [16], the recently proposed Soft Confidence Weighted algorithms (SCW) [17], the Adaptive Regularization of Weight Vectors (AROW) [18], the Confidence-Weighted (CW) learning algorithm [19]. Here, the BODL-Base algorithm is regarded as an online learning approach without the bilevel optimization strategy.

## 3.2 Datasets

The learning performance of BODL algorithm is numerically validated on stationary and non-stationary data, but evolving data stream usually characterize non-stationary properties in real-word task. Thus, in our experiments, we select three non-stationary datasets and two stationary datasets for experimental comparison. Here, the datasets are obtained from UCI repositories and the properties are shown in details in Table 1.

**Table 1.** Batch datasets properties.

| Dataset | Size | Features | Type |
|---------|------|----------|------|
| MNIST | 70000 | 786 | Stationary |
| Magic | 19020 | 10 | Stationary |
| PIMA | 768 | 8 | Non-stationary |
| Weather | 18140 | 8 | Non-stationary |
| KDDCUP | 1036241 | 127 | Non-stationary |

## 3.3 Experimental Results

In this section, the experimental comparative results of all baselines and the proposed BODL algorithm with four different metric criteria: average accuracy, average precision, F1-Score and recall-score are reported in Table 2. In additional, in order to study the contribution of each component, a complete ablation studies are conducted in our work where BODL-2: the model is trained using the bilevel learning and the similar constrain, BODL-1: the model is trained using the similar constrain alone, BODL-Base: the model is trained without the bilevel learning and the similar constrain.

The experiment results show that our BODL-2 algorithm enjoys competitive performance on different datasets implementing different evaluation criteria. BODL-2 is slightly better than BODL-1 with the help of bilevel learning since it can alleviate the catastrophic forget when the concept drift occurs. BODL-Base have lower accuracy

**Table 2.** Numerical results of different algorithms on different datasets.

| Method | Average accuracy | | | | |
|---|---|---|---|---|---|
| | MNIST | Magic | PIMA | Weather | KDDCUP |
| **BODL-2** | **92.00%** | **78.73%** | **74.36%** | 74.90% | **99.68%** |
| **BODL-1** | 91.99% | **78.49%** | **73.84%** | 73.28% | 99.44% |
| **BODL-Base** | 90.80% | 78.31% | 71.69% | 72.34% | 99.35% |
| Perceptron | 84.77% | 70.60% | 64.45% | 65.85% | 99.31% |
| ROMMA | 83.22% | 66.67% | 64.45% | 65.63% | 99.34% |
| OGD | 90.10% | 78.72% | 72.78% | 72.70% | 99.61% |
| SCW | 88.98% | 78.64% | 70.31% | **76.12%** | 99.75% |
| AROW | 89.04% | 78.71% | 72.14% | 75.15% | 99.58% |
| CW | 86.88% | 67.90% | 63.41% | 36.81% | 99.62% |
| PA | 85.68% | 70.13% | 66.41% | 65.74% | 99.41% |
| Method | Average precision | | | | |
| | MNIST | Magic | PIMA | Weather | KDDCUP |
| **BODL-2** | **91.91%** | 74.65% | 54.83% | **77.35%** | 98.55% |
| **BODL-1** | 91.89% | 73.96% | 54.38% | **75.76%** | 97.46% |
| **BODL-Base** | 90.70% | 73.80% | 51.88% | 76.06% | 96.99% |
| Perceptron | 84.61% | 67.77% | 64.03% | 60.78% | 98.96% |
| ROMMA | 82.99% | 64.16% | 63.74% | 60.69% | 99.08% |
| OGD | 89.99% | **77.66%** | **71.77%** | 67.91% | 99.35% |
| SCW | 88.83% | 76.75% | 69.18% | 74.90% | **99.55%** |
| AROW | 88.92% | 77.62% | 70.84% | 71.13% | 99.31% |
| CW | 86.70% | 64.75% | 62.55% | 53.55% | 99.56% |
| PA | 85.45% | 67.19% | 65.06% | 59.95% | 99.01% |
| Method | F1-score | | | | |
| | MNIST | Magic | PIMA | Weather | KDDCUP |
| **BODL-2** | **91.97%** | 65.81% | 60.83% | **82.62%** | 99.21% |
| **BODL-1** | **91.97%** | 65.73% | 63.30% | **81.80%** | 98.61% |
| **BODL-Base** | 90.78% | 65.70% | 59.66% | 81.69% | 98.38% |
| Perceptron | 84.78% | 70.61% | 65.27% | 66.07% | 99.31% |
| ROMMA | 83.21% | 67.05% | 65.27% | 65.95% | 99.33% |
| OGD | 90.08% | 78.02% | **73.39%** | 71.04% | 99.61% |
| SCW | 88.97% | **78.41%** | 70.96% | 77.53% | **99.75%** |
| AROW | 88.98% | 78.16% | 72.73% | 74.28% | 99.66% |
| CW | 86.87% | 67.86% | 64.24% | 29.00% | 99.67% |
| PA | 85.66% | 70.08% | 67.12% | 65.58% | 99.41% |

than BODL-1, which means the similar constrain would be beneficial to generate the favorable feature representations.

Compared to the state-of-the-art methods, we can draw several conclusions. In terms of average accuracy, first but not surprise, traditional online learning techniques, such as Perceptron and CW, achieve relatively poor performance on almost all datasets. Next, we also note that the algorithms, such as OGD, could obtain relatively competitive numerical results on MNIST datasets. However, lacked the ability to further explore the power of depth or adaptively adjust the model parameters when concept drift occurs, so they receive poor performance on weather and PIMA dataset. SCW and AROW achieve favorable accuracy in concept drift datasets such as weather and KDDCUP, but they product poor results in PIMA dataset which features highly imbalance and non-stationary. In contrary, our BODL-2 algorithm can exploit the different-level favorable feature representation base on the deep learning framework, besides, when the concept drift is observed, the learner can adaptively adjust the model parameters via bilevel optimization strategy based on memory replay and then encourage positive transfer and prevent the large drift.

In additional, BODL-2 algorithm outperform all other approaches on Magic, MNIST and KDDCUP dataset under accuracy evaluation criteria. It is noted that our method can produce good performance from highly imbalance data streams with concept drift, such as PIMA. Only 1.22% less than the highest one in terms of accuracy on weather dataset but achieve highest results under the average precision, F1-Score and recall-score evaluation criteria and so on. To conclude, the experimental results demonstrate that our BODL-2 algorithm is a promising online learning approach comparing to the state-of-the-art online methods.

# 4   Related Works

Recent years we have witnessed enormous success in the deep neural network. Compared to traditional off-line learning, online learning is more suitable in many real-word tasks. Online learning algorithms represents a class of scalable algorithms which are devised to optimize the models incrementally where the data instance comes gradually. Perceptron based on maximum-margin classification is the earliest online learning algorithm, which is primarily developed to learn linear models. However, the class of perceptron algorithm is fragile to the samples that are linearly inseparable. Thus, perceptron algorithm with the kernel functions are developed [20], which give a solution to online learning techniques with nonlinear models. While such approaches are able to solve the non-linear classification, determining the type and number of kernel function is an open challenge. Moreover, these approaches are not explicitly built to extract the different-depth feature representations for the data instances. Base on this fact, Sahoo et al. present an online algorithm with different depth network for evolving data streams [4]. However, they neglect the intractable problem of catastrophic forgetting, or cannot cope with the non-stationary environment very well. Recently, there are some specific algorithms handle for concept drift in non-stationary environment. These methods concentrate on incrementally update the model as long as the data instance arrives in a stream, such as dynamic combination model; the online Gradient Descent Algorithm (OGD) [16]; the relaxed online maximum margin algorithm and its aggressive version aROMMA, ROMMA, and aROMMA [15]; the Adaptive Regularization of Weight Vectors (aROW) [18]; the Confidence-Weighted (CW) learning algorithm [19]; The recently proposed Soft Confidence Weighted algorithms(SCW) [17]. However, these methods characterize the constant updating of their models, which would make the model evolve in an extremely regular manner regardless of the concept drift.

## 5    Conclusion and Future Work

Concept drift is an inevitable problem with learning from evolving data streams, which must be handled for data instances to be practically useful. In this work, we proposed a novel Bilevel Online Deep Learning (BODL) framework to learn in non-stationary environment in an online manner. BODL creates an ensemble classifier using the different depth feature representations, where the important weights of each classifier would be updated by online exponential gradient descent strategy. In order to make the deeper layers converge faster and generate the favorable feature representation, we impose the similar constraint between the shallower and the deeper layer's features. Besides, a concept drift detected mechanism is devised according to the error rate of classifier. When the concept drift is detected, our BODL algorithm can adaptively update the model parameters via bilevel optimization based on tiny episodic memory and then prevent the large drift and encourage positive transfer.

At last, we validated the proposed BODL algorithm through extensive experiments on various stationary and non-stationary datasets and the competitive numerical results show our BODL algorithm is a promising online learning approach.

In the future work, we would consider the online learning problem for class incremental learning. Besides, in order to obtain the more favorable feature representation, we also consider incorporating the recently proposed self-supervised learning and data augment methods.

**Acknowledgements.** This work was supported by the Science Foundation of China University of Petroleum, Beijing (No. 2462020YXZZ023).

## References

1. Bengio, Y., Courville, A., Vincent, P.: Representation learning: a review and new perspectives. IEEE Trans. Pattern Anal. Mach. Intell. **35**, 1798–1828 (2013)
2. Chen, T., Goodfellow, I.J., Shlens, J.: Net2Net: accelerating learning via knowledge transfer. In: BT - 4th International Conference on Learning Representations, ICLR 2016, San Juan, Puerto Rico, 2–4 May 2016, Conference Track Proceedings (2016)
3. Cesa-Bianchi, N., Lugosi, G.: Prediction, Learning, and Games. Cambridge University Press, Cambridge (2006). https://doi.org/10.1017/CBO9780511546921
4. Sahoo, D., Pham, Q., Lu, J., Hoi, S.C.H.: Online deep learning: learning deep neural networks on the fly. In: BT - Proceedings of the 27th International Joint Conference on Artificial Intelligence, IJCAI 2018, Stockholm, Sweden, 13–19 July 2018, pp. 2660–2666 (2018). https://doi.org/10.24963/ijcai.2018/369

5. Hoi, S.C.H., Lu, J.: Online Learning: A Comprehensive Survey, vol. 1, pp. 1–100 (2018)
6. Kirkpatrick, J., et al.: Overcoming catastrophic forgetting in neural networks. CoRR vol. abs/1612.00796 (2016)
7. Chaudhry, A., Dokania, P.K., Ajanthan, T., Torr, P.H.S.: Riemannian walk for incremental learning: understanding forgetting and intransigence. In: Ferrari, V., Hebert, M., Sminchisescu, C., Weiss, Y. (eds.) ECCV 2018. LNCS, vol. 11215, pp. 556–572. Springer, Cham (2018). https://doi.org/10.1007/978-3-030-01252-6_33
8. Jenni, S., Favaro, P.: Deep bilevel learning. In: Ferrari, V., Hebert, M., Sminchisescu, C., Weiss, Y. (eds.) ECCV 2018. LNCS, vol. 11214, pp. 632–648. Springer, Cham (2018). https://doi.org/10.1007/978-3-030-01249-6_38
9. Shalev-Shwartz, S.: Online learning and online convex optimization. Found. Trends Mach. Learn. **4**, 107–194 (2012)
10. Kifer, D., Ben-David, S., Gehrke, J.: Detecting change in data streams. In: BT - (e)Proceedings of the Thirtieth International Conference on Very Large Data Bases, VLDB 2004, Toronto, Canada, 31 August–3 September 2004, pp. 180–191 (2004)
11. Pham, Q., Sahoo, D., Liu, C., Hoi, S.C.H.: Bilevel Continual Learning. CoRR vol. abs/2007.15553 (2020)
12. Nichol, A., Achiam, J., Schulman, J.: On First-Order Meta-Learning Algorithms. CoRR vol. abs/1803.02999 (2018)
13. Zhang, M.R., Lucas, J., Ba, J., Hinton, G.E.: Lookahead optimizer: k steps forward, 1 step back. In: BT - Advances in Neural Information Processing Systems 32: Annual Conference on Neural Information Processing Systems 2019, NeurIPS 2019, Vancouver, BC, Canada, 8–14 December 2019, pp. 9593–9604 (2019)
14. Chaudhry, A., et al.: Continual Learning with Tiny Episodic Memories. CoRR vol. abs/1902.10486 (2019)
15. Li, Y., Long, P.M.: The relaxed online maximum margin algorithm. Mach. Learn. **46**, 361–387 (2002)
16. Zinkevich, M.: Online convex programming and generalized infinitesimal gradient ascent. In: BT - Machine Learning, Proceedings of the Twentieth International Conference (ICML 2003), Washington, DC, USA, 21–24 August 2003, pp. 928–936 (2003)
17. Hoi, S.C.H., Wang, J., Zhao, P.: Exact soft confidence-weighted learning. In: BT - Proceedings of the 29th International Conference on Machine Learning, ICML 2012, Edinburgh, Scotland, UK, 26 June–1 July 2012 (2012)
18. Crammer, K., Kulesza, A., Dredze, M.: Adaptive regularization of weight vectors. Mach. Learn. **91**(2), 155–187 (2013). https://doi.org/10.1007/s10994-013-5327-x
19. Crammer, K., Dredze, M., Pereira, F.: Exact convex confidence-weighted learning. In: BT - Advances in Neural Information Processing Systems 21, Proceedings of the Twenty-Second Annual Conference on Neural Information Processing Systems, Vancouver, British Columbia, Canada, 8–11 December 2008, pp. 345–352 (2008)
20. Kivinen, J., Smola, A.J., Williamson, R.C.: Online learning with kernels. IEEE Trans. Signal Process. **52**, 2165–2176 (2004)

# A Blockchain Based Decentralized Gradient Aggregation Design for Federated Learning

Jian Zhao[1], Xin Wu[2], Yan Zhang[3], Yu Wu[3], and Zhi Wang[2(✉)]

[1] Shenzhen Technology University, Shenzhen, China
`zhaojian@sztu.edu.cn`
[2] Tsinghua University, Beijing, China
`wux17@mails.tsinghua.edu.cn`, `wangzhi@sz.tsinghua.edu.cn`
[3] School of Cyberspace Security, Dongguan University of Technology,
Dongguan, China
`yzha1032@asu.edu`, `wuyu@dgut.edu.cn`

**Abstract.** Based on the concept of letting training organizations only exchange their partial gradients instead of the proprietary datasets owned by them, federated learning has become a promising approach for organizations to train deep learning models collaboratively. However, conventional federated learning based on a centralized parameter server is susceptible to "recovery" attacks, in which the original data can be recovered if the attacker can collect enough gradients from the organizations. To solve the problem, we first propose a blockchain-based decentralized model training architecture for federated learning, which is more robust than the centralized architecture. Based on this architecture, we develop a joint efficiency and randomness aware gradient aggregation approach. Our real-world experiments show that our design is not affected by a single point of failure. Moreover, it can increase the model accuracy of the participating organization, while mitigating the data privacy disclosure risk and improving the gradient aggregation performance.

**Keywords:** Federated learning · Blockchain · Smart contract

## 1 Introduction

In recent years, artificial intelligence technology has attracted tremendous attention from both academia and industry. The availability of high-quality data is the key to the success of the various machine learning algorithms [8]. As the amount and dimensions of the data increase, the machine learning algorithm training performance is greatly improved [3]. However, data, *e.g.*, financial data or medical data is usually owned by different organizations. The General Data Protection Regulation (GDPR) limits organizations not to take a risk of data privacy disclosure. Hence, organizations are not willing to contribute their data for training.

---

J. Zhao and X. Wu—Contributed equally to this work.

ⓒ Springer Nature Switzerland AG 2021
I. Farkaš et al. (Eds.): ICANN 2021, LNCS 12892, pp. 359–371, 2021.
https://doi.org/10.1007/978-3-030-86340-1_29

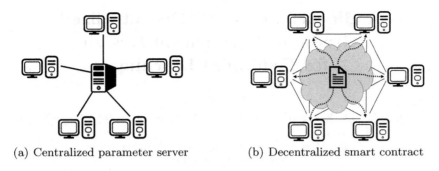

(a) Centralized parameter server    (b) Decentralized smart contract

**Fig. 1.** Comparison of two different architectures.

Based on the concept of letting organizations only exchange their partial gradients instead of the proprietary datasets owned by them, federated learning has become a promising approach for organizations to train deep learning models collaboratively [12]. Existing federated learning is mainly based on a centralized architecture. It uses third-party collaborators to enable each worker node to perform encryption training. The collaborators aggregate and decrypt the encrypted gradients, and then pass the gradients back to corresponding worker nodes. Finally, the worker nodes update the parameters of the local model according to the gradients. This architecture relies on a centralized third-party aggregator, as illustrated in Fig. 1a, which is similar as the traditional parameter server architecture [11]. Conventional federated learnings based a centralized "parameter server" is vulnerable to "recovery" attacks, in which the original data can be recovered if the attacker can collect enough gradients from the organizations. Third-party collaborators in federal learning are a centralized structure that captures the full gradient information of the entire training process. However, researchers have proved that the important information about the training data can be inferred through the intermediate gradient information [2,9]. Therefore, when the collaborator is "curious", it will threaten the data privacy of the worker nodes, and the worker nodes cannot verify whether third-party collaborators have used the gradient information to collect data privacy.

In order to solve the above problems due to centralized "parameter servers", we propose a blockchain-based decentralized approach. Blockchain is appropriate for this application scenario of connecting multiple independent entities together for cooperation. Developers can write smart contracts and deploy them on the blockchain platform for specific application services. As illustrated in Fig. 1(b), our design utilizes smart contracts [5] on the blockchain to achieve the aggregation and control logic in the training process, replacing the traditional centralized architecture. Because of the openness and transparency of the blockchain, the control logic of the entire federated learning process is also open and transparent, and can be audited by any organization, ensuring that the entire process is safe and reliable. Besides, the blockchain-based smart contract is executed on all nodes participating in federated learning, and any single node cannot affect its operation. Even if any node quits or fails, other nodes can continue to train their models. Our contributions can be summarized as follows:

First, we build a federated learning system coordinated by the blockchain platform. Compared to conventional architecture, our architecture is completely decentralized and does not require third-party aggregators or collaborators. In consideration of blockchain not suitable for large data transmission and storage, we design an architecture including control and data layer. The control layer is based on smart contracts for coordinating the training process such as gradient aggregation. The data layer is for transmitting data. The architecture inherits the characteristics of blockchain technology and provides a mathematical and cryptographic based trust mechanism for organizations participating in the training. Most importantly, the architecture is very robust and unaffected by a single point of failure.

Second, by reducing the risk of data privacy disclosure, this architecture ensures the effectiveness of the federated training. This approach can help organizations involved in the training get a model with higher accuracy than training alone. The embedded gradient aggregation algorithm with random enforcement strategy considers both randomness and system performance, improving data privacy security and time performance of the system.

Finally, our real-world experiments demonstrate the effectiveness of our architecture design. When any node fails and exits, other nodes can still continue training. In the case of sparse data, our approach increases the model accuracy by up to 8.40%. For the indicator of randomness, our strategy is 90.19% higher than the conventional centralized approach, and 53.43% higher than a performance priority approach. For the time to accomplish an aggregation in the case of synchronous training, our approach saves up to 66.52% of the time compared to the centralized approach, and up to 35.32% of the time compared to the completely random approach.

The remainder of this paper is organized as follows: Sect. 2 describes research background. Sect. 3 presents system design and workflow of our proposed architecture. Sect. 4 proposes a gradient aggregation algorithm with random enforcement for our architecture. Sect. 5 evaluates the architecture and the proposed algorithm. Sect. 6 concludes our paper.

## 2   Background

### 2.1   Studies on Federated Learning

The number of studies on federated learning is increasing. Many studies have pointed out the data privacy problem of federated learning with centralized "parameter server". The gradient information transmitted in the training process can be used to infer the original data itself or important information about the original data. Aono *et al.* [2] proved that an honest but curious centralized server can even partially recover the original data based on the gradient information under certain conditions. To enhance the protection of data privacy, Shokri *et al.* [14] used differential privacy techniques to add noise to gradient information. However, Hitaj *et al.* [9] demonstrated that the centralized server can still obtain private data from the gradient information after differential privacy by using generative adversarial network. In order to protect gradient information from the central node, Phong *et al.* [13] applied homomorphic encryption to the gradient information, and they assume that all training nodes are not curious about the privacy of other nodes. Some researchers tried to transmit part of the model parameters instead of the gradients, but this is even more likely to learn data privacy. Song *et al.* [15] proved that model parameters can contain important information about original training data. Carlini *et al.* [6] showed that when a deep learning based sequence generation model is trained based on text data, it unintentionally memorizes the training data information that can be extracted from the model. Emerging federated learning technologies have used third-party collaborators to encrypt and decrypt intermediate information [4]. However, once the third-party collaborator is curious, the intermediate information it holds is sufficient to infer the privacy of the original data.

In contrast, there are very few studies on the system architecture of decentralized federated learning. The existing federated learning still mainly adopts the centralized parameter server architecture, which is similar to traditional distributed computing [11].

### 2.2 Enforcement by Smart Contract Platform - Blockchain

Blockchain has three categories: public blockchain, private blockchain and consortium blockchain. Here we use the consortium blockchain for connecting multiple cooperated organizations. The consortium blockchain also supports smart contracts for developing specific applications, such as hyperledger fabric [10].

Blockchain is a platform that every participating node synchronizes data and runs according to the same codes. Hence, it is a suitable platform for multiple independent entities that want to cooperate and keep their own data, as every entity can have one copy of the shared data and run the same codes to process the data.

A smart contract is a message-driven program deployed on a blockchain [5]. It is automatically executed according to pre-defined rules that are transparent to all entities. We introduce smart contract technology into coordinating the model training in deep learning. The decentralization feature of smart contracts provides a mechanism without the need for centralized collaborators or servers. This mitigates the risk of data privacy disclosure due to "recovery" attacks through gradient information.

## 3    System Design and Workflow

In this section, we present the design of our blockchain-based federated learning system. Figure 2 shows our system architecture.

### 3.1    Terms and Entities

Some key terms and entities in Fig. 2 are listed below:

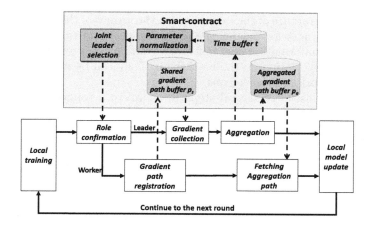

**Fig. 2.** System architecture.

**Round:** Each node will upload a local encrypted path from time to time to share the gradient information once. When all the nodes participating in the collaborative training have uploaded the path and realized the gradient information sharing, this process is called a round.

**Node:** Each node in the system has its corresponding organization, which is authorized to enter the blockchain. These institutions have a stake in each other, and have a similar industry background to maintain the chain's operations. These nodes access the blockchain and interact with the smart contract. Each node may play two different roles in different rounds of the federated training process.

**NodeID:** This is a string of numbers. Each node has its corresponding nodeID. The nodeID of each node is different as their identity.

**Worker:** One of the roles played by the node. When a node works as such a role, it uses local data to calculate the gradient to update the model. On the other hand, it also uses aggregated gradient information to update the local model.

**Leader:** One of the roles played by the node. In each round, only the selected node can play this role. Worker nodes use the public key of the leader node to encrypt the gradient path and upload the encrypted path to the blockchain. The leader node decrypts these paths. Based on these paths, the gradient information is acquired, and aggregated locally. The aggregated gradient path is encrypted and uploaded to the blockchain, through the key generated by our encrypted communication mechanism for the current round, thereby ensuring the consistency and confidentiality of the path information.

## 3.2 System Workflow

Each participating node needs to negotiate in advance before the training begins. The content of the negotiation includes the number $N$ of nodes participating in the training, the structure of the target model, the format of the training samples, and a balance factor $\lambda$ for balancing the randomness and time performance of the training. This information does not involve data privacy and does not require communication negotiation on the blockchain. They can be negotiated over the peer-to-peer network or other means.

Our system consists of several steps to complete a round of training. The specific steps are as follows.

**Local Training:** The nodes cyclically use local data for training and update the local models. It should be noted that in the first round, nodes need to initialize the parameters of the agreed model structure. When the nodes think that gradient sharing is needed, it stores the gradient information generated by the training at this time, generates a shared gradient information file, and sends a query request to the smart contract deployed on the blockchain. Although the file is for sharing, only the leader node of this round can parse its content due to the encryption mechanism. The timing of gradient information sharing is determined by each node.

**Role Confirmation:** The smart contract returns a response each time it receives a query request. The response message contains the nodeID of leader in this round. The leader node is selected by varying randomness, and will be re-selected in the next round, which is performed by the smart contract. The selection takes into account the randomness and time performance. Since the selection process is done by the smart contract, it also inherits the decentralization of the smart contract. This method guarantees that it cannot be controlled by any node within the system, so its result is credible for all nodes. The specific selection algorithm will be introduced in the next section. Nodes know their roles in the current round by querying the nodeID of leader, and perform the corresponding operations in the subsequent steps.

**Gradient Collection and Aggregation:** Each worker node encrypts the shared gradient file path and sends a request to the smart contract to register the encrypted path. When all the worker nodes have been registered, the leader node will obtain these encrypted paths from the smart contract and decrypt them. The decrypted paths are used by the leader node to obtain corresponding shared gradient information from the peer-to-peer network.

The leader node aggregates the shared gradient information of this round, which also contains its own shared gradient information. The method of gradient aggregation is not limited, and is determined by the leader node [16]. The simplest method is to take the average of all the shared gradient information in this round, and this method still helps all the nodes involved in the training to improve the model accuracy a lot. The aggregated gradient information is stored as a new file, and its path is encrypted and registered by the leader node to the smart contract. In addition, the smart contract deployed on the blockchain automatically records the time that it takes for the current leader to complete the aggregation process, which is used as one of the reference factors for selecting the leader node in subsequent rounds. It is worth noting that during gradient collection and aggregation, worker nodes can continue to train with local data in parallel. This approach helps to increase the efficiency of the entire system and avoids wasted performance due to waiting for aggregated information.

**Local Model Update with Aggregated Gradient:** The leader node directly updates the local model with locally stored aggregated gradient information. In terms of worker nodes, they get the encrypted path of the aggregated gradient from the smart contract. After decrypting it, the aggregated gradient information is acquired by the worker nodes through the peer-to-peer network and then used to update their local models. After completing the update, each node can continue to the next round of training, or apply to quit training.

**Exit:** When the node reaches its predefined conditions, it sends an exit request to the smart contract and completely withdraws from the training in the next round. The predefined conditions may be that the number of shared rounds reaches a threshold set in advance, the local model accuracy satisfies its own target value, or the number of nodes participating in the current round is less than the expected value. In addition, for a training process, the nodes may choose to quit midway through training, but the nodes that are not involved in this training cannot join in the middle.

## 4    Aggregation Algorithm with Random Enforcement

We design a leader selection algorithm that combines performance and randomness. The algorithm is implemented through a transparent and decentralized smart contract, rather than a third-party organization, ensuring that no node can control the generation of subsequent leaders. The selection of the leader node is random, which makes the gradient aggregation process random and decentralized. Such a method enables no node to continuously obtain gradient information of other nodes. Under the premise of ensuring randomness, the advantages of higher performance nodes are utilized, to improve the efficiency of the whole system. The specific algorithm is as Algorithm 1.

Before the start of the training, the smart contract will store the nodeID of nodes that will participate in this training, and select the nodeID $l$ of leader in the first round randomly. In every round, when all workers complete the registration of the encrypted gradient path, the smart contract will automatically start timing, which is achieved by a counter in the smart contract. After the leader node performs the gradient aggregation and registers the aggregated gradient path on the smart contract, the smart contract stops timing. The time is recorded as $t$, which is the sum of the communication time $t_c$ and the aggregation time $t_a$. For the entire system, it only cares about the value of $t$. If $t$ corresponds to the leader node of the first round, it will be used to initialize the time mapping $T$. This mapping stores the time recorded by each node when it was last selected as the leader. Next, the values in mapping $T$ will be normalized and stored in weight mapping $W$:

$$W[l] = \log(1 + \lambda/t)$$

**Algorithm 1.** Leader selection based on randomness and performance

1: Select leader node $l$ of the first round randomly
2: Initialize balance factor $\lambda$
3: **for all** round $i$ **do**
4:     Record the aggregation time $t$ of $l$
5:     **if** $i$ is 1 **then**
6:         Initialize time mapping $T$ with $t$
7:         $w \leftarrow \log(1 + \lambda/t)$
8:         Initialize weight mapping $W$ with $w$
9:     **else**
10:         $T[l] \leftarrow t$
11:         $W[l] \leftarrow \log(1 + \lambda/t)$
12:     **end if**
13:     Initialize $w_s$ to 0
14:     **for all** node $j$ that participates in the next round **do**
15:         $w_s \leftarrow w_s + W[j]$
16:     **end for**
17:     Initialize probability mapping $P$
18:     **for all** node $j$ that participates in the next round **do**
19:         $P[j] \leftarrow W[j]/w_s$
20:     **end for**
21:     Select leader node $l$ of the next round according to probability $P$
22: **end for**

$l$ is the nodeID of the current leader. The weights stored in mapping $W$ are used to calculate the probability mapping $P$. Mapping $P$ stores the probability that each node will be selected as the leader in the next round. The specific calculation steps are as follows:

$$w_s = \sum_{W[j] \in W} W[j]$$

$$P[j] = W[j]/w_s$$

The smart contract selects the leader node of the next round, according to the probability $P[j]$ corresponding to the nodeID $j$.

## 5    Evaluation

In this section, we carry out several experiments based on our decentralized training system. We demonstrate the effectiveness of the system in enhancing robustness, improving the accuracy of local models for each node, and striking a balance between system performance and randomness.

## 5.1 Experiment Setup

In our system, the blockchain and smart contract are implemented based on Hyperledger Fabric. Hyperledger Fabric is an open source collaborative effort hosted by The Linux Foundation, created to advance cross-industry blockchain technologies.

The system we design and implement is based on the sharing of gradient information, so it is applicable to almost all deep learning models. To demonstrate the effectiveness of the system, we use the MNIST dataset that is widely used and researched. More importantly, current research on federated learning is mainly based on the MNIST dataset [1,7], which allows us to compare with other methods. We have 5,500 training samples for each node participating in federated training in the system. For each node, the class distribution of the training samples is random. For the deep learning model, we choose a commonly used CNN model, which contains two convolutional layers, two fully connected layers and one output layer.

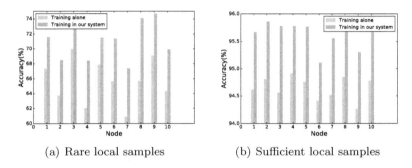

(a) Rare local samples            (b) Sufficient local samples

**Fig. 3.** Training accuracy with ten nodes.

## 5.2 Baselines and Metrics

We compare our training method to the following baselines in our experiments. 1) *Training alone*, in which each node only trains the local model with locally owned data. 2) *Federated training based on completely random selection*, in which the leader nodes of each round are completely randomly selected, regardless of the time performance requirements of the federated training. 3) *Federated training based on performance priority selection*, in which the probability that a node is selected as a leader is directly proportional to its performance, and it is possible that the selection of the leader node is almost monopolized. 4) *Federated training based on centralized parameter server*, in which the training process relies on a centralized node.

## 5.3   Results

**Training Accuracy.** First, we validate the accuracy of our training approach. We compare the accuracy of ten nodes with federated training. The conventional centralized training approach not only shares a large amount of gradient information, but also synchronizes the model parameters. In order to show the impact of differences in the original data owned by different organizations, our training approach only shares part of the gradient information. In our system, the accuracy of the model is still improved compared to that of training alone. When each node has 5,000 samples, the accuracy of federated training in our system is 1.22% higher than training alone. However, when the node has only 50 samples, the accuracy of the improvement is as high as 8.40%, as shown in Fig. 3. At the same time, for the node with higher quality and more number of local samples, the final training model will tend to be better than other nodes, while the final model obtained by each node is exactly the same through the centralized approach. Our training approach is more fair and drives nodes to use more and better samples for federated training.

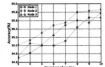

**Fig. 4.** Model accuracy increases as No. of joining nodes increases.

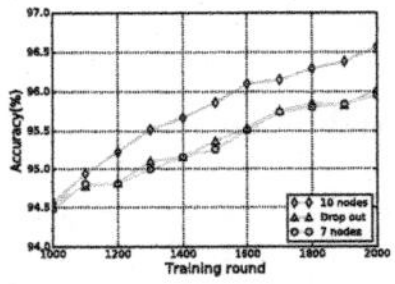

**Fig. 5.** Model accuracy is still improved after the dropout occurs.

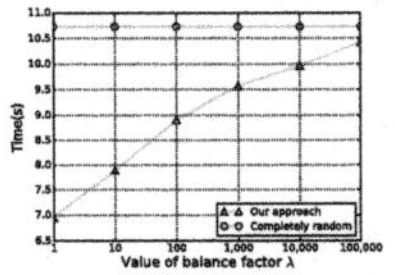

**Fig. 6.** Time comparison among completely random approach & ours.

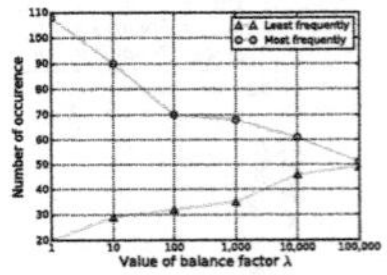

**Fig. 7.** Difference in the No. of times the node is selected as leader.

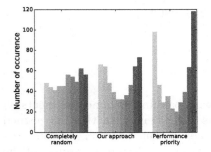

**Fig. 8.** The distribution of leader node.

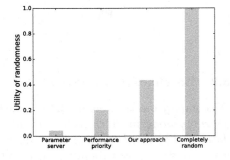

**Fig. 9.** The utility of randomness.

In addition, we choose three nodes for observation. When they perform federated training with different numbers of nodes, the accuracy of their local models changes as shown in Fig. 4. An increase in the number of federated nodes can be observed, which helps each training node to achieve higher model accuracy, motivating more nodes to participate in our federated training together.

**System Robustness.** We select ten nodes to perform 1000 rounds of training. At this time, three nodes dropout, and the model accuracy after 1000 rounds is shown in Fig. 5. It can be seen that the federated learning continues, and the model accuracy is slightly higher than the training with seven nodes throughout. This shows the extremely robustness of the system.

**Time Performance.** The training approach we designed considers system performance. In Fig. 6, we show the variation of the gradient aggregation time of the system as the balance factor $\lambda$ changes. The results show that our training approach can save up to 35% of the time, compared to a completely random approach. Even when the balance factor $\lambda$ is taken as 100, it can still save about 17% of the time. We assign balance factor $\lambda$ to different values and compare the corresponding aggregation time with other approaches. The specific time for aggregation is listed in Table 1. In terms of the centralized approach, the worst performing node becomes a bottleneck. For the time required to complete an aggregation in the case of synchronous training, our approach saves up to 66.52% of the time compared to the centralized approach, and up to 35.32% of the time compared to the completely random approach.

**Table 1.** Aggregation time

| Approach | $\lambda = 1$ | $\lambda = 100$ | Completely random | Parameter server |
|---|---|---|---|---|
| Aggregation time (s) | 6.96 | 8.91 | 10.73 | 20.79 |

**Randomness for Gradient Aggregation.** We introduce randomness into the training process by weighted random selection of the leader nodes. This selection requires the balance factor $\lambda$, which is negotiated by the participating nodes before training to balance randomness and system performance. In our approach, let $\lambda$ be 100 to compare with other approaches. We count the number of occurrences of the most frequently selected node and the least frequently selected node in the 500 rounds of training, with the different values of the balance factor $\lambda$, as shown in Fig. 7. The larger the balance factor is, the more average the probability that each node is selected. When the balance factor $\lambda$ approaches infinity, the selection approximates a completely random election.

In Fig. 8, we also compare our approach to performance priority selection. In the performance priority selection approach, the probability that each node is selected is proportional to its performance, while our approach only guarantees that the probability is positively correlated with the performance. The parameter normalization of the logarithmic function prevents the probability of each node from being too large. It can be seen that in the performance priority approach, the sum of the two most frequently selected nodes is close to half of the total number. This creates the possibility of monopolizing the leader role through the performance advantages of the node. Once a node in the system has performance far exceeding that of other nodes, such a selection will result in the system degenerating into a centralized parameter server architecture.

Finally, we calculated the standard deviations for the different approaches, and divided them by the standard deviation of the completely random method, as the corresponding utility value to measure the randomness. The results are shown in Fig. 9. It can be observed that our approach is not much different from completely random selection, while far superior to the other two methods. For the utility of randomness, our design is 90.19% higher than the conventional centralized approach, and 53.43% higher than the performance priority approach.

# 6    Conclusion

We design and implement a blockchain-based federated learning system through deploying smart contract on the blockchain, and develop corresponding random enforcement training approach. In our system, the organizations involved in training trust the mathematics and cryptography rather than third-party organizations. All participating organizations are equal. They participate in the model training of federated learning, and jointly maintain the normal conduct of federated learning. Compared with existing centralized systems and methods, our design is more robust and avoids the threat of a single point of failure.

**Acknowledgments.** This work is supported in part by NSFC (Grant No. 61872215), Shenzhen Science and Technology Program (Grant No. RCYX20200714114523079), Shenzhen Nanshan District Ling-Hang Team Project (Grant No. LHTD20170005), Featured Innovation Project of Guangdong Education Department (Grant No. 2020 KTSCX126), and Natural Science Foundation of Top Talent of SZTU (Grant No. 2018010801008).

# References

1. Abadi, M., et al.: Deep learning with differential privacy. In: Proceedings of the 2016 ACM SIGSAC Conference on CCS, pp. 308–318 (2016)
2. Phong, L.T., Aono, Y., Hayashi, T., Wang, L., Moriai, S.: Privacy-preserving deep learning: revisited and enhanced. In: Batten, L., Kim, D.S., Zhang, X., Li, G. (eds.) ATIS 2017. CCIS, vol. 719, pp. 100–110. Springer, Singapore (2017). https://doi.org/10.1007/978-981-10-5421-1_9
3. Banko, M., Brill, E.: Scaling to very very large corpora for natural language disambiguation. In: Proceedings of the 39th Annual Meeting on Association for Computational Linguistics, pp. 26–33. Association for Computational Linguistics (2001)
4. Bonawitz, K., et al.: Towards federated learning at scale: System design. arXiv preprint arXiv:1902.01046 (2019)
5. Buterin, V., et al.: A next-generation smart contract and decentralized application platform. White Paper, vol. 3, no. 37 (2014)
6. Carlini, N., Liu, C., Kos, J., Erlingsson, Ú., Song, D.: The secret sharer: measuring unintended neural network memorization & extracting secrets. arXiv preprint arXiv:1802.08232 (2018)
7. Geyer, R.C., Klein, T., Nabi, M.: Differentially private federated learning: a client level perspective. arXiv preprint arXiv:1712.07557 (2017)
8. Halevy, A., Norvig, P., Pereira, F.: The unreasonable effectiveness of data (2009)

9. Hitaj, B., Ateniese, G., Perez-Cruz, F.: Deep models under the GAN: information leakage from collaborative deep learning. In: Proceedings of the 2017 ACM SIGSAC Conference on Computer and Communications Security, pp. 603–618. ACM (2017)
10. HyperLedger Fabric. https://www.hyperledger.org
11. Li, M., et al.: Scaling distributed machine learning with the parameter server. In: 11th {USENIX} Symposium on Operating Systems Design and Implementation ({OSDI} 2014), pp. 583–598 (2014)
12. McMahan, B., Ramage, D.: Federated learning: collaborative machine learning without centralized training data. Google Research Blog 3 (2017)
13. Phong, L.T., Aono, Y., Hayashi, T., Wang, L., Moriai, S.: Privacy-preserving deep learning via additively homomorphic encryption. IEEE Trans. Inf. Forensics Secur. **13**(5), 1333–1345 (2018)
14. Shokri, R., Shmatikov, V.: Privacy-preserving deep learning. In: Proceedings of the 22nd ACM SIGSAC Conference on CCS, pp. 1310–1321. ACM (2015)
15. Song, C., Ristenpart, T., Shmatikov, V.: Machine learning models that remember too much. In: Proceedings of the 2017 ACM SIGSAC Conference on Computer and Communications Security, pp. 587–601. ACM (2017)
16. Yu, M., et al.: Gradiveq: vector quantization for bandwidth-efficient gradient aggregation in distributed CNN training. In: Advances in Neural Information Processing Systems, pp. 5123–5133 (2018)

# Continual Learning for Fake News Detection from Social Media

Yi Han$^{(\boxtimes)}$ iD, Shanika Karunasekera iD, and Christopher Leckie iD

School of Computing and Information Systems, The University of Melbourne,
Melbourne, Australia
{yi.han,karus,caleckie}@unimelb.edu.au

**Abstract.** The prevalence of fake news over social media has a profound impact on justice, public trust and society as a whole. Although significant effort has been applied to mitigate its negative impact, our study shows that existing fake news detection algorithms may perform poorly on new data. In other words, the performance of a model trained on one dataset degrades on another and potentially vastly different dataset. Considering that in practice a deployed fake news detection system is likely to observe unseen data, it is crucial to solve this problem without re-training the model on the entire data from scratch, which would become prohibitively expensive as the data volumes grow. An intuitive solution is to further train the model on the new dataset, but our results show that this direct incremental training approach does not work, as the model only performs well on the latest dataset it is trained on, which is similar to the problem of catastrophic forgetting in the field of continual learning. Instead, in this work, (1) we first demonstrate that with only minor computational overhead, balanced performance can be restored on both existing and new datasets, by utilising Gradient Episodic Memory (GEM) and Elastic Weight Consolidation (EWC)—two techniques from continual learning. (2) We improve the algorithm of GEM so that the drop in model performance on the previous task can be further minimised. Specifically, we investigate different techniques to optimise the sampling process for GEM, as an improvement over random selection as originally designed. (3) We conduct extensive experiments on two datasets with thousands of labelled news items to verify our results.

**Keywords:** Fake news detection · Continual learning · Social media

## 1 Introduction

A series of incidents over recent years have demonstrated the profound damage fake news can cause to society, and it has become an urgent challenge to study how to automatically and accurately identify fake news[1] before it is widespread.

---

[1] Here we use the definition in [38]: *fake news is intentionally and verifiably false news published by a news outlet.*

© Springer Nature Switzerland AG 2021
I. Farkaš et al. (Eds.): ICANN 2021, LNCS 12892, pp. 372–384, 2021.
https://doi.org/10.1007/978-3-030-86340-1_30

A variety of techniques have been proposed for fake news detection [17,38], including *content-based approaches* that use news headlines and body content to verify the validity of the news, *context-based approaches* that rely on the interactions between users, *e.g.*, tweet, retweet, reply, mention and follow, and *mixed approaches*. However, we find that **even though these methods may achieve satisfactory results on the dataset on which they are trained, their performance often degrades considerably on another and potentially vastly different dataset.** In practice, a deployed fake news detection system is likely to observe new, unseen data. Therefore, it is crucial to solve this problem without re-training the model from scratch every time a new dataset is obtained, which would become prohibitively expensive as the data volumes grow.

Specifically, we start with the most intuitive approach of direct incremental training—further train the model on the new dataset. However, our results suggest that using this approach the obtained model only performs well on the latest dataset it is trained on. This is similar to the problem of catastrophic forgetting [12] in the field of continual learning: when a deep neural network is trained to learn a sequence of tasks (in this case, a new dataset represents a different task), its performance degrades on the earlier tasks after it learns new tasks, as the new tasks override the weights. Therefore, in this work:

- We first demonstrate that with only minor computational overhead, balanced performance can be restored on both existing and new datasets, by utilising GEM [9] and EWC [7]—two popular techniques from continual learning, although GEM-trained models perform better in general.
- We improve GEM so that the drop in model performance on the previous task can be further minimised. GEM keeps a certain number of samples from the previous task when training a model on the new task. In contrast to existing approaches that use uniform random sampling, we investigate more sophisticated sampling techniques—maximum entropy sampling and support samples—so that the chosen instances are more informative.
- We conduct extensive experiments on two datasets with thousands of labelled news items. Specifically, our experimental results show that after the above sampling techniques are applied, the trained models can achieve better performance on the previous task, while maintaining their performance on the new task.

The remainder of this paper is organised as follows: Sect. 2 briefly reviews existing work on fake news detection; Sect. 3 describes the problem with current detection algorithms when facing new, unseen data; Sect. 4 investigates how to restore balanced performance on both existing and new data using GEM and EWC, as well as how to improve GEM; and finally Sect. 5 concludes the paper and offers directions for future work.

## 2    Background: Fake News Detection Algorithms and Datasets

Detecting fake news on social media has been a popular research problem over recent years. In this section, we briefly review the prior work on this topic, and introduce the datasets chosen in our experiments. Specifically, similar to [17, 24], we classify existing work into three categories: content-based approaches, context-based approaches and mixed approaches.

**Content-Based Approaches.** Content-based approaches use news headlines and body content to verify the validity of the news. It can be further classified into two categories [24,38]: (1) *knowledge-based detection.* In order for this type of method to work, a knowledge base or knowledge graph [15] has to be built first. Here, knowledge can be represented in the form of a triple: (Subject, Predicate, Object), *i.e.*, SPO triple. Then, to verify an item of news, knowledge extracted from its content is compared with the facts in the knowledge graph [3]. (2) *Style-based detection.* Since the purpose of fake news is to mislead the public, it often exhibits unique writing styles that are rarely seen in real news. Therefore, style-based methods aim to identify these characteristics [19,27,29].

In addition to textual information, images posted in social media have also been investigated to facilitate the detection of fake news [5,30,33,37].

**Context-Based Approaches.** Social context here refers to the interactions between users, including tweet, retweet, reply, mention and follow. These engagements provide valuable information for identifying fake news spread on social media. For example, Jin *et al.* [6] build a stance network where the weight of an edge represents how much each pair of posts support or contradict each other. Then fake news detection is based on estimating the credibility of all the posts related to the news item. Tacchini *et al.* [26] propose to detect fake news based on user interactions, *i.e.*, users who liked them on Facebook.

Unlike the above supervised methods, an unsupervised approach is proposed in Yang *et al.* [32]. It builds a Bayesian graphical model to capture the generative process among the validity of news, user opinions and user credibility.

**Mixed Approaches.** Mixed approaches use both news content and associated user interactions over social media to differentiate between fake news and real news. Ruchansky *et al.* [20] design a three-module architecture that combines the text of a news article, the received user response and the source of the news. Other methods that fall into this category include [25,36]

In addition to the above work, a few recent papers have started to work on explainability, *i.e.*, why their model labels certain news items as fake [10,18,21].

**Datasets.** A number of datasets covering different domains have been collected for fake news detection. In our work, we use the dataset of FakeNews-Net [22], which contains labelled news from two websites: politifact.com and gossipcop.com. The news content includes both linguistic and visual information, all the tweets and retweets for each item of news, and the information of the corresponding Twitter users (please refer to [22] for more details).

# 3   Problem Description

In previous work on fake news detection, most proposed methods were evaluated on multiple datasets separately. However, our experimental results on several detection algorithms suggest that models trained on one dataset, *e.g.*, PolitiFact, do not perform well on another dataset, *e.g.*, GossipCop. Note that these two datasets are chosen for demonstration purpose only. Similar findings can be made on other datasets as well, *e.g.*, recently collected COVID-19 datasets, or from two splits of the same dataset that are temporally far away from each other.

A natural thought is to re-train the model on both datasets, but this may not be feasible, or at least not ideal in practice: there will always be new data that our model has not seen before, and it does not make sense to re-train the model from scratch on the entire data every time a new dataset is obtained, especially since as the data size grows, this can become prohibitively expensive.

Therefore, we aim to **find an incremental training method to address the issue of dealing with new, unseen data in fake news detection.** Specifically, let one dataset, *e.g.*, PolitiFact, represent the existing data that our model has been trained on, and the other dataset, *e.g.*, GossipCop, represent the unknown data that our model will face in the future, we investigate how to train models incrementally so that balanced performance can be achieved on both datasets.

To answer the above question, we choose a widely-cited content-based app-roach HAN [34], and design a context-based method that applies graph neural networks (GNNs) to differentiate between the propagation patterns of fake and real news on social media. More details are given in the next subsection.

## 3.1   Propagation Patterns for Fake News Detection

Empirical evidence suggests that fake news and real news spread differently online [28], and the idea of using propagation patterns to detect fake news has been explored in a number of previous studies [1,8,10,11,14,23,31,39]. However, considering the capability of graph neural networks (GNNs) in dealing with non-Euclidean data, we use GNNs to differentiate between the propagation patterns of fake and real news on social media. In addition, given that machine learning models are vulnerable to adversarial attacks [4], we decide not to rely on any text information, *e.g.*, news content or tweet content, so that our model can be less susceptible to the manipulation of advanced fake news fabricators.

**Notation in GNNs.** Consider a graph $G = (A, F)$ with $n$ vertices/nodes and $m$ edges, where $A \in \{0, 1\}^{n \times n}$ is the adjacency matrix. $A_{i,j} = 1$ if there is an edge from node $i$ to node $j$, and $A_{i,j} = 0$ otherwise; $F \in R^{n \times d}$ is the feature matrix, *i.e.*, each node has $d$ features. Given $A$ and $F$ as inputs, the output of a GNN after the $k^{th}$ step is: $H^{(k)} = f\left(A, H^{(k-1)}; \theta^{(k)}\right) \in R^{n \times d}$, where $f$ is the propagation function parameterised by $\theta$, and $H^0 = F$. $H^{(k)}$ can be used for node- or graph-level classification. There have been a number of implementations for the propagation function. In our work, since the goal is to label the propagation pattern of each item of news, which is a graph, we choose the algorithm of DiffPool [35] that is specifically designed for graph classification.

Below we explain how we define the adjacency matrix and the feature matrix in our model, and then present a brief performance comparison.

**Adjacency Matrix.** Once an item of news is published, it may be tweeted by multiple users. We call these tweets that directly reference the news URL *root* tweets. Each of them and their retweets form a separate cascade [28], and all the cascades form the propagation pattern of an item of news.

Each propagation pattern is a graph, where a node refers to a tweet (including the corresponding user)—either the root tweet that references the news or its retweets. A special case is that an extra node representing the news is added to connect all cascades together. All the feature values for this node are set to zero. Edges here represent information flow, *i.e.,* how the news transfers from one person to another. However, since Twitter APIs do not provide the immediate source of a retweet, we first sort the tweets by their timestamps within each cascade, and then search for the potential source of a retweet from all the tweets published earlier. Specifically, there is an edge from node $i$ to node $j$[2] if:

- The user of node $i$ mentions the user of node $j$ in the tweet, *e.g.,* user $i$ retweets a news item and also recommends it to user $j$ via mentioning;
- Tweet $i$ is public and tweet $j$ is posted within a certain period of time after tweet $i$. We set the time limit to ten hours in our experiments.

Note that edges only exist between nodes within the same cascade. We have also further considered the follower and following relations, but our results demonstrate that there is no significant improvement. In addition, since Twitter applies a much stricter rate limit on corresponding APIs, these types of information may not be available in real time, especially if a number of news items need to be validated at the same time and within a detection deadline.

**Feature Matrix.** Since our method does not rely on any textual information, we only choose the following information from user profiles as the features for each node: (1) whether the user is verified, (2) the timestamp when the user was created, encoded as the number of months since March 2006—the time when Twitter was founded, (3) the number of followers, (4) the number of friends, (5) the number of lists, (6) the number of favourites; (7) the number of statuses, (8) the timestamp of the tweet, encoded as the number of seconds since the first tweet that references the news is posted. Another important reason why we choose the above features is that they are easily accessible—they are directly available within the tweet object, which is preferable for online detection.

**Performance Comparison.** We compare our method with the content-based approach HAN [34] and a state-of-the-art algorithm dEFEND [21]. To make our results comparable with those reported in [21] (as they also tested fake news detection algorithms on the same dataset), we follow the same procedure to train

---

[2] Node $i$ is published before node $j$, and the information goes from user $i$ to user $j$.

and test the GNNs: randomly choose 75% of the news as the training data while keeping the rest as the test data, and the final result is the average performance over five repeats. The model is evaluated with the following commonly used metrics: accuracy, precision, recall and F1 score.

For our method, the hyper-parameters for the DiffPool algorithm are set as follows: 2 pooling layers, 64 hidden dimensions and 64 embedding dimensions. In addition, **since it is more critical to detect fake news at an early stage before it becomes widespread, we train GNNs on a clipped dataset that only contains the first $K = 100$ tweets for each news item**[3].

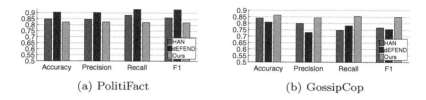

(a) PolitiFact                          (b) GossipCop

**Fig. 1.** Performance comparison on the datasets of PolitiFact and GossipCop.

As can be seen from Fig. 1, by only relying on the limited set of non-textual features and the clipped dataset, our model can achieve comparable performance on PolitiFact, and the best result on GossipCop.

## 4    Dealing with Degraded Performance on New Data

As mentioned in the problem description, we have tested several fake news detection algorithms and find that models trained on PolitiFact perform poorly on GossipCop, and vice versa, where all four metrics drop to around 0.6 or below. An examination of the news content and the generated graphs reveals that (1) since PolitiFact is mainly about political news while GossipCop is more about entertainment news, the writing style, the commonly discussed subjects and topics are vastly different; (2) the graphs generated from PolitiFact and GossipCop are also distinct from each other, in terms of the numbers of nodes and edges.

Similar observations can also be made between PolitiFact/GossipCop and other datasets, or from two splits of one dataset that are temporally far away from each other. In practice, no matter how much data a model has been trained on, it is likely that it will face unknown, different data in the future. This section investigates effective incremental training techniques so that balanced performance can be achieved on both existing and new data for fake news detection.

---

[3] We have also tested $K = 200, 500, 1000, \infty$ (not clipped). Those results are omitted due to space limits (the results are better under those settings).

## 4.1   Incremental Training Reverses the Model Performance

We first test incremental training, *i.e.*, further train the model obtained from PolitiFact (or GossipCop) on the other dataset of GossipCop (or PolitiFact). However, then the models only perform well on the latest dataset on which they are trained, while achieving degraded results on the former dataset. Note that during incremental training, we still randomly choose 75% of news as the training data and the rest as the test data.

This is similar to the problem of catastrophic forgetting which was first recognised in [12]: a neural network tends to forget the information learned in the previous tasks when training on new tasks. In our case, each new dataset can be considered as a new task. In the next subsection, we investigate how to solve the problem by proposing techniques based on continual learning.

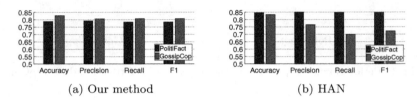

(a) Our method                        (b) HAN

**Fig. 2.** Performance of models first trained on PolitiFact and then on GossipCop using GEM ($|\mathcal{M}| = 300$).

## 4.2   Continual Learning Restores Balanced Performance

In order to deal with catastrophic forgetting, a number of approaches have been proposed, which can be roughly classified into three types [16]: (1) regularisation-based approaches that add extra constraints to the loss function to prevent the loss of previous knowledge; (2) architecture-based approaches that selectively train a part of the network for each task, and expand the network when necessary for new tasks; (3) dual-memory-based approaches that build on top of complementary learning systems (CLS) theory, and replay samples for memory consolidation. In this paper, we consider the following two popular methods:

- Gradient Episodic Memory (GEM)—GEM uses episodic memory to store a number of samples from previous tasks, and when learning a new task $t$, it does not allow the loss over those samples held in memory to increase compared to when the learning of task $t - 1$ is finished;
- Elastic Weight Consolidation (EWC)—its loss function consists of a quadratic penalty term on the change of the parameters, in order to prevent drastic updates to those parameters that are important to the old tasks.

In our case, the learning on the two datasets ($\mathcal{D}_1$ and $\mathcal{D}_2$) are considered as two tasks. When the model learns the first task, it is trained as usual; then during the learning of the second task, we incorporate GEM and EWC:

- Let $C$ be the model, $\theta_1$ be the parameters after the first task, and $\mathcal{M}$ be the set of instances sampled from the first dataset, then the optimisation problem under GEM becomes:

$$min_\theta \sum_{(x_i,y_i)\in\mathcal{D}_2} loss\,(C(x_i;\theta),y_i)$$

$$\text{subject to} \sum_{(x_j,y_j)\in\mathcal{M}} loss\,(C(x_j;\theta),y_j) \leq \sum_{(x_j,y_j)\in\mathcal{M}} loss\,(C(x_j;\theta_1),y_j)$$

- Let $\lambda$ be the regularisation weight, $F$ be the Fisher information matrix, and $\theta^*_{\mathcal{D}_1}$ be the parameters of the Gaussian distribution used by EWC to approximate the posterior of $p(\theta|\mathcal{D}_1)$, then the loss function under EWC is:

$$\sum_{(x_i,y_i)\in\mathcal{D}_2} loss\,(C(x_i;\theta),y_i) + \frac{\lambda}{2}F(\theta - \theta^*_{\mathcal{D}_1})^2$$

**Table 1.** Performance of models first trained on GossipCop and then on PolitiFact using EWC ($|\mathcal{M}| = 300, \lambda = 10^3 \sim 10^5$, the other results are omitted).

| $\lambda$ | Our method | | | | | | | | HAN | | | | | | | |
|---|---|---|---|---|---|---|---|---|---|---|---|---|---|---|---|---|
| | PolitiFact | | | | GossipCop | | | | PolitiFact | | | | GossipCop | | | |
| | Acc | Pre | Rec | F1 | Acc | Pre | Rec | F1 | Acc | Pre | Rec | F1 | Acc | Pre | Rec | F1 |
| $10^3$ | 0.71 | 0.71 | 0.71 | 0.71 | 0.76 | 0.74 | 0.68 | 0.69 | 0.72 | 0.72 | 0.72 | 0.72 | 0.69 | 0.65 | 0.71 | 0.64 |
| $3\times10^3$ | 0.72 | 0.72 | 0.72 | 0.72 | 0.73 | 0.70 | 0.66 | 0.67 | 0.73 | 0.73 | 0.73 | 0.72 | 0.68 | 0.65 | 0.71 | 0.64 |
| $10^4$ | **0.72** | **0.72** | **0.71** | **0.71** | **0.79** | **0.77** | **0.73** | **0.74** | 0.73 | 0.72 | 0.72 | 0.72 | 0.71 | 0.66 | 0.73 | 0.66 |
| $3\times10^4$ | 0.72 | 0.72 | 0.72 | 0.72 | 0.76 | 0.74 | 0.71 | 0.72 | **0.72** | **0.73** | **0.72** | **0.72** | **0.73** | **0.68** | **0.74** | **0.68** |
| $10^5$ | 0.71 | 0.71 | 0.71 | 0.71 | 0.77 | 0.75 | 0.71 | 0.72 | 0.73 | 0.73 | 0.72 | 0.72 | 0.72 | 0.67 | 0.74 | 0.67 |

Note that when estimating the Fisher information matrix $F$, we sample a set of instances ($\mathcal{M}$) and compare the model performance under different sample sizes.

In terms of parameters, we test sample size $|\mathcal{M}| = 100, 200, 300$ (all the samples are chosen randomly), and $\lambda = 1, 3, 10, 30, 10^2, 3 \times 10^2, 10^3, 3 \times 10^3, 10^4, 3 \times 10^4, 10^5$ (for EWC only). Figure 2 shows the results of models first trained on PolitiFact and then on GossipCop using GEM when $|\mathcal{M}| = 300$, and Table 1 presents the performance of models first trained on GossipCop and then on PolitiFact using EWC when $|\mathcal{M}| = 300, \lambda = 10^3, 3 \times 10^3, 10^4, 3 \times 10^4, 10^5$ (the other results are omitted due to space limits). The results demonstrate that both methods can achieve relatively balanced performance over the two datasets, although GEM trained models work better in general. Comparing Figs. 1 and 2, we can see that the GEM-trained models almost restore their performance on the previous task, where the drop in all four metrics is below 3% in most cases.

**Efficiency.** In terms of efficiency, we observe that: (1) compared with the normal training process, training with GEM and EWC requires slightly more time: 5% to 10%—this is a significant improvement over re-training from scratch, the time of which grows linearly with the number of nodes and edges in our case; (2) there is no significant difference in training time between GEM and EWC; and (3) the impact of the parameters on the training time is also not significant.

### 4.3 Optimise the Sampling Process to Further Minimise Performance Drop

In the above experiments, the set of instances $\mathcal{M}$ from the previous task is chosen randomly. In this section, we explore other techniques so that the selected samples are more informative about the data of the previous task. Note that all the experiments below are conducted using the propagation-based approach introduced in Sect. 3.1 with GEM (which outperforms EWC) and $|\mathcal{M}| = 300$, while we leave the improvement of content-based approaches for future work.

**Technique I: Maximum Entropy Sampling (MES).** We first consider maximum entropy sampling, which aims to select a subset $\mathcal{S}$ from the entire dataset $\mathcal{N}$ such that the obtained information of $\mathcal{N}$ is maximised. According to the principle of MES, the entropy of the remaining data points $\mathcal{N} \backslash \mathcal{S}$ must be minimised, while the entropy of $\mathcal{S}$ must be maximised, i.e.,

$$\mathcal{M} = \underset{\mathcal{S}}{\operatorname{argmax}} \mathcal{H}(\mathcal{S}) = \underset{\mathcal{S}}{\operatorname{argmax}} - \sum_{x_i} p(x_i) log_2 p(x_i), x_i \in \mathcal{S}$$

In our case, considering that the graphs generated from the two datasets have quite different numbers of nodes, we **calculate the entropy over the graph size**.

The MES problem is NP-hard [13]. A quasi-optimal solution adopts a greedy strategy: it starts with an empty set $\mathcal{S} = \emptyset$, and in each step, a new sample is chosen that maximises the marginal gain, i.e., $x = \operatorname{argmax}_{x_i \notin \mathcal{S}} \mathcal{H}(\mathcal{S} \cup \{x_i\}) - \mathcal{H}(\mathcal{S})$. However, this greedy algorithm is computationally expensive, and is not suitable for large datasets. We explain our approaches later in this section.

**Technique II: Support Samples.** A similar idea has been explored in [2], which is inspired by margins in SVMs. For SVMs the support vectors determine the decision boundary, and in our case, we can define the margin as $Margin(x) = C(x, y) - C(x, 1 - y)$, where $C$ is the classifier, $x$ is the input, and $y \in \{0(real), 1(fake)\}$ is the label. A negative margin means that $x$ is misclassified, while a larger margin suggests that the classifier is more confident of the prediction. Since the purpose of sampling instances from the previous task is to ensure that the model performance does not degrade, it does not make sense to choose misclassified instances, nor would it be efficient to select samples with large margins.

**Proposed Sampling Approaches.** Our sampling approaches combine the above two techniques—(1) first we calculate the margin for each graph in the previous task, and initialise $S$ with the graphs whose margin is within the range of $(0, \delta)$, $\delta \in [0, 1]$. Three values, $0.05, 0.1, 0.2$, are tested and we finally set $\delta = 0.1$. Note that the size of this initialised set is normally much smaller than the sample size of 300. (2) Then we propose the following two strategies (Algorithm 1):

- **Strategy I** goes through the graphs in $N \backslash S$ ordered by their margin values, and add one graph $x_i$ if the entropy increases, *i.e.*, $\mathcal{H}(S \cup \{x_i\}) > \mathcal{H}(S)$;
- **Strategy II** adopts a stochastic greedy method [13], where in each step we randomly sample a set of graphs $(\mathcal{R})$ from $N \backslash S$, and find $x_i \in \mathcal{R}$ that maximises the marginal gain, *i.e.*, $x = \text{argmax}_{x_i \in \mathcal{R}} \mathcal{H}(S \cup \{x_i\}) - \mathcal{H}(S)$. Please refer to [13] for how to choose the size of $\mathcal{R}$. In our experiments, we set $|\mathcal{R}| = max(\frac{|N|}{|M|}, 20)$.

In addition, we design another two strategies as baselines: (1) choose the graphs with the top $|M| = 300$ smallest margin values, and (2) initialise $S = \{x | 0 < Margin(x) \leq \delta = 0.1\}$, sort the remaining graphs $N \backslash S$ by size, and sample uniformly at random.

Figure 3 compares the five sampling strategies—(1) random as originally designed, (2) Baseline 1, (3) Baseline 2, (4) Strategy I, (5) Strategy II—for models first trained on PolitiFact and then on GossipCop using GEM with $|M| = 300$ (results for models first trained on GossipCop and then on PolitiFact are omitted due to space limits). We can see that while all models perform similarly on GossipCop (*i.e.*, the new task), Strategy II can improve the results on PolitiFact (*i.e.*, the previous task), which indicates the effectiveness of this sampling method. However, Strategy I does not work well—a comparison reveals that the selected samples differ significantly from those under Strategy II.

---

**Algorithm 1:** Sampling Strategies

---

**Input**  : Sample size $|M|$; The number of instances from the previous task $|N|$
**Output** : Samples, $S$

1  Initialise $S = \{x | 0 < Margin(x) \leq \delta = 0.1\}$
2  **Strategy I:**
3  Sort $N \backslash S$ by their margin values from smallest to largest
4  **while** $|S| < |M|$ **do**
5      **for** $x_i \in N \backslash S$ **do**
6          **if** $\mathcal{H}(S \cup \{x_i\}) > \mathcal{H}(S)$ **then**
7              $S = S \cup \{x_i\}$

8  **Strategy II:**
9  **while** $|S| < |M|$ **do**
10     $\mathcal{R} =$ randomly sample $max(\frac{|N|}{|M|}, 20)$ instances from $N \backslash S$
11     $x = \text{argmax}_{x_i \in \mathcal{R}} \mathcal{H}(S \cup \{x_i\}) - \mathcal{H}(S)$
12     $S = S \cup \{x\}$
13 **return** $S$

---

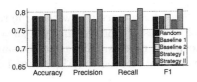
(a) Performance on PolitiFact

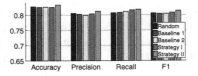
(b) Performance on GossipCop

**Fig. 3.** Comparison of different sampling strategies for models first trained on Politi-Fact and then on GossipCop using GEM ($|\mathcal{M}| = 300$).

## 5    Conclusions and Future Work

The prevalence of fake news over social media has become a serious social problem. Although a number of detection methods have been proposed, we identify the problem that models trained on a given dataset may not perform well on new data, and direct incremental training cannot solve the issue. Since this is similar to catastrophic forgetting in continual learning, we propose to apply two popular approaches, GEM and EWC, during the incremental training, so that balanced performance can be achieved on both existing and new data. This avoids retraining on the entire data, which becomes prohibitively expensive as data size grows. In addition, we further improve the results by optimising the sampling process with maximum entropy sampling and support samples.

For future work, we will investigate whether Algorithm 1 also improves the performance of content-based approaches. Specifically, entropy needs to be redefined, and one possibility is to calculate it over the topic of each news item.

## References

1. Bian, T., et al.: Rumor detection on social media with bi-directional graph convolutional networks. arXiv:2001.06362 (2020)
2. Chen, Z., Lin, T.: Revisiting gradient episodic memory for continual learning (2019). https://openreview.net/pdf?id=H1g79ySYvB
3. Cui, L., Seo, H., Tabar, M., Ma, F., Wang, S., Lee, D.: DETERRENT: knowledge guided graph attention network for detecting healthcare misinformation. In: 26th ACM SIGKDD, KDD 2020, pp. 492–502 (2020)
4. Goodfellow, I.J., Shlens, J., Szegedy, C.: Explaining and harnessing adversarial examples. eprint arXiv:1412.6572 (2014)
5. Jin, Z., Cao, J., Zhang, Y., Zhou, J., Tian, Q.: Novel visual and statistical image features for microblogs news verification. IEEE Trans. Multimedia **19**(3), 598–608 (2017)
6. Jin, Z., Cao, J., Zhang, Y., Luo, J.: News verification by exploiting conflicting social viewpoints in microblogs. In: 30th AAAI, pp. 2972–2978 (2016)
7. Kirkpatrick, J., et al.: Overcoming catastrophic forgetting in neural networks. NAS **114**(13), 3521 (2017)
8. Liu, Y., Wu, Y.F.B.: Early detection of fake news on social media through propagation path classification with recurrent and convolutional networks. In: 32nd AAAI, pp. 354–361 (2018)

9. Lopez-Paz, D., Ranzato, M.: Gradient episodic memory for continual learning. In: 31st NeurIPS, pp. 6467–6476. Curran Associates, Inc. (2017)
10. Lu, Y.J., Li, C.T.: GCAN: graph-aware co-attention networks for explainable fake news detection on social media. arXiv:2004.11648 (2020)
11. Ma, J., Gao, W., Wong, K.F.: Detect rumors in microblog posts using propagation structure via kernel learning. In: 55th ACL, pp. 708–717 (2017)
12. McCloskey, M., Cohen, N.J.: Catastrophic interference in connectionist networks: The sequential learning problem. In: Psychology of Learning and Motivation, vol. 24, pp. 109–165. Academic Press (1989)
13. Mirzasoleiman, B., Badanidiyuru, A., Karbasi, A., Vondrák, J., Krause, A.: Lazier than lazy greedy. In: 29th AAAI, pp. 1812–1818 (2015)
14. Monti, F., Frasca, F., Eynard, D., Mannion, D., Bronstein, M.M.: Fake news detection on social media using geometric deep learning. arXiv:1902.06673
15. Nickel, M., Murphy, K., Tresp, V., Gabrilovich, E.: A review of relational machine learning for knowledge graphs. IEEE **104**(1), 11–33 (2016)
16. Parisi, G.I., Kemker, R., Part, J.L., Kanan, C., Wermter, S.: Continual lifelong learning with neural networks: a review. arXiv:1802.07569 (2018)
17. Pierri, F., Ceri, S.: False news on social media: a data-driven survey. SIGMOD Rec. **48**(2), 18–27 (2019)
18. Popat, K., Mukherjee, S., Yates, A., Weikum, G.: Debunking fake news and false claims using evidence-aware deep learning. arXiv:1809.06416 (2018)
19. Pérez-Rosas, V., Kleinberg, B., Lefevre, A., Mihalcea, R.: Automatic detection of fake news. In: 27th COLING, pp. 3391–3401 (2018)
20. Ruchansky, N., Seo, S., Liu, Y.: CSI: a hybrid deep model for fake news detection. In: 26th CIKM, pp. 797–806 (2017)
21. Shu, K., Cui, L., Wang, S., Lee, D., Liu, H.: DEFEND: explainable fake news detection. In: 25th KDD, pp. 395–405 (2019)
22. Shu, K., Mahudeswaran, D., Wang, S., Lee, D., Liu, H.: FakeNewsNet: a data repository with news content, social context and spatialtemporal information for studying fake news on social media. arXiv:1809.01286 (2018)
23. Shu, K., Mahudeswaran, D., Wang, S., Liu, H.: Hierarchical propagation networks for fake news detection: investigation and exploitation. arXiv e-prints arXiv:1903.09196 (2019)
24. Shu, K., Sliva, A., Wang, S., Tang, J., Liu, H.: Fake news detection on social media: a data mining perspective. SIGKDD Explor. **19**(1), 22–36 (2017)
25. Shu, K., Wang, S., Liu, H.: Beyond news contents: the role of social context for fake news detection. In: 12th WSDM, pp. 312–320 (2019)
26. Tacchini, E., Ballarin, G., Della Vedova, M.L., Moret, S., de Alfaro, L.: Some like it hoax: Automated fake news detection in social networks. arXiv e-prints arXiv:1704.07506 (2017)
27. Volkova, S., Shaffer, K., Jang, J.Y., Hodas, N.: Separating facts from fiction: linguistic models to classify suspicious and trusted news posts on twitter. In: 55th ACL, pp. 647–653 (2017)
28. Vosoughi, S., Roy, D., Aral, S.: The spread of true and false news online. Science **359**(6380), 1146–1151 (2018)
29. Wang, W.Y.: "Liar, liar pants on fire": a new benchmark dataset for fake news detection. In: 55th ACL, pp. 422–426 (2017)
30. Wang, Y., et al.: EANN: event adversarial neural networks for multi-modal fake news detection. In: 24th KDD, pp. 849–857 (2018)
31. Wu, K., Yang, S., Zhu, K.Q.: False rumors detection on Sina Weibo by propagation structures. In: 31st ICDE, pp. 651–662 (2015)

32. Yang, S., Shu, K., Wang, S., Gu, R., Wu, F., Liu, H.: Unsupervised fake news detection on social media: a generative approach. In: 33rd AAAI, vol. 33, pp. 5644–5651 (2019)
33. Yang, Y., Zheng, L., Zhang, J., Cui, Q., Li, Z., Yu, P.S.: TI-CNN: convolutional neural networks for fake news detection. arXiv:1806.00749 (2018)
34. Yang, Z., Yang, D., Dyer, C., He, X., Smola, A., Hovy, E.: Hierarchical attention networks for document classification. In: 2016 NAACL, pp. 1480–1489 (2016)
35. Ying, R., You, J., Morris, C., Ren, X., Hamilton, W.L., Leskovec, J.: Hierarchical graph representation learning with differentiable pooling. In: 32nd NeurIPS, pp. 4805–4815 (2018)
36. Zhang, J., Dong, B., Yu, P.S.: FAKEDETECTOR: effective fake news detection with deep diffusive neural network. arXiv:1805.08751 (2018)
37. Zhou, X., Wu, J., Zafarani, R.: SAFE: similarity-aware multi-modal fake news detection. In: 24th PAKDD, pp. 354–367 (2020)
38. Zhou, X., Zafarani, R.: Fake news: a survey of research, detection methods, and opportunities. arXiv:1812.00315 [cs] (2018)
39. Zhou, X., Zafarani, R.: Network-based fake news detection: a pattern-driven approach. arXiv e-prints arXiv:1906.04210 (2019)

# Balanced Softmax Cross-Entropy
# for Incremental Learning

Quentin Jodelet[1,3]([⊠]), Xin Liu[2,3], and Tsuyoshi Murata[1,3]

[1] Department of Computer Science, Tokyo Institute of Technology, Tokyo, Japan
jodelet@net.c.titech.ac.jp, murata@c.titech.ac.jp
[2] Artificial Intelligence Research Center, AIST, Tokyo, Japan
xin.liu@aist.go.jp
[3] AIST-Tokyo Tech RWBC-OIL, Tokyo, Japan

**Abstract.** Deep neural networks are prone to catastrophic forgetting when incrementally trained on new classes or new tasks as adaptation to the new data leads to a drastic decrease of the performance on the old classes and tasks. By using a small memory for rehearsal and knowledge distillation, recent methods have proven to be effective to mitigate catastrophic forgetting. However due to the limited size of the memory, large imbalance between the amount of data available for the old and new classes still remains which results in a deterioration of the overall accuracy of the model. To address this problem, we propose the use of the Balanced Softmax Cross-Entropy loss and show that it can be combined with exiting methods for incremental learning to improve their performances while also decreasing the computational cost of the training procedure in some cases. Experiments on the competitive ImageNet, subImageNet and CIFAR100 datasets show states-of-the-art results.

**Keywords:** Incremental learning · Continual learning

## 1 Introduction

In a class incremental learning scenario, the complete training dataset is not available at once. Instead, the training samples are gradually available, few classes at a time. The model has to be trained on new classes in a sequential manner similarly to some real world scenarios where it is not possible to either store all the data for training due to memory constraints or re-train the model from scratch each time new samples are available due to time and computational power limitations. For example, a robot learning new objects while interacting with its environment may not have enough memory to store images of all past encountered objects and may not be able to be re-trained on the complete dataset each time a new object is discovered due to the limited computational power.

This work is partly supported by JST CREST (Grant Number JPMJCR1687), JSPS Grant-in-Aid for Scientific Research (Grant Number 21K12042, 17H01785), and the New Energy and Industrial Technology Development Organization (Grant Number JPNP20006).

I. Farkaš et al. (Eds.): ICANN 2021, LNCS 12892, pp. 385–396, 2021.
https://doi.org/10.1007/978-3-030-86340-1_31

Although deep neural networks achieve state-of-the-art performance for many problems in computer vision, it is challenging to use them in an incremental learning scenario due to their high propensity to steeply forget previously learned classes while learning new ones. This situation is known as catastrophic forgetting [10, 24, 26].

In this context, replay has proven to be an effective solution to mitigate catastrophic forgetting. A small memory buffer is used to store examples from previously encountered classes which are then used for rehearsal while learning new classes. However, a large imbalance problem appears due to the limited size of the memory buffer: at a given incremental step, the model will mainly see data from the new classes and only few from the previous classes. This leads the model to be biased toward the new classes which greatly deteriorates its overall performance. Methods designed to tackle this issue mainly rely on using some finetuning steps on a small balanced dataset after the main training process or using specifically designed classifiers.

In this work, we propose a novel approach to address the bias toward new classes in the context of incremental learning using a rehearsal memory. Our proposed method relies on the use of the Balanced Softmax activation function [28] for the Cross-Entropy loss instead of the commonly used Softmax function during the training procedure. When combining the Balanced Softmax Cross-Entropy loss with recent advanced methods in incremental learning, the average incremental accuracy of the models can be improved which enables us to reach state-of-the-art performances on competitive datasets. Moreover, the computational cost of the training procedure can also decrease as using the Balanced Softmax Cross-Entropy loss does not require any additional balanced finetuning step. Finally, we also investigate the use of a meta-learning algorithm to further improve the accuracy of the models.

## 2   Related Work

Various scenarios for continual learning can be considered [17, 23]. In this work we will mostly consider the class incremental scenario. When applied on large scale datasets, methods for this scenario usually rely on three components: constraints to preserve past knowledge, a memory for rehearsal and bias correction methods.

The distillation loss [15] initially proposed by Hinton *et al.* for transferring knowledge from a large teacher model into a smaller student model has been adapted to continual learning by Li *et al.* [21] to distill the knowledge of the model learned during the previous step into the next step one using the output logits. This method was applied by several authors [6, 27, 32]. Recently, several proposal have been made to improve the distillation for incremental learning. Hou *et al.* [16] proposed a novel distillation loss applied on the final class embeddings instead of the output logits. Dhar *et al.* [8] proposed to penalize changes in the attention maps of the classifiers. Douillard *et al.* [9] proposed a new distillation loss using a pooling function and applied it to several intermediate layers of the neural network in addition to the final class embedding. Tao *et al.* [30] proposed to model the class embedding topology using an elastic Hebbian graph and then used a topology-preserving loss to constrain the change of the neighboring relationships of the graph during each incremental step. Similarly, Lei *et al.* [20] adopted a feature-graph preservation approach and proposed the weighted-Euclidean regularization to preserve the knowledge.

Rehearsal using a small memory [7] containing sample data from previously learned classes has been shown to be an effective method to mitigate catastrophic forgetting. The output logits can be stored instead of the true labels for distillation if the model from the previous step is not available [4]. Using compressed versions [5] or intermediate representations as proposed by Hayes *et al.* [13] instead of the input images allows the memory to store more samples for a fixed size compared to other methods. Liu *et al.* [22] proposed to parameterize the exemplars of the memory and to learn them in an end-to-end manner.

However, using a small memory results in an unbalanced training set mainly composed of examples from the new classes. Several recent works highlighted this problem and proposed methods to address it. Rebuffi *et al.* [27] introduced iCaRL which relies on a nearest-mean-of-exemplars (NME) classifier. Castro *et al.* [6] proposed to use more data augmentation on the training set and to then finetune the model on a small balanced dataset. Wu *et al.* [32] proposed to learn a two parameters linear model on a small balanced dataset to correct the bias of the last fully connected layer while Hou *et al.* [16] proposed to use cosine normalization on the classifier and finetuning on a balanced dataset. A recent work [1] proposed to use oversampling of old classes and to separately compute the softmax probabilities of the new and old classes for the Cross-Entropy loss.

In this work, we propose a new method to address the issue of unbalanced training set in incremental learning by using the Balanced Softmax Cross-Entropy loss. Compared to the previously presented methods, it does not require oversampling or any finetuning step while achieving similar or higher accuracy.

## 3    Proposed Method

The objective of class-incremental learning is to learn an unified classifier (also denoted single-head classifier) from a sequence of training steps, each containing new previously unseen classes, as described on Fig. 1. The first step, named base step, is followed by several incremental training step, numbered from 1 to $T$, each composed of the training set $\mathcal{X}_t$ containing samples of the classes from set $C_t$. Each incremental step contains different classes such that $\bigcap_{t=0}^{T} C_t = \emptyset$. In addition to $\mathcal{X}_t$, at each incremental step, the model also has access to the small replay memory $\mathcal{X}_M$ which contains samples from classes encountered during previous incremental steps. The number of classes learned up to the incremental step $t$ included is denoted $N_t$.

### 3.1    Incremental Learning Baseline

To highlight the strengths of our method, we use a simple baseline for incremental learning, denoted IL-baseline, initially proposed in [32]. This baseline consists

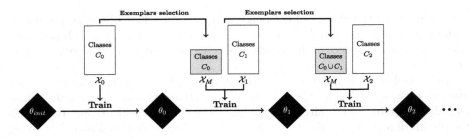

**Fig. 1.** Illustration of the class incremental training procedure. At each incremental step $i$, the model has access for the training to the new data $\mathcal{X}_i$ containing samples from new classes $C_i$ and the memory $\mathcal{X}_M$ containing few samples from previously encountered classes $\bigcup_{t=0}^{i-1} C_t$. The step 0, named the base step, contains the base classes.

in a deep neural network combined with a small replay memory and optimized using the Softmax Cross-Entropy loss and the distillation loss.

The total loss $\mathcal{L}$ used to train the model, is defined as a weighed sum of the distillation loss $\mathcal{L}_d$ and the Softmax Cross-Entropy loss $\mathcal{L}_c$:

$$\mathcal{L} = \rho \mathcal{L}_d + (1 - \rho)\mathcal{L}_c \tag{1}$$

where $\rho$ is defined as $\frac{N_{t-1}}{N_t}$ with $N_t$ the total number of classes at incremental step $t$ and is used to balance the importance of the two losses.

At the beginning of each incremental step $t$, the previous step parameters $\theta_{t-1}$ are first copied to initialize the new parameters $\theta_t$ and are then used to maintain the knowledge of previously learned classes using the distillation loss [15, 21]:

$$\mathcal{L}_d(x) = \sum_{k=1}^{N_{t-1}} -\hat{p}_k(x) \log(p_k(x)) \, T^2 \, ,$$

$$\hat{p}_k(x) = \frac{e^{\hat{z}_k(x)/T}}{\sum_{j=1}^{N_{t-1}} e^{\hat{z}_j(x)/T}}, \quad p_k(x) = \frac{e^{z_k(x)/T}}{\sum_{j=1}^{N_{t-1}} e^{z_j(x)/T}} \tag{2}$$

where $(x, y) \in \mathcal{X}_t \cup \mathcal{X}_M$ are the input image and the associated ground truth label, $z(x) = [z_1(x), ..., z_{N_t}(x)]$ is the output logits of the current model $\theta_t$, $\hat{z}(x) = [\hat{z}_1(x), ..., \hat{z}_{N_{t-1}}(x)]$ is the output logits of the model at the previous incremental step $\theta_{t-1}$ and $T$ is the temperature.

The replay memory used is a growing memory: the number of stored samples per class is fixed so the total size of the memory increases at each incremental step. The herding selection [31] is used to select the samples as it has been shown to be more efficient than the random selection [3].

## 3.2  Balanced Softmax Cross-Entropy

Due to the limited size of the replay memory, the training set $\mathcal{X}_t \cup \mathcal{X}_M$ contains only few tens of samples for each of the old classes while containing hundreds or thousands of samples for each of the new classes at each incremental step. The discrepancy in the classes frequency between the training and testing sets, as the latter contains the same number of samples for each classes, induces a bias toward the most recently learned classes [2,16,32]. It appears that the model tends to predict the classes which had the largest number of samples in the training set during the last incremental steps (the new classes) rather than the old classes. This situation is similar to the Long-Tailed Visual Recognition problem where a model is evaluated on a balanced test dataset after being trained on a dataset composed of few classes which are over-represented (the head classes) and a large number of classes which are under-represented (the tail classes).

Based on this observation, we propose to replace the Softmax activation function by the Balanced Softmax for the Cross-Entropy loss during the training procedure. This activation function has been initially introduced by Ren *et al.* [28] to address the label distribution shift between the training and testing in Long-Tailed Visual Recognition. The Balanced Softmax is defined as:

$$q_k(x) = \frac{\lambda_k e^{z_k(x)}}{\sum_{j=1}^{N_t} \lambda_j e^{z_j(x)}} \qquad \text{with } \lambda_i = n_i \tag{3}$$

where $x$ is the input, $z(x) = [z_1(x), ..., z_{N_t}(x)]$ is the output logits of the current model and $n_i$ is the number of samples in the training set for the $i^{\text{th}}$ class.

The new classification loss $\mathcal{L}_c$ is then defined as the Cross-Entropy loss using the Balanced Softmax instead of the Softmax:

$$\mathcal{L}_c(x) = \sum_{k=1}^{N_t} - \delta_{k=y} \log(q_k(x)) \tag{4}$$

The Balanced Softmax Cross-Entropy loss, denoted BalancedS-CE, can be used as replacement of the Softmax Cross-Entropy loss in the previously defined IL-Baseline or in any other model for incremental learning.

### 3.3   Meta Balanced Softmax Cross-Entropy

The expression of the Balanced Softmax presented in Eq. (3) allows for a direct control on the importance of each class by selecting a dedicated weighting coefficient $\lambda_i$ for each of them, which may be different from the number of samples for this class in the training dataset, similarly to [18]. In the context of large scale incremental learning, the modification of these weighting coefficients offers a new method for controlling the plasticity-rigidity trade-off of the trained model but also for controlling separately the importance of each individual class.

We propose to extend the Balanced Softmax by introducing a new global weighting coefficient $\alpha$ to control the importance of the past classes:

$$q_k(x) = \frac{\lambda_k e^{z_k(x)}}{\sum_{j=1}^{N_t} \lambda_j e^{z_j(x)}} \qquad \text{with } \lambda_i = n_i \left(\delta_{i \notin P} + \alpha \, \delta_{i \in P}\right) \tag{5}$$

where $P$ is the set of old classes, $\delta$ is the indicator function and the weighting coefficient $\alpha$ is a real number, usually between 0 and 1. This expression is equivalent to Eq. (3) for $\alpha$ equal to 1.0 .

In practice, it appears that 1.0 may not be the optimal value for $\alpha$ when only considering the average incremental accuracy of the model. However, it is difficult to determine beforehand a satisfying value for $\alpha$ without performing several trials with different values. Therefore, to further improve the accuracy of Balanced Softmax Cross-Entropy for Incremental Learning, we propose a new training procedure, named Meta Balanced Softmax Cross-Entropy (Meta BalancedS-CE), in order to slightly adjust the weighting coefficient $\alpha$ of the Balanced Softmax during the training as described by Algorithm 1.

---

**Algorithm 1:** Meta Balanced Softmax Cross-Entropy training procedure

---

Initialize parameters $\theta$ and function $Z$ of the model ; Initialize memory $\mathcal{X}_M$

**for** $t \leftarrow 1$ **to** $T$ **do**

    $\alpha \leftarrow 1.0$

    $D_t, B_t \leftarrow \text{split}(\mathcal{X}_t \cup \mathcal{X}_M)$

    **for** $r \leftarrow 1$ **to** $R$ **do**

        **for** $(X, Y) \sim D_t$ **do**

            $\theta^* \leftarrow \theta - \nabla_\theta \text{balancedLoss}(Z(\theta, X), Y)$

            $(\bar{X}, \bar{Y}) \sim B_t$

            $\alpha \leftarrow \alpha - \nabla_\alpha \text{softmax\_CE}(Z(\theta^*, \bar{X}), \bar{Y})$

            $\theta \leftarrow \theta - \nabla_\theta \text{balancedLoss}(Z(\theta, X), Y)$

    $\mathcal{X}_M \leftarrow \text{updateMemory}(\mathcal{X}_t)$

---

Instead of using the same fixed weighting coefficient $\alpha$ during the complete training procedure, we propose to jointly learn $\alpha$ during the training of the deep neural network. To achieve this, we propose a meta-learning algorithm which estimates at each optimization step the optimal value of $\alpha$ using a balanced validation set $B_t$. At the beginning of each incremental step, the unbalanced training set $\mathcal{X}_t \cup \mathcal{X}_M$ composed of the samples from the new classes and the samples of old classes stored in the memory is split into a training set $D_t$ and a validation set $B_t$. Unlike $D_t$ which is a large unbalanced dataset, $B_t$ is a smaller set containing the same number of samples for every classes. At each optimization step, a temporary model $\theta^*$ is created by training the current model $\theta$ on the incoming batch of data $(X, Y)$ from $D_t$ using the balanced loss which is the sum of the Balanced Softmax Cross-Entropy loss and secondary losses (such as the distillation loss). By using a batch $(\bar{X}, \bar{Y})$ from the balanced validation set $B_t$, the value of $\alpha$ is then updated using the gradient of the standard Softmax Cross-Entropy loss of $(Z(\theta^*, \bar{X}), \bar{Y})$ with respect to $\alpha$. Finally we update the current model $\theta$ on the batch $(X, Y)$ previously sampled from $D_t$ using the balanced loss with the newly learned value of $\alpha$.

Unlike the Balanced Softmax Cross-Entropy which does not modify the computational cost of the training procedure compared to the Softmax Cross-

Entropy, the Meta Balanced Softmax Cross-Entropy have an impact on the training procedure. The method requires to compute gradients through the optimization process. One of the main drawbacks is a large increase of the memory requirement which makes it more difficult to combine this approach with some existing methods for incremental learning.

## 4  Experiments

### 4.1  Experimental Setups

**Datasets.** Experiments are conducted on three competitive datasets for large scale incremental learning: CIFAR100, subImageNet and ImageNet. We used the experimental settings defined in [16] by initially training the models on the first half of the classes of the dataset (referred as the base classes) before learning the remaining classes during the next 5 or 10 incremental steps. Following [16,27], the class order is defined by NumPy using the random seed 1993.

- **CIFAR100** [19] is composed of 60,000 $32 \times 32$ RGB images equally divided among 100 classes. There are 50 base classes and the remaining ones are learned by groups of 5 or 10 depending on the number of incremental steps.
- **ImageNet** (ILSVRC 2012) [29] is composed of about 1.3 million high-resolution RGB images divided among 1,000 classes. There are 500 base classes and the remaining classes are learned by groups of 50 or 100 depending on the number of incremental steps.
- **SubImageNet** is a subset of ImageNet only containing the first 100 classes. There are 50 base classes and the remaining classes are learned by groups of 5 or 10 depending on the number of incremental steps.

**Baselines.** The IL-Baseline which uses the Softmax Cross-Entropy loss is considered as the lower-bound method and used to highlight the impact of the Balanced Softmax Cross-Entropy loss function for incremental learning. Furthermore, the proposed models are compared with iCaRL [27], LUCIR [16], Mnemonics [22], PODNet [9] and Topology-Preserving Class-Incremental Learning (TPCIL) [30].

To measure the performance of the different models and compare them, the average incremental accuracy is used following [27]. It is defined as the average of the Top-1 accuracy of the model on the test dataset at the end of each training step, including the initial base step.

**Implementation Details.** All compared methods use the 32-layer ResNet [14] for CIFAR100 and the 18-layers ResNet for ImageNet and SubImageNet. The input images are normalized, randomly horizontally flipped and cropped with no further augmentation applied. For a fair comparison, each method uses a growing memory containing exactly 20 samples per class.

The Balanced Softmax Cross-Entropy is used with $\alpha$ equal to 1.0 and when combined with other methods, the same hyper-parameters as those reported in their respective original publications are used. Meta-Balanced Softmax Cross-Entropy is implemented using Higher [12] and 10% of the memory size is used for the balanced validation set $B_t$. To decrease the training cost of the method, $\alpha$ is only updated every 10 optimization steps instead of every optimization step.

## 4.2   Comparison Results

**Table 1.** Average incremental accuracy (Top-1) on CIFAR100, SubImageNet and ImageNet with 5 incremental steps and 10 incremental steps settings, using a growing memory of 20 samples per class for all methods. Results for iCaRL and LUCIR are reported from [16] ; results for Mnemonics and BiC are reported from [22]; results for PODNet and TPCIL are reported from their respective paper. Results marked with "*" correspond to our own experiments. Results on CIFAR-100 averaged over 3 random runs. Results on ImageNet and SubImageNet are reported as a single run.

| Number of incremental steps | CIFAR100 | | SubImageNet | | Imagenet | |
|---|---|---|---|---|---|---|
| | 5 | 10 | 5 | 10 | 5 | 10 |
| iCaRL [27] | 57.17 | 52.57 | 65.04 | 59.53 | 51.36 | 46.72 |
| BiC [32] | 59.36 | 54.20 | 70.07 | 64.96 | 62.65 | 58.72 |
| LUCIR [16] | 63.42 | 60.18 | 70.47 | 68.09 | 64.34 | 61.28 |
| LUCIR w/ Mnemonics [22] | 63.34 | 62.28 | 72.58 | 71.37 | 64.54 | 63.01 |
| PODNet [9] | 64.83 | 63.19 | 75.54 | 74.33 | 66.95 | 64.13 |
| TPCIL [30] | 65.34 | 63.58 | **76.27** | 74.81 | 64.89 | 62.88 |
| IL-Baseline* | 43.80 | 37.00 | 51.52 | 42.22 | 43.23 | 36.70 |
| IL-Baseline w/BalancedS-CE (ours) | 62.22 | 58.32 | 72.57 | 68.25 | 66.45 | 62.14 |
| IL-Baseline w/Meta BalancedS-CE (ours) | 64.11 | 60.08 | 72.88 | 69.26 | 66.15 | 61.59 |
| LUCIR* | 63.37 | 60.88 | 70.25 | 67.84 | 66.69 | 64.06 |
| LUCIR w/BalancedS-CE (ours) | 64.83 | 62.36 | 71.18 | 70.66 | 67.81 | 66.47 |
| PODNet* | 64.46 | 62.69 | 74.97 | 71.57 | 65.20 | 62.87 |
| PODNet w/BalancedS-CE (ours) | **67.67** | **66.63** | 76.08 | **74.93** | **69.67** | **68.65** |

The average incremental accuracy on CIFAR100, SubImageNet and ImageNet for our methods and the different baselines are reported in Table 1.

First, we use the IL-Baseline to precisely compare the Balanced Softmax Cross-Entropy loss with the standard Softmax Cross-Entropy loss. On every dataset and in every settings, IL-Baseline trained using the Balanced Softmax Cross-Entropy loss outperforms the IL-Baseline trained using the standard Softmax Cross-Entropy by a large margin. Moreover, by meta-learning the weighting coefficient $\alpha$ instead of using the fixed value of 1.0, it is possible to further improve the accuracy of the Balanced Softmax Cross-Entropy loss.

Then, to demonstrate the flexibility of the proposed loss function, we combined it with both LUCIR and PODNet. By using the Balanced Softmax Cross-Entropy loss instead of the NCA loss [11,25] used by PODNet and the Softmax Cross-Entropy loss used by LUCIR, we were able to significantly improve the performance of both methods while decreasing the computation cost of the training procedure by removing the need of a balanced finetuning step without modifying any hyper-parameters. On every dataset and in every settings, using the Balanced Softmax Cross-Entropy significantly improves the average incremental accuracy of both LUCIR and PODNet, this improvement is especially important in the challenging 10 incremental steps settings. It improves the average incremental accuracy from 0.93% up to 2.82% for LUCIR and from 1.11% up to 5.78% for PODNet depending on the setting and the dataset considered. On ImageNet with 5 incremental steps, PODNet with Balanced Softmax Cross-Entropy reaches a final overall Top-1 accuracy of 64.4% which is only about 6% below the theoretical Top-1 accuracy of the model trained on the whole dataset at once.

### 4.3   Ablation Study

**Effect of the Memory Size.** The average incremental accuracy of the IL-Baseline trained with different losses on the CIFAR100 using the 5 incremental steps settings is reported in Table 2 for various number of exemplars per class stored in the replay memory. The Meta Balanced Softmax Cross-Entropy appears to be especially efficient in scenarios with highly restricted memory.

**Table 2.** Average incremental accuracy on the test set of CIFAR100 with 5 incremental steps of the Incremental Learning Baseline depending on the number of samples stored in memory for each class and the training loss. Results averaged over 3 random runs.

| Training procedure | Memory size | | | | |
|---|---|---|---|---|---|
| | 1 | 5 | 10 | 20 | 50 |
| IL-Baseline w/Softmax Cross-Entropy | 24.83 | 30.59 | 37.27 | 43.80 | 52.99 |
| IL-Baseline w/BalancedS-CE (ours) | **51.55** | 56.93 | 60.11 | 62.22 | 64.44 |
| IL-Baseline w/Meta BalancedS-CE (ours) | – | **62.13** | **63.02** | **64.11** | **65.60** |

**Impact of the Weighting Coefficient Alpha.** The accuracy of the IL-Baseline trained using the Balanced Softmax Cross-Entropy loss on CIFAR100 is reported in Table 3 depending on the value of the weighting coefficient $\alpha$. It appears that decreasing the value of the weighting coefficient $\alpha$ induces an increase of the accuracy of the old classes at the end of the incremental training. The impact on the final overall accuracy of the model remains marginal compared to the impact on the base classes accuracy: by decreasing the weighting coefficient $\alpha$ from 1.0 to 0.1, the accuracy on the 50 base classes increases by 16.3% while the final overall accuracy of the model only decreases by 3.01%. While using the weighting coefficient $\alpha$ equal to 1.0 achieves in both 5 and 10 steps settings the most balanced models between base classes and new classes,

**Table 3.** Accuracy on the test set of CIFAR100 with 5 and 10 incremental steps of the Incremental Learning Baseline depending on the value used for the weighing coefficient $\alpha$ of the Balanced Softmax Cross-Entropy; using a growing memory of 20 samples per class. Results averaged over 3 random runs.

| | Final base acc. | Final overall acc. | Average inc. acc. | | Final base acc. | Final overall acc. | Average inc. acc. |
|---|---|---|---|---|---|---|---|
| $\alpha = 0.1$ | **68.38** | 51.54 | 62.68 | $\alpha = 0.1$ | **63.43** | 44.71 | 57.68 |
| $\alpha = 0.25$ | 63.99 | 54.88 | 64.09 | $\alpha = 0.25$ | 60.28 | 47.86 | 59.40 |
| $\alpha = 0.5$ | 58.78 | **55.44** | 63.80 | $\alpha = 0.5$ | 56.48 | 49.62 | 59.52 |
| $\alpha = 1.0$ | 52.08 | 54.55 | 62.22 | $\alpha = 1.0$ | 51.01 | 49.57 | 58.32 |
| Meta $\alpha$ | 61.20 | 55.21 | **64.11** | Meta $\alpha$ | 60.39 | **49.65** | **60.08** |

(a) CIFAR100 - 5 incremental steps    (b) CIFAR100 - 10 incremental steps

it does not achieve the highest average incremental accuracy. Carefully selecting the value of $\alpha$ can improve the average incremental accuracy on CIFAR100 by up to 1.87% for 5 incremental steps settings and by 1.2% for 10 incremental steps settings. The proposed meta-learning procedure achieves the highest average incremental accuracy in both setting. This shows the strength of this method for determining an efficient value for the weighting coefficient $\alpha$ without conducting several trials.

**Table 4.** Accuracy on the test set of CIFAR100 with 5 incremental steps of the Incremental Learning Baseline depending on the bias correction method used; using a growing memory of 20 samples per class. Results averaged over 3 random runs.

| Training procedure | Average incremental accuracy |
|---|---|
| IL-Baseline | 43.80 |
| IL-Baseline w/memory oversampling | 49.75 |
| IL-Baseline w/class oversampling | 55.95 |
| IL-Baseline w/loss rescaling | 57.01 |
| IL-Baseline w/balanced finetuning | 59.46 |
| IL-Baseline w/Separated Softmax [1] + oversampling | 61.21 |
| IL-Baseline w/BalancedS-CE (ours) | 62.22 |
| IL-Baseline w/Meta BalancedS-CE (ours) | **64.11** |

**Mitigation of Imbalance.** In Table 4, different bias correction procedures are compared on CIFAR100 with 5 incremental steps. Memory oversampling and class oversampling are both types of replay memory oversampling but the former ensures that each mini-batch theoretically contains the same number of sample from new and old classes while the latter ensures that each class has the same probability of appearing in each mini-batch. For Loss rescaling, the loss for each sample is rescaled in inverse proportion to the number of samples corresponding to this label in the train dataset. For Balanced finetuning, the model is finetuned after each incremental step on a small balanced set similar to PODNet and LUCIR. Our proposed methods achieve the highest average incremental accuracy without requiring a two steps training procedure or oversampling.

## 5   Conclusion

In this work, we proposed to replace the Softmax Cross-Entropy loss by the Balanced Softmax Cross-Entropy loss in order to mitigate the bias toward new classes in large scale incremental learning. We propose a simple, yet efficient, training procedure to meta-learn the balance between old and new classes using this new loss. Experiments show that by combining the Balanced Softmax Cross-Entropy with advanced methods for incremental learning, it is possible to further increase the accuracy of those methods while decreasing the computational cost of the training procedure by removing the need for a balanced finetuning step.

## References

1. Ahn, H., Moon, T.: A simple class decision balancing for incremental learning. arXiv preprint arXiv:2003.13947 (2020)
2. Belouadah, E., Popescu, A.: Il2m: class incremental learning with dual memory. In: IEEE/CVF International Conference on Computer Vision (2019)
3. Belouadah, E., Popescu, A., Kanellos, I.: A comprehensive study of class incremental learning algorithms for visual tasks. Neural Netw. **135**, 38–54 (2020)
4. Buzzega, P., Boschini, M., Porrello, A., Abati, D., Calderara, S.: Dark experience for general continual learning: a strong, simple baseline (2020)
5. Caccia, L., Belilovsky, E., Caccia, M., Pineau, J.: Online learned continual compression with adaptive quantization modules. In: International Conference on Machine Learning (2020)
6. Castro, F.M., Marín-Jiménez, M.J., Guil, N., Schmid, C., Alahari, K.: End-to-end incremental learning. In: Ferrari, V., Hebert, M., Sminchisescu, C., Weiss, Y. (eds.) ECCV 2018. LNCS, vol. 11216, pp. 241–257. Springer, Cham (2018). https://doi.org/10.1007/978-3-030-01258-8_15
7. Chaudhry, A., et al.: On tiny episodic memories in continual learning (2019)
8. Dhar, P., Singh, R.V., Peng, K.C., Wu, Z., Chellappa, R.: Learning without memorizing. IEEE/CVF Conference on Computer Vision and Pattern Recognition (2019)
9. Douillard, A., Cord, M., Ollion, C., Robert, T., Valle, E.: PODNet: pooled outputs distillation for small-tasks incremental learning. In: Vedaldi, A., Bischof, H., Brox, T., Frahm, J.-M. (eds.) ECCV 2020. LNCS, vol. 12365, pp. 86–102. Springer, Cham (2020). https://doi.org/10.1007/978-3-030-58565-5_6
10. French, R.M.: Catastrophic forgetting in connectionist networks. Trends Cogn. Sci. **3**(4), 128–135 (1999)
11. Goldberger, J., Hinton, G.E., Roweis, S., Salakhutdinov, R.R.: Neighbourhood components analysis. Adv. Neural. Inf. Process. Syst. **17**, 513–520 (2004)

12. Grefenstette, E., et al.: Generalized inner loop meta-learning. arXiv preprint arXiv:1910.01727 (2019)
13. Hayes, T.L., Kafle, K., Shrestha, R., Acharya, M., Kanan, C.: REMIND your neural network to prevent catastrophic forgetting. In: Vedaldi, A., Bischof, H., Brox, T., Frahm, J.-M. (eds.) ECCV 2020. LNCS, vol. 12353, pp. 466–483. Springer, Cham (2020). https://doi.org/10.1007/978-3-030-58598-3_28
14. He, K., Zhang, X., Ren, S., Sun, J.: Deep residual learning for image recognition. In: IEEE Conference on Computer Vision and Pattern Recognition (2016)
15. Hinton, G., Vinyals, O., Dean, J.: Distilling the knowledge in a neural network (2015)
16. Hou, S., Pan, X., Loy, C.C., Wang, Z., Lin, D.: Learning a unified classifier incrementally via rebalancing. In: IEEE Conference on Computer Vision and Pattern Recognition (2019)
17. Hsu, Y.C., Liu, Y.C., Ramasamy, A., Kira, Z.: Re-evaluating continual learning scenarios: a categorization and case for strong baselines. arXiv preprint arXiv:1810.12488 (2018)
18. Khan, S.H., Hayat, M., Bennamoun, M., Sohel, F.A., Togneri, R.: Cost-sensitive learning of deep feature representations from imbalanced data. IEEE Trans. Neural Netw. Learn. Syst. **29**(8), 3573–3587 (2017)
19. Krizhevsky, A., et al.: Learning multiple layers of features from tiny images (2009)
20. Lei, C.H., Chen, Y.H., Peng, W.H., Chiu, W.C.: Class-incremental learning with rectified feature-graph preservation. In: Proceedings of the Asian Conference on Computer Vision (2020)
21. Li, Z., Hoiem, D.: Learning without forgetting. IEEE Trans. Pattern Anal. Mach. Intell. **40**(12), 2935–2947 (2017)
22. Liu, Y., Su, Y., Liu, A.A., Schiele, B., Sun, Q.: Mnemonics training: multi-class incremental learning without forgetting. In: IEEE/CVF Conference on Computer Vision and Pattern Recognition, pp. 12245–12254 (2020)
23. Lomonaco, V., Maltoni, D.: Core50: a new dataset and benchmark for continuous object recognition. In: Conference on Robot Learning, pp. 17–26. PMLR (2017)
24. McCloskey, M., Cohen, N.J.: Catastrophic interference in connectionist networks: the sequential learning problem. Psychol. Learn. Motiv. **24**, 109–165 (1989)
25. Movshovitz-Attias, Y., Toshev, A., Leung, T.K., Ioffe, S., Singh, S.: No fuss distance metric learning using proxies. IEEE International Conference on Computer Vision (2017)
26. Parisi, G.I., Kemker, R., Part, J.L., Kanan, C., Wermter, S.: Continual lifelong learning with neural networks: a review. Neural Netw. **113**, 54–71 (2019)
27. Rebuffi, S.A., Kolesnikov, A., Sperl, G., Lampert, C.H.: ICARL: incremental classifier and representation learning. In: IEEE Conference on Computer Vision and Pattern Recognition (2017)
28. Ren, J., Yu, C., Sheng, S., Ma, X., Zhao, H., Yi, S., Li, H.: Balanced meta-softmax for long-tailed visual recognition. arXiv preprint arXiv:2007.10740 (2020)
29. Russakovsky, O., et al.: ImageNet large scale visual recognition challenge (2015)
30. Tao, X., Chang, X., Hong, X., Wei, X., Gong, Y.: Topology-preserving class-incremental learning. In: Vedaldi, A., Bischof, H., Brox, T., Frahm, J.-M. (eds.) ECCV 2020. LNCS, vol. 12364, pp. 254–270. Springer, Cham (2020). https://doi.org/10.1007/978-3-030-58529-7_16
31. Welling, M.: Herding dynamical weights to learn. In: Proceedings of the 26th Annual International Conference on Machine Learning, pp. 1121–1128 (2009)
32. Wu, Y., et al.: Large scale incremental learning. In: IEEE/CVF Conference on Computer Vision and Pattern Recognition (2019)

# Generalised Controller Design Using Continual Learning

Diana Benavides-Prado[1]([✉]), Chathura Wanigasekara[2], and Akshya Swain[2]

[1] Auckland University of Technology, Auckland, New Zealand
diana.benavides.prado@aut.ac.nz
[2] The University of Auckland, Auckland, New Zealand
{c.wanigasekara,a.swain}@auckland.ac.nz

**Abstract.** In control systems applications, controllers for different plants are usually designed with different methods. Although plants may share common characteristics, these controllers are generally designed in isolation. The problem of continually learning a sequence of related tasks has been extensively studied recently. A challenge in continual learning is the phenomenon of catastrophic forgetting of knowledge of previous tasks which have been integrated into a neural network model. In this paper we evaluate the feasibility of modelling different controllers using continual learning. We explore regression versions of state-of-the-art methods and demonstrate that even the simplest continual learning approach decreases the overall Mean Average Error (MAE) by 39% of the MAE achieved by a non-continual strategy. Furthermore, a method based on dynamically expanding the network can achieve an overall MAE which is only 18% of the non-continual MAE. We also propose a set of new metrics that allow us to characterise the nature of catastrophic forgetting experienced while using different continual learning methods.

**Keywords:** Continual learning · Catastrophic forgetting

## 1 Introduction

Many control methods are available for controlling a wide variety of systems (plants) [5,9]. Typical control schemes include PID control, feedback control, sliding mode control among others [22,23]. Most of these systems usually have similar characteristics and can be reduced to standard forms such as state-space models, since they are subjected to similar variations due to various factors such as heat, dust, wear and tear. However, control methods are commonly designed in isolation for each system. This results in redesign/tuning/re-calibration of existing controllers, which is a time-consuming and tedious task that in practice might need to be carried out a few times each year.

An alternative strategy to avoid redesign is by treating these plant control schemes as tasks learned continually. Reusing knowledge acquired in previously learned plant control schemes may help to avoid the need for learning different

© Springer Nature Switzerland AG 2021
I. Farkaš et al. (Eds.): ICANN 2021, LNCS 12892, pp. 397–408, 2021.
https://doi.org/10.1007/978-3-030-86340-1_32

plants from scratch. Therefore, a single neural network can be used in a wide range of similar problems in the context of plant control. An example of this approach is depicted in Fig. 1.

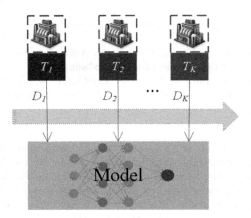

**Fig. 1.** Generalised controller modelled as a continual learning problem. Different plants correspond to different tasks $\mathcal{T} = \{T_1, T_2, \ldots, T_K\}$ with different distributions $D_1, D_2, \ldots, D_K$. Those tasks are learned sequentially.

Continual learning has been an increasingly active area of research in deep neural networks [6,13]. In continual learning, a machine learning system observes a sequence of tasks from a particular domain. Training examples of these tasks are observed sequentially, with limited or no access to training data from previously learned tasks. A long-standing challenge in continual learning is the problem of catastrophic forgetting of knowledge since new tasks may interfere with knowledge acquired for previous tasks. This is related to the *stability-plasticity dilemma* which has been studied for decades in the context of connectionist systems [3]. A single network that is used to learn a sequence of tasks should be *plastic* or *adaptive* enough to accommodate knowledge of new tasks, while also stable enough to not forget knowledge of previous tasks.

A range of methods have been proposed to tackle the problem of catastrophic forgetting in supervised continual learning systems [6]. Memory replay methods rely on storing or generating some training examples of previous tasks which are reused in future tasks. Regularisation-based methods regularise the objective function to be optimised for each incoming task, therefore controlling how parameters or weights learned for previous tasks change. Parameter-isolation methods allocate sub-networks to specific tasks, by possibly changing the network size as more tasks are sequentially observed. Hybrid methods combine two or more of these strategies.

In this paper we study the problem of designing a generalised controller using a continual learning approach. We explore three existing state-of-the-art continual learning methods which are based on memory replay, regularisation and parameter-isolation. We propose regression versions of these algorithms for the generalised controller domain. We also define two new metrics to characterise the amount and the type of catastrophic forgetting occurring in this system. Our main contributions are:

1. We propose an approximation to the problem of optimising multiple controllers using continual learning. Each of these problems is treated as a learning task with training examples observed sequentially.
2. We perform a systematic evaluation of continual learning methods for learning a generalised controller, which includes state-of-the-art metrics in continual learning such as overall accuracy, accuracy per task and time complexity. For this we cast existing continual learning methods which are originally designed for classification problems as regression tasks.
3. We propose two new metrics for better characterising the levels and the types of catastrophic forgetting occurring in the continual learning system under exploration.

## 2   Existing Research

The challenge of learning systems that learn a sequence of tasks was first studied more than two decades ago [20]. Several approaches from transfer, multitask, and lifelong learning have been categorised as alternatives for learning a sequence of tasks [21]. These approaches explored the ability of a learning system to improve the performance while more training examples were observed and tasks were learned. Silver [19] described lifelong learning systems that retain knowledge and use it to learn new tasks more efficiently and effectively. Silver and Mercer [18] studied lifelong learning in the context of neural networks. More recently, three core properties of lifelong learning systems were identified [4]: 1) learning new tasks by leveraging knowledge from previous tasks, 2) learning continuously and incrementally, 3) retaining knowledge acquired during previous tasks.

Continual learning tackles the problem of lifelong learning of a sequence of tasks using a deep neural network. This area has recently gained extraordinary interest. A vast of continual learning research has focused on the problem of catastrophic forgetting of knowledge of previous tasks. Parisi et al. [13] and De Lange et al. [6] described methods that tackle the problem of catastrophic forgetting. These methods are typically categorised into: 1) regularisation-based methods to impose constraints on how the network changes as new tasks are observed [10], 2) memory management and dual-memories for memory replay, e.g. long-term and short-term memories [12,14] and, 3) dynamic network architectures that change as more tasks are observed, e.g. by expanding or shrinking sub-networks [17,24]. The problem of catastrophic forgetting was also studied in the context of knowledge consolidation in neural networks [15,16]. Recent research has also explored the problem of improving existing knowledge as tasks are learned sequentially [1,2].

Besides catastrophic forgetting, a latent challenge in continual learning systems is how to measure their performance. Although general metrics such as accuracy may be applicable, it is of interest to understand the performance per task and the forgetting behaviour for each task. Diaz-Rodriguez et al. [7] surveyed and proposed a set of metrics for a variety of characteristics of continual learning systems, including accuracy, backward transfer of knowledge, and forward transfer of knowledge [12]. Other studies have proposed metrics to determine the ratio of catastrophic forgetting at the end of learning [11].

# 3   Methodology

Continual learning systems are composed of a set of $\mathcal{T} = \{T_1, T_2, \ldots, T_K\}$ tasks observed in a sequence of consecutive time steps. In supervised learning, a task $T_k$ is about learning a mapping from an input feature space $\mathcal{X}_k$ to an output feature space $\mathcal{Y}_k$. This mapping is represented by a function $f_k : \mathcal{X}_k \to \mathcal{Y}_k$. A training sample $\mathcal{D}_k$ is available for learning a task $T_k$, where $\mathcal{D}_k = \{(x_{k,1}, y_{k,1}), (x_{k,2}, y_{k,2}), \ldots, (x_{k,n}, y_{k,n})\}$ contains training vectors $x_k$ sampled from the input feature space $\mathcal{X}_k$ and their corresponding outputs or labels $y_k$ sampled from the output feature space $\mathcal{Y}_k$. The challenge in supervised continual learning is when the distributions of multiple tasks differ, i.e. $\mathcal{D}_1 \neq \mathcal{D}_2 \neq \ldots \mathcal{D}_K$, therefore making it hard for a single neural network to perform well for examples from all these distributions.

The phenomenon of catastrophic forgetting is experienced when a deep neural network diminishes its ability to retain knowledge of previous tasks while more tasks are learned, therefore affecting their accuracy. A number of approaches have been proposed to deal with this problem, including regularisation-based methods to protect existing knowledge, replay-based methods to retain and replay data from previous tasks, and parameter-isolation methods to dynamically expand a network [6,13]. Section 2 points to existing research in these three settings.

We experiment with three existing methods for the problem of catastrophic forgetting: 1) Elastic Weight Consolidation (EWC) [10], which regularises learning of network weights for new tasks with respect to existing weights, 2) Orthogonal Weight Modification (OWM) [25], which combines regularisation and retention of data from previous tasks for replay and, 3) Dynamically Expandable Networks (DEN) [24], a method that allows to dynamically expand a network as new tasks are learned. We explore variants of these methods for our sequence of regression tasks for multiple controllers. We then propose two new metrics to characterise the level and the type of forgetting experienced by each of these approaches in the context of a generalised controller.

## 3.1   Methods

EWC [10] is a regularisation-based method for continual learning. The problem of EWC at a current task $T_k$ is to find a set of parameters $\boldsymbol{\theta}_{T_k}$ that are optimal for that task while avoiding interference with the set of optimal parameters $\boldsymbol{\theta}^*_{T_{k-1}}$ learned for previous tasks. The loss function $\mathcal{L}$ to be minimised at task $T_k$ is given by:

$$\mathcal{L}(\boldsymbol{\theta}_{T_k}) = \mathcal{L}(\boldsymbol{\theta}_{T_k}) + \sum_i \frac{\lambda}{2} F_i(\theta_{T_k,i} - \theta^*_{T_{k-1},i}) \tag{1}$$

where $F_i$ is a cell of the Fisher information matrix for a network weight value for the current task, $\theta_{T_k,i}$, and the corresponding network weight value for previous tasks, $\theta^*_{T_{k-1},i}$. The parameter $\lambda$ controls the influence of previous tasks. In our regression version of EWC, named EWCReg, the function $\mathcal{L}$ is a loss function for regression such as Mean Absolute Error (MAE).

OWM regularises learning of new network weights by forcing these to be orthogonal to the subspace spanned by inputs from previous tasks. This ensures that new weights do not interact with previous inputs, therefore avoiding interference with past tasks. To determine the orthogonal direction to these inputs, OWM finds a projector $\mathbf{P}_{T_k} = \mathbf{I} - \mathbf{A}_{T_{k-1}}(\mathbf{A}^T_{T_{k-1}}\mathbf{A}_{T_{k-1}} + \alpha\mathbf{I})^{-1}\mathbf{A}_{T_{k-1}}$, where the columns of $\mathbf{A}_{T_{k-1}}$, such that $\mathbf{A}_{T_{k-1}} = \{\mathbf{x}_{k-1,1}, \mathbf{x}_{k-1,2}, \dots, \mathbf{x}_{k-1,n}\}$, consist of past inputs from tasks $\mathcal{T} = \{T_1, \dots T_{k-1}\}$, $\mathbf{I}$ is the unit matrix and $\alpha$ is a small constant. Note that $\mathbf{A}^T_{T_{k-1}}$ denotes the transpose of $\mathbf{A}_{T_{k-1}}$. During gradient descent at a learning task $T_k$, the vector of weights $\boldsymbol{\theta}_{T_k}$ is modified according to:

$$\boldsymbol{\theta}_{T_k} = \eta\mathbf{P}_{T_k}\boldsymbol{\theta}_{T_k} \tag{2}$$

where $\mathbf{P}_{T_k}$ is the projector of previously learned inputs for previous tasks up to task $T_{k-1}$. The parameter $\eta$ is the learning rate. Similar to OWM for classification problems, the loss function of the proposed regression variant, named OWMReg, can be any loss function used for regression such as MAE.

DEN is a dynamic network expansion method that tackles the problem of catastrophic forgetting during learning of a new task in three steps: 1) selective retraining of parameters affected by the new task, 2) dynamic expansion of selected layers and units of the network, 3) split and duplication of selected units of the network. A new task is first trained on the current version of the network while enforcing sparsity. Then, in the first step, a sub-network $S$ is identified. This sub-network contains parameters that are connected to the outputs of the current task. Re-training of this sub-network is performed by minimising:

$$\min_{\boldsymbol{\theta}^S_{T_k}} \mathcal{L}(\boldsymbol{\theta}^S_{T_k}; \boldsymbol{\theta}^S_{T_{k-1}}, \mathcal{D}_{T_k}) + \mu \left\|\boldsymbol{\theta}^S_{T_k}\right\|_2 \tag{3}$$

where $\boldsymbol{\theta}^S_{T_k}$ are the parameters for the sub-network $S$ on the current task $T_k$, $\boldsymbol{\theta}^S_{T_{k-1}}$ is the set of parameters for this sub-network on the previous task and $\mathcal{D}_{T_k}$ is the training data for the current task. $\mu$ is a regularisation parameter.

The second step uses group sparse regularisation to dynamically decide the number of neurons to be added to a particular layer $L$, by minimising:

$$\min_{\boldsymbol{\theta}^L_{T_k,\mathcal{N}}} \mathcal{L}(\boldsymbol{\theta}^L_{T_k,\mathcal{N}}; \boldsymbol{\theta}^L_{T_{k-1}}, \mathcal{D}_{T_k}) + \mu \left\|\boldsymbol{\theta}^L_{T_k,\mathcal{N}}\right\|_1 + \gamma \sum_g \left\|\boldsymbol{\theta}^{L,g}_{T_k,\mathcal{N}}\right\|_2 \tag{4}$$

where $\boldsymbol{\theta}^L_{T_k, \mathcal{N}}$ is the expanded set of parameters for task $T_k$ at layer $L$, and $g \in \mathcal{G}$ is a group defined on the parameters for each neuron. The network is expanded using (4), when the loss is above a user-specified threshold. In that case, the network is expanded by $u$ units, with $u$ a user-defined parameter.

In the final step, the network is split/duplicated by solving:

$$\min_{\boldsymbol{\theta}_{T_k}} \mathcal{L}(\boldsymbol{\theta}_{T_k}; \mathcal{D}_{T_k}) + \lambda \left\| \boldsymbol{\theta}_{T_k} - \boldsymbol{\theta}_{T_{k-1}} \right\|^2_2 \tag{5}$$

where $\lambda$ is the $L_2$ regularisation parameter. In our regression version of DEN, named DENReg, the loss functions $\mathcal{L}$ used in (3), (4) and (5) can be any typical loss function for regression problems such as MAE.

## 3.2   Metrics to Characterise Catastrophic Forgetting

In this section, we propose two new metrics that aim to provide more insights into the behaviour of a continual learning system. Our first metric determines the level of forgetting of a task once the full sequence of tasks has been learned. This metric is similar in nature to the catastrophic forgetting ratio proposed by Lee et al. [11], which measures the final performance on a task with respect to the best performance that can be achieved for that particular task. In our proposed metric, the final performance of a task once all tasks in a sequence have been learned is compared to the performance of that task when it was learned for the first time. This helps to identify the level of forgetting derived from including that task as part of a continual learning system rather than learning it in isolation, in a non-continual manner. For a given sequence of $K$ tasks, the forgetting level $FL_{T_k}$ for a task $T_k$ is formally defined as:

$$FL_{T_k} = P^K_{T_k} - P^t_{T_k} \tag{6}$$

where the overall level of forgetting of task $T_k$, $FL_{T_k}$ is the difference between the performance $P$ at the final time step of the sequence $K$ and the performance $P$ on that task when that task was originally learned for the first time, $t$. Note that the level of forgetting behaves differently depending on the type of performance metric used. For example, for performance metrics measuring accuracy, a task experiencing a low level of forgetting has an $FL_{T_k}$ close to zero. Small negative values denote low levels of forgetting, while positive values would denote a gain in performance. Similarly, for performance metrics measuring error, such as MAE, a task experiencing low levels of forgetting should have an $FL_{T_k}$ close to zero. However, in this case small positive values denote low levels of forgetting, while negative values for this metric will denote gain in performance.

The forgetting level metric can effectively help quantify the degree to which forgetting is occurring. However, it is also interesting to look at various types of forgetting which may often occur in a continual learning system. Gama et al. [8] provide some ideas into a useful categorisation about changes or *drifts* in dynamic learning systems. Similar to online learning, in the context of continual learning it is important to understand the nature of changes in performance,

which could occur: 1) abruptly (i.e. when tasks experience high levels of forgetting suddenly at a single time step in the sequence), 2) incrementally (i.e. when
tasks experience and accumulate forgetting across several consecutive time steps
of the sequence) or 3) gradually (i.e. when forgetting levels are experienced
across several time steps with a *seasonal* pattern of performance increasing and
decreasing over consecutive time steps). This categorisation would help to better
profile forgetting, and therefore to react to this more appropriately for different
tasks.

To determine if abrupt forgetting is occurring for a task, we first need to
determine the maximum level of forgetting for that task at any pair of consecu-
tive time steps using: $MF_{T_k} = \max{(P_{T_k}^t - P_{T_k}^{t-1})}, \forall t \in \{0, 1, \ldots, K\}$[1]. Given a
fixed threshold $\tau_a$, a task $T_k$ is said to be experiencing abrupt forgetting if:

$$\frac{MF_{T_k}}{FL_{T_k}} \leq \tau_a \quad \text{and} \quad MF_{T_k} \times FL_{T_k} > 0 \tag{7}$$

To determine if a task is experiencing incremental forgetting up to some level
$\tau_i$ for $l_i$ consecutive time steps, we first need to determine the number of times
that:

$$\frac{P_{T_k}^t - P_{T_k}^{t-1}}{FL_{T_k}} \leq \tau_i, \forall t \in \{0, 1, \ldots, K\} \tag{8}$$

If this number of times is above some fixed threshold $l_i$ then task $T_k$ is experiencing incremental forgetting, since we can say that large fractions of forgetting
are continuously observed for that task as the sequence of tasks progresses.

Finally, to determine whether a task is experiencing gradual forgetting up to
some level $\tau_g$ for up to $l_g$ consecutive time steps, we need to determine the
number of times that:

$$\left| \frac{P_{T_k}^t - P_{T_k}^{t-1}}{FL_{T_k}} \right| \leq \tau_g, \forall t \in \{0, 1, \ldots, K\} \tag{9}$$

If this number of times is above some fixed threshold $l_g$ then task $T_k$ experiences
gradual forgetting, since we can say that forgetting occurs for that task at a
number of consecutive time steps.

## 4   Experiments and Results

We evaluate the feasibility of various methods described in earlier sections for
an example of controlling a DC motor. We investigate learning a sequence of
plant control schemes using the three continual learning methods explained in
Sect. 3: EWCReg, OWMReg and DENReg. The performance of these learning
methods are compared with Vanilla CL and Vanilla NonCL. Vanilla CL learns

---

[1] Note that we make a common assumption of the number of time steps being the
same as the number of tasks.

**Table 1.** Mean MAE and total training time after training all 20 tasks sequentially, averaged across task orders.

| Method | Mean MAE | Training time (sec.) |
|---|---|---|
| DENReg | $0.252 \pm 0.001$ | $501.0 \pm 18.3$ |
| EWCReg | $0.401 \pm 0.048$ | $6,330.0 \pm 190.34$ |
| OWMReg | $0.364 \pm 0.038$ | $276.0 \pm 12.4$ |
| Vanilla CL | $0.538 \pm 0.106$ | $179.00 \pm 19.1$ |
| Vanilla NonCL | $1.36 \pm 0.068$ | $7.18 \pm 0.34$ |

tasks sequentially without considering the effects of catastrophic forgetting while Vanilla NonCL learns all tasks jointly. We also measure the level and nature of forgetting using the metrics proposed in Sect. 3.

Experiments are carried out by generating data for 20 tasks. For each task, we generated values of input parameters of the DC such as for example inertia, inductance, resistance. A dataset for a specific task is generated by making a DC motor to follow a fixed trajectory. Each task is composed of $7,500$ training examples, $1,500$ validation examples and $1,500$ test examples, and 21 input features. One of the input features corresponds to previously observed speeds of a DC motor, while the other 20 features correspond to the values of their corresponding output feature ($y$) in the previous 20 times. This output feature for each task corresponds to the speed of the DC motor. For Vanilla NonCL, all training examples available for each task were used. For the other methods, we used only the first $1,000$ training examples, to simulate real-world continual learning scenarios where training data is scarce. We arranged 30 randomly selected task orders, ensuring that each task is the first task of the sequence for at least one of these orders. Results are averaged across task orders, unless stated otherwise. To make these tasks more varied, we added random noise to 50% of the training examples. Furthermore, the order of the input features was shuffled randomly for each task, except for Vanilla NonCL which is not subject to any of the above types of noise.

For all methods under evaluation, we train a two-layer fully-connected deep neural network with 200 units in each layer. We use $1,000$ epochs for batches containing 128 training examples per batch. The learning rate is set to 0.001 in all cases. In all cases except OWMReg, we use gradient descent to optimise MAE. For OWMReg, a momentum optimiser of value 0.99 is used, while also optimising for MAE. For the remaining hyperparameters of each method, we set their corresponding values according to previous studies. EWC $\lambda$ parameter is set to the number of tasks, 20. We use 200 validation examples from each previous tasks to construct the Fisher information matrix in EWCReg. For OWMReg, $\alpha$ parameter is set to 10. For DENReg, we set the lambda sparsity parameter $L_1$ to 0.001 and $L_2$ to 0.0001. The group LASSO lambda is set to 0.001, the number of units to be increased in the expansion process is set to 5, the threshold for dynamic expansion is 0.1 and the threshold for split and duplication is set to 0.1.

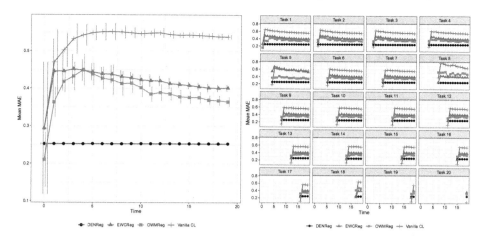

**Fig. 2.** Mean MAE of tasks learned sequentially, at each timestep, across all task orders, overall (left) and per task (right).

## 4.1 Overall Performance

Table 1 presents the MAE after all tasks are learned sequentially and the total training time at the end of the sequence of tasks, averaged across task orders. A naive method such as Vanilla CL, with no control for catastrophic forgetting, outperforms the approach of Vanilla NonCL, which possibly indicates relatedness of these tasks. EWCReg and OWMReg achieve lower MAE than Vanilla CL, demonstrating the ability of these methods to avoid catastrophic forgetting. However, the training time of EWCReg is approximately 35 times higher compared to Vanilla CL. DENReg clearly outperforms counterparts with a final MAE of 0.252, which is only 18% of Vanilla NonCL and 47% of Vanilla CL. DENReg requires only 3 times more training time than Vanilla CL. Figure 2 (left) presents the mean MAE averaged across task orders at each timestep of the sequence, for DENReg, EWCReg, OWMReg and Vanilla CL. Although the MAE of Vanilla CL decreases with increasing number of tasks, its performance is poorer compared to other methods such as DENReg, OWMReg and EWCReg.

## 4.2 Performance per Task

Figure 2 (right) shows MAE of each task during the learning sequence, for one of the task orders used in the experiments. Vanilla CL achieves a low MAE for each of the tasks when these are learned for the first time. However, high levels of catastrophic forgetting are experienced as new tasks are learned. EWCReg also experiences forgetting after a task is learned for the first time, although at a lower rate than Vanilla CL. OWMReg experiences forgetting during the initial task (Task 1). However, this method is capable of retaining knowledge of previous tasks with small forgetting later in the sequence. DENReg is stable for

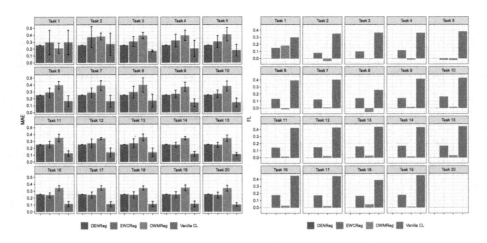

**Fig. 3.** Left: Mean MAE of tasks when tasks are learned for the first time, for all task orders. Right: Forgetting level for each task, measured as the difference of MAE at the last timestep of the sequence and the MAE on the first time a task was learned, for a specific task order.

the full sequence of 20 tasks. The result for DENReg is consistent with previous findings for this method, where it has been shown that DEN is able to maintain its performance for the full sequence when the number of tasks is relatively small [2].

Similarly, Fig. 3 (left) explores MAE of each task when these are learned for the first time, averaged across task orders. Vanilla CL achieves a low MAE when a task is learned for the first time. However, contrasting to Fig. 3 (right), tasks learned using this method are always affected in their performance in the next timestep. On the other hand, OWMReg tends to perform worse than other methods while learning tasks for the first time. However, as depicted in Fig. 3 (right), this allows the method to control catastrophic forgetting later in the sequence. EWCReg and DENReg achieve values of MAE which are more similar to Vanilla CL when a task is learned for the first time.

### 4.3   Characterisation of Catastrophic Forgetting

Figure 3 (right) shows levels of forgetting for tasks presented in Fig. 3 (left). Overall forgetting levels for all tasks in this sequence are: Vanilla CL, 0.376, EWCReg, 0.129, OWMReg, 0.0137, and DENReg, 0.0. Consistent with previous results, DENReg does not experience forgetting once the sequence of tasks is finished. Table 2 shows the types of forgetting experienced by each method and task, for a specific task order. The abrupt forgetting threshold $\tau_a$ was set to 0.95. Incremental forgetting would occur if the level of forgetting is at least $\tau_i = 0.05$ of the level of forgetting for that task for at least 3 consecutive timesteps. Similarly, gradual forgetting would occur if the level of forgetting is at least $\tau_g = 0.01$ of

**Table 2.** Number of tasks that experience each type of forgetting, for a specific task order.

| Type of drift | DENReg | EWCReg | OWMReg | Vanilla CL |
|---|---|---|---|---|
| Abrupt | 0 | 19 | 11 | 19 |
| Incremental | 0 | 0 | 1 | 0 |
| Gradual | 0 | 0 | 1 | 0 |
| No/Unclassified | 20 | 1 | 7 | 1 |

the level of forgetting for that task for at least 2 consecutive timesteps. Methods such as EWCReg and Vanilla CL experience abrupt forgetting for all the tasks. OWMReg, on the contrary, experiences different kinds of forgetting for different tasks. DENReg experiences no forgetting at all, a result that is consistent with findings in Fig. 2 (right).

## 5    Conclusions

We investigated the problem of learning a sequence of controllers continually. We explored a variety of state-of-the-art continual machine learning methods. Experiments demonstrated that formulating this problem as a continual learning problem results in much lower error compared to learning all these controllers jointly. Dynamic network expansion methods showed a potential to retain knowledge of previous controller tasks thus helping to avoid the problem of catastrophic forgetting in this context for a small number of tasks. An important future work derived from these results is the exploration of scenarios using real-world data. More complex problems of controllers that are designed to systems such as generic classes of linear systems, T-S fuzzy nonlinear systems, or control systems composed of a larger number of tasks could also be potentially explored.

## References

1. Benavides-Prado, D., Koh, Y.S., Riddle, P.: Selective hypothesis transfer for lifelong learning. In: 2019 International Joint Conference on Neural Networks (IJCNN), pp. 1–10. IEEE (2019)
2. Benavides-Prado, D., Koh, Y.S., Riddle, P.: Towards knowledgeable supervised lifelong learning systems. J. Artif. Intell. Res. **68**, 159–224 (2020)
3. Carpenter, G.A., Grossberg, S.: The ART of adaptive pattern recognition by a self-organizing neural network. Computer **21**(3), 77–88 (1988)
4. Chen, Z., Liu, B.: Lifelong machine learning. In: Synthesis Lectures on Artificial Intelligence and Machine Learning, vol. 12, no. (3), pp. 1–207 (2018)
5. Cloosterman, M.B.G., Hetel, L., Van De Wouw, N., Heemels, W.P.M.H., Daafouz, J., Nijmeijer, H.: Controller synthesis for networked control systems. Automatica **46**(10), 1584–1594 (2010)
6. Delange, M., et al.: A continual learning survey: defying forgetting in classification tasks. IEEE Trans. Pattern Anal. Mach. Intell. (2021)

7. Díaz-Rodríguez, N., Lomonaco, V., Filliat, D., Maltoni, D.: Don't Forget, There is More than Forgetting: New Metrics for Continual Learning. arXiv preprint arXiv:1810.13166 (2018)

8. Gama, J., Žliobaitė, I., Bifet, A., Pechenizkiy, M., Bouchachia, A.: A survey on concept drift adaptation. ACM Comput. Surv. (CSUR) **46**(4), 1–37 (2014)

9. Heij, C., Ran, A.C., Schagen, F.V.: Introduction to Mathematical Systems Theory: Linear Systems, Identification and Control. Birkhäuser, Basel (2007)

10. Kirkpatrick, J., et al.: Overcoming catastrophic forgetting in neural networks. Proc. Nat. Acad. Sci. **114**(13), 3521–3526 (2017)

11. Lee, S., Stokes, J., Eaton, E.: Learning shared knowledge for deep lifelong learning using deconvolutional networks. In: IJCAI, pp. 2837–2844 (2019)

12. Lopez-Paz, D., Ranzato, M.: Gradient episodic memory for continual learning. In: Advances in Neural Information Processing Systems, pp. 6467–6476 (2017)

13. Parisi, G.I., Kemker, R., Part, J.L., Kanan, C., Wermter, S.: Continual lifelong learning with neural networks: a review. Neural Netw. **113**, 54–71 (2019)

14. Rebuffi, S.A., Kolesnikov, A., Sperl, G., Lampert, C.H.: ICARL: incremental classifier and representation learning. In: Proceedings of the IEEE Conference on Computer Vision and Pattern Recognition, pp. 2001–2010 (2017)

15. Robins, A.: Catastrophic forgetting, rehearsal and pseudorehearsal. Connection Sci. **7**(2), 123–146 (1995)

16. Robins, A.: Consolidation in neural networks and in the sleeping brain. Connection Sci. **8**(2), 259–276 (1996)

17. Rusu, A.A., et al.: Progressive neural networks. arXiv preprint arXiv:1606.04671 (2016)

18. Silver, D.L., Mercer, R.E.: Selective Transfer of Neural Network Task Knowledge. The University of Western Ontario (Canada) (2000)

19. Silver, D.L., Yang, Q., Li, L.: Lifelong machine learning systems: beyond learning algorithms. In: AAAI Spring Symposium: Lifelong Machine Learning, vol. 13, pp. 49–53 (2013)

20. Thrun, S.: Is learning the n-th thing any easier than learning the first? In: Advances in Neural Information Processing Systems, pp. 640–646 (1996)

21. Thrun, S., Pratt, L.: Learning to Learn: Introduction and Overview. In: Thrun, S., Pratt, L. (eds.) Learning to Learn, pp. 3–17. Springer, Boston (1998). https://doi.org/10.1007/978-1-4615-5529-2_1

22. Wanigasekara, C., Almakhles, D., Swain, A., Nguang, S.K.: Delta-modulator-based quantised output feedback controller for linear networked control systems. IEEE Access **8**(1), 175169–175179 (2020)

23. Wanigasekara, C., Almakhles, D., Swain, A., Zhou, L.: Design of dynamic fuzzy Q-learning controller for networked wind energy conversion systems. In: Proceedings of 20th International Conference on Environment and Electrical Engineering (EEEIC) (2020)

24. Yoon, J., Yang, E., Lee, J., Hwang, S.J.: Lifelong Learning with Dynamically Expandable Networks. arXiv e-prints (2017)

25. Zeng, G., Chen, Y., Cui, B., Yu, S.: Continual learning of context-dependent processing in neural networks. Nat. Mach. Intell. **1**(8), 364–372 (2019)

# DRILL: Dynamic Representations
# for Imbalanced Lifelong Learning

Kyra Ahrens[(⊠)], Fares Abawi, and Stefan Wermter

Knowledge Technology, Department of Informatics, University of Hamburg,
Hamburg, Germany
{kyra.ahrens,fares.abawi,stefan.wermter}@uni-hamburg.de
http://www.informatik.uni-hamburg.de/WTM

**Abstract.** Continual or lifelong learning has been a long-standing challenge in machine learning to date, especially in natural language processing (NLP). Although state-of-the-art language models such as BERT have ushered in a new era in this field due to their outstanding performance in multitask learning scenarios, they suffer from forgetting when being exposed to a continuous stream of non-stationary data. In this paper, we introduce DRILL, a novel lifelong learning architecture for open-domain sequence classification. DRILL leverages a biologically inspired self-organizing neural architecture to selectively gate latent language representations from BERT in a domain-incremental fashion. We demonstrate in our experiments that DRILL outperforms current methods in a realistic scenario of imbalanced classification from a data stream without prior knowledge about task or dataset boundaries. To the best of our knowledge, DRILL is the first of its kind to use a self-organizing neural architecture for open-domain lifelong learning in NLP.

**Keywords:** Continual learning · NLP · Imbalanced learning ·
Self-organization · BERT

## 1 Introduction

Humans possess the ability to continuously acquire, reorganize, integrate, and enrich linguistic concepts throughout their lives. As early as infancy and based on an innate inference capability, the conventional symbols of language are learned within a socio-communicative context. The underlying neuro-cognitive mechanisms involved in human language acquisition are still far from being fully understood. However, they offer great potential for computational models that are inspired by the neuroanatomical mechanisms in the mammalian brain, enabling the continual integration of consolidated linguistic knowledge with current experience [27].

With the advent of deep learning and the surge of computational resources and data collection, state-of-the-art transformer-based language models (LM) such as BERT [5] and OpenAI GPT [20] have gradually moved away from the

© Springer Nature Switzerland AG 2021
I. Farkaš et al. (Eds.): ICANN 2021, LNCS 12892, pp. 409–420, 2021.
https://doi.org/10.1007/978-3-030-86340-1_33

symbolic level and given way to *isolated learning* solutions revealing an outstanding performance on downstream NLP tasks in a multitask set-up [4]. Yet when being exposed to a sequence of tasks, *catastrophic forgetting* or *catastrophic interference* of previously learned concepts was observed [17]. As re-training on all prior data would be inefficient both in terms of computational cost and memory capacity, this observation motivated the introduction of *continual* or *lifelong language learning* (LLL).

Despite recent advances in LLL, most current methods make overly simplistic assumptions that are in stark contrast to realistic, biologically inspired learning settings. This includes enabling multiple passes over the input data stream instead of single-epoch training, resulting in a surge of computational cost. Such methods further rely on perfectly balanced and annotated data, arranged in a way that the assumption of independent and identically distributed samples holds. As a consequence, they are poorly applicable to few-shot, unsupervised, or self-supervised learning scenarios [2].

Thus, striving for a more biologically grounded model architecture and training set-up, we introduce DRILL, a text classification model applicable to CL settings that involve the presence of a continuous stream of imbalanced data without prior knowledge about task boundaries or probability distributions. DRILL is a hybrid architectural and rehearsal-based CL method that uses meta-learning and a self-organizing neural architecture to enable rapid adaptation to novel data while minimizing catastrophic forgetting.

Due to the lack of a continual text classification benchmark of imbalanced data, we introduce two sampling strategies to induce class imbalance artificially. These strategies are evaluated on five text classification datasets presented by Zhang et al. [30], commonly used as CL benchmarks in NLP. With this setting, we show in our experiments that our model outperforms current baselines while better generalizing to unseen data.

## 2    Related Work

### 2.1    Continual Learning

Striving for a balance between memory consolidation and generalization to new input data from non-stationary distributions, also referred to as the *stability-plasticity dilemma* [7], paved the way for various LLL approaches in recent years. These approaches can be fully or partially categorized into regularization, rehearsal, and dynamic architectures:

*Regularization-based* approaches constrain the plasticity of a learning model either by introducing additional loss terms for weight adaptation at a fixed model capacity [13,29], or by setting an additional constraint on prior tasks' predictions to be kept invariant using *knowledge distillation* [15]. This fixed-capacity paradigm contrasts with *architecture-based* CL models that assign some model capacity to each task and therefore dynamically expand in response to novel input [18,22]. Inspired by the concept of memory consolidation, *rehearsal-based* (or *memory replay*) approaches maintain performance on prior tasks by storing and retraining the model on old training samples from an episodic memory [3,16,21].

To limit the associated memory overhead with an increasing number of tasks, *pseudo-rehearsal* approaches employing generative network architectures have been proposed. Such models rely on experience replay of task-representative samples or latent representations based on statistical properties learned from old training data [11,19]. Two such generative replay approaches based on GPT-2 [20], i.e. Language Modelling for Lifelong Language Learning (LAMOL) [24] and Distill and Replay (DnR) [25] view LLL through the lens of question answering. DnR deviates from LAMOL in that it bounds model complexity through knowledge distillation following a teacher-student strategy. Although both approaches are the current performance leaders on datasets benchmarked in this work, they require multiple epochs of training and explicit knowledge about task boundaries. Such preconditions deviate from the realistic CL scenario we advocate for in this work.

## 2.2 Meta-Learning

Meta-learning [26] has become increasingly popular in recent years as it paved the way for sophisticated algorithms capable of quickly adapting to new data. Online aware Meta-Learning (OML) [10] combines the common meta-learning objective of maximizing fast adaptation to new tasks with the CL objective of minimizing catastrophic interference during training. A Neuromodulated Meta-Learning Algorithm (ANML) [1] extends OML by an independent representation learning stream to selectively gate latent activations. Holla et al. [8] introduce a sparse experience replay mechanism to OML and ANML, denoting their two novel methods by OML-ER and ANML-ER respectively. Both extensions outperform state-of-the-art methods for text classification and question answering benchmarks under a training set-up in which data becomes only available over time and a lack of information about when a dataset or task boundary is crossed.

## 2.3 Growing Memory and Self-organization

In an attempt to mimic the explicit memory formation in the mammalian brain, early artificial neural networks based on competitive learning mechanisms and self-organization have been developed and refined [6,14]. One more recent extension to such topology learning methods is the Self-organizing Incremental Neural Network (SOINN) algorithm, which regulates plasticity in unsupervised learning tasks by means of dynamically creating, adapting, and deleting neurons [23]. SOINN+ [28] extends the original SOINN algorithm by introducing a novel node deletion mechanism based on (i) idle time, (ii) trustworthiness, and (iii) non-usage of a network unit. Given that SOINN+ successfully demonstrates its resilience to noisy data and its ability to learn a high-quality topology from the input domain while keeping the number of nodes small, we utilize it as a semantic memory component in our DRILL architecture.

# 3   Methods

With the challenge of achieving LLL from unbalanced data in mind, we lay the theoretical foundation for our proposed DRILL method.

## 3.1   Task Formulation

Consider an ordered sequence of tasks $\mathcal{T} = \{T_1, T_2, \ldots, T_N\}$, where we observe $n_k$ annotated input samples from the $k$-th task, i.e. $T_k = \{(\boldsymbol{x}_k^i, y_k^i)\}_{i=1}^{n_k}$ drawn from the distribution $P_k(\mathcal{X}, \mathcal{Y})$. Assuming a realistic scenario of missing task and dataset descriptors, we have no knowledge about which task each input sample belongs to. Following prior work [8], we define task in terms of text classification domain, i.e. sentiment, news topic, question-and-answer, and ontology. Our objective is to learn a model $f_\theta : \mathcal{X} \rightarrow \mathcal{Y}$ with parameters $\theta$ to minimize the negative log-likelihood averaged across all $N$ tasks

$$\mathcal{L}(\theta) = -\frac{1}{N} \sum_{k=1}^{N} \ln P(\boldsymbol{x}_k \,|\, y_k \,;\, \theta) \tag{1}$$

## 3.2   Progressive Imbalancing

Prior work on lifelong text classification [8,16,24,25] has traditionally deployed the perfectly balanced version of the five NLP datasets by Zhang et al. [30]. Following the idea of d'Autume et al. [16], we introduce two sampling techniques called *progressive reduction* ($R$) and *progressive expansion* ($E$), which exponentially increase or decrease the number of samples for each incoming task, such that

$$n_{k+1}^R \leftarrow \left\lfloor \frac{n_k^R}{2} \right\rfloor \tag{2}$$

with progressive reduction and

$$n_{k+1}^E \leftarrow 2 \cdot n_k^E \tag{3}$$

with progressive expansion respectively, and $k \in \{1, \ldots, N\}$. Both sampling techniques allow us to simulate two opposite LLL settings in which data at an early or late stage are significantly less present.

## 3.3   Episode Generation

For the construction of training episodes and experience rehearsal from episodic memory, we follow a commonly adopted set-up [8,16]:

Under the assumption that samples arrive in batches of size $s$ and are written into episodic memory module $\mathcal{M}_\mathcal{E}$ with probability $p_\mathcal{E}$, we construct the $i$-th episode from $b$ batches, where the first $b-1$ batches denote support set $\mathcal{S}_i$ and the $b$-th batch denotes query set $\mathcal{Q}_i$.

After having observed $R_I$ samples from the stream, $\lfloor r \cdot R_I \rfloor$ samples from $\mathcal{M_E}$ are randomly being drawn for rehearsal, where $r \in [0, 1]$ denotes the predefined replay ratio.

Aligned with the episodic fashion of meta-learning, we calculate the replay frequency

$$R_F = \left\lceil \frac{R_I/s + 1}{b} \right\rceil \tag{4}$$

Thus, every $R_F$-th episode can be considered as replay episode in a way that its query set does not consist of data from the stream, but from the episodic memory module $\mathcal{M_E}$.

## 3.4   DRILL

The DRILL architecture comprises four main elements, namely a dual-memory system of (1) an episodic memory module $\mathcal{M_E}$ and (2) a semantic memory module $\mathcal{M_S}$, and, following the original OML algorithm [10], (3) a representation learning network (RLN) $h_\phi$ as well as (4) a prediction learning network (PLN) $g_W$.

We use the SOINN+ [28] algorithm as semantic memory module $\mathcal{M_S}$. Each neural unit is a $d$-dimensional real-valued vector. The network is parameterized by a pull factor $\eta$ denoting the influence of a new observation on neighboring nodes. For the sake of simplicity and as proposed by Wiwatcharakoses and Berrar [28], we set the pull factor to a constant value $\eta = 50$. Thus, our model $f_\theta$ optimizes for the set of parameters $\theta = \phi \cup W$, consisting of parametrization $\phi$ from $\mathcal{X} \rightarrow \mathbb{R}^d$ of the RLN $h_\phi$ and $W$ from $\mathbb{R}^d \rightarrow \mathcal{Y}$ of the PLN $g_W$ respectively.

Taking inspiration from the mammalian thalamus as a 'gate to consciousness', we propose two DRILL variants that differ in how latent representations from the RLN are integrated with signals from the semantic memory $\mathcal{M_S}$, translating its internal selective plasticity to the entire learning process.

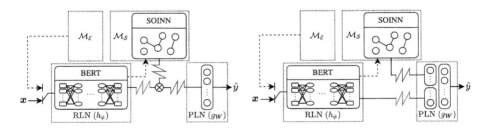

**Fig. 1.** Overview of the two variants DRILL$_M$ (left) and DRILL$_C$ (right). Latent representation signals retrieved from RLN are integrated with neural weight signals from $\mathcal{M_S}$ either by multiplication (DRILL$_M$) or concatenation (DRILL$_C$). Input to the model is either an new observation $x$ from the stream or an episodic replay sample from $\mathcal{M_E}$.

The first variant, called *Integration by Multiplication* (DRILL$_M$), can be described as follows: On receiving input $\boldsymbol{x}$, the model gates the activations $h_\phi(\boldsymbol{x})$ arriving from the RLN by multiplying them element-wise with a set of neural weights $\boldsymbol{w}_S$ drawn from $\mathcal{M}_S$ in a procedure described in Subsect. 3.5. We express the model variant DRILL$_M$ as

$$f_\theta^M(\boldsymbol{x}) = g_{\boldsymbol{W}}\left(\boldsymbol{w}_S \cdot h_\phi(\boldsymbol{x})\right) \tag{5}$$

For the second variant called *Integration by Concatenation* (DRILL$_C$), each of the $d$-dimensional signals $\boldsymbol{w}_S$ and $h_\phi(\boldsymbol{x})$ retrieved from $\mathcal{M}_S$ and the RLN respectively are reduced to half of their dimension $\frac{d}{2}$ and subsequently concatenated in a $d$-dimensional linear layer that is allocated to the PLN, as shown in Fig. 1. Thus, we derive the following model

$$f_\theta^C(\boldsymbol{x}) = g_{\boldsymbol{W}}\left(\,[\boldsymbol{w}_S, h_\phi(\boldsymbol{x})]\,\right) \tag{6}$$

where $[\cdot, \cdot]$ denotes the concatenation operator. The meta-learning procedure for both DRILL variants works as follows: During inner-loop optimization of the $i$-th episode, the RLN is kept frozen while the PLN is fine-tuned using SGD with an inner-loop learning rate $\alpha$, such that

$$\boldsymbol{W}' \leftarrow \mathrm{SGD}(\mathcal{L}_i(\phi, \boldsymbol{W}), \mathcal{S}_i, \alpha) \tag{7}$$

Subsequently, both RLN and PLN are fine-tuned on the query set $\mathcal{Q}_i$ during outer-loop optimization, such that all model parameters are updated using the Adam optimizer [12] with an outer-loop learning rate $\beta$ to give

$$\theta' \leftarrow \mathrm{Adam}(\mathcal{L}_i(\phi, \boldsymbol{W}'), \mathcal{Q}_i, \beta) \tag{8}$$

For the RLN, we use the state-of-the-art transformer-based language model BERT$_{\mathrm{BASE}}$ [5] with 12 transformer layers and $d = 768$ hidden dimensions. With DRILL$_M$, the PLN is a single linear layer with softmax activation that outputs the class probabilities, while a linear concatenation layer additionally precedes this layer with DRILL$_C$.

## 3.5   Self-supervised Sampling

In contrast to the episodic memory $\mathcal{M}_\mathcal{E}$ that we solely use for experience replay, we use the semantic memory $\mathcal{M}_S$ for generating high-quality representations, which influence the fine-tuning of the PLN. For every input sample $(\boldsymbol{x}_i, y_i)$, we initiate a competitive voting mechanism among all nodes in $\mathcal{M}_S$ to determine the two neurons with neural weights $\boldsymbol{w}_S^1$ and $\boldsymbol{w}_S^2$ that have most frequently been best-matching units (BMUs) for class $y_i$. According to the original SOINN+ algorithm [28], the network node that lies closest to the input in Euclidean space is denoted as BMU.

The two winners are then either multiplied element-wise (DRILL$_M$) or concatenated (DRILL$_C$) with the activations of the latent representation $h_\phi(\boldsymbol{x}_i)$ coming from the RLN, thus generating two inputs to the PLN from one output of the RLN. During the evaluation phase, only one signal from the winning node $\boldsymbol{w}_S$ is retrieved from $\mathcal{M}_S$ for the purpose of unambiguous label prediction by the PLN.

# 4    Experiments

## 4.1    Benchmark Datasets

We train our model sequentially on five text classification datasets by Zhang et al. [30] covering four different tasks: Sentiment analysis, news topic detection, question-and-answer classification, and ontology categorization. We summarize them in Table 1. Following d'Autume et al. [16], the datasets are arranged in four randomized permutations reflecting the significant impact of task ordering on evaluation results.

**Table 1.** The five balanced text classification datasets as in Zhang et al. [30], each containing 7,600 test samples randomly drawn from the original datasets. The number of training samples differs depending on order position and imbalanced sampling strategy.

| Classification domain | Dataset | Classes | Order position | | | |
|---|---|---|---|---|---|---|
| | | | I | II | III | IV |
| Sentiment | Amazon | 5 | 4 | 4 | 3 | 3 |
| | Yelp | (merged) | 1 | 5 | 1 | 2 |
| News Topic | AGNews | 4 | 2 | 3 | 5 | 1 |
| Question Topic | Yahoo | 10 | 5 | 2 | 2 | 4 |
| Ontology | DBPedia | 14 | 3 | 1 | 4 | 5 |
| **Total:** | | **33** | | | | |

For evaluation, we follow prior work [8,16,24,25] and randomly draw 7,600 samples from each of the five datasets, yielding a total test size of 38,000. However, we depart from the perfectly balanced and thus poorly realistic scenario of 115,000 training samples per dataset and instead apply progressive imbalancing as described in Subsect. 3.2 with $n_0^R = 115,000$ and $n_0^E = 7,187$, thus providing a total training size of $222,812$ for either sampling strategy.

## 4.2    Baselines

For performance evaluation, we compare our two proposed model variations **DRILL$_M$** and **DRILL$_C$** with the two performance leaders given a realistic single-epoch set-up without prior task-specific knowledge, i.e. **ANML-ER** and **OML-ER** [8]. Just like our method, they use a pretrained BERT$_{BASE}$ language encoder. We further implement the lower bound for CL model performance, **SEQ**, in which we fine-tune both RLN and PLN on all tasks sequentially without any rehearsal. We also compare our methods with **REPLAY**, an extension of SEQ towards experience rehearsal with samples stored in an episodic memory. Finally, we train RLN and PLN jointly in a multitask set-up **MTL**, which we consider as an upper bound for CL model performance. For a fair comparison, we choose the same memory-write and rehearsal policies for REPLAY, ANML-ER, and OML-ER, as well as our two proposed DRILL variants.

### 4.3   Implementation Details

Our experimental set-up consists of three independent runs on seeds 42–44, each run performed on the four order permutations and two sampling strategies respectively. Accordingly, the comparison results are averaged over all three runs.

Due to computational limitations, we train all baseline models on normalized batches of size $s = 8$ following the procedure of Ioffe and Szegedy [9] and optimize based on the cross-entropy loss on all 33 classes. We truncate the $BERT_{BASE}$ input sequences to length 448 and set the buffer size $b = 6$. The inner-loop and outer-loop learning rates of the four meta-learning-based models $DRILL_M$, $DRILL_C$, OML-ER, and ANML-ER are set to $\alpha = 8e-3$ and $\beta = 1.5e-5$ respectively. The learning rate of all remaining baselines SEQ, REPLAY, and MTL is set to $1e-5$.

All models are trained for a single epoch, whereas MTL is trained for two epochs. The probability of storing an observation in the episodic memory module $\mathcal{M}_\mathcal{E}$ is governed by the maximum write probability $p_\mathcal{E} = 0.8$. The $p_\mathcal{E}$ is inversely proportional to the expansion or reduction for all rehearsal-based models, restoring class balance within $\mathcal{M}_\mathcal{E}$. The learning rates and $p_\mathcal{E}$ are derived using a Parzen–Rosenblatt estimator[1]. The hyperparameter optimization is applied to OML-ER as the representative model for all meta-learning-based approaches and SEQ for inferring the learning rate of the remaining models. Both OML and SEQ are trained on the full dataset (without expansion or reduction) with order I and random seed 42. With both DRILL architectures, the unsupervised SOINN+ algorithm is performed as described in the original paper [28], including setting the pull factor $\eta = 50$.

We follow the rehearsal and evaluation strategies adopted by Holla et al. [8], setting $R_I = 9,600$ and $r = 1\%$, such that we draw 96 samples from $\mathcal{M}_\mathcal{E}$ after observing 9,600 samples from the data stream. The evaluation of the four meta-learning models is performed by generating five episodes, each containing the test datasets as query sets. All baseline models were trained on an NVIDIA TITAN RTX with 24 GB VRAM and 64 GB RAM. The training time ranges between 1 and 7 h, depending on the model and number of observations.

## 5   Results

### 5.1   Imbalanced Lifelong Text Classification

Unlike prior work, we report $F_1$ scores rather than macro-averaged classification accuracy due to the unbalanced nature of the training data. Our main results are summarized in Table 2.

---

[1] CometML Hyperparameter Optimizer: https://www.comet.ml/.

**Table 2.** Text classification $F_1$ scores on four permutations of task orders and progressive expansion $(E)$ and progressive reduction $(R)$ sampling respectively. The two rightmost columns denote the macro-average and standard deviation across all orderings and sampling strategies.

| Method | Order (E) | | | | Order (R) | | | | $\mu$ | $\sigma$ |
|---|---|---|---|---|---|---|---|---|---|---|
| | I | II | III | IV | I | II | III | IV | | |
| SEQ | 17.4 | 27.6 | 26.6 | 21.0 | 23.7 | 32.7 | 28.8 | 25.0 | 25.4 | 4.9 |
| REPLAY | 55.3 | 67.9 | 58.6 | **65.7** | 44.2 | 57.7 | 53.5 | 37.0 | 55.0 | 10.5 |
| ANML-ER | 66.7 | **70.5** | 55.0 | 62.9 | 57.0 | 58.6 | 62.7 | 45.2 | 59.8 | 8.8 |
| OML-ER | **70.2** | 64.9 | 52.2 | 64.4 | 56.0 | **62.0** | 66.5 | 48.7 | 60.6 | 8.1 |
| DRILL$_M$ | 23.2 | 36.5 | 37.1 | 37.6 | 58.0 | 51.7 | 41.0 | **50.4** | 41.9 | 13.7 |
| DRILL$_C$ | 68.4 | 68.1 | **59.1** | 65.5 | **61.8** | 61.6 | 62.9 | 49.5 | **62.1** | 6.2 |
| MTL | 77.9 | 78.7 | 76.2 | 76.7 | 77.7 | 76.4 | 78.3 | 78.2 | 77.5 | 1.0 |

Our DRILL$_C$ variant outperforms existing methods in terms of higher overall average performance and higher median under equal conditions (the latter is depicted in Fig. 2). In addition, it has a significantly smaller variance than all other replay-based comparison methods, thus demonstrating its robustness to the order of training data and the imbalancing strategy. Consequently, it narrows the gap to the upper bound of multitask learning.

Interestingly, the DRILL$_M$ method is trailing the current models with respect to absolute performance. Yet, it provides a smaller variance for progressively expanded data than all other baselines except SEQ, exhibiting robustness against undersampled classes at the beginning of training. The enormous performance difference of our two DRILL variants motivates a more detailed analysis of the impact of knowledge integration mechanisms from RLN and $\mathcal{M}_\mathcal{S}$.

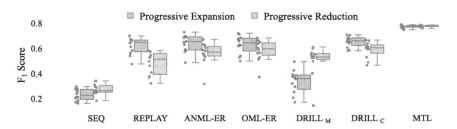

**Fig. 2.** $F_1$ scores of all comparison models aggregated across three seeds and four orderings. Sequential (SEQ) and multitask (MTL) learning can be viewed as lower and upper bound for model performance respectively.

## 5.2   Knowledge Integration Mechanisms

Although the introduction of class-representative signals drawn from semantic memory yields greater robustness under a realistic training scenario, the overall model performance varies greatly depending on how the latent signals retrieved are integrated during training. The relatively poor performance of $DRILL_M$ could be attributed to the multiplicative gating mechanism that we adopted from the original ANML algorithm [1]. The ANML is designed so that 'gating parameters' of preceding layers are learned in a supervised fashion, which is in contrast to the unsupervised nature of SOINN+.

Conversely, with $DRILL_C$, signals from RLN are enriched with those from the SOINN rather than fused, allowing for better linear separation, thus resulting in an increase of model performance. From this, we conclude that the concatenation of modalities in our training scenario provides a better knowledge retention strategy.

## 5.3   Self-organized Networks in NLP

A generally known problem of self-organizing networks is that they capture the entire evolution of hidden representations in feature space along with obsolete knowledge and are therefore unsuitable for training on shifting latent distributions. With the DRILL architecture, we overcome this problem by freezing the RLN parameters during inner-loop optimization and by the choice of our retrieval strategy for neural weight signals coming from the SOINN. The former leads to a more stable latent data distribution over a longer period. The latter ensures that neural units residing in the current input distribution are more likely to be considered as high-quality class representatives.

As this is the first work to combine a self-organizing neural architecture with a transformer-based language model in a CL setting, we advocate further exploring such set-ups in future work. This is due to the intrinsic ability of the SOINN and its various extensions to be applicable in an infinite learning setting with an unlimited number of tasks. The model can additionally handle partially annotated data, setting the basis for semi-supervised LLL scenarios.

## 6   Conclusion and Future Work

In this work, we introduce a novel, more challenging continual learning set-up with imbalanced data. We further propose Dynamic Representations for Imbalanced Lifelong Learning (DRILL), a neuroanatomically inspired CL method which combines a state-of-the-art language model with a self-organizing neural architecture. It outperforms current baselines, yet is more stable against data ordering and imbalancing. Thus, the fusion of supervised language models with unsupervised clustering algorithms has proven effective for lifelong learning methods, further narrowing the gap to multitask learning approaches. DRILL achieves the best results on imbalanced data, with the least overall variance in comparison to other meta-learning-based lifelong learning approaches. For future work, we plan to extend our model towards infinite learning of an unknown number of tasks as well as sequence-to-sequence learning.

**Acknowledgements.** We would like to thank Dr. Cornelius Weber (University of Hamburg) and Katja Kösters (University of Hamburg) for their feedback and suggestions. The authors gratefully acknowledge partial support from the German Research Foundation (DFG) under Project CML (TRR-169).

# References

1. Beaulieu, S., et al.: Learning to continually learn. In: 24th European Conference on Artificial Intelligence, vol. 325, pp. 992–1001. IOS Press (2020)
2. Biesialska, M., Biesialska, K., Costa-jussá, M.R.: Continual lifelong learning in natural language processing: a survey. In: 28th International Conference on Computational Linguistics, pp. 6523–6541. International Committee on Computational Linguistics (2020)
3. Chaudhry, A., Marc'Aurelio, R., Rohrbach, M., Elhoseiny, M.: Efficient lifelong learning with A-GEM. In: 7th International Conference on Learning Representations (2019)
4. Chen, Z., Liu, B.: Lifelong machine learning. Synth. Lect. Artif. Intell. Mach. Learn. **12**(3), 1–207 (2018)
5. Devlin, J., Chang, M.W., Lee, K., Toutanova, K.: BERT: pre-training of deep bidirectional transformers for language understanding. In: Proceedings of the 2019 Conference of the North American Chapter of the Association for Computational Linguistics, pp. 4171–4186. Association for Computational Linguistics (2019)
6. Fritzke, B., et al.: A growing neural gas network learns topologies. Adv. Neural. Inf. Process. Syst. **7**, 625–632 (1995)
7. Grossberg, S.: How does a brain build a cognitive code? Stud. Mind Brain 1–52 (1982)
8. Holla, N., Mishra, P., Yannakoudakis, H., Shutova, E.: Meta-Learning with Sparse Experience Replay for Lifelong Language Learning. arXiv preprint arXiv:2009.04891 (2020)
9. Ioffe, S., Szegedy, C.: Batch normalization: accelerating deep network training by reducing internal covariate shift. In: 32nd International Conference on Machine Learning, vol. 37, pp. 448–456. PMLR (2015)
10. Javed, K., White, M.: Meta-learning representations for continual learning. Adv. Neural. Inf. Process. Syst. **32**, 1820–1830 (2019)
11. Kemker, R., Kanan, C.: FearNet: brain-inspired model for incremental learning. In: 6th International Conference on Learning Representations (2018)
12. Kingma, D.P., Ba, J.L.: Adam: a method for stochastic optimization. In: 3rd International Conference on Learning Representations (2015)
13. Kirkpatrick, J., et al.: Overcoming catastrophic forgetting in neural networks. Proc. Natl. Acad. Sci. U.S.A. **114**(13), 3521–3526 (2017)
14. Kohonen, T.: The self-organizing map. Proc. IEEE **78**(9), 1464–1480 (1990)
15. Li, Z., Hoiem, D.: Learning without forgetting. IEEE Trans. Pattern Anal. Mach. Intell. **40**(12), 2935–2947 (2017)
16. de Masson d'Autume, C., Ruder, S., Kong, L., Yogatama, D.: Episodic memory in lifelong language learning. In: Advances in Neural Information Processing Systems 32 (2019)

17. McCloskey, M., Cohen, N.J.: Catastrophic interference in connectionist networks: the sequential learning problem. In: Bower, G.H. (ed.) Psychology of Learning and Motivation, Psychology of Learning and Motivation, vol. 24, pp. 109–165. Academic Press (1989)

18. Parisi, G.I., Kemker, R., Part, J.L., Kanan, C., Wermter, S.: Continual lifelong learning with neural networks: a review. Neural Netw. **113**, 54–71 (2019)

19. Parisi, G.I., Tani, J., Weber, C., Wermter, S.: Lifelong learning of spatiotemporal representations with dual-memory recurrent self-organization. Front. Neurorobot. **12**, 78 (2018)

20. Radford, A., Narasimhan, K., Salimans, T., Sutskever, I.: Improving Language Understanding by Generative Pre-Training. OpenAI (2018)

21. Rebuffi, S.A., Kolesnikov, A., Sperl, G., Lampert, C.H.: iCaRL: incremental classifier and representation learning. In: Proceedings of the IEEE Conference on Computer Vision and Pattern Recognition (2017)

22. Rusu, A.A., et al.: Progressive neural networks. arXiv preprint arXiv:1606.04671 (2016)

23. Shen, F., Hasegawa, O.: Self-organizing incremental neural network and its application. In: Diamantaras, K., Duch, W., Iliadis, L.S. (eds.) ICANN 2010. LNCS, vol. 6354, pp. 535–540. Springer, Heidelberg (2010). https://doi.org/10.1007/978-3-642-15825-4_74

24. Sun, F.K., Ho, C.H., Lee, H.Y.: LAMOL: LAnguage MOdeling for lifelong language learning. In: 8th International Conference on Learning Representations (2020)

25. Sun, J., Wang, S., Zhang, J., Zong, C.: Distill and replay for continual language learning. In: 28th International Conference on Computational Linguistics, pp. 3569–3579. International Committee on Computational Linguistics, Barcelona (2020)

26. Thrun, S., Pratt, L.: Learning to learn: introduction and overview. In: Thrun, S., Pratt, L. (eds.) Learning to Learn, pp. 3–17. Springer, Boston (1998). https://doi.org/10.1007/978-1-4615-5529-2_1

27. Tomasello, M.: The social bases of language acquisition. Soc. Dev. **1**(1), 67–87 (1992)

28. Wiwatcharakoses, C., Berrar, D.: SOINN+, a self-organizing incremental neural network for unsupervised learning from noisy data streams. Expert Syst. Appl. **143**, 113069 (2020)

29. Zenke, F., Poole, B., Ganguli, S.: Continual learning through synaptic intelligence. In: 34th International Conference on Machine Learning. Proceedings of Machine Learning Research, vol. 70, pp. 3987–3995. PMLR (2017)

30. Zhang, X., Zhao, J., LeCun, Y.: Character-level convolutional networks for text classification. In: 28th International Conference on Neural Information Processing Systems, pp. 649–657. MIT Press (2015)

# Principal Gradient Direction and Confidence Reservoir Sampling for Continual Learning

Zhiyi Chen[1] and Tong Lin[2,3]([✉])

[1] Georgia Institute of Technology, Atlanta, USA
zchen798@gatech.edu
[2] The Key Laboratory of Machine Perception (MOE), School of EECS,
Peking University, Beijing, China
lintong@pku.edu.cn
[3] Peng Cheng Laboratory, Shenzhen, China

**Abstract.** Task-free online continual learning aims to alleviate catastrophic forgetting of the learner on a non-iid data stream. Experience Replay (ER) is a SOTA continual learning method, which is broadly used as the backbone algorithm for other replay-based methods. However, the training strategy of ER is too simple to take full advantage of replayed examples and its reservoir sampling strategy is also suboptimal. In this work, we propose a general proximal gradient framework so that ER can be viewed as a special case. We further propose two improvements accordingly: **Principal Gradient Direction** (PGD) and **Confidence Reservoir Sampling** (CRS). In Principal Gradient Direction, we optimize a target gradient that not only represents the major contribution of past gradients, but also retains the new knowledge of the current gradient. We then present Confidence Reservoir Sampling for maintaining a more informative memory buffer based on a margin-based metric that measures the value of stored examples. Experiments substantiate the effectiveness of both our improvements and our new algorithm consistently boosts the performance of MIR-replay, a SOTA ER-based method: our algorithm increases the average accuracy up to 7.9% and reduces forgetting up to 15.4% on four datasets.

**Keywords:** Continual learning · Principal gradient direction · Confidence reservoir sampling

## 1 Introduction

Primates and humans can continually learn new skills and accumulate knowledge throughout their lifetime [5]. However, in machine learning, the agents hardly have a steady good performance when they learn a data stream. *Catastrophic forgetting* [10] is a common challenge when training a single neural network

This work was supported by NSFC Tianyuan Fund for Mathematics (No. 12026606), and National Key R&D Program of China (No. 2018AAA0100300).

I. Farkaš et al. (Eds.): ICANN 2021, LNCS 12892, pp. 421–432, 2021.
https://doi.org/10.1007/978-3-030-86340-1_34

model on consecutive tasks: the model may perform well over the first task but suffers a serious accuracy decay along with the training process on the next tasks. *Continual learning* [14], also known as *lifelong learning* [16], is a special field in machine learning that focuses on avoiding or alleviating catastrophic forgetting.

The primary setting of continual learning (CL) is the task-incremental setting [17], which assumes the stream of data can be clearly divided into sequential tasks and learnt offline. However, task-free online has received increasing attention recently, which is more practical: not only each sample can be merely observed once (single pass setting) but also the data stream is non-iid without any task information to assist the process of continual learning.

There are three major families of architecture in CL: expansion-based methods, regularization-based methods and replay-based methods. In this paper, we focus on the last one, which store the previous raw data and replay some of them when learning current data to alleviate forgetting. Experience Replay (ER) [4] is one of the most representative methods, and has been proven as a strong baseline. Because of its superior performance, ER becomes the backbone algorithm for many recent replay-based methods, such as ER-MIR [1], GSS [2], etc.

However, there is still room for improvement: on the one hand, the training strategy of ER is too simple to make full use of examples. On the other hand, reservoir sampling, which is a commonly used memory update strategy, can only ensure the equilibrium of previous samples but not good enough to maintain a more informative memory buffer. Our paper aims to tackle these defects and produces a stronger backbone algorithm for other continual learning methods based on ER.

In this paper, we firstly present a new algorithm for the training strategy called Principal Gradient Direction (PGD), which attempts to optimize a new gradient that not only represents the past data better but also retains the new knowledge of the current example. Secondly, we define a margin-based metric to measure the value of stored data and propose Confidence Reservoir Sampling (CRS), which helps to maintain a more informative memory buffer.

Under the online CL setting, our experimental results show that both of our two approaches improve ER and also boost the performance of other ER-based CL methods, such as MIR [1], which achieve the best accuracy and forgetting measure among all the replay-based methods.

## 2   Methods

In this section, we will first discuss the setup of task-free online continual learning and replay-based methods in Sect. 2.1, and then propose a proximal gradient framework to analyze the training strategy of ER from a new perspective in Sect. 2.2. Finally, we elaborate our two methods: Principal Gradient Direction and Confidence Reservoir Sampling in Sect. 2.3 and 2.4.

### 2.1   Setup

In task-free online continual learning setting, there is a stream of non-iid data: $..., (x_t, y_t), ...$, which doesn't contain any task information to identify the specific task that one example belongs to. The learner $f(.; \theta^t)$ can only observe $(x_t, y_t)$ at the $t^{th}$ training step due to the single pass constraint.

For replay-based methods, a space-limited memory buffer $\mathcal{M}$ can be used to store some examples to help provide information of past data. The learner should try to maximize the overall performance of all data, i.e., the average accuracy, and minimize the forgetting of past knowledge.

Many methods [1, 2] have addressed their improvements on the simple random selection used in ER, which is orthogonal to our improvements. In the following subsections, we will analyze the shortcomings of ER on training strategy and storage strategy and present our improvements in Sect. 2.3 and 2.4 accordingly.

## 2.2 Proximal Gradient Framework

In this subsection, we use *Proximal operator* [12], a well-studied numerical method in optimization, to build a proximal gradient framework, which is the foundation of our Principal Gradient Direction and also provides a new perspective to the training strategy of ER.

The proximal operator of a function $f(\cdot)$ with a scalar parameter $\lambda \ (> 0)$ is defined by

$$\text{prox}_{\lambda f}(v) := \arg\min_x f(x) + \frac{1}{2\lambda}\|x - v\|_2^2, \tag{1}$$

where $x \in \mathbb{R}^n, v \in \mathbb{R}^n$ are two $n$ dimensional vectors and $f : \mathbb{R}^n \to \mathbb{R}$ is a closed proper convex function. Proximal operators can be interpreted as modified gradient steps:

$$\text{prox}_{\lambda f}(v) = v - \lambda \nabla M_{\lambda f}(v), \tag{2}$$

where $M_{\lambda f}$ is a smoothed or regularized form of $f$ termed as Moreau envelop $M_{\lambda f}(v) := \inf_x f(x) + \frac{1}{2\lambda}\|x - v\|_2^2$.

As shown in [9], continual learning can be formulated as a minimization problem that finds a new gradient close enough to the gradient of the new data and satisfies some constraints at the same time. In other words, the new gradient should still be beneficial to the current task and also takes the past tasks into consideration.

Based on this insight, we introduce the proximal operator into the setting of continual learning:

$$\text{prox}_{\lambda f}(g) = \arg\min_w f(w) + \frac{1}{2\lambda}\|g - w\|_2^2, \tag{3}$$

where $g$ is the gradient vector calculated on the new data, and $w$ is the target gradient to update the network weights. $f(\cdot)$ is the convex function we need to design which characterizes the relation between the target gradient and gradients of past examples selected from the memory.

The training strategy of ER is simple: the learner randomly samples a small batch of past data from memory and directly uses the sampled data $B_t$ as well as the new input data $(x_t, y_t)$ to co-train the network. From the perspective of proximal gradient framework, the constraint function $f(\cdot)$ of ER is the inner product of the target gradient and the average gradient of selected past data without $\lambda$:

$$\min_w \frac{1}{2}\|g - w\|_2^2 - \langle g_{ref}, w\rangle, \tag{4}$$

where $g_{ref}$ is the reference gradient of $B_t$. The Eq. (4) has an analytic solution as follows, which is the actual training strategy of ER:

$$w^* = g + g_{ref}. \tag{5}$$

However, this strategy ignores the difference of sampled examples and it also regards new data and past data equally weighted, which is suboptimal.

### 2.3 Principal Gradient Direction

A more reasonable idea of utilizing the new data and selected examples is to find a target gradient that not only represents the overall contribution of the sampled past examples, but also maintains the knowledge of new data. Such a gradient can be found in the neighbor of $g$, which should also follow the principal direction of all past gradients. In this way, the new gradient will not violate the past knowledge for the reason that principal direction ensures a gradient descent towards a overall decrease on losses of past examples. In addition, the gradient also promotes the memorization of new data because it is a near neighbour of $g$.

To find the principal direction, we attempt to minimize the sum of solid angles between the new gradient vector and the past gradients, i.e., maximize the sum of cosine value. Besides, the length of a gradient should also be taken into consideration, because the "short" gradient vector means that current model $f(.; \theta^t)$ can learn it well and hence is less important than a "long" gradient. So we apply *sigmoid* function on length of the gradient as weight. We can also set a small threshold $\epsilon$ for the length of gradient: $\|g_i\|_\epsilon = max(\epsilon, \|g_i\|)$ to further decrease the impact of the short one.

Under the proximal gradient framework, we formulate a optimization problem as follows:

$$\min_w -\sum_{i=0}^{K} \frac{\langle w, g_i\rangle}{\|w\|\,\|g_i\|_\epsilon} sigmoid(\|g_i\|) + \frac{1}{2\alpha}\|w - g\|_2^2, \tag{6}$$

where $w$ is the target gradient, $g$ is the gradient of the new input, $g_i$ is the gradient of the sampled past example, $\alpha$ is a hyperparameter to balance the two parts and $K$ is the size of sampled batch $B_n$.

To solve this optimization problem, we choose *Proximal Gradient Method* [12] to get an iterative solution of the proximal problem. Considering a general optimization problem:

$$\text{minimize} \quad f(x) + h(x), \tag{7}$$

where $f : \mathbb{R}^n \to \mathbb{R}$ and $h : \mathbb{R}^n \to \mathbb{R} \cup \{+\infty\}$ are two closed proper convex functions and $f$ is differentiable. The *Proximal Gradient Method* is formulated as follows:

$$x^{(k+1)} = prox_{\beta h}(x^{(k)} - \beta \nabla f(x^{(k)})). \tag{8}$$

As for our problem, we regard the target gradient $w$ as the optimization variable, the principal direction term in (6) as function $f$ and the distance constraint term as function $h$.

After substituting the variables and expanding the formulation of (8), we get the standard form of proximal gradient method for our optimization problem:

$$w^{(k+1)} = \arg\min_w \frac{1}{2\beta} \|w - (w^{(k)} - \beta \nabla f(w^{(k)}))\|_2^2$$
$$+ \frac{1}{2\alpha} \|w - g\|_2^2. \tag{9}$$

To find the solution, we need to set the derivative of (9) to zero. Note that we can ignore the constant term, e.g. $g^T g$, so we can get:

$$w^{(k+1)} = \frac{\alpha(w^{(k)} - \beta \nabla f(w^{(k)})) + \beta g}{\alpha + \beta}. \tag{10}$$

For the gradient $\nabla f(w^{(k)})$, with the rule of derivation for fraction, the solution is:

$$\nabla f(w^{(k)}) = -\sum_{i=0}^{K} \left( \frac{g_i}{\|w^{(k)}\| \|g_i\|_\epsilon} sigmoid(\|g_i\|) \right.$$
$$\left. - \frac{\langle w^{(k)}, g_i \rangle w^{(k)}}{\|w^{(k)}\|_2^3 \|g_i\|_\epsilon} sigmoid(\|g_i\|) \right). \tag{11}$$

Here we choose the gradient of new input data $g$ as $w^{(0)}$ for the reason that the new gradient should be a neighbor of $g$. From empirical observation, we find that just one step optimization is good enough, so an approximate solution is:

$$w^{(1)} = g - \frac{\alpha\beta}{\alpha + \beta} \nabla f(g). \tag{12}$$

We replace the fraction $\alpha\beta/(\alpha + \beta)$ in (12) with a single hyperparameter $\lambda$ in experiment, which makes it look like one step gradient descent from $g$ on our principal direction function $f$. In practice, we can choose to group the examples averagely to decrease the number of backward propagation to obtain an appropriate computational complexity.

## 2.4   Confidence Reservoir Sampling

In this subsection, we focus on the storage strategy about how to update the memory with the new example $(x_t, y_t)$.

**Algorithm 1. Reservoir sampling**

**Procedure:** $\mathcal{M}$, mem_sz, $t$, $(x_t, y_t)$
**if** $|\mathcal{M}| \leq$ mem_sz **then**
    $\mathcal{M}$.append($(x_t, y_t)$)
**else**
    $i = \text{randint}(0, t)$
    **if** $i \leq$ mem_sz **then**
        $\mathcal{M}[i] \leftarrow (x_t, y_t)$
    **end if**
**end if**

ER and many other replay-based methods apply reservoir sampling strategy (Algorithm 1) [18], where mem_sz is the total memory size of $\mathcal{M}$ and $t$ is the order number of input $(x_t, y_t)$.

Though this strategy can ensure the equilibrium for memory buffer, the random replacement (the blue row in Algorithm 1) still has a room for improvement considering the limited memory space. We aspire to maintain a more informative memory buffer by replacing the less useful examples, which can improve continual learning no matter which subset is selected to consolidate the past knowledge.

Just like the exploration and exploitation dilemma in reinforcement learning, the same situation also exists in online continual learning: exploration is replacing the old data with the new one to explore the new knowledge, while exploitation is keeping the old data intact. Actually, only when an example is selected, it is really exploited by the learner.

Inspired by the idea of Upper-Confidence Bound (UCB) algorithm, which balances the uncertainty and reward of a certain action to choose one from the action set, we use a similar strategy to calculate a score for each example in memory buffer and choose the appropriate one to be replaced.

The exploitation rate, denoted as $EX$, is the first part of the metric, which is calculated by a division from the times $n$ that the example is selected into $B_t$ and the age of the example $a$: $EX = n/a$. We intend to replace the highly exploited one, which is more likely to be overfitted by the learner.

Then we define *margin* [8] based on the prediction probability from the forward propagation: the output prediction $p(x; \theta)$ on an example $(x, y)$ is computed through a softmax activation function, and we formulate margin, denoted as $m$, as:

$$m := p_y(x; \theta) - \max_{y' \neq y} p_{y'}(x; \theta). \tag{13}$$

When the model makes a correct prediction, the margin of the certain input is positive, otherwise, we get a negative margin. Margin value indicates the confidence of the prediction: larger the margin is in magnitude, more confidence we have in the prediction.

At the $t^{th}$ training step, we can first get $m_t$ of $(x_t, y_t)$ from model $f(.; \theta^t)$ and then $m_{t+1}$ from the new model $f(.; \theta^{t+1})$ that executes one step gradient descent. Then we define margin increment: $MI = m_{t+1} - m_t$, which measures

**Algorithm 2. Confidence Reservoir sampling**

**Procedure:** $\mathcal{M}$, mem_sz, $t$, $(x_t, y_t)$
**if** $|\mathcal{M}| \leq$ mem_sz **then**
    $\mathcal{M}$.append($(x_t, y_t)$)
**else**
    $i = \text{randint}(0, t)$
    **if** $i \leq$ mem_sz **then**
        **if** Using strategy $s_1$ **then**
            $j \leftarrow \max(\mathcal{S}(\mathcal{M}))$
        **else if** Using strategy $s_2$ **then**
            $j \sim P(j) = \mathcal{S}_j / \sum_k \mathcal{S}_k$
        **end if**
        $\mathcal{M}[j] \leftarrow (x_t, y_t)$
    **end if**
**end if**

the importance of a certain example at one training step. If margin increment is large, it means that this training step has learnt the example very well, in other words, the example is simple and less informative for the model.

So we can calculate our metric, denoted as $\mathcal{S}$, for all the examples in memory buffer:

$$\mathcal{S} := EX + c \cdot MI, \tag{14}$$

where $EX$ is the exploitation rate, $MI$ is the margin increment and $c$ is a weight hyperparameter. For a high score, the example is either over-exploited or less informative, which is more appropriate to be replaced.

We have two strategies to replace examples based on $\mathcal{S}$: $s_1$ directly chooses the biggest score, and $s_2$ replaces each example with a probability $P(i) = \mathcal{S}_i / \sum_j \mathcal{S}_j$, which applies to different datasets.

So far, we complete the definition of our margin-based metric and implement it on reservoir sampling as Confidence Reservoir Sampling (Algorithm 2). In this way, Confidence Reservoir Sampling not only satisfies the requirment of equal storage, but also maintains a more informative memory buffer. Note that our margin-based metric can also be extended to other storage strategy.

## 3 Experiments

In this section, we report the details of experiments and the performance of our two improvements. We apply PGD and CRS on ER and conduct ablation study. We also use the renewed backbone algorithm over MIR-replay [1] to demonstrate the effectiveness of our approaches.

### 3.1 Datasets and Architectures

We consider four commonly used datasets:

**Table 1.** Average accuracy (%) of ablation Study (↑)

| Method | ER | ER-P | ER-C | ER-PC |
|---|---|---|---|---|
| MNIST-S | 79.8 ± 3.2 | 82.4 ± 2.1 | 81.5 ± 2.1 | **84.0 ± 2.3** |
| MNIST-P | 79.1 ± 0.7 | 80.9 ± 0.3 | 79.9 ± 0.5 | **81.7 ± 0.6** |
| CIFAR10-S | 30.7 ± 2.0 | 36.1 ± 1.8 | 38.5 ± 1.1 | **40.0 ± 2.1** |
| Mini-S | 23.0 ± 1.2 | 25.5 ± 0.6 | 25.2 ± 0.8 | **25.8 ± 1.0** |

**Table 2.** Forgetting measure (%) of ablation Study (↓)

| Method | ER | ER-P | ER-C | ER-PC |
|---|---|---|---|---|
| MNIST-S | 19.2 ± 4.0 | 13.2 ± 3.1 | 17.3 ± 3.2 | **9.6 ± 1.9** |
| MNIST-P | 4.3 ± 0.5 | 2.6 ± 0.5 | 4.0 ± 0.6 | **2.4 ± 0.4** |
| CIFAR10-S | 63.3 ± 2.7 | 56.6 ± 3.7 | **49.4 ± 1.7** | 49.7 ± 3.3 |
| Mini-S | 32.1 ± 2.0 | 25.7 ± 1.4 | 28.5 ± 1.1 | **25.7 ± 1.1** |

(1) **MNIST Split** is derived from MNIST, the famous dataset on handwritten digits, which directly splits 10 classes of MNIST into 5 non-overlapping different tasks.

(2) **MNIST Permutations** is also derived from MNIST, which randomly generates different pattern of pixel permutation for each task to exchange the position of the original images of MNIST. For both MNIST Split and MNIST Permutations, we use the similar benchmark setting as [9] that each task consists of 1000 examples.

(3) **CIFAR10 Split** is derived from CIFAR10, which averagely divides the whole classes in CIFAR10 into 5 tasks, where each task has 9750 samples and 250 retained for validation just as [1].

(4) **MiniImageNet Split** is derived from miniImageNet, a subset of ImageNet with 100 classes and 600 images per class, which averagely divides the whole classes into 20 tasks.

For MNIST-S and MNIST-P, all baselines use fully-connected neural networks with two hidden layers of 100 ReLU units. A smaller version of ResNet18 [6] is used for CIFAR10-S and MINI-S, which has three times less feature maps for each layer than the original ResNet18.

## 3.2   Metrics

We use *Average Accuracy* and *Forgetting Measure* [3] to evaluate the performances of the baselines over four datasets. For *Average Accuracy*, the higher the number (indicated by ↑) the better is the model. For *Forgetting Measure*, the lower the number (indicated by ↓) the better is the model. We run 10 times to get each result.

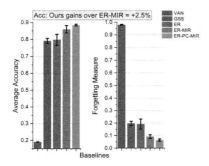

**Fig. 1.** Performances on MNIST-S

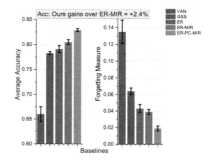

**Fig. 2.** Performances on MNIST-P

### 3.3   Ablation Study

We conduct ablation study on four datasets by combining our two approaches with ER, and the resulting algorithms are as follows: basic ER (noted as ER), ER pluses PGD (noted as ER-P), ER pluses CRS (noted as ER-C) and ER pluses both PGD and CRS (noted as ER-PC). We store 50 examples per class and select 10 past examples for $B_t$ on MNIST-S, MNIST-P and CIFAR10-S while store 100 examples per class and select 20 examples on MINI-S. The results are showed in Table 1 and 2.

**Effectiveness of PGD and CRS.** From the results, we can observe that both PGD and CRS can improve the performance of ER on all four datasets: the two methods can boost the average accuracy up to 7.7% and reduce the forgetting measure up to 13.9%. On MNIST-S and MNIST-P, whose size are relatively small and network is simpler, PGD contributes more than CRS. The situation reverses on CIFAR10-S. MINI-S has the longest task sequence (20 tasks) and the biggest input size, where our two approaches have similar contribution in average accuracy. The comparative relations are same in forgetting measure.

**Joint Improvement of PGD and CRS.** The results also demonstrate that PGD and CRS can always jointly render a further improvement. On all four datasets, ER-PC is the best algorithm in terms of average accuracy which outperforms ER from 2.6% to 9.3%. ER-PC also achieves least forgetting on the first three datasets, which only performs slightly worse than ER-C on CIFAR10-S.

Our aim is to produce a stronger backbone algorithm for other ER-based methods, so we use ER-PC as a renewed backbone algorithm for the following comparison.

### 3.4   Performance of ER-PC

In this subsection, we will show the performance of ER-PC, where we use it as the new backbone algorithm by overlying MIR-replay [1] on it, which is an example-selection strategy for replay and is SOTA replay-based method so far. We note the new method as **ER-PC-MIR**.

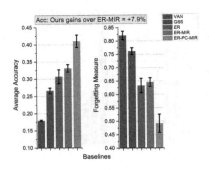

**Fig. 3.** Performances on CIFAR10-S

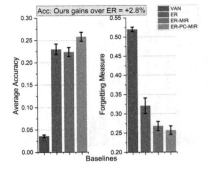

**Fig. 4.** Performances on MINI-S

**Basic Comparison.** We take the following four baselines into comparison: **VAN** (a vanilla method that a single predictor for all the tasks without any continual learning strategy), **ER** [4], **ER-MIR** [1] (the basic version of MIR-replay based on ER) and **GSS** [2].

For the reason that the training time of GSS on MINI-S is unacceptable, we don't take GSS into comparison on this dataset. We also don't take GEM [9] and A-GEM [3] into comparison because they all need the task information to update the memory and train the network, which violate the task-free online CL setting. Prior works show that ER and ER-MIR outperform GEM-like algorithms. The settings of memory size are same as our ablation study. The results are reported in Figs. 1, 2, 3 and 4.

First, ER-PC-MIR achieves the best average accuracy on all four datasets. On MNIST-S, MNIST-P and CIFAR10-S, ER-PC-MIR achieves better average accuracy than ER-MIR, the best baseline on these datasets, with improvements up to 7.9%. In MINI-S, our method is better than ER, the best baseline, with improvement 2.8%.

Second, our method also forgets least knowledge among the baselines on all four datasets: ER-PC-MIR reduces forgetting than ER-MIR with improvements from 1.1% to 15.4%. On CIFAR10-S, ER is the best baseline in terms of forgetting measure, and ER-PC-MIR is better than it with 13.6%.

The results show that our method ER-PC is a stronger backbone algorithm than vanilla ER: after combining with MIR-replay, ER-PC-MIR not only outperforms than ER-MIR, but also achieves the best performance among all other replay-based methods.

**Comparison in Different Memory Size.** As MNIST-P and CIFAR10-S are two representative datasets in domain-incremental and class-incremental datasets, we run ER-MIR and ER-PC-MIR on them in different memory size. We store 100, 50, 25 and 10 examples per class, which means that the total size of memory buffer is 1000, 500, 250, 100 on two datasets. We report the average accuracy and forgetting measure in Tables 3 and 4.

**Table 3.** Average accuracy (%) on MNIST-P and CIFAR10-S in different memory size (↑)

| MNIST-P | 1000 | 500 | 250 | 100 |
|---|---|---|---|---|
| ER-MIR | $82.7 \pm 0.4$ | $80.5 \pm 0.5$ | $77.5 \pm 0.9$ | $73.6 \pm 1.0$ |
| ER-PC-MIR | $\mathbf{84.4 \pm 0.4}$ | $\mathbf{82.9 \pm 0.3}$ | $\mathbf{79.6 \pm 0.6}$ | $\mathbf{76.1 \pm 0.4}$ |
| CIFAR10-S | 1000 | 500 | 250 | 100 |
| ER-MIR | $43.5 \pm 1.7$ | $33.1 \pm 1.1$ | $27.1 \pm 2.3$ | $22.0 \pm 2.2$ |
| ER-PC-MIR | $\mathbf{48.9 \pm 2.5}$ | $\mathbf{41.0 \pm 1.8}$ | $\mathbf{33.7 \pm 1.9}$ | $\mathbf{26.6 \pm 3.0}$ |

**Table 4.** Forgetting measure (%) on MNIST-P and CIFAR10-S in different memory size (↓)

| MNIST-P | 1000 | 500 | 250 | 100 |
|---|---|---|---|---|
| ER-MIR | $2.3 \pm 0.4$ | $3.9 \pm 0.3$ | $6.0 \pm 0.6$ | $8.8 \pm 0.9$ |
| ER-PC-MIR | $\mathbf{1.2 \pm 0.3}$ | $\mathbf{1.9 \pm 0.3}$ | $\mathbf{4.4 \pm 0.5}$ | $\mathbf{7.0 \pm 0.7}$ |
| CIFAR10-S | 1000 | 500 | 250 | 100 |
| ER-MIR | $46.4 \pm 5.1$ | $64.6 \pm 1.6$ | $72.2 \pm 4.3$ | $77.0 \pm 2.5$ |
| ER-PC-MIR | $\mathbf{36.0 \pm 4.8}$ | $\mathbf{49.2 \pm 3.4}$ | $\mathbf{54.6 \pm 3.8}$ | $\mathbf{69.1 \pm 5.3}$ |

In all memory size, ER-PC-MIR consistently improves the performance of ER-MIR. ER-PC-MIR achieves more average accuracy than ER-MIR from 1.7% to 2.5% on MNIST-P. On CIFAR10-S, ER-PC-MIR gains over ER-MIR from 4.6% to 7.9% in average accuracy. The results show the reliability of our renewed backbone algorithm in different memory size.

## 4   Conclusion

In this paper, we firstly focus on the training strategy of CL and present a proximal gradient framework. Based on it, **Principal Gradient Direction** is proposed to take full advantage of replayed examples and new data. Then we pay attention to memory updating strategy: we define a new margin-based metric to measure the value of stored data and propose **Confidence Reservoir Sampling** based on it to maintain a more informative memory buffer. The experiments demonstrate that our two approaches are both beneficial and can jointly give a further improvement. After applied with PGD and CRS, the renewed backbone algorithm can boost the performance of MIR-replay and always achieves the best performance among other replay-based baselines on four datasets. On task-incremental and domain-incremental datasets, our method also consistently outperforms ER-MIR in different memory size. The experiments show that our method is a reliable and stronger backbone algorithm than vanilla ER.

# References

1. Aljundi, R., Caccia, L., Belilovsky, E., et al.: Online continual learning with maximally interfered retrieval. In: NeurIPS (2019)
2. Aljundi, R., Lin, M., Goujaud, B., Bengio, Y.: Gradient based sample selection for online continual learning. In: NeurIPS (2019)
3. Chaudhry, A., Ranzato, M.A., Rohrbach, M., Elhoseiny, M.: Efficient lifelong learning with A-GEM. In: ICLR (2019)
4. Chaudhry, A., Rohrbach, M., Elhoseiny, M., et al.: Continual Learning with Tiny Episodic Memories. arXiv, abs/1902.10486 (2019)
5. Fagot, J., Cook, R.G.: Evidence for large long-term memory capacities in baboons and pigeons and its implications for learning and the evolution of cognition. Proc. Natl. Acad. Sci. **103**(46), 17564–17567 (2006)
6. He, K., Zhang, X., Ren, S., Sun, J.: Deep residual learning for image recognition. In: CVPR (2016)
7. Hsu, Y.-C., Liu, Y.-C., Kira, Z.: Re-evaluating Continual Learning Scenarios: A Categorization and Case for Strong Baselines. CoRR, abs/1810.12488 (2018)
8. Koltchinskii, V., Panchenko, D.: Empirical margin distributions and bounding the generalization error of combined classifiers. Ann. Stat. **30**(1), 1–50 (2002)
9. Lopez-Paz, D., Ranzato, M.A.: Gradient episodic memory for continual learning. In: NeurIPS (2017)
10. McCloskey, M., Cohen, N.J.: Catastrophic interference in connectionist networks: the sequential learning problem. In: Psychology of Learning and Motivation (1989)
11. Oquab, M., Bottou, L., Laptev, I., Sivic, J.: Learning and transferring mid-level image representations using convolutional neural networks. In: CVPR (2014)
12. Parikh, N., Boyd, S.: Proximal algorithms. Found. Trends Optim. **1**(3), 123–231 (2014)
13. Riemer, M., Cases, I., Ajemian, R., et al.: Learning to learn without forgetting by maximizing transfer and minimizing interference. In: ICLR (2019)
14. Ring, M.B.: Continual Learning in Reinforcement Environments. University of Texas at Austin (1994)
15. Sener, O., Koltun, V.: Multi-task learning as multi-objective optimization. In: NeurIPS (2018)
16. Thrun, S.: A lifelong learning perspective for mobile robot control. In: IEEE/RSJ/GI International Conference on Intelligent Robots and Systems (1994)
17. Van de Ven, G.M., Tolias, A.S.: Three scenarios for continual learning. CoRR: abs/1904.07734 (2019)
18. Vitter, J.S.: Random sampling with a reservoir. ACM Trans. Math. Softw. **11**(1), 37–57 (1985)

# Explainable Methods

# Spontaneous Symmetry Breaking in Data Visualization

Cilie W. Feldager$^{(\boxtimes)}$, Søren Hauberg, and Lars Kai Hansen

Section for Cognitive Systems, Technical University of Denmark,
Kongens Lyngby, Denmark
{cife,sohau,lkai}@dtu.dk

**Abstract.** Data visualization tools should create low-dimensional representations of data that emphasize structure and suppress noise. However, such non-linear amplifications of structural differences can have side effects like spurious clustering in t-SNE [1]. We present a more general class of spurious structure, namely broken symmetry, defined as visualizations that lack symmetry present in the underlying data. We develop a simple workflow for detection of broken symmetry and give examples of spontaneous symmetry breaking in t-SNE and other well-known algorithms such as GPLVM and kPCA. Our extensive, quantitative study shows that these algorithms frequently break symmetry, thereby highlighting new shortcomings of current visualization tools.

## 1 Motivation

*Data visualization* is a core tool in the machine learning toolbox. Data sets are visualized for exploration, to formulate hypotheses and to make modeling decisions. Visualization is commonly used for interpretation of learned models, e.g. visualization of latent variables of a generative model to understand representations. Data visualization is also very useful for debugging. For these applications *faithfulness* is a concern—can we trust the structure revealed in a visualization?

Most data of interest is high dimensional, hence can not be directly visualized. Rather, some form of dimensionality reduction is required, which inevitably will lead to loss of information. Popular schemes such as t-SNE [27], aim at two or three-dimensional representations that capture both local and global structure in data. Figure 1 shows a two-dimensional t-SNE visualization of images from the COIL-20 dataset [20]; the given example concerns a wooden object on a turntable that is viewed from multiple, equidistant angles forming full 360° rotation. Such an incremental physical rotation leads to a set of images with a simple topological structure which can be quantified by the neighborhood graph. More specifically, we form a graph with the images as nodes and connect neighboring nodes along the rotation path to obtain the graph of a circle. The neighborhood graph presents us with a strong physical symmetry and we naturally expect a visualization of the data to reveal this pattern by a structure which is topologically equivalent to a circle. Evidently, this does not happen: The visualization has broken the symmetry and "invented" a difference between neighboring points that is non-physical.

© Springer Nature Switzerland AG 2021
I. Farkaš et al. (Eds.): ICANN 2021, LNCS 12892, pp. 435–446, 2021.
https://doi.org/10.1007/978-3-030-86340-1_35

The significance of transformations and the ensuing question of symmetry preservation goes beyond the physical rotations of the COIL data set. Parameterized transformations are key to modern data augmentation strategies. The question of preservation of symmetries in augmented data sets is then related to whether given symmetries are successfully represented during learning.

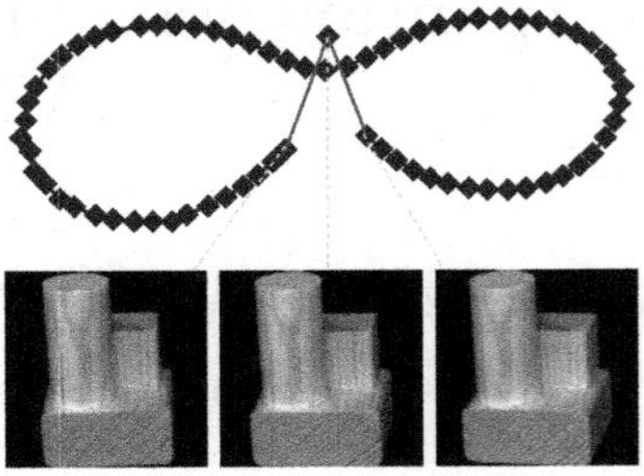

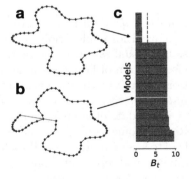

**Our contribution** is to identify a new, general class of spurious structures in data visualization, namely spontaneously broken symmetry, defined as representations that lack symmetry present in the underlying data. We provide a topological,

**Fig. 1.** We analyse a set of images of an object subject to a 360° rotation on a turntable. The nearest neighbor graph forms a simple circle, however when the set is visualized using t-SNE the symmetry is lost.

quantitative measure to detect broken symmetry (Sect. 2) allowing for a systematic study. Our empirical studies (Sect. 3) show that widely used visualization techniques break simple symmetries like rotations, hence, challenging the notion that they conserve global structure.

## 2   Symmetries, Graphs, and Persistent Homology

*Symmetry Groups.* We consider symmetries, i.e. a property of a system that remains unchanged under a given transformation. The images of the wooden toy in Fig. 1 are formally *equivariant* when the toy is rotated physically on the turn-table, while the outputs of a deep network for image based object classification ideally would be invariant (symmetric) under rotation.

Mathematically, such transformations and symmetries are described by Lie groups [11]. A real Lie group is a smooth differentiable manifold on which points are connected through a group operation and its inverse. For instance, rotation matrices form a smooth group with the matrix multiplication group operation. The unit circle can then be generated by a

**Fig. 2.** The latent space of a model that preserves symmetry (*a*) and one that does not (*b*). (c) A *barcode* as a function of thresholds $B_t$.

single unit vector and its multiplication with all members of the group of rotation matrices. If the rotation group governs a physical phenomenon then we expect to observe data along a path that topologically is a circle, disregarding observation noise.

This paper focus on situations where the governing group is known and investigate if its structure is preserved by common visualization techniques. This is achieved by verifying if the group topology remains intact under visualizations.

*Discrete Approximations.* In practice, we only observe a finite number of data points, rather than the entirety of a group. We can, however, approximate the path spanned by the observations with a graph, where points are connected if their generating group elements are close under the group metric. For instance, we may connect rotated images in a graph if their rotation angles are similar.

*Measuring Broken Symmetry.* For visualization, we map data to a low-dimensional space (typically $\mathbb{R}^2$); we let $X = \{x_i\}$ denote data coordinates in this low-dimensional space. We can now determine if a symmetry has been preserved under visualization by asking if the associated graph can be recovered from the low-dimensional coordinates. As the graph informs as to which points should be neighbors, we measure for each set of neighbors the radius of the ball needed to include one in the other's neighborhood graph. To compare across methods, we scale all distances by their median

$$B_{\text{median}} = \underset{(x_i, x_j) \in G}{\text{median}} (\|x_i - x_j\|), \tag{1}$$

where $G$ denotes the graph associated with the generating group. We rely on the median due to its high breakdown point [15]. We, thus, measure

$$B_{ij} = \frac{\|x_i - x_j\|}{B_{\text{median}}}. \tag{2}$$

We can then threshold this measure such that, we say that a symmetry has been broken if $B_{ij} > B_t$ for any pair or equivalently, $\max(B_{ij}) > B_t$. We define $B_{\max} := \max(B_{ij})$. Note that this measure does not distinguish between one or multiple instances of broken symmetry.

*Persistent Homology.* The measure above is linked with *persistent homology* [12]. This is a key mathematical tool in topological data analysis that has been shown to be robust to perturbations of the input data [6]. Following Carlsson [5], we place balls on each data point with radius $\epsilon$ and points falling within this ball defines a neighborhood. This defines a topological space $\Omega_\epsilon$. By varying $\epsilon$, we can create multiple topological spaces and let the Betti numbers $b_i(\Omega_\epsilon)$ quantify the structure of the topological space. The number $b_0$ represents the approximate number of connected components and $b_1$ the number of circles or holes.

In persistent homology, we study a spectrum of neighborhood sizes. For a *known* generating group, we would know its Betti numbers, and may ask which (if any) $\epsilon$ yield the given Betti numbers in the visualization point set. This allows us to consider multiple thresholds of our measure (2) of symmetry.

*Barcodes.* A broken symmetry is defined by the maximum of the normalized pairwise distances $B_{\max}$ being greater than a threshold $B_t$. This we can represent by a bar ranging from zero to $B_{\max}$ that visualizes the birth and death of symmetry. Stacking such bars (as in Fig. 2) yields a *barcode*. This lets us inspect the sensitivity of a chosen threshold for multiple models visually as each bar corresponds to a model [10]. The 'sharper' the transition from short bars to long bars is, the more robust the conclusion is. The barcode in Fig. 2 suggests that a choice of $B_t = 3$ is robust as any value in $B_t \in [2, 8]$ yields the same conclusions. For quantitative comparisons across experiments we consistently use $B_t = 3$ though this may be suboptimal for some models.

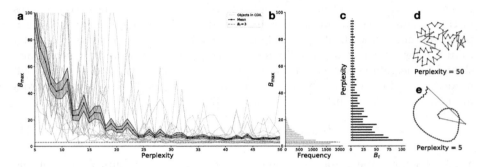

**Fig. 3.** (*a*) $B_{\max}$ vs. the perplexity for t-SNE. Each blue line represents the mean over 30 repeats for an object in COIL-20. The dotted, red line marks $B_t = 3$ and the black lines represent mean and standard error over all objects. (*b*) Histogram of models. (*c*) Barcode for the mean (black lines in (*a*) of objects. (*d*) Latent space in model with perplexities 50 ($B_{\max}$ is small). (*e*) Latent space in model with perplexities 5 ($B_{\max}$ is large).

## 3    Experiments

We consider four methods representing the spectrum of visualization techniques:

**t-SNE** matches an exponential distribution of pairwise distances in data space with a t-distribution of pairwise distances in the latent space [27]. The visualization is controlled by a *perplexity* parameter that quantifies the effective number of neighbors used in the exponential distribution over pairwise distances. This is a randomized model as implemented in scikit learn [22].

**TriMap** [2] is a recent method that relies on an elaborate triplet weighting scheme such that point triplets are weighted with their pairwise distance before obtaining the final triplet weight $\omega_{ijk} = \zeta_\gamma \left( \delta + \tilde{\omega}_{ijk}/\omega_{\max} \right)$. Here $\zeta_\gamma(u) = \log(1 + \gamma u)$, where the the *locality* parameter $\gamma$ is said to place focus on either local or global structure. The method is randomized and experiments were performed using software provided by Amid and Warmuth [2] where the default value is $\gamma = 500$.

**Kernel principle component analysis (kPCA)** [25] extends classic PCA through the kernel trick. We use the squared exponential kernel $k(x_i, x_j) = \exp\left(-||x_i - x_j||^2/\lambda\right)$, which is controlled by the *scale* parameter $\lambda$. The model is deterministic and experiments were performed using scikit learn [22].

**Gaussian process latent variable model (GPLVM)** [17] visualizes data using a latent representation with a Gaussian process prior with covariance function $k_{ij} = \theta \exp\left(-1/2||x_i - x_j||^2\right) + \sigma^2 \delta_{ij}$, where $x_i, x_j$ denote latent points. The model is deterministic for a given *initial condition* of the hyperparameters $\theta$ and $\sigma^2$, $\theta_0$ and $\sigma_0^2$. Experiments were performed using Pyro [4].

**In all experiments**, we vary method parameters over a large range, and randomized methods are repeated multiple times and reported numbers are averages. Experimentally, we focus on the most elementary symmetry of interest: *the rotation group*. We consider images from (1) *COIL-20* where objects are rotated $360°$ in 72 steps and (2) *MNIST* where we synthetically rotate images with up to $360°$ and 5% Gaussian noise is added to the pixel intensities. We perform a detailed analysis of each model's behavior, and quantitatively compare and summarize in Sect. 3.5.

## 3.1   t-Distributed Stochastic Neighborhood Embedding (t-SNE)

To investigate possible symmetry breaking in t-SNE, we fit 30 t-SNE models to images of each COIL-20 object over a large span of *perplexity* parameters. We measure $B_{\max} = \max B_{ij}$ and report averages over the 30 models (the blue lines in Fig. 3a).[1] As perplexity increase, $B_{\max}$ becomes smaller. This is to be expected as perplexity controls the smoothness of the t-SNE model. In 73% of all models, we observe broken symmetry ($B_{\max} > 3$). The barcodes reveal that this percentage is not particular sensitive to the choice of threshold (the red dotted line correspond to $B_t = 3$). On MNIST, we observe a similar pattern (omitted due to space constraints) with 96.5% of all models having a broken symmetry.

In our experience, t-SNE tends to amplify small gaps in the data, leading to broken symmetry. This is linked to the 'spurious clustering' effect observed by Amid and Warmuth [1]. We generally observe that random initialization of t-SNE seems to better preserve symmetries than initialization by other methods such as PCA or Isomap. This former approach requires multiple restarts and choosing the embedding with lowest KL divergence.

## 3.2   TriMap

Amid and Warmuth [2] developed TriMap motivated by the spurious clustering effect in t-SNE, and we hypothesized that TriMap would lead to less symmetry breaking. However, the evidence in Fig. 4 does not support that conclusion. As before, each blue line shows the average $B_{\max}$ for 30 randomly initialized models for each object in COIL-20 over a wide span of the $\gamma$ parameter. Here 77% of all models are estimated to show broken symmetry, which is roughly on par with

---

[1] $B_{\max}$ axis is cut off intentionally as the value for some object diverge.

t-SNE. The barcode indicates that the choice of threshold is robust, though we find some inter-object variability (omitted). Our findings for MNIST are similar with 93.32% estimated symmetry breaking.

## 3.3    Kernel Principal Component Analysis (kPCA)

In kPCA, we examine symmetries as a function of the kernel scale parameter $\lambda$. The barcode (Fig. 5) shows the robustness of the conclusion of preserved symmetry for the mean across COIL-20 objects. For large values of the scale parameter, the conclusion is robust as $B_t$ can vary, but for smaller values, our conclusions become sensitive to the specific choice of $B_t$.

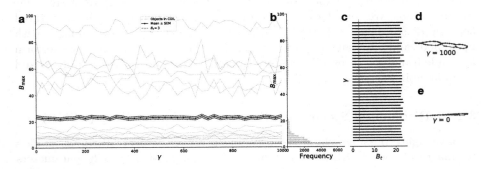

**Fig. 4.** ($a$) $B_{\max}$ vs. the locality parameter $\gamma$ for TriMap. Each blue line represents the mean over 30 repeats for an object in COIL-20. The dotted, red line marks $B_t = 3$ and the black lines represent mean and standard error over all objects. ($b$) Histogram of models. ($c$) Barcode for the mean (black lines in ($a$) of objects. ($d$) Latent space in model with $\gamma = 1000$. ($e$) Latent space in model with $\gamma = 0$.

In the non-linear regime (small values of $\lambda$), $B_{\text{median}}$ (1) is driven to small values (Fig. 5d) and $B_{\max}$ diverges. In the linear regime (large values of $\lambda$), the model approaches PCA which explains the flattening (Fig. 5e).

In 42% of models, we observe broken symmetry and note that five objects in COIL-20 give rise to broken symmetries: Object 2 (wooden toy), object 16 (round bottle), object 16 (ceramic vase), object 18 (tea cup) and object 20 (round container). Of these, four are rotationally symmetric in the plane of rotation, supporting our hypothesis that additional symmetry can induce symmetry breaking.

On MNIST data, the rate of broken symmetries was 7.23%. One possible explanation for this reduction, is that if PCA on the MNIST data does not induce symmetry breaking then fewer models will break the symmetry because kPCA converges to PCA in the linear regime.

## 3.4    Gaussian Process Latent Variable Model (GPLVM)

We investigated the GPLVM design space by varying the initial values of the kernel hyperparameters, $\theta_0$ and $\sigma_0^2$ all with identical initialization of the latent space (isomap [26]). In Fig. 6a, $\theta_0$ is fixed and $\sigma_0^2$ is varying and in Fig. 6b, $\sigma_0^2$ is fixed while $\theta_0$ varies. An interesting thing to notice is while we mostly get consistent results, sometimes a small change in the initial condition induces a large change in the $B_{\max}$ leading to somewhat complex behavior.

The loss is often an indicator of broken symmetry as we saw with the KL divergence for t-SNE. If the parameter space contains symmetry-preserving models then these generally have lower loss than models that break symmetry.

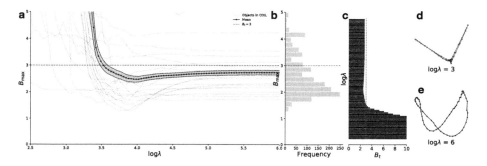

**Fig. 5.** (a) $B_{\max}$ vs. the scale parameter $\lambda$ for kPCA. Each blue line represents an object in COIL-20. The dotted, red line marks $B_t = 3$ and the black lines represent mean and standard error over all objects. (b) Histogram of models. (c) Barcode for the mean of objects (black lines in (a)). (d) Latent space of model with $\log \lambda = 3$ ($B_{\max}$ is large). (e) Latent space of model with $\log \lambda = 6$ ($B_{\max}$ is small).

The hyperparameters $\theta$ and $\sigma^2$ converge to the final values independent of the model preserving the symmetry. This means that the difference in loss between symmetry-preserving and symmetry-breaking models must be accounted for by the latent variables. It also means that it is not possible to detect a broken symmetry from the optimized hyperparameters but rather, one have to consider the latent variables to detect a broken symmetry.

Like in kPCA, we find broken symmetries in the most symmetric objects. In the GPLVM, this is linked to the choice of initialization of the latent space. Overall, we found broken symmetries in 65.48% of the models and similarly in MNIST (46.32%).

### 3.5   Summary of Experiments

We found broken symmetry in all models with a high prevalence as summarized in Fig. 7. Note that we did not tune the parameters but varied important parameters across large ranges and used default parameters for others.

All objects in COIL-20 are indeed symmetric in data space according to our estimator. One may expect that high-level features may be less susceptible to broken symmetry than raw data. To investigate we extracted features using ResNet18 [13] and found no broken symmetries in the extracted features and no consistent, significant difference when looking at symmetry in the models trained on extracted features. We noticed that the most symmetric objects generally experienced more broken symmetry across models.

## 4    Related Works

**Data visualization** is important at many steps in the machine learning process. Visualization is used exploratively to form hypotheses [3], for understanding latent representations in supervised learning [8] and generative models [9].

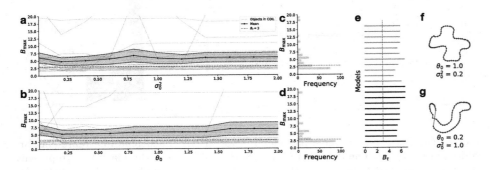

**Fig. 6.** (*a*) $B_{\max}$ vs. the initial value of the noise variance $\sigma_0^2$ for GPLVM. (*b*) $B_{\max}$ vs. the initial value of the kernel variance $\theta_0$ for GPLVM. Each blue line represents an object in COIL-20. The dotted, red line marks $B_t = 3$ and the black lines represent mean and standard error over all objects. (*a*) Parameter space in $\sigma_0^2$ with fixed $\theta_0$. (*b*) Parameter space in $\theta_0$ with fixed $\sigma_0^2$. (*c*) Histogram of models in *a*. (*d*) Histogram of models in *b*. (*e*) Barcode for the mean of objects (black lines in (*a*) and (*b*)). (*f*) Latent space of model with $\theta_0 = 1$ and $\sigma_0^2 = 0.2$. (*g*) Latent space of model with $\theta_0 = 0.2$ and $\sigma_0^2 = 0.2$.

The desiderata of visualization are discussed by Kaski et al. [16] and Venna et al. [28], who argue that visualizations should be trustworthy, meaning that samples appearing similar (e.g., neighbors) in the visualization should be similar in a physical sense. Also, they point out that data points close in a physical sense should be close in visualization. They noted the similarity with the concepts of precision and recall in information retrieval. Our concept of broken symmetry is related to the "recall" dimension, i.e., data that are physical neighbors, should also be visualized as such. The precision and recall criteria together measure the faithfulness of the visualization, see also Najim [19] for a related quantitative measure of the preservation of neighborhood relations in visualizations.

The immensely popular visualization scheme t-SNE [27] is constructed with the aim of representing both global and local structure. The original motivation for t-SNE included a critique of its predecessor SNE [14] for creating crowded visualizations, i.e., visualizations that did not show a clear separation of known clusters. Crowding is closely related to the trustworthiness concept of [16,28].

By using a long-tailed distribution of the representations, t-SNE aims to fix the crowding problem. However, this emphasis of local dissimilarity comes at a price as noted in [18], simple manifolds like lines and sheets are broken apart in clusters. These clustering problems are examples of broken symmetry in our definition. Motivated by the problem of over-fitting cluster structure Amid and Warmuth [2] proposed TriMap. We observed, however, that TriMap cannot heal the problem of broken symmetry.

For detecting symmetries, we used topological data analysis [5], specifically persistent homology. Using this, we examined all values of thresholds simultaneously rather than study just a single threshold. Conveniently, Cohen-Steiner et al. [6] showed that the persistent homology tool is robust under pertubations of the data. [23] used persistent homology in its classical form whereas we have adapted it slightly as we knew which Betti numbers were required to preserve the symmetry. Our work exploits the coordinate and deformation invariances in topology and these properties aid in detecting symmetries as various deformations of the "circle" graph.

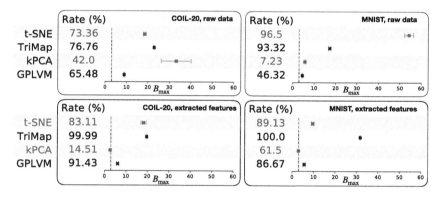

**Fig. 7.** Each panel shows the rate of broken symmetries in percent at $B_t = 3$ with the mean and standard error plotted displayed on the axis for t-SNE, TriMap, kPCA, and GPLVM. *Top, left pane)* Summary of results on COIL-20. *Top, right pane)* Summary of results on MNIST. *Bottom, left pane)* Summary of results on features extract from COIL-20 using ResNet-18. *Bottom, right pane)* Summary of results on features extracted from MNIST using ResNet-18.

## 5   Discussion

We have investigated to which extend common visualization techniques are able to preserve simple symmetries, and have largely found the answer to be negative.

### 5.1   Empirical Findings

We have investigated four popular algorithms that also represent different branches of the literature, namely t-SNE [27], TriMap [2], kPCA [25] and the

GPLVM [17]. We have performed a systematic study of the influence of parameter choices in these methods by training more than 85.000 models over a wide parameter span. To quantitatively summarize these models' performance, we have introduced a simple scheme for detecting whether known symmetries are broken. Tools from persistent homology verify that this scheme is generally reliable, with some deviations for kPCA (see below).

**t-SNE** was found to be particularly sensitive to local optima and generally we found a need for multiple restarts. Fortunately, we generally observe that smaller KL reported values imply less symmetry breaking. Even with such mechanisms in place, we still see an overwhelming number of broken symmetries. Symmetry breaking can, to some extend, be reduced by increasing the perplexity parameter, but this also limits the flexibility and expressivity of the model.

**TriMap**, which was developed in part to alleviate problems with t-SNE, overall had comparable behavior to t-SNE with regards to broken symmetry. The $\gamma$ parameter, that controls the trade-off between capturing local or global structure, was found to have practically no effect with regards to symmetry breaking. We did not expect this, but have manually verified that broken symmetry is prevalent across large spans of $\gamma$.

**kPCA** was in a sense the most successful method according to our estimator. Kernel PCA, however, has a tendency to collapse points on to each other when mapping only two latent dimensions in the non-linear regime leading to strong symmetry breaking. On the other hand, kPCA reduces to conventional PCA in the limit of large kernel length scales, showing less symmetry breaking.

**GPLVM** was generally found to be sensitive to choice of initial parameters. While we have found it helpful to consider multiple restarts and choosing the model with highest likelihood, broken symmetries remain rather prevalent.

**High-Level Features.** One could suspect that symmetries are broken more commonly when working with raw data than with high-level abstract features, e.g., as those extracted by deep neural networks. We found no broken symmetries directly in the high-level features though when applying visualization algorithms, the prevalence was indeed high.

**Summary.** Our general finding is that symmetries are broken consistently across the studied methods. It is generally possible to manually tweak parameters to enforce that a known symmetry remains intact, but such strategies are not possible when the symmetry is unknown,[2] e.g. for knowledge discovery. We also note that default parameters of publicly available implementations of the studied methods generally perform poorly with regards to broken symmetry.

## 5.2   Faithful Representations

At the heart of our study is the quest for *faithful representations*, i.e. representations that reflect the underlying physics of the data generating process. These have wider applicability than just visualization as studied here. For instance, a

---

[2] It should be emphasized that while we consider known symmetries, we only do so in order to make quantitative statements.

representation that is not faithful will most likely not result in a fair prediction. A broken symmetry can be viewed as model that violates the Lipschitz continuity condition. *Individual fairness* [7] can then no longer be ensured as *similar individuals should be treated similarly.*

Similar statements can be made for interpretable models, where 'almost discontinuous' models are generally difficult to interpret. From a purely predictive point of view, it is strictly not required that representations are faithful, though there is some evidence in that direction [24].

Finally, we note that visualization may be particularly sensitive to symmetry breaking as we tend to embed onto $\mathbb{R}^2$. While it is well-known that only few graphs (namely the *planar* ones) can be embedded in $\mathbb{R}^2$, then *all* graphs can be embedded in $\mathbb{R}^3$ [21]. This suggests that symmetries are likely to be broken when data is forced onto a two-dimensional view (as is often the case in visualization), and indeed our experiments indicate that symmetry breaking is less frequent when embedding into three or more dimensions (omitted due to space constraints).

### 5.3   Concluding Remarks

We have here pointed to a previously unnoticed problem in visualizations, namely *broken symmetries*. Through a systematic study of more than 85.000 trained models, we have found an alarming rate at which even the most simple symmetries are spontaneously broken during data visualizations. This suggest a need for both new methods that can reliably visualize high-dimensional data, but also for more systematic and quantitative evaluations of visualization techniques.

We have purposefully not investigated more complex symmetries as these raise complications that are beyond existing techniques; for instance, the two-dimensional torus is mathematically impossible to embed in $\mathbb{R}^2$ without breaking the underlying symmetry. This calls for visualization techniques that embed onto curved surfaces in order to preserve symmetries, just as we use a sphere when we visualize global geoinformatics patterns.

**Acknowledgements.** This work received funding from the European Research Council (ERC) under the European Unions Horizon 2020 research and innovation programme (757360). SH were supported in part by a research grant (15334) from VILLUM FONDEN.

## References

1. Amid, E., Warmuth, M.K.: A more globally accurate dimensionality reduction method using triplets. arXiv:1803.00854, March 2018
2. Amid, E., Warmuth, M.K.: TriMap: large-scale dimensionality reduction using triplets. arXiv:1910.00204, October 2019
3. Arora, S., Hu, W., Kothari, P.K.: An analysis of the t-SNE algorithm for data visualization. arXiv preprint arXiv:1803.01768 (2018)
4. Bingham, E., et al.: Pyro: deep universal probabilistic programming. J. Mach. Learn. Res. **20**(1), 973–978 (2019)

5. Carlsson, G.: Topology and data. Bull. Am. Math. Soc. **46**(2), 255–308 (2009)
6. Cohen-Steiner, D., Edelsbrunner, H., Harer, J.: Stability of persistence diagrams. Discrete Comput. Geom. **37**(1), 103–120 (2006). https://doi.org/10.1007/s00454-006-1276-5
7. Dwork, C., Hardt, M., Pitassi, T., Reingold, O., Zemel, R.: Fairness through awareness. arXiv:1104.3913, November 2011
8. Esteva, A., et al.: Dermatologist-level classification of skin cancer with deep neural networks. Nature **542**(7639), 115–118 (2017)
9. Frid-Adar, M., Diamant, I., Klang, E., Amitai, M., Goldberger, J., Greenspan, H.: Gan-based synthetic medical image augmentation for increased CNN performance in liver lesion classification. Neurocomputing **321**, 321–331 (2018)
10. Ghrist, R.: Barcodes: the persistent topology of data. Bull. Am. Math. Soc. **45**(1), 61–75 (2008)
11. Hall, B.C.: Lie Groups, Lie Algebras, and Representations. GTM, vol. 222. Springer, Cham (2015). https://doi.org/10.1007/978-3-319-13467-3
12. Hatcher, A.: Algebraic Topology. Cambridge University Press, Cambridge (2005)
13. He, K., Zhang, X., Ren, S., Sun, J.: Deep residual learning for image recognition. arXiv:1512.03385, December 2015
14. Hinton, G.E., Roweis, S.T.: Stochastic neighbor embedding. In: Advances in Neural Information Processing Systems, pp. 857–864 (2003)
15. Huber, P.J.: Robust Statistics, vol. 523. Wiley, New York (2004)
16. Kaski, S., et al.: Trustworthiness and metrics in visualizing similarity of gene expression. BMC Bioinform. **4**, 48 (2003)
17. Lawrence, N.D.: Probabilistic non-linear principal component analysis with Gaussian process latent variable models. J. Mach. Learn. Res. **6**, 1783–1816 (2005)
18. Linderman, G.C., Steinerberger, S.: Clustering with t-SNE, provably. arXiv:1706.02582, June 2017
19. Najim, S.A.: Information visualization by dimensionality reduction: a review. J. Adv. Comput. Sci. Technol. **3**(2), 101 (2014)
20. Nene, S.A., Nayar, S.K., Murase, H.: Columbia Object Image Library (COIL-20). Technical Report CUCS-006-96, p. 6 (1996)
21. Nishizeki, T., Chiba, N.: Planar Graphs: Theory and Algorithms. Elsevier, Amsterdam (1988)
22. Pedregosa, F., et al.: Scikit-learn: machine learning in Python. J. Mach. Learn. Res. **12**, 2825–2830 (2011)
23. Pokorny, F.T., Kjellström, H., Kragic, D., Ek, C.: Persistent homology for learning densities with bounded support. In: Pereira, F., Burges, C.J.C., Bottou, L., Weinberger, K.Q. (eds.) Advances in Neural Information Processing Systems, vol. 25, pp. 1817–1825. Curran Associates, Inc. (2012)
24. Rieger, L., Singh, C., Murdoch, W.J., Yu, B.: Interpretations are useful: penalizing explanations to align neural networks with prior knowledge. arXiv preprint arXiv:1909.13584 (2019)
25. Schölkopf, B., Smola, A., Müller, K.R.: Nonlinear component analysis as a Kernel eigenvalue problem. Neural Comput. **10**(5), 1299–1319 (1998)
26. Tenenbaum, J.B.: A global geometric framework for nonlinear dimensionality reduction. Science **290**(5500), 2319–2323 (2000)
27. van der Maaten, L., Hinton, G.: Visualizing Data using t-SNE. J. Mach. Learn. Res. **9**, 2579–2605 (2008)
28. Venna, J., Peltonen, J., Nybo, K., Aidos, H., Kaski, S.: Information retrieval perspective to nonlinear dimensionality reduction for data visualization. J. Mach. Learn. Res. **11**(13), 451–490 (2010)

# Deep NLP Explainer: Using Prediction Slope to Explain NLP Models

Reza Marzban$^{(\boxtimes)}$ and Christopher Crick

Computer Science Department, Oklahoma State University, Stillwater, OK, USA
reza.marzban@okstate.edu

**Abstract.** Natural Language Processing models have been increasingly used for many tasks, from sentiment analysis to text summarization. Most of these models are reaching the performance of human experts. Unfortunately, not only are these models not intuitive to the end-user, but they are also not even interpretable to highly-skilled Machine Learning scientists. We need explainable artificial intelligence to be able to trust models in high-stakes scenarios, and also to develop insights to optimize them by removing existing limitations and biases. In this paper, we devise a new tool called "Prediction Slope" that can be applied to any NLP model, extracting the importance rate of the component words and thereby helping to explain the model. It uses the average effect each word has on the final prediction slope as the word importance rate. We compared our technique with preceding approaches and observed that although they perform similarly, the earlier approaches do not generalize as well. Our method is independent of the model's architecture and details.

**Keywords:** Natural language processing · Deep learning · Artificial neural networks · Explainable artificial intelligence · Transformers

## 1 Introduction

The rapid growth in the amount of data available has provided both opportunities and challenges. It has helped us to build and optimize new models like different architectures of deep learning models. On the other hand, much of the available data cannot be processed by traditional statistical models and machine learning algorithms. These algorithms are desirable when we have small to medium-sized formatted data in tables inserted by a domain expert, but they are not able to handle modern tasks that require analyzing unstructured data (e.g. texts, movies, pictures). Neural networks are not a new technology – perceptrons were invented in 1958 – but they were not terribly successful until recently, due to the small amount of available data and weak computing power. However, both of these conditions have changed recently, and deep artificial neural networks have become the superhero of each and every Artificial Intelligence (AI) task from Natural Language Processing (NLP) to voice recognition and machine vision.

© Springer Nature Switzerland AG 2021
I. Farkaš et al. (Eds.): ICANN 2021, LNCS 12892, pp. 447–458, 2021.
https://doi.org/10.1007/978-3-030-86340-1_36

Although we have seen a huge jump in deep learning models' performance, they are not without drawbacks. The most important is that they are not as intuitive as basic machine learning models like decision trees. These models are more like black boxes, in that we throw data at them, use the output, and hope for the best, but we do not understand how or why. If the user does not understand the logic behind a model's decision, it will cause distrust, especially in high-stakes situations like autonomous vehicles. As a result, recently researchers have made large efforts toward explainable artificial intelligence. Not only should this boost the users' trust, but interpretability also helps developers, ML experts, and data scientists learn the defects of their models, detect bias, and tune them for further improvement.

In the relevant literature, many papers have contributed toward making deep learning models interpretable and intuitive, although they have mostly concentrated on image processing problems, as 2D pictures are much easier to visualize. They use a broad range of techniques like segmentation or creating heatmaps and saliency maps to highlight the pixels that are critical to a specific final model decision. Such approaches help users to understand the logic behind each decision, as humans can digest 2-dimensional images and find patterns in them. On the other hand, there is a huge gap in the literature on explainable AI in other contexts like NLP. Natural Language Processing is the science of enabling machines to communicate (understand and generate) in human languages. Textual data that is consisted of sentences, words, and letters are very hard to visualize, especially in a 2d space where humans can find patterns, even though accessible visualization is a key component of explainable AI.

Deep learning models come in various flavors with different architectures. Convolutional neural networks (CNNs) were originally designed for image classification but can be applied to other types of data like texts. Recurrent neural networks (RNNs) are assumed to be a natural choice for time-series data; Long Short Term Memory (LSTMs) and Gated Recurrent Units (GRUs) are common types of RNN. LSTMs are believed to be one of the most effective options in NLP tasks, as they are constructed with time series in mind. Each word or token can be looked at as a time step in a sentence. CNNs (1-dimensional versions) can also be used on textual data. Their performance is comparable with LSTM on well-known textual benchmarks for various tasks like sentiment analysis. They are also much faster than LSTMs.

Our contribution in this paper creates a brand new explainable AI technique that can be applied to any type of NLP model. Our technique uses a model's inner logic to come up with an importance rate for each and every unique word in the corpus. This has many benefits: we can take a look at the model's most important words to understand its overall general logic. It also can be used to inject insights into future models for further performance improvements. We observed that using our technique, models that were trained on just the 5% most important words perform equally as well as baseline models that have access to 100% of data. However, because only a small fraction of words are used, the model's speed is much greater. In order to create an importance rate for all words, we use and compare the mean significance of the effect of each unique word to the overall sentence prediction. In other words, we compare the change in the prediction of all sentences that contain a specific word with and without that word and use the average prediction change throughout all sentences in the corpus to create an importance rate.

Previously there has been some related work on finding and targeting the most important words to a model, but they mainly suffer from a couple of disadvantages. They provide the most important words locally, in a single output to a specific decision, which is useful but does not help in understanding the logic of the model in general. In addition, the techniques that are used for extracting the most important words are highly dependent on the architecture of the model and are thus limited to specific types of NLP models (e.g. CNNs). However, our technique can be applied to all types of NLP models and provides general explainability for the overall model.

## 2   Related Work

If we want users to understand and trust deep learning models we should provide justifications along with predictions. Explainable artificial intelligence (XAI) [10] attempts to address this problem, as well as helping data scientists to find the models' weaknesses, biases, and blind spots and thereby improve them.

XAI enables models to explain themselves to satisfy non-technical users [9], and helps developers to justify and improve them. XAI approaches can have various flavors [1]; they can provide local explanations of each and every prediction or globally explain the logic of the model as a whole. Layer-wise relevance propagation (LRP) [3, 21] matches each prediction in the model to the input features that have a significant effect on the prediction. LIME [26] is a technique for providing local interpretable model-agnostic explanations. These tools and techniques help us to trust deep learning models.

Almost all deep learning researchers working toward XAI have concentrated on image processing and machine vision, as humans find it easy to understand and find patterns in visual data. This research has created heat maps, saliency maps [27] and attention networks [29]. However, other artificial intelligence fields, such as NLP, have seen far fewer research efforts. NLP has made many significant improvements in model performance on various types of tasks and data in recent years [7], but very few of them concentrate on creating self-explanatory models.

Arras [2] identified the words that support or contradict a specific classification using LRP, highlighting them to create a visual aid for the user to understand the reasoning behind each model's decisions and predictions. This can help identify when a model arrives at a correct prediction through incorrect logic or bias, and provide clues toward fixing such errors. This technique is local, which helps to confirm single model predictions, but in order to improve and optimize models, we need tools for understanding their global logic.

RNNs and LSTMs [11] are efficient architectures for NLP tasks and textual data; however, 1-dimensional CNNs are also used for common NLP tasks like sentence classification [13] and modeling [12]. Le [14] demonstrates how CNN depth affects performance in sentiment analysis. Yin [32] compares RNN and CNN performance on various NLP tasks. Wood [30] proves that CNNs might outperform RNNs on textual data, in addition to being faster.

In 2017, a new generation of NLP models appeared, starting with Vaswani's first Transformer attention-based architecture [28]. Instead of remembering an entire text, it assigns an attention weight to each token, which allows it to process much longer texts. The attention technique enabled the creation of much more advanced transformer-based models like BERT [8], RoBERTa [16], and GPT-3 [5]. All of these models have tried to overcome their predecessor models' limitations. Some researchers have changed the inner architecture of these models and others have created auto-encoders to overcome the sequence length limitation of these models [19], adding a custom encoder layer to compress the input so that models like LSTM and BERT can accept and process longer texts.

Many researchers have tried to interpret and visualize CNN models, often on famous visual object recognition databases and benchmarks like ImageNet [34]. There are four basic techniques to visualize models in image processing tasks: activation maximization, network inversion, deconvolutional neural networks, and network dissection [23]. Yosinski [33] has devised tools to visualize features of a CNN model at each layer in image space. Model explanation, visualization, and interpretation for other types of data, such as text, are nowhere near as well-developed, but there have been a few attempts. Choi [6] attempted to explain a CNN model that classifies genres of music, and showed that deeper layers capture textures. Xu [31] used attention-based models to describe the contents of images in natural language, showing saliency relationships between image contents and word generation.

One of the hardest challenges in NLP is visualizing data after tokenizing textual data with available tools like NLTK [4]. Each token or word is represented by an embedding [17, 20, 25]. An embedding is a vector of numbers that represent a word's semantic relationship to other words. Pre-trained embeddings like GloVe [22] are available that are trained on a huge corpus. However, they are not understandable by humans, and it is very challenging to explain models that use them. Li [15] created methods to illustrate the saliency of word embeddings and their contribution to the overall model's comprehension. Rajwadi [24] trained a 1-dimensional CNN for a sentiment analysis task and used a deconvolution method to explain text classification. They estimate the importance of each word to the overall decision by masking it and checking its effect on the final prediction score.

Activation Maximization (AM) is a technique that can be applied on CNN models trained on textual data; some research has focused on creating an importance rate for each unique word in a corpus using AM on CNNs by analyzing the convolution filter weights [18]. However, instead of creating a local explanation for each prediction and decision, they used this technique to describe the whole model's logic and tried to explain it in a layer-wise manner by studying the filters of the trained model. They used the IMDb dataset [17] as their benchmark. It is very useful as their result is not dependent on every prediction, but provides a general justification for overall model logic. However, it is limited to CNN models, while we need a technique that is independent of the model architecture.

In this paper, we created a brand new tool to generate a word importance rate for an entire model, for all unique words in a corpus. This is similar to previous tools, except that this new technique is independent of the models' inner details and architecture. In other words, it can be applied to any type of NLP model.

## 3   Technical Description

### 3.1   Dataset Introduction and Preprocessing

In this research, we used two benchmark datasets with different tasks. The first is the IMDb review dataset [17],[1] which contains movie reviews and a binary target value (no neutral reviews are included). The task of this benchmark is sentiment analysis, one of the basic but crucial NLP tasks. The second dataset is the Stack Overflow dataset[2], in which each question is tagged with one of 20 possible tags. In other words, it is a multinomial classification. Obviously, the first task is easier for models as it contains only two classes.

Both of these benchmark datasets were preprocessed by removing all stop-words, special characters, numbers, HTML tags, and hapax legomena (words that appear only once in an entire corpus). All characters were converted to lower case. We used NLTK [4] to tokenize the reviews. Word2Vec [25] was used to generate 100-dimensional embeddings for each word. In the final results, our IMDb dataset had around 43,000 documents and 23,000 unique words while the Stack Overflow dataset had around 40,000 documents and 28,000 unique words. Our final step was splitting them into training and test sets.

### 3.2   Overview of the Latest Importance Rate (Activation Maximization)

Most of the work on XAI in NLP fields concentrates on providing local interpretability or justifying each and every prediction for all inputs. In contrast, we need a global explainability technique or tool to understand the overall logic of a model. Recently, some research has tried to handle that issue by identifying the most important words to the whole model [18].

They used a 1-d CNN model and activation maximization to create an importance rate with Eq. 1. They used this technique to inject insights into newer models. They proved that new models that use only a tiny fraction of the most

---

[1] https://ai.stanford.edu/~amaas/data/sentiment/.
[2] https://console.cloud.google.com/marketplace/product/stack-exchange/stack-overflow.

important words (extracted with the help of their equation) result in no significant accuracy change and dramatic increase in speed.

$$importance = \left\{ \sum_{f=1}^{F} \sum_{s=1}^{S} \sum_{i=1}^{I} |w_i * Filter_{f*s*i}| \, | w \in Corpus, Filter \right\} \quad (1)$$

In Eq. 1, $F$ is the number of filters in the CNN layer, $S$ is the size of the filters, and $I$ is the embedding length. $w$ is a word embedding vector with a length of $I$. Corpus is a matrix of the entire word embedding of size $m * I$, in which $m$ is the count of unique words in our corpus dictionary. Filter is a 3-D tensor of size $F * S * I$. This equation calculates the sum of activations of all filters caused by a single word from the Corpus.

While this technique (which will be referred to as **"activation maximization"** in this paper) is innovative, providing as it does a global interpretability rather than a local justification, it has one main limitation. The equation is highly dependent on CNN filters, and it can only be used on CNN models trained on textual data. We need similar tools that can be applied to any type of model inner architecture. In this paper, our contribution is to create a brand new technique for choosing the most important words, that is independent of the NLP model architecture.

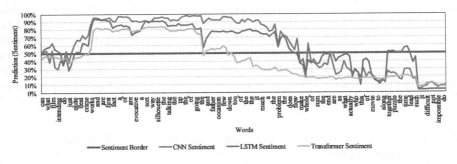

**Fig. 1.** Effect of each word in an IMDb document on the binary prediction of 3 different models (CNN, LSTM, and Transformer). Predictions above 50% represent positive sentiment and below 50% represent negative sentiment.

### 3.3   Introduction of Prediction Slope

In order to create an importance rate that is independent of the model's inner architecture and details, we created the concept of the prediction slope, which will be defined and clarified in this section. In all machine learning models, and specifically in Artificial Neural Networks (ANNs), there is a final prediction (a.k.a. output layer), where the model's decisions are found. In NLP our inputs consist of words or tokens. To understand the significance of each of these words on the final prediction, we can feed them one by one into our model and observe the effect of each word on the final prediction.

In Fig. 1, an IMDb document with negative sentiment is randomly chosen to visualize the prediction slope in a binary classification problem. In a multiclass task like the Stack Overflow dataset, we would have 20 predictions due to the fact that there are 20 classes, and the highest probability output is taken as the model's decision. We observe this maximum probability class and the effect of adding new words.

$$S_i = F(x_0, x_1, x_2, ..., x_{i-1}, x_i) - F(x_0, x_1, x_2, ..., x_{i-1}) \qquad (2)$$

In Eq. 2, $S_i$ is the prediction slope of the $i^{\text{th}}$ word in a document, and $F$ is simply the function defined by the model, which receives a sentence as input and produces a prediction. $x_n$ is the $n^{\text{th}}$ word in a document.

### 3.4 Extracting Word Importance Rate from the Prediction Slope

The prediction slope technique is not entirely new; it has been used in the literature to map a prediction to the most important words in a single input, and is sometimes also known as the temporal score. However, until now it has not been considered as a tool to perform a similar technique to an entire model, and this is where our contribution comes into play.

In each document of our corpus, we can monitor the local significance and effect of each word on the final prediction slope, but we needed a way to find the global importance rate of each unique word to the whole model. In order to do so, we use Eq. 3, in which $S_i$ is extracted from Eq. 2, $D_j$ is all documents in our corpus that contain the $j^{\text{th}}$ unique word, and $|D_j|$ is the count of those documents. Notice that the $j^{\text{th}}$ unique word in our corpus is the $i^{\text{th}}$ word that appears in a document. After applying this equation, we will a global importance rate for all unique words applicable to the whole model rather than just a single prediction. This importance rate is the mean value of the prediction slope of a particular word in all sentences containing it.

$$importance_j = \frac{\sum_{D_j} S_i}{|D_j|} \qquad (3)$$

### 3.5 Comparing Importance Rates

The prediction slope importance rate technique can be applied to any type of model, but we chose to use it on a basic Transformer model, as it is one of the hardest models to interpret and understand. Now that we have two importance rates at hand, one generated by activation maximization and the other created by prediction slope, we performed experiments to compare them. As a result, we created several brand new models that were trained on a subset of the unique words which were selected by one of our two importance rates, and we examined their respective performances.

## 4    Experimental Results

In order to test our hypothesis on both of our datasets, and compare the performance of each of the two importance rates extracted, we designed new models that were just trained on the most important words based on three different algorithms: **Activation Maximization, Prediction Slope, Random**. In the random technique, words are chosen randomly as a naive baseline for comparison with our two other models. We also compare them against the **Base Model** that uses all 100% of the words. The final model is called **Hybrid**, and it averages the importance rates for each word generated by each of the two techniques.

We created a threshold that identified the percentage of the most important words that our models would train on. We tested different threshold values: 10%, 5%, 2%, 1%, 0.5%.

### 4.1    Comparing Importance Rates on the IMDb Dataset

In our IMDb dataset, as it is a sentiment analysis problem with a binary target value, the prediction accuracy starts from 50% and the baseline accuracy with access to all words was 84%. Results are shown in Fig. 2.

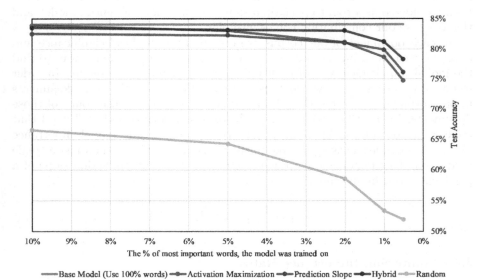

**Fig. 2.** Comparison of different importance rate techniques on IMDb dataset.

Both models are interchangeable, with no significant difference in their performance. In addition, both perform superbly while using just 2% of the data. Accuracies are very similar to the base model while they are much faster. The random model performs poorly as expected.

## 4.2    Comparing Importance Rates on the Stack Overflow Dataset

The Stack Overflow dataset presents a multinomial task with 20 possible classes or tags. Accuracy, therefore, starts at 5%, and the accuracy of the base model with access to all words is 74%.

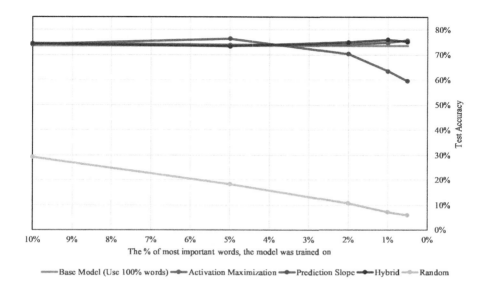

**Fig. 3.** Comparison of different importance rate techniques on Stack Overflow dataset.

Figure 3 shows that both models are still very similar, although the prediction slope technique has lower performance at thresholds smaller than 2%. The activation maximization model, however, has very good performance – even slightly better than the baseline model – even when training on only 0.5% of words. The model focuses on critical keywords, and it turns out that in this task, they are extremely predictive. Both models still perform well overall, even when they have access to a small subset of the data. Again, they are much faster than the baseline model. Also as in the previous experiment, the random model performs weakly as expected.

## 4.3    Analysis of the Result

It was observed that both techniques have quite similar performance (They performed equally in the IMDb dataset, Activation Maximization was slightly better in the Stack Overflow dataset), and both are much faster than the base model as they are just using a small subset of the input. However, the Activation Maximization can just be applied on CNN models and is very dependent on the model architecture, while the Prediction Slope can be applied on any type of NLP model architecture (In our case it was applied on a transformer model). This is very beneficial to have a tool that can analyze the model independent of the inner architecture or details and gives us insights from the model's global logic.

(a) Activation Maximization          (b) Prediction Slope

**Fig. 4.** Wordcloud of the top 100 most important words in IMDb dataset

These techniques can be used to generate insights to improve future models, and we can also use them to visualize the most important words to a model to make it more explainable and understandable. Figure 4 shows the top 100 most important words extracted from both techniques in the IMDb dataset. The size of the word represents its importance rate. The most important words according to the activation maximization technique exhibited higher document frequencies.

## 5  Conclusion

Now that many AI models, for many tasks, have reached acceptable performance levels, and often even surpass human experts, it is time to focus on other aspects of machine learning models beyond their raw accuracies. Machine learning models raise many challenging questions about AI fairness, ethical issues, and biases. In order to answer all these questions, we need to develop infrastructure and tools that make our models explainable in order to justify their decisions. Our contribution in this paper was to generate a new method for explaining NLP models' logic. Our experiments show that our method is as accurate as previous ones, while it is much more generalized. Our technique is not dependent on the NLP architecture and type and can be applied to any NLP model and task.

## References

1. Adadi, A., Berrada, M.: Peeking inside the black-box: a survey on explainable artificial intelligence (XAI). IEEE Access **6**, 52138–52160 (2018)
2. Arras, L., Horn, F., Montavon, G., Müller, K.R., Samek, W.: "What is relevant in a text document?": an interpretable machine learning approach. PLoS ONE **12**(8), e0181142 (2017)

3. Bach, S., et al.: On pixel-wise explanations for non-linear classifier decisions by layer-wise relevance propagation. PLoS ONE **10**(7), e0130140 (2015)
4. Bird, S., Klein, E., Loper, E.: Natural Language Processing with Python: Analyzing Text with the Natural Language Toolkit. O'Reilly Media Inc., Sebastopol (2009)
5. Brown, T.B., et al.: Language models are few-shot learners. arXiv preprint arXiv:2005.14165 (2020)
6. Choi, K., Fazekas, G., Sandler, M.: Explaining deep convolutional neural networks on music classification. arXiv preprint arXiv:1607.02444 (2016)
7. Collobert, R., Weston, J., Bottou, L., Karlen, M., Kavukcuoglu, K., Kuksa, P.: Natural language processing (almost) from scratch. J. Mach. Learn. Res. **12**(Aug), 2493–2537 (2011)
8. Devlin, J., Chang, M.W., Lee, K., Toutanova, K.: Bert: pre-training of deep bidirectional transformers for language understanding. arXiv preprint arXiv:1810.04805 (2018)
9. Du, M., Liu, N., Hu, X.: Techniques for interpretable machine learning. Commun. ACM **63**(1), 68–77 (2019)
10. Gunning, D.: Explainable artificial intelligence (XAI). Defense Advanced Research Projects Agency (DARPA), nd Web 2 (2017)
11. Hochreiter, S., Schmidhuber, J.: Long short-term memory. Neural Comput. **9**(8), 1735–1780 (1997)
12. Kalchbrenner, N., Grefenstette, E., Blunsom, P.: A convolutional neural network for modelling sentences. arXiv preprint arXiv:1404.2188 (2014)
13. Kim, Y.: Convolutional neural networks for sentence classification. arXiv preprint arXiv:1408.5882 (2014)
14. Le, H.T., Cerisara, C., Denis, A.: Do convolutional networks need to be deep for text classification? In: Workshops at the Thirty-Second AAAI Conference on Artificial Intelligence (2018)
15. Li, J., Chen, X., Hovy, E., Jurafsky, D.: Visualizing and understanding neural models in NLP. arXiv preprint arXiv:1506.01066 (2015)
16. Liu, Y., et al.: Roberta: a robustly optimized bert pretraining approach. arXiv preprint arXiv:1907.11692 (2019)
17. Maas, A.L., Daly, R.E., Pham, P.T., Huang, D., Ng, A.Y., Potts, C.: Learning word vectors for sentiment analysis. In: Proceedings of the 49th Annual Meeting of the Association for Computational Linguistics: Human Language Technologies, vol. 1, pp. 142–150. Association for Computational Linguistics (2011)
18. Marzban, R., Crick., C.: Interpreting convolutional networks trained on textual data. In: Proceedings of the 10th International Conference on Pattern Recognition Applications and Methods, ICPRAM, vol. 1, pp. 196–203. INSTICC, SciTePress (2021). https://doi.org/10.5220/0010205901960203
19. Marzban, R., Crick., C.: Lifting sequence length limitations of NLP models using autoencoders. In: Proceedings of the 10th International Conference on Pattern Recognition Applications and Methods, ICPRAM, vol. 1, pp. 228–235. INSTICC, SciTePress (2021). https://doi.org/10.5220/0010239502280235
20. Mikolov, T., Sutskever, I., Chen, K., Corrado, G.S., Dean, J.: Distributed representations of words and phrases and their compositionality. In: Advances in Neural Information Processing Systems, pp. 3111–3119 (2013)
21. Montavon, G., Samek, W., Müller, K.R.: Methods for interpreting and understanding deep neural networks. Digit. Signal Process. **73**, 1–15 (2018)
22. Pennington, J., Socher, R., Manning, C.D.: Glove: global vectors for word representation. In: Proceedings of the 2014 Conference on Empirical Methods in Natural Language Processing (EMNLP), pp. 1532–1543 (2014)

23. Qin, Z., Yu, F., Liu, C., Chen, X.: How convolutional neural network see the world-a survey of convolutional neural network visualization methods. arXiv preprint arXiv:1804.11191 (2018)

24. Rajwadi, M., Glackin, C., Wall, J., Chollet, G., Cannings, N.: Explaining sentiment classification. In: Interspeech 2019, pp. 56–60 (2019)

25. Rehurek, R., Sojka, P.: Software framework for topic modelling with large corpora. In: In Proceedings of the LREC 2010 Workshop on New Challenges for NLP Frameworks. Citeseer (2010)

26. Ribeiro, M.T., Singh, S., Guestrin, C.: "Why should i trust you?" explaining the predictions of any classifier. In: Proceedings of the 22nd ACM SIGKDD International Conference on Knowledge Discovery and Data Mining, pp. 1135–1144 (2016)

27. Simonyan, K., Vedaldi, A., Zisserman, A.: Deep inside convolutional networks: visualising image classification models and saliency maps. arXiv preprint arXiv:1312.6034 (2013)

28. Vaswani, A., et al.: Attention is all you need. In: Advances in Neural Information Processing Systems, pp. 5998–6008 (2017)

29. Wang, F., et al.: Residual attention network for image classification. In: Proceedings of the IEEE Conference on Computer Vision and Pattern Recognition, pp. 3156–3164 (2017)

30. Wood-Doughty, Z., Andrews, N., Dredze, M.: Convolutions are all you need (for classifying character sequences). In: Proceedings of the 2018 EMNLP Workshop W-NUT: The 4th Workshop on Noisy User-generated Text, pp. 208–213 (2018)

31. Xu, K., et al.: Show, attend and tell: neural image caption generation with visual attention. In: International Conference on Machine Learning, pp. 2048–2057 (2015)

32. Yin, W., Kann, K., Yu, M., Schütze, H.: Comparative study of CNN and RNN for natural language processing. arXiv preprint arXiv:1702.01923 (2017)

33. Yosinski, J., Clune, J., Nguyen, A., Fuchs, T., Lipson, H.: Understanding neural networks through deep visualization. arXiv preprint arXiv:1506.06579 (2015)

34. Zeiler, M.D., Fergus, R.: Visualizing and understanding convolutional networks. In: Fleet, D., Pajdla, T., Schiele, B., Tuytelaars, T. (eds.) ECCV 2014. LNCS, vol. 8689, pp. 818–833. Springer, Cham (2014). https://doi.org/10.1007/978-3-319-10590-1_53

# Empirically Explaining SGD from a Line Search Perspective

Maximus Mutschler$^{(\boxtimes)}$ and Andreas Zell$^{(\boxtimes)}$

University of Tübingen, Sand 1, 72076 Tübingen, Germany
{maximus.mutschler,andreas.zell}@uni-tuebingen.de

**Abstract.** Optimization in Deep Learning is mainly guided by vague intuitions and strong assumptions, with a limited understanding how and why these work in practice. To shed more light on this, our work provides some deeper understandings of how SGD behaves by empirically analyzing the trajectory taken by SGD from a line search perspective. Specifically, a costly quantitative analysis of the full-batch loss along SGD trajectories from common used models trained on a subset of CIFAR-10 is performed. Our core results include that the full-batch loss along lines in update step direction is highly parabolically. Further on, we show that there exists a learning rate with which SGD always performs almost exact line searches on the full-batch loss. Finally, we provide a different perspective why increasing the batch size has almost the same effect as decreasing the learning rate by the same factor.

**Keywords:** Empirical analysis · Optimization · Line search · SGD

## 1  Introduction

Although the field of Deep Learning has made impressive progress in recent years both in theory and application, little is known about why and how approaches work in detail. In general, Deep Learning approaches are based on vague intuitions in practice or rather strong assumptions in theory, without providing comprehensive empirical evidence that their intuitions and assumptions hold (e.g.: [1, 8, 10, 11, 22, 23, 25, 26, 28]).[1] Consequently, empirical analyses that search for a deeper understanding and try to explain in detail why specific approaches work, are rare to find.

This is in particular valid for optimization, which, in this domain, is optimizing the mean of a stochastic loss function with an extremely high-dimensional parameter space. The landscape of such a loss function is generally assumed to be highly non-convex, however, recent works [2, 5–7, 15, 17, 19, 29] claim that loss landscapes look rather simplistic for common Deep Learning benchmarks used in optimization.[2] This is shown to be valid for the full-batch loss with low evidence and for

---

[1] Better performance does not imply that the assumptions used are correct.
[2] Image classification on MNIST, SVHN, CIFAR-10, CIFAR-100 and ImageNet.

© Springer Nature Switzerland AG 2021
I. Farkaš et al. (Eds.): ICANN 2021, LNCS 12892, pp. 459–471, 2021.
https://doi.org/10.1007/978-3-030-86340-1_37

mini-batch losses with higher evidence. So far there exists no detailed analysis of the relation of mini-batch losses to the full-batch loss to be optimized as well as of the exact performance of approaches using mini-batches on the full-batch loss. Globally, such an empirical analysis is not feasible in terms of resources and time, even if performed for a single model only. To nevertheless shed light on the subject, this work focuses on the quantitative analysis of full-batch and mini-batch losses along lines in SGD update step directions of a ResNet-20, a ResNet-18 [8] and a MobileNet-V2 [24] trained on a subset of CIFAR-10 [14]. Since the evaluation on each of the models supports our claims, we concentrate on the results of ResNet-20.[3]

Our core results are: **1.** We provide further quantitative evidence that the full-batch loss along lines in update step direction behaves locally to a high degree parabolically (Sects. 3,4). **2.** We analyze the behavior of SGD [23], PAL [19] and further approaches on the full-batch loss when trained on mini-batch losses (Sect. 5). We show empirically that there exists a leaning rate for which SGD always performs almost exact line searches on the full-batch loss. This is since the optimal update step size on the full-batch loss and the norm of the gradient of the mini-batch loss behave approximately proportional. **3.** We consider the behavior of optimization approaches for different batch sizes (Sect. 6) and, from a different perspective, can quantitatively explain why increasing the batch size has virtually the same effect as decreasing the learning rate by the same factor, as experienced by [27].

## 2    Related Work

*SGD Trajectories:* Similar to this work [29] analyzes the loss along SGD trajectories, but with less focus on line searches and the exact shape of the full-batch loss. [12] and [16] consider second order information along SGD trajectories. Where [12] investigates the spectral norm of the Hessian (highest curvature) along the SGD trajectory and shows, inter alia, that it initially visits increasingly sharp regions. [16] investigates the dynamics and generalization of SGD based on the Hessian of the loss. They show, among other things, that the primary subspace of the second momentum of stochastic gradients overlaps substantially with that of the Hessian. Thus, to an extent, SGD uses second order information.

*The Simple Loss Landscape:* Loss landscapes of Deep Learning problems can generally be highly non-convex, and thus, hard to optimize. In practice, however, loss landscapes tend to be simple: [15] suggests that loss landscapes of networks with skip connections behave smoothly. [29] shows that the full-batch loss along SGD update step directions is roughly convex and that SGD bounces of walls of a *valley like structure*. [2,19] reveal that the batch loss along the update step direction is almost parabolically and [19] suggests with weak

---

[3] See the GitHub link in Sect. 7 for further analyses and code. We are aware that our analysis of a small set of problems provides low evidence. Nevertheless, we consider it to be guiding. With the code published with this paper, it is simple to run our experiments on further problems.

empirical evidence that this holds also for the full-batch loss. Regarding this, [17] claims that the full-batch loss can be fitted by cubic splines along negative gradient directions. [7] points out that on a straight path from initialization to solution optimizers do not encounter any significant obstacles on the loss landscape. [6] models the loss landscape as a set of high-dimensional wedges and demonstrates the existence of a low loss subspace connecting a set of minima. Similarly [5] constructs continuous low-loss paths between minima and suggests that minima are best seen as points on single connected low-loss manifolds.

*Line Searches:* Recently, line searches have gained attention for optimization in Deep Learning. [19] shows empirically that a parabolic approximation line search on batch losses performs well across models and datasets. [28] proposes a simple, well performing backtracking line search on mini-batch losses based on the interpolation assumption. The latter states that, if the full-batch loss has zero gradient, then each mini-batch loss has zero gradient. [17] builds a local model of the full-batch loss along the update direction based on a Gaussian Process.

*Batch Size and Learning Rate:* Besides choosing the learning rate, selecting an appropriate batch size remains an important choice for SGD. [18] introduces the empirically based "gradient noise scale", which predicts the largest useful batch size over datasets and models. [3] adaptively increases the batch size over update steps to assure that the negative gradient is a descent direction. [27] claims that decreasing the learning rate has virtually the same effect as increasing the batch size by the same factor.

# 3   The Empirical Method

For the empirical analysis, a Deep Learning problem has to be chosen which is (a) computationally so cheap that the analysis of the full-batch loss can be performed in a reasonable amount of time and (b) still is representative for common Deep Learning benchmarks used in optimization. Therefore, this work considers the problem of training a ResNet-20 [8] on eight percent of the CIFAR-10 dataset [14]. ResNet-like architectures are widely used in practice and CIFAR-10 is a commonly used baseline. The dataset is scaled down, so that computations for one training process take less than three weeks. Typical data augmentation is applied.[4] Using PyTorch [20], the model is trained with SGD [21] with learning rate $\lambda = 0.1$,[5] batch size 128 and momentum $\beta$ of 0 and 0.9 for 10000 steps.

---

[4] Cropping, horizontal flipping and normalization with mean and standard deviation.
[5] Best performing $\lambda$ chosen of a grid search over $\{10^{-i}|i \in \{0, 1, 1.3, 2, 3, 4\}\}$.

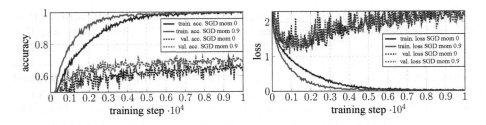

**Fig. 1.** Training processes of a ResNet-20 trained on 8% of CIFAR-10 with SGD with momentum 0 and 0.9. In the course of this work these processes will be analyzed in significant deeper details.

Figure 1 shows the results of these SGD trainings. We note that the shown accuracies and losses do not provide much insight on what is happening on a deeper level. E.g. it does not provide much information why SGD performs well. To deal with this and further issues, the full-batch loss for each SGD update step is measured along lines in update step direction. This loss $l$ along direction $\mathbf{d}$ through the current parameters $\theta_0$ is given by:

$$l(s) = \mathcal{L}(\theta_0 + s\mathbf{d}) = \frac{1}{|T|} \sum_{t \in T} L(t; \theta_0 + s\mathbf{d}), \tag{1}$$

where $s$ is the step size along the line, $\mathcal{L}$ is the full batch loss, $L$ is the sample loss and $T$ is the dataset. In the case of SGD without momentum, $\mathbf{d}$ is the negative unit gradient $-\mathbf{g}/\|\mathbf{g}\|$ of the original SGD trajectory whereas, in the case of SGD with momentum, $\mathbf{d}$ is the negative unit momentum direction $-\mathbf{m}/\|\mathbf{m}\|$.

For each of the 10000 update steps, we analyze the full-batch loss along the corresponding line in the interval $s \in [-0.5, 0.5]$ with a fine grained resolution of 0.006. For each of the 167 sample step sizes along the line the sample loss of each element in the dataset is calculated and then all losses at a step size are averaged. All in all, this procedure requires more than 52 million inferences or 1.67 million epochs.

Representative visualizations of mini- and full-batch losses along such lines are given in Fig. 2. The following is observed considering all 10000 visualizations: The full-batch loss along lines has a simple almost parabolic shape and does not change substantially across all lines. Further on is the slope of the direction defining mini-batch around $s = 0$ is always steeper than the full-batch loss. The following sections provide further quantitative evidence that these observations hold.

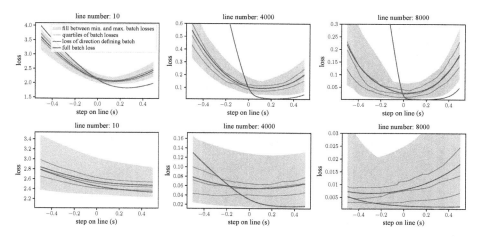

**Fig. 2.** Losses along lines of the SGD training processes exhibit a simple shape. There is a significant difference between the full batch loss (red) and the loss of the direction defining batch (green). The loss of the direction defining batch is always steeper around 0. A mini-batch size of 128 is used. **Row 1:** SGD with momentum 0.0. **Row 2:** SGD with momentum 0.9. The mini-batch loss distributions exclude the direction defining mini batch. (Color figure online)

In addition, we found the following interesting observations, but do not investigate them further. There is a significant difference between the full-batch loss and the loss of the direction defining batch. Further, the loss of the direction defining batch does not follow the distribution of any other mini-batch loss along the line, especially for SGD without momentum. In addition, for SGD without momentum this loss is always lower and steeper as the other mini-batch losses.

## 4   On the Similarity of the Shape of Full-Batch Losses Along Lines

The visualization of the full-batch loss along 10000 lines suggests that the shape of this loss does not vary significantly during the training process. For a more detailed investigation, the Mean Absolute Error (MAE) of the full-batch loss between each pair of lines is analyzed on a relevant interval. Since solely the shape of the loss is of interest and not the offset, each loss along a line is shifted along the y-axis, such that the minimum is at zero. The interval from $s \in [-0.2, 0.2]$ is considered for SGD and from $s \in [-0.5, 0.5]$ for SGD with momentum. This ensures that the minimum position and the origin are always included. The resulting distance matrices are depicted in Fig. 3. They show that **only the shapes of the full-batch loss of the very first lines vary strongly, whereas, later shapes behave more alike. In particular, the full-batch loss along consecutive lines behave similarly.** This favors optimization with fixed step sizes, since the optimal update step does not change

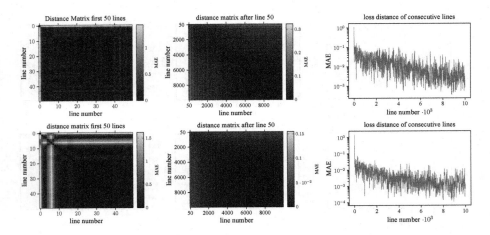

**Fig. 3.** Distances of the shape of full-batch losses along lines in a window around the current position $s = 0$. **Row 1:** SGD without momentum. **Row 2:** SGD with momentum. Since the offset is not of interest the minimum is shifted to 0 on the y-axis. The distances are rather high for the first 10 lines (left). For the following lines the distances are less than 0.3 MAE (middle) and concentrate around 0.01. The MAEs of the full-batch loss of pairs of consecutive lines are given on the right.

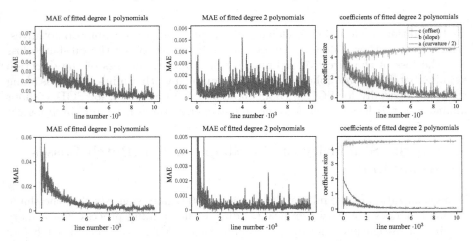

**Fig. 4.** MAE of polynomial approximations of the full-batch loss of degree 1 and 2. **Row 1:** SGD without momentum. **Row 2:** SGD with momentum. Full-batch losses along lines can be well fitted by polynomials of degree 2. The slope of the approximation stays roughly constant whereas the curvature decreases.

much. These results are also valid for the full-batch loss along each line in multiple noisy gradient directions starting from the same position in parameter space (Appendix Fig. 8). This implies from an optimization point of view that it does not matter which of the descent directions is taken.

Figure 2 also indicates that **the full-batch loss along lines exhibits an almost parabolic shape locally** (core result 1). Figure 4 shows in detail that this is valid since the fitting error of a parabola is always low. In addition, we can see that the curvature of the fitted parabolas (i.e. the second directional derivative) decreases during training, whereas, the slope stays roughly constant. This implies that **the approximated loss becomes flatter and suggests that SGD follows a simple valley like structure which becomes continuously wider**. Considering the even faster decreasing curvature of SGD with momentum, its valley becomes even wider (see also Fig. 2). This might be a reason why SGD with momentum optimizes and generalizes better [9,13]. In accordance to [12], we also found that the curvature is increasing rapidly during the very first steps and then decreases.

## 5 On the Behavior of Line Search Approaches on the Full-Batch Loss

The previous section showed that the full-batch loss along lines in update step direction behaves parabolically and exhibits positive curvature. This means that $l(s) \approx as^2 + bs + c$ with $a > 0$ (see Eq. 1). In the following the performance of several parabolic approximation line searches applied on the direction defining mini-batch loss are analyzed. From now on, we concentrate on SGD without momentum, but, Fig. 9 (appendix) shows that the upcoming results for SGD with momentum support the same derivations.

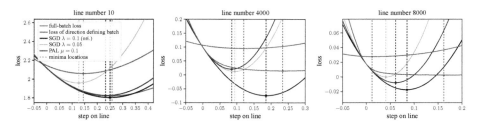

**Fig. 5.** Several parabolic line approximations and their minimum positions on representative losses along lines. The optimal update step, from a local perspective, is depicted by the red dashed line. The other update steps are derived from the direction defining mini-batch loss. (Color figure online)

For SGD the mini-batch loss and its gradient $\mathbf{g}$ are given at the origin ($s = 0$) of a line. In addition, the directional derivative, which is the negative norm of $\mathbf{g}$, can be computed easily ($-\mathbf{g}/\|\mathbf{g}\| \cdot \mathbf{g}^T = -\|\mathbf{g}\|$). To perform a parabolic approximation, either one additional loss along the line has to be considered or the curvature has to be estimated. The first approach is proposed by [19]. The default update step of their optimizer PAL is given as:

$$s_{pal} = -\frac{b}{2a} = -\frac{l'_m(0)\mu^2}{2(l_m(\mu) - l_m(0) - l'_m(0)\mu)}, \qquad (2)$$

where $l_m$ is the mini-batch loss along a line in the direction of $\mathbf{g}$ and $\mu$ is the sample step size for the second loss. The second approach is a reinterpretation of SGD as a parabolic approximation line search with estimated curvature. SGD's update step is given as $-\lambda\mathbf{g}$, where $\lambda$ is the learning rate. Considering a normalized gradient and defining $k = \frac{1}{\lambda}$ as the curvature, we get

$$-\lambda\mathbf{g} = \lambda\|\mathbf{g}\|\cdot\frac{-\mathbf{g}}{\|\mathbf{g}\|} = \frac{\|\mathbf{g}\|}{k}\cdot\frac{-\mathbf{g}}{\|\mathbf{g}\|} = -\frac{\frac{-\mathbf{g}}{\|\mathbf{g}\|}\mathbf{g}^T}{k}\cdot\frac{-\mathbf{g}}{\|\mathbf{g}\|} = -\frac{\text{first directional derivative}}{\text{second directional derivative}}\cdot\text{direction}$$

(3)

Note that the latter is a Newton update step.

To get a first intuition of how these approaches operate, several parabolic approximations and their resulting update steps on representative lines are shown in Fig. 5.

The next step is to compare several update step strategies using three metrics. Beforehand, we have to define $s_{opt}$ as the step size to the minimum of the full-batch loss along a line, which is the optimal update step size from a local perspective. $s_{upd}$ is the update step size of an arbitrary optimization strategy considered. The metrics are: the update step size $s_{upd}$, the distance of $s_{upd}$ to the minimum of the full-batch loss $(s_{opt} - s_{upd})$, and the loss improvement per step, given as: $l(0) - l(s_{upd})$, where $l$ is the full-batch loss along a line (see Eq. 1). Note that this improvement measure does not represent actual training performance, since the next considered line is independent of the previous update step size for all strategies except for SGD. which training process we are considering. However, it does represent the performance on full-batch losses along lines, which are likely to occur during training.

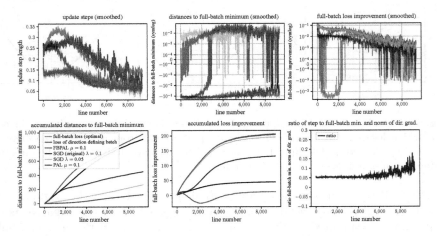

**Fig. 6.** Several metrics to compare update step strategies: 1. update step sizes. 2. the distance to the minimum of the full batch loss $(s_{opt} - s_{upd})$, which is the optimal update step from a local perspective. 3. the loss improvement per step given as: $l(0) - l(s_{upd})$ where $s_{upd}$ is the update step of a strategy. Average smoothing with a kernel size of 25 is applied. The right lower plot shows almost proportional behavior between $s_{opt}$ and the directional derivative of the direction defining mini-batch loss.

Figure 6 shows that some strategies exhibit varying behavior on the metrics. To strengthen our previous observation, a parabolic approximation on the full-batch loss (FBPAL) yields almost optimal performance. Surprisingly, SGD with $\lambda = 0.05$ estimates the minima of the full-batch loss almost as well. This is because **the step to the minimum of the full-batch loss $s_{opt}$ is almost proportional to the directional derivative ($-\|g\|$) of the direction defining mini-batch loss** (core result 2), as shown in the lower plot of Fig. 6. Observe that the variance becomes larger during the end of the training and thus the proportionality holds less. **This almost proportional behavior explains why a constant learning rate can lead to a good performance, since it is sufficient to control the update step size with the norm of the noisy mini-batch gradient.** In practice, however, this locally optimal learning rate is unknown. The globally best performing learning rate of 0.1 always does a step far beyond the locally optimal step. This is what [29] described as *bouncing off walls of a valley-like structure*. Contrary to their intuition, we have not found any boundaries at all in the valley. Finally, Fig. 6 suggests that **exact line searches on the mini-batch loss perform poorly.** For SGD with momentum, similar results are obtained (Appendix Fig. 9).

Combining the last core results suggest that **the locally optimal step size $s_{opt}$ can be well approximated by a Newton step on the full-batch loss or by a simple proportionality:**

$$s_{opt} \approx -\frac{-\|\mathbf{g}_{fbl}\|}{\mathbf{g}_{fbl} H_{fbl} \mathbf{g}_{fbl}^T} \approx c \cdot -\|\mathbf{g}_{dl}\| \tag{4}$$

where $fbl$ stands for the full-batch loss and $dl$ for the loss of the direction defining mini-batch. However, **on a global perspective a step size larger than $s_{opt}$, can perform better, although it yields locally lower improvement** (Appendix Fig. 10 ).

# 6    On the Influence of the Batch Size on Update Steps

This section analyzes to which extent the performance of SGD and PAL changes with varying batch sizes. In addition, we show why, on the losses along lines measured, increasing the batch size has almost the same effect as decreasing the learning rate by the same factor, as suggested by [27].

The presented results are simplified assuming that the SGD trajectory keeps identical with changing batch size. Thus, the same losses over lines can be considered. The original batch size is 128. For larger batch sizes additional sample losses from the set of all measured losses are drawn without replacement. For smaller batch sizes, the sample losses with the highest directional derivatives are removed, assuming that for smaller batch sizes steeper steepest directions are found.

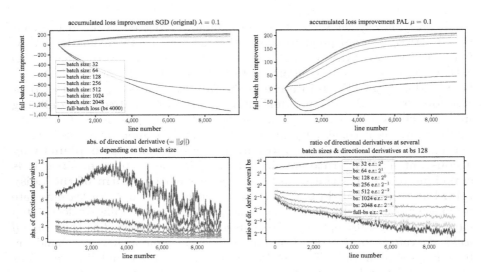

**Fig. 7. Row 1** Comparing the influence of the batch size on the loss improvement. Left: SGD with the original learning rate of 0.1. Right: parabolic approximation line search (PAL). **Row 2:** Analysis of the relation of the batch size to the absolute directional derivative (=gradient norm) which shows in detail that increasing the batch size has a similar effect as decreasing the learning rate by the same factor. **e.r.** stands for expected ratio.

The upper plots of Fig. 7 show that SGD performs significantly worse for smaller batch sizes than PAL does. Both approaches become significantly more accurate at larger batch sizes. A batch size of 512 is already sufficient to perform almost optimally.

[27] shows that when training a ResNet-50 [8] on ImageNet [4], increasing the batch size has virtually the same effect as decreasing the learning rate by the same factor. Their interpretation is based on the noise on the full-batch gradient introduced by mini-batches whereas, we argue from the perspective of mini-batch losses. The SGD update step length on losses along a line is the absolute of the learning rate times the directional derivative ($\lambda \cdot |l'_m(0)| = \lambda \cdot ||\mathbf{g}||$). The lower left plot of Fig. 7 shows that with higher batch sizes the absolute of the directional derivative, and thus the step size, decreases. This can be figuratively explained with the help of Fig. 2. As the batch size increases, the loss of the direction defining batch becomes more similar to the full-batch loss, consequently, the absolute of the directional derivative decreases. The lower plot of Fig. 7 shows by which factor the directional derivative is divided when the batch size is multiplied by a factor. **For batch size 32 to 256 the assumption that if the batch size is increased by a factor, then the update step size decreases by the same factor, is valid during the whole training** (core result 3). For larger batch sizes the directional derivative is divided by a lower factor, at the beginning of the training, then the batch size is multiplied but converges towards the same

factor during the training. Based on the data collected, we cannot estimate the momentum term for a different batch size for each line, therefore, this analysis was not performed for SGD with momentum.

## 7    Discussion and Outlook

With this work, we provided a better understanding of what happens in detail during SGD training from a line search perspective. In short, we quantitatively showed that the full-batch loss along lines in update step direction locally is highly parabolically. Further on, we found a learning rate for which SGD always performs an almost optimal line search. This questions the usefulness of line searches for deep learning in general. Finally, we quantitatively analyzed the relation of learning rate and batch size in detail and provide a different perspective on why increasing the batch size has almost the same effect as decreasing the learning rate by the same factor.

We have to emphasize that this work focused on a small set of representative problems only.[6] Therefore, our results have to be handled with care. To get a more general view about the behavior of SGD and other optimizers across models and datasets, we propose to repeat these or similar experiments for as many as possible. This can be easily done with the published code, but is extraordinarily time consuming (see https://github.com/cogsys-tuebingen/empirically_explaining_sgd_from_a_line_search_perspective).

In general, we want to emphasize that a prospective goal of future studies in Deep Learning should be, beyond reporting of good results, to provide empirical evidence that the assumptions used hold.

## 8    Appendix

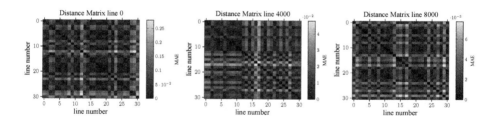

**Fig. 8.** Distances (MAE) of the shape of full-batch losses along lines in multiple noisy gradient direction in a window of 0.3 around the line origin $s = 0$. The minimum is shifted to 0 on the y-axis. At fixed positions in parameter space the full-batch loss along lines in several noisy gradient directions reveals low distances. Those plots are representative for 100 positions we analyzed.

---

[6] Note that we have done the same evaluation for a ResNet-18 [8] and a MobileNetV2 [24] trained on the same data and obtained results supporting our claims. See GitHub link.

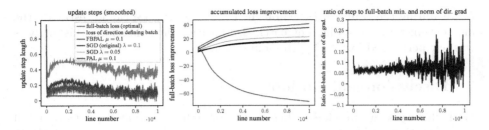

**Fig. 9. SGD training process with momentum 0.9.** See Fig. 6 for explanations. The core differences are, that for the proportionality, the noise is higher than in the SGD case. In addition, SGD with momentum overshoots the locally optimal step size less and does not perform an as exact line search.

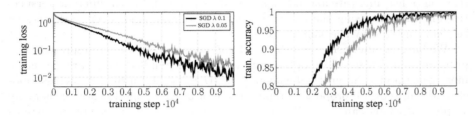

**Fig. 10.** SGD with a locally optimal learning rate of 0.05 performs worse than SGD with a globally optimal learning rate of 0.01. Trainings are performed on a ResNet-20 and 8% of CIFAR-10 with SGD without momentum.

# References

1. Berrada, L., Zisserman, A., Kumar, M.P.: Training neural networks for and by interpolation. In: ICML (2020)
2. Chae, Y., Wilke, D.N.: Empirical study towards understanding line search approximations for training neural networks. arXiv (2019)
3. De, S., Yadav, A.K., Jacobs, D.W., Goldstein, T.: Big batch SGD: automated inference using adaptive batch sizes. arXiv (2016)
4. Deng, J., Dong, W., Socher, R., Li, L.J., Li, K., Fei-Fei, L.: ImageNet: a large-scale hierarchical image database. In: CVPR (2009)
5. Draxler, F., Veschgini, K., Salmhofer, M., Hamprecht, F.A.: Essentially no barriers in neural network energy landscape. In: ICML (2018)
6. Fort, S., Jastrzebski, S.: Large scale structure of neural network loss landscapes. In: NeurIPS (2019)
7. Goodfellow, I.J., Vinyals, O., Saxe, A.M.: Qualitatively characterizing neural network optimization problems. In: ICLR (2015)
8. He, K., Zhang, X., Ren, S., Sun, J.: Deep residual learning for image recognition. In: CVPR (2016)
9. Hochreiter, S., Schmidhuber, J.: Simplifying neural nets by discovering flat minima. In: NeurIPS (1994)
10. Huang, G., Liu, Z., Van Der Maaten, L., Weinberger, K.Q.: Densely connected convolutional networks. In: CVPR (2017)

11. Ioffe, S., Szegedy, C.: Batch normalization: accelerating deep network training by reducing internal covariate shift. In: ICML (2015)
12. Jastrzebski, S., Kenton, Z., Ballas, N., Fischer, A., Bengio, Y., Storkey, A.J.: On the relation between the sharpest directions of DNN loss and the SGD step length. In: ICLR (2019)
13. Keskar, N.S., Mudigere, D., Nocedal, J., Smelyanskiy, M., Tang, P.T.P.: On large-batch training for deep learning: generalization gap and sharp minima. In: ICLR (2017)
14. Krizhevsky, A., Hinton, G.: Learning multiple layers of features from tiny images. Technical report, Citeseer (2009)
15. Li, H., Xu, Z., Taylor, G., Goldstein, T.: Visualizing the loss landscape of neural nets. In: NeurIPS (2018)
16. Li, X., Gu, Q., Zhou, Y., Chen, T., Banerjee, A.: Hessian based analysis of SGD for deep nets: dynamics and generalization. In: SDM21 (2020)
17. Mahsereci, M., Hennig, P.: Probabilistic line searches for stochastic optimization. J. Mach. Learn. Res. **18**(1), 4262–4320 (2017)
18. McCandlish, S., Kaplan, J., Amodei, D., Team, O.D.: An empirical model of large-batch training. arXiv (2018)
19. Mutschler, M., Zell, A.: Parabolic approximation line search for dnns. In: NeurIPS (2020)
20. Paszke, A., et al.: Pytorch: an imperative style, high-performance deep learning library. In: NeurIPS (2019)
21. Robbins, H., Monro, S.: A stochastic approximation method. Ann. Math. Stat. **22**, 400–407 (1951)
22. Rolinek, M., Martius, G.: L4: Practical loss-based stepsize adaptation for deep learning. In: NeurIPS (2018)
23. Rumelhart, D.E., Hinton, G.E., Williams, R.J.: Learning representations by back-propagating errors. Nature **323**(6088), 533 (1986)
24. Sandler, M., Howard, A.G., Zhu, M., Zhmoginov, A., Chen, L.C.: Mobilenetv 2: inverted residuals and linear bottlenecks. In: CVPR (2018)
25. Simonyan, K., Zisserman, A.: Very deep convolutional networks for large-scale image recognition. In: ICLR (2015)
26. Smith, L.N.: Cyclical learning rates for training neural networks. In: WACV (2017)
27. Smith, S.L., Kindermans, P., Ying, C., Le, Q.V.: Don't decay the learning rate, increase the batch size. In: ICLR (2018)
28. Vaswani, S., Mishkin, A., Laradji, I., Schmidt, M., Gidel, G., Lacoste-Julien, S.: Painless stochastic gradient: Interpolation, line-search, and convergence rates. In: NeurIPS (2019)
29. Xing, C., Arpit, D., Tsirigotis, C., Bengio, Y.: A walk with sgd. arXiv (2018)

# Towards Ontologically Explainable Classifiers

Grégory Bourguin$^{(\boxtimes)}$, Arnaud Lewandowski, Mourad Bouneffa,
and Adeel Ahmad

LISIC, Université du Littoral Côte d'Opale, 62228 Calais, France
`gregory.bourguin@univ-littoral.fr`

**Abstract.** In order to meet the explainability requirement of AI using Deep Learning (DL), this paper explores the contributions and feasibility of a process designed to create ontologically explainable classifiers while using domain ontologies. The approach is illustrated with the help of the Pizzas ontology that is used to create a synthetic image classifier that is able to provide visual explanations concerning a selection of ontological features. The approach is implemented by completing a DL model with ontological tensors that are generated from the ontology expressed in Description Logic.

**Keywords:** Machine learning · Ontology · Explainability · Classifier

## 1 Introduction

The last years have been characterized by a large democratization of solutions using Machine Learning (ML), and particularly Deep Learning (DL). This wide spread has been accompanied by questions regarding their trustworthiness. Many research papers have recently underlined the problem of the opacity of DL algorithms. This issue is at the heart of the XAI [1] initiative.

As stated in [8], *"clearly explaining a rationale for a classification decision to an end-user can be as important as the decision itself"*. It is thus necessary to create AI solutions that are able to provide explanations regarding their decisions, but moreover, these explanations also need to be understandable by the users, i.e. while using the adequate abstraction level. The users' abstraction level mainly depends on their knowledge, their expertise, or even their viewpoint.

Widely used in the Knowledge Management and Engineering research domains, the ontologies aim at reifying the knowledge of users involved in specific domains, thus allowing algorithms to use it. Taking note of the crucial need for explainable AI, the purpose of this paper is to explore a process for creating automatic classifiers that are able to provide explanations founded on an ontology. We do not focus here on new means for improving classification, but on the contributions of ontologies for explainable AI. We also explore the feasibility of such an approach while using the classical ML tools, and propose a solution that

© Springer Nature Switzerland AG 2021
I. Farkaš et al. (Eds.): ICANN 2021, LNCS 12892, pp. 472–484, 2021.
https://doi.org/10.1007/978-3-030-86340-1_38

allows to complement a DL model with a graph of tensors that is automatically generated from description logic assertions coming from the targeted ontology.

The 2nd part of the paper proposes a state of the art concerning solutions for providing explainable AI. The 3rd part of the paper illustrates the benefits expected from a process involving ontological reasoning for explainability, and introduces the generic approach we propose. The 4th part presents its application through the implementation of an ontologically explainable image classifier. The 5th part presents our conclusions resulting from this experiment.

## 2   Explainability

The systems using ML are more and more efficient, but also more and more complex and opaque. They appear as black-boxes [6] making problematic for human to step in and understand their decisions, and to control their deployment, execution, and evolution [1,9]. As a consequence, the need for transparency, and moreover, AI explainability has been revealed crucial.

### 2.1   Post-hoc Model Explanation

The tools for explaining decisions of DL systems mainly follow post-hoc approaches designed to provide explanations about pre-existing models. Most of theses methods are also called agnostic because they can be applied to any DL algorithm.

Most explanation techniques rely on the idea of associating each input feature with a value representing its importance for highlighting the key factors participating in the final prediction. It is thus possible to get explanations concerning a particular prediction, or more global ones represented with different graphics associating features, importance factors and predictions. One of the domains where this type of works is the best represented is Computer Vision (CV). In CV, the raw input features correspond to the image's pixels. The propositions consist in making a correspondence between the predictions and the pixels that leaded to a classification. Diverse approaches have been adopted and one of the most representative is the Grad-CAM [20] method (and derivatives) that uses the gradient of a targeted class to produce a *heatmap* highlighting the image's regions that most participated to its prediction. The techniques using input features to explain a model are not limited to CV. Tools like LIME [15] allow to identify some pixels in an image in a CV problem, but also to highlight the terms most participating in a prediction in a NLP (Natural Language Processing) model. In the same idea, while using different methods, we can also cite SHAP (SHapely Additive exPlanation) [11], or *What-If* [13].

All these techniques and tools have already proved to be really useful for explaining AI models. However, as it was underlined by [10], and as we will show in part 3.2, these approaches do not guarantee that the provided explanations are in fact understandable by the users.

## 2.2  Explainablity, Semantics and Ontologies

As recalled by [2]: *"Concept-based explanation approach is a popular model interpertability tool because it expresses the reasons for a model's predictions in terms of concepts that are meaningful for the domain experts"*. The benefits from ontologies for providing explanations have already been proven. For many authors, it is obvious that ontologies can help in providing adequate explanations about the decision process of DL models [3].

Following this idea, the concept of *semantic bottleneck* has recently been formalized in [10] and further developed in [12]: a classifier is built while integrating semantic layers in its very conception in order to extract *semantic features*. These latter are then used to compute the final classification. The pondered contribution of each semantic feature helps in providing explanations regarding a prediction, and in understanding misclassification errors. However, it should be noted that even if these interesting works speak about semantics, none of them use an ontological approach.

Research works like [4] are dedicated to image interpretations while using ontologies. A DL process (e.g. object detection) is used to extract features corresponding to ontological concepts. These features are then used to infer predictions at a higher abstraction level. Such approach implies reasoning while using description logic for enabling complex classification tasks. Even if they do not explicitly focus on the explainability issue, such reasoning is intrinsically explainable, and these solutions should indeed be able to provide explanations at the users' ontological abstraction level.

## 2.3  Positioning

As in Grad-CAM or LIME, our goal is to provide explanations while highlighting in the raw data the features that leaded to a classification. However, our approach is not agnostic: the explanations we want to provide are intimately bound to the targeted domain, and the features we want to highlight need to be at the user's abstraction level, i.e., from our viewpoint, ontological features.

Our approach is neither post-hoc because we need the ontology to be directly involved in the very process of the classifier creation. We follow a *semantic bottleneck* approach, with the difference that the semantics is here provided by an ontology which moreover is itself directly used to compute the predictions.

From this viewpoint, we are inspired by the research works implying ontologies for high abstraction level image interpretation. Our approach is however somehow different while definitely focusing on the explainability issue, and by advocating for explainable classifiers that involve ontologies in classification tasks that would *a priori* not need it.

# 3  Ontological Explainability Approach

## 3.1  Illustration Domain: Pizzas

To illustrate our approach, we choose to reuse the Pizzas ontology (Manchester University). The reasons are multiple, but the main one is the fact that this ontology is accessible and really famous, and thus already known by many researchers.

The Pizzas ontology defines a set of pizzas classes (e.g. Napoletana), that are subclasses of the NamedPizza class (being itself a subclass of Pizza). The pizzas definitions mainly involve the hasTopping object property whose domain is the Pizza class, and whose range is the PizzaTopping class which is the superclass of diverse toppings concepts like anchovies (AnchoviesTopping), etc.

We will then for example find the Napoletana pizza defined by:

Napoletana ≡ Pizza

⊓ (∃ hasTopping . AnchoviesTopping)

⊓ (∃ hasTopping . OliveTopping)

⊓ (∀ hasTopping . (AnchoviesTopping ⊔ OliveTopping))

As our aim is to link the results of an image classifier with the ontological definitions, we built a dataset in which the samples are labeled with the subclasses of NamedPizza. Other searchers have already created some pizzas images datasets [14]: to our knowledge, none of them corresponds to the definitions of the Pizzas ontology. Moreover, our goal in this experiment is not to enhance the classification performance (in terms of accuracy, etc.), but rather to study the benefits and the feasibility of an approach that implies an ontology for enhancing a classifier's explainability. Inspired by [14] in which the authors generate synthetic pizzas images to constitute a controlled dataset, we generated synthetic images of ontological pizzas by combining toppings cliparts (cf. Fig. 1).

The Pizza ontology defines 22 subclasses of NamedPizza while using 36 subclasses of PizzaTopping. To simplify the construction of our dataset, we decided to focus on 14 subclasses of NamedPizza involving 16 subclasses of PizzaTopping, thus keeping diversity while removing the pizzas made of toppings like TobascoPepperSauce that are hard do illustrate with cliparts, and that are not essential to our demonstration.

The generated images voluntary use the same "pizza base": only the toppings distribution is varying in number, position and orientation, in order to force any (non-ontological) classifier to focus on the toppings for classifying the pizzas. The classification task for these synthetic pizza images being relatively simple, we only generated a "small" and totally balanced dataset containing 200 pizzas per each of the 14 NamedPizza subclasses.

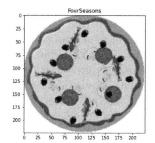 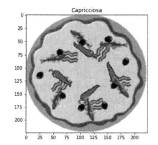

**Fig. 1.** Generating synthetic images of ontological pizzas.

## 3.2   Problems of a Non-ontological Approach

To illustrate our thoughts about the problems of post-hoc tools for explainability, we built and trained a "classical" image classifier based on a VGG19 [19] CNN architecture, we used transfer learning by reusing the weights of VGG19 pretrained on Imagenet, and complemented it by a Dense (256) and a SoftMax (14 pizzas classes) layers. The images data being simple, we were able to train this classifier while achieving 100% accuracy on a test set constituted by 20% of our samples.

We then used tools implementing the LIME [15] and Grad-CAM [18] methods which both explain a specific prediction by generating a heatmap highlighting the image's pixels that most participated to the classification. As our images were generated in a way to let the toppings being the sole elements that can help in differentiating the pizzas classes, we can expect the heatmaps to focus on the toppings' corresponding pixels.

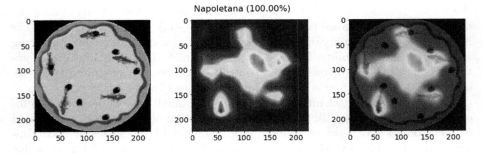

**Fig. 2.** Grad-CAM explanations for a specific pizza classification.

The Fig. 2 shows the explanations provided by Grad-CAM for a pizza predicted as Napoletana, i.e. a pizza only containing olive and anchovies toppings (cf. definition in part 3.1). We only show Grad-CAM's results here, but the explanations provided by LIME and Grad-CAM are similar. We can notice that the CNN focuses well on the anchovies. However, it ignores the olives while also focusing on a part of the pizza base (empty of toppings). We can thus consider that for this DL model, this pizza is a Napoletana because it has some anchovies and some void: this of course does not correspond to the definition we expected.

Nevertheless, the Pizzas ontology can help in explaining this phenomenon if it is used to generate an ontological correlation matrix regarding the toppings. This matrix reveals to what extent the toppings are correlated in the pizzas definitions: we can notice that the anchovies (AnchoviesTopping) always appear with olives (OliveTopping). On the other hand, the olives frequently appear with other toppings. As a result, for the CNN, on a Napolitana only made of anchovies and olives, the discriminant is the presence of anchovies.

The purpose of these remarks is not to discredit tools like Grad-CAM and LIME at all. As we just showed it, they are truly useful for explaining a classifier. However, these explanations can generally only be interpreted by an AI specialist and, as in works trying to associate some semantics to CNN filters [7], this example demonstrates that the abstraction level of the discriminants emerging from the training of a CNN does not coincide with the abstraction level of a pizza specialist. As a result, these tools do not seem to be the most adequate for providing explanations that are easily understandable by domain experts.

### 3.3   Proposed Approach

Our proposition aims at creating classifiers that are able to provide explanations at the domain experts' abstraction level, i.e. using the terms of their ontology. The steps for this realization are:

($a$) Build a set $C$ of the classes from the ontology that will be predicted as output of the classifier.

($b$) Consider $D$: the set of definitions in the ontology such as
$D = \{d \mid \exists\ c \in C,\ d \equiv c$ is an axiom of the ontology$\}$.
Consider $P$: the set of properties in the ontology involved in $D$.
Consider $R$: the set of ranges such as $R = \{r \mid r = \mathrm{range}(p),\ p \in P\}$
Build the set $F$ of the ontological features $f \in F$, i.e. the triplets $(c, p, r)$ involved in $D$ and that will be used while explaining the predictions.

($c$) Implement a DL technique to build the set $FI \subseteq F$ of the identified ontological features (satisfied assertions) in a data sent to the classifier such as
$FI = \{fi \in F \mid fi \equiv \exists\ p.r\ \}$

($d$) Implement an ontological reasoning using $D$ and $FI$ for calculating $CI \subseteq C$, the set of the $ci$ classes predicted for a data.

($e$) Use the set $DI \subseteq D$ such as $DI = \{di \equiv ci\}$ and the set $FI$ for explaining the $CI$ classification.

One can note that the ($b$) and ($c$) steps are tightly linked because it would be useless to build $F$ with ontological features that cannot be extracted from the data. In our example, we focus on the hasTopping object property because it defines the pizzas, but also because the presence of toppings (elements of $R$) can be deduced from the image.

We also want to underline that the abstraction level of the explanations is intrinsically linked to the abstraction level of the ontological features. Indeed, if in our example it will be possible to explain that an image represents a Napoletana because it contains anchovies and olives, the classifier will not be able to explain how it decided that an image region corresponds to a specific topping. We need to recall that any approach for explainability is facing the fact that, at some abstraction level, one considers not having to provide deeper explanations. We for example can cite [8] that proposes a birds species classifier while marrying a CNN and NLP for providing explanations: the system can explain that an image represents an Albatross because it contains a yellow beak, etc., but it does not try to demonstrate what is a yellow beak.

# 4   Ontological Classifier

This section presents the implementation of our approach with the pizzas example. This implementation is mainly constituted by 2 modules (Fig. 3): a semantic segmentation (DL) module designed to extract the ontological features from an image, and an ontological reasoning module called OntoClassifier designed to compute the CI classes that can be deduced from FI, while being able to provide explanations. These 2 modules are implemented in Tensorflow 2.

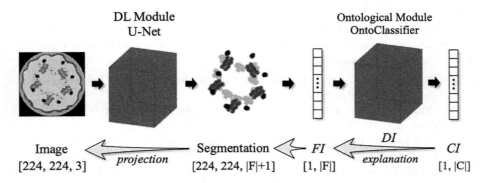

**Fig. 3.** Architecture of the ontologically explainable classifier.

## 4.1   DL Module: Semantic Segmentation

The first part of our classification pipeline aims at extracting the ontological features from an image, i.e. the satisfiability of the assertions corresponding to the triplets of $F$, considering that here:

$$F = \{(c \sqsubseteq \text{Pizza}, \text{hasTopping}, r \sqsubseteq \text{PizzaTopping})\}$$

We choose to use a semantic segmentation technique whose purpose is to label each pixel of an image with the classes from $R = \{r \sqsubseteq \text{PizzaTopping}\}$. We use a model architecture based on U-Net [16] and, as our dataset is fully controlled, we generate the segmentation masks (that are necessary to train the model) during the image generation process.

This U-Net implementation (based on MobileNetV2 [17] with the Imagenet weights) has for input 3 channels (RGB) pizzas images ($224 \times 224 \times 3$), and for output an image segmentation with 17 channels ($224 \times 224 \times 17$): each channel corresponds to one of the 16 PizzaTopping subclasses, excepted for 1 channel that is intended to receive the pixels not corresponding to any topping.

The central part of Fig. 3 shows how an image sent to the DL module is segmented: to represent this segmentation here, we have overlaid the different channels while associating each of them with a different color.

## 4.2   Ontological Module: OntoClassifier

The presence of pixels in a segmentation layer can be interpreted as the presence of an ontological feature ($\exists$ hasTopping . topping), topping $\in R$, thus letting to deduce the set *FI* of the satisfied assertions for each image treated by this model. It then remains to reason from *FI* while using the set of definitions *D* to deduce the set of classes *CI* that can label the image.

This reasoning process using properties extracted from an image is similar to those that can be found in diverse works merging DL and ontologies to propose interpretations at high abstraction level. A classical approach would be to populate the ontology with instances representing the samples to be classified (using their identified ontological features), and then to start an ontological reasoner like Jena, Hermit or Pellet to obtain a classification. However, as it was underlined in [5], this process is costly because it needs to complement the DL model with external tools, and these tools that are designed to reason in globality about an ontology are much slower that the DL pipelines nowadays used to create classifiers.

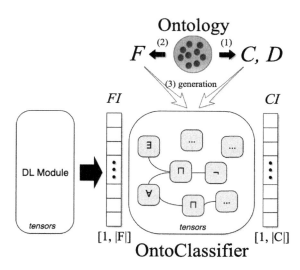

**Fig. 4.** Generating an OntoClassifier.

In our proposed approach, we do not need the full power of a classic ontological reasoner to deduce *CI* from *FI* and *D*. We thus created the OntoClassifier module whose constructor generates a set of tensors directly from the ontology, and in particular from *C*, *D* and *F*. This process is illustrated in Fig. 4: after the selection of the targeted classes and definitions constituting *C* and *D* (1), and of the ontological features constituting *F* (2), a graph of tensors is automatically generated (3): these tensors are typed and interconnected thanks to the decomposition of the OWL (Web Ontology Language) definitions found in

*D*. The resulting OntoClassifier is then ready to complement the classification pipeline directly after the output of the DL module (right part of Fig. 3). This assemblage is able to compute the satisfiability of ontological assertions like the definition of a Napoletana (cf. Sect. 3.1), or more complex assertions for example implying toppings' superclasses (using inheritance) like in:

$$\text{CheesyPizza} \equiv \exists \text{ hasTopping . CheeseTopping}$$
$$\text{VegetarianPizza} \equiv \neg (\exists \text{ hasTopping . FishTopping}) \sqcap$$
$$\neg (\exists \text{ hasTopping . MeatTopping})$$

Moreover, the OntoClassifier being implemented as a graph of tensors that represents the decomposition of the elements of *D*, this module allows to trace back the graph to identify the elements of *FI* that satisfied each assertion for a given data.

## 4.3   Results

Generating the OntoClassifier under the form of tensors allows the integration of the ontological dimension directly inside the classification pipeline. The resulting global model is then truly faster than in the case where the ontological reasoning is delegated to an external "classic" inference engine. For instance, using our semantic segmentation (DL) module combined with the Hermit reasoner on our computers (I9-10850K 3.6 GHz, 32 Go DDR4 3200 MHz, GPU RTX 3080), the classification of 100 pizzas images takes on average 130s. With the OntoClassifier, on the same computers, this classification only takes on average 1,6 s. As in Sect. 3.2, we were able to train this pipeline to achieve 100% accuracy on the test set.

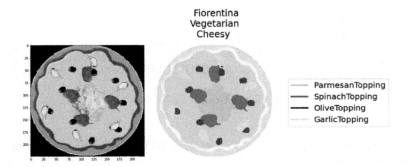

**Fig. 5.** Classification and ontological segmentation.

The Fig. 5 shows the example of an image of Fiorentina. The classifier predicts the set of classes that can label this image (Fiorentina, Vegetarian, Cheesy). The segmentation mask highlights the set of identified toppings. One can notice that in contrast to the example presented in Sect. 3.2, the abstraction level of this heatmap is in line with the ontology: no topping is ignored by the classifier, the highlighted entities correspond to the class definitions, and each topping is differentiated and identifiable thanks to a color code.

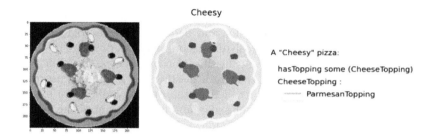

**Fig. 6.** Classification and visual ontological explanations.

The Fig. 6 illustrates the fact that this system also allows to focus on a specific identified class (here focusing on the Cheesy class identified for the image classified in Fig. 5), and to use the OntoClassifier's introspection mechanism to explain this classification. This focus reuses the ontological segmentation mask, and adds (in the right part), an explanation that binds the OWL definition of the targeted class with the parts of the image that satisfied the (sub-)assertions. Here, the binding is represented using a heatmap color code, but we can imagine more interactive means like dynamically highlighting the original image while moving the cursor over parts of the definition.

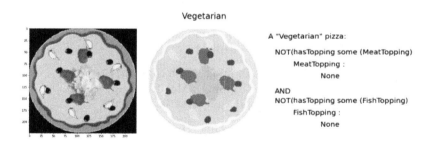

**Fig. 7.** Explanations for classification due to missing features.

The Fig. 7 shows that the OntoClassifier can focus on an identified class and also explain a classification due to the absence of elements.

## 5   Conclusion

Accounting the need for explainable AI, we explored the benefits and the feasibility of a process for creating classifiers that are ontologically explainable, i.e. providing explanations at the abstraction level for their domain users. We proposed a generic approach that results in an architecture mainly constituted by 2 modules: a DL module dedicated to the ontological features extraction, and another module named OntoClassifier and dedicated to ontological reasoning. In order to integrate the ontological dimension in the very heart of the classifier without burdening the resulting classification pipeline, we have introduced a tool for automatically generating the OntoClassifier as a graph of tensors directly built from the class definitions provided in the ontology. We have exemplified our approach by creating an image classifier and have illustrated the possibilities for ontological classification, as well as for visual explanation.

It is true that this approach involves additional work around the creation of an ontology that reifies the users' abstraction level, the construction of the sets $C$, $D$, and $F$, and also the use of a DL technique that is more complex than for a "simple" classification. One can however also notice that this approach not only results in an ontologically explainable classifier, but also presents other benefits. As long as the set of ontological features ($F$) does not change, it is easily possible to evolve the classifier, for example by adding new classes/definitions, and to integrate this evolution into the pipeline without having to retrain the DL model. The sole thing to do is to automatically re-generate the OntoClassifier. As underlined in [21], the notion of viewpoint is important too, even while considering ontologies. Our proposed approach and tools can offer a solution to the need for multi-viewpoints because it is easily possible to generate different OntoClassifier modules, each one dedicated to a specific viewpoint on the same domain. Our approach also allows to introduce the notion of viewpoints in the explanations themselves. Indeed, for the same $C$ set, it is possible to build different $D$ sets, and then to generate different explainable classifiers focusing on different ontological definitions for the same classes. For example, in the Pizza ontology, a Vegetarian pizza can be defined as:

(1)   $\text{VegetarianPizza} \equiv \neg (\exists \text{ hasTopping . FishTopping}) \sqcap$
$\neg (\exists \text{ hasTopping . MeatTopping})$

(2)   $\text{VegetarianPizza} \equiv \forall \text{ hasTopping . VegetarianTopping}$

If these 2 definitions lead to the same classification, the associated visual explanations correspond to different viewpoints focusing on (or highlighting) (1) the fish or meat toppings (cf. Fig. 7), or (2) the vegetarian toppings.

These approach and tools are still in development. In this paper, the visual explanations directly use the OWL expressions: this representation needs to be improved, and then evaluated through experiments while involving end-users. We also are working on the human-machine interfaces that will allow end-users to manipulate and explore the provided explanations. The presented elements however already let imagine functionalities that are promising, and even necessary in the frame of projects involving actors with different cultures and viewpoints.

# References

1. Arrieta, A., et al.: Explainable artificial intelligence (XAI): concepts, taxonomies, opportunities and challenges toward responsible AI. ArXiv abs/1910.10045 (2020)
2. Bahadori, M.T., Heckerman, D.: Debiasing concept bottleneck models with a causal analysis technique (2020)
3. Confalonieri, R., Besold, T.R.: Trepan reloaded: a knowledge-driven approach to explaining black-box models. In: ECAI (2020)
4. Conigliaro, D., Ferrario, R., Hudelot, C., Porello, D.: Integrating computer vision algorithms and ontologies for spectator crowd behavior analysis. In: Group and Crowd Behavior for Computer Vision (2017)
5. Ding, Z., Yao, L., Liu, B., Wu, J.: Review of the application of ontology in the field of image object recognition. In: ICCMS 2019 (2019)
6. Dosilovic, F.K., Brčič, M., Hlupic, N.: Explainable artificial intelligence: a survey. In: 2018 41st International Convention on Information and Communication Technology, Electronics and Microelectronics (MIPRO), pp. 0210–0215 (2018)
7. Gonzalez-Garcia, A., Modolo, D., Ferrari, V.: Do semantic parts emerge in convolutional neural networks? Int. J. Comput. Vis. **126**, 476–494 (2017)
8. Hendricks, L.A., Akata, Z., Rohrbach, M., Donahue, J., Schiele, B., Darrell, T.: Generating visual explanations. In: Leibe, B., Matas, J., Sebe, N., Welling, M. (eds.) ECCV 2016, Part IV. LNCS, vol. 9908, pp. 3–19. Springer, Cham (2016). https://doi.org/10.1007/978-3-319-46493-0_1
9. Lipton, Z.C.: The mythos of model interpretability. Queue **16**, 31–57 (2018)
10. Losch, M., Fritz, M., Schiele, B.: Interpretability beyond classification output: semantic bottleneck networks. ArXiv abs/1907.10882 (2019)
11. Lundberg, S.M., Lee, S.I.: A unified approach to interpreting model predictions. In: NIPS (2017)
12. Marcos, D., Lobry, S., Tuia, D.: Semantically interpretable activation maps: what-where-how explanations within CNNs. In: 2019 IEEE/CVF International Conference on Computer Vision Workshop (ICCVW), pp. 4207–4215 (2019)
13. Martens, D., Provost, F.: Explaining data-driven document classifications. MIS Q. **38**, 73–99 (2014)
14. Papadopoulos, D.P., Tamaazousti, Y., Ofli, F., Weber, I., Torralba, A.: How to make a pizza: learning a compositional layer-based GAN model. In: 2019 IEEE/CVF Conference on Computer Vision and Pattern Recognition (CVPR), pp. 7994–8003 (2019)
15. Ribeiro, M.T., Singh, S., Guestrin, C.: "why should i trust you?": explaining the predictions of any classifier. In: Proceedings of the 22nd ACM SIGKDD International Conference on Knowledge Discovery and Data Mining (2016)
16. Ronneberger, O., Fischer, P., Brox, T.: U-net: convolutional networks for biomedical image segmentation. ArXiv abs/1505.04597 (2015)
17. Sandler, M., Howard, A., Zhu, M., Zhmoginov, A., Chen, L.C.: MobileNetV2: inverted residuals and linear bottlenecks. In: 2018 IEEE/CVF Conference on Computer Vision and Pattern Recognition, pp. 4510–4520 (2018)
18. Selvaraju, R.R., Das, A., Vedantam, R., Cogswell, M., Parikh, D., Batra, D.: Grad-CAM: visual explanations from deep networks via gradient-based localization. Int. J. Comput. Vis. **128**, 336–359 (2019)
19. Simonyan, K., Zisserman, A.: Very deep convolutional networks for large-scale image recognition. CoRR abs/1409.1556 (2015)

20. Zhang, Q., Wu, Y., Zhu, S.: Interpretable convolutional neural networks. In: 2018 IEEE/CVF Conference on Computer Vision and Pattern Recognition, pp. 8827–8836 (2018)
21. Zhitomirsky-Geffet, M., Erez, E.S., Bar-Ilan, J.: Toward multiviewpoint ontology construction by collaboration of non-experts and crowdsourcing: the case of the effect of diet on health. J. Assoc. Inf. Sci. Technol. **68**, 681–694 (2017)

# Few-shot Learning

# Leveraging the Feature Distribution in Transfer-Based Few-Shot Learning

Yuqing Hu[1,2]([⊠]) [iD], Vincent Gripon[1] [iD], and Stéphane Pateux[2] [iD]

[1] Electronics Department, IMT Atlantique, Brest, France
`yuqing.hu@imt-atlantique.fr`
[2] Orange Labs, Cesson-Sévigné, France

**Abstract.** Few-shot classification is a challenging problem due to the uncertainty caused by using few labelled samples. In the past few years, methods have been proposed to solve few-shot classification, among which transfer-based methods have consistently proved to achieve the best performance. Following this vein, in this paper we propose a novel transfer-based method that builds on two successive steps: 1) preprocessing the feature vectors so that they become closer to Gaussian-like distributions, and 2) leveraging this preprocessing using an optimal-transport inspired algorithm. Using standardized vision benchmarks, we prove the ability of the proposed methodology to achieve state-of-the-art accuracy with various datasets, backbone architectures and few-shot settings.

**Keywords:** Few-shot classification · Transfer learning · Semi-supervised learning

## 1 Introduction

Thanks to their outstanding performance, Deep Learning methods have been widely considered for vision tasks such as image classification and object detection. In order to reach top performance, these systems are typically trained using very large labelled datasets that are representative enough of the inputs to be processed afterwards.

However, in many applications, it is costly to acquire or to annotate data, resulting in the impossibility to create such large labelled datasets. In this context, it is challenging to optimize Deep Learning architectures considering the fact they typically are made of way more parameters than the dataset contains. This is the reason why in the past few years, few-shot learning (i.e. the problem of learning with few labelled examples) has become a trending research subject in the field. In more details, there are two settings that authors often consider: a) "inductive few-shot", where only a few labelled samples are available during training and prediction is performed on each test input independently, and b) "transductive few-shot", where prediction is performed on a batch of (non-labelled) test inputs, allowing to take into account their joint distribution.

Many works in the domain are built based on a "learning to learn" guidance, where the pipeline is to train an optimizer [8,18] with different tasks of limited

© Springer Nature Switzerland AG 2021
I. Farkaš et al. (Eds.): ICANN 2021, LNCS 12892, pp. 487–499, 2021.
https://doi.org/10.1007/978-3-030-86340-1_39

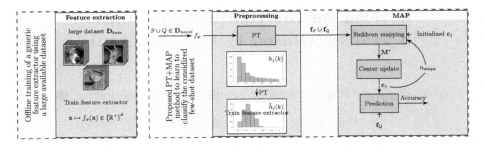

**Fig. 1.** Illustration of the proposed method. First we train a feature extractor $f_\varphi$ using $\mathbf{D}_{base}$ that has a large number of labelled data, then we extract feature vectors of all the inputs (support set $S$ and query set $Q$) in $\mathbf{D}_{novel}$ (the considered few-shot dataset) and preprocess them with Power Transform (PT), which has the effect of mapping a skewed feature distribution into a gaussian-like distribution ($h_j(k)$ denotes the histogram of feature $k$ in class $j$), to obtain the corresponding feature vectors $\mathbf{f}_S \cup \mathbf{f}_Q$. In the next step, we perform Sinkhorn mapping with class center $\mathbf{c}_j$ initialized on labelled feature vectors $\mathbf{f}_S$ to obtain the class allocation matrix $\mathbf{M}^*$ for unlabelled $\mathbf{f}_Q$, and we update the class centers for the next iteration. After $n_{steps}$ we evaluate the accuracy on $\mathbf{f}_Q$.

data so that the model is able to learn generic experience for novel tasks. Namely, the model learns a set of initialization parameters that are in an advantageous position for the model to adapt to a new (small) dataset. Recently, the trend evolved towards using well-thought-out transfer architectures (backbones) [3, 6, 17, 24] trained one time on the same training data, but seen as a unique large dataset.

A main problem of using feature vectors extracted using a backbone architecture is that their distribution is likely to be complex, as the problem the backbone has been optimized for most of the time differs from the considered task. As such, methods that rely on strong assumptions about the data distributions are likely to fail in leveraging the quality of features. In this paper, we tackle the problem of transfer-based few-shot learning with a twofold strategy: 1) preprocessing the data extracted from the backbone so that it fits a Gaussian-like distribution and 2) leveraging this specific distribution thanks to a well-thought proposed algorithm based on maximum a posteriori and optimal transport (only in the case of transductive few-shot). Using standardized benchmarks in the field, we demonstrate the ability of the proposed method to obtain state-of-the-art accuracy, for various problems and backbone architectures in some inductive settings and most transductive ones.

## 2   Related Work

A large volume of works in few-shot classification is based on meta learning [23] methods, where the training data is transformed into few-shot learning episodes to better fit in the context of few examples. In this branch, optimization based methods [8, 18, 23] train a well-initialized optimizer so that it quickly adapts to unseen classes with a few epochs of training. Other works [4,31] utilize data augmentation techniques to artificially increase the size of the training datasets.

In the past few years, there have been a growing interest in transfer-based methods. The main idea consists in training feature extractors able to efficiently segregate novel classes it never saw before. For example, in [3] the authors train the backbone with a distance-based classifier that takes into account the inter-class distance. In [17], the authors utilize self-supervised learning techniques [2] to co-train an extra rotation classifier for the output features. Many approaches are built on top of a feature extractor. For instance, in [29] the authors implement a nearest class mean classifier to associate an input with a class whose centroid is the closest in terms of the $\ell_2$ distance. In [14] an iterative approach is used to adjust the class centers. In [10] the authors build a graph neural network to gather the feature information from similar samples. Transfer-based techniques typically reach the best performance on standardized benchmarks.

Although many works involve feature extraction, few have explored the features in terms of their distribution. Often, assumptions are made that the features in a class align to a certain distribution, even though these assumptions are rarely experimentally discussed. In our work, we take into account the impact of the features distributions and how they can be transformed for better processing and accuracy. We also introduce a new algorithm to improve the quality of the association between input features and corresponding classes.

**Contributions.** Let us highlight the main contributions of this work. (1) We propose to preprocess the raw extracted features in order to make them more aligned with Gaussian assumptions. Namely we introduce transforms of the features so that they become less skewed. (2) We use a wasserstein-based method to better align the distribution of features with that of the considered classes. (3) We show that the proposed method can bring large increase in accuracy with a variety of feature extractors and datasets, leading to state-of-the-art results in the considered benchmarks.

# 3    Methodology

In this section we introduce the problem settings. We discuss the training of the feature extractors, the preprocessing steps that we apply on the trained features and the final classification algorithm. A summary of our proposed method is depicted in Fig. 1.

## 3.1    Problem Statement

We consider a typical few-shot learning problem. We are given a *base* dataset $\mathbf{D}_{base}$ and a *novel* dataset $\mathbf{D}_{novel}$ such that $\mathbf{D}_{base} \cap \mathbf{D}_{novel} = \emptyset$. $\mathbf{D}_{base}$ contains a large number of labelled examples from $K$ different classes. $\mathbf{D}_{novel}$, also referred to as a task in other works, contains a small number of labelled examples (support set $S$), along with some unlabelled ones (query set $Q$), all from $w$ *new* classes. Our goal is to predict the class of the unlabelled examples in the query set.

The following parameters are of particular importance to define such a few-shot problem: the number of classes in the novel dataset $w$ (called $w$-way), the number of labelled samples per class $s$ (called $s$-shot) and the number of unlabelled samples per class $q$. So the novel dataset contains a total of $w(s + q)$ samples, $ws$ of them being labelled, and $wq$ of them being those to classify. Note that here, as it is standard in the field, the query set is well balanced among classes. In the case of inductive few-shot, the prediction is performed independently on each one of the $wq$ samples. In the case of transductive few-shot [14,16], the prediction is performed considering all $wq$ samples together.

## 3.2   Feature Extraction

The first step is to train a neural network backbone model using only the base dataset. In this work we consider multiple backbones, with various training procedures. Once the considered backbone is trained, we obtain robust embeddings that should generalize well to novel classes. We denote by $f_\varphi$ the backbone function, obtained by extracting the output of the penultimate layer from the considered architecture, with $\varphi$ being the trained architecture parameters. Note that importantly, in all backbone architectures used in the experiments of this work, the penultimate layers are obtained by applying a ReLU function, so that all feature components coming out of $f_\varphi$ are nonnegative.

## 3.3   Feature Preprocessing

As mentioned in Sect. 2, many works hypothesize, explicitly or not, that the features from the same class are aligned with a specific distribution (often Gaussian-like). But this aspect is rarely experimentally verified. In fact, it is very likely that features obtained using the backbone architecture are not Gaussian. Indeed, usually the features are obtained after applying a relu function, and exhibit a positive distribution mostly concentrated around 0.

Multiple works in the domain [14,29] discuss the different statistical methods (e.g. normalization) to better fit the features into a model. Although these methods may have provable assets for some distributions, they could worsen the process if applied to an unexpected input distribution. This is why we propose to preprocess the obtained feature vectors so that they better align with typical distribution assumptions in the field. Namely, we use a power transform as follows.

**Power Transform (PT).** Denote $\mathbf{v} = f_\varphi(\mathbf{x}) \in (\mathbb{R}^+)^d, \mathbf{x} \in \mathbf{D}_{novel}$ as the obtained features on $\mathbf{D}_{novel}$. We hereby perform a power transformation method, which is similar to Tukey's Transformation Ladder [25], on the features. This process is then followed by a unit variance projection, the formula is given by:

$$f(\mathbf{v}) = \begin{cases} \frac{(\mathbf{v}+\epsilon)^\beta}{\|(\mathbf{v}+\epsilon)^\beta\|_2} & \text{if } \beta \neq 0 \\ \frac{\log(\mathbf{v}+\epsilon)}{\|\log(\mathbf{v}+\epsilon)\|_2} & \text{if } \beta = 0 \end{cases}, \tag{1}$$

where $\epsilon = 1e - 6$ is used to make sure that $\mathbf{v} + \epsilon$ is strictly positive and $\beta$ is a hyper-parameter. The rationales of the preprocessing above are: (1) Power transforms have the functionality of reducing the skew of a distribution, adjusted by $\beta$, (2) Unit variance projection scales the features to the same area so that large variance features do not predominate the others. This preprocessing step is often able to map data from any distribution to a close-to-Gaussian distribution.

Note that $\beta = 1$ leads to almost no effect. More generally, the skew of the obtained distribution changes when $\beta$ varies. For instance, if a raw distribution is right-skewed, decreasing $\beta$ phases out the right skew, and phases into a left-skewed distribution when $\beta$ becomes negative. After experiments, we found that $\beta = 0.5$ gives the most consistent results for our considered experiments. This first step of feature preprocessing can be performed in both inductive and transductive settings. We observed that it typically brings more benefits compared with other preprocessing methods such as batch normalisation. More details based on our considered experiments are available in Sect. 4.

### 3.4 MAP

Let us assume that the preprocessed feature distribution for each class is Gaussian or Gaussian-like. As such, a well-positioned class center is crucial to a good prediction. In this section we discuss how to best estimate the class centers when the number of samples is very limited and classes are only partially labelled. In more details, we propose an Expectation–Maximization [7]-like algorithm that iteratively finds the Maximum A Posteriori (MAP) estimates of the class centers.

We firstly show that estimating these centers through MAP is similar to the minimization of Wasserstein distance. Then, an iterative procedure based on a Wasserstein distance estimation, using the sinkhorn algorithm [5,11,26], is designed to estimate the optimal transport from the initial distribution of the feature vectors to one that would correspond to the draw of samples from Gaussian distributions. Note that here we consider the transductive setting, as in many other few shot learning works (e.g. [10,14–16]), where we exploit unlabelled samples during the procedure and priors about their relative proportions.

To better explain our proposed method, here we denote by $\mathbf{f}_S$ the set of feature vectors corresponding to labelled inputs and by $\mathbf{f}_Q$ the set of feature vectors corresponding to unlabelled inputs. For a feature vector $\mathbf{f} \in \mathbf{f}_S \cup \mathbf{f}_Q$, we denote by $\ell(\mathbf{f})$ the corresponding label. The set of admissible labellings will be denoted $\mathcal{C}$. We use $0 < i \leq wq$ to denote the index of an unlabelled sample, so that $\mathbf{f}_Q = (\mathbf{f}_i)_i$, and we denote $\mathbf{c}_j, 0 < j \leq w$ the estimated center for feature vectors that correspond to class $j$.

Our algorithm consists of several steps in which we estimate class centers from a soft allocation matrix $\mathbf{M}^*$, then we update the allocation matrix based on the newly found class centers and iterate the process. More details are provided in the following paragraphs to illustrate the algorithm.

**Sinkhorn Mapping.** Considering using MAP estimation for the class centers, and assuming a Gaussian distribution for each class, we typically aim at solving:

$$\begin{aligned}
\{\hat{l}(\mathbf{f}_i)\}, \{\hat{\mathbf{c}}_j\} &= \arg\max_{\{\ell(\mathbf{f}_i)\} \in \mathcal{C}, \{\mathbf{c}_j\}} \prod_i P(\mathbf{f}_i | j = \ell(\mathbf{f}_i)) \\
&= \arg\min_{\{\ell(\mathbf{f}_i)\} \in \mathcal{C}, \{\mathbf{c}_j\}} \sum_i (\mathbf{f}_i - \mathbf{c}_{\ell(\mathbf{f}_i)})^2,
\end{aligned} \tag{2}$$

Let us point out that the last term corresponds exactly to the Wasserstein distance used in the Optimal Transport problem formulation [5, 26].

Therefore, in this step we find the class mapping matrix that minimizes the Wasserstein distance. Inspired by the Sinkhorn algorithm [5, 26], we define the mapping matrix $\mathbf{M}^*$ as follows:

$$
\begin{aligned}
\mathbf{M}^* &= Sinkhorn(\mathbf{L}, \mathbf{p}, \mathbf{q}, \lambda) \\
&= \arg \min_{\mathbf{M} \in \mathbb{U}(\mathbf{p},\mathbf{q})} \sum_{ij} \mathbf{M}_{ij} \mathbf{L}_{ij} + \lambda H(\mathbf{M}),
\end{aligned}
\tag{3}
$$

where $\mathbb{U}(\mathbf{p}, \mathbf{q}) \in \mathbb{R}_+^{wq \times w}$ is a set of positive matrices for which the rows sum to $\mathbf{p}$ and the columns sum to $\mathbf{q}$. Formally, $\mathbb{U}(\mathbf{p}, \mathbf{q})$ can be written as: $\mathbb{U}(\mathbf{p}, \mathbf{q}) = \{\mathbf{M} \in \mathbb{R}_+^{wq \times w} | \mathbf{M}\mathbf{1}_w = \mathbf{p}, \mathbf{M}^T\mathbf{1}_{wq} = \mathbf{q}\}$, where $\mathbf{p}$ denotes the distribution of the amount that each unlabelled example uses for class allocation, and $\mathbf{q}$ denotes the distribution of the amount of unlabelled examples allocated to each class. Therefore, $\mathbb{U}(\mathbf{p}, \mathbf{q})$ contains all the possible ways of allocating examples to classes. The cost function $\mathbf{L} \in \mathbb{R}^{wq \times w}$ in Eq. (3) consists of the euclidean distances between unlabelled examples and class centers, hence $\mathbf{L}_{ij}$ denotes the euclidean distance between example $i$ and class center $j$. It is worth noting that here we assume a soft class mapping, meaning that each example can be "sliced" into different classes.

The second term on the right of Eq. (3) denotes the entropy of $\mathbf{M}$: $H(\mathbf{M}) = -\sum_{ij} \mathbf{M}_{ij} \log \mathbf{M}_{ij}$, regularized by a hyper-parameter $\lambda$. Increasing $\lambda$ would force the entropy to become smaller, so that the mapping is less homogeneous. This term also makes the objective function strictly convex [5] and thus a practical and effective computation. From lemma 2 in [5], the result of this Sinkhorn mapping has the typical form $\mathbf{M}^* = \text{diag}(\mathbf{u}) \cdot \exp(-\mathbf{L}/\lambda) \cdot \text{diag}(\mathbf{v})$.

**Iterative Center Estimation.** In this step, our aim is to estimate class centers. As shown in Algorithm 1, we initialize $\mathbf{c}_j$ as the average of labelled samples belonging to class $j$. Then $\mathbf{c}_j$ is iteratively re-estimated. At each iteration, we compute a mapping matrix $\mathbf{M}^*$ on the unlabelled examples using Sinkhorn mapping introduced in the previous step. Along with labelled examples, we re-estimate $\mathbf{c}_j$ (temporarily denoted $\boldsymbol{\mu}_j$) by weighted-averaging the feature vectors with their allocated portions for class $j$:

$$
\boldsymbol{\mu}_j = g(\mathbf{M}^*, j) = \frac{\sum_{i=1}^{wq} \mathbf{M}^*_{ij} \mathbf{f}_i + \sum_{\mathbf{f} \in \mathbf{f}_s, \ell(\mathbf{f})=j} \mathbf{f}}{s + \sum_{i=1}^{wq} \mathbf{M}^*_{ij}}.
\tag{4}
$$

This formula corresponds to the minimization of Eq. (3). Note that labelled examples do not participate in the mapping process. Since their labels are known, we instead set allocations for their belonging classes to be 1 and to the others to be 0. Therefore, labelled examples have the largest possible weight when re-estimating the class centers.

**Proportioned Center Update.** To avoid taking risky harsh decisions in early iterations of the algorithm, we propose to proportionate the update of class centers using an inertia parameter. More specifically, we update the center with

---

**Algorithm 1.** Proposed algorithm

---

   **Parameters:** $w, s, q, \lambda, \alpha, n_{steps}$
   **Initialization:** $\mathbf{c}_j = \frac{1}{s} \cdot \sum_{\mathbf{f} \in \mathbf{f}_S, \ell(\mathbf{f}) = j} \mathbf{f}$
   **for** $i = 1$ **to** $n_{steps}$ **do**
      $\mathbf{L}_{ij} = \|\mathbf{f}_i - \mathbf{c}_j\|^2, \forall i, j$
      $\mathbf{M}^* = Sinkhorn(\mathbf{L}, \mathbf{p} = \mathbf{1}_{wq}, \mathbf{q} = q\mathbf{1}_w, \lambda)$
      $\boldsymbol{\mu}_j = g(\mathbf{M}^*, j)$
      $\mathbf{c}_j \leftarrow \mathbf{c}_j + \alpha(\boldsymbol{\mu}_j - \mathbf{c}_j)$
   **end for**
   **return** $\hat{\ell}(\mathbf{f}_i) = \arg\max_j(\mathbf{M}^*[i, j])$

---

a learning rate $0 < \alpha \leq 1$. When $\alpha$ is close to 0, the update becomes very slow, whereas $\alpha = 1$ corresponds to directly allocating the newly found class centers:

$$\mathbf{c}_j \leftarrow \mathbf{c}_j + \alpha(\boldsymbol{\mu}_j - \mathbf{c}_j). \tag{5}$$

**Final Decision.** After a fixed number of steps $n_{steps}$, the rows of $\mathbf{M}^*$ are interpreted as the probabilities of examples belonging to each class. Therefore, the maximal value corresponds to the decision of the algorithm. A summary of our proposed algorithm is presented in Algorithm 1.

# 4 Experiments

## 4.1 Datasets

We evaluate the performance of the proposed method using standardized few-shot classification datasets: miniImageNet [27], tieredImageNet [19], CUB [28] and CIFAR-FS [1]. The **miniImageNet** dataset contains 100 classes randomly chosen from ILSVRC- 2012 [20] and 600 images of size $84 \times 84$ pixels per class. It is split into 64 base classes, 16 validation classes and 20 novel classes. The **tiered-ImageNet** dataset is another subset of ImageNet, it consists of 34 high-level categories with 608 classes in total. These categories are split into 20 meta-training superclasses, 6 meta-validation superclasses and 8 meta-test superclasses, which corresponds to 351 base classes, 97 validation classes and 160 novel classes respectively. The **CUB** dataset contains 200 classes and has 11,788 images of size $84 \times 84$ pixels in total, it is split into 100 base classes, 50 validation classes and 50 novel classes. The **CIFAR-FS** dataset has 100 classes, each class contains 600 images of size $32 \times 32$ pixels. The splits of this dataset are the same as those in miniImageNet.

## 4.2 Implementation Details

In order to stress the genericity of our proposed method with regards to the chosen backbone architecture and training strategy, we perform experiments using **WRN** [30], **ResNet18** and **ResNet12** [9], along with some other pretrained backbones (e.g. DenseNet [12, 29]). For each dataset we train the feature extractor with base classes, tune the hyperparameters with validation classes and test the performance using novel classes. Therefore, for each test run, $w$ classes are drawn uniformly at random among novel classes. Among these $w$ classes, $s$ labelled examples and $q$ unlabelled examples per class are uniformly drawn at random to form $\mathbf{D}_{novel}$. The WRN and ResNet are trained following [17]. In the inductive setting, MAP is not suitable since there is only one unlabelled sample, therefore we use our proposed Power Transform followed by a basic Nearest Class Mean (NCM) classifier. In the transductive setting, the MAP or an alternative is applied after PT. In order to better segregate between feature vectors of corresponding classes for each task, we implement the "trans-mean-sub" [14] before MAP where we separately subtract inputs by the means of labelled and unlabelled examples, followed by a unit hypersphere projection. All our experiments are performed using $w = 5, q = 15, s = 1$ or 5. We run 10,000 random draws to obtain mean accuracy score and indicate confidence scores (95%) when relevant. The tuned hyperparameters for miniImageNet are $\beta = 0.5, \lambda = 10, \alpha = 0.4$ and $n_{steps} = 30$ for $s = 1$; $\beta = 0.5, \lambda = 10, \alpha = 0.2$ and $n_{steps} = 20$ for $s = 5$. Hyperparameters for other datasets are detailed below.

### 4.3   Comparison with State-of-the-Art Methods

In the first experiment, we conduct our proposed method on different benchmarks and compare the performance with other state-of-the-art solutions. The results are presented in Table 1, we observe that our method with WRN as backbone reaches the state-of-the-art performance for most cases in both inductive and transductive settings on all the benchmarks. In Table 2 we also implement our proposed method on tieredImageNet based on a pre-trained DenseNet121 backbone following the procedure described in [29]. From these experiments we conclude that the proposed method can bring gain with a variety of backbones and datasets, leading to competitive performance. In terms of execution time, we measured an average of $0.002s$ per run, which is relatively efficient.

### 4.4   Other Experiments

**Ablation Study.** To further stress the interest of the ingredients on the proposed method in order to reach top performance, we report in Tables 3 and 4 the results of ablation studies. In Table 3, we first investigate the impact of changing the backbone architecture. Together with previous experiments, we observe that the proposed method consistently achieves the best results for any fixed backbone architecture. We also report performance in the case of inductive few-shot using a simple Nearest-Class Mean (NCM) classifier instead of the iterative MAP procedure described in Sect. 3. We perform another experiment where we replace the MAP algorithm with a standard K-Means algorithm where centroids are initialized with the available labelled samples for each class. We can observe significant drops in accuracy, emphasizing the interest of the proposed MAP procedure to better estimate the class centers.

**Table 1.** 1-shot and 5-shot accuracy of state-of-the-art methods in the literature, compared with the proposed solution. We present results using WRN as the backbone for our proposed solutions.

| Setting | Method | Backbone | miniImageNet | |
|---|---|---|---|---|
| | | | 1-shot | 5-shot |
| Inductive | Baseline++ [3] | ResNet18 | $51.87 \pm 0.77\%$ | $75.68 \pm 0.63\%$ |
| | MAML [8] | ResNet18 | $49.61 \pm 0.92\%$ | $65.72 \pm 0.77\%$ |
| | ProtoNet [22] | WRN | $62.60 \pm 0.20\%$ | $79.97 \pm 0.14\%$ |
| | Matching Networks [27] | WRN | $64.03 \pm 0.20\%$ | $76.32 \pm 0.16\%$ |
| | SimpleShot [29] | DenseNet121 | $64.29 \pm 0.20\%$ | $81.50 \pm 0.14\%$ |
| | S2M2_R [17] | WRN | $64.93 \pm 0.18\%$ | $83.18 \pm 0.11\%$ |
| | PT+NCM(ours) | WRN | $\mathbf{65.35 \pm 0.20\%}$ | $\mathbf{83.87 \pm 0.13\%}$ |
| Transductive | BD-CSPN [15] | WRN | $70.31 \pm 0.93\%$ | $81.89 \pm 0.60\%$ |
| | Transfer+SGC [10] | WRN | $76.47 \pm 0.23\%$ | $85.23 \pm 0.13\%$ |
| | TAFSSL [14] | DenseNet121 | $77.06 \pm 0.26\%$ | $84.99 \pm 0.14\%$ |
| | DFMN-MCT [13] | ResNet12 | $78.55 \pm 0.86\%$ | $86.03 \pm 0.42\%$ |
| | PT+MAP(ours) | WRN | $\mathbf{82.92 \pm 0.26\%}$ | $\mathbf{88.82 \pm 0.13\%}$ |

| Setting | Method | Backbone | CUB | |
|---|---|---|---|---|
| | | | 1-shot | 5-shot |
| Inductive | Baseline++ [3] | ResNet10 | $69.55 \pm 0.89\%$ | $85.17 \pm 0.50\%$ |
| | MAML [8] | ResNet10 | $70.32 \pm 0.99\%$ | $80.93 \pm 0.71\%$ |
| | ProtoNet [22] | ResNet18 | $72.99 \pm 0.88\%$ | $86.64 \pm 0.51\%$ |
| | Matching Networks [27] | ResNet18 | $73.49 \pm 0.89\%$ | $84.45 \pm 0.58\%$ |
| | S2M2_R [17] | WRN | $\mathbf{80.68 \pm 0.81\%}$ | $90.85 \pm 0.44\%$ |
| | PT+NCM(ours) | WRN | $80.57 \pm 0.20\%$ | $\mathbf{91.15 \pm 0.10\%}$ |
| Transductive | BD-CSPN [15] | WRN | $87.45\%$ | $91.74\%$ |
| | Transfer+SGC [10] | WRN | $88.35 \pm 0.19\%$ | $92.14 \pm 0.10\%$ |
| | PT+MAP(ours) | WRN | $\mathbf{91.55 \pm 0.19\%}$ | $\mathbf{93.99 \pm 0.10\%}$ |

| Setting | Method | Backbone | CIFAR-FS | |
|---|---|---|---|---|
| | | | 1-shot | 5-shot |
| Inductive | ProtoNet [22] | ConvNet64 | $55.50 \pm 0.70\%$ | $72.00 \pm 0.60\%$ |
| | MAML [8] | ConvNet32 | $58.90 \pm 1.90\%$ | $71.50 \pm 1.00\%$ |
| | S2M2_R [17] | WRN | $\mathbf{74.81 \pm 0.19\%}$ | $87.47 \pm 0.13\%$ |
| | PT+NCM(ours) | WRN | $74.64 \pm 0.21\%$ | $\mathbf{87.64 \pm 0.15\%}$ |
| Transductive | Transfer+SGC [10] | WRN | $83.90 \pm 0.22\%$ | $88.76 \pm 0.15\%$ |
| | PT+MAP(ours) | WRN | $\mathbf{87.69 \pm 0.23\%}$ | $\mathbf{90.68 \pm 0.15\%}$ |

**Table 2.** 1-shot and 5-shot accuracy of state-of-the-art methods on tieredImageNet.

| Method | Backbone | tieredImageNet | |
|---|---|---|---|
| | | 1-shot | 5-shot |
| ProtoNet [22][a] | ConvNet4 | $53.31 \pm 0.89\%$ | $72.69 \pm 0.74\%$ |
| LEO [21][a] | WRN | $66.33 \pm 0.05\%$ | $81.44 \pm 0.09\%$ |
| SimpleShot [29][a] | DenseNet121 | $\mathbf{71.32 \pm 0.22\%}$ | $\mathbf{86.66 \pm 0.15\%}$ |
| PT+NCM(ours)[a] | DenseNet121 | $69.96 \pm 0.22\%$ | $86.45 \pm 0.15\%$ |
| DFMN-MCT [13][b] | ResNet12 | $80.89 \pm 0.84\%$ | $87.30 \pm 0.49\%$ |
| TAFSSL [14][b] | DenseNet121 | $84.29 \pm 0.25\%$ | $89.31 \pm 0.15\%$ |
| PT+MAP(ours)[b] | DenseNet121 | $\mathbf{85.67 \pm 0.26\%}$ | $\mathbf{90.45 \pm 0.14\%}$ |

[a]: Inductive setting.
[b]: Transductive setting.

**Table 3.** Accuracy of the proposed method in inductive and transductive settings, with different backbones, and comparison with K-Means and NCM baselines.

| Setting | | Inductive | | Transductive | | | |
|---|---|---|---|---|---|---|---|
| Dataset | Backbone | (NCM baseline) Proposed PT+NCM | | PT+K-Means | | Proposed PT+MAP | |
| | | 1-shot | 5-shot | 1-shot | 5-shot | 1-shot | 5-shot |
| miniImageNet | ResNet12 | (49.08) $62.68 \pm 0.20\%$ | (70.85) $81.99 \pm 0.14\%$ | $72.73 \pm 0.23\%$ | $84.05 \pm 0.14\%$ | $78.47 \pm 0.28\%$ | $85.84 \pm 0.15\%$ |
| | ResNet18 | (47.63) $62.50 \pm 0.20\%$ | (72.89) $82.17 \pm 0.14\%$ | $73.08 \pm 0.22\%$ | $84.67 \pm 0.14\%$ | $80.00 \pm 0.27\%$ | $86.96 \pm 0.14\%$ |
| | WRN | (55.31) $\mathbf{65.35 \pm 0.20\%}$ | (78.33) $\mathbf{83.87 \pm 0.13\%}$ | $76.67 \pm 0.22\%$ | $\mathbf{86.73 \pm 0.13\%}$ | $82.92 \pm 0.26\%$ | $\mathbf{88.82 \pm 0.13\%}$ |
| CUB | ResNet12 | (61.30) $78.40 \pm 0.20\%$ | (82.83) $91.12 \pm 0.10\%$ | $87.35 \pm 0.19\%$ | $92.31 \pm 0.10\%$ | $90.96 \pm 0.20\%$ | $93.77 \pm 0.09\%$ |
| | ResNet18 | (58.92) $76.98 \pm 0.20\%$ | (82.69) $90.56 \pm 0.10\%$ | $87.16 \pm 0.19\%$ | $91.97 \pm 0.09\%$ | $91.10 \pm 0.20\%$ | $93.78 \pm 0.09\%$ |
| | WRN | (69.21) $\mathbf{80.57 \pm 0.20\%}$ | (88.33) $\mathbf{91.15 \pm 0.10\%}$ | $88.28 \pm 0.19\%$ | $\mathbf{92.37 \pm 0.10\%}$ | $91.55 \pm 0.19\%$ | $\mathbf{93.99 \pm 0.10\%}$ |
| CIFAR-FS | ResNet12 | (52.50) $71.02 \pm 0.22\%$ | (74.16) $84.68 \pm 0.16\%$ | $78.39 \pm 0.24\%$ | $85.73 \pm 0.16\%$ | $82.45 \pm 0.27\%$ | $87.33 \pm 0.17\%$ |
| | ResNet18 | (56.40) $71.41 \pm 0.22\%$ | (78.30) $85.50 \pm 0.15\%$ | $79.95 \pm 0.23\%$ | $86.74 \pm 0.16\%$ | $84.80 \pm 0.25\%$ | $88.55 \pm 0.16\%$ |
| | WRN | (68.93) $\mathbf{74.64 \pm 0.21\%}$ | (86.81) $\mathbf{87.64 \pm 0.15\%}$ | $83.69 \pm 0.22\%$ | $\mathbf{89.19 \pm 0.15\%}$ | $87.69 \pm 0.23\%$ | $\mathbf{90.68 \pm 0.15\%}$ |

In Table 4 we show the impact of PT in the transductive setting, where we can see about 6% gain for 1-shot and 4% gain for 5-shot in terms of accuracy.

**Influence of the Number of Unlabelled Samples.** To better understand the gain in accuracy with access to more unlabelled samples, we depict in Fig. 2 (1) the evolution of accuracy as a function of $q$, when $w = 5$ is fixed. Interestingly, the accuracy quickly reaches a close-to-asymptotical plateau, emphasizing the ability of the method to soon exploit available information in the task.

**Hyperparameter Tuning.** We also tune $\beta$, $\lambda$ and $\alpha$ on the validation classes of each dataset, and then apply them to test our model on novel classes. We vary each hyperparamter in a certain range and observe the evolution of accuracy to choose the peak that corresponds to the highest prediction. For example, the evolving curve for $\beta$, $\lambda$ and $\alpha$ with miniImageNet are presented in Fig. 2 (2) to (4). In comparison, we also trace the corresponding curves on novel classes. We draw a dash line on the hyperparameter values where the accuracy on the validation classes peaks, meaning that this is the chosen value resulting in Table 1. Overall, it is interesting to point out the little sensitivity of the proposed method accuracy with regards to hyperparameter tuning.

We followed this procedure to find the tuned hyperparameters for each dataset. Therefore, we obtained that working with CUB leads to the same hyperparameters as miniImageNet. For tieredImageNet and CIFAR-FS, the best accuracy are obtained on validation classes when $\beta = 0.5, \lambda = 10, \alpha = 0.3$ for $s = 1$; $\beta = 0.5, \lambda = 10, \alpha = 0.2$ for $s = 5$.

**Table 4.** Influence of Power Transform in the transductive setting with different backbones on miniImageNet.

| PT | MAP | WRN | | ResNet18 | | ResNet12 | |
|---|---|---|---|---|---|---|---|
| | | 1-shot | 5-shot | 1-shot | 5-shot | 1-shot | 5-shot |
| | ✓ | $75.60 \pm 0.29\%$ | $84.13 \pm 0.16\%$ | $74.48 \pm 0.29\%$ | $82.88 \pm 0.17\%$ | $72.04 \pm 0.30\%$ | $80.98 \pm 0.18\%$ |
| ✓ | ✓ | $\mathbf{82.92 \pm 0.26\%}$ | $\mathbf{88.82 \pm 0.13\%}$ | $\mathbf{80.00 \pm 0.27\%}$ | $\mathbf{86.96 \pm 0.14\%}$ | $\mathbf{78.47 \pm 0.28\%}$ | $\mathbf{85.84 \pm 0.15\%}$ |

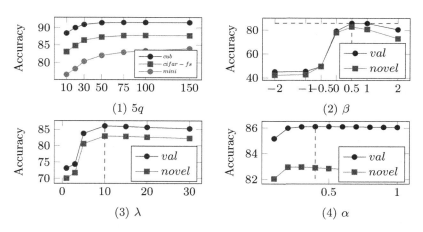

**Fig. 2.** (1) represents 5-way 1-shot accuracy on miniImagenet, CUB and CIFAR-FS (backbone: WRN) as a function of $q$. (2), (3) and (4) represent 1-shot accuracy on miniImageNet (backbone: WRN) as a function of $\beta, \lambda$ and $\alpha$ respectively.

## 5   Conclusion

In this paper we introduced a new pipeline to solve the few-shot classification problem. Namely, we proposed to firstly preprocess the raw feature vectors to better align to a Gaussian distribution and then we designed an optimal-transport inspired iterative algorithm to estimate the class centers. Our experimental results on standard vision benchmarks reach state-of-the-art accuracy, with important gains in both 1-shot and 5-shot classification. Moreover, the proposed method can bring gains with a variety of feature extractors, with few hyperparameters. Thus we believe that the proposed method is applicable to many practical problems.

# References

1. Bertinetto, L., Henriques, J.F., Torr, P.H., Vedaldi, A.: Meta-learning with differentiable closed-form solvers. arXiv preprint arXiv:1805.08136 (2018)
2. Chapelle, O., Scholkopf, B., Zien, A.: Semi-supervised learning. IEEE Trans. Neural Netw. **20**(3), 542–542 (2009)
3. Chen, W.Y., Liu, Y.C., Kira, Z., Wang, Y.C.F., Huang, J.B.: A closer look at few-shot classification (2019)
4. Chen, Z., Fu, Y., Wang, Y.X., Ma, L., Liu, W., Hebert, M.: Image deformation meta-networks for one-shot learning. In: Proceedings of the IEEE Conference on Computer Vision and Pattern Recognition, pp. 8680–8689 (2019)
5. Cuturi, M.: Sinkhorn distances: lightspeed computation of optimal transport. In: Advances in Neural Information Processing Systems, pp. 2292–2300 (2013)
6. Das, D., Lee, C.G.: A two-stage approach to few-shot learning for image recognition. IEEE Trans. Image Process. **29**, 3336–3350 (2019)
7. Dempster, A.P., Laird, N.M., Rubin, D.B.: Maximum likelihood from incomplete data via the EM algorithm. J. Roy. Stat. Soc.: Ser. B (Methodol.) **39**(1), 1–22 (1977)
8. Finn, C., Abbeel, P., Levine, S.: Model-agnostic meta-learning for fast adaptation of deep networks. In: Proceedings of the 34th International Conference on Machine Learning, vol. 70, pp. 1126–1135. JMLR.org (2017)
9. He, K., Zhang, X., Ren, S., Sun, J.: Deep residual learning for image recognition. In: IEEE Conference on Computer Vision and Pattern Recognition, pp. 770–778 (2016)
10. Hu, Y., Gripon, V., Pateux, S.: Exploiting unsupervised inputs for accurate few-shot classification. arXiv preprint arXiv:2001.09849 (2020)
11. Huang, G., Larochelle, H., Lacoste-Julien, S.: Are few-shot learning benchmarks too simple? arXiv preprint arXiv:1902.08605 (2019)
12. Huang, G., Liu, Z., Van Der Maaten, L., Weinberger, K.Q.: Densely connected convolutional networks. In: Proceedings of the IEEE Conference on Computer Vision and Pattern Recognition, pp. 4700–4708 (2017)
13. Kye, S.M., Lee, H.B., Kim, H., Hwang, S.J.: Transductive few-shot learning with meta-learned confidence. arXiv preprint arXiv:2002.12017 (2020)
14. Lichtenstein, M., Sattigeri, P., Feris, R., Giryes, R., Karlinsky, L.: Tafssl: task-adaptive feature sub-space learning for few-shot classification. arXiv preprint arXiv:2003.06670 (2020)
15. Liu, J., Song, L., Qin, Y.: Prototype rectification for few-shot learning. arXiv preprint arXiv:1911.10713 (2019)
16. Liu, Y., et al.: Learning to propagate labels: transductive propagation network for few-shot learning. arXiv preprint arXiv:1805.10002 (2018)
17. Mangla, P., Kumari, N., Sinha, A., Singh, M., Krishnamurthy, B., Balasubramanian, V.N.: Charting the right manifold: manifold mixup for few-shot learning. In: The IEEE Winter Conference on Applications of Computer Vision, pp. 2218–2227 (2020)
18. Ravi, S., Larochelle, H.: Optimization as a model for few-shot learning (2016)
19. Ren, M., et al.: Meta-learning for semi-supervised few-shot classification. arXiv preprint arXiv:1803.00676 (2018)
20. Russakovsky, O., et al.: Imagenet large scale visual recognition challenge. Int. J. Comput. Vision **115**(3), 211–252 (2015)

21. Rusu, A.A., et al.: Meta-learning with latent embedding optimization. arXiv preprint arXiv:1807.05960 (2018)
22. Snell, J., Swersky, K., Zemel, R.: Prototypical networks for few-shot learning. In: Advances in Neural Information Processing Systems, pp. 4077–4087 (2017)
23. Thrun, S., Pratt, L.: Learning to Learn. Springer, Boston (2012). https://doi.org/10.1007/978-1-4615-5529-2
24. Torrey, L., Shavlik, J.: Transfer learning. In: Handbook of Research on Machine Learning Applications and Trends: Algorithms, Methods, and Techniques, pp. 242–264. IGI Global (2010)
25. Tukey, J.W.: Exploratory Data Analysis, vol. 2. Addison-Wesley, Reading (1977)
26. Villani, C.: Optimal Transport: Old and New, vol. 338. Springer, Heidelberg (2008). https://doi.org/10.1007/978-3-540-71050-9
27. Vinyals, O., Blundell, C., Lillicrap, T., Wierstra, D., et al.: Matching networks for one shot learning. In: Advances in Neural Information Processing Systems, pp. 3630–3638 (2016)
28. Wah, C., Branson, S., Welinder, P., Perona, P., Belongie, S.: The caltech-ucsd birds-200-2011 dataset (2011)
29. Wang, Y., Chao, W.L., Weinberger, K.Q., van der Maaten, L.: Simpleshot: revisiting nearest-neighbor classification for few-shot learning. arXiv preprint arXiv:1911.04623 (2019)
30. Zagoruyko, S., Komodakis, N.: Wide residual networks. arXiv preprint arXiv:1605.07146 (2016)
31. Zhang, H., Zhang, J., Koniusz, P.: Few-shot learning via saliency-guided hallucination of samples. In: Proceedings of the IEEE Conference on Computer Vision and Pattern Recognition, pp. 2770–2779 (2019)

# One-Shot Meta-learning for Radar-Based Gesture Sequences Recognition

Gianfranco Mauro[1,2(✉)], Mateusz Chmurski[1,4], Muhammad Arsalan[1,3],
Mariusz Zubert[4], and Vadim Issakov[1,3]

[1] Infineon Technologies AG, Neubiberg, Germany
gianfranco.mauro@infineon.com
[2] Universidad de Granada, Granada, Spain
[3] Technische Universität Braunschweig, Braunschweig, Germany
[4] Lodz University of Technology, Lodz, Poland

**Abstract.** Radar-based gesture recognition constitutes an intuitive way
for enhancing human-computer interaction (HCI). However, training algorithms for HCI capable of adapting to gesture recognition often require a
large dataset with many task examples. In this work, we propose for the
first time on radar sensed hand-poses, the use of optimization-based meta-
techniques applied on a convolutional neural network (CNN) to distinguish 16 gesture sequences with only one sample per class (shot) in 2-ways,
4-ways and 5-ways experiments. We make use of a frequency-modulated
continuous-wave (FMCW) 60 GHz radar to capture the sequences of four
basic hand gestures, which are processed and stacked in the form of temporal projections of the radar range information (Range-Time Map - RTM).
The experimental results demonstrate how the use of optimization-based
meta-techniques leads to an accuracy greater than 94% in a 5-ways 1-shot
classification problem, even on sequences containing a type of basic gesture
never observed in the training phase. Additionally, thanks to the generalization capabilities of the proposed approach, the required training time
on new sequences is reduced by a factor of 8,000 in comparison to a typical
deep CNN.

**Keywords:** Gesture recognition · Meta learning · Millimeter wave radar

## 1 Introduction

Gesture sensing technology represents a very direct and intuitive method of
human-computer interaction (HCI). Under the needs of users and system interface architectures, hand movements can be identified and tracked through the
use of a wide variety of sensors and detection algorithms [21]. Conventional methods for the classification of gestures involve the employment of camera sensors
for optical images or time of flight (ToF) images for depth information. These
sensors allow a complete and touchless understanding of the performed gestures,
but they usually lead to privacy issues and poor performance in the presence of

© Springer Nature Switzerland AG 2021
I. Farkaš et al. (Eds.): ICANN 2021, LNCS 12892, pp. 500–511, 2021.
https://doi.org/10.1007/978-3-030-86340-1_40

intense light [10,17,18]. In contrast, Radio-based sensing can be efficiently used to estimate movements and poses of subjects even through walls and obstructions [14]. Through Wi-Fi technology, the hand-pose estimation can be addressed with very high performance even in a cross-domain application, where the user's location, orientation, and environment can vary considerably [23]. However, Wi-Fi-based sensing systems require often to develop high output power in the RF range and a module in continuous working operation to exploit the functionalities. To overcome these challenges, the use of radar sensors for this application is becoming a widely adopted practice [2]. Among the various radar modulation techniques, FMCW is a particularly suitable approach, thanks to its capability of providing simultaneously accurate range and Doppler information of objects and people located in the field of view [8,11,19,22]. Excellent results in the classification of gestures through range-Doppler images are achieved in [12], using the *BGT60TR13C* FMCW radar sensor [20]. The authors in [12] use the domain adaption applied to a CNN to minimize the differences among users' gestures in both learning and application stages. Through this approach, an average accuracy of 98.8% is achieved on seven gestures performed by ten different users. Even though the state-of-the-art deep learning methods like [12] achieve excellent accuracy and robustness on radar-based gestures recognition, they demand a large amount of data to successfully train the detection algorithms [15]. This suggests that an interface based on such systems, would not be able to learn promptly how to distinguish new types of movements.

In contrast to the conventional deep learning approach, the meta-learning (Meta-L) is designed to counter the problem of huge data demand. It is based on multiple-episode few-shot optimization (tasks), which considers different learning objectives in many training steps, to extract general information from available data and efficiently solve series of problems by learning how to learn [7,9]. The class of optimization-based Meta-L algorithms exploits the model's parameters and gradient propagation among several tasks (meta-iterations) to accomplish the generalization goal. In the inner loop of each meta-iteration, a model tries to solve an $N$-ways task, where $N$ is the number of classes, that are randomly sampled from a training set of data. An example (1-shot) called *support* is then sampled for each class and used for the training. Some algorithms such as Model Agnostic Meta-Learning (MAML) [6], require additional examples per class called *query* for the evaluation of inter-tasks generalization performance after every meta-iteration.

In this paper, we suggest for the first time, the application of optimization-based meta-learning techniques to classify sequences of hand gestures using only one sample per class. We make use of the radar range information only, in the form of RTMs of four different basic gestures, to minimize preprocessing and the CNN input data complexity. We evaluate the models with a common in-training procedure (Fig. 1) and test them on a sufficient number of new tasks to prove the robustness of the approach. With the use of only one sequence of gestures instance and over 50 test examples per class, we achieve an accuracy of 94% even in the 5-ways experiments. Finally, we compare the performance results of the Meta-L approach with the ones of a conventional CNN trained on a configuration of

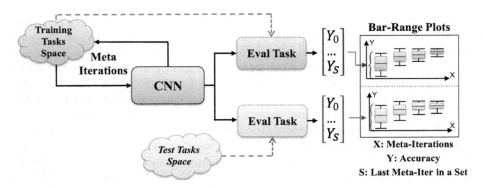

**Fig. 1.** The in-training evaluation of the meta-model is performed after each meta-iteration (adaptation of the CNN to the new extracted information) on both a train and a test sampled tasks. Network generalization capability is assessed through bar plots built on batches of tasks as the meta-iterations progress.

gesture sequences. We report how the potential offline adaptation to new gesture sequences with the Meta-L model leads, in comparison with the traditional CNN, to an average training time reduction of 4 orders of magnitude.

## 2    FMCW Radar Processing

### 2.1    Radar Sensor

To capture gestures, we use the *BGT60TR13C* FMCW radar sensor [20]. The *BGT60TR13C* is equipped with one transmit (TX) and three receive (RX) channels including antennas integrated in package. During operations, the instantaneous local oscillator and reflected signals from targets are mixed and provide a resulting signal called intermediate frequency (IF) signal. As an outcome of its system power mode management and operation optimized duty-cycle, the device can run at less than 5 mW for a detection range up to 5 m in smart presence detection uses. Thanks to the center frequency of 60 GHz and a bandwidth of 7 GHz, this radar sensor enables a very high range resolution sensing ($\approx$2 cm). Moreover, time and micro-Doppler [4] analysis of the IF signal enable the discrimination of elaborate hand gestures with millimeter accuracy. The *BGT60TR13C* represents hence, a low-power and small-size solution for short-range sensing applications.

### 2.2    Time-Range Preprocessing

The data is gathered with the 60 GHz radar and then processed. It consists of RTM of four basic gestures [Down/Up, Left/Right, Rubbing, Up/Down] with a shape of $62 \times 32$ pixels per sample. We used a single RX antenna and extracted only the range information to reduce the power consumption and to simplify the preprocessing pipeline. To obtain the representative RTMs of the gestures starting from the IF signal, we performed the following preprocessing steps. First of all, we subtracted the mean chirp value from every data frame (set of chirps). In the next step, to resolve targets over the range, we computed the first order Fast Fourier Transform (FFT) in the fast time direction. Then, to derive the Doppler information, we performed the second-order FFT in the slow time direction.

The steps mentioned above allowed us to generate the sequence of the range-Doppler images (RDI) for every gesture. RDIs were then employed to produce the range-time images. The procedure of obtaining the range-time image is as follows:

1. identify the point with the highest intensity in the RDI;
2. cut the row in which the point with the highest intensity is localized. This row corresponds to the distance of the object from the radar in the given time step;
3. transpose each row and stack them together to form the range-time image.

The adopted preprocessing procedure in its steps is shown graphically in Fig. 2.

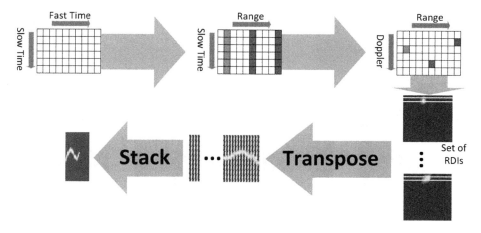

**Fig. 2.** The Range Doppler images (RDI) are obtained through radar frames (IF signal) preprocessing. The lines of the RDIs with the greatest intensity are then transposed and stacked in time sequence, to obtain the RTMs.

To ensure a high level of variance of the dataset, the gestures were performed by five different persons and collected in multiple environments. The experimental setup and the employed sensor ($BGT60TR13C$) are shown in Fig. 3.

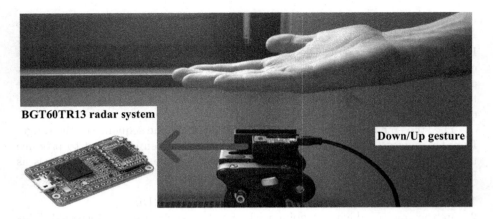

**Fig. 3.** Experimental Setup (Down/Up gesture) and *BGT60TR13C*.

Each gesture was recorded independently, in a timeslot of 3.1 s. To diversify the gesture occurrence within the recording window, a random shift in time and range was also applied to every RTM. An example of RTM for each of the four basic gestures is shown in Fig. 4. Single gestures were then stacked in channels to make sequences of two and used to generate the meta-dataset for our experiments (Sect. 3.2).

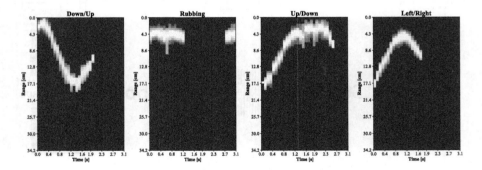

**Fig. 4.** Examples of generated RTMs corresponding to the four gestures.

# 3    Meta-learning Based Network

## 3.1    Models and Training Procedure

As mentioned previously, we propose using an optimization-based meta-approach applied on a CNN topology, to recognize hand gesture sequences with only one sample per class in the 1-shot 2-ways, 1-shot 4-ways and 1-shot 5-ways experiments. For all the experiments, we used a CNN topology with four convolution layers of 128 filters each, for the extraction of the visual features, a kernel size $3 \times 3$ and a stride of size 2. All convolutional layers are followed by BatchNormalization, to speed up the deep network training, and by rectified linear unit (ReLu) activation function. The classification is then performed by a fully connected layer with a Softmax activation function. The chosen cost function is Sparse Categorical Crossentropy while the optimizer is Adam. For each set of experiments, belonging to a defined number of ways, we employed three traditional optimization-based meta algorithms: Reptile [16], MAML second-order [6] and MAML first-order approximation. Additionally, we adopted a version of the second-order MAML algorithm that uses Multi-Step Loss Optimization (MSL), Derivative-Order Annealing (DA) and Cosine Annealing (CA) to stabilize inter-tasks training, as defined by the authors in [3]. The evaluation of the models is done after each meta-iteration, on a task sampled from the training set and another one sampled from a set of classes never seen by the model (test). For each $S$ number of meta-iterations, a box-plot is built on the distribution of the obtained accuracy values. The trend of inter-tasks accuracy values in the form of box plots for sets of meta-iterations facilitates estimating the in-training learning capability of the algorithm. The employed in-training evaluation procedure is shown as part of the meta-approach schema in Fig. 1.

### 3.2 Meta-dataset and Tasks Definition

Starting from the dataset $D$, containing the gathered data of the four basic gestures [Down/Up, Left/Right, Rubbing, Up/Down] (Sect. 2), we generated a meta dataset $D^m$ with 16 classes, i.e. all the possible combinations of the four initial classes. $D^m$ consists of 51 samples per class, where every instance is a sequence of two RTMs that are randomly sampled from $D$, augmented and then stacked in the $3^{rd}$ dimension (channels). $D^m$ is then split into two sub-datasets, $D^{m\text{-train}}$ and $D^{m\text{-test}}$. All the examples of the 7 classes that contain the basic 'Left/Right' move are included in $D^{m\text{-test}}$ so that they never appear in the training phase and therefore can be used to test the algorithm on never seen before gestures. $D^{m\text{-train}}$ contains instead all data belonging to the other 9 classes, which correspond to all the combinations of the other three basic gestures. An example of possible training and test tasks in the 1-shot 2-ways experiments, sampled respectively from $D^{m\text{-train}}$ and $D^{m\text{-test}}$, is shown in Fig. 5.

## 4     Experimental Results

### 4.1 Models Performance

For each task in every experiment, the convolutional networks were trained for 4 epochs with inner-loop batches of size 2. The best performance results were obtained with a meta-batch of size 1 in the outer loops (inter-tasks training).

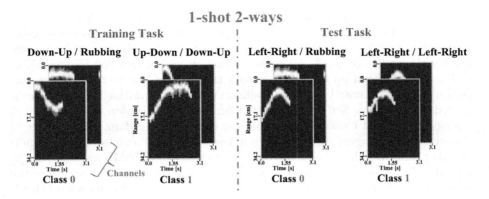

**Fig. 5.** 1-shot 2-ways meta-experiments. Training and test tasks examples.

An internal learning rate in the range $[5 - 10]e^{-4}$ and an external one of $1e^{-4}$ were adopted for all MAML experiments. For the MAML version that uses cosine annealing (CA), an initial outer learning rate of $2.5e^{-4}$ with a decay step every $1/4$ of the total meta iterations was used. For all the Reptile simulations instead, an internal learning rate of $1e^{-3}$ and a meta step-size for the outer loop of 0.25 have been employed. All hyperparameters, except for the outer learning rate in MAML + CA + MSL + DA, were kept constant throughout the entire meta-training procedure. The chosen number of meta-iterations was respectively 100 for the 2-way experiments, 3,000 for the 4-ways, and 10,000 for the 5-ways. Only the Reptile algorithm required 15,000 meta-iterations in the 5-way configuration to achieve a stationary inter-tasks accuracy. The inter-task generalization capacity during training was evaluated at the end of each meta-iteration following the procedure described in Sect. 3.1. All experiments were performed using a Tesla P4 GPU [1,5] and the performance of the models in terms of inter-task generalization was evaluated as the average percentage classification accuracy. All experiments were reproduced 3 times each.

Table 1 and Table 2 present respectively, the inter-task percentage median accuracy and interquartile range (IQR) values achieved with all the combinations of employed algorithms and chosen number of ways. The listed values in all the tables represent the mean values obtained over all the reproductions of each experiment for the first and last meta-tasks batches.

Figure 6 shows the accuracy trend over meta-iterations as a sequence of box plots of 1,000 samples each, for the MAML + CA + MSL + DA 1-shot 5-ways experiment. The evaluation done on the training tasks is shown in red in the upper subplot of Fig. 6, while the evaluation on test tasks is shown in blue in the bottom subplot. The lighter colored lines in the box plots represent the median value of the accuracy ($50^{\text{th}}$ percentile) in the set of meta-iterations, while the green triangles indicate the average value.

**MAML+CA+MSL+DA Seq. of 2 Gestures (Channels) - Box Plots**

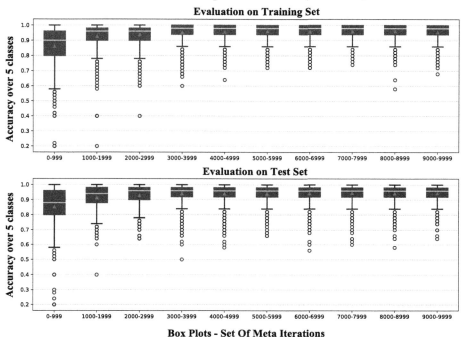

**Fig. 6.** In-training evaluation of the inter-task generalization capacity for MAML + CA + MSL + DA in the 5-ways experiment. Evaluation on training tasks (upper subplot) and test tasks (bottom subplot).

All the trained models were further tested on 250 tasks sampled from $D^{\text{m-test}}$. For each task, one sample per class was used to train the model and 10 for the test. This means that e.g. in the 5-ways experiments, 5 training samples and 50 test samples were used. The achieved percentage inter-task mean accuracy values, averaged over 3 experiments reproductions are presented in Table 3.

As can be seen numerically from the tables, the MAML + CA + MSL + DA algorithm achieves the best performances regardless of the number of ways. The application of the second gradient in MAML favors the achievement of a greater generalization and therefore of higher inter-task accuracy compared to the first-order algorithms. Furthermore, the outer-loop update, done on a query sample, increases the algorithm's robustness thus reducing the dependence on individual tasks. First-order algorithms (Reptile and MAML 1st order) on the other hand, achieve very good results in the 2-way experiments but lead to significantly lower results in more complex experiments (4-ways and 5-ways). This is due to the first-order approximation of the gradient and therefore to the lack of part of the information, which becomes significant in more complex experiments.

**Table 1.** Inter-task percentage median accuracy obtained on test tasks, on an average of 3 experiment reproductions for the first and last meta tasks batches. * In the Reptile 5-ways experiments (first batch: 0–1,499, last batch: 13,500–14,999).

| 1-shot experiments - median accuracy | | | | | | |
|---|---|---|---|---|---|---|
| Algorithm | 2-ways | | 4-ways | | 5-ways* | |
| | 0–24 | 75–99 | 0–299 | 2700–2999 | 0–999 | 9000–9999 |
| Reptile | 91.67% | 94% | 81% | 90% | 70.67% | 72.67% |
| MAML 1st Ord | 94.67% | 97% | 76% | 90.67% | 72% | 85% |
| MAML 2nd Ord | 95.67% | 98% | 78% | 92.67% | 86% | 96% |
| MAML 2nd CA+MSL+DA | 96.33% | 98% | 82.67% | 96% | 87.33% | 96% |

**Table 2.** Inter-task interquartile range (IQR) measures, obtained on test tasks, on an average of 3 experiment reproductions for the first and last meta tasks batches. * In the Reptile 5-ways experiments (first batch: 0–1,499, last batch: 13,500–14,999).

| 1-shot experiments - interquartile ranges | | | | | | |
|---|---|---|---|---|---|---|
| Algorithm | 2-ways | | 4-ways | | 5-ways* | |
| | 0–24 | 75–99 | 0–299 | 2700–2999 | 0–999 | 9000–9999 |
| Reptile | 12.33% | 6.33% | 16% | 12.33% | 19.33% | 16.67% |
| MAML 1st Ord | 5% | 1.67% | 20% | 13.33% | 20% | 18.33% |
| MAML 2nd Ord | 4.33% | 1% | 12.33% | 9% | 16.67% | 8% |
| MAML 2nd CA+MSL+DA | 3.67% | 1% | 30% | 9.33% | 16% | 6% |

**Table 3.** Inter-task percentage mean accuracy obtained on 250 test tasks for each experiment and number of ways on an average of 3 reproductions.

| Algorithm | 1-shot experiments - test accuracy | | |
|---|---|---|---|
| | 2-ways | 4-ways | 5-ways |
| Reptile | 92.59% | 86.22% | 72.36% |
| MAML 1st Ord. | 96.81% | 89.37% | 84.88% |
| MAML 2nd Ord. | 96.87% | 91.09% | 93.20% |
| MAML 2nd Ord. CA+MSL+DA | 97.12% | 94.67% | 94.12% |

For all the experiments, the increment in the median and mean accuracy (Table 1), and the reduction of whiskers and quartiles of box plots with progressing of meta-iterations (Table 2), represent the models' ability to learn faster to solve new tasks. This means that with time, the CNN learns how to solve new tasks with better performance than before, thanks to the context information extracted from the previously faced tasks.

To exhibit the versatility of the meta-approach in adapting to new tasks, we compared our best model in the 1-shot 4-ways, with the optimized CNN defined in [13], that has been used to classify the four basic gestures dataset employing a conventional deep learning approach. In our case, we trained this traditional CNN on tasks sampled from $D^{m\text{-test}}$, using 1,000 sequences of two gestures for training and 200 for testing. Through a transfer learning approach on new tasks, this model fails to reach an appreciable accuracy value (over 85%) despite the significant amount of training data. Consequently, each new training is done starting from a random initialization of the model parameters.

In Table 4, the average performance values of 3 independent tests of the traditional CNN are compared with the ones achieved by testing the best MAML + CA + MSL + DA model on 50 samples per class and over 250 tasks. The training of both models in this case has been done using a 5 cores CPU. The performance values achieved by the traditional CNN are presented in the relative two sub-columns of the table. The maximum achieved test accuracy and its required training time are listed in the first sub-column. The second sub-column shows instead, the time required to reach an average test accuracy comparable to that of the 1-shot Meta-L CNN. Besides, we also tested how many training shots per class are needed for the meta-model to achieve a prediction accuracy in the order of the traditional CNN.

**Table 4.** Performance comparison of traditional and Meta-L CNNs for the 4-ways tasks. Training of both models done on a five cores CPU.

|                   | Trad. CNN |         | Meta-L CNN |           |
|-------------------|-----------|---------|------------|-----------|
| Training samples  | 1000      |         | 4          | 8         |
| Test samples      | 200       |         | 200        | 200       |
| Avg. train. time  | 56 min    | 39 min  | 400 ms     | 1,580 ms  |
| Test accuracy     | 98.85%    | 93.67%  | 93.47%     | 98.32%    |

As can be observed, the optimized CNN achieves greater accuracy on the test samples, at the expense of a large amount of data and a long adaptation time to new tasks. The meta-model, on the other hand, thanks to the pre-acquired knowledge during training, is capable of adapting to new contexts with only one sample per class and in a very short time.

## 5    Conclusion

This paper demonstrates that the use of optimization-based meta-techniques can bring significant benefits for the recognition of FMCW radar-based hand gesture sequences. The inter-tasks learning approach considerably enhances the model's ability to adapt to new potential gestures or performing users. The experimental results show how even with a single sample per sequence, it is possible to achieve an inter-task accuracy of over 94% in the 5-way setup on new test tasks. The outcomes also highlight how the Meta-L approach can lead to an accuracy comparable to that of a traditional CNN with only a few more samples per class. Furthermore, it is shown how the adaptation of the obtained models to new tasks can take less than half of a second when performing the experiments on a 5 cores CPU. Future work will focus on the application of meta-learning for the recognition of a greater set of gestures and on an online demonstrator to test the approach.

# References

1. Awan, A.A., Subramoni, H., Panda, D.K.: An in-depth performance characterization of CPU-and GPU-based DNN training on modern architectures. In: Proceedings of the Machine Learning on HPC Environments, pp. 1–8 (2017)
2. Ahmed, S., Kallu, K.D., Ahmed, S., Cho, S.H.: Hand gestures recognition using radar sensors for human-computer-interaction: a review. Remote Sens. **13**(3), 527 (2021)
3. Antoniou, A., Edwards, H., Storkey, A.: How to train your MAML. arXiv preprint arXiv:1810.09502 (2018)
4. Chen, V.C.: The micro-Doppler Effect in Radar. Artech House (2019)
5. Lindholm, E., Nickolls, J., Oberman, S., Montrym, J.: Nvidia tesla: a unified graphics and computing architecture. IEEE Micro **28**(2), 39–55 (2008)
6. Finn, C., Abbeel, P., Levine, S.: Model-agnostic meta-learning for fast adaptation of deep networks. In: International Conference on Machine Learning, pp. 1126–1135. PMLR (2017)
7. Hospedales, T., Antoniou, A., Micaelli, P., Storkey, A.: Meta-learning in neural networks: a survey. arXiv preprint arXiv:2004.05439 (2020)
8. Issakov, V., Bilato, A., Kurz, V., Englisch, D., Geiselbrechtinger, A.: A highly integrated D-Band multi-channel transceiver chip for radar applications. In: 2019 IEEE BiCMOS and Compound Semiconductor Integrated Circuits and Technology Symposium (BCICTS), pp. 1–4. IEEE (2019)
9. Vanschoren, J.: Meta-learning: a survey. arXiv preprint arXiv:1810.03548 (2018)
10. Khari, M., Garg, A.K., Crespo, R.G., Verdú, E.: Gesture recognition of RGB and RGB-D static images using convolutional neural networks. Int. J. Interact. Multimedia Artif. Intell. **5**(7) (2019)
11. Lammert, V., Achatz, S., Weigel, R., Issakov, V.: A 122 GHz ISM-band FMCW radar transceiver. In: 2020 German Microwave Conference (GeMiC), pp. 96–99. IEEE (2020)
12. Lee, H.R., Park, J., Suh, Y.J.: Improving classification accuracy of hand gesture recognition based on 60 GHz FMCW radar with deep learning domain adaptation. Electronics **9**(12), 2140 (2020)
13. Chmurski, M., Zubert, M., Bierzynski, K., Santra, A.: Analysis of edge-optimized deep learning classifiers for radar-based gesture recognition. IEEE Access (2021)
14. Zhao, M., et al.: Through-wall human pose estimation using radio signals. In: Proceedings of the IEEE Conference on Computer Vision and Pattern Recognition, pp. 7356–7365 (2018)
15. Marcus, G.: Deep learning: a critical appraisal. arXiv preprint arXiv:1801.00631 (2018)
16. Nichol, A., Achiam, J., Schulman, J.: On first-order meta-learning algorithms. arXiv preprint arXiv:1803.02999 (2018)

17. Oudah, M., Al-Naji, A., Chahl, J.: Hand gesture recognition based on computer vision: a review of techniques. J. Imaging **6**(8), 73 (2020)
18. Augustauskas, R., Lipnickas, A.: Robust hand detection using arm segmentation from depth data and static palm gesture recognition. In: 2017 9th IEEE International Conference on Intelligent Data Acquisition and Advanced Computing Systems: Technology and Applications (IDAACS), vol. 2, pp. 664–667. IEEE (2017)
19. Rimmelspacher, J., Ciocoveanu, R., Steffan, G., Bassi, M., Issakov, V.: Low power low phase noise 60 GHz multichannel transceiver in 28 nm CMOS for radar applications. In: 2020 IEEE Radio Frequency Integrated Circuits Symposium (RFIC), pp. 19–22. IEEE (2020)
20. Trotta, S., et al.: Soli: a tiny device for a new human machine interface. In: 2021 IEEE International Solid-State Circuits Conference (ISSCC), vol. 64, pp. 42–44. IEEE (2021)
21. Yasen, M., Jusoh, S.: A systematic review on hand gesture recognition techniques, challenges and applications. PeerJ Comput. Sci. **5**, e218 (2019)
22. Wang, Y., Ren, A., Zhou, M., Wang, W., Yang, X.: A novel detection and recognition method for continuous hand gesture using FMCW radar. IEEE Access **8**, 167 264–167 275 (2020)
23. Zheng, Y., et al.: Zero-effort cross-domain gesture recognition with wi-fi. In: Proceedings of the 17th Annual International Conference on Mobile Systems, Applications, and Services, pp. 313–325 (2019)

# Few-Shot Learning with Random Erasing and Task-Relevant Feature Transforming

Xin Wang[1,2], Shouhong Wan[1,2], and Peiquan Jin[1,2(✉)]

[1] University of Science and Technology of China, Hefei, China
wx3435@mail.ustc.edu.cn, {wansh,jpq}@ustc.edu.cn
[2] Key Laboratory of Electromagnetic Space Information, CAS, Hefei, China

**Abstract.** Few-shot learning for visual recognition aims to classify images from unseen classes with only a few labeled samples. Many previous works address such a challenge by using a base set consisting of massive labeled samples to learn a feature extractor, which is transferred to categorize unseen classes from a novel set. However, a challenging issue is how to make the learned feature extractor transferable in few-shot learning because the categories extracted from the base set are different from those in the novel set. To address this issue, this paper proposes a novel *Random Erasing Network(RENet)* to make the network better utilize the full context of the input image, yielding a more transferable network than previous networks that only use the most discriminative features. Further, we present a *Task-Relevant Feature Transforming(TRFT)* framework based on CrossTransformers to generate embedding that can better exploit the information within the current task. Then, we combine RENet and TRFT to implement a cooperative training model *RE-TRFT* for the episodic training. We conduct extensive experiments on two benchmarks and the results show that our approach outperforms recent state-of-the-art methods.

**Keywords:** Few-shot learning · Random erasing · Feature transforming

## 1 Introduction

Deep learning-based methods have made significant achievements on a variety of computer vision tasks, such as image classification [1,2], object detection [3,4] and semantic segmentation [5,6]. However, these supervised methods commonly rely on a large number of labeled samples, which are scarce or expensive in many practical applications. In contrast, humans are good at learning new visual concepts from very little direct supervision. Few-shot learning (FSL) aims to computationally mimic human perception systems with the help of deep learning. Conventionally, there are two fundamental data sets in few-shot learning problem, namely base set(seen classes) and novel set(unseen classes). Each class in

© Springer Nature Switzerland AG 2021
I. Farkaš et al. (Eds.): ICANN 2021, LNCS 12892, pp. 512–524, 2021.
https://doi.org/10.1007/978-3-030-86340-1_41

the base set contains abundant labeled samples, while the class in the novel set has only a few labeled samples. Note that there is no class overlap between the base and novel sets. The main idea of FSL is to discover transferable visual knowledge in the seen classes, and leverage it to construct a desired classifier that can correctly categorize the unseen query samples from the novel set.

Compared to traditional image classification, few-shot learning has two major challenges. The first challenge is the non-overlap categories between the base and novel set, and the second is the low-data problem. A straightforward method to solve FSL is to train a model with base set and fine-tune it with few labeled novel set samples. However, with too little labeled data for each class, such a system empirically performs poorly. Recently, the episodic training strategy [7] is proposed to take place of the ineffective fine-tuning approach. As a typical meta-learning paradigm, it samples a number of classification tasks from the base set by imitating the settings in the test phase, which we call episodes, to narrow the gap between the training and test settings and enhance the generalization ability of the model. With the help of episodic training, many methods have been proposed to solve the challenging few-shot classification problem by building a good metric function and encouraging the network to learn transferable knowledge that can effectively compare the feature similarity of different samples in a shared feature space [16–19, 22].

While promising, such approaches suffer from an important limitation: Assuming the test features extracted by the embedding function trained on the seen classes are generalizable enough to represent the true distributions of the unseen classes. However, since the feature extractor never sees the categories in the novel set, it focuses much more likely on the discriminative visual knowledge that will be useful for base classes recognition rather than novel ones and may occasionally ignore the critical concepts for unseen classes. For the pre-trained classification model, the classifier usually determines the category of an image by only exploiting the discriminative information from part of target objects [8]. By contrast, extracting features that contain the intact target object [28] and exploiting the full context of the whole image can be more transferable.

In this work, we propose a novel random-erasing network called RENet to enhance the transferability of the feature embedding function. While we could specifically remove important visual features from the input image with supervised information(e.g., Class Activation Map), we choose to randomly remove regions of a fixed size as Cutout [9] due to its inherent simplicity and similar effectiveness. Then, based on RENet, we further present a task-relevant feature transforming framework to explore the latent task-relevant information within the current episode. Intuitively, the most useful features for distinguishing "cat" versus "fish" could be quite different and noise compared to the task of distinguishing "cat" versus "dog". Therefore, it is necessary to make use of such useful latent information especially when data is scarce. To summarize, we make the following contributions in this paper:

(1) We propose a new *Random-Erasing Network* (*RENet*) to enhance the transferability of the feature extractor by exploiting the full context of the image in

the base set. RENet presents a random erasing method to force the network to concentrate on part of the areas for each image by removing regions repeatedly. Such a mechanism is helpful to exploit the extra subordinate information for the input image and improve the model's robustness.

(2) We establish a *Task-Relevant Feature Transforming (TRFT)* framework to modulate features and reduce the feature similarity among different classes within the current episode. TRFT can better utilize the potential correlation information among different samples within a task and adapt the feature embedding to the current task, which can enhance the effectiveness of the feature learning.

(3) We combine *RENet* and *TRFT* to implement a cooperative training model *RE-TRFT* for the episodic training, and conduct comprehensive experiments on two datasets to verify the performance of our proposal. The results suggest the effectiveness of *RE-TRFT*.

## 2    Related Work

According to the adopted techniques, existing few-shot learning methods can be categorized into two groups, namely optimization-based methods and metric learning-based methods.

### 2.1    Optimization-Based Methods

Optimization-based methods focus on quickly adapting the model parameters to current tasks with a few fine-tuning updates [10,12–15]. Typical approaches like MAML [10] and Reptile [12] target to learn a good way of parameters initialization that makes the model easy to fine-tune. MetaLSTM [11] adopts Long Short-Term Memory(LSTM) as an optimizer and propose to treat the model parameters as its hidden state. LEO [15] decoupled the gradient-based adaptation procedure of the model parameters and performed meta-learning to find suitable parameters for the current task in the low-dimensional latent space. These methods commonly rely on simple base learners such as nearest neighbor classifiers. Lee *et al.* [14] argued that discriminatively trained linear predictors could offer better generalization than simple base learners. Specifically, this approach exploited two properties of linear classifiers to use high-dimensional embedding with improved generalization.

### 2.2    Metric Learning-Based Methods

Metric learning-based methods aim at learning representations that minimize the intra-class distances within the same class while maximize the inter-class distances among different classes. These approaches first learned an embedding space with feature extractor and then employed a distance function to determine the category of the input test samples [16–22,27,28]. For example, Prototypical Network [16] viewed the learned features as the class prototype and performed nearest neighbor classification based on the Euclidean distance. Relation Network [17] proposed to construct a learnable metric module to take place of specific distance functions such as cosine similarity and Euclidean distance. These approaches conducted image-level feature comparison by performing global pooling to the final features. DN4 [18] adopted a local descriptor-based image-to-class measure instead of the image-level measure for the first time to calculate the distance among different samples. This measure was conducted via a k-nearest neighbor search over local descriptors of the feature maps. Similarly, Lifchitz *et al.* [20] viewed each of the local representations as a single classification unit and proposed dense classification among all the positions of the features. Hou *et al.* [19] proposed a Cross Attention Module between a query set and a support set to enhance the feature discriminability. Simon *et al.* [21] formulated FSL as a two-stage learning paradigm and proposed an extension of existing dynamic classifiers by using subspace.

Our approach is related to metric learning-based methods. We focus on how to obtain good generalization ability for the feature extractor and exploit the feature semantic relevance among the current task.

## 3   Methodology

In this section, we first formulate the FSL problem. Then, we detail the proposed RENet and the TRFT framework.

### 3.1   Problem Statement

In the standard formulation of few-shot learning, we are given a large labeled data set $D_{base}$, test support set $S^{test}$ with typically 1–5 labeled examples each class and test query set $Q^{test}$ which has the same label space with test support set. We call the test task with $C$ categories and $K$ labeled examples per class in $S^{test}$ as $C$-way $K$-shot task. Our goal is to use $D_{base}$ and $S^{test}$ to correctly classify the samples in the test query set.

Following [7, 16, 19, 22], we adopt episodic training mechanism and construct training episodes by simulating the test process in the training stage. Specifically, in each training episode, we sample a training support set $S^{train}$ and a training query set $Q^{train}$ from $D_{base}$, which are formulated as $S^{train} = \{S_i\}_{i=1}^{N_s}$ and $Q^{train} = \{Q_j\}_{j=1}^{N_q}$ respectively, where $N_s = C \times K$ and $N_q = C \times M$. $M$ here denotes the number of query samples per class in $Q^{train}$. How to represent each training support class and query sample and accurately measure the distance between them is the key issue for FSL.

### 3.2   Random Erasing Network (RENet)

The first challenge in our approach is to improve the generalization ability of the embedding function to extract better features for unseen classes. Motivated by Cutout [9], we adopt the simple yet effective image-level random erasing approach to better exploit the full context of the input image rather than the most discriminative features for the seen classes. Empirically, networks trained in this way can be more sensitive to transferable semantic information.

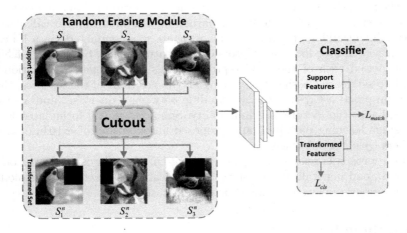

**Fig. 1.** Illustration of the proposed RENet.

To this end, we randomly convert part of the training episodes into random erasing episodes and retain the left episodes to imitate the test settings as before. Specifically, let $S^{train} = \{S_i\}_{i=1}^{N_s}$ be the training support set in each episode, and $\rho(\cdot)$ denote the random erasing operation, as shown in Fig. 1. Note that we directly discard the query set in each random erasing episode since samples in support set are enough for our purpose. We transform each sample in $S^{train}$ with $\rho(\cdot)$ for $r$ times to generate a new support set formulated as $S^n = \{S_j^n\}_{j=1}^{N_s}$, where $n \in \{1, 2, ..., r\}$. The label for each new image in the random erasing episode is its index in the original support set. Then, the original support set and new transformed set are fed into a weight shared feature extractor to generate feature embeddings, which denoted as $\{F_{S_i}\}_{i=1}^{N_s}$ and $\{F_{S_j^n}\}_{j=1}^{N_s}$. Finally, we conduct a $N_s - way$ match task and a global classification for the new support features.

To be specific, the $N_s - way$ match loss is defined as the negative log-probability according to the corresponding class index, as shown in Eq. 1 and Eq. 2. Here, $d$ represents the squared Euclidean distance.

$$L_{match} = -\sum_{n=1}^{r} \sum_{i=1}^{N_s} \log p(y = i | F_{S_i^n}) \tag{1}$$

$$p(y = i | F_{S_i^n}) = \frac{\exp(-d(GAP(F_{S_i^n}), GAP(F_{S_i})))}{\sum_{j=1}^{N_s} \exp(-d(GAP(F_{S_i^n}), GAP(F_{S_j})))} \tag{2}$$

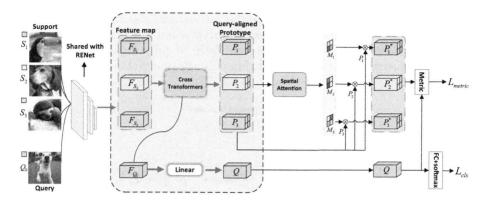

**Fig. 2.** Overview of the proposed TRFT framework. Here we take 3-way 1-shot as an example. The symbol $\otimes$ denotes the pointwise multiplication.

In addition, the global classification loss $L_{cls}$ is the regular CrossEntropy loss generated by a learned linear layer $W_1$ followed by a softmax operation (Eq. 3).

$$L_{cls} = -\sum_{n=1}^{r}\sum_{i=1}^{N_s} \log p(softmax(W_1(F_{S_i^n}))) \tag{3}$$

To sum up, the overall loss function for RENet is defined by Eq. 4, where $\lambda$ is the weight to balance the effects of different losses.

$$L_{RE} = L_{cls} + \lambda L_{match} \tag{4}$$

### 3.3  Task-Relevant Feature Transforming (TRFT)

For the regular training episodes, support and query samples commonly get their features independently, thus may well ignore the semantic relevance between the class and query features. Recently, an effective feature fusion approach is proposed in [22], which is called CrossTransformers. As shown in Fig. 2, CrossTransformers gets input the support and query features and outputs the query-aligned prototype for each class. Specifically, we denote the input support features as $F_S = \{F_{S_i}\}_{i=1}^{C \times K}$, where $C$ and $K$ represent $C$ categories and $K$ samples per class in an episode. The query feature is defined as $F_{Q_0}$. Following Transformer, key-value pairs are generated for each image in support set using two different linear maps, and a query linear map is adopted for the query feature. Then a dot-product attention map can be obtained with key and query features, followed by a softmax across all the spatial locations in $F_S^c$ for category $c$. The attention map is used to align features in a support class with the query feature $F_{Q_0}$. By using CrossTransformers, we can effectively aggregate the information among support and query samples. However, the obtained query-aligned prototypes get closer with each other in the embedding space since all of them are aligned with the same query feature, which may confuse the downstream classifier. To reduce the feature similarity among different class prototypes and in the meantime exploit the relevant information within the current task, we propose a spatial attention module as illustrated in Fig. 3 by utilizing only the query-aligned prototypes.

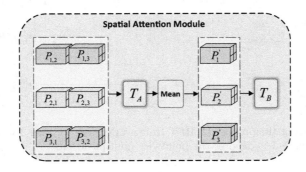

**Fig. 3.** Illustration of our proposed spatial attention modulation. Here $T_A$ and $T_B$ are two nonlinear transformation. The output channel of $T_B$ equals one to get a spatial weight mask.

Assuming that we have got the query-aligned prototypes $P = \{P_i\}_{i=1}^C$ and the query feature $Q$, we first adopt a pointwise subtraction among $P$ and denote the output as $P_{i,j} = P_i - P_j$, which represents the difference between $P_i$ and $P_j$. Then, we conduct a nonlinear transformation $T_A$ for each $P_{i,j}$ to aggregate the local information in the difference maps. After that, we get the mean of the transformed difference maps for the same class $P_i' = \sum_{j=1, j \neq i}^C P_{i,j}$, followed by another nonlinear transformation $T_B$. At last, the spatial attention masks $\{M_i\}_{i=1}^C$ are obtained which indicate the weight of each spatial location for $P$. Note that $T_A$ and $T_B$ are both convolution operations.

Similarly, we build a $C - way$ classification loss $L_{metric}$ and a global classification loss $L_{cls}$ as in the random erasing episodes. The difference is, we conduct the form of dense classification like CAN [20]. As shown in Eq. 5, Eq. 6, and Eq. 7.

$$L_{metric} = -\sum_{j=1}^M \sum_{i=1}^{H \times W} \log p(y = k | Q_j^i) \tag{5}$$

$$p(y = k | Q_j^i) = \frac{\exp(sim(Q_j^i, GAP(P_k^*)))}{\sum_{m=1}^C \exp(sim(Q_j^i, GAP(P_m^*)))} \tag{6}$$

$$L_{cls} = -\sum_{j=1}^M \sum_{i=1}^{H \times W} \log p(softmax(W_2(Q_j^i))) \tag{7}$$

Here, $Q_j^i$ represents the $i^{th}$ spatial position for the $j^{th}$ query feature, $k$ is the corresponding class for $Q_j$, $M$ denotes the query numbers in a task, $H$ and $W$ are the height and width of the final query feature. We choose cosine similarity as the metric function $sim$.

Finally, the overall classification loss for TRFT episodes can be defined by Eq. 8.

$$L_{TRFT} = L_{cls} + \beta L_{metric} \tag{8}$$

where $\beta$ denotes the weight hyperparameter.

### 3.4   RE-TRFT: Integration of RENet and TRFT

To better use the transferable and task-relevant properties, we incorporate RENet and TRFT into the episodic training procedure to construct a cooperative training modulation. Specifically, we randomly convert 50% of the training episodes into random erasing episodes namely the RENet training process. The feature extractor trained with RENet can capture generalized visual knowledge that may transfer well to the unseen classes. Then, for the left 50% training episodes, we perform the regular feature matching tasks with TRFT framework. Note that, TRFT framework shares the same feature extractor with RENet. With such a training strategy, the TRFT framework can acquire both transferable meta-knowledge and task-relevant feature modulating ability in the episodic training procedure, which are critical for novel set samples in the test phase.

## 4   Performance Evaluation

### 4.1   Implementation Details

Following the setting in [20, 21, 25], we use *mini*ImageNet and *tired*ImageNet to evaluate our proposed methods. The miniImageNet contains 100 classes with 600 images per class. These 100 classes are divided into 64 training classes, 16 validation classes, and 20 test classes, respectively. The tiredImageNet is a much larger dataset, which consists of 34 categories(608 classes) and 779,165 images in total. These are divided into 20 categories for training, 6 categories for validation, and 8 categories for testing. Note that the base set is formed by training classes while the novel set is sampled from validation and test classes. We resize the original images to 84 × 84 pixels and conduct basic image augmentation as in [26].

We use ResNet-12 as our embedding model, and we stack two convolutional layers to construct the non-linear transformation $T_A$ and $T_B$. In random erasing training episodes, we conduct different erasing manners following the operations in [9] and we choose to cutout $r = 2$ times for each support image. The feature extractor is pre-trained by conducting a traditional classification task(e.g., 64 classes in the miniImageNet) on the training set. The initial learning rate is 0.002 and decreased by half every 40 epochs. The weight hyperparameter $\lambda$ and

$\beta$ are set to 0.5 and 0.1 respectively. At test time, each test task is fed into the TRFT framework to modulate features without performing the random erasing operation. We report the performance of our method using the mean accuracy and the 95% confidence interval on 600 randomly generated episodes. PyTorch and NVIDIA 2080Ti GPUs are used throughout our experiments.

## 4.2   Comparison with State-of-the-Arts

Table 1 and Table 2 show the results of our method and other state-of-the-art methods on miniImageNet and tiredImageNet. We can observe from the results that our proposed model achieves the best performance in both 1-shot and 5-shot among those competitive methods on two commonly used datasets. Especially in the 1-shot setting, we significantly improve the accuracy by 1.6% compared to ConstellationNet [27] on miniImageNet and 1.3% than E$^3$BM [25] on tiredImageNet. This might due to the improved generalization ability of the model, and a better way to exploit extra information within a task, which could be vital in the extremely low data regime. In addition, our method achieves similar result compared to the recently proposed CSEI [28] with the superiority of simplicity and efficiency without complicated image pre-processing steps. It is worth mentioning that we achieve relatively stable test accuracy compared with other competitive methods.

**Table 1.** The 5-way, 1-shot and 5-shot classification testing accuracy(%) on mini-ImageNet with 95% confidence intervals. These methods are divided into two types: Optimization-based methods(**O**) and Metric-based methods(**M**). "†": Results re-implemented by ourselves.

| Method | Type | Backbone | 1-shot | 5-shot |
|---|---|---|---|---|
| MAML [10] | O | Conv-32F | 48.70 ± 1.84 | 63.11 ± 0.92 |
| Meta-SGD [13] | O | Conv-32F | 50.47 ± 1.87 | 64.03 ± 0.94 |
| LEO [15] | O | WRN-28-10 | 61.76 ± 0.08 | 77.59 ± 0.12 |
| ProtoNet [16] | M | Conv-64F | 49.42 ± 0.78 | 68.20 ± 0.66 |
| DN4 [18] | M | Conv-64F | 51.24 ± 0.74 | 71.02 ± 0.64 |
| CAN [19] | M | ResNet-12 | 63.85 ± 0.48 | 79.44 ± 0.34 |
| DSN-MR [21] | M | ResNet-12 | 64.60 ± 0.72 | 79.51 ± 0.50 |
| E$^3$BM [25] | M | ResNet-12 | 63.8 ± 0.4 | 80.1 ± 0.3 |
| FEAT [26] | M | ResNet-12 | 62.96 ± 0.2 | 78.49 ± 0.15 |
| ConstellationNet [27] | M | ResNet-12 | 64.89 ± 0.23 | 79.95 ± 0.37 |
| CSEI$^†$ [28] | M | ResNet-12 | **66.70 ± 0.65** | **81.41 ± 0.72** |
| **RE-TRFT(Ours)** | M | ResNet-12 | **66.48 ± 0.32** | **81.24 ± 0.57** |

**Table 2.** The 5-way, 1-shot and 5-shot classification testing accuracy(%) on tiredImageNet with 95% confidence intervals.

| Method | Type | Backbone | 1 shot | 5 shot |
|--------|------|----------|--------|--------|
| ProtoNet [16] | M | Conv-64F | 53.31 ± 0.89 | 72.69 ± 0.74 |
| CAN [19] | M | ResNet-12 | 69.89 ± 0.51 | 84.23 ± 0.37 |
| DSN-MR [21] | M | ResNet-12 | 67.39 ± 0.82 | 82.85 ± 0.56 |
| E³BM [25] | M | ResNet-12 | 71.2 ± 0.4 | 85.3 ± 0.3 |
| FEAT [26] | M | ResNet-12 | 70.80 ± 0.23 | 84.79 ± 0.16 |
| **RE-TRFT(Ours)** | M | ResNet-12 | **72.49 ± 0.57** | **85.90 ± 0.43** |

### 4.3   Ablation Study

**Effect of Different Modules.** We evaluate the effectiveness of each component of our method on miniImageNet with 5-way 1-shot and 5-shot settings. We adopt ProtoNet [16] implemented by ourselves as the baseline for comparison. Table 3 gives the results, we can observe that both RENet and TRFT are critical for the accuracy gain. Specifically, CrossTransformers [22] together with our proposed spatial attention module achieves a great improvement in test accuracy and stability compared with baseline. Besides, the RENet improves the performance by more than 1% compared with baseline, which shows the importance of capturing transferable features in few-shot classification task. When we use RENet and TRFT together, we can get the best performance.

**Table 3.** Effect of RENet and each components of TRFT. TRFT is the combination of CrossTransformers and Spatial Attention module.

| Method | 1 shot Acc(%) | 5 shot Acc(%) |
|--------|---------------|---------------|
| ProtoNet | 60.37 ± 0.83 | 78.02 ± 0.74 |
| ProtoNet+Spatial Attention | 60.91 ± 0.87 | 78.15 ± 0.81 |
| ProtoNet+CrossTransformers | 64.57 ± 0.43 | 79.20 ± 0.59 |
| ProtoNet+TRFT | 65.73 ± 0.36 | 80.59 ± 0.52 |
| ProtoNet+RENet | 65.31 ± 0.45 | 80.34 ± 0.63 |
| ProtoNet+RENet+TRFT | **66.48 ± 0.32** | **81.24 ± 0.57** |

**Effect of Different Erasing Manners.** We conduct more experiments to deeply investigate the influence of different erasing manners, i.e., size, shape, and the inpainting content of the erasing region on miniImageNet with 5-way 5-shot setting. Figure 4 gives the results. We can observe from Fig. 4(a) that a proper patch length makes a big difference to the result. When the patch

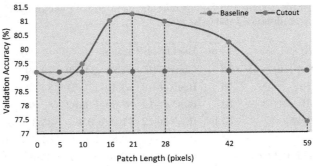

(a) Result with different patch lengths.

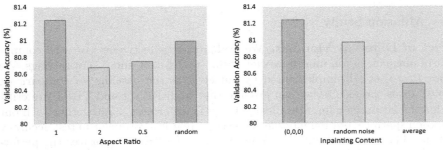

(b) Result with different aspect ratios.     (c) Result with different inpainting contents.

**Fig. 4.** Effect of different erasing manners. (a) The input image size is $84 \times 84$, we random erase $\left\{ \frac{1}{2}, \frac{1}{4}, \frac{1}{9}, \frac{1}{16}, \frac{1}{25} \right\}$ and a few other small patches of the input image. Baseline is a model trained without random erasing. (b) "*random*" denotes a randomly generated width with height calculated by the fixed area. (c) (0,0,0) represents the pure black color inpainting. "*average*" indicates painting with the mean value of the input image.

length is about a quarter of the image width, we can get the best performance. As the patch length increasing continuously, the validation accuracy decreases rapidly. This might due to the vast information loss which could confuse the global classifier in the random erasing episode. In Fig. 4(b) and Fig. 4(c), we can observe that the simple square erasing and zero-padding can yield effective results compared with other special operations. The square shape in the cutout operation is compatible with the input image which is beneficial for erasing part of the discriminative area and the zero-padding can easily eliminate the impact of this region.

## 5   Conclusion

In this paper, we propose a novel random erasing training strategy to exploit extra subordinate information for the input image to improve the robustness and transferability of the model. To be specific, we adopt the simple yet effective Cutout operation as our erasing method and conduct a few times to better explore information within the current image. Besides, we propose a task-relevant feature transforming framework to adapt generated features to the current task base on CrossTransformers. Extensive experiments show that our method can achieve better performance than recent competitive few-shot learning approaches.

**Acknowledgments.** This paper is supported by the National Science Foundation of China (grant no. 62072419).

# References

1. Tian, Q., Wan, S., Jin, P., et al.: A novel feature fusion with self-adaptive weight method based on deep learning for image classification. In: PCM, pp. 426–436 (2018)
2. Yang, X., Wan, S., Jin, P., et al.: MHEF-TripNet: mixed triplet loss with hard example feedback network for image retrieval. In: ICIG, pp. 35–46 (2019)
3. Yang, X., Wan, S., Jin, P.: Domain-invariant region proposal network for cross-domain detection. In: ICME, pp. 1–6 (2020)
4. Redmon, J., Divvala, S., Girshick, R., et al.: You only look once: unified, real-time object detection. In: CVPR, pp. 779–788 (2016)
5. Long, J., Shelhamer, E., Darrell, T.: Fully convolutional networks for semantic segmentation. In: CVPR, pp. 3431–3440 (2015)
6. Chen, L.C., Papandreou, G., et al.: Deeplab: semantic image segmentation with deep convolutional nets, atrous convolution, and fully connected crfs. IEEE Trans. Pattern Anal. Mach. Intell. **40**(4), 834–848 (2017)
7. Vinyals, O., Blundell, C., Lillicrap, T., et al.: Matching networks for one shot learning. In: NeurIPS, pp. 3630–3638 (2016)
8. Wei, Y., Feng, J., Liang, X., et al.: Object region mining with adversarial erasing: a simple classification to semantic segmentation approach. In: CVPR, pp. 6488–6496 (2017)
9. DeVries, T., Taylor, G.: Improved regularization of convolutional neural networks with cutout. arXiv preprint arXiv:1708.04552 (2017)
10. Finn, C., Abbeel, P., Levine, S.: Model-agnostic meta-learning for fast adaptation of deep networks. In: International Conference on Machine Learning, PMLR, pp. 1126–1135 (2017)
11. Ravi, S., Larochelle, H.: Optimization as a model for few-shot learning. In: ICLR (2016)
12. Nichol, A., Achiam, J., Schulman, J.: On first-order meta-learning algorithms. arXiv preprint arXiv:1803.02999 (2018)
13. Li, Z., Zhou, F., Chen, F., et al.: Meta-sgd: Learning to learn quickly for few-shot learning. arXiv preprint arXiv:1707.09835 (2017)
14. Lee, K., Maji, S., Ravichandran, A., et al.: Meta-learning with differentiable convex optimization. In: CVPR, pp. 10657–10665 (2019)
15. Rusu, A., Rao, D., Sygnowski, J., et al.: Meta-learning with latent embedding optimization. In: International Conference on Learning Representations (2018)
16. Snell, J., Swersky, K., Zemel, R.: Prototypical networks for few-shot learning. In: NeurIPS, pp. 4080–4090 (2017)

17. Sung, F., Yang, Y., Zhang, L., et al.: Learning to compare: relation network for few-shot learning. In: CVPR, pp. 1199–1208 (2018)
18. Li, W., Wang, L., Xu, J., et al.: Revisiting local descriptor based image-to-class measure for few-shot learning. In: CVPR, pp. 7260–7268 (2019)
19. Hou, R., Chang, H., Ma, B., et al.: Cross attention network for few-shot classification. In: NeurIPS, pp. 4005–4016 (2019)
20. Lifchitz, Y., Avrithis, Y., Picard, S., et al.: Dense classification and implanting for few-shot learning. In: CVPR, pp. 9258–9267 (2019)
21. Simon, C., Koniusz, P., Nock, R., et al.: Adaptive subspaces for few-shot learning. In: CVPR, pp. 4136–4145 (2020)
22. Doersch, C., Gupta, A., Zisserman, A.: CrossTransformers: spatially-aware few-shot transfer. In: NeurIPS (2020)
23. Wang, Y.K., Xu, C.M., et al.: Instance credibility inference for few-shot learning. In: CVPR, pp. 12836–12845 (2020)
24. Li, K., Zhang, Y., Li, K., et al.: Adversarial feature hallucination networks for few-shot learning. In: CVPR, pp. 13470–13479 (2020)
25. Liu, Y., Schiele, B., Sun, Q.: An ensemble of epoch-wise empirical bayes for few-shot learning. In: ECCV, pp. 404–421 (2020)
26. Ye, H., Hu, H., Zhan, D., et al.: Few-shot learning via embedding adaptation with set-to-set functions. In: CVPR, pp. 8808–8817 (2020)
27. Xu, W., Xu, Y., Wang, H., et al.: Attentional constellation nets for few-shot learning. In: ICLR (2021)
28. Li, J., Wang, Z., Hu, X.: learning intact features by erasing-inpainting for few-shot classification. In: AAAI (2021)

# Fostering Compositionality in Latent, Generative Encodings to Solve the Omniglot Challenge

Sarah Fabi(✉)[ID], Sebastian Otte[ID], and Martin V. Butz[ID]

Neuro-Cognitive Modeling Group, University of Tübingen, Tübingen, Germany
sarah.fabi@uni-tuebingen.de

**Abstract.** The ability to develop representations of components and to recombine them in a new but compositionally meaningful manner is considered a hallmark of human cognition, which has not been reached by machines, yet. The Omniglot challenge taps into this deficit by posing several one-shot/few-shot generation and classification tasks of handwritten character trajectories. In contrast to the original approach of providing character components, we investigated how compositional representations can develop naturally within a generative LSTM model. The network's performance and the underlying mechanisms are examined on the original Omniglot dataset and on our own more representative dataset. We show that solving the challenge becomes possible, because, during training, the designed LSTM network fosters the learning of compositional representations, which it can quickly reassemble into new, unseen but related character trajectories. Evidence is provided by several experiments, including an analysis of the latent states of the system, revealing the emergent compositional structures with t-SNE, and the evaluation of the network's performance, when training and test alphabets do or do not share components. Overall, we show how compositionality can be fostered in latent, generative encodings, thus improving machine learning by further aligning technical methods to cognitive mechanisms in humans.

**Keywords:** Omniglot challenge · Characters challenge · Compositionality · Efficient learning · Generative RNN · LSTM · One-shot inference mechanism

## 1 Introduction

Since the introduction of the first connectionist models, it has been debated whether artificial neural networks were able to develop compositional representations [16]. With our investigations of their inner working mechanisms, we show that generative long short-term memory (LSTM) [15] networks are indeed able to recombine components of previously learned concepts, thereby enabling one- and few-shot learning. However, an embedding layer as well as inverse latent

© Springer Nature Switzerland AG 2021
I. Farkaš et al. (Eds.): ICANN 2021, LNCS 12892, pp. 525–536, 2021.
https://doi.org/10.1007/978-3-030-86340-1_42

state inference is required to enable the flexible recombination of previously learned compositional encodings, such as circles, dots, and lines, when facing handwritten character trajectories.

We build on Partee's [24] definition of compositionality from linguistics: 'The meaning of a whole is a function of the meanings of the parts and of the way they are syntactically combined.' When children learn new concepts, for example, the concept of a 'bird', they only need very few examples in order to generalize to other types of birds. One explanation for this efficient learning is that, when viewing, for example, a blackbird, children decompose it into its components, like wings, beak, feet etc. As a result, they recognize these components in other blackbirds, and even other bird species, resulting in the correct classification of 'bird'. Furthermore, children can rearrange these components in creative ways, imagine new blackbirds, or even invent fictitious bird types that only exist in their imagination [9].

For machine learning systems, on the other hand, the ability of combinatorial generalization, that is, the construction of new things by recombining known building blocks, is still a major challenge. Therefore, the demand to include compositional capabilities into machines becomes more and more apparent [7,9, 20]. Battaglia et al. [1] even go as far as to 'suggest that a key path forward for modern AI is to commit to combinatorial generalization as a top priority'.

In order to motivate researchers to investigate how human-like efficient learning based on compositionality can be realized within machine learning algorithms, the Omniglot challenge has been introduced six years ago [18]. It consists of the following generation and classification tasks of handwritten character trajectories: (i) one-shot regeneration of a character, (ii) one-shot generation of concept variants, (iii) one-shot classification, (iv) and few-shot generation of new concepts. In the same work [18], the researchers provided a model with a general idea on how to draw a character, by providing basic motor components, like half circles or straight lines, using Bayesian program learning. Since the release of the Omniglot challenge, lots of researchers from Google DeepMind, the MIT, and other universities aimed at solving the challenge without providing such basic components [3,4,6,8,11,13,18,25–28]. Nevertheless, in a summary about the progress on the Omniglot challenge within the last years, Lake et al. [19] concluded that models' performance on one-shot classification had been largely improved [26–28], but the progress on the other tasks had been very limited. Various generated examples of the same concept or of new concepts were either very similar or too dissimilar, so that one could not recognize them any more [8,13,25]. In other cases, only single tasks were tackled with no model being able to perform all the tasks at once [3,4,11]. What seemed promising for solving the Omniglot challenge, though, was putting strong inductive biases about compositional structures into the models [6,18]. In their overview article, Lake et al. [19] encourage the inclusion of causality (by applying sequential instead of pictorial data) and compositionality into more neurally-grounded architectures that can perform all instead of just some of the tasks.

Since LSTMs had proved to be successful in generating handwritten letters [10], in Fabi et al. [5], we presented a way to tackle the Omniglot challenge on sequential drawing data with a simple LSTM network and the *one-shot inference mechanism* without providing basic motor components. In the current paper, we investigate precisely how the algorithm accomplishes this and which role compositionality plays. Our main hypothesis is that the LSTM network is able to recombine previously learned components in a meaningful manner when confronted with new concepts. Following Jensen [17], who demanded that researchers should investigate the underlying mechanisms of algorithms instead of just comparing which system performs better, we apply methods from empirical research. We formulate hypotheses that are falsifiable and conduct experiments to evaluate the hypotheses, effectively addressing explainability and circumventing reproducibility issues of Machine Learning research [12].

In detail, we perform two experiments to investigate the mechanisms in our model thoroughly. In Experiment 1, the tasks of the Omniglot challenge are solved on an own dataset and the cell and hidden states of the LSTM layer are analysed. With t-distributed stochastic neighbour embedding (t-SNE) we test our hypotheses that compositional representations are the reason for the success on the Omniglot challenge and that they develop within the LSTM network. In Experiment 2, we finally test the mechanism on alphabets of the Omniglot dataset. This allows for experiments in which the model is provided with learning stimuli of the same alphabet as the test stimuli, with stimuli of different alphabets, and even with ones that do not share all components that are necessary for the recombination, when presented with new characters. In short, we aim at rendering our model explainable on two accounts: By providing post-hoc interpretations of its performance on several experiments, and by rendering the model transparent by analyzing the hidden LSTM states.

## 2 Method

### 2.1 Model and *one-shot Inference Mechanism*

In order to solve the Omniglot challenge's tasks, we applied a generative RNN as shown in Fig. 1. This RNN consists of a variable-sized input layer, a linear latent embedding layer with 100 neurons, a recurrent generator module with 100 LSTM units [15], and a linear output layer with two neurons. The input layer represents particular characters in form of one-hot encoded vectors. Each input neuron projects its activity onto the next layer with its own set of weights. Thus, a concept indicator induces a specific activity pattern within the latent code layer. This code, which can be seen as the motor program encoding of the network, seeds and continuously shapes the unfolding dynamics within the recurrent generator. Eventually, the hidden dynamics are mapped onto the output layer, generating a change in x and y position at every timestep.

During training, the model learned to generate trajectories out of one-hot encoded inputs for a subgroup of characters. Since the examples per character varied, the training resulted in the generation of average characters. When tackling the Omniglot challenge, the tasks should be solved with very few examples, which is why, after training, the model was presented with one example of a new

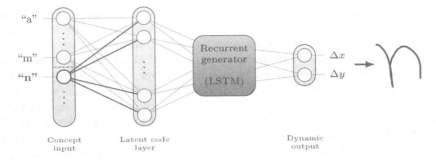

**Fig. 1.** Illustration of the *one-shot inference mechanism*. Only the blue weights that map the concept indicator (here of the new concept "n") onto a generative latent code are trained. The other parts of the network remain unchanged. Thus, if dynamical primitives are indeed learned from previously shown concepts, this mechanism should reassemble them to generate the new trajectory.

character that had not been part of the training. If it had learned components during training as expected, it should be able to reassemble these representations compositionally in order to generate new trajectories. Therefore, we allowed only the first weights into the first feedforward layer (cf. blue weights in Fig. 1) to adapt for several iterations in order to re-arrange the already learned representations of components, leaving the remaining parts of the network, including the recurrent layer, untouched. Note that this is conceptually equivalent to inversely inferring (guided by prediction error-induced gradient signals) the latent activity pattern (cf. [2,23]), plus persisting the inferred code within the respective weights. All learning was performed using the L2 loss function, the Adam optimizer with standard parameters ($\eta = 0.001$, $\beta_1 = 0.9$, $\beta_2 = 0.999$), and a batch size of 1.

## 2.2 Dataset

The Omniglot data, which underlies the Omniglot challenge, was originally pictorial data containing 50 alphabets, with 20 variants per character [18]. To include stronger forms of compositionality and causality, Lake et al. [19] added a sequential stroke dataset, for which 20 Amazon Mechanical Turk participants traced the pictures of the original characters. Even though the introduction of the Omniglot challenge and datasets was of tremendous importance, we want to criticize the sequential dataset in a certain regard: When looking at Fig. 2, it becomes apparent that the characters were not naturally drawn with a pen, but traced with a computer mouse, leading to "a"s and "beta"s that are composed of three or four different and rather arbitrary strokes (different colors) instead of just one, which would resemble a natural writing movement. This problem might be even larger for unknown alphabets, about whose generation the Amazon Mechanical Turk participants had no background knowledge. It was most problematic for

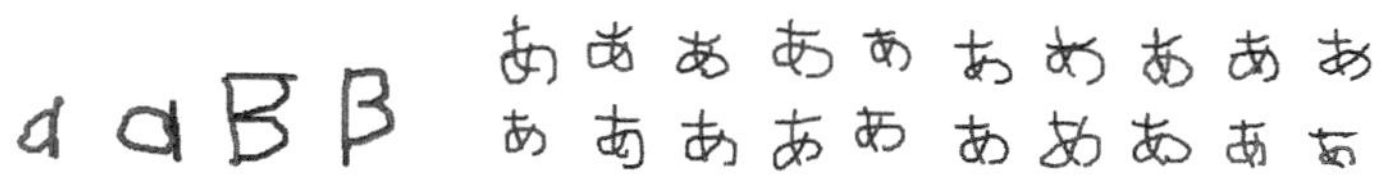

**Fig. 2.** Examples of the sequential Omniglot dataset provided by Lake et al. [19]. Colors represent consecutive strokes in the following order: red, green, blue, purple, turquoise. Note how "a" and "beta" as well as the first character of the Japanese Hiragana alphabet are drawn with unusually many strokes and in an inconsistent sequential manner.

alphabets with a manifold of different strokes instead of just a few, which is illustrated by the heterogeneous stroke orders of the first character of the Japanese alphabet (cf. right handside of Fig. 2).

Because of these shortcomings, in Experiment 1, we applied a dataset of handwritten character trajectories of the Latin alphabet that we had recorded ourselves. With this, we wanted to ensure that the characters were produced by experts of the alphabet, that they were generated freely instead of tracing previously drawn characters, leading to consistent, natural, and correct trajectories. Furthermore, instead of a rather imprecise computer mouse, the participants of our dataset used a dedicated pen on a touch-sensitive surface, making their writing more realistic. Furthermore, the 20 variants of the Omniglot dataset are very similar, whereas our dataset provides more natural variability in 440 examples per character from 10 different subjects, including script and print characters.

Nevertheless, to provide comparability, additionally to the analyses on our dataset, we furthermore applied our network architecture to the sequential Omniglot dataset [19] in Experiment 2. To do this, we transformed the trajectory data into difference values of x and y positions. We furthermore deleted the information about when a new stroke ended in order not to prime the network, but to let it develop its own compositional representations. Because of the shortcomings of the sequential Omniglot dataset described above, which are worse in characters that are composed of lots of different strokes, we selected alphabets that are complex, but originally not composed of too many strokes.

## 3   Results

### 3.1   Experiment 1

The five generative LSTM models that were trained for 10 epochs on the first half of the Latin alphabet ("a" to "m"), together with the *one-shot inference mechanism* for 1000 iterations per new character "n" to "z", were able to regenerate new character trajectories, which have not been part of the training set and of which only one example was presented (cf. Fig. 3a). Applying the *one-shot inference mechanism* on untrained models did not lead to readable character generations (Fig. 3b), showing how important the training was and supporting our hypothesis that sequence components are learned that can later on be recombined in a compositional manner. It led to even worse results than the

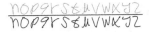

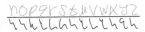

(a) Pre-trained model plus *one-shot inference mechanism*

(b) *one-shot inference mechanism* without pre-trained model

(c) Pre-trained model without *one-shot inference mechanism*

**Fig. 3.** Human handwritten (blue) and regenerated trajectories (black) (Color figure online)

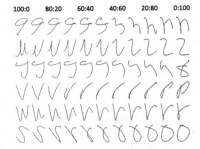

(a) Generation of character variants out of the original one (first row).

(b) Generation of new concepts through blended input vectors.

**Fig. 4.** Generation tasks of the Omniglot challenge

trained models without the *one-shot inference mechanism* (Fig. 3c), showing that the *one-shot inference mechanism* cannot be viewed as a generic training of the network. Rather, it compositionally rearranges previously encoded sequence dynamics (Dynamic Time Warping distances [22]: $M = 0.320, SD = 0.063$ vs. $M = 1.554, SD = 0.219$ vs. $M = 0.650, SD = 0.124$).

**Tackling the Tasks of the Omniglot Challenge.** To generate new variants of a character concept (cf. Fig. 4a), after having applied the *one-shot inference mechanism*, we added normally-distributed noise with a scale between 0.009 and 0.15 onto the one-hot encoded input vectors. For the classification task, instead of a one-hot encoded input, the network got a zero vector of length 26 for every timestep. The error between the generated and the trajectory of the presented variant was calculated and the gradient was backpropagated onto the input vector, which was then passed forward through the network again. This was repeated 10 000 times for every variant. The highest input activation represented the network's classification. If tested on the variants of Fig. 4a, the mechanism classified 96, 7% correctly (88 out of 91 characters). Looking at the three mistakes more closely, they were not even implausible (e.g., the second "u" was classified as an "f"). For the last generation task of new concepts, the model was confronted with blended input vectors that indicated which character should be included into the mixture to which extent. The results (Fig. 4b) show no abrupt changes, but very smooth blendings between two characters, supporting our hypothesis

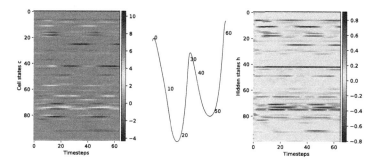

**Fig. 5.** Cell (left) and hidden states (right) of the corresponding trajectory of "w" with timesteps (middle) show a repetition of similar activation patterns.

of compositionality. In short, the generative LSTM model, together with the *one-shot inference mechanism*, was able to solve the tasks of the Omniglot challenge, advancing previous attempts to solve the Omniglot challenge which used large amounts of background alphabets, complex algorithms, or tackled only one instead of all tasks [3,19,25].

**Analysis of the LSTM Cell and Hidden States.** We wanted to more thoroughly investigate our hypothesis that solving the challenge was possible because the model learned compositional structures during training, which it recombined when generating new characters. Looking at the cell and hidden state activation patterns of the LSTM layer provided hints that similar components were indeed represented by similar hidden state activation patterns. This is illustrated exemplarily for the character "w" in Fig. 5, where the repetition of a similar component applied when writing a "w" is represented in the cell as well as the hidden states.

For a more systematic analysis, we analyzed the respective cell and hidden states when generating characters "n" to "z" with t-SNE [14,21] with 1.000 iterations. Via a gradient-based procedure, t-SNE projects the relations between data points from a high dimensional space onto a two-dimensional space, making their interpretation a lot easier. For visualizing the corresponding trajectory parts, clustering was applied with 2 as the maximum distance between two points to be considered as in the same neighborhood. Furthermore, for a point to be considered as a core point, 5 samples needed to be in a neighborhood.

The 2d-representations of the cell states are clearly clustered with respect to their corresponding character (Fig. 6). Thus, the c-states might be an important indicator for the network to stay in this attractor and generate this one character. Focusing on the "w", the spiral reflects the two similar components of which the trajectory is made. Other components shared between characters can also be identified in close proximity, like the half circle and downwards stroke in "q" and "y", or the stroke from bottom to top in "r" and "p" that look very similar in the current trajectory variants. The projection of the hidden states h onto the 2d

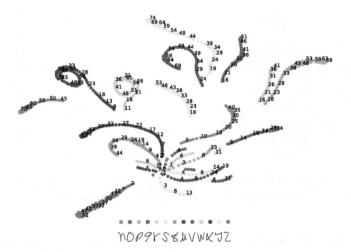

**Fig. 6.** Results of the t-SNE analysis of the cell states c with the corresponding timesteps when generating different characters.

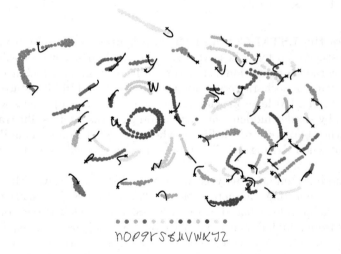

**Fig. 7.** Results of the t-SNE analysis of the hidden states h. The corresponding trajectory parts are drawn in black with a cross marking their beginning. The respective trajectory plots are centered on the first respective cluster position. Note that the size of the trajectory parts is not representative.

space identifies clear character components, since the end of one sequence represents a significant change in the hidden values from one timestep to another. It is important to note, though, that the network forms its own representations that might differ from components humans would identify. Nevertheless, most often similar components led to sequences in close proximity (Fig. 7). For example, on

**Fig. 8.** Original (blue) and generated (black) character trajectories of the second half of the Greek (top), Balinese (center), and Burmese (bottom) alphabets, after being trained on the respective first halves. (Color figure online)

the left, there is a group of bottom to top trajectory parts, curves in specific directions are clustered next to each other, and the "u" encoding in the middle reflects the fact that it is generated by two very similar components, which are encoded in the almost overlapping red circles. This speaks for our hypothesis that components are represented in the LSTM hidden states.

### 3.2   Experiment 2

In Experiment 2, we applied the generative LSTM model together with the *one-shot inference mechanism* onto alphabets of the Omniglot dataset. When tackling the Omniglot challenge, most researchers applied 30 or more background alphabets for training [13,25]. Since humans do not need as many background alphabets and since most of the components are already represented in very few alphabets, we hypothesized that our compositional approach does not need training on that many character concepts. Therefore, we decided to train on only one alphabet, giving us the additional opportunity to perform experiments with different alphabet combinations, that either do or do not share components. Nevertheless, it must be mentioned that the variants of one character concept are unnaturally similar in the Omniglot dataset, whereas humans are confronted with more varying examples (as represented in our dataset of Experiment 1).

In Experiment 2a, we tested whether the LSTM model and the *one-shot inference mechanism* performed well on single alphabets of the Omniglot dataset. Therefore, we trained the models on the first half of the Greek, the Balinese, or the Burmese alphabet for 500 epochs. Then, we provided 2000 iterations of the *one-shot inference mechanism* per character of the second half of these alphabets. Even though in this experiment, the network was only trained on 20 similar variants instead of 440 varying ones per character, the results for the one-shot regeneration of the characters of the second half of these alphabets look quite promising, as can be seen in Fig. 8, as well as in the DTW values: 0.356 (Greek), 0.378 (Balinese), 0.241 (Burmese).

To investigate further whether recombining previously learned compositional representations leads to success in learning new characters efficiently, in Experiment 2b, we selected alphabets of the original Omniglot dataset for training and

(a) Training on first half of the Balinese alphabet provided all necessary components leading to best regeneration.

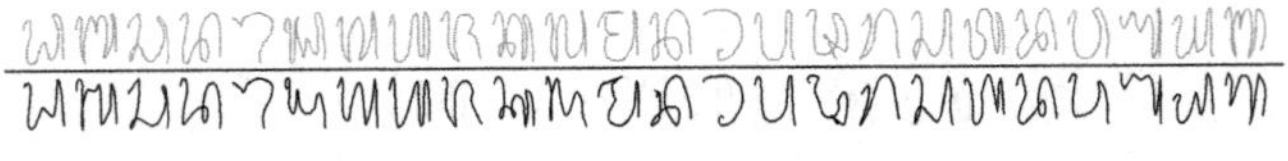

(b) Training on the Burmese alphabet provided most necessary components leading to good regeneration.

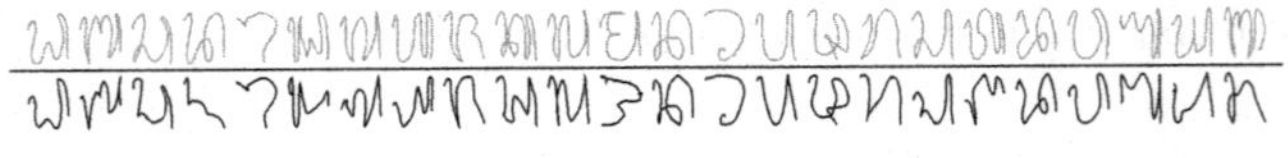

(c) Training on the Latin alphabet did not provide all necessary components leading to worse regeneration.

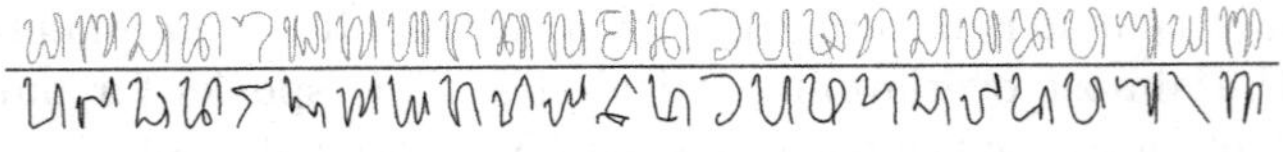

(d) Training on the Greek alphabet provided even less components leading to worst regeneration.

**Fig. 9.** Original (blue) and generated (black) character trajectories of the Balinese alphabet, trained on the first half of the Balinese, or the whole Burmese, Latin, or Greek alphabet. Supporting our hypothesis, the quality of the results decreases with the dissimilarity between the components of the training and test alphabets. (Color figure online)

test with similar or differing components. For 500 epochs, we trained the generative LSTM network on the Burmese, Greek, or Latin alphabet, or the first half of the Balinese alphabet and tested its performance when confronted with one variant of the characters of the Balinese alphabet. Since the components of the first and the second half of the Balinese alphabet should be the most similar, we expected best performance for this combination, followed by the Burmese-Balinese combination, since their characters share lots of components. Not so many components are shared between the Balinese and the Latin, or Greek alphabets, which is why we expected worst performance here, assuming our compositionality hypothesis is true. Supporting our hypothesis, the *one-shot inference mechanism* led to the best performance for training on the first half of the Balinese alphabet (Fig. 9a), followed by the Burmese (Fig. 9b), Latin (Fig. 9c), and Greek (Fig. 9d) alphabet (DTW distances: 0.378 vs. 0.384 vs. 0.427 vs. 0.509)[1]. Note as well that the Burmese alphabet contains more characters than the Latin and the Greek alphabet, which probably led to more variability in the compositional representations.

---

[1] Similar results were found for other test alphabets. A deeper interaction analysis goes beyond the scope of this paper. Test Burmese: Training Balinese (0.273) < Greek (0.280) < Latin (0.299); Test Latin: Training Greek / Burmese (0.230) < Balinese (0.251); Test Greek: Training Latin (0.329) < Burmese (0.334) < Balinese (0.339).

# 4  Conclusion

The Omniglot challenge can be solved with a generative LSTM model without providing it any knowledge about specific motor components. We show how compositional structures that develop within such models can later on be recombined when confronted with a new character. This provides explainable insights into the inner working mechanisms of the models and advances previous work like Lake et al. [18], who predefined the components that the model was supposed to use. Ultimately, this research is a step towards bringing specific Machine Learning architectures towards closer resemblance to human cognitive mechanisms, by introducing compositionality as an inductive bias into a simple LSTM network.

**Acknowledgements.** We thank Marcel Molière for help with the t-SNE plots, Thilo Hagendorff for helpful comments on the manuscript, and Maximus Mutschler for maintaining the GPU cluster of the BMBF funded project Training Center for Machine Learning, on which the results were computed. This research was funded by the German Research Foundation (DFG) within Priority-Program SPP 2134 - project "Development of the agentive self" (BU 1335/11-1, EL 253/8-1). MB is part of the Machine Learning Cluster of Excellence, EXC number 2064/1 – Project number 390727645.

# References

1. Battaglia, P.W., et al.: Relational inductive biases, deep learning, and graph networks. arXiv:1806.01261 (2018)
2. Butz, M.V., Bilkey, D., Humaidan, D., Knott, A., Otte, S.: Learning, planning, and control in a monolithic neural event inference architecture. Neural Netw. **117**, 135–144 (2019)
3. Edwards, H., Storkey, A.: Towards a neural statistician. In: Advances in Neural Information Processing Systems (NeurIPS) (2016)
4. Eslami, S., et al.: Attend, infer, repeat: fast scene understanding with generative models. In: Advances in Neural Information Processing Systems (NeurIPS) (2016)
5. Fabi, S., Otte, S., Wiese, J.G., Butz, M.V.: Investigating efficient learning and compositionality in generative LSTM networks. In: Farkaš, I., Masulli, P., Wermter, S. (eds.) ICANN 2020. LNCS, vol. 12396, pp. 143–154. Springer, Cham (2020). https://doi.org/10.1007/978-3-030-61609-0_12
6. Feinman, R., Lake, B.M.: Learning task-general representations with generative neuro-symbolic modeling. arXiv:2006.14448 (2020)
7. Franklin, N.T., Norman, K.A., Ranganath, C., Zacks, J.M., Gershman, S.J.: Structured event memory: a neuro-symbolic model of event cognition. Psychol. Rev. **127**, 327–361 (2020)
8. George, D., et al.: A generative vision model that trains with high data efficiency and breaks text-based CAPTCHAs. Science **358**, 6368 (2017)
9. Gopnik, A.: AIs versus four-year-olds. In: Brockman, J. (ed.) Possible Minds: Twenty-five ways of looking at AI. Penguin Press, New York (2019)
10. Graves, A.: Generating sequences with recurrent neural networks. arXiv:1308.0850 (2013)
11. Gregor, K., Besse, F., Rezende, D.J., Danihelka, I., Wierstra, D.: Towards conceptual compression. In: Advances in Neural Information Processing Systems (NeurIPS) (2016)

12. Haibe-Kains, B., et al.: Transparency and reproducibility in artificial intelligence. Nature **586**, 1–7 (2020)
13. Hewitt, L.B., Nye, M.I., Gane, A., Jaakkola, T., Tenenbaum, J.B.: The variational homoencoder: Learning to learn high capacity generative models from few examples. In: Uncertainty in Artificial Intelligence (2018)
14. Hinton, G.E., Roweis, S.: Stochastic neighbor embedding. In: Advances in Neural Information Processing Systems (NeurIPS) (2003)
15. Hochreiter, S., Schmidhuber, J.: Long short-term memory. Neural Comput. **9**, 1735–1780 (1997)
16. Hupkes, D., Dankers, V., Mul, M., Bruni, E.: Compositionality decomposed: how do neural networks generalise? J. Artif. Intell. Res. **67**, 757–795 (2020)
17. Jensen, D.: Empirical research in machine learning: perspectives and strategies. In: Advances in Neural Information Processing Systems (NeurIPS) (2020)
18. Lake, B.M., Salakhutdinov, R., Tenenbaum, J.B.: Human-level concept learning through probabilistic program induction. Science **350**, 1332–1338 (2015)
19. Lake, B.M., Salakhutdinov, R., Tenenbaum, J.B.: The omniglot challenge: a 3-year progress report. Curr. Opin. Behav. Sci. **29**, 97–104 (2019)
20. Lake, B.M., Ullman, T.D., Tenenbaum, J.B., Gershman, S.J.: Building machines that learn and think like people. Behav. Brain Sci. **40**, e253 (2017)
21. van der Maaten, L., Hinton, G.: Visualizing data using t-SNE. J. Mach. Learn. Res. **9**, 2579–2605 (2008)
22. Niels, R., Vuurpijl, L.: Using dynamic time warping for intuitive handwriting recognition. In: Proceedings of the 12th Conference of the Internatonal Graphonomics Society (2005)
23. Otte, S., Karlbauer, M., Butz, M.V.: Active tuning. arXiv:2010.03958 (2020)
24. Partee, B.: Lexical semantics and compositionality. Invitation Cogn. Sci. Lang. **1**, 311–360 (1995)
25. Rezende, D., Danihelka, I., Gregor, K., Wierstra, D., et al.: One-shot generalization in deep generative models. In: International Conference on Machine Learning (2016)
26. Shyam, P., Gupta, S., Dukkipati, A.: Attentive recurrent comparators. In: International Conference on Machine Learning (2017)
27. Snell, J., Swersky, K., Zemel, R.S.: Prototypical networks for few-shot learning. In: Advances in Neural Information Processing Systems (NeurIPS) (2017)
28. Vinyals, O., Blundell, C., Lillicrap, T., Kavukcuoglu, K., Wierstra, D.: Matching networks for one shot learning. In: Advances in Neural Information Processing Systems (NeurIPS) (2016)

# Better Few-Shot Text Classification with Pre-trained Language Model

Zheng Chen[✉] and Yunchen Zhang

School of Information and Software Engineering, University of Electronic Science and
Technology of China, Chengdu, China
zchen@uestc.edu.cn, yunchenz@std.uestc.edu.cn

**Abstract.** Recently, pre-trained language models achieve extraordinary
performance on numerous benchmarks. By learning the general language
knowledge from a large pre-train corpus, the language models could fit
for a specific downstream task with a relatively small amount of labeled
training data in the fine-tuning stage. More remarkably, the GPT-3 with
175 B parameters performs well in specific tasks by leveraging natural-
language prompts and few demonstrations of the task. Inspired by the
success of GPT-3, we desire to know whether smaller language models
could still have a similarly few-shot learning ability. Unlike the various
delicately designed tasks in previous few-shot learning research works, we
do it more practically. We present a question-answering-based method
to help the language model better understand the text classification task
by concatenating a label-related question to each candidate sentence.
By leveraging the label-related language knowledge, which the language
model has learned during the pre-trained stage, our QA model can outperform the traditional binary and multi-class classification approaches
over both English and Chinese datasets. Afterward, we test our QA
model by performing few-shot learning experiments on multiple pre-
trained language models of different sizes that range from the Distil-
BERT to the RoBERTa-large. We are surprised to find that even the
DistilBERT, which is the smallest language model we tested with only 66
M parameters, still holds undeniable few-shot learning ability. Moreover,
the RoBERTa-large with 355 M parameter could achieve a remarkable
high accuracy rate of 92.18% with only 100 labeled training data. This
result gives people a practical guideline that when a new category of
labeled data is needed, only as few as 100 data need to be labeled. Then
cooperate with an appropriate pre-training model and classification algorithm, reliable classification results can be obtained. Even without any
labeled training data, that is, under the zero-shot learning setup, the
RoBERTa-large still achieves a solid accuracy rate of 84.84%. Our code
is available at https://github.com/ZhangYunchenY/BetterFs.

**Keywords:** Few-shot learning · Text classification · Pre-trained
language model

Supported by the Sichuan Science and Technology Plan Project 2020YFG0009.

I. Farkaš et al. (Eds.): ICANN 2021, LNCS 12892, pp. 537–548, 2021.
https://doi.org/10.1007/978-3-030-86340-1_43

# 1   Introduction

With the evolution of deep learning, various pre-trained language models (PLMs) have been widely used to solve Natural Language Processing tasks. The first-generation PLMs, such as Skip-Gram and GloVe, aim to learn context-free word embeddings that fail to capture higher-level semantic concepts. The second-generation PLMs, such as ELMo, BERT, and GPT, represent words in context. By pre-trained over a large corpus in a self-supervised way, the PLMs only need to be fine-tuned over a small amount of labeled data for specific downstream tasks. Since then, the pre-training and fine-tuning paradigm started dominating NLP. With 175 billion parameters trained on 400 billion tokens, GPT-3, introduced by Brown et al. [3] in 2020, has pushed the PLMs to the next level. When provided with only a description and few examples of the task, the GPT-3 model could make accurate predictions without gradient updates or fine-tuning. Even though remarkable few-shot learning capabilities have been obtained, it is also prominent that the massive amount of parameters underlying GPT-3 makes it challenging to apply it to real-world applications.

As a machine learning problem, few-shot learning has a longer history than PLMs [5]. Humans are capable of learning new tasks rapidly by utilizing what they learned in the past. Hence, researchers believed that designing an efficient few-shot learning algorithm could let machines achieve the same intelligence level as human beings [9]. However, inspired by GPT-3, we argue that few-shot learning is a capability of a pre-trained language model itself, rather than being considered as a task. Undoubtedly, language models with few-shot learning abilities should have large parameters and be pre-trained over large corpora. Nevertheless, how big is enough? So in this work, we conduct experiments to explore the few-shot learning ability of various language models by doing text classification. We design a question-answering-based text classification method that the label information in the question can make good use of the pre-trained model's semantic knowledge, hence, help the model learn with few samples. The pre-trained language models that we tested include DistilBERT [15], BERT [4], and RoBERTa-large [11], which have 66M, 110M, and 355M parameters , respectively. Extending a regular-sized auto encoder language model's few-shot ability within text classification is appealing since (1) text classification is a downstream task that the model can grasp with ease; (2) a few labeled samples are easy to access; (3) such models can be fine-tuned on general hardware. So we propose a feasible scenario to make a better few-shot text classifier and study the impact of the language model scale on its few-shot learning ability. Specifically, the main contributions of this paper are as follows.

- We propose a question-answering-based classification method that outperforms traditional binary and multi-class classification approaches over both English and Chinese datasets.
- We perform a series of few-shot learning experiments on multiple pre-trained language models of different sizes that range from the DistilBERT to the RoBERTa-large. The results illustrate that all these models exhibit varying levels of few-shot learning capability. Some even realize zero-shot learning.

- We report detailed accuracy rates of each model with different training samples. The results can be used as a guideline for people to label samples in practice.
- We also provide an in-depth illustration and discussion of the attention mechanism of the pre-trained language models. By which, we attempt to uncover the mystery of the few-shot learning ability.

## 2   Related Work

### 2.1   Language Models

The evolution of language models can be divided into three periods, the statistical language model, the neural language model, and pre-trained language model. Statistical language models dominated from the 1960 s to 2010 s, such as Hidden Markov Model [1] and Conditional Random Field [8]. Since 2010, the advent of deep learning models makes remarkable progress in text classification. Neural models, such as CNN [7] and LSTM [23], are only data driven and avoid doing feature engineering. However, they cannot deal with few-shot learning.

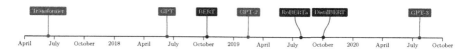

**Fig. 1.** The language models in recent years (GPT series are in purple; BERT series are in blue; Transformer, which is the basis of BERTs and GPTs, is in green).

Following the advances of the Transformer, pre-trained language models spring up in recent years (Fig. 1). Remarkably, the GPT-like auto-regressive language model [3,12,13] performs surprisingly well with a carefully chosen prompt and only a few examples in many downstream tasks. Being attracted by these few-shot learning ability, researchers start to explore BERT-like auto-encoder language model [4,11,15], and find it also has the few-shot learning ability.

### 2.2   Traditional Few-Shot Learning

Over the years, deep learning has been hugely successful in data-bound industries, but it is often infeasible when the amount of data is small [22]. Therefore, training a well-performed model with insufficient data is naturally seen as a challenging task. Various methods are presented to tackle the few-shot learning task, including Data argumentation [19] which uses the accessible data to generate more samples, siamese neural network [2] which calculates the similarities between features, and meta-learning [14] which learns many datasets to learn several examples. These approaches seem to be ways to 'mechanically' use the knowledge. Motivated by GPT series, however, we argue that few-shot should be considered as an inherent property of language models.

## 2.3   Few-Shot Learning Based on Pre-trained LM

Employing prompts to let language models do better inferences seems to be more 'humanized'. The pretraining on a large corpus endows language models with strong linguistic skills, thus need only be finetuned within a small amount of labeled data for specific downstream tasks. The auto-regressive language models, such as GPTs and CPM [21], can make predictions by generating the subsequent text, with an literal definition of the task in the context, which is called prompt. In recent works [6,16], they use a delicate-construct template to make language models do cloze tasks, which helps LMs understand a specific task. It seems effectual, but the limitation of the template makes these above approaches cannot adapt to any tasks. Deviated from these studies, however, we focus on the few-shot learning capability of the language model itself, and proposed a task-agnostic method called QA classification.

## 3   Methodology

### 3.1   Text Classification

In this paper, we conduct experiments by doing text classification (see Fig. 2) since text classification is a downstream task that is easy for a language model to learn. Hence doing text classification makes the language model easier to show the few-shot learning ability. Then we adopt the idea of doing questions and answering could help language models better leverage the knowledge since we give more information to the models. As a result, we transform multi-class text classification to question and answering (QA), which provides prior information to the language model and turn a the task into a simple binary classification.

We fine-tune a BERT $\mathcal{M}$ on the dataset $\mathcal{D}$ with label space $\mathcal{Y}$. $\mathcal{M}$ takes an input of a sequence $x_{in}$ and outputs the representation of the sequence. The first of the output is always [CLS] which we take as the representation of the whole sequence [17], and fine-tuning $\mathcal{M}$ to minimize the cross entropy. We take $\mathcal{M}'$ as the representation of $\mathcal{M}$ with a fully connected layer and the output of $\mathcal{M}'$ is $\mathbf{P}$ which consists of the probability corresponding to the class and $dim(\mathbf{P}) = |\mathcal{Y}|$.

**Binary Classification.** In binary classification, we just add a fully connected layer with activation function *sigmoid* at the top of $\mathcal{M}$ to predict the label $y_{predict}$, and the probability of the $y_{predict}$ is:

$$p(y|x_{in}) = \frac{1}{1 + exp(-W \cdot \mathbf{h}_{[CLS]})} \tag{1}$$

where $\mathbf{h}_{[CLS]}$ is the hidden state of the [CLS], and $W$ is the task-special matrix.

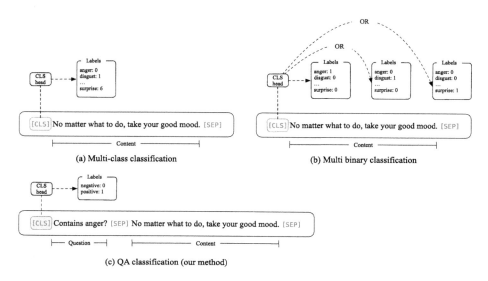

**Fig. 2.** An illustration of approaches we used (a) multi-class classification, (b) multi binary classification, (c) transforming multi-class classification to question answering.

In binary classification, $dim(\mathbf{P}) = 1$. So for each sequence, the output of $\mathcal{M}'$ is a constant. We use a threshold to determine which category the sequence belongs to. So the class is:

$$class = \begin{cases} positive, & p \geq threshold \\ negative, & p < threshold \end{cases} \qquad (2)$$

**Multi-class Classification.** In the multi-class classification, the inputs are the same as the binary classification. The difference is we put a *softmax* layer on the top of $\mathcal{M}$, and the probability of the label $y$ is:

$$p(y|x_{in}) = softmax(W \cdot \mathbf{h}_{[\text{CLS}]}) \qquad (3)$$

where $W$ is the task-specific matrix. We fine-tune the parameters from BERT and $W$ jointly by maximizing the probability of the correct label.

**Classification Based on QA.** In terms of results, QA classification is a binary classification. The difference between QA classification and binary classification is the input $x_{in}$. In QA classification, the input $x_{in}$ as:

$$x_{qa-in} = [\text{CLS}]question[\text{SEP}]content[\text{SEP}]$$

We also take the [CLS] as the presentation of the whole sequence, and the process of the classification is the same as the binary classification. For questions, we construct questions manually as simple as possible to avoid too much redundancy(e.g. For one content, we can ask 'does this sentence contain anger?' or 'contains anger?'. We choose the letter one). We will ask $|\mathcal{Y}|$ questions for each sentence, and determine the class of the sentence by using a threshold. So in this case, it could have multi answers in one sentence or no answers at all.

## 3.2 Few-Shot Classification

We conduct the few-shot text classification experiment based on our QA classification method. The input is as same as QA classification, the only difference is how we use the data (see Fig. 3).

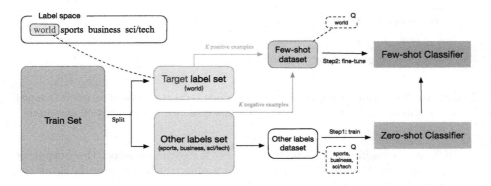

**Fig. 3.** An illustration of how we do few-shot learning with an example.

When doing few-shot learning, (1) we choose one class as the target to do few-shot learning; (2) according to the class we have chosen, we split the train set into target set (contains only one class) and the other set (contains the rest classes); (3) we pick **K** positive examples from the target set and **K** negative examples from the other data randomly, questioned by the class we have chosen to form the few-shot dataset. But we use a constant random seed $\mathcal{S}$ to sample, ensuring samples are the same when changing the size of language model; (4) we use the whole other data, questioned by the rest classed to form the other dataset; (5) we use the other dataset to train a plain classifier to get a zero-shot classifier; (6) we use **2K** examples from few-shot dataset to fine-tune the zero-shot classifier to obtain a few-shot classifier.

## 4    Problem Setup

### 4.1    Datasets

We conduct a systematic study across 2 tasks (Table 1), a Chinese Sentiment classification task (**OCEMOTION**[10] ) and a English Topic classification task (**AG's News** [20]).

**Table 1.** Statistics of two datasets

| Dataset | Classes | Samples | | Labels |
|---------|---------|---------|------|--------|
| | | Train | Test | |
| OCEMOTION | 7 | 32,124 | 3,570 | Anger, Disgust, Fear, Like, Happiness, Sadness, Surprise |
| AG's News | 4 | 120,000 | 7,600 | World, Sports, Business, Sci/Tech |

All datasets we have chosen are single-sentence text classification tasks. Our goal is to make predictions based on $x_{in}$ and $x_{qa-in}$. The tasks are range from sentiment analysis to topic classification, from Chinese to English.

### 4.2 Evaluation Protocol

**Text Classification.** We take $\mathcal{D}_{train}$ and $\mathcal{D}_{test}$ as the train set and the test set of traditional classification respectively. We split each dataset $\mathcal{D}$ into a train set $\mathcal{D}_{train}$ and a test set $\mathcal{D}_{test}$ or the dataset has already been split. To evaluate a classifier's performance, we choose *accuracy, micro-precision, micro-recall, micro-f1* [18] of the classifier as performance metrics. And calculate these metrics on $\mathcal{D}_{test}$, as the performance of the classifier.

**Few-Shot Learning.** We take $\mathcal{D}'_{train}$ and $\mathcal{D}'_{test}$ as the train set and the test set of QA classification respectively. The data given to the zero-shot classifier have balanced data between positive samples (target-label samples) and negative samples. In other words, the dataset $\mathcal{D}'_{train}$ we give to the zero-shot classifier has the same number of the positive samples and the negative samples. It is worth to mention that the negative samples in dataset $\mathcal{D}'_{train}$ have been seen by the zero-shot classifier. In the test set $\mathcal{D}'_{test}$, we choose all target-related samples from $\mathcal{D}_{test}$ as the positive (target-label) samples and the same number of the other samples from $\mathcal{D}_{test}$ as the negative samples. Meanwhile, we use a constant seed $\mathcal{S}$ to sample the negative examples, ensuring the $\mathcal{D}'_{test}$ is same when evaluate the performance of the classifier. And we take average accuracy between each target label as the performance metric of the few-shot classifier.

## 5 Experiments

### 5.1 Analysis of Text Classification

In general, the *f1 scores* get higher when the language models become lager under the condition of the same approach we train the classifier. It reflects that the lager model can learn more knowledge. It must to be mentioned is that the **OCEMOTION** is a fine-grained emotion classification dataset, and **AG's News** is a news classification dataset. Hence the **OCEMOTION** dataset is

**Table 2.** The results(*precision, recall and f1 scores*) of the multi binary classifications, the multi-class classification, and the QA classification

| Models | OCEMOTION | | | AG's News | | |
|---|---|---|---|---|---|---|
| | P | R | F | P | R | F |
| DistilBERT-binary | 50.82 | 52.72 | 51.75 | 92.21 | 95.07 | 93.62 |
| DistilBERT-multi | 53.05 | 53.05 | 53.05 | 93.83 | 93.83 | 93.83 |
| **DistilBERT-QA** | 50.78 | 53.61 | 52.16 | 92.45 | 94.09 | 93.26 |
| BERT-base-binary | 66.30 | 56.75 | 61.15 | 92.75 | 94.66 | 93.70 |
| BERT-base-multi | 62.07 | 62.07 | 62.07 | 93.64 | 93.64 | 93.64 |
| **BERT-base-QA** | 61.10 | 64.68 | **62.84** | 93.08 | 94.17 | 93.62 |
| RoBERTa-large-binary | 60.96 | 65.91 | 63.34 | 92.73 | 94.91 | 93.81 |
| RoBERTa-large-multi | 62.72 | 62.72 | 62.72 | 94.08 | 94.08 | 94.08 |
| **RoBERTa-large-QA** | 62.37 | 64.96 | **63.64** | 93.94 | 94.08 | 94.01 |

relatively difficult for the language model to learn. Meanwhile, we can see Table 2, in the same model, the *f1 scores* of **OCEMOTION** is lower than **AG's News**.

By comparing different scales of the language model, we can easily find out that the larger model has better performance in the same situation. Especially in the **OCEMOTION** dataset, from DistilBERT to BERT-base, the performance improves 9.7% on average. However, the *f1 scores* in **AG's News** dataset are awfully close. As a result, increase the scale of the language model could improve the performance of the classifier, especially on the harder dataset.

Furthermore, under the same scale model condition, the performance of the QA classification is close to the other two methods in the **AG's News** dataset, while notably better than the other two methods in the **OCEMOTION** dataset. In addition, the QA models' *f1 scores* surpass the multi models when the models become larger. In terms of this phenomenon, we think the prior knowledge we provide is effective, since most of the performance of QA classification is better than the binary classification. And the questions we add to the models can help them to better understand the task, especially beneficial to the large-scale model and the fine-grained task.

Besides that, we noticed that in most of the QA classification, the value of the *recall* is higher than *precision*. We think the cause of this phenomenon is that the prior knowledge sometimes will confuse the QA models. So the QA language model will turn negative samples into positive samples more easily, which resulted in the value of *recall* is higher than *precision*.

## 5.2    Analysis of Few-Shot Learning

We collected the average accuracy of each label as the indicator of few-shot learning. In Table 3, we believe the language model is not working when the *acc-avg* is around **50.00%**, since the task is a binary classification.

For the comparison of the number of the learning samples, we can see that the performances of the few-shot models are better as the number of the samples

**Table 3.** The result of few-shot learning

| Task | K | DistilBERT (avg-acc) | BERT-base (avg-acc) | RoBERTa-large (avg-acc) |
|---|---|---|---|---|
| OCEMOTION | 0 | 52.39 | 54.02 | 57.26 |
| | 10 | 61.55 | 69.68 | 71.50 |
| | 20 | 62.59 | 70.67 | 71.86 |
| | 50 | 62.65 | 71.25 | 72.37 |
| | 100 | 62.99 | 71.47 | 73.43 |
| AG's News | 0 | 61.32 | 62.09 | **84.84** |
| | 10 | 63.18 | 65.61 | 89.54 |
| | 20 | 65.41 | 66.19 | 89.88 |
| | 50 | 66.97 | 72.05 | 89.13 |
| | 100 | 70.86 | 81.47 | 92.18 |

increases. Apparently, the more samples are given, the more knowledge the language models can learn. However, with the increase of the number of samples, the performances of these models are not grown linearly. From 0 samples to 10 samples, the performance increased **8.91%**, but from 50 samples to 100 samples, it is only 2.98%. We think it is because that the language model we trained can easily learn some new things but not master them, so the increasing value of 0 to 10 is higher than 50 to 100. According to our experiment, 10 labeled samples is the most cost-effective number to train a few-shot classifier.

For the comparison of the scales of the models, we can see that larger language models have higher scores. We have mentioned this phenomenon in Sect. 5.1, that larger models can better leverage the prompts. Especially, the average accuracy of RoBERT-large's zero-shot classifier in AG's News dataset is **84.84%**, which is higher than the average accuracy of DistilBERT's and BERT-base's 100-shot classifier. It strengthen the idea that the larger model could better understand the task by leveraging the additional prompts. On the other hand, this value means that the classifier of the RoBERTa-large realizes zero-shot learning. It also approves our opinion that when a language model is strong enough, it will realize few-shot learning, even zero-shot learning.

### 5.3 Visualization of Attention

Comparing the multi-class classification to the QA classification, we noticed that the performance of QA classification is slightly superior to the multi-class classification or on a par with multi-class classification. More wonderfully, the QA method can help language models do few-shot learning. To figure out what the reason is here, we associate it with the attention mechanism.

So in this section, we make visualizations of attention to explain the work of the question. As shown in Fig. 4, we randomly chose a sample from the **AG's News** dataset, and generated four questions, according to the labels.

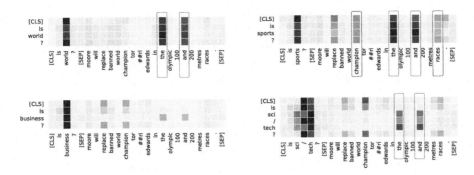

**Fig. 4.** Visualizations of attention of a fine-tuned QA classifier based on BERT-base. The content is: "Moore will replace banned world champion Torri Edwards in the Olympic 100 and 200 m races", which belongs to the **sports** class.

As we can see, when we ask "is sports?", the word **sports** in the question notice the **champion** and the **races** in the content (in blue boxes), which are words representative of certain classes. Then the question helps the [CLS] notice these keywords, so we use the [CLS] as the representation of the content is logical. But when we ask other questions, it seems not well, the question noticed other inconsequential words. Interestingly, the questions almost noticed the word **the** and the word **and** (in green boxes), which have nothing to do with classification.

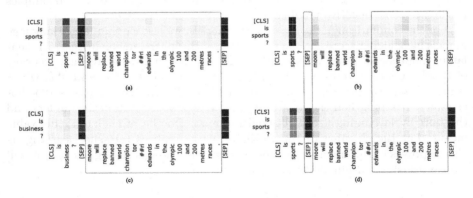

**Fig. 5.** An illustration of visualizations of the BERT-base's attention, (a) a model have never seen the **sports** class; (b) a model just have seen 10 examples of the **sports** class; (c) the same model as (a), ask "is business?" which it has seen; (d) a model have seen 50 examples of the visualization class. All of the models have not seen the content.

In Fig. 5, comparing (a) and (c), (c) is much cleaner in the green box. We can notice that the model of (a) pay some attention to the 'edwards', '100' and '200', and when we ask a different question that has already been seen, the model knows it doesn't need to pay attention to anything. The content is nothing to do with the business class, so it is logical that the attention weight of the content in (c) is close to 0. But in (a), the language model guesses the words that should be attention to. To some extent, the language model can identify and leverage the prompt. In (b) and (d), the significant difference is in the blue box and the purple box. In purple box, we think more training samples led to changes in attention, that the question pay less attention to the content, while more attention to the special token [SEP]. This phenomenon needs further discussion.

## 6    Conclusion

In this paper we present a QA-based method, helping language models do text classification and exploring the few-shot learning ability of a language model, which is simple but effective. This method enables the language model to demonstrate the ability of a few-shot learning ability that only using 100 labeled data, the average accuracy could reach 92.18%, some even achieve zero-shot learning. In future work, we focus on the few-shot capability of the language model itself and why it exists.

## References

1. Baum, L.E., Petrie, T.: Statistical inference for probabilistic functions of finite state markov chains. Ann. Math. Stat. **37**(6), 1554–1563 (1966)
2. Bromley, J., Guyon, I., LeCun, Y., Säckinger, E., Shah, R.: Signature verification using a "siamese" time delay neural network. In: Advances in Neural Information Processing Systems, pp. 737–737 (1994)
3. Brown, T., et al.: Language models are few-shot learners. In: Advances in Neural Information Processing Systems, vol. 33, pp. 1877–1901 (2020)
4. Devlin, J., Chang, M.W., Lee, K., Toutanova, K.: BERT: pre-training of deep bidirectional transformers for language understanding. In: Proceedings of the 2019 Conference of the North American Chapter of the Association for Computational Linguistics: Human Language Technologies, vol. 1, pp. 4171–4186 (2019)
5. Fei-Fei, L., Fergus, R., Perona, P.: One-shot learning of object categories. IEEE Trans. Pattern Anal. Mach. Intell. **28**(4), 594–611 (2006)
6. Gao, T., Fisch, A., Chen, D.: Making pre-trained language models better few-shot learners. In: Association for Computational Linguistics (ACL) (2021)
7. Kalchbrenner, N., Grefenstette, E., Blunsom, P.: A convolutional neural network for modelling sentences. In: Proceedings of the 52nd Annual Meeting of the Association for Computational Linguistics, vol. 1, pp. 655–665 (2014)
8. Lafferty, J.D., McCallum, A., Pereira, F.C.N.: Conditional random fields: probabilistic models for segmenting and labeling sequence data. In: Proceedings of the Eighteenth International Conference on Machine Learning (ICML 2001), Williams College, Williamstown, MA, USA, June 28 - July 1, 2001, pp. 282–289 (2001)
9. Lake, B.M., Ullman, T.D., Tenenbaum, J.B., Gershman, S.J.: Building machines that learn and think like people. Behavioral Brain Sciences, vol. 40 (2017)
10. Li, M., Long, Y., Qin, L., Li, W.: Emotion corpus construction based on selection from hashtags. In: Proceedings of the Tenth International Conference on Language Resources and Evaluation (LREC'16), pp. 1845–1849. European Language Resources Association (ELRA), Portorož, Slovenia (2016)

11. Liu, Y., et al.: Roberta: A robustly optimized bert pretraining approach. arXiv preprint arXiv:1907.11692 (2019)
12. Radford, A., Narasimhan, K., Salimans, T., Sutskever, I.: Improving language understanding by generative pre-training (2018)
13. Radford, A., Wu, J., Child, R., Luan, D., Amodei, D., Sutskever, I.: Language models are unsupervised multitask learners. OpenAI Blog **1**(8), 9 (2019)
14. Ravi, S., Larochelle, H.: Optimization as a model for few-shot learning. In: 5th International Conference on Learning Representations, ICLR 2017, Toulon, France, April 24–26, 2017, Conference Track Proceedings (2017)
15. Sanh, V., Debut, L., Chaumond, J., Wolf, T.: Distilbert, a distilled version of bert: smaller, faster, cheaper and lighter. arXiv preprint arXiv:1910.01108 (2019)
16. Schick, T., Schütze, H.: Exploiting cloze-questions for few-shot text classification and natural language inference. In: Proceedings of the 16th Conference of the European Chapter of the Association for Computational Linguistics: Main Volume, pp. 255–269. Online (2021)
17. Sun, C., Qiu, X., Xu, Y., Huang, X.: How to fine-tune BERT for text classification? In: Sun, M., Huang, X., Ji, H., Liu, Z., Liu, Y. (eds.) CCL 2019. LNCS (LNAI), vol. 11856, pp. 194–206. Springer, Cham (2019). https://doi.org/10.1007/978-3-030-32381-3_16
18. Tharwat, A.: Classification assessment methods. Applied Computing and Informatics (2020)
19. Wei, J., Zou, K.: EDA: easy data augmentation techniques for boosting performance on text classification tasks. In: Proceedings of the 2019 Conference on Empirical Methods in Natural Language Processing and the 9th International Joint Conference on Natural Language Processing (EMNLP-IJCNLP), pp. 6382–6388. Hong Kong, China (2019)
20. Zhang, X., Zhao, J.J., LeCun, Y.: Character-level convolutional networks for text classification. In: Cortes, C., Lawrence, N.D., Lee, D.D., Sugiyama, M., Garnett, R. (eds.) Advances in Neural Information Processing Systems 28: Annual Conference on Neural Information Processing Systems 2015, December 7–12, 2015, Montreal, Quebec, Canada, pp. 649–657 (2015)
21. Zhang, Z., et al.: Cpm: A large-scale generative chinese pre-trained language model. arXiv preprint arXiv:2012.00413 (2020)
22. Zhao, T., Yan, Z., Cao, Y., Li, Z.: Asking effective and diverse questions: a machine reading comprehension based framework for joint entity-relation extraction. In: Bessiere, C. (ed.) Proceedings of the Twenty-Ninth International Joint Conference on Artificial Intelligence, IJCAI 2020, pp. 3948–3954 (2020)
23. Zhou, P., Qi, Z., Zheng, S., Xu, J., Bao, H., Xu, B.: Text classification improved by integrating bidirectional LSTM with two-dimensional max pooling. In: Proceedings of COLING 2016, the 26th International Conference on Computational Linguistics: Technical Papers, pp. 3485–3495 (2016)

# Generative Adversarial Networks

# Leveraging GANs via Non-local Features

Xuyang Peng[1], Weifeng Liu[2(✉)], Baodi Liu[2], Kai Zhang[3], Xiaoping Lu[4], and Yicong Zhou[5]

[1] College of Oceanography and Space Informatics,
China University of Petroleum (East China), Qingdao, China
`pengxuyang19972@163.com`
[2] College of Control Science and Engineering,
China University of Petroleum (East China), Qingdao, China
`liuwf@upc.edu.cn, thu.liubaodi@gmail.com`
[3] School of Petroleum Engineering, China University of Petroleum (East China),
Qingdao, China
`zhangkai@upc.edu.cn`
[4] Haier Industrial Intelligence Institute Co., Ltd., Qingdao, China
`luxiaoping@haier.com`
[5] University of Macau, Macau, China
`yicongzhou@um.edu.mo`

**Abstract.** Recent years, Generative Adversarial Networks (GANs) have achieved tremendous success in image synthesis, which usually employ the convolutional operation to extract image features. However, most existing convolutional GANs only extract features in a local neighborhood at a time, which may often cause a lack of non-local information resulting in generating the wrong semantic object in the wrong position. In this paper, we propose a Graph Convolutional Architecture (GCA) for GANs to tackle this problem. GCA constructs a pixel-level graph structure between image regions through an attention mechanism and leverages Graph Convolutional Networks (GCNs) to extract non-local features. GCA extracts the connections between different regions of the image through GCNs, which is a more effective method of using relationship information than directly adding long-range dependencies to the model. We implement the GCA into Deep Convolutional Generative Adversarial Networks (DCGAN), Self-Attention Generative Adversarial Networks (SAGAN), and Concurrent-Single-Image-GAN (ConSinGAN). Extensive experiments are conducted to verify the performance of GCA. The results demonstrate that the GCA can significantly boost the quality of the generated image with more non-local features.

**Keywords:** Generative adversarial networks · Non-local features · Attention mechanism

© Springer Nature Switzerland AG 2021
I. Farkaš et al. (Eds.): ICANN 2021, LNCS 12892, pp. 551–562, 2021.
https://doi.org/10.1007/978-3-030-86340-1_44

# 1   Introduction

Recent years, GANs attract much attention for their prodigious performance in image synthesis. And many GANs variants are reported in most of all aspects of the image generating such as single image super-resolution reconstruction [13,25,26], text-to-image synthesis [20,21,29], image-to-image translation [9,30], single image synthesis [8,22] and multi-class image synthesis [17,28], etc. The early GANs models only design straight-forward discriminators and generators [3,5,19], which usually causes some problems such as unstable training and mode collapse. To improve the performance, many varieties of GANs are reported and can briefly divide into three categories, i.e. (1) Hierarchical Methods, (2) Iterative Methods, and (3) Loss Methods.

Hierarchical methods aim to modify the architecture of discriminators and generators with some specific modules to assist GANs for better image generating [16–18]. Wang et al. propose a Style and Structure Generative Adversarial Network (S2-GAN) by generating a surface normal map to encode the texture on the objects and the illumination with two GANs [24]. Karras et al. propose an Alternative Generator Architecture for Generative Adversarial Networks (Sytle-GAN) by employing a style transfer module to control the high-level attributes, such as hairstyles, freckles [11]. Odena et al. propose Auxiliary Classifier Generative Adversarial Networks (AC-GAN) which deploys an auxiliary classifier in the discriminator to exhibiting global coherence in GANs [18].

Iterative methods aim to design a skillful training process of GANs to drive generating photorealistic images [8,10,22]. Karras et al. propose a progressive growing method for GANs (ProgressiveGAN) by gradually increasing the layers of generator and discriminator to generate images from a low resolution to high resolution [10]. Shaham et al. propose a method for GANs in single image synthesis (SinGAN) by exploiting the pyramid structure to learn the whole image features from a single image [22]. Hinz et al. draw the pyramid structure of SinGAN and adopt parallel computing to reduce training time while improving the performance of the model [8].

Loss methods aim to apply suitable loss functions to stabilize the GANs training and improve generation performance [1,6,17]. Arjovsky et al. propose Wasserstein Generative Adversarial Networks (WGAN) by adopting the Wasserstein distance loss function instead of the Min-Max loss function to achieve a more stable training process [1]. Gulrajani et al. propose an improved method for WGAN by using a gradient penalty instead of a parameter clip [6]. Miyato et al. propose a regularization method for GANs (SN-GAN) by limiting the spectral norm of the parameters of the discriminator to constrain the Lipschitz constant [17].

Most GANs mentioned above are based on Convolutional Neural Networks (CNNs). However, traditional CNNs only capture the local spatial features in the receptive field and can't cover enough non-local information. The non-local information e.g. long-range dependencies can reflect the relationship between image regions and complement the neural network. Therefore, ignoring non-local information will often make the convolutional GANs generate the wrong semantic objects in the wrong positions. To alleviate the lack of non-local information in the convolutional operation, Wang et al. propose a self-attention-mechanism-based module called Non-Local (NL) block to capture long-range dependencies in CNNs [23]. Han et al. introduce the NL block into GANs, proposing Self-Attention Generative Adversarial Networks (SAGAN) to alleviate the lack of non-local information in GANs [28]. SAGAN takes the long-range dependencies captured by the NL block as the weight and performs a weighted summation with the convolution feature maps to supplement the non-local information for the convolution GAN. Although SAGAN has supplemented convolutional GANs with long-range dependencies, it has great research potential on utilizing non-local information rather than simply adding long-range dependencies into models.

In this paper, we propose a Graph Convolutional Architecture (GCA) for GANs. GCA constructs a pixel-level graph structure between image regions by the self-attention mechanism and leverages GCNs to capture non-local features. Specifically, GCA employs an attention mechanism for pixel-level graph structure construction. Compared with the NL block directly adding long-distance dependencies to models, the non-local features extracted by GCNs in GCA further refine the non-local relationship information contained in long-distance dependencies. And the non-local features also have higher generalization, because GCNs are a kind of generalized form of CNNs. Equipped with GCA, the generator and the discriminator can successfully supplement non-local information for GANs to generate more realistic images. Furthermore, GCA can be easily applied to most convolutional GANs to improve the quality of the generated images. We show the flow chart of GCA in Fig. 1.

To evaluate the generalization of GCA, we implement the GCA into DCGAN, SAGAN, and ConSinGAN. And we conduct extensive experiments on these models. In addition, we also compare the NL block with GCA. The comparative results demonstrate the superiority of GCA in both quantitative and qualitative analysis. Briefly, the contribution of this paper can be summarized as the following:

(1) A Graph Convolutional Architecture (GCA) is proposed to model non-local information to GANs.

(2) The GCA is implemented into three GANs and extensive experiments are conducted to show the superiority of the proposed GCA.

The rest of this paper is arranged as follows. Section 2 briefly introduces the related work. Section 3 describes the details of GCA including the construction of pixel-level global graph structure. Section 4, reports the experimental results and provides some analysis. And finally, Sect. 5 concludes this paper.

## 2  Related Work

### 2.1  Generative Adversarial Networks

Ian et al. first propose Generative Adversarial Networks (GANs), which can only generate gray-scale images by two fully-connected networks [5]. Inspired by

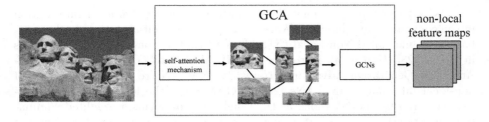

**Fig. 1.** GCA constructs a pixel-level graph structure among image regions through self-attention mechanism and exploits GCNs to extract non-local features.

Convolutional Neural Networks (CNNs), DCGAN introduces convolution into GANs and succeeds in unsupervised image synthesis [19]. The generator in DCGAN is constructed by transposed convolution, batch normalization, and ReLU activation, and the discriminator is constructed by convolution, batch normalization, and LeakyReLU activation. SAGAN introduces an NL block that models the long-range dependencies [28]. The NL block uses the weighted sum of all features to construct the relationship between image regions. SAGAN deploys the NL block in both the generator and discriminator, achieving great success in multi-classes image synthesis. ConSinGAN is currently the state-of-the-art GANs-based single image synthesis model [8]. ConSinGAN is an improvement of the Single Natural Image Generative Adversarial Network (SinGAN). Unlike SinGAN, ConSinGAN trains several stages in a sequential multi-stage manner, allowing the model to learn the whole features of a single image with fewer stages of increasing image resolution.

## 2.2   Graph Convolutional Networks

Graph Convolutional Networks (GCNs) are networks that can extract information in a more general domain, especially structural information. The early GCNs are dedicated to generalizing CNNs to enable them to work on high-dimensional irregular domains (for example, social networks, brain connection groups, or reference networks) [2,16]. Bruna et al. propose two constructions, one based on a clustering of the domain, and the other based on the spectrum of the graph Laplacian [2]. Defferrard et al. propose a graph convolution method that is based on the spectrogram theory and design fast localized convolutional filters on the graph [16]. Kipf et al. propose a scalable method for semi-supervised learning of graph-structured data, which is based on the spectrum of the graph Laplacian, and the convolution kernel is approximated by shifted Chebyshev polynomials to reduce the algorithm complexity [12].

## 2.3   Attention Mechanism

The attention mechanism in the neural networks mainly models the relationship between neural elements based on their correlation, which is a key component of

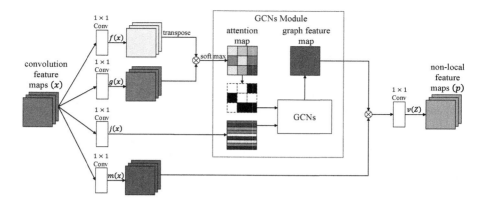

**Fig. 2.** The whole structure of GCA. The $\otimes$ denotes matrix multiplication.

various natural language processing and computer vision tasks. Attention mechanisms can process variable-sized inputs, focusing on the most relevant parts of the input to assist the model to make decisions. Attention mechanisms used to be adapted in many sequence-based tasks, such as machine reading [4] and learning sentence representations [14]. In image generation, the long-distance relationship modeling through the attention mechanism has proved effective for learning high-dimensional and complex image distribution. Wang et al. propose a self-attention-mechanism-based module for video processing called Non-Local (NL) block [23]. The NL block can capture long-range dependencies about image regions, and it can be inserted into many CNNs. In addition to being deployed in image processing, this non-local structure is also applicable for sequence and video problems. In addition to modeling the relationship between neural elements, the attention mechanism can also be used to construct graph structure in a graph domain. GCA employs a self-attention mechanism to construct a pixel-level global graph structure.

## 3    Graph Convolutional Architecture

The GCA employs an attention mechanism to construct a pixel-level graph structure and exploit GCNs to extract the non-local features. GCA is a complement to the convolutional GANs, alleviating the disadvantage of convolution that only captures local features. The whole structure of GCA is shown in Fig. 2.

The convolutional feature maps $x \in \mathbb{R}^{C \times H \times W}$ obtained by the previous network are mapped into four feature spaces in GCA by $f, g, j, m$. Here, $f, g, j, m$ are all $1 \times 1$ convolutions and $W_f \in \mathbb{R}^{\bar{c} \times c}, W_g \in \mathbb{R}^{\bar{c} \times c}, W_j \in \mathbb{R}^{\bar{c} \times 1}, W_m \in \mathbb{R}^{c \times c}, \bar{c} = \frac{c}{k}, k = 1, 2, 4, 8$. Because $\bar{c}$ does not influence the essential characteristics of the attention maps, we choose $k = 8$ for memory efficiency. Among them, $f$ and $g$ are used to calculate the attention map,

$$a_{j,i} = \frac{\exp(r_{i,j})}{\sum_{i=1}^{N} \exp(r_{i,j})} \quad (1)$$

where $r_{i,j} = f(x_i)^T g(x_j), N = H \times W$, and $a_{j,i}$ indicates the attention value of the $j^{th}$ region to the $i^{th}$ region. The whole attention map $A \in \mathbb{R}^{N \times N}$ is assembled by $a_{j,i}$, containing the relations between all the regions in $x$. Based on these relations, $A$ can directly consider as an adjacency matrix in a graph domain. Also, according to different GANs models and GCNs algorithms, some methods can be used to operate $A$ to make GCA obtain better performance, e.g. binarization, which is marked as a dotted box in Fig. 2.

$J \in \mathbb{R}^{N \times N}$ is the feature matrix in a graph domain according to $A$. $A$ and $J$ constitute the main input of GCNs, and the calculation formula of GCNs is

$$Y = \tilde{D}^{-\frac{1}{2}} \tilde{A} \tilde{D}^{-\frac{1}{2}} J \Theta \quad (2)$$

where $\tilde{A} = A + I_N, \tilde{D}_{ii} = \sum_j \tilde{A}_{i,j}, J = W_j x$ and $\Theta \in \mathbb{R}^{N \times N}$ which is the parameter matrix. The output of GCNs $Y \in R^{N \times N}$ is the graph feature map.

To make the input and output of GCA have the same dimensions, GCA leverages convolution and matrix multiplication to adjust the size of the graph feature map, the formula is

$$Z = MY \quad (3)$$

where $M = W_j x$, and $Z \in \mathbb{R}^{C \times H \times W}$. The property that GCA doesn't change the dimensions making it a plug-and-play module. The final convolution v is deployed at the end of the model. This convolution allows GCA to map the features to non-local features, the formula is

$$p = W_v Z \quad (4)$$

where $v$ is a $1 \times 1$ convolution and $W_v \in \mathbb{R}^{c \times c}$.

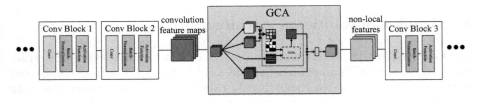

**Fig. 3.** The way GCA works in convolutional GANs. GCA can be easily embedded between two convolutional blocks.

To start training from easy to hard, we multiply the output of the GCNs model by a learnable scale parameter $\alpha$ and add back the input feature map. The $\alpha$ is initialized as 0. Therefore, the final output is given by

$$o = \alpha p + x \tag{5}$$

where $x$ represents the previous convolutional feature maps.

The way GCA works in the convolutional GANs is shown in Fig. 3.

## 4   Experiments

We implement the GCA into DCGAN, SAGAN, and ConSinGAN. Two datasets are adopted, including CelebA [15], and LSUN (church) [27]. Besides, we also conduct single image synthesis experiments. We deploy the NL block in the same position in DCGAN and SAGAN for comparison experiments. All models adopt the same hyperparameters, loss function, and training method.

The GCA and NL block deployed in DCGAN, SAGAN adopt $8 \times 8$ convolutional feature maps as input, and DCGAN and SAGAN are trained to generate $64 \times 64$ resolution images. The GCA deployed in ConSinGAN only works in the first stage of training. It should be noted that the GCA deployed in SAGAN replaces its original NL block instead of being equipped with an additional GCA module. All models are trained on NVIDIA Tesla V100 GPU. Quantitative and qualitative analyses are applied to the experimental results.

We quantitatively analyze the quality of the images generated by the above model. We chose the Fréchet Inception Distance (FID) [7] and Single Image Fréchet Inception Distance (SIFID) [22] to evaluate the generated images. FID compares the distribution of a pre-trained network's activations between a set of generated and real images. Especially, SIFID is an adaptation of the FID to the single image domain. The generated on CelebA and LSUN (church) synthesized by DCGAN, DCGAN + NL, and DCGAN + GCA are shown in Fig. 4. The FID scores of all models are shown in Table 1 (The real images for calculating FID are the original images in datasets sampled to $64 \times 64$. All FID scores are calculated on 50,000 generated images). We show the heatmap of convolutional operation, NL block, and GCA in Fig. 5. The heatmap shows that GCA captures more non-local information than the NL block.

Visually, when models are equipped with GCA, they can generate more realistic images. In quantitative analysis, the lower FID scores indicate that GCA can bring significant enhancement to GANs. However, the NL block doesn't improve the performance, causing a side effect instead. This contrast shows that the long-range dependencies captured by NL block are not generalized information in GANs, simply adding them to the model will even bring negative effects. In contrast, the non-local features modeled by GCA are extracted by GCNs. GCNs are a generalized form of CNNs, so non-local features are more generalized than long-range dependencies.

DCGAN          DCGAN + NL

DCGAN + GCA

**Fig. 4.** Generated images of CelebA and LSUN (church) synthesized by DCGAN, DCGAN + NL, and DCGAN + GCA.

Conv          NL          GCA

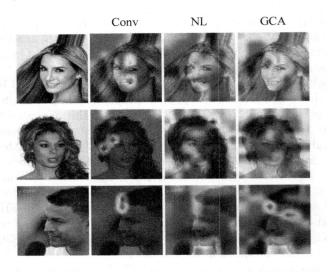

**Fig. 5.** Heatmaps of convolutional operation, NL block, and GCA. GCA and NL block can significantly increase the high activation regions. GCA and NL block enable CNNs to have high activation values for multiple regions at the same time instead of being limited to local regions. In addition, compared to NL block, GCA has more high activation regions. This means that GCA captures more non-local information.

**Table 1.** The FID scores of DCGAN, DCGAN + NL, DCGAN + GCA, SAGAN and SAGAN + GCA.

| Model | Dataset | |
|---|---|---|
| | CelebA | LSUN (church) |
| DCGAN [19] | 33.39 | 33.59 |
| DCGAN + NL | 34.56 | 54.36 |
| **DCGAN + GCA** | **25.75** | **22.15** |
| SAGAN [28] | 54.75 | 36.56 |
| **SAGAN + GCA** | **37.39** | **28.74** |

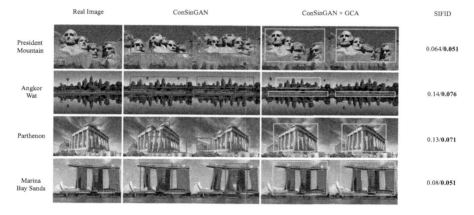

**Fig. 6.** Results of single image synthesis. The semantics that ConSinGAN fails to model are marked with red boxes and the improvements of GCA are marked with green boxes. The left side of the fourth column is the SIFID scores of ConSinGAN, and the right side is the SIFID scores of ConSinGAN deployed with GCA.

Single image synthesis can intuitively reflect the improvement of GCA to the GANs. However, SIFID itself has a large variance, qualitative analysis is more intuitive in single image synthesis. The results of the experiments are shown in Fig. 6 (All SIFID scores are the average of the scores of 10 generated samples).

Intuitively, after GCA is equipped, the semantics of the generated images are significantly improved in space, structure, and texture. For example, in the President Mountain image, GCA can correctly model the positional relation between semantics. The generative model can correctly generate the position of each semantic object, avoiding the defect that the semantic objects are mixed. The improvements confirm that the pixel-level graph structure constructed by GCA can indeed successfully model the relationship information between the various features of the image. ConSinGAN uses a phased training method similar to ProgressiveGAN. In Fig. 6, we show the results of different training phases of

Stage    1    2    3    4    5    6

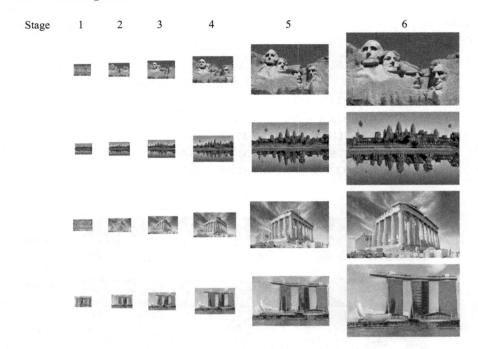

**Fig. 7.** The results of ConSinGAN + GCA in different training stages. The GCA helps ConSinGAN to model the image semantics early in the training.

ConSinGAN after deploying GCA. The results of each stage of the ConSinGAN deployed with GCA are shown in Fig. 7.

# 5    Conclusion

In this paper, we propose the Graph Convolutional Architecture (GCA) for GANs. The GCA employs the self-attention mechanism to construct a pixel-level graph structure and then incorporates the GCNs into the GANs. With the captured graph structure, GCA successfully supplements non-local feature extraction of GANs. Finally, we embed it into three representative GANs i.e. DCGAN, SAGAN, and ConSinGAN for evaluation. Experimental results verify the superiority of GCNs and show that GCA can significantly improve the performance of the convolutional GANs.

**Acknowledgment.** The paper was supported by the National Natural Science Foundation of China (Grant No. 61671480), the Major Scientific and Technological Projects of CNPC under Grant ZD2019-183-008, the Open Project Program of the National Laboratory of Pattern Recognition (NLPR) (Grant No. 20200009).

# References

1. Arjovsky, M., Chintala, S., Bottou, L.: Wasserstein generative adversarial networks. In: International Conference on Machine Learning, pp. 214–223 (2017)
2. Bruna, J., Zaremba, W., Szlam, A., Lecun, Y.: Spectral networks and locally connected networks on graphs. In: International Conference on Learning Representations (2014)
3. Chen, X., Duan, Y., Houthooft, R., Schulman, J., Sutskever, I., Abbeel, P.: InfoGAN: interpretable representation learning by information maximizing generative adversarial nets. In: Advances in Neural Information Processing Systems, pp. 2180–2188 (2016)
4. Cheng, J., Dong, L., Lapata, M.: Long short-term memory-networks for machine reading. In: Conference on Empirical Methods in Natural Language Processing, pp. 551–561 (2016)
5. Goodfellow, I., et al.: Generative adversarial nets. In: Advances in Neural Information Processing Systems, pp. 2672–2680 (2014)
6. Gulrajani, I., Ahmed, F., Arjovsky, M., Dumoulin, V., Courville, A.: Improved training of Wasserstein GANs. In: Advances in Neural Information Processing Systems, pp. 5769–5779 (2017)
7. Heusel, M., Ramsauer, H., Unterthiner, T., Nessler, B., Hochreiter, S.: Gans trained by a two time-scale update rule converge to a local Nash equilibrium. In: Advances in Neural Information Processing Systems, pp. 6626–6637 (2017)
8. Hinz, T., Fisher, M., Wang, O., Wermter, S.: Improved techniques for training single-image GANs. In: IEEE Winter Conference on Applications of Computer Vision, pp. 1300–1309 (2021)
9. Isola, P., Zhu, J., Zhou, T., Efros, A.A.: Image-to-image translation with conditional adversarial networks. In: IEEE Conference on Computer Vision and Pattern Recognition, pp. 5967–5976 (2017)
10. Karras, T., Aila, T., Laine, S., Lehtinen, J.: Progressive growing of GANs for improved quality, stability, and variation. In: International Conference on Learning Representations (2018)
11. Karras, T., Laine, S., Aila, T.: A style-based generator architecture for generative adversarial networks. In: IEEE Conference on Computer Vision and Pattern Recognition, pp. 4401–4410 (2019)
12. Kipf, T., Welling, M.: Semi-supervised classification with graph convolutional networks. In: International Conference on Learning Representations (2017)
13. Ledig, C., Theis, L., Huszar, F., Caballero, J., Cunningham, A., Acosta, A.: Photorealistic single image super-resolution using a generative adversarial network. In: IEEE Conference on Computer Vision and Pattern Recognition, pp. 105–114 (2017)
14. Lin, Z., et al.: A structured self-attentive sentence embedding. In: International Conference on Learning Representations (2017)
15. Liu, Z., Luo, P., Wang, X., Tang, X.: Deep learning face attributes in the wild. In: IEEE International Conference on Computer Vision, pp. 3730–3738 (2015)
16. Defferrard, M., Bresson, X., Vandergheynst, P.: Convolutional neural networks on graphs with fast localized spectral filtering. In: Advances in Neural Information Processing Systems, pp. 3844–3852 (2016)
17. Miyato, T., Kataoka, T., Koyama, M., Yoshida, Y.: Spectral normalization for generative adversarial networks. In: International Conference on Learning Representations (2018)

18. Odena, A., Olah, C., Shlens, J.: Conditional image synthesis with auxiliary classifier GANs. In: International Conference on Machine Learning, pp. 2642–2651 (2017)
19. Radford, A., Metz, L., Chintala, S.: Unsupervised representation learning with deep convolutional generative adversarial networks. In: International Conference on Learning Representations (2016)
20. Reed, S., Akata, Z., Mohan, S., Tenka, S., Schiele, B., Lee, H.: Learning what and where to draw. In: Advances in Neural Information Processing Systems, pp. 217–225 (2016)
21. Reed, S., Akata, Z., Yan, X., Logeswaran, L., Schiele, B., Lee, H.: Generative adversarial text to image synthesis. In: International Conference on Machine Learning, pp. 1060–1069 (2016)
22. Shaham, T.R., Dekel, T., Michaeli, T.: SinGAN: learning a generative model from a single natural image. In: IEEE International Conference on Computer Vision, pp. 4570–4580 (2019)
23. Wang, X., Girshick, R., Gupta, A., He, K.: Non-local neural networks. In: IEEE Conference on Computer Vision and Pattern Recognition, pp. 7794–7803 (2018)
24. Wang, X., Gupta, A.: Generative image modeling using style and structure adversarial networks. In: European Conference on Computer Vision, pp. 318–335 (2016)
25. Wang, X., Yu, K., Dong, C., Loy, C.C.: Recovering realistic texture in image super-resolution by deep spatial feature transform. In: IEEE Conference on Computer Vision and Pattern Recognition, pp. 606–615 (2018)
26. Wang, X., et al.: ESRGAN: enhanced super-resolution generative adversarial networks. In: Leal-Taixé, L., Roth, S. (eds.) ECCV 2018. LNCS, vol. 11133, pp. 63–79. Springer, Cham (2019). https://doi.org/10.1007/978-3-030-11021-5_5
27. Yu, F., Zhang, Y., Song, S., Seff, A., Xiao, J.: LSUN: construction of a large-scale image dataset using deep learning with humans in the loop. arXiv preprint arXiv: 1411.7766 (2014)
28. Zhang, H., Goodfellow, I., Metaxas, D.N., Odena, A.: Self-attention generative adversarial networks. In: International Conference on Machine Learning, pp. 7354–7363 (2019)
29. Zhang, H., Xu, T., Li, H.: StackGAN: text to photo-realistic image synthesis with stacked generative adversarial networks. In: IEEE International Conference on Computer Vision, pp. 1060–1069 (2016)
30. Zhu, J., Park, T., Isola, P., Efros, A.A.: Unpaired image-to-image translation using cycle-consistent adversarial networks. In: IEEE International Conference on Computer Vision, pp. 2242–2251 (2017)

# On Mode Collapse in Generative Adversarial Networks

Kaifeng Zhang$^{(\boxtimes)}$

Nanjing, China

**Abstract.** Generative adversarial networks (GANs) have shown extraordinary performance in generating high quality samples in domains including image, video, and text. GANs therefore have great potential in learning complex probability distributions in high dimensional spaces. However, current methods often miss capturing some of the modes in the examples, known as the mode collapse problem. The reason for this issue can be traced to that the initial generated manifold fails to cover the whole data manifold, while the training process is hard to recover from this failure. In this paper, we propose GANs with supervision signal (SSGAN), which introduces a supervision signal to alleviate this issue. The supervision signal tells the generator an approximate output corresponding to the input noise, which ensures the generated manifold to be close to the data manifold. Therefore, the generator could be able to better capture the whole data distribution. We have conducted experiments on MNIST, CIFAR 10 and CelebA datasets. The results show that our method outperforms several SoTA approaches measured by the inception score, mode score, and the newly proposed *matching score*.

## 1 Introduction

Learning probability distribution in high dimensional space is a fundamental yet difficult task in artificial intelligence (e.g., [11]). Generative adversarial networks (GANs) [6] have shown great successes in generating vivid objects in high dimensional space, such as image [5], video [13], and 3D model [20], by training a generator $G$ together with an adversarial discriminator $D$. These successes disclose the great potential of GANs in learning complex probability distribution in high dimensional space.

The original study [6] has shown that, when the discriminator capacity and the number of samples are both sufficient, the convergence of GANs implies that the learned distribution $P_{gen}$ will be very close to the ground-truth distribution $P_{real}$. However, it is usually not the case in practice. The mode collapse issue is often observed (e.g., [3]), which appears as that a significant part of the training data is hard to be generated by the learned generative model. This observation means that the learned distribution shifts away from the real distribution. Therefore, the learned distribution by GANs could have a large error, e.g., especially for imitation learning [8].

---

K. Zhang—Independent Researcher.

© Springer Nature Switzerland AG 2021
I. Farkaš et al. (Eds.): ICANN 2021, LNCS 12892, pp. 563–574, 2021.
https://doi.org/10.1007/978-3-030-86340-1_45

The reason that some modes in the training data are missed can be traced to the initialization of GANs. In high dimensional sample space, it is hard for the initial generated manifold to cover all the modes with limited training examples. Meanwhile, some theoretical results also indicate that the gradients on the generator cannot lead the generated manifold to cover all the examples. Therefore, training generative adversarial networks always suffers from the problem of mode collapse.

In this paper, we introduce a supervision signal to formal GANs in order to alleviate the mode collapse issue, which aims at drawing the generated manifold close to the real data manifold. The intuition of our work is summarized as follows. We add an inverse generator to the formal GAN, which learns a mapping from high dimensional sample space to low dimensional noise space. Therefore, we can use these data pairs to guide the generated manifold being close to the real data manifold. Experiment results show that our method outperforms several SoTA methods in training GANs with the measure: inception score, mode score and newly proposed matching score.

The contributions of our work are threefold.

– We re-analyzes the reasons for mode collapse in GANs theoretically;
– We extend formal GAN to SSGAN in order to alleviate the mode collapse issue in GANs;
– We introduce a new evaluation metric: *matching score* which can better measure the performance on modes capturing.
– Experiments show that our SSGAN outperforms several SoTA methods in both image quality and modes capturing.

## 2   Related Work

Mode collapse problem always occurs in training GANs. And there are also some SoTA methods for alleviating this issue as follows.

WGAN [1] and WGAN-GP [7] use Wasserstein metric to avoid gradient vanishing when the discriminator trains to be optimal. It also shows that the mode collapse in GANs is somehow alleviated in its experiments.

Unrolled GAN [14] defines the generator objective with respect to an unrolled optimization of the discriminator. With more information from surrogate loss function, the training for generator and discriminator can be more balanced. This technique might be ideal for mode collapse issue in GANs but not feasible in practice.

AdaGAN [19] is inspired by boosting algorithm. At every step of AdaGAN procedure, a new component will be added into a mixture model by running a GAN algorithm on a re-weighted training data set. Theoretical results show that such an incremental procedure will lead the generated data distribution converge to the real data distribution.

Spectral normalization generative adversarial networks (SNGAN) [15] propose to use spectral normalization to stabilize the training of the discriminator. With such an operation to the discriminator at each iteration, Lipschitz constant for the discriminator can be bounded. So the training stability for the discriminator can be better than before and the mode collapse problem can also be alleviated.

Mode regularized GAN [3] introduces two regularizers to regularize the objective: geometric metrics regularizer and mode regularizer. And the proposed manifold-diffusion training for GANs divides the training procedure into two parts: a manifold step and a diffusion step. In the manifold step, the generated manifold and the real data manifold can be matched. And in the diffusion step, the probability mass on the generation manifold can be distributed according to the real data distribution.

Variational encoder enhancement to generative adversarial networks (VEE-GAN) [18] introduces a reconstructor network which reverses the action of the generator by mapping the data distribution to noise distribution (a Gaussian). Once the reconstructor learns to be an inverse of the generator network and the mapping from data distribution to noise distribution, this will help to encourage the generator to cover all the examples in real data distributions.

## 3   Reasons for Mode Collapse in GANs

Although minimizing the distance (e.g. JSD) between generated manifold and real data manifold do help us to obtain a mapping from noise space to sample space, there still exists some limitations in training GANs. Mode collapse is one of severest problems. The reasons for mode collapse in GANs can be traced to that the initial generated manifold cannot cover all the examples, and the training process is hard to recover from this failure. In this section, we will analyze the reasons for mode collapse phenomenon theoretically.

Firstly, we suppose the generator is a function composed by affine transformations and point-wise nonlinearities. Here we consider the nonlinearities are rectifiers or leaky rectifiers of the form $\delta(x) = 1[x < 0]c_1 x + 1[x \geq 0]c_2 x$ for some $c_1, c_2 \in R$. Therefore, the generator network can be represented as:

$$g(z) = M_n W_n \cdots M_1 W_1 z, \tag{1}$$

where $M_i$ are some diagonal matrices dependent on $z$ that have diagonal entries $c_1$ or $c_2$ and $W_i$ are affine transformations.

Suppose $M$ is the set of all diagonal matrices with diagonal entries $c_1$ or $c_2$, then:

$$g(\mathcal{Z}) \subseteq \bigcup_{M_i \in M} M_n W_n \cdots M_1 W_1 \mathcal{Z}, \tag{2}$$

which is a finite union of linear manifolds. Denote that in the singular value decomposition, $W = U\Sigma V$, the operations (multiplying by $\Sigma$ and applying a change of basis are diffeomorphisms, and adding 0s to new coordinates) indicate a manifold embedding. Thus, the generated manifold will be projected onto a subset of the coordinates. So the generated manifold $g(\mathcal{Z})$ will be contained in a countable union of low dimensional manifolds. Therefore, the generated manifold has measure 0 in $\mathcal{X}$.

The illustrations above tell that the generated manifold will be contained in a countable union of low dimensional manifolds. At the same time, the real data manifold might be full of the sample space. Therefore, it is hard for the generator to cover all the examples, especially in the beginning of the training procedure. And it also points out the first reason for mode collapse in training GANs: the initial generated manifold cannot cover all the examples.

Secondly, we consider the generalization in GANs which means that the population distance between the generated distribution and real data distribution is close to the empirical distance between the empirical distributions.

We first assume the training objective function for GANs is $E_{x \sim P_r}[\phi(D(x))] + E_{z \sim P_g}[\phi(1 - D(G(z)))]$. Meanwhile we also assume the measuring function ranges from $-\Delta$ to $\Delta$, $\mathcal{F} = \{D_v, v \in \mathcal{V}\}$ is the class of discriminators that is $L$-Lipschitz with respect to the parameters $v$ and $p$ is to denote the number of parameters in $v$.

Let $\mu$, $v$ be two distributions and $\hat{\mu}$, $\hat{v}$ be empirical versions each with at least $m$ samples. We show that with high probability, for every discriminator $D_v$, there exists:

$$|E_{x \sim \mu}[\phi(D_v(x))] - E_{x \sim \hat{\mu}}[\phi(D_v(x))]| \leq \epsilon/2 \qquad (3)$$

$$|E_{x \sim v}[\phi(1 - D_v(x))] - E_{x \sim \hat{v}}[\phi(1 - D_v(x))]| \leq \epsilon/2 \qquad (4)$$

The proof can be seen in [2] in detail.

Therefore, we can obtain a conclusion that if $\hat{\mu}$ is the empirical version of distribution $\mu$ with $m$ samples. There is a universal constant $c$ such that when $m \geq (cp^2 \Delta^2 log(LL_{\phi}p/\epsilon))/\epsilon^2$, we have that with probability at least $1 - exp(-p)$, $d_{F,\Phi}(\mu, \hat{\mu}) \leq \epsilon$.

It shows that a discriminator net with $p$ parameters cannot distinguish a distribution $\mu$ and a distribution with support $\tilde{O}(p/\epsilon^2)$. That is, the low capacity discriminator cannot detect the lack of sample diversity. Actually, the training examples is very sparse and the sample space has a high dimensionality. That's why mode collapse occurs in GANs. It also leads to a conclusion that in GANs training procedure, the gradients on the generator cannot lead the generated manifold to cover all the examples. Therefore, it points out the second reason for mode collapse in GANs: the training procedure for GANs cannot recover from mode collapse failure.

Overall, the interpretations above show the reasons for mode collapse in training GANs which also motivate us to design a new training architecture for GANs.

## 4   Our Method

Our method to deal with mode collapse in GANs is to introduce a supervision signal to alleviate this issue. Therefore, the supervision signal will keep the generated manifold and the real data manifold close even in the initialization.

Inspired by variational auto-encoder, we set an encoder to learn the low dimensional representation for training examples. Thus, we can train the generator to ensure the generated manifold to be close to the real data manifold.

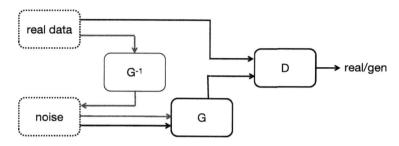

**Fig. 1.** Architecture for our model sGAN. Note that the red lines represents that using the encoder to learn the low dimensional representations for high dimensional training examples; Therefore, a supervision signal is added to typical GANs model. (Color figure online)

Figure 1 shows the architecture of our model SSGAN. In SSGAN, we use an encoder network (inverse generator) to learn the low dimensional representations for the training data. Meanwhile, the encoder can also restrict the low dimensional distribution to be some distribution (e.g. a Gaussian). Thus, the noise input for generator can be sampled from this distribution. Therefore, the generated manifold can be trained to be close to the real data manifold via such a supervision signal. The training paradigm is shown in the following paragraphs in detail.

The encoder in our training architecture is actually an inverse generator which can map the training examples to low dimensional representations. Therefore, this low dimensional representation can be used to make the generated manifold and real data manifold closely.

In our model, we regularizes the encoder by imposing a prior $z \sim \mathcal{N}(0, I)$ over the latent distribution. Thus the latent distribution can be restricted to a Gaussian by $\mathcal{L}_{prior} = KL(\mathcal{N}(\mu(x), \Sigma(x))\|\mathcal{N}(0, I))$. The training objective function for the encoder network can be shown as:

$$\mathcal{L}_E = \mathcal{L}_{prior} + \|G \circ E(x) - x\|_2^2 \tag{5}$$

where minimizing $\|G \circ E(x) - x\|_2^2$ is actually reducing the reconstruction error for the encoder-generator networks.

In the typical setting of GANs, it consists of two components: a generator and a discriminator. The discriminator tries to distinguish the real data examples and generated samples while the generator tries to confuse the discriminator. Here we assume the training objective function for GANs is:

$$\mathcal{L}_{GAN} = E_{x \sim P_r}[\phi(D(x))] + E_{z \sim P_g}[\phi(1 - D(G(z)))] \tag{6}$$

In SSGAN, the generated manifold is kept close to the real data manifold via a supervision signal. Meanwhile, the generator should still be trained to confuse the discriminator. By trading off these two motivations, we can obtain the objective function for the generator:

$$\mathcal{L}_G = E_{z \sim p_g}[\phi(1 - D(G(z)))] + \gamma \|G \circ E(x) - x\|_2^2 \tag{7}$$

On the other hand, the discriminator still tries to distinguish the real samples and the generated samples. So the training objective function for the discriminator can be shown as:

$$\mathcal{L}_D = E_{x \sim p_r}[\phi(D(x))] + E_{z \sim p_g}[\phi(1 - D(G(z)))] \tag{8}$$

By iteratively training the inverse generator, the generator and the discriminator, a supervision signal will be added to the GANs model to help the generated manifold capture more modes in examples.

## 5   Evaluation Metrics

To evaluate both the sample quality and modes capturing phenomenon in GANs, we use several different metrics for different experiments.

To estimate the sample quality, the inception score [17] is a very good assessment. The expression of inception score can be shown as:

$$I = exp(E_x KL(p(y|\mathbf{x}) \| p^*(y))) \tag{9}$$

Here, $\mathbf{x}$ represents one generated sample, $p(y|\mathbf{x})$ is the soft-max output of a strong classifier of the labels for a generated sample $\mathbf{x}$, and $p^*(y)$ is the overall label distribution for the generated examples. Considered that the strong classifier always has a high confidence for good samples, the higher inception score insures better sample quality.

However, the inception score do not consider the distribution of the training data. So once the GAN model is not very good, the inception score can still be very large for generated samples. [3] propose a new metric (mode score) to avoid this issue. The expression for mode score is shown as:

$$M = \exp(E_x KL(p(y|\mathbf{x}) \| p(y)) - KL(p^*(y) \| p(y))) \tag{10}$$

Here, $p(y)$ is the overall distributions for training samples. This metric considers the human evaluation experiences. The former part of mode score insures the sample quality and the latter part insures the sample diversity. However, the overall distribution for training data might has a very high entropy which will make the former part loss its efficacy.

The shortcomings of these two evaluation metrics motivate us to design a new metric to evaluate the performance for different GAN models on mode capturing.

**Definition 1 (Matching Score).** Given two datasets $D_1 = \{x_1, \cdots, x_n\}$ and $D_2 = \{g_1, \cdots, g_n\}$ in the same sample space, and a similarity function between two samples $s(\cdot, \cdot)$, the matching score between the two datasets w.r.t. $s$ is

$$MS = \frac{1}{n} \max_{\pi \in \Pi} \sum_{i=1}^{n} s(x_i, g_{\pi(i)}),$$

where $\Pi$ is all the permutations of $\{1, \cdots, n\}$.

Definition 1 tells that the matching score is the average value of similarity for generated samples and real samples with maximum matching. To calculate the matching score directly demands a large computational cost. In practice, we use maximum bipartite matching algorithm to search the optimal permutation of generated samples corresponding to some permutation of training examples. Therefore, the matching score can be obtained. Owing to that the matching score considers the optimal matching of generated samples and real samples, higher matching score insures more modes in generated manifold. That is why we use it to evaluate the performance of GANs on mode collapse problem. Besides, cosine similarity is chosen in our experiments.

# 6 Experiments

In order to show the efficacy of our newly proposed SSGAN, we conducted a set of experiments on MNIST [10], CIFAR10 [9], and CelebA face dataset [12]. The compared algorithms consist: DCGAN [16], improved Wasserstein GAN [7], VEEGAN [18], MDGAN [3], AdaGAN [19], and InfoGAN [4]. Meanwhile, we also provide the performance on metrics include: inception score, mode score and matching score.

In detail, we set the architecture from DCGAN as the architecture for our SSGAN and also the compared models. Besides, in the setting of SSGAN, we use the following standard objective function for training GANs:

$$\mathcal{L} = E_{x \sim p_r}[log(D(x))] + E_{z \sim p_g}[log(1 - D(G(z)))] \tag{11}$$

In the following paragraphs, we will provide the performance for different GANs on different datasets respectively.

## 6.1 Ablation Study

We conduct ablation studies on MNIST dataset compared with WGAN [1] and WGAN-GP [7]. MNIST is a dataset for hand written digits with 60,000 training examples and 10,000 test examples. The digits have been size normalized and centered in a fixed-size image. And these examples are from approximately 250 writers. Besides, we have made sure that the sets of writers for the training set and test set are disjoint.

For MNIST dataset, we borrow the architecture from DCGAN with three de-convolutional layers for the generator network and three convolutional layers for

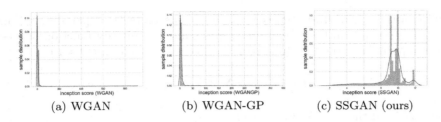

(a) WGAN                (b) WGAN-GP              (c) SSGAN (ours)

**Fig. 2.** Comparison on the histogram of inception score for generated samples.

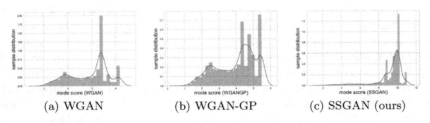

(a) WGAN                (b) WGAN-GP              (c) SSGAN (ours)

**Fig. 3.** Comparison on the histogram of mode score for generated samples.

the discriminator network. We also assume the data generating distribution can be approximated with ten dominant modes. So we train a regular three layers convolutional neural network to classify the generated samples into 10 classes. Therefore, we can get the inception score and the mode score respectively.

In Fig. 2, we use the histogram of inception score to evaluate the sample visual quality. Clearly, our proposed model SSGAN improves the inception scores and thus show the benefits of our model to improve the sample qualities. At the same time, we also use the histogram of mode score to evaluate the modes dropping phenomenon with these three models. In Fig. 3, the distribution of mode score of our model shows that our model can capture more modes than other two models.

**Table 1.** The proportion of digits for generated samples with 10,000 samples (%).

| Method | 0 | 1 | 2 | 3 | 4 | 5 | 6 | 7 | 8 | 9 |
|---|---|---|---|---|---|---|---|---|---|---|
| WGAN | 0.72 | 5.21 | 8.12 | 0.38 | 0.24 | 36.76 | 0.49 | 48.03 | 0.01 | 0.04 |
| WGAN-GP | 3.86 | 17.55 | 12.80 | 6.36 | 5.83 | 26.92 | 2.87 | 23.36 | 0.32 | 0.13 |
| SSGAN (ours) | 9.62 | 11.11 | 10.32 | 10.65 | 9.36 | 8.90 | 9.74 | 10.65 | 9.75 | 9.90 |

Table 1 shows the proportion of digits for generated samples with 10,000 samples. Clearly, the proposed SSGAN captures all the digits and the distribution for generated samples is almost the ground truth distribution of training data. On the other hand, WGAN missed a digit "8" and the digit distribution for WGAN and WGAN-GP is far away from the ground truth distribution.

**Table 2.** The inception score, mode score with 10,000 generated samples and the results of matching score for different models.

| Method | Inception score | Mode score | Matching score |
|---|---|---|---|
| WGAN | 5.158 | 3.390 | 0.025 |
| WGAN-GP | 5.800 | 3.765 | 0.159 |
| SSGAN (ours) | 9.364 | 9.296 | 0.737 |

In Table 2, we show the inception score, mode score and matching score for different GAN models. The former two evaluation metrics are calculated via 10,000 generated samples. These results show that our model SSGAN has better visual quality (higher inception score and mode score) and capture more modes in generated manifold (higher mode score and matching score). Meanwhile, the evaluation of matching score also shows that our model SSGAN can better match the training examples.

Overall, by these three evaluation metrics and the histogram of inception score and mode score, the proposed SSGAN outperforms WGAN and WGAN-GP with better sample quality and more modes captured.

Owing to that the training data distribution for MNIST is uniform, it is hard to evaluate the performance on mode collapse for different models. So we synthesized a new unbalanced MNIST dataset for better evaluation on modes dropping problem.

**Table 3.** The proportion of digits for generated samples with 10,000 samples (%).

| Method | 0 | 1 | 2 | 3 | 4 | 5 | 6 | 7 | 8 | 9 | KL |
|---|---|---|---|---|---|---|---|---|---|---|---|
| Ground truth | 0.48 | 0.48 | 0.96 | 2.39 | 4.78 | 9.57 | 14.35 | 19.14 | 23.92 | 23.92 | – |
| WGAN | 0.38 | 0.81 | 1.31 | 7.26 | 5.78 | 4.08 | 0.85 | 12.48 | 34.48 | 32.57 | 36.77 |
| WGAN-GP | 1.31 | 0.15 | 0.18 | 1.93 | 1.82 | 2.09 | 12.13 | 16.14 | 32.56 | 31.69 | 12.92 |
| SSGAN (ours) | 0.49 | 0.51 | 0.92 | 2.27 | 4.74 | 9.65 | 14.33 | 19.23 | 23.91 | 23.85 | 0.10 |

Table 3 shows the proportion for different digits in generated samples with our new synthetic unbalanced MNIST dataset. According to the results of KL divergence between the ground truth distribution and distribution generated by different models, the distribution of our model SSGAN is more close to the ground truth.

Table 4 shows the comparison on inception score, mode score and matching score for different models. The results show that our model SSGAN has higher inception score, mode score and matching score which ensures better visual quality and modes capturing.

**Table 4.** The inception score, mode score with 10,000 generated samples and the matching score results for different models.

| Method | Inception score | Mode score | Matching score |
|---|---|---|---|
| WGAN | 4.103 | 3.987 | 0.076 |
| WGAN-GP | 5.475 | 4.776 | 0.175 |
| SSGAN (ours) | 9.043 | 8.975 | 0.832 |

Owing to the distribution of training data is not a uniform, the experiments on MNIST dataset and synthetic unbalanced MNIST dataset can better evaluate the capacity on modes capturing for different modes.

In CIFAR 10 dataset, there are 60,000 images (10 classes) with 6,000 images per class. The dataset consists a training dataset with 50,000 images and a test dataset with 10,000 images. The images are drawn randomly from the entire dataset. And this dataset involve high quality and diverse images.

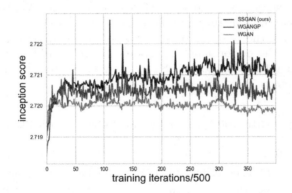

**Fig. 4.** Comparison on inception score for different models.

Figure 4 shows the comparison on inception score compared with WGAN and WGAN-GP. By applying an inception network [17] to classify the images, the inception score and mode score can be calculated. With the results for inception score, we can observe that our model SSGAN is higher than the other two methods. This indicates that SSGAN can generate better looking samples.

Overall, our proposed SSGAN outperforms WGAN and WGAN-GP on both visual quality and modes capturing.

## 6.2   SoTA Comparison

In this section, we conduct the experiments on CelebA dataset. CelebA is a large scale face dataset with more than 200,000 celebrity images. Each image has 40 attribute annotations. So CelebA images are very diverse with large pose variations and background clutter. For the experiments involving CelebA face dataset, we reshaped the images into $32 \times 32 \times 3$. At the same time, we borrow the architecture from DCGAN [16] for training GANs.

**Table 5.** The results of matching score for different models.

| Method | DCGAN | WGAN | WGAN-GP | VEEGAN |
|---|---|---|---|---|
| Matching score | 0.002 | 0.002 | 0.053 | 0.267 |
| Method | MDGAN | AdaGAN | InfoGAN | SSGAN |
| Matching score | 0.317 | 0.402 | 0.393 | 0.456 |

Table 5 shows the results of the matching score for different GAN models. Our model SSGAN achieves 0.456 on CelebA face dataset which is much better than other SoTA methods.

Overall, the SoTA comparison experiments tell that the proposed SSGAN is not only capable of facing large scale dataset but also better capture more modes in training examples.

## 7 Conclusions

GANs is known as one of the most popular generative models. However, some limitations in training GANs unlock its power to be applied into more areas. One of the most severest problem is mode collapse. In this paper, we blame the mode collapse problem for the initial generated manifold cannot cover all the examples, and the training process is hard to recover from this failure. Therefore, we bring a supervision signal to GANs to keep the generated manifold being close to the real data manifold even at the initialization. Experiment results show that our method could outperform several SoTA methods in training GANs on both visual quality and modes capturing.

## References

1. Arjovsky, M., Chintala, S., Bottou, L.: Wasserstein GAN. In: International Conference on Machine Learning (ICML) (2017)
2. Arora, S., Ge, R., Liang, Y., Ma, T., Zhang, Y.: Generalization and equilibrium in generative adversarial nets. In: International Conference on Machine Learning (ICML) (2017)
3. Che, T., Li, Y., Jacob, A.P., Bengio, Y., Li, W.: Mode regularized generative adversarial networks. In: International Conference on Learning Representation (ICLR) (2017)

4. Chen, X., Duan, Y., Houthooft, R., Schulman, J., Sutskever, I., Abbeel, P.: Info-GAN: interpretable representation learning by information maximizing generative adversarial nets. In: Advances in Neural Information Processing Systems (NIPS) (2016)
5. Denton, E.L., Chintala, S., Fergus, R., et al.: Deep generative image models using a Laplacian pyramid of adversarial networks. In: Advances in Neural Information Processing Systems (NIPS), pp. 1486–1494 (2015)
6. Goodfellow, I.J., et al.: Generative adversarial nets. In: Advances in Neural Information Processing Systems (NIPS), pp. 2672–2680 (2014)
7. Gulrajani, I., Ahmed, F., Arjovsky, M., Dumoulin, V., Courville, A.: Improved training of wasserstein GANs. In: Advances in Neural Information Processing Systems (NIPS) (2017)
8. Ho, J., Ermon, S.: Generative adversarial imitation learning. In: Advances in Neural Information Processing Systems (NIPS), pp. 4565–4573 (2016)
9. Krizhevsky, A., Hinton, G.: Learning multiple layers of features from tiny images (2009)
10. LeCun, Y., Bottou, L., Bengio, Y., Haffner, P.: Gradient-based learning applied to document recognition. Proc. IEEE 86(11), 2278–2324 (1998)
11. Liu, H., Lafferty, J.D., Wasserman, L.A.: Sparse nonparametric density estimation in high dimensions using the rodeo. In: Proceedings of the 11th International Conference on Artificial Intelligence and Statistics, (AISTATS), pp. 283–290 (2007)
12. Liu, Z., Luo, P., Wang, X., Tang, X.: Deep learning face attributes in the wild. In: Proceedings of International Conference on Computer Vision (ICCV) (2015)
13. Mathieu, M., Couprie, C., LeCun, Y.: Deep multi-scale video prediction beyond mean square error. International Conference on Learning Representation (ICLR) (2016)
14. Metz, L., Poole, B., Pfau, D., Sohl-Dickstein, J.: Unrolled generative adversarial networks. In: International Conference on Learning Representation (ICLR) (2017)
15. Miyato, T., Kataoka, T., Koyama, M., Yoshida, Y.: Spectral normalization for generative adversarial networks. In: International Conference on Learning Representation (ICLR) (2018)
16. Radford, A., Metz, L., Chintala, S.: Unsupervised representation learning with deep convolutional generative adversarial networks. In: International Conference on Learning Representation (ICLR) (2016)
17. Salimans, T., Goodfellow, I., Zaremba, W., Cheung, V., Radford, A., Chen, X.: Improved techniques for training GANs. In: Advances in Neural Information Processing Systems (NIPS), pp. 2234–2242 (2016)
18. Srivastava, A., Valkov, L., Russell, C., Gutmann, M.U.: VEEGAN: reducing mode collapse in GANs using implicit variational learning. In: Advances in Neural Information Processing Systems (NIPS), pp. 3310–3320 (2017)
19. Tolstikhin, I., Gelly, S., Bousquet, O., Simon-Gabriel, C.J., Schölkopf, B.: Ada-GAN: boosting generative models. In: Advances in Neural Information Processing Systems (NIPS) (2017)
20. Wu, J., Zhang, C., Xue, T., Freeman, B., Tenenbaum, J.: Learning a probabilistic latent space of object shapes via 3D generative-adversarial modeling. In: Advances in Neural Information Processing Systems (NIPS), pp. 82–90 (2016)

# Image Inpainting Using Wasserstein Generative Adversarial Imputation Network

Daniel Vašata[ID], Tomáš Halama[ID], and Magda Friedjungová[(✉)][ID]

Faculty of Information Technology, Czech Technical University in Prague,
Prague, Czech Republic
{daniel.vasata,halamto2,magda.friedjungova}@fit.cvut.cz

**Abstract.** Image inpainting is one of the important tasks in computer vision which focuses on the reconstruction of missing regions in an image. The aim of this paper is to introduce an image inpainting model based on Wasserstein Generative Adversarial Imputation Network. The generator network of the model uses building blocks of convolutional layers with different dilation rates, together with skip connections that help the model reproduce fine details of the output. This combination yields a universal imputation model that is able to handle various scenarios of missingness with sufficient quality. To show this experimentally, the model is simultaneously trained to deal with three scenarios given by missing pixels at random, missing various smaller square regions, and one missing square placed in the center of the image. It turns out that our model achieves high-quality inpainting results on all scenarios. Performance is evaluated using peak signal-to-noise ratio and structural similarity index on two real-world benchmark datasets, CelebA faces and Paris StreetView. The results of our model are compared to biharmonic imputation and to some of the other state-of-the-art image inpainting methods.

**Keywords:** Imputation methods · Missing data · Image inpainting · Generative models · Wasserstein GAIN · Wasserstein GAN

## 1 Introduction

In computer vision, one of the most important tasks being solved is image inpainting, also known as image completion, which aims to restore missing pixels in a damaged image. The aim is to estimate and impute the pixel information in missing locations based on the context from non-missing parts of the image. Since locations of missingness can appear in many ways such as random noise or entire connected regions of various size and shape, it may not be easy to have a universal model that can handle most of these scenarios. Image inpainting can also be used for replacing unwanted by a realistically looking output.

Conventional approaches understand pixel imputation as a smooth function extension problem, see e.g. [2, 4, 7, 19]. These methods work well for cases where

© Springer Nature Switzerland AG 2021
I. Farkaš et al. (Eds.): ICANN 2021, LNCS 12892, pp. 575–586, 2021.
https://doi.org/10.1007/978-3-030-86340-1_46

image corruption is minor or straightforward to fill in, but not so well for cases with more significant damage, failing to produce reasonable or plausible outcomes [16]. Recently, the most successful methods (e.g. [13,18,25,26]) combine convolutional neural networks and generative adversarial networks which yield improvements such as higher sharpness, matching colours and general shapes of imputed objects in missing regions. Typically these models have the common advantage that one does not need to know which pixels are missing in advance. However, the most successful ones are often of high-complexity and with complicated loss functions often based on pretrained networks for visual classification.

The aim of this work is to address image inpainting task using Wasserstein Generative Adversarial Imputation Network (WGAIN) that was recently introduced by the authors in [9] as a general imputation model. It is a generative imputation model which, for non-visual imputation tasks, performs comparatively to other state-of-the-art methods. It beneficially incorporates the Wasserstein metric to adversarial training which does not suffer from vanishing gradients.

For the image inpainting domain one needs to adjust the model for the scenario of image data, namely make use of convolutional layers. In our WGAIN model, we adopt the architecture from [13] and extend it by using building blocks composed from parallel convolutional layers with multiple dilation rates. This leads to different sizes of the layers' receptive fields which improves the ability of the model to focus on both the local and global structure of the image hence obtaining universality in terms of variable missing pixel regions. Moreover we use skip connections allowing the model to propagate high resolution features in the hourglass network topology of the generator in a sandwich like way which helps the model reproduce the fine details.

Our aim is to research the ability of our WGAIN model to perform well even without the highly complicated pre-trained elements. We experimentally show that our model is able to perform well in three different scenarios of missingness when trained for all of them at once. These scenarios are given by missing pixels at random, missing various smaller square regions, and one missing square placed in the center of the image. Hence the model is able to react properly on large missing areas as well as on many missing small areas simultaneously. This shows the universality of the proposed WGAIN model. The performance is evaluated using peak signal-to-noise ratio (PSNR) and structural similarity index (SSIM). The results are compared to conventional methods of inpainting by biharmonic functions used e.g. in [1,3,6,7]. We also discuss the comparison to other state-of-the art methods [11,13,16,18,25,26] where possible.

## 2    Related Work

Most conventional methods such as [2,4,7,8,19,20] used to perform computer-aided inpainting rely on local features such as colours and textures, but they fail to consider the global semantics of the image. These methods work well for cases where image corruption is minor or scattered across the image in small regions, but not so well for cases with more significant regions to fill, failing to produce reasonable or plausible outcomes [16].

A significant number of state-of-the-art methods use deep generative neural networks with very promising results. One of the ways of creating globally well-organized and coherent images is by introducing a second neural network, an adversary, that tries to decide whether the produced results look artificial or genuine. The original generating network can learn to produce results that are much less likely to be discarded as artificial using information from this adversary network. Such networks are called generator and discriminator. This type of architecture is called generative adversarial network (GAN) [10].

Let us briefly mention some of state-of-the-art methods. A very inspiring work handling inpainting using deep neural networks with an adversary discriminative network is Context Encoders (CE) [16]. Based on the autoencoder architecture and using only convolutional layers, they achieved superior results in a semantic inpainting task. In [25] introduced contextual attention layer enables distant areas of the image to influence each other. When combined with two discriminating losses, one for determining whether the entirety of the resulting image is real-looking and one only for the generated patch, the work achieved more plausible results than other methods in a human evaluated test. Hui et al. in [12] mitigated the problem of blurred outputs using a one-stage model called dense multi-scale fusion network (DMFN), which utilizes dense combinations of dilated convolutions to obtain larger and more effective receptive fields. They designed a novel self-guided regression loss for concentrating on uncertain areas and enhancing semantic details. In [26] presented network contains reconstructive and generative parts, both represented by GANs, and a new short+long term attention layer improving appearance consistency. This network is able to generate multi-modal results. The PiiGAN [5] based on [25] also adopted the idea of producing multiple reasonable result. The recently proposed Symmetric Skip Connection Wasserstein Generative Adversarial Network [13] contains encoder-decoder with convolutional blocks, linked by skip connections, together with a Wasserstein-Perceptual loss function to preserve colour and maintain realism on a reconstructed image. PEPSI and Diet-PEPSI [18] are another recent very successful GAN-based models incorporating parallel extended-decoder path for semantic inpainting, which aims at reducing the number of convolution operations as well as improving the inpainting performance.

## 3    Wasserstein Generative Imputation Network

Here we introduce the WGAIN following [9] closely. Let us denote by $\mathcal{X} = \mathbb{R}^{m,n,3}$ the space of all possible images of size $m \times n$ and three color channels (RGB) and let $\boldsymbol{X}$ be a random element of $\mathcal{X}$ whose distribution is denoted by $\mathrm{P}(\boldsymbol{X})$. The identification of missing/damaged pixels is stored in a mask boolean matrix $\boldsymbol{M} \in \{0,1\}^{m,n}$, where:

$$\boldsymbol{M}_{i,j} = \begin{cases} 1, & \text{if } ij\text{th pixel of } \boldsymbol{X} \text{ is valid,} \\ 0, & \text{if } ij\text{th pixel of } \boldsymbol{X} \text{ is missing.} \end{cases}$$

The distribution of $\boldsymbol{M}$ corresponds to the distribution of missingness in the data. Let us further denote by $\tilde{\boldsymbol{X}}$ the image $\boldsymbol{X}$ having zeros in place of missing pixels given by

$$\tilde{X} = X \odot M,$$

where $\odot$ denotes element-wise multiplication performed along all three color channels.

The next step is to prepare the input that can be used to replace the missing pixels in $\tilde{X}$ by random values drawn independently from the normal distribution. Formally, let $Z \in \mathbb{R}^{m,n,3}$ be a random tensor with independent and identically distributed components having normal distribution $\mathcal{N}(0, \sigma^2)$ with variance $\sigma^2$ and define

$$\tilde{Z} = Z \odot (1 - M).$$

To impute missing pixels in $\tilde{X}$ based on the information from non-missing pixels, we want the model to learn the conditional distribution $P(X | \tilde{X}, M)$ of $X$ given $\tilde{X}$ and $M$.

The generator $g$ of the WGAIN model is a mapping $g : \mathcal{X} \times \mathcal{X} \times \{0, 1\}^{m,n} \to \mathcal{X}$ represented by a deep convolutional network that is fed by $\tilde{X}$, $\tilde{Z}$, and by $M$. It produces a new random image $g(\tilde{X}, \tilde{Z}, M)$ corresponding to $\tilde{X}$ with all pixels imputed. The final image where only the missing pixels are imputed is then given by

$$\hat{X}_Z = g(\tilde{X}, \tilde{Z}, M) \odot (1 - M) + \tilde{X} \odot M$$

and it is a random image whose conditional distribution $P(\hat{X}_Z | \tilde{X}, M)$ is given by the distribution $P(Z)$ of $Z$ and should be as close as possible to $P(X | \tilde{X}, M)$.

The critic part $f$ of the WGAIN model is a Lipschitz mapping $f : \mathcal{X} \times \{0, 1\}^{m,n} \to \mathbb{R}$ represented by a deep convolutional network with norm restricted weights and fed by images and masks trained to maximize

$$E_{X \sim P(X), M \sim P(M)}\big(f(X, M) - E_{Z \sim P(Z)}f(\hat{X}_Z, M)\big)$$

which is estimated by sample means from mini-batches. This corresponds to the estimate of the expectation with respect to $M$ and $X$ of the Earth-Mover's or Wasserstein distance [17, 21] between the two conditional distributions $P(\hat{X}_Z | \tilde{X}, M)$ and $P(X | \tilde{X}, M)$.

### 3.1 Training

The critic $f$ is used in adversarial training of both the generator $g$ and the critic itself. There the generator and the critic play an iterative two-player minimax game where the critic wants to recognize the imputed values from the real ones and the goal of the generator is to trick the critic so it cannot recognize them. Moreover, the generator's output is tightened to the correct image by the absolute error loss function $\mathcal{L}_{\mathrm{MAE}}$.

Therefore, there are two objective functions to minimize. The first corresponds to training of the critic given by

$$J(f) = E_{X \sim P(X), M \sim P(M)} \lambda_f \big(f(X, M) - E_{Z \sim P(Z)}f(\hat{X}_Z, M)\big),$$

---

**Algorithm 1:** WGAIN training pseudo-code.

---

**Input**: $\alpha$ - the learning rate; $w_{\max}$ - maximal norm of critic weights used in clipping; $m$ - the mini-batch size; $\lambda_f, \lambda_g, \lambda_{\mathrm{MAE}}$ - weights of the objectives

Draw $m$ samples $\{x_j\}_{j=1}^m$ from the dataset;

Draw $m$ samples $\{m_j\}_{j=1}^m$ from the mask distribution;

Draw $m$ samples $\{z_j\}_{j=1}^m$ from the normal distribution of $Z$;

**while** *not converged* **do**

$\quad$ $\tilde{x}_{z_j} \leftarrow z_j \odot (1 - m_j) + x_j \odot m_j$;

$\quad$ $\hat{x}_{z_j} \leftarrow g(\tilde{x}_{z_j}, m_j) \odot (1 - m_j) + x_j \odot m_j$;

$\quad$ Update weights $w$ of $f$ using Adam optimizer with learning rate $\alpha$ and gradient

$\quad$ $\nabla J(f) = \lambda_f \nabla \left[ \frac{1}{m} \sum_{j=1}^m f(\hat{x}_{z_j}, m_j) - \frac{1}{m} \sum_{j=1}^m f(x_j, m_j) \right]$;

$\quad$ Clip the norm of $w$ by $w_{\max}$;

$\quad$ Update weights of $g$ using Adam optimizer with learning rate $\alpha$ and gradient

$\quad$ $\nabla J(g) = \nabla \left[ -\lambda_g \frac{1}{m} \sum_{j=1}^m f(\hat{x}_{z_j}, m_j) + \lambda_{\mathrm{MAE}} \frac{1}{m} \sum_{j=1}^m \|\hat{x}_{z_j} - x_j\|^2 \right]$;

**end**

---

where the weight $\lambda_f$ enables one to increase or decrease the influence of the corresponding gradient. Second is the objective for the generator,

$$J(g) = \mathrm{E}_{X \sim \mathrm{P}(X), Z \sim \mathrm{P}(Z), M \sim \mathrm{P}(M)} \left( -\lambda_g f(\hat{X}_Z, M) + \lambda_{\mathrm{MAE}} \mathcal{L}_{\mathrm{MAE}}(\hat{X}_Z, X) \right),$$

where $\lambda_g$ and $\lambda_{\mathrm{MAE}}$ are weights enabling one to strengthen or weaken the influence of the absolute error loss function.

The pseudo-code of the WGAIN training is given in Algorithm 1. The values of the objective functions are estimated from mini-batches. The optimization is done via alternating gradient descent, where the first step is updating the critic $f$ and the second step is updating the generator $g$. Hence, when perfectly trained, the discriminator gives negative values for cases with imputed features and positive values for cases with true features. On the other hand, the generator entering the critic will be pushed to obtain large positive values of the critic as it gives to real values.

## 3.2 Architecture of Networks

Both the generator and the critic networks are based on convolutional layers. The architecture of the generator $g$, as shown in Fig. 1, is composed of building blocks of convolutional or deconvolutional layers with different dilation rates. Those building blocks are then combined in the encoder-decoder bottleneck topology with sandwich like skip connections as introduced in [13].

The skip connections allow the model to propagate high resolution features from layers of the encoder into layers of the decoder (in reverse order) which helps the model transfer the fine details in every depth better. The first skip connection is fed by the concatenation of the network's input $(\tilde{X}, \tilde{Z}, M)$. The subsequent ones by the outputs of the encoder's blocks.

The building blocks are composed of three parallel convolutional (for encoder) or deconvolutional (for decoder) layers with the same kernel size of $5 \times 5$ but with different dilation rates $0, 2, 5$ corresponding to different sizes of the layer's receptive field [24]. The layers use padding and no strides so that the same dimension of the output is guaranteed. The numbers of channels for the three layers are of the form $(n/2, n/4, n/4)$ with increasing numbers in the encoder as $n = 128, 128, 256, 512$ and decreasing in the decoder as $n = 256, 128, 128$. All three layers of the block have ELU activation functions and are concatenated into a single output. In the case of the encoder the output goes into the outgoing skip connection and also into the next block. If the next block belongs to encoder the max-pooling of pool size $2 \times 2$ is applied before entering it. In the case of the decoder the input into the block is given by a concatenation of the previous block output and the incoming skip connection. The output of the decoder's block is followed by an up-sampling operation of factor $2 \times 2$.

The final block of the decoder is not up-sampled but only concatenated with the first skip connection and fed into the one other deconvolutional layer with 8 channels, kernel size of $3 \times 3$, and ELU activation which is then followed by the last deconvolutional layer with 3 channels, kernel size of $3 \times 3$, and hard-sigmoid activation function, defined by

$$h(x) = \begin{cases} 0 & \text{for } x < -2.5, \\ 0.2x + 0.5 & \text{for } x \in [-2.5, 2.5], \\ 1 & \text{for } x > 2.5, \end{cases}$$

that is responsible for collection of the final output.

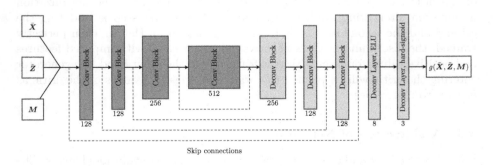

**Fig. 1.** The architecture of the generator.

The critic $f$ has a simple funnel topology with 5 convolutional layers with kernel size of $5 \times 5$, 2 strides, and channel numbers $64, 128, 256, 256, 512$. The layers have Leaky ReLU activation function. The final output is produced by a single neuron connected to the flattened output of the last convolutional layer with linear activation. The norm restriction needed for the Lipschitz property of the critic is achieved by clipping the $L_2$ norm of each layer weights tensor to 1.

# 4   Experiments

The experiments were performed on two benchmark datasets: Paris StreetView [16] and CelebA faces [15]. For the CelebA faces dataset the aligned and cropped variant which has faces aligned in the central position was used. In the preprocessing step images from both datasets were cropped to be square shaped and have a common size of $128 \times 128$ pixels.

## 4.1   Scenarios of Missingness

In order to analyze the performance of the inpainting model we focus on three scenarios of missingness, i.e. on three probability distributions of the mask $M$. These three scenarios can be taken as representatives of three qualitatively different situations of how the missing pixels might be distributed across the image.

**Noise** corresponds to the situation when each pixel of the mask $M$ is sampled independently on other pixels with a probability $p$ of having value 0 which corresponds to the portion of missingness. In this scenario, we choose three different values of $p$ to simulate various damage portions. The simplest case is when 50% of the pixels are dropped. The more severe damages are represented by 75% and 95%.

In the training phase, the values of $p$ for each sample are generated randomly with a uniform distribution in the interval $[0.5, 0.95]$.

**Single square in the center** represents a demanding task with a large continuous region missing in the image, as there are no hints left inside the area. To test this scenario, we fixed $M$ to represent a centered square of missing pixels. One side of the missing square is as long as half of the side of the original image, thus the missing portion is 25%.

In the training phase the square is centered but its side is a randomly (uniformly) chosen integer in the interval $[\ell/2.5, \ell/1.6]$, where $\ell$ is the side of the original image.

**Randomly located multiple squares** is a compromise between the previous two types of region mask. There are multiple smaller squares uniformly independently distributed across the image. The number of randomly located squares is fixed to 5 and the squares have a fixed size of $31 \times 31$ pixels. Because of the overlapping it yields the final missing portion approximately equal to 25%.

In the training phase the number of squares, their positions, and their sizes are chosen randomly. To be precise, we generate 30 squares with lower left corners uniformly distributed in the 2D interval $[-2\ell, 3\ell]^2$ and with their sides uniformly distributed in the interval $[\ell/5, \ell/3]$. The final mask for the sample is then given by the intersection of those squares with the 2D interval $[1, \ell]^2$.

During the training phase the model learns all these scenarios at once. This means that each training sample randomly choses which scenario it belongs to and then it generates the mask matrix as described above. In the evaluation phase each of these scenarios is evaluated separately.

## 4.2  Implementation Details

We perform a global normalization on all channels of the images to set the intensity values of the pixels in the range $[0, 1]$. The hyperparameters for the experiment were empirically set as $\lambda_f = 1$, $\lambda_g = 0.005$, and $\lambda_{\mathrm{MAE}} = 1$. The training procedure was optimized using Adam optimizer with learning rate $\alpha = 0.00005$. The mini-batch size was $m = 32$. The model for the Paris StreetView dataset was trained in 2000 epochs and the model for the CelebA dataset in 200 epochs. This corresponds to a similar number of training steps and training time for both datasets.

The source code of our experiments is available at Github repository[1]. We used the `TensorFlow` library[2] running on a nVidia Tesla V100-PCIE-32GB. It took approximately 3 days to train each model. For the implementation of biharmonic function inpainting we used the scikit-image[3] library.

## 4.3  Results

The examples of the experimental results are shown in Figs. 2 and 3. Our model performs well for both datasets in all scenarios of missingness. Moreover, in all cases it visually outperforms the results of inpainting by biharmonic functions. Interesting results can be observed in Fig. 3 in the single centered square scenario. Here the inpainted face looks quite realistic but differs from the original image. The person on the original image is looking to the left with eyes wide open whereas the face generated by our model is looking to the center with less open eyes. We may say that the inpainting result is satisfactory since one is not able to determine this information from the non-missing part of the image.

As a quantitative evaluation the peak signal-to-noise ratio (PSNR) [22] and the structural similarity index measure (SSIM) [23] were used. Both metrics are common for image inpainting evaluation [5,12,18,25]. In Table 1 the results are presented together with biharmonic function inpainting results in the same setup. In all evaluation scenarios the WGAIN outperformed biharmonic inpainting.

To be able to compare the results to other state of the art methods, we used the single square in the center scenario. The values of the PSNR and SSIM measures for PiiGAN, DMFN, and CE compared to our method are summarized in Table 2. It shows that on the Paris StreetView dataset the WGAIN outperforms CE and also the DMFN in SSIM with equal PSNR. On the CelebA faces dataset

---

[1] https://github.com/vasatdan/wgain-inpaint.
[2] https://www.tensorflow.org.
[3] https://scikit-image.org/.

**Fig. 2.** Demonstration of inpainting scenarios and results for Paris StreetView dataset.

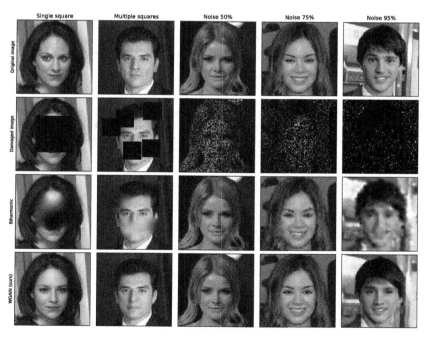

**Fig. 3.** Demonstration of inpainting scenarios and results for CelebA dataset.

**Table 1.** Results on Paris StreetView and CelebA datasets.

| Damage type | | Paris StreetView | | | | CelebA | | | |
|---|---|---|---|---|---|---|---|---|---|
| | | WGAIN | | Biharmonic | | WGAIN | | Biharmonic | |
| | | PSNR | SSIM | PSNR | SSIM | PSNR | SSIM | PSNR | SSIM |
| Singlesquare 25% | | **25.00** | **0.88** | 21.12 | 0.85 | **25.96** | **0.92** | 17.94 | 0.83 |
| Multisquare 25% | | **26.51** | **0.90** | 22.67 | 0.86 | **26.75** | **0.93** | 23.34 | 0.89 |
| Noise | 50% | **31.48** | **0.96** | 30.11 | 0.95 | **34.00** | **0.98** | 33.37 | 0.98 |
| | 75% | **27.73** | **0.90** | 25.90 | 0.87 | **29.96** | **0.95** | 28.73 | 0.93 |
| | 95% | **22.72** | **0.74** | 21.13 | 0.67 | **23.86** | **0.83** | 22.52 | 0.79 |

in comparison to the DMFN our model has lower PSNR and higher SSIM. Both WGAIN and DMFN, however, are outperformed by the PiiGAN for this dataset.

To interpret this comparison correctly one should note that the results of the experiments presented for the other methods were often obtained with different resolutions of images, for different target tasks, and some of them actually on different datasets - instead of the CelebA dataset, the CelebA-HQ dataset collected from CelebA and post-processed (for details see [14]) was used in both [5,12]. Especially the different target tasks are of high importance. The presented results for the competitive models are obtained under the scenario where the corresponding imputation method is trained on the same task where it is evaluated. It means that the models are trained to impute the centered square of fixed size only. On the other hand, our model is trained for all the scenarios of missingness together and performs quite well on all of them. Hence, on one specific subtask, it might be outperformed by a specialized model trained for that subtask only.

**Table 2.** Comparison of inpainting methods on the single square in the center scenario of missingness, where 25% of pixels are missing. The values of PSNR and SSIM are taken from the papers cited in the table. Note that PiiGAN and DMFN used CelebA-HQ dataset, and that DMFN used images of size 256 × 256.

| Method | CelebA dataset | | Paris StreetView dataset | |
|---|---|---|---|---|
| | PSNR | SSIM | PSNR | SSIM |
| PiiGAN [5] | 34.99 | 0.99 | – | – |
| DMFN [12] | 26.50 | 0.89 | 25.00 | 0.86 |
| CE [16] | – | – | 18.58 | – |
| WGAIN (ours) | 25.96 | 0.92 | 25.00 | 0.88 |

# 5 Conclusion

In this paper we present an image inpainting model based on Wasserstein Generative Adversarial Imputation Network where the generator network uses convolutional building blocks and skip connections. The combination of convolutional layers with different dilation rates enables each building block to focus on both the global (large range) and the local (small range) structure of the input, and skip connections help the model reproduce fine details of the output.

This yields a universal imputation model that is able to handle various scenarios of missingness with sufficient quality. We tested three scenarios given by missing pixels at random, missing various smaller square regions, and one missing square placed in the center of the image. The model was trained simultaneously for all of the scenarios. The performance was evaluated using peak signal-to-noise ratio and structural similarity index on two real-world benchmark datasets, CelebA faces and Paris StreetView. The results were compared to biharmonic imputation and to three other state-of-the-art methods. It turns out that our WGAIN image inpainting model achieves high-quality inpainting results which outperform the conventional inpainting by biharmonic functions and is comparable to state-of-the-art method DMFN [12]. The superiority of PiiGAN [5] on the CelebA dataset compared to our model is assumed to be caused by focusing on only one scenario of missingness.

**Acknowledgements.** This research has been supported by SGS grant No. SGS20/213/OHK3/3T/18, by GACR grant No. GA18-18080S, and by the Student Summer Research Program 2020 of FIT CTU in Prague, Czech Republic.

# References

1. Amrani, N., Serra-Sagristà, J., Peter, P., Weickert, J.: Diffusion-based inpainting for coding remote-sensing data. IEEE Geosci. Remote Sens. Lett. **14**(8), 1203–1207 (2017)
2. Ballester, C., Bertalmio, M., Caselles, V., Sapiro, G., Verdera, J.: Filling-in by joint interpolation of vector fields and gray levels. IEEE Trans. Image Process. **10**(8), 1200–1211 (2001)
3. Barnum, A., Jiao, J.: Adaptive biharmonic in-painting for sparse acquisition using variance frames. Microsc. Microanal. **23**(S1), 148–149 (2017). https://doi.org/10.1017/S1431927617001428
4. Bertalmio, M., Sapiro, G., Caselles, V., Ballester, C.: Image inpainting. In: Proceedings of the 27th annual conference on Computer graphics and interactive techniques, pp. 417–424 (2000)
5. Cai, W., Wei, Z.: PiiGAN: generative adversarial networks for pluralistic image inpainting. IEEE Access **8**, 48451–48463 (2020)
6. Chen, Y., Ranftl, R., Pock, T.: A bi-level view of inpainting-based image compression. arXiv preprint arXiv:1401.4112 (2014)
7. Damelin, S.B., Hoang, N.S.: On surface completion and image inpainting by biharmonic functions: numerical aspects. Int. J. Math. Math. Sci. **2018**, 1–8 (2018)

8.  Efros, A.A., Freeman, W.T.: Image quilting for texture synthesis and transfer. In: Proceedings of the 28th Annual Conference on Computer Graphics and Interactive Techniques, pp. 341–346 (2001)
9.  Friedjungová, M., Vašata, D., Balatsko, M., Jiřina, M.: Missing features reconstruction using a Wasserstein generative adversarial imputation network. In: Krzhizhanovskaya, V.V., et al. (eds.) ICCS 2020. LNCS, vol. 12140, pp. 225–239. Springer, Cham (2020). https://doi.org/10.1007/978-3-030-50423-6_17
10. Goodfellow, I., et al.: Generative adversarial nets. In: Advances in Neural Information Processing Systems, vol. 27, pp. 2672–2680. Curran Associates, Inc. (2014)
11. Hua, P., Liu, X., Liu, M., Dong, L., Hui, M., Zhao, Y.: Image inpainting using Wasserstein generative adversarial network. In: Optics and Photonics for Information Processing XII, vol. 10751, pp. 183–194. SPIE (2018). https://doi.org/10.1117/12.2320212
12. Hui, Z., Li, J., Wang, X., Gao, X.: Image fine-grained inpainting. arXiv preprint arXiv:2002.02609 (2020)
13. Jam, J., Kendrick, C., Drouard, V., Walker, K., Hsu, G.S., Yap, M.H.: Symmetric skip connection Wasserstein GAN for high-resolution facial image inpainting. arXiv preprint arXiv:2001.03725 (2020)
14. Karras, T., Aila, T., Laine, S., Lehtinen, J.: Progressive growing of GANs for improved quality, stability, and variation. arXiv preprint arXiv:1710.10196 (2017)
15. Liu, Z., Luo, P., Wang, X., Tang, X.: Deep learning face attributes in the wild. In: Proceedings of International Conference on Computer Vision (ICCV) (2015)
16. Pathak, D., Krahenbuhl, P., Donahue, J., Darrell, T., Efros, A.A.: Context encoders: feature learning by inpainting. In: 2016 IEEE Conference on Computer Vision and Pattern Recognition (CVPR). IEEE (2016). https://doi.org/10.1109/cvpr.2016.278
17. Rubner, Y., Guibas, L.J., Tomasi, C.: The earth mover's distance, multidimensional scaling, and color-based image retrieval. In: Proceedings of the ARPA Image Understanding Workshop, vol. 661, p. 668 (1997)
18. Shin, Y.G., Sagong, M.C., Yeo, Y.J., Kim, S.W., Ko, S.J.: Pepsi++: fast and lightweight network for image inpainting. IEEE Trans. Neural Netw. Learn. Syst. (2020)
19. Simakov, D., Caspi, Y., Shechtman, E., Irani, M.: Summarizing visual data using bidirectional similarity. In: 2008 IEEE Conference on Computer Vision and Pattern Recognition, pp. 1–8. IEEE (2008)
20. Telea, A.: An image inpainting technique based on the fast marching method. J. Graph. Tools 9(1), 23–34 (2004). https://doi.org/10.1080/10867651.2004.10487596
21. Villani, C.: Optimal Transport: Old and New, vol. 338. Springer, Heidelberg (2008)
22. Wang, Z., Bovik, A.C.: Mean squared error: love it or leave it? a new look at signal fidelity measures. IEEE Signal Process. Mag. 26(1), 98–117 (2009)
23. Wang, Z., Bovik, A.C., Sheikh, H.R., Simoncelli, E.P.: Image quality assessment: from error visibility to structural similarity. IEEE Trans. Image Process. 13(4), 600–612 (2004)
24. Yu, F., Koltun, V.: Multi-scale context aggregation by dilated convolutions. CoRR abs/1511.07122 (2016)
25. Yu, J., Lin, Z., Yang, J., Shen, X., Lu, X., Huang, T.S.: Generative image inpainting with contextual attention. In: Proceedings of the IEEE Conference on Computer Vision and Pattern Recognition, pp. 5505–5514 (2018)
26. Zheng, C., Cham, T.J., Cai, J.: Pluralistic image completion. In: Proceedings of the IEEE Conference on Computer Vision and Pattern Recognition, pp. 1438–1447 (2019)

# COViT-GAN: Vision Transformer for COVID-19 Detection in CT Scan Images with Self-Attention GAN for Data Augmentation

Ara Abigail E. Ambita$^{(\boxtimes)}$ (iD), Eujene Nikka V. Boquio$^{(\boxtimes)}$ (iD), and Prospero C. Naval Jr.$^{(\boxtimes)}$ (iD)

Computer Vision and Machine Intelligence Group Department of Computer Science, University of the Philippines Diliman, Quezon City, Philippines
{aeambita,evboquio,pcnaval}@up.edu.ph

**Abstract.** The Vision Transformer (ViT) is currently gaining popularity in computer vision circles due to its record-breaking performance and faster training time achieved without relying on convolution operations found in CNN architectures. In this study, the Vision Transformer is applied to the task of COVID-19 detection from computed tomography (CT) scan images, specifically on the COVID-CT and Sars-CoV-2 datasets. Using a model pretrained on the mid-sized ImageNet-21k dataset, results show that even the smallest ViT variant that uses small input patch sizes outperformed cutting-edge CNNs especially on the smaller COVID-CT dataset with only a few hundred training images. Furthermore, generation of synthetic images using a ResNet-based Self-Attention Generative Adversarial Network (SAGAN-ResNet) was employed as a data augmentation method to alleviate the problem of limited data and was found to further improve accuracy by approximately 3% and 2% on the COVID-CT and Sars-CoV-2 datasets, respectively. In addition to being more computationally efficient and scalable than CNNs, ViT also provides representations that allow visualization of areas that are semantically relevant for detection.

**Keywords:** GANs · Vision transformers · COVID-19

## 1 Introduction

Due to the recent and ongoing pandemic caused by the infectious Coronavirus disease (COVID-19), there are numerous efforts to automate detection of this highly infectious disease using computer vision techniques. Many of these studies focused on detection from chest x-ray images since chest x-ray COVID-19 datasets are more accessible [7,13,26]. Some studies also proposed detection methods for computed tomography (CT) scan images [2,12,16]. These have also been shown to be very useful for COVID-19 detection and can provide more detailed information than x-ray images such as the shape, size, density of internal lung structures.

© Springer Nature Switzerland AG 2021
I. Farkaš et al. (Eds.): ICANN 2021, LNCS 12892, pp. 587–598, 2021.
https://doi.org/10.1007/978-3-030-86340-1_47

Moreover, most of the methods proposed for the automated detection of the virus make use of the widely popular convolutional neural networks (CNN) [7,9,11,16,25,26]. While it has been shown that CNNs are very powerful in computer vision tasks and can obtain very accurate results, they require a large amount of computational resources to train. Recently, a new method that does not rely on convolution operations for computer vision tasks was proposed. This method, called the Vision Transformer (ViT), was shown to achieve excellent results compared to state-of-the-art CNNs especially when pre-trained on very large datasets [3].

Based on the transformer architecture originally designed for NLP tasks, the ViT is computationally efficient and scalable. They pre-trained on different datasets such as the ImageNet-21k [1] and the JFT-300M [22] and then fine-tuned the model on several benchmark tasks. It was shown to outperform ResNets with the same computational budget [3,24]. Unlike in CNNs where only the local features are present in the lowest layers, ViT employs the self-attention mechanism, which integrates both global and local feature information across the whole image even in the lowest layers consequently improving its generalization capabilities. Furthermore, using the attention weights in the ViT, it is possible for us to visualize the areas that are semantically relevant for image classification, which could be especially beneficial for examining closely these areas in the image.

However, with the scarcity of medical datasets made available to researchers for experimentation, not to mention the COVID-19 outbreak occurring relatively recently and the shortage of experts for accurate data labeling, publicly available COVID-19 CT-scan datasets are very limited in size. To address this, several studies have also explored the use of GANs for data augmentation in chest x-ray images [9,25] and CT-scan images [8,11] and observed improvements in the detection of COVID-19.

Motivated by the mentioned studies, we employ the Vision Transformer for COVID-19 detection in CT scan images and GANs for data augmentation. To the best of our knowledge, this is the first study to apply ViT to this problem. For data augmentation, we use a ResNet-based self-attention GAN, which we refer to as the SAGAN-ResNet. Furthermore, we present how the ViT provides visualization for the images by showing what parts of the input image the model focuses its attention in the different layers.

## 2   Methodology

In this section, we describe our proposed method using Vision Transformer for COVID-19 detection in CT-scan images coupled with SAGAN-ResNet for data augmentation. Figure 1 shows the flowchart of the proposed method. To generate synthetic images that will be combined with the original training sets for training the ViT, we use the ResNet-based SAGAN (SAGAN-ResNet). In addition, we compare the classification performance with other common GAN architectures, such as the Auxiliary Classifier GAN (ACGAN) [15], Balancing GAN

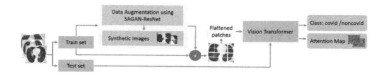

**Fig. 1.** General flowchart of COViT-GAN.

**Table 1.** GAN Hyperparameters

| PARAMETER | ACGAN | BAGAN | SAGAN | SAGAN-RESNET |
|---|---|---|---|---|
| EPOCHS | 600 | 100 | 1000 | 2000 |
| LEARNING RATE | 0.001 | 0.002 | G: $1^{-4}$, D: $/4^{-4}$ | G: $1^{-4}$, d: $4^{-4}$ |
| BATCH SIZE | 32 | 32 | 64 | 64 |
| $\beta$ | (0.5,0.99) | (0.5,0.99) | (0,0.9) | (0,0.9) |
| IMG SIZE | 64 | 64 | 128 | 128 |

(BAGAN) [14], and the original Self-Attention GAN (SAGAN) [27]. For the image classification of the COVID CT-scan images, we implement the different variants of the ViT: ViT-B_16, ViT-B_32, ViT-L_16, ViT-L_32, and ViT-H_14. We also compare the performance of the ViT models with various CNN architectures such as the ResNet-18, ResNet-50, ResNet-101, ResNet-152 [4], DenseNet-121 [6], VGG-16 [19], EfficientNet (EN) [23], and the deeper EfficientCovidNet (ECN) [18]. For all the ViT and CNN models, we implement transfer learning by using the ImageNet-21k [1] pre-trained models.

### 2.1 GANs for Data Augmentation

GANs are known for its powerful image generation capabilities, which is ideal for data augmentation as it provides very realistic and unseen image samples. We propose SAGAN-ResNet which is based on the SAGAN proposed in [27]. It also employs the self-attention mechanism, which helps model long-range dependencies in the image and amplify relevant signals in the input images. SAGAN uses spectral normalization on both the generator and the discriminator, resulting in better conditioning with the two-time-scale-update rule (TTUR) providing a more stable training [5].

In SAGAN-ResNet, both the discriminator and generator networks are based on Residual Networks (ResNet) that employs skip connections [4]. By skipping some layers, the network can build more layers that can deal with more complex image patterns without sacrificing accuracy degradation caused by vanishing gradients. We used an imbalanced 1:5 learning schedule rate for the generator versus the discriminator that results in a more stable learning schedule. We use the SAGAN-ResNet implementation provided in GitHub[1]. Table 1 shows the hyperparameters used for the image generation process of the SAGAN-ResNet and the three other GANs.

---

[1] https://github.com/rosinality/sagan-pytorch.

## 2.2   Image Classification

**Vision Transformer (ViT).** ViT [3] uses a standard Transformer [24] applied directly to image patches. The process, shown in Fig. 2, is as follows: the input image is split into fixed-sized patches, which are then flattened and mapped to one dimension with trainable linear projection to generate patch embeddings. Then, a learnable embedding is prepended to the sequence of patch embeddings, resulting in a 1D sequence of token embeddings. In order to retain positional information, position embeddings are also added to the patch embeddings, which are then fed to the transformer encoder as input. A classification head that is implemented by a Multilayer Perceptron (MLP) is attached to the output of the transformer encoder. COViT-GAN refers to the combination of the Vision Transformer and SAGAN-ResNet as a data augmentation method applied to the task of COVID-19 detection from CT scans.

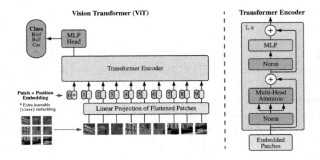

**Fig. 2.** The vision transformer model. Image is from [3]

**Training and Implementation Details.** We train the different ViT[2] model variants on the two datasets for binary image classification. We use the following baseline hyperparameters: batch size 32, learning rate of 0.03, and cosine scheduler trained on 5000 epochs. The model that achieves the best validation accuracy is used for testing. For the CNN models, the hyperparameters were standardized across the experiments (Adam optimizer, cross-entropy loss function, learning rate of 0.001, batch size 32, and minimum epochs of 50).

To evaluate the performance of the ViT models and other CNN models for comparison, we compute the accuracy ($Acc$), COVID-19 positive prediction ($+P_C$) or precision, COVID-19 sensitivity ($Se_C$) or recall, and F1-score ($F1$). All experiments were performed in Google Colab Notebooks using Pytorch.

## 3   Results and Discussion

**Datasets.** We use two publicly available datasets, the first one is the COVID-CT[28] dataset[3], which contains CT-scan images collected from several scientific

---

[2] https://github.com/jeonsworld/ViT-pytorch.
[3] https://github.com/UCSD-AI4H/COVID-CT.

articles. We used a total of 746 images, 349 of which belong to 216 patients diagnosed with COVID-19. We use the data split provided, with 425 training, 118 validation, and 203 test images.

The Sars-CoV-2 [20] multi-class dataset[4] contains 4173 CT scans for 210 patients from hospitals from Sao Paulo, Brazil who are healthy, infected with Sars-CoV-2, and infected with other pulmonary diseases. We categorize the images from healthy patients and patients with other non-COVID-19 diseases under one class (noncovid). While this makes it much more difficult to classify, we use this dataset for the main reason that it separates the images by patient, thus ensuring that no data leaking will occur. We use a 70/10/20 train/validation/test split of for a total of 2921 training, 417 validation, and 835 test images.

All input images have size $224 \times 224$, obtained by resizing all training images to $256 \times 256$, then getting sample random crops of size $224 \times 224$. To ensure that all pixels range from 0 to 1, we also perform simple image normalization to help the model converge during training.

**Performance of ViT Model Variants.** Figure 3 displays the performance of different ViT models on COVID-CT and Sars-Cov-2 datasets trained with the baseline hyperparameters. For COVID-CT, ViT-H_14 has the best accuracy of 84.24% but ViT-B_16 also shows great promise with good performance in terms of the metrics, considering that it is the smallest model. Meanwhile, Sars-CoV-2 has achieved the best accuracy and sensitivity of 94.01% and 98.68% respectively with just the ViT-B_16.

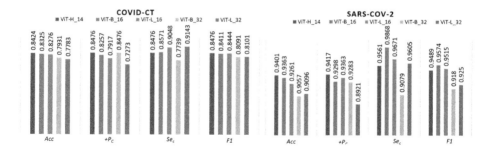

**Fig. 3.** Baseline performance of ViT model variants on COVID-CT and Sars-CoV-2 Datasets.

**Performance of ViT with GANs.** Figure 4 displays the accuracy of ViT models with data augmentation using GANs. The models were trained with the original training set combined with the generated synthetic images, samples of which are displayed on Fig. 5. We added 1000 and 500 random images for each class to the COVID-CT and Sars-CoV-2 training sets, respectively. The declining accuracy is observed as the model's input patch size is increasing.

---

[4] https://www.kaggle.com/plameneduardo/a-covid-multiclass-dataset-of-ct-scans.

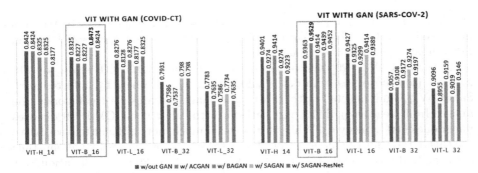

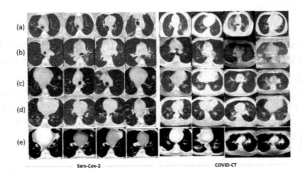

**Fig. 4.** Accuracy of ViT model variants with and without GAN on COVID-CT and Sars-CoV-2 Datasets. The results enclosed in a box corresponds to the variant that obtained the best accuracy for each dataset.

**Fig. 5.** Sample GAN-generated images. (a) Images from the original distribution, (b) SAGAN, (c) BAGAN, (d) ACGAN, (e) SAGAN-ResNet

For the COVID-CT dataset, ViT-H_14 and ViT-L_32 did not improve with any of the GAN models. ViT-L_16 only improved with SAGAN-ResNet. The base models, ViT-B_16 and ViT-B_32, have both improved with SAGAN and SAGAN-ResNet. These slight improvements demonstrate the potential of using data augmentation with GANs, especially the GANs that employ the self-attention mechanism. Overall, the best accuracy obtained is with ViT-B_16 with SAGAN-ResNet. No model has improved with BAGAN. Nevertheless, it is still important to note that the performance are still close to the performance without the GAN. Meanwhile, on the Sars-CoV-2, we observed some performance improvements with GAN for all the ViT models except ViT-L_16, wherein the accuracy degraded with the addition of GAN-generated images. The best accuracy was also obtained with ViT-B_16 but with ACGAN.

Our findings in Sect. 3 show that ViT_H14 is the best performing ViT variant without GAN. However, when we incorporate the GAN, ViT_B16 has produced better results than that of ViT_H14, with a resulting accuracy of 0.9529 and 0.9414, respectively. In fact, this result of ViT_B16 (with GAN) is still better than ViT_H14 (without GAN) which has only produced an accuracy of 0.9401. Due to these findings, we further fine-tune on COVID-CT and Sars-CoV-2 with the ViT-B_16 model.

**Fine-Tuning of Parameters.** We perform hyperparameter tuning on the best model (ViT-B_16) for each dataset (with and without GANs) by exploring several values of the learning rate (0.001, 0.008, 0.01, 0.02, 0.03, 0.04), batch size (16, 32, 64), number of augmented images per class (500, 1000), and attention dropout rate (0, 0.1, 0.2). Here, the attention dropout rate corresponds to dropout regularization applied in the self-attention module. We do not show all of the results obtained from the fine-tuning, but instead report the two best performing models for each the two datasets in terms of accuracy in Table 2.

**Table 2.** Best COViT-GAN Models and Parameters. (LR, BS, #synthetic, DR, ADR) refers to (learning rate, batch size, number of augmented synthetic images from GAN, dropout rate, attention dropout rate). Values in bold are the best values for each dataset.

| DATASET | COViT-GAN MODEL | LR | BS | # SYNTHETIC | DR | ADR | Acc | SE$_c$ | + P$_c$ | F1 |
|---|---|---|---|---|---|---|---|---|---|---|
| COVID-CT | ViT_B-16 + SAGAN-RESNET | 0.01 | 16 | 1000 | 0.1 | 0.2 | **0.8719** | 0.8571 | **0.8911** | **0.8738** |
| COVID-CT | ViT_B-16 + SAGAN-RESNET | 0.01 | 32 | 1000 | 0.1 | 0.1 | 0.8473 | **0.8667** | 0.8426 | 0.8545 |
| SARS-CoV-2 | ViT_B-16 + SAGAN-RESNET | 0.04 | 32 | 500 | 0.1 | 0.0 | 0.9529 | **0.9868** | 0.9356 | 0.9605 |
| SARS-CoV-2 | ViT_B-16 + SAGAN-RESNET | 0.01 | 32 | 500 | 0.1 | 0.0 | **0.9541** | 0.9803 | **0.9430** | **0.9613** |

In Fig. 4, we can observe that ACGAN and SAGAN performed better than SAGAN-ResNet but after performing hyperparameter tuning, we have found the best results with SAGAN-ResNet, as shown in Table 2. We were able to get the best values for learning rate (0.1 and 0.4) and batch sizes (16, 32) for each of the datasets. For the COVID-CT dataset, the results seem to improve when 1000 images per class were added to the original training set. Considering the original training set only has 425 images, the best performance achieved by our model (87.19% accuracy, 85.71% sensitivity, and 89.11% COVID-19 positive precision) is impressive since the training data is comprised of about 82.5% synthetic images generated by the SAGAN-ResNet. For the Sars-CoV-2 dataset, we were able to get better performance when only 500 synthetic images per class were added instead of 1000. This may be because the original train set already has a lot of images (3021) and the addition of a lot more synthetic images could not be beneficial. Another reason could be due to the fact that the noncovid class contains both CT scans that are healthy cases or cases with other pulmonary diseases, which makes it more difficult for the GAN. Nevertheless, the addition of 500 images per class still gave better performance than when no synthetic images were added.

In addition, when we increased the attention dropout rate, we observed some performance improvements on the COVID-CT dataset. We believe this is because the attention dropout regularization helped avoid overfitting in the smaller dataset by not limiting its "attention" to a smaller amount of feature cues from the patches of the input image.

**Performance Comparison of ViT and CNN Models.** We compare the performance of the ViT model or the ViT_B16 (without GAN), the fine-tuned CoViT-GAN model obtained, and the other CNN models on the original datasets in Table 3 using the base hyperparameters. We note that the COVIT-GAN uses the fine-tuned ViT_B16 as a classifier and SAGAN-Resnet as a data augmentation technique.

**Table 3.** Performance Comparison of the best performing ViT, COViT-GAN model, and other CNNs for the COVID-CT and Sars-CoV-2 datasets.

| Architecture | COVID-CT | | | | Sars-CoV-2 | | | |
|---|---|---|---|---|---|---|---|---|
| | Acc | Sec | +Pc | F1 | Acc | Sec | +Pc | F1 |
| DENSENET-121 | 0.8226 | 0.8227 | 0.8252 | 0.8219 | 0.9248 | 0.9248 | 0.9324 | 0.9253 |
| VGG-16 | 0.7537 | 0.7537 | 0.7537 | 0.7537 | 0.9299 | 0.9299 | 0.9299 | 0.9299 |
| RESNET-152 | 0.7833 | 0.7881 | 0.7829 | 0.7833 | 0.9121 | 0.9229 | 0.9121 | 0.9127 |
| RESNET-101 | 0.8030 | 0.8096 | 0.8012 | 0.8030 | 0.9567 | 0.9567 | 0.9573 | 0.9568 |
| RESNET-18 | 0.7783 | 0.7782 | 0.7780 | 0.7783 | 0.9159 | 0.9159 | 0.9159 | 0.9159 |
| RESNET-50 | 0.8177 | 0.8208 | 0.8169 | 0.8177 | **0.9580** | 0.9579 | **0.9580** | 0.9580 |
| EN | 0.8177 | 0.7810 | 0.8542 | 0.8159 | 0.9299 | 0.9452 | 0.9349 | 0.9400 |
| ECN | 0.7488 | 0.7048 | 0.7872 | 0.7437 | 0.9465 | 0.9846 | 0.9277 | 0.9553 |
| **ViT (w/o GAN)** | 0.8424 | 0.8476 | 0.8476 | 0.8476 | 0.9363 | 0.9781 | 0.9177 | 0.9469 |
| **COViT-GAN** | **0.8719** | **0.8571** | **0.8911** | **0.8738** | 0.9541 | **0.9803** | 0.9430 | **0.9613** |

For the smaller COVID-CT dataset, it can be seen that the ViT alone has outperformed all of the CNNs in all the metrics despite the small size of the dataset with only a few hundred training images and thus are more difficult to classify. Moreover, with the addition of synthetic images using COViT-GAN, we can see the improvements over all the metrics (almost 3% improvement in accuracy over ViT). For the Sars-CoV-2 dataset, we obtained the best accuracy and positive prediction with ResNet-50. However, we also note that the ViT model has competitive performance to ResNet-50. The COViT-GAN is also very competitive, outperforming all of the CNN models except the ResNet-50 and ResNet-101 in some of the metrics. Furthermore, compared to the ViT model, all the metrics are better for COViT-GAN, with more competitive results than the ResNet-50 (95.41% accuracy compared to 95.80%). With almost 2% accuracy improvement compared to the best ViT without GAN, COViT-GAN demonstrates its effectiveness on a larger yet still challenging dataset.

These observations are consistent with that of [3], wherein they observed that when pretrained with a mid-sized dataset such as ImageNet, the performance of the ViT is similar to ResNets. However, when pretrained on a much larger dataset like the JFT-300M, we can see the full benefit of the ViT and COViT-GAN models, especially the larger ones. We wish to emphasize that there is a more significant performance improvement on the smaller dataset, despite only using the smallest ViT variant. This shows that applying COViT-GAN to limited datasets can be very advantageous.

**Visualization of the Salient Parts in COVID CT Images.** In this section, we offer insights on how the model arrives at such predictions by investigating the attention maps produced by the model. We used images from journals [10, 17, 21] and websites that investigate the detection of COVID-19 in CT scan images and tested it on ViT-B_16 trained on Sars-CoV-2. All the images are correctly classified and the relevant portions of the image are appropriately highlighted in the attention map as seen in Fig. 6 *(a)–(b)*. We compared the radiological features that are indicative of COVID in the original images pointed by the arrows (first column) with the salient portions in its corresponding attention map (third column). We can observe that the prominent blue areas in the attention maps match the portions of the original image that are indicative of COVID-19.

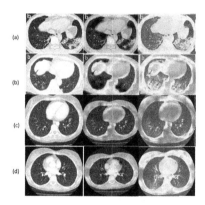

**Fig. 6.** (a-b) contain covid and (c–d) noncovid images. In (a–b), the prominent blue areas in the attention maps match the ground glass opacities, characterized by its white lung appearance, in the original image indicating COVID-19. In column 2, heatmap is applied on the attention before fusing with the input image but salient portions are clearer in column 3 where it is applied after fusing attention with input image.

We also investigated the attention maps of normal chest CT images (c) in Fig. 6. Based on our observations, the amount of blue areas that are prominent on COVID-19 images are reduced. According to literature [17], the COVID-19 indications are characterized by ground glass opacities which gives a white lung appearance in CT images. Since these (c) are normal images, the ground glass opacities are absent which explains why no large blue sections are present.

However, note that we do not claim these observations as clinically correct since we did not consult with a radiologist. Although, these visualized results could assist the radiologists on the analysis of the scans.

**Attention Maps per Layer.** In this section, we visualize how attention progresses across the different layers of the network (Fig. 7). Since ViT-B_16 has 12 attention heads, we only look at layers 1, 6, and 12 for simplicity on randomly sampled images from Sars-CoV-2 (a–b) and other images with labeled indications of COVID-19 (c–d). As observed on the figure, the earlier layers have saturated monotonous colors but the relevant parts of the image are already slightly emphasized. As discussed in [27], the model is able to integrate the global information in the image which is shown in the image where some heads already attend to the image in the earlier layers. As the attention develops from one layer to another, some elements are getting ignored while others are emphasized. As we can see, the more pixels that are ignored, the better the relevant parts are isolated and highlighted. These observations are more pronounced in images with labeled COVID-19 indications. Starting from layers 8, the ground lung opacities are more emphasized in the attention maps.

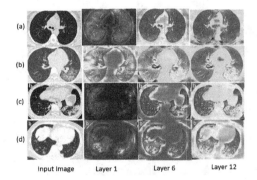

Fig. 7. Visualization of attention flows from one layer to another. (a-b) noncovid images from Sars-Cov-2, (c-d) covid image with labeled COVID-19 indications. As the layer deepens, the better the relevant parts are isolated, as observed on the more emphasized white lung appearances in COVID images (c-d).

## 4   Conclusions

We present COViT-GAN, a method that combines the Vision Transformer and a ResNet-based Self-Attention GAN (SAGAN-ResNet) for data augmentation for the detection of COVID-19 from CT scan images. We also confirm the capabilities of the self-attention mechanism to capture global and local features.

With the use of pre-trained models on a mid-sized ImageNet dataset, we showed that the ViT is competitive against high-performing CNNs, outperforming these models when tested on the much smaller COVID-CT dataset. Since the datasets we used are limited, we further improved our results by employing a ResNet-based GAN to generate synthetic images for data augmentation. With the self-attention mechanism, the SAGAN-ResNet was able to produce additional training images that helped improve the performance of ViT, with about 3% and 2% accuracy improvements on the COVID-CT and Sars-CoV-2 datasets, respectively. With fine-tuning, our COVïT-GAN was able to obtain a classification accuracy of about 87.19% and 95.41%, respectively.

As a disclaimer, we emphasize that we do not intend to use GAN for the generation of realistic medical CT-scan images, but for the performance improvement of ViT for COVID-19 detection. Visualizations generated could be used to verify the effectiveness of the ViT by showing the areas of the image that are semantically relevant for classification in each model layer. This visualization feature might be essential for radiologists for the analysis of the CT scans. In the future, we hope to further improve our results by evaluating the proposed method in other datasets and modifying the architecture of transformers or GANs.

# References

1. Deng, J., Dong, W., Socher, R., Li, L.J., Li, K., Fei-Fei, L.: ImageNet: a large-scale hierarchical image database. In: 2009 IEEE Conference on Computer Vision and Pattern Recognition, pp. 248–255. IEEE (2009)
2. Do, C., Vu, L.: An approach for recognizing covid-19 cases using convolutional neural networks applied to CT scan images. In: Applications of Digital Image Processing XLIII, vol. 11510, p. 1151034. International Society for Optics and Photonics (2020)
3. Dosovitskiy, A., et al.: An image is worth $16 \times 16$ words: transformers for image recognition at scale. arXiv preprint arXiv:2010.11929 (2020)
4. He, K., Zhang, X., Ren, S., Sun, J.: Deep residual learning for image recognition. In: Proceedings of the IEEE Conference on Computer Vision and Pattern Recognition, pp. 770–778 (2016)
5. Heusel, M., Ramsauer, H., Unterthiner, T., Nessler, B., Hochreiter, S.: GANs trained by a two time-scale update rule converge to a local nash equilibrium. arXiv preprint arXiv:1706.08500 (2017)
6. Huang, G., Liu, Z., Van Der Maaten, L., Weinberger, K.Q.: Densely connected convolutional networks. In: Proceedings of the IEEE Conference on Computer Vision and Pattern Recognition, pp. 4700–4708 (2017)
7. Ismael, A.M., Şengür, A.: Deep learning approaches for covid-19 detection based on chest x-ray images. Expert Syst. Appl. **164**, 114054 (2020)
8. Jiang, Y., Chen, H., Loew, M., Ko, H.: Covid-19 CT image synthesis with a conditional generative adversarial network. IEEE J. Biomed. Health Inf. (2020)
9. Khalifa, N.E.M., Taha, M.H.N., Hassanien, A.E., Elghamrawy, S.: Detection of coronavirus (covid-19) associated pneumonia based on generative adversarial networks and a fine-tuned deep transfer learning model using chest x-ray dataset. arXiv preprint arXiv:2004.01184 (2020)

10. Li, X., et al.: CT imaging changes of corona virus disease 2019(COVID-19): a multi-center study in Southwest China. J. Transl. Med. **18**(1), 154 (2020)
11. Loey, M., Manogaran, G., Khalifa, N.E.M.: A deep transfer learning model with classical data augmentation and CGAN to detect COVID-19 from chest CT radiography digital images. Neural Comput. Appl. (2020)
12. Maghdid, H.S., Asaad, A.T., Ghafoor, K.Z., Sadiq, A.S., Khan, M.K.: Diagnosing covid-19 pneumonia from x-ray and CT images using deep learning and transfer learning algorithms. arXiv preprint arXiv:2004.00038 (2020)
13. Mahmud, T., Rahman, M.A., Fattah, S.A.: CovxNet: a multi-dilation convolutional neural network for automatic covid-19 and other pneumonia detection from chest x-ray images with transferable multi-receptive feature optimization. Comput. Biol. Med. **122**, 103869 (2020)
14. Mariani, G., Scheidegger, F., Istrate, R., Bekas, C., Malossi, C.: BAGAN: data augmentation with balancing GAN. arXiv preprint arXiv:1803.09655 (2018)
15. Odena, A., Olah, C., Shlens, J.: Conditional image synthesis with auxiliary classifier GANs. In: International Conference on Machine Learning, pp. 2642–2651. PMLR (2017)
16. Polsinelli, M., Cinque, L., Placidi, G.: A light CNN for detecting covid-19 from CT scans of the chest. arXiv preprint arXiv:2004.12837 (2020)
17. Shi, H., et al.: Radiological findings from 81 patients with COVID-19 pneumonia in Wuhan, China: a descriptive study. Lancet Infect. Dis. **20**(4), 425–434 (2020)
18. Silva, P., et al.: COVID-19 detection in CT images with deep learning: a voting-based scheme and cross-datasets analysis. Inf. Med. Unlocked **20**, 100427 (2020)
19. Simonyan, K., Zisserman, A.: Very deep convolutional networks for large-scale image recognition. arXiv preprint arXiv:1409.1556 (2014)
20. Soares, E., Angelov, P., Biaso, S., Higa Froes, M., Kanda Abe, D.: SARS-CoV-2 CT-scan dataset: a large dataset of real patients CT scans for SARS-CoV-2 identification. preprint, Health Informatics, April 2020. https://doi.org/10.1101/2020.04.24.20078584
21. Sultan, O.M., et al.: Pulmonary CT manifestations of COVID-19: changes within 2 weeks duration from presentation. Egyptian J. Radiol. Nuclear Med. **51**(1), 105, December 2020
22. Sun, C., Shrivastava, A., Singh, S., Gupta, A.: Revisiting unreasonable effectiveness of data in deep learning era. In: Proceedings of the IEEE International Conference on Computer Vision, pp. 843–852 (2017)
23. Tan, M., Le, Q.V.: EfficientNet: rethinking model scaling for convolutional neural networks. arXiv preprint arXiv:1905.11946 (2019)
24. Vaswani, A., et al.: Attention is all you need. arXiv preprint arXiv:1706.03762 (2017)
25. Waheed, A., Goyal, M., Gupta, D., Khanna, A., Al-Turjman, F., Pinheiro, P.R.: CovidGAN: data augmentation using auxiliary classifier GAN for improved Covid-19 detection. IEEE Access **8**, 91916–91923 (2020)
26. Wang, L., Wong, A.: Covid-net: a tailored deep convolutional neural network design for detection of covid-19 cases from chest x-ray images. arXiv preprint arXiv:2003.09871 (2020)
27. Zhang, H., Goodfellow, I., Metaxas, D., Odena, A.: Self-attention generative adversarial networks. In: International Conference on Machine Learning, pp. 7354–7363. PMLR (2019)
28. Zhao, J., Zhang, Y., He, X., Xie, P.: Covid-CT-dataset: a CT scan dataset about covid-19. arXiv preprint arXiv:2003.13865 (2020)

# PhonicsGAN: Synthesizing Graphical Videos from Phonics Songs

Nuha Aldausari[✉], Arcot Sowmya, Nadine Marcus, and Gelareh Mohammadi

University of New South Wales, Kensington, Australia
{n.aldausari,a.sowmya,nadinem,g.mohammadi}@unsw.edu.au

**Abstract.** Content creation is a growing field in Artificial Intelligence (AI) that achieves promising results using generative models. With recent advances in generative models such as Generative Adversarial Networks (GAN), videos can be generated according to specific conditions or even without any conditional settings. In this paper, we propose an end-to-end model that generates videos according to audio signals using both transcript and music. We call our model phonicsGAN since it draws a graphical alphabetic video and animate it given a phonics song. PhonicsGAN is among the first attempts to create preliminary graphical videos which can inspire and support graphical designers and educators to save time and effort. Since available graphical datasets lack acoustic signals, a suitable candidate domain for our proposed application is the phonic videos for children. PhonicsGAN deals with diverse videos in terms of content, motion and soundtrack by employing Gated Recurrent Units (GRU) layers to encode the soundtrack. A Convolutional Neural Network (CNN) is then used to generate a phonics video based on the encoded audio signal and the provided label. The preliminary results are promising and show improvements over LSTM and MoCoGAN which are state-of-the-art frameworks in the video generation domain.

**Keywords:** Video synthesis · Generative Adversarial Network · Audio-to-video mapping

## 1 Introduction

In 2017, video consumption represents 70% of the internet traffic, and this number is expected to be increased by 4 folds by 2022 [6]. This trend is supported by the increase in internet speed, which facilitates using videos in fields such as education and marketing, in addition to entertainment. However, creating video content is also more demanding than other forms of media in multiple aspects such as time, cost, and skills. Thus, there have been increasing efforts that aim at utilizing generative models to automate the process of generating videos. The current applications of video generative models range from video predication, video re-targeting, video synchronization, to reverse video captioning. Meanwhile, this paper aims at building a model that draws graphical videos according

© Springer Nature Switzerland AG 2021
I. Farkaš et al. (Eds.): ICANN 2021, LNCS 12892, pp. 599–610, 2021.
https://doi.org/10.1007/978-3-030-86340-1_48

to audio signals. Audio signals are not descriptive in general cases and may lack detailed description of a scene. Thus, it is not feasible to train a model on just an audio signal to draw the content of the frames. However, we chose a domain where the acoustic signals are effectively conveying the illustrated objects in the videos. This domain is phonics songs videos. One application for phonicsGAN is to help teachers in creating customized phonics videos based on children's preferences. They can also be used to inspire graphical designers by incorporating different styles and format. In addition, the model can be a baseline for other video generative models that trained on descriptive audio signals.

GAN is one of few content creation models that synthesize realistic-looking examples [9]. While generation of images using GAN is quite advanced, video generation is still at an early stage. The reason is that videos consist of multiple images with temporal dynamics and it is essential to maintain the coherence between frames when generating videos. Thus, video creation is more complex when compared with image synthesis. In video GAN frameworks, random synthesized videos can be generated from noise vectors in unconditional settings, whereas in conditional settings, input signals such as texts, audios, videos or images are provided, and videos are created based on the given condition. Generating videos according to audio files has given rise to several applications. One such application is the conversion of speech to a synchronized moving head [17,30,35]. Transforming a music file to a video of a person playing a specific musical instrument [5,7] or to a video of a person dancing to the music [2,8,14,20,27,33] is another application. A preliminary application could use an audio signal to generate a video for non-human artefacts such as fireworks or beach waves [16]. The music-to-dance applications rely on key points or optical flow to facilitate maintenance of the coherence between sound and motion in the generation process. In non-guided motion applications, the dataset is homogeneous which means that the data samples are from the same category, and in some datasets, target objects are centered around the same pixels in all samples. In this work, we build an application that synthesizes animated videos from a dataset of videos collected from YouTube. Our model synthesizes animated letters videos based on phonics songs. Our proposed dataset has a variety of objects, as illustrated in Fig. 1. Thus, training a GAN model on such a dataset can be more challenging especially without key points.

A factor common to video synthesis models is that the models are trained on photographed datasets such as Kinetics-600 [23], UCF-101 [24], Mug facial expression [3], Solo-Dancer [34], FaceForensics [21], and YouTube dancing videos [31]. However, there is relatively little work on graphical video datasets. A related work that utilizes a graphical dataset is storyGAN [15]. However, StoryGAN cannot be directly applied to our problem, namely song-to-video generation, due to some substantial differences as follows; StoryGAN generates animated image sequences that represent stories based on text descriptions, whereas our proposed work synthesizes videos based on songs, which can be a more challenging task. This is because a song creates a multimodal dataset that contains lyrics and music, and music in turn can be divided into sub-elements such as beat, rhythm, melody, and harmony. Besides, songs do not necessarily illustrate the scenes in detail, unlike text descriptions. Another difference is that StoryGAN's dataset, Pororo-SV, is

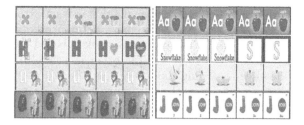

**Fig. 1.** Eight samples from the collected dataset. For demonstration purpose, each clip was sampled 5 Hz to produce 5 frames per second.

collected from a single anime series where all the clips contain a subset of the same characters, objects and backgrounds [13]. The dataset in phonicsGAN, on the other hand, was gathered from YouTube. Thus, data samples vary in styles, motions, backgrounds, and objects. Therefore, song-to-video generation models require additional attention to the music content as well as varieties in the scene characters. This paper presents a preliminary model, phonicGAN, to tackle this problem in the context of phonics song videos.

The main contributions of this paper are as follows. First, collecting a suitable graphical dataset that has an adequate number of samples. The chosen domain of the dataset is that of nursery rhyme videos on YouTube. Second, proposing a framework, namely phonicsGAN, that generates animated videos content from songs and captures the relationship between the music and the motion of videos. PhonicsGAN utilizes GRU-blocks to model the changes in the audio signals over time. The output of the GRU-based audio encoder is used to generate the video frames that are evaluated by the image discriminator and the video discriminator. Lastly, the resulting videos from the novel framework phonicsGAN is compared against LSTM and MoCoGAN. Section 2 categorizes recent models that are conditioned on audio signals. In Sect. 3, a description of phonicsGAN is provided. Section 4 illustrates the generated videos and discuss the result. Finally, the research paper is concluded in Sect. 5, with the provision of possible applications.

## 2 Background

GAN is a generative deep neural network model introduced in 2014 which surpassed other generative models by producing high-quality images [12]. GAN models are not limited to image synthesis, they can also produce videos. Aldausari et al. [4] review the state-of-the-art GAN in the video realm and categorise video GAN models based on the existence and type of the conditional signals in detail. Motion Content GAN (MoCoGAN) [29] is one of unconditional models using N noise vectors to produce N frames. MoCoGAN traverse the noise vectors first to generate the motion vectors to be combined with a fixed content vector. Then, the combined representation is utilized to generate the video frames. MoCoGAN effective framework has been extended in multiple architectures such as storyGAN [15]. The main difference between MoCoGAN and the proposed framework is that our framework is based on two conditions: one is changing according to a song and the other is a label based on the content. Audio-to-video deep learning models are another category of conditional video synthesis that need to keep the coherence between frames and maintain synchronization between motions and input audio signals. Following subsections review the recent relevant audio-to-video generation studies.

## 2.1  Speech to Moving Face

Speech synchronization generative models deal differently with the audio signals. Vougioukas et al. [30] choose to input to the Facial Synthesizer model the entire audio waveform file. In contrast, the Disentangled Audio-Visual System (DAVS) [35] disentangles the audios into subject-related information and speech-related information while Mittal et al. [17] disentangle the audio signals into content, emotion, and noise using Variational Autoencoder (VAE). These models [17,30,35] were trained on datasets of talking persons and the data samples cropped to fit on the desired dataset template. In contrast, our dataset was collected from YouTube, with objects scattered around the frames, which makes the learning process more complex. Another difference is that the earlier models [17,30,35] are conditioned on the first frame, which can be seen as a prediction problem, while phonicsGAN synthesizes videos without conditioning on the initial frame.

## 2.2  Music to Moving Body

Music-to-dance mapping has multiple applications such as virtual reality, games and robotics. The moving body generative models in the literature can be divided into four families: unsupervised, semi-supervised, weakly-supervised and self-supervised.

Many approaches are based on self-supervised methods. An early attempt [27] uses traditional Long Short-Term Memory (LSTM) based autoencoders. The model first encodes the music signals, then a predictor is employed to produce the pose features. More recent papers use adversarial learning. Lee et al. [14] proposed a two-stage model where the first stage is to synthesize the basic dance movements using VAE, then the second stage organizes the movements based on the audio signals using GAN. Ren et al. [20] encode acoustic features using bidirectional Gated Recurrent Unit (GRU). The poses are generated using a multilayered perceptron according to the hidden states of the music. Sun et al. [25] also use RNN architecture not only to encode the music features but also to decode the poses given the hidden states and the initial frame. Zhuang et al. [36] borrow WaveNet [18], which is a generative adversarial model that was originally introduced for speech generation, to synthesise dance movements.

Yalta et al. [33] provide weakly supervised signals to a deep RNN to help the training process with fewer data samples and less effort. The weak labels reflect whether there are significant changes between consecutive audio frames to direct the motion.

Another model [8] uses semi-supervised methods where in the first pre-training stage, the model is trained on unlabelled data. The model in the first stage encodes Mel Spectrogram representations and then decodes it into Mel Spectrogram, melody and rhythm. The second stage uses the pre-trained encoder and music embedding to generate the skeletons. Ahn et al. [2] also use the first layers in the pre-trained music genre classifier to produce the music representations. Then they use dilated convolution layers to generate the skeleton sequences.

All the previous models [2, 8, 14, 20, 25, 27, 33, 36] use the extracted pose frames, since these skeletons are a way to emphasize motions. The correlation between the acoustic features and the motions of the skeletons can be built easily in the training process. However, in phonicsGAN, it is difficult to extract skeletons for the objects because there are multiple objects in a frame and the objects are varied. Thus, phonicsGAN deals with a challenging problem, namely generation of frames with motion in pixel space rather than in skeleton space.

### 2.3   Audio to Moving Object

While many methods for generating the moving body are based on key-points, there are some datasets where it is difficult to detect key-points, such as sea waves or fireworks. Qiu et al. [19] generate only one photographed image such as sky, water, mountain or desert based on the sound of that scene. Their model starts with an GRU structure to extract the features, then DCGAN [28] to generate one image. Tsuchiya et al. [28] proposed a bidirectional LSTM sound encoder that is followed by a GAN to generate videos of photographed scenes such as fireworks and beach waves. The generator is U-net and there are two discriminators for the image level and the video level. While the model [28] is trained separately on each dataset that represents one object, phonicsGAN is trained on a dataset with 26 categories, with each category containing multiple sub-objects.

## 3   PhonicsGAN

### 3.1   Dataset Construction

The goal of this work is to construct a model that can draw graphical video frames based on songs. The available datasets are either not graphical datasets, or lack soundtracks or both. One potential domain is phonics songs with their videos. This domain satisfies specific criteria which are graphics-based videos, a synchronized soundtrack for each video, and a sufficient number of samples.

The videos were collected based on keywords from YouTube. Possible keywords are "alphabets songs", "letters song", and "phonic songs". Only videos that have a segment that consists of a letter and an object that represents that letter are chosen. Examples of the selected video transcriptions could be "a is for apple" or "q q q queen", and Fig. 1 illustrates different examples of the dataset samples. The chosen videos were downloaded with the corresponding English captions where available and otherwise speech-to-text Google API [1] is used to generate the transcripts. The videos were then trimmed based on the transcripts, where each trimmed clip contains a letter and an object. The metadata for the clips was saved in a JSON file. The saved information for a clip consists of the name of the clip, the name of the main file, the category of the clip, the transcript, and the ID of the video in YouTube. The category of the clip refers to the letter that is displayed in the clip frames. The total number of collected videos from YouTube is 150 videos. After trimming the videos using the procedure described, the total number of clips is 1176.

### 3.2    Problem Formalization

PhonicsGAN maps phonics songs and the target letters to frames while maintaining the correlation between the changes in the audio signal and the changes in the motion between the generated frames. PhonicsGAN is trained on a dataset $D = \{(V_1, A_1, L_1), (V_2, A_2, L_2), (V_3, A_3, L_3), \ldots, (V_M, A_M, L_M)\}$, where $Vi = \{v_1, v_2, v_3, \ldots, v_N\}$ is clip i containing a sequence of frames $v_j$ , $j = 1, \ldots, N$. The corresponding audio segment is $A_i = \{a_1, a_2, a_3, \ldots, a_N\}$, where $a_j$ , $j = 1, \ldots, N$. is the audio segment. It is important to note here that the video frame $v_j$ is aligned with the audio features in $a_j, j = 1, \ldots, N$. The category of the clip $L_i \subseteq S = \{"A", "B", "C", \ldots, "Z"\}$ where $|L_i| = 1$ and $|S| = 26$. The main aim of this paper is to train phonicsGAN to generate a clip $V`_i = \{v`_1, v`_2, v`_3, \ldots.v`_N\}$ that conforms to the audio segment $A_i = \{a_1, a_2, a_3, \ldots, a_N\}$ and similar to the ground truth clip $V_i = \{v_1, v_2, v_3, \ldots, v_N\}$.

### 3.3    Model Architecture

The overall architecture of phonicsGAN is illustrated in Fig. 2. It can be divided into three main components: audio encoder, generator, two-level discriminators.

**Audio Encoder.** The audio signal $A_i = \{a_1, a_2, a_3, \ldots, a_N\}$ is first converted to a Mel Spectrogram because the latter can represent musical information effectively [8,11,32]. The Mel spectrogram tensors are input into fully connected layers to downscale the dimensions, then the encoded vectors are concatenated with Gaussian noise vectors $E = \{e_1, e_2, e_3, \ldots, e_N\}$ to feed the GRU layer as described in equation (1). Then another GRU layer receives the hidden states from the lower layer with the labels as illustrated in equation (2).

$$o_t = GRU((a_t, e_t), o_{t-1}) \tag{1}$$

$$s_t = GRU((L, o_t), s_{t-1}) \tag{2}$$

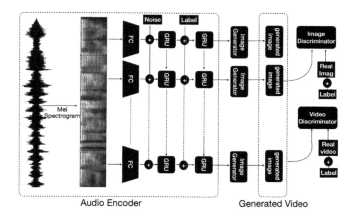

**Fig. 2.** PhonicsGAN: it consists of two encoders and two-level discriminators

In equation (1), $(a_t, e_t)$ represents a concatenated vector that consists of a noise vector $e_t$ and an audio segment $a_t$ at time step t, while $o_{t-1}$ is the hidden state from the previous state. In equation (2), the label of the clip L is concatenated with $o_t$, which is the hidden state of the lower layer. The vector $s_{t-1}$ is accumulated from the previous GRU cells.

**Video and Image Generators.** The video generator can sequentially map the encoded audio vectors to a set of frames. It consists of a deep convolutional neural network to upscale the audio vectors to video frames. The image generator follows the same architecture as the video generator. However, instead of receiving multiple encoding vectors based on the desired length of the video frames, the generator receives one encoding audio vector to generate one frame.

**Video and Image Discriminators.** The image discriminator judges the static generated images from the image generator. The image discriminator is trained to distinguish between a real image i from a fake one i'. The video discriminator extends the task of the image discriminator to judge not only the realism of the generated frames, but also their motion. While the video discriminator criticizes both the content and motion in the generated frames, the importance of the image discriminator lies in its facilitating the adversarial training convergence [29]. Both discriminators are implemented as CNN networks.

**Training.** The overall loss function $\mathcal{L}$ for phonicsGAN is:

$$min_G max_D \mathcal{L} = \mathcal{L}_{ImageGAN} + \mathcal{L}_{VideoGAN} + \mathcal{L}_{reconstruction} \tag{3}$$

The terms $\mathcal{L}_{ImageGAN}$, $\mathcal{L}_{VideoGAN}$ are the adversarial loss functions for Image GAN and Video GAN, and their defined equations are (4) and (5) respectively.

$$\mathcal{L}_{ImageGAN}(D, G) = E_{i \sim p_i}[log D(i|c)] + E_{i' \sim p_{i'}}[log(1 - D(G(i'|c)))] \tag{4}$$

Generated Samples        Ground Truth Samples

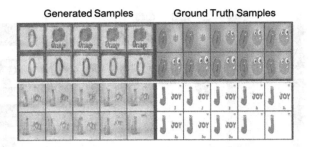

**Fig. 3.** Generated videos from phonicsGAN and the real frames. The lyrics for the top sample is "o o o orange" and for the bottom sample is "j is for joy".

$$\mathcal{L}_{VideoGAN}(D, G) = E_{v \sim p_v}[logD(v|c)] + E_{v' \sim p_{v'}}[log(1 - D(G(v'|c)))] \quad (5)$$

In equation (4) and (5), i and v are the real images and videos in the datasets, while i' and v' are the synthesized images and videos. Both Image GAN and Video GAN are conditional GANs [16] where c is the condition added to the model. The condition in the image and video generators are the audio signal and the category of the clip or image that are added at different stages. The reconstruction loss $\mathcal{L}_{reconstruction}$ is the $\mathcal{L}_1$ loss between the generated frames and real frames.

### 3.4   Implementation

We used PyTorch to implement the model. The length of the generated videos is 15 frames due to our computational power limitations. However, in theory it can be set to any video length. The video frames are resized to $64 \times 64$. The frames are sampled 5 Hz by timestamp (equivalent to a step size of 200 msec). The corresponding audio segment of the 15-frame video clip is converted to log Mel Spectrogram, then the overall Mel Spectrogram is divided into $64 \times 64$ audio segments, and two consecutive segments have $17 \times 64$ pixels overlap. Because the dataset contains categorical data, each letter is assigned to an integer value, i.e. 1 is for letter A, 2 is for letter B and so on. One-Hot Encoding is used to encode the letter labels using 26 bits (one per each letter). In the training phase, a batch size of 10, and Adam optimizer with learning rate 0.0002 are applied.

## 4   Results and Discussion

PhonicsGAN is able to generate videos that have the same content as the ground truth videos but with a different style. For example, in Fig. 3, the song of the first example is transcribed as "o is for orange" and the generated frames has the same letter "o" and "orange" as in the training frames but with a style similar to other training samples. In addition, we notice that phonicsGAN can successfully

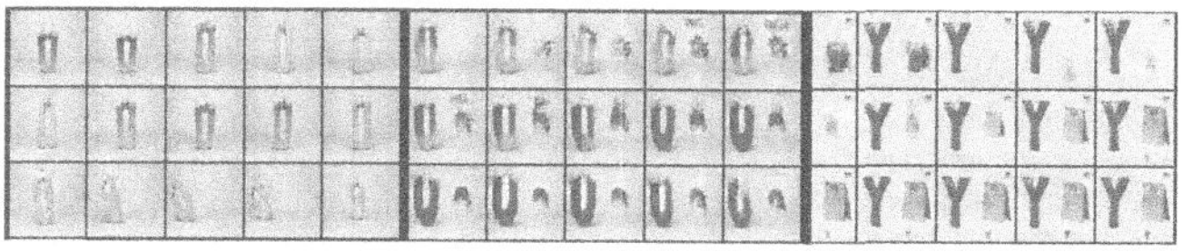

**Fig. 4.** The generated videos reflect different motion styles such as bending, changing colour, and appearing/disappearing (left to right).

generate different motion styles such as moving around the image, appearing, fading, swivelling and changing colour, as illustrated in Fig. 4.

One strategy to evaluate the proposed model is to compare it with mainstream models. As in works [14,25], the outputs of our model are compared with generated videos from baseline models such as LSTM and MoCoGAN. MoCoGAN [29] is first input a number of noise vectors that represent the changes in the motion to a GRU layer. Then, the result is concatenated with a fixed vector that acts as content. Thus, the generated frames of a video have the same content with different motion in each frame. We use the original implementation of MoCoGAN while replacing the motion vectors by audio vectors and the content vector by labels, we called this model Audio MoCoGAN. In addition, as in Lee et al. [14], we compared our results with LSTM's outputs that generates frames based on the audio signal and label. However, we did not present the generated samples from LSTM because of poor generated frames. Figure 5 illustrates the generated frames from Audio MoCoGAN and phonicsGAN.

Inception Score (IS) [22] is a quantitative measure that evaluates whether the images is correctly classified and whether each class has equal proportion in the generated samples. The main drawback of IS is that it only evaluates the distribution of the generated samples. In contrast, Fréchet Inception Distance (FID) [10] can be used in GAN to compute the distance between two distributions, in this instance the real and fake distributions. The IS and FID score depends heavily on the number of samples. Fewer samples may yield an inconsistent IS and FID score. A pre-trained Inception-v3 [26] is used to extract the spatial-temporal features to calculate FID and IS. We used 75 samples (due to memory limitation, we could not test it with larger number of samples) based on randomly selected songs. The averaged scores of 5 trials and their standard deviation are reported in Table 1. The quality of the generated images using PhonicsGAN surpasses MoCoGAN and LSTM as shown by the IS and FID score, as a lower FID score indicated closer distributions, and higher IS means better quality and diversity. However, since IS is based on ImageNet embeddings which is different than our dataset's representation, the overall IS scores are low. LSTM shows the lowest results as it lacks having discriminator network and adversarial loss proven to enhance the generated result. In addition, our model employs three layers to encode the conditional signals and reserve the changes of the signal over time while in Audio MoCoGAN the encoding procedure is done through one layer. Simple concatenation between encoded audio features and the label in Audio MoCoGAN cannot convey the importance of the encoded features at each time

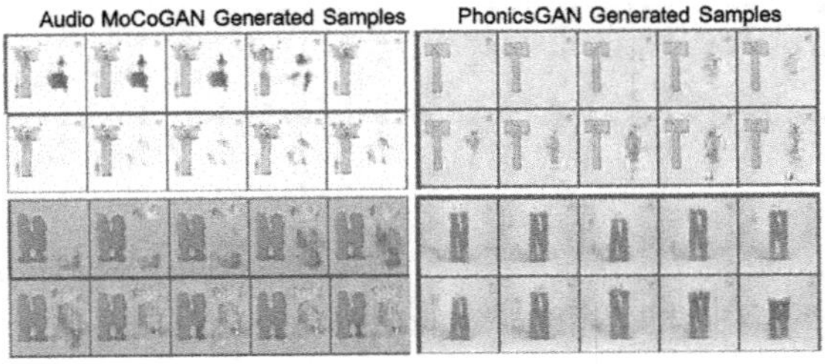

**Fig. 5.** The generated videos using Audio MoCoGAN (left column) and PhonicsGAN (right column) conditioned on labels from T (top) and N (bottom).

**Table 1.** The average IS and FID scores for LSTM, MoCoGAN, and PhonicsGAN at the standard deviations.

|  | IS | FID |
|---|---|---|
| LSTM | 0.0005 ($\pm$ 0.00006) | 146.0 ($\pm$ 2.0) |
| MoCoGAN | 0.0005 ($\pm$ 0.00000) | 62.2 ($\pm$ 0.4) |
| PhonicsGAN | 0.0008 ($\pm$ 0.00002) | 46.0 ($\pm$ 0.2) |

step. Even though the IS and FID score is comparable with human evaluation, the need for subjective evaluation is still necessary since individuals are more sensitive to undesired motions and artifacts, and that will be addressed in our future works.

One limitation of the proposed model is that the generated frames do not illustrate the correct object that is in the song, and sometimes the correct object is generated but not clear. One reason for this problem is the lack of a sufficient number of samples of each object in the dataset. The proposed dataset has 26 letters, and each letter has 18 objects on average. The average number of samples for each object is 3 samples. Besides, each object might be represented differently. For example, for "p is for purple", the object might appear as a paintbrush while in another video as a purple rectangle. We believe enriching the framework by conditioning on the first frame, the category of the object, or t lyric of the songs can help to address the issue with not having clear objects in the synthesized examples which we plan to address in the future extension of this work.

## 5    Conclusion

Generative models imitate multiple tasks in different domains. In the video realm, these models automate time-consuming processes such as generating videos, editing videos, changing the style of videos and predicting future frames. This research aims to contribute to synthesizing videos based on songs. The literature provides audio-to-video mapping models that rely on pose extractor models, initial frames or pre-processing steps. However, phonicsGAN is an end-to-end model that generates videos that vary in style, motion and objects according to multimodal data input such as songs. In addition, the emphasis of previous studies is the training of generative models on photographed datasets while phonicsGAN is trained on a graphical dataset. Several techniques are integrated in developing phonicsGAN, including using GRU layers to represent changes in the music signal and map it to changes in the motion. Adoption of two-level discriminators facilitates maintaining the coherence and realism in the generated frames. The proposed GAN was evaluated with IS and FID metrics and compared with LSTM and MoCoGAN. This work can be a first step towards song-to-graphical content systems where scenes are created based on musical composition.

**Acknowledgments.** The first author is supported by a scholarship from Princess Nourah bint Abdulrahman University, KSA.

# References

1. https://cloud.google.com/speech-to-text
2. Ahn, H., Kim, J., et al.: Generative autoregressive networks for 3D dancing move synthesis from music. IEEE Robot. Autom. Lett. **5**(2), 3500–3507 (2020)
3. Aifanti, N., Papachristou, C., et al.: The mug facial expression database. In: 11th International Workshop on Image Analysis for Multimedia Interactive Services WIAMIS 2010, pp. 1–4. IEEE (2010)
4. Aldausari, N., Sowmya, A., et al.: Video generative adversarial networks: a review. arXiv preprint arXiv:2011.02250 (2020)
5. Chen, L., Srivastava, S., et al.: Deep cross-modal audio-visual generation. In: Proceedings of the on Thematic Workshops of ACM Multimedia 2017, pp. 349–357. ACM (2017)
6. CISCO: VNI complete forecast highlights. Report shorturl.at/tDGV2
7. Duan, B., Wang, W., et al.: Cascade attention guided residue learning gan for cross-modal translation. arXiv preprint arXiv:1907.01826 (2019)
8. Duan, Y., Shi, T., et al.: Semi-supervised learning for in-game expert-level music-to-dance translation. arXiv preprint arXiv:2009.12763 (2020)
9. Goodfellow, I., Pouget-Abadie, J., et al.: Generative adversarial nets. In: Advances in Neural Information Processing Systems, pp. 2672–2680 (2014)
10. Heusel, M., Ramsauer, H., et al.: GANs trained by a two time-scale update rule converge to a local nash equilibrium. In: Advances in Neural Information Processing Systems, pp. 6626–6637 (2017)
11. Kaneko, T., Takaki, S., et al.: Generative adversarial network-based postfilter for STFT spectrograms. In: Interspeech, pp. 3389–3393
12. Karras, T., Aila, T., et al.: Progressive growing of GANs for improved quality, stability, and variation. arXiv preprint arXiv:1710.10196 (2017)
13. Kim, K.M., Heo, M.O., et al.: Deepstory: video story QA by deep embedded memory networks. arXiv preprint arXiv:1707.00836 (2017)
14. Lee, H.Y., Yang, X., et al.: Dancing to music. arXiv preprint arXiv:1911.02001 (2019)
15. Li, Y., Gan, Z., et al.: StoryGAN: a sequential conditional GAN for story visualization. In: Proceedings of the IEEE/CVF Conference on Computer Vision and Pattern Recognition, pp. 6329–6338 (2019)

16. Mirza, M., Osindero, S.: Conditional generative adversarial nets. arXiv preprint arXiv:1411.1784 (2014)
17. Mittal, G., Wang, B.: Animating face using disentangled audio representations. In: The IEEE Winter Conference on Applications of Computer Vision, pp. 3290–3298 (2019)
18. van den Oord, A., Dieleman, S., Zen, H., et al.: WaveNet: a generative model for raw audio. arXiv preprint arXiv:1609.03499 (2016)
19. Qiu, Y., Kataoka, H.: Image generation associated with music data. In: Proceedings of the IEEE Conference on Computer Vision and Pattern Recognition Workshops, pp. 2510–2513 (2018)
20. Ren, X., Li, H., et al.: Self-supervised dance video synthesis conditioned on music. In: Proceedings of the 28th ACM International Conference on Multimedia, pp. 46–54 (2020)
21. Rössler, A., Cozzolino, D., et al.: FaceForensics: a large-scale video dataset for forgery detection in human faces. arXiv preprint arXiv:1803.09179 (2018)
22. Salimans, T., Goodfellow, I., et al.: Improved techniques for training GANs. arXiv preprint arXiv:1606.03498 (2016)
23. Schuldt, C., Laptev, I., et al.: Recognizing human actions: a local SVM approach. In: Proceedings of the 17th International Conference on Pattern Recognition, ICPR 2004, vol. 3, pp. 32–36. IEEE (2004)
24. Soomro, K., Zamir, A.R., et al.: UCF101: a dataset of 101 human actions classes from videos in the wild. arXiv preprint arXiv:1212.0402 (2012)
25. Sun, G., Wong, Y., et al.: DeepDance: music-to-dance motion choreography with adversarial learning. IEEE Trans. Multimed. **23**, 497–509 (2020)
26. Szegedy, C., Liu, W., et al.: Going deeper with convolutions. In: Proceedings of the IEEE Conference on Computer Vision and Pattern Recognition, pp. 1–9 (2015)
27. Tang, T., Jia, J., et al.: Dance with melody: an LSTM-autoencoder approach to music-oriented dance synthesis. In: Proceedings of the 26th ACM International Conference on Multimedia, pp. 1598–1606 (2018)
28. Tsuchiya, Y., Itazuri, T., et al.: Generating video from single image and sound. In: CVPR Workshops, pp. 17–20 (2019)
29. Tulyakov, S., Liu, M.Y., et al.: MoCoGAN: decomposing motion and content for video generation. In: Proceedings of the IEEE Conference on Computer Vision and Pattern Recognition, pp. 1526–1535 (2017)
30. Vougioukas, K., Petridis, S., et al.: End-to-end speech-driven facial animation with temporal GANs. arXiv preprint arXiv:1805.09313 (2018)
31. Wang, T.C., Liu, M.Y., et al.: Video-to-video synthesis. arXiv preprint arXiv:1808.06601 (2018)
32. Wang, Y., Skerry-Ryan, R., et al.: Tacotron: towards end-to-end speech synthesis. arXiv preprint arXiv:1703.10135 (2017)
33. Yalta, N., Watanabe, S., et al.: Weakly-supervised deep recurrent neural networks for basic dance step generation. In: 2019 International Joint Conference on Neural Networks (IJCNN), pp. 1–8. IEEE (2019)
34. Yang, Z., Zhu, W., et al.: TransMoMo: invariance-driven unsupervised video motion retargeting. In: Proceedings of the IEEE/CVF Conference on Computer Vision and Pattern Recognition, pp. 5306–5315 (2020)
35. Zhou, H., Liu, Y., et al.: Talking face generation by adversarially disentangled audio-visual representation. In: Proceedings of the AAAI Conference on Artificial Intelligence, vol. 33, pp. 9299–9306 (2019)
36. Zhuang, W., Wang, C., et al.: Music2dance: music-driven dance generation using Wavenet. arXiv preprint arXiv:2002.03761 (2020)

# A Progressive Image Inpainting Algorithm with a Mask Auto-update Branch

Liang Nie[1], Wenxin Yu[1(✉)], Xuewen Zhang[1], Siyuan Li[1], Ning Jiang[1], and Zhiqiang Zhang[2]

[1] Southwest University of Science and Technology,
Mianyang, Sichuan, China
yuwenxin@swust.edu.cn
[2] Hosei University, Koganei, Tokyo, Japan

**Abstract.** Recently, learning-based image inpainting methods have made inspiring progress with squared or irregular holes. The generative adversarial networks (GANs) have been able to produce visually realistic and semantically correct results. However, most existing methods generate the results by one stage. They may have a slight advantage in computation time, but more information is lost during the inpainting process. Due to the lack of sufficient context information, these inpainting approaches cannot inpaint large holes in natural images very well. This paper proposes a progressive image inpainting algorithm for solving the above problem. This algorithm synthesizes different image components in a parallel manner within one stage. Moreover, this paper design a branch, which transmits the image features to the generative model iteratively. In each iteration, we adopt a mask auto-updating mechanism to shrink the boundary of a hole. Finally, the generative component can shrink the large corrupted regions in natural images and yield promising inpainting results.

**Keywords:** Progressive image inpainting · Generative adversarial networks · Multi-column convolutional

## 1 Introduction

Image inpainting (also named image completion) targets using the known information of the images and a specific algorithm to reconstruct missing areas in corrupted images. This technique is used in various applications such as object removal, error concealment, image denoising, etc. A significant inpainted result should exhibit consistency in both structure and texture between the inferential pixels and the known area. Hence, it is still challenging for a computer to recover the details coherent with the human eyes' visual experience.

There were various solutions for the inpainting task that have been proposed in nearly two decades. One is traditional diffusion-based methods. They

---

L. Nie, W. Yu—These authors have contributed equally to this work.

I. Farkaš et al. (Eds.): ICANN 2021, LNCS 12892, pp. 611–622, 2021.
https://doi.org/10.1007/978-3-030-86340-1_49

can utilize the high smoothness assumption of images to reconstruct missing regions from the known areas. This kind of approach is not suitable for recovering large corrupted regions as they cannot synthesize semantic content. The others are patches-based approaches. They complete images by copying patches from known areas. As the high consumption of calculation, they may not suit for inpainting high-resolution images. In short, the above two kinds of methods cannot generative pleasantly visible results.

Recently, due to the development of deep learning techniques such as convolutional neural networks (CNN) and generative adversarial networks (GAN). The semantic image inpainting work has caught the eye of the researchers again. Such as a Context Encoder is proposed by Pathak et al. [8]. This work aims at reconstructing the semantic information in a large proportion of missing regions. It uses an encoder-decoder pipeline with an adversarial loss and a pixel-wise loss to fill the hole in the pictures. A convolutional neural network's robust feature learning capability gained remarkable results in restoring corrupted images even when the missing holes are quite large. Furthermore, on account of an adversarial training strategy, the generated regions are often visually more realistic than those generated using diffusion-based approaches and example-based methods. Soon after this work, Yang et al. [13], Yeh et al. [14], and Iizuka et al. [2] extended this strategy to other semantic inpainting scenarios and achieved good results.

Despite significant progress made by these learning-based approaches in recent years, most of them are one-stage inpainting methods. So there are two problems; one is lacking constraints for the hole center. Because the damaged areas become large and the distances between known and unknown pixels increase, these correlations are weakened. This problem leads to difficultly fill in large continuous holes. Another one is that the hole center cannot obtain sufficient valid context for generating visually pleasing results. Hence, the center area will use some invalid information for inpainting. Finally, the networks generate semantically ambiguous results. This paper adopts a scheme that progressively is to inpaint from the hole boundary to the center to tackle these issues (see Fig. 1). Our method is analogous

**Fig. 1.** Given an image with a large missing region to inpaint, the exterior subregion (marked with the red rectangle) is undoubtedly much more accessible than to inpaint the interior subregion (marked with the green rectangle). (Color figure online)

to how humans solve puzzles (i.e., first solve the more accessible parts and then use the results as additional information to solve complex parts). This paper uses the implicit diversified Markov random field (ID-MRF) term to strengthen the central part's constraint and a multi-column convolution structure to extract image features in various scales. Finally, this paper came up with a mask auto-update branch in the test phase, which is our main contribution to solving the above problems.

## 2    Related Work

### 2.1    Image Inpainting

Recently, the learning-based approaches have attracted interest in researchers again. Iizuka et al. [2] introduced an extra discriminator to ensure local image coherency and used Poisson blending to refine the image, which achieved more detailed and sharper results. Yan et al. [12] and Yu et al. [15] devised feature shift and contextual attention operations, respectively, to allow the model to borrow feature patches from distant areas of the image. Liu et al. [4] and Yu et al. [16] devised particular convolutional layers to enable the network to reconstruct on irregularly masked images. In the aspect of feature extraction, wang et al. [10] proposed a multi-column convolutional neural network, it has three branches to capture image features in a different level. The multi-column structure can decompose the image into components with different receptive fields and feature resolution. However, as they try to recover the whole target with inadequate constraints, these methods fail to address the semantic ambiguity.

### 2.2    Progressive Inpainting

Progressive image inpainting has recently been investigated. Li et al. [3] added the gradually reconstructed boundary map as an additional training target to assist the inpainting process of U-net. Zhang et al. [17] used a cascade generator to fill in the image progressively. Guo et al. [1] used a single-stage feed-forward network to draw the image of the original size directly. Xiong et al. [11] and Nazeri et al. [6] completed the contour of the images step by step to ensure structural consistency. Oh et al. [7] used an onion-peel scheme that progressively embedded video data using content from reference frames, allowing precise content borrowing.

These approaches attempted to add structural constraints for inpainting missions, but they still lack information for restoring deeper pixels in holes. Furthermore, as these methods do not use recurrent designs and render redundant models, computational costs make these methods less practical. And these methods trained an excellent model with a progressive repair strategy in the training stage. However, in the application stage, the model still cannot capture enough context information. Hence, this paper design a recurrent method with a mask auto-update branch in the test stage. So, the trained generator can acquire more boundary information by mask shrinkage in the iterative process and finally complete a remarkable result.

# 3   Our Method

## 3.1   Network Structure

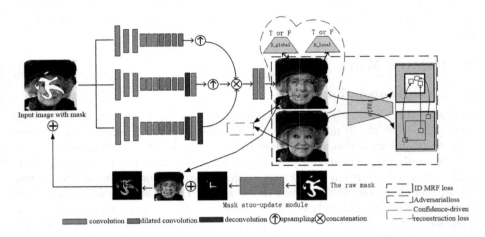

**Fig. 2.** The network with a mask auto-update branch

Suppose we have an original image **X** from a training dataset. And then, it is degraded by a mask M (1 for the known areas, 0 for the missing areas) named **Y** (contain the valid and invalid pixels). The aim is to reconstruct the invalid regions with valid pixels. Meanwhile, the completion images **Ŷ** are required semantically reasonable and visually realistic. In order to achieve this goal, this paper improve the Generative Multi-column Convolutional Neural Network (GMCNN) [10] and propose a new progressive repair method. The network structure is shown in Fig. 2. It consists of three sub-networks and a mask auto-update branch: a generator to produce results, global and local discriminators for adversarial training, and a pretrained VGG network [9] to calculate ID-MRF loss. In the testing phase, only the generator network and the branch are used.

There are n(here n = 3) parallel encoder-decoder branches to extract features in different levels from input **X** with mask M. And then follow a shared decoder module to transform in-depth features into natural image space. The diverse branches have various receptive fields to capture different levels of information. These encoder-decoder branches are trained in a data-driven manner to generate a better feature. These features are then up-sampled (bilinearly) to the original resolution and are concatenated into feature map F. The network further transform features F into image space via a shared decoding module with two convolutional layers.

By minimizing the difference between **Ŷ** and **Y** with a local and a global discriminator, the encoder-decoder branches can capture the more appropriate feature for inpainting. The pretrained VGG network plays the role of the ID-MRF loss calculator to strengthen the center hole constraint in a picture. It is helpful for the encoder-decoder network to select suitable patches for inpainting. Finally, when the model converges, this paper uses the mask auto-update module to fill in the missing area's boundary gradually. This process mainly offers more context supply for generators to achieve the results we desire.

## 3.2  ID-MRF Regularization

For semantic structure matching, the scheme takes MRF-like regularization, which is calculated by the pretrained VGG network only in the training phase. To calculate ID-MRF loss here is not to directly use cosine similarity measure. Instead, adopt a relative distance measure [5] to model the relation between local features and target feature sets. It can inpaint subtle details, as shown in Fig. 3.

(a)                                        (b)

**Fig. 3.** Using different similarity measures to search the nearest neighbors. (a) Inpainting results using cosine similarity. (b) Inpainting results using the relative similarity.

The left picture shows that directly use cosine similarity measure to calculate ID-MRF loss. It can be easily observed that the holes are quickly filled with a patch around them due to the background's smooth texture. It results in a blurry hole area that does not produce a sharp texture. Based on the relative position similarity strategy, the image on the right shows that it can select similar patches to fill in the missing areas. For example, according to the calculation, the figure's white area will be filled with different patches around it instead of one.

Let $\hat{\mathbf{Y}}_g$ be the generated content for the missing regions, $\hat{\mathbf{Y}}_g^L$ and $\mathbf{Y}^L$ are the features generated by the $L_{th}$ feature layer of a pretrained deep model. For neural patches $\mathbf{v}$ and $\mathbf{s}$ extracted from $\hat{\mathbf{Y}}_g^L$ and $\mathbf{Y}^L$ respectively, the relative similarity from $\mathbf{v}$ to $\mathbf{s}$ is defined as

$$\mathrm{RS}(\mathbf{v}, \mathbf{s}) = \exp\left(\left(\frac{\mu(\mathbf{v}, \mathbf{s})}{\max_{\mathbf{r} \in \rho_{\mathbf{v}}(\mathbf{Y}^L)} \mu(\mathbf{v}, \mathbf{r}) + \epsilon}\right) / h\right) \tag{1}$$

where $\mu(.,.)$ is the cosine similarity. $\mathbf{r} \in \rho_{\mathbf{v}}\left(\mathbf{Y}^L\right)$ means r belongs to $\mathbf{Y}^L$ excluding $\mathbf{v}$. $\epsilon$ and h are two positive constants. For details, please refer to the ID-MRF loss of GMCNN [10].

The method proposed in this paper can offer more candidates for inpainting the hole areas. Since ID-MRF regularization can prevent the missing area from being quickly filled by a similar patch, the incremental repair strategy proposed in this paper can provide more accurate information selection for reconstructing.

### 3.3   Spatial Variant Reconstruction Loss

Pixel-wise reconstruction loss is important for inpainting [15]. The network design the confidence-driven reconstruction loss to impose constraints based on spatial position. And we use a Gaussian filter g to convolve $\overline{\mathbf{M}}$ to create a loss weight mask $M_w$ as

$$\mathbf{M}_w^i = \left(g * \overline{\mathbf{M}}^i\right) \odot \mathbf{M} \tag{2}$$

where $\mathbf{g}$ is with size $64 \times 64$ and its standard deviation is 40. $\overline{\mathbf{M}}^i = 1 - \mathbf{M} + \mathbf{M}_w^{i-1}$ and $\mathbf{M}_w^0 = \mathbf{0}$. $\odot$ is the Hadamard product operator. The final reconstruction loss is

$$\mathcal{L}_c = \|(\mathbf{Y} - G([\mathbf{X}, \mathbf{M}]; \theta)) \odot \mathbf{M}_w\|_1 \tag{3}$$

where $G([\mathbf{X}, \mathbf{M}]; \theta)$ is the output of the generative model G, and $\theta$ denotes learnable parameters. This loss function exploits spatial locations and their relative order by considering confidence in both known and unknown pixels. It results in the effect of gradually shifting learning focus from filling the border to the center and smoothing the learning curve.

### 3.4   Mask Auto-update Module

The confidence-driven reconstruction loss makes unknown pixels close to the filling boundary are more strongly constrained than those away from it. The above work mainly solves the optimization problem of the network in the training process. Therefore, this method can get a more reasonable generation model in image reconstruction. And in the test phase, the generator uses the learned distribution to repair the hole areas. It can inference the appropriate location where the hole may most like to borrow. However, the location may also be in unknown regions. So, the generator has to choose the second-best solution to fill the corresponding missing area.

On account of this problem, this paper proposed the mask auto-update module using in the test stage for progressive inpainting (shown in Fig. 4). In the test phase, the model can make a rough prediction (the prediction result for the first time) of the broken image $\hat{\mathbf{Y}}$ based on the learned distribution. Meanwhile, the mask update branch will reduce the mask's coverage area through image erosion technology. Then, add the shrank mask to the complete result. Hence, there is a residual of the boundary between known and unknown areas(the residual is shown in Fig. 5). It helps the generator achieve semantically richer results.

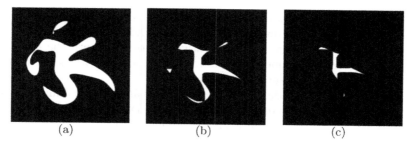

**Fig. 4.** The set of pictures shows a process of mask-updating though our mask shrink module. (a) The raw mask have not passed the module. (b) The mask have passed the module three times. (c) The mask have passed the module five times.

Finally, we combine the residual with raw input as a new input transmitting to the generator again. This residual image will provide the generator with more context, allowing it always to fill the hole with the optimal solution patch. By iterating the above process, we can finally get the result we desire in a progressive way.

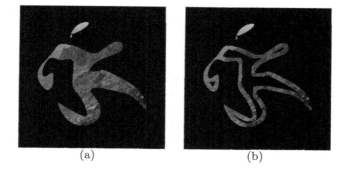

**Fig. 5.** Here are the generated content in the hole areas and the residual with a three-times shrunk mask. (a) the generated content. (b) the residual context from (a). Which can offer the generator more information of the hole boundary.

## 4    Experiments

### 4.1    Training Procedure

First, we scaled and cropped the original dataset to get the data samples of $128 \times 128$. These samples are then enhanced by flipping and other operations. The mask is also generated randomly. The samples are then fed into the inpainting network along with the mask. These pictures damaged by the mask are repaired by encoding and decoding through the generator. The completed results and the real images are fed into the discriminator. Through adversarial learning strategy, the generator and discriminator are iteratively optimized until the model converges. Subsequently, the model's initial inpainting results and the initial masks are fed into the mask auto-update branch.

In this branch, the initial mask is shrunk by an edge etc.hing operation. The cutdown mask is then combined with the original repair result to get a new damaged image. The new one has a smaller damage area than the initial damage image. Therefore, when put it into the model for inference, the model can obtain more practical information to generate better predict results. By iterating the above steps, the final inpainting results are obtained.

### 4.2   Quantitative Evaluation

Table 1. Quantitative results on three testing datasets.

| Method | Pairs street view | Places2 | CelebA-HQ |
|--------|-------------------|---------|-----------|
|        | PSNR              | PSNR    | PSNR      |
| CA [15] | 23.78 | 20.03 | 23.98 |
| GMCNN [10] | 24.65 | 20.16 | 25.70 |
| Ours | **24.77** | **20.33** | **25.92** |

In the Quantitative Evaluation, the peak signal-to-noise ratio (PSNR) score is used to evaluate the different methods' repair results. This paper evaluates our method on three datasets of Paris street view, Places2, and CelebA-HQ. CA and GMCNN also executed on the same conditions for reference and completeness. The comparison results are shown in Table 1. The method presented in this paper is superior to other methods in PSNR. The progressive inpainting strategy based on automatic update of the mask has excellent advantages for detailed information repair, and the results can verify the effectiveness of this method in Figs. 6 and 7. The results in Table 1 show that the enhancement of the face dataset by this method is the largest among the three datasets. Because in the face data set, the face structure is much simpler than that of the building. The gradual repair strategy can make the transition smoother. However, other methods ignore the edge filling information which can help repair the center of the missing area. Moreover, in the experiment, by adding a mask auto-update branch, there is little effect on the time elapsed.

### 4.3   Qualitative Evaluation

This paper added the mask auto-update module to GMCNN and the test results as shown in Figs. 6 and 7. When the mask is not updated by the module automatically, most one-stage repair methods (such as GMCNN) will produce fuzzy image repair results because the missing area is large and the hole center cannot get enough sufficient context information.

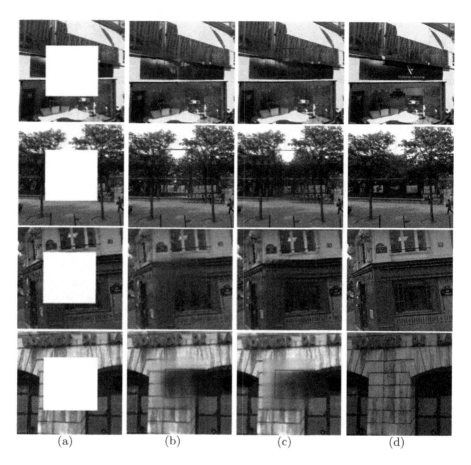

**Fig. 6.** Visual comparisons on Paris street view. (a) Input image with mask. (b) Inpainting results of GMCNN. (c) Our inpainting results. (d) Ground truth image.

Figure 6 are the inpainting results of the Paris street view. Column (b) are the results of GMCCN, and column (c) represents the results of this paper. In the first row, (b) has apparent artifacts in the red box that make the picture seemingly unrealistic. In contrast, (c) has more nature content, smoother line, and no artifacts. Hence, (c) making up a more realistic image. In the second row, (c) shows a more great texture in the center of the mask, making the result closer to the original appearance. In the third row, (b) shows that the method failed to restore the whole region, with a severe artifact in the mask area. The picture is too smooth, especially with only a blur in the center of the mask. However, (c)

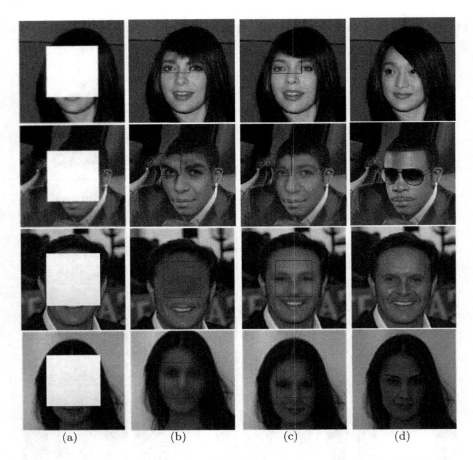

(a)          (b)          (c)          (d)

**Fig. 7.** Visual comparisons on CelebA. (a) Input image with mask. (b) Inpainting results of GMCNN. (c) Our inpainting results. (d) Ground truth image. (Color figure online)

performs better in the face of such complex conditions, and (c) can reconstruct more structural information based on successfully restoring the image. In a few rare cases, (c) although produce the same failure results show in the last row. Comparing the middle of the two missing areas, one can observe that (c) still managed to generate some lines (gaps between the bricks), but (b) only have a patch.

Figure 7 shows the two methods' repair results on the Celeba dataset, reflecting the phenomenon similar to the Paris street view dataset results. Columns (b) and (c) represent GMCNN and the inpainting method in this paper, respectively. In the red box in the first row, column (b), a prominent black artifact appears between the woman's eyebrows and hair. Nevertheless, in the same position, the result of (c) is accurate and credible. In the second row, the contours of the man's face (column (b)) are distorted to make him look like a monster. By contrast, (c) can get a more realistic, smooth, and natural facial contour. In the last two lines, the results of (b) are a complete failure. The reconstruction results of (c), though not particularly satisfactory, are still much better than that of (b). At least (c) produces the correct semantic information.

The above examples have two things in common. The first one is that the method proposed in this paper can achieve better results in terms of texture and structure. The second point is that, whether or not the method successfully restores the image in the central area of the mask, the method produces better results in terms of detail. Because the automatic update branch of the mask is used to carry out progressive image restoration, the center of the mask region can get more information step by step, which is the advantage of this method.

## 5   Conclusion

By analyzing the image repair results of GMCNN, we can find unreasonable pixels obviously in the inpainting area. Because during the testing phase, the generator's talents are still limited by insufficient information. Although the generator learns an excellent image information distribution with reasonable constraints, the location of the best similar patches that the generator surmised may distribute in the missing region, especially when the missing region was too large. Furthermore, the generator had to borrow other similar patches from the known region to finish the inpainting work. That is why it results in semantic conflicts.

The paper proposes a progressive repair module with an automatic mask update mechanism used in the model testing phase to solve this problem. We capture the inpainting content from the generator by our module. Then, we utilize the module shrinking the raw mask by an erosion operation. Finally, we combine the updated mask with the generated content to get a residual image of the boundary of hole areas and transmit the residual image to the generator again with the initial input image. The new input can provide more information for the generator. Hence, we can achieve more remarkable inpainting results at the semantic level.

Because the mask-updating rules are simple, the generator will still borrow a small fraction of the wrong pixels for inpainting. Hence, our next step can be to optimize the mask update rules. The application of the progressive repair method in the testing stage has a promising prospect.

**Acknowledgment.** This research is supported by Sichuan Science and Technology Program (No. 2020YFS0307, No. 2020YFG0430, No. 2019YFS0146), Mianyang Science and Technology Program (No. 2020YFZJ016).

## References

1. Guo, Z., Chen, Z., Yu, T., Chen, J., Liu, S.: Progressive image inpainting with full-resolution residual network. In: Proceedings of the 27th ACM International Conference on Multimedia, pp. 2496–2504 (2019)

2. Iizuka, S., Simo-Serra, E., Ishikawa, H.: Globally and locally consistent image completion. ACM Trans. Graph. **36**(4), 107:1–107:14 (2017)
3. Li, J., He, F., Zhang, L., Du, B., Tao, D.: Progressive reconstruction of visual structure for image inpainting. In: Proceedings of the IEEE/CVF International Conference on Computer Vision, pp. 5962–5971 (2019)
4. Liu, G., Reda, F.A., Shih, K.J., Wang, T.C., Tao, A., Catanzaro, B.: Image inpainting for irregular holes using partial convolutions. In: Proceedings of the European Conference on Computer Vision (ECCV), pp. 85–100 (2018)
5. Mechrez, R., Talmi, I., Zelnik-Manor, L.: The contextual loss for image transformation with non-aligned data. In: European Conference on Computer Vision (2018)
6. Nazeri, K., Ng, E., Joseph, T., Qureshi, F.Z., Ebrahimi, M.: EdgeConnect: Structure guided image inpainting using edge prediction. In: 2019 IEEE/CVF International Conference on Computer Vision Workshops, ICCV Workshops 2019, Seoul, Korea (South), 27–28 October 2019, pp. 3265–3274. IEEE (2019)
7. Oh, S.W., Lee, S., Lee, J.Y., Kim, S.J.: Onion-peel networks for deep video completion. In: Proceedings of the IEEE/CVF International Conference on Computer Vision, pp. 4403–4412 (2019)
8. Pathak, D., Krahenbuhl, P., Donahue, J., Darrell, T., Efros, A.A.: Context encoders: feature learning by inpainting. IEEE (2016)
9. Simonyan, K., Zisserman, A.: Very deep convolutional networks for large-scale image recognition (2015)
10. Wang, Y., Tao, X., Qi, X., Shen, X., Jia, J.: Image inpainting via generative multi-column convolutional neural networks. In: NeurIPS (2018)
11. Xiong, W., et al.: Foreground-aware image inpainting. In: Proceedings of the IEEE/CVF Conference on Computer Vision and Pattern Recognition, pp. 5840–5848 (2019)
12. Yan, Z., Li, X., Li, M., Zuo, W., Shan, S.: Shift-Net: image inpainting via deep feature rearrangement. In: Proceedings of the European Conference on Computer Vision (ECCV), pp. 1–17 (2018)
13. Yang, C., Lu, X., Lin, Z., Shechtman, E., Wang, O., Li, H.: High-resolution image inpainting using multi-scale neural patch synthesis. IEEE (2017)
14. Yeh, R.A., Chen, C., Lim, T.Y., Schwing, A.G., Do, M.N.: Semantic image inpainting with deep generative models. In: 2017 IEEE Conference on Computer Vision and Pattern Recognition (CVPR) (2017)
15. Yu, J., Lin, Z., Yang, J., Shen, X., Lu, X., Huang, T.S.: Generative image inpainting with contextual attention. In: 2018 IEEE Conference on Computer Vision and Pattern Recognition, CVPR 2018, Salt Lake City, UT, 18–22 June 2018, pp. 5505–5514. IEEE Computer Society (2018)
16. Yu, J., Lin, Z., Yang, J., Shen, X., Lu, X., Huang, T.S.: Free-form image inpainting with gated convolution. In: 2019 IEEE/CVF International Conference on Computer Vision, ICCV 2019, Seoul, Korea (South), 27 October–2 November 2019, pp. 4470–4479. IEEE (2019)
17. Zhang, H., Hu, Z., Luo, C., Zuo, W., Wang, M.: Semantic image inpainting with progressive generative networks. In: Proceedings of the 26th ACM International Conference on Multimedia, pp. 1939–1947 (2018)

# Hybrid Generative Models
# for Two-Dimensional Datasets

Hoda Shajari$^{(\boxtimes)}$, Jaemoon Lee, Sanjay Ranka, and Anand Rangarajan

University of Florida, Gainesville, FL 32611-6120, USA
{shajaris,j.lee1,sranka,anandr}@ufl.edu

**Abstract.** Two-dimensional array-based datasets are pervasive in a variety of domains. Current approaches for generative modeling have typically been limited to conventional image datasets and performed in the pixel domain which does not explicitly capture the correlation between pixels. Additionally, these approaches do not extend to scientific and other applications where each element value is continuous and is not limited to a fixed range. In this paper, we propose a novel approach for generating two-dimensional datasets by moving the computations to the space of representation bases and show its usefulness for two different datasets, one from imaging and another from scientific computing. The proposed approach is general and can be applied to any dataset, representation basis, or generative model. We provide a comprehensive performance comparison of various combinations of generative models and representation basis spaces. We also propose a new evaluation metric which captures the deficiency of generating images in pixel space.

**Keywords:** Generative models · Image representation bases · Normalizing flows · Independent component analysis · Generative adversarial networks

## 1 Introduction

The high volume and unique requirements of scientific image datasets necessitate the development of novel approaches for data modeling. The bedrock assumption of all modeling methodologies is the existence of spatiotemporal homogeneities in the data which can be exploited. However, in contrast to two-dimensional image modeling, scientific data are underpinned by unusual geometries and topologies. This "exotic setting" has to be leveraged and addressed by machine learning methods in their quest to find homogeneities which in turn can be efficiently exploited using representation bases. Additionally, unlike image datasets where pixel values are discrete and within a certain range, the elements of scientific datasets are continuous and can vary for each data point. In this paper, we propose a novel approach for modeling the probability distribution of two-dimensional datasets while developing a new measure for evaluating the models. The proposed approach can be applied to image and scientific datasets, with elements that are either discrete or continuous valued. Generative models

© Springer Nature Switzerland AG 2021
I. Farkaš et al. (Eds.): ICANN 2021, LNCS 12892, pp. 623–636, 2021.
https://doi.org/10.1007/978-3-030-86340-1_50

in machine learning have drawn significant attention with many applications in different fields, including, but not limited to, computer vision, and physics-based simulations for scientific datasets. The importance of generative modeling and approximating data distributions stems from the fact that unlabeled data are relatively abundant compared to labeled data, and this has applications in density estimation, outlier detection, and reinforcement learning. Deep generative modeling also has emerged during the bloom of deep learning and takes advantage of advances in computational power [16,18]. However, these models have not leveraged classical methods of data representation. These models usually learn the probability distribution of the images directly in pixel space, which is costly and inefficient while ignoring 50 years of image representation bases used in the compression literature. Furthermore, learning the distribution of the data in pixel space does not leverage the correlation information among pixels.

Representation basis techniques aim to transform data in such a way that useful aspects of data, for example statistical properties, are captured in the transformed space. Principal Component Analysis (PCA), Independent Component Analysis (ICA), and tensor decompositions using the higher order SVD (which we henceforth encapsulate as the Tucker decomposition for the sake of convenience) are among the widely used methods in this area. The other utility of representation bases is dimensionality reduction, which can be considered as a kind of lossy compression, i.e., it is possible to represent the data with a subset of coefficients with desired accuracy. Therefore, dimensionality reduction also brings a compression aspect into our approach.

We propose an approach to integrate image representation basis techniques in generative image modeling and perform a comparison among three generative models—generative adversarial networks (GANs), normalizing flows (NFs), and Gaussian mixture modeling (GMM)—and analyze their performance. The results suggest that this is a promising direction to pursue for efficient two-dimensional dataset generative modeling, in particular for applications where resources are scarce and speed of training matters. We summarize the contributions of our work below:

- We propose an approach for two-dimensional datasets which exploits representation bases to capture the correlation among elements explicitly and therefore makes the generation process fast and efficient. This approach is general and can be applied to image and scientific datasets where the underlying data are respectively discrete with a fixed range and continuous with a free range.
- We propose a new quantitative metric to compare the performance of our approach for different choices of generative models and representation bases. This metric seems to capture the quality of the learned probability distribution better than conventional metrics, especially for scientific data.

The rest of the paper is outlined as follows. In Sect. 2, we cover previous work on generative models utilizing representation bases or compression concepts. In Sect. 3, we provide an overview of representation basis approaches used in this work. In Sect. 4, our methodology for hybrid generative modeling is outlined. Implementation details and experiments are discussed in Sect. 5. Section 6 concludes the paper.

## 2    Previous Work

Learning the probability distribution of datasets is a long-standing problem, and generative models in machine learning constitute an important class of models with a rich literature. The Gaussian mixture model (GMM) is one of the important and classical models for generative modeling [21] while deep generative models rely on multilayer perceptrons (with deep architectures) for learning the data distribution.

Despite the importance of image representation bases and their abundant application in the compression literature, there are very few approaches which learn image probability distributions by marrying image representation bases (thereby moving away from pixel space) and deep learning-based generative models. Our proposed work therefore bridges the gap between image representation and deep learning-based image generation. As we will demonstrate in Sect. 4, our approach combines parametric and nonparametric modules where the parametric component is based on representation bases, while the nonparametric module is based on machine learning methods.

Generative Latent Optimization (GLO) [3] was proposed as a deep generative model which learns a deep CNN generator to map latent vectors to data by a Laplacian pyramid loss function while forcing latent representations to lie on a unit sphere. In this model, however, it is not possible for the generator to randomly sample from a known distribution. Implicit Maximum Likelihood Estimation (IMLE) [20] uses a non-adversarial approach for discovering the mapping between two densities. In this model, latent variables are mapped into image space via a generator and for each training image, the nearest generated image is found such that the $\ell_2$ distance between the image and mapping is minimized and the generator is repeatedly optimized via a nearest neighbor-based loss. IMLE optimization is costly and the generated images are typically blurry. The work in [12] proposed the idea of combining GLO and IMLE to learn a mapping for projecting images into a spherical latent space and learning a network for mapping sampled points from latent space to pixel image space in a non-adversarial fashion. Generative Latent Flow [25] learns the latent space of data via an autoencoder and then maps the distribution of latent variables to i.i.d. noise distributions. In the wavelet domain, SWAGAN [8] proposed a wavelet-based progressive GAN for image generation which improves visual quality by enforcing a frequency-aware latent representation. Our proposed method is different from the aforementioned approaches because it can be incorporated into any generative model and therefore allows for sampling from a known distribution whenever necessary. Furthermore, it has a parametric module and when used within a GAN architecture, it is trained via an adversarial loss.

At the intersection of compression and deep generative models, Agustsson et al. [2] proposed a framework based on GANs for generating images at lower bitrates. The model learns an encoder which includes a quantization module which is trained in combination with a multiscale discriminator. Kang et al. [16] proposed a framework for generating JPEG images via GANs. They proposed a generator with different layers for chroma sampling and residual blocks. Our approach is also different from these approaches because image compression concepts are directly used in the form of representation bases (like Tucker etc.) coupled with dimensionality reduction.

The Tucker decomposition [23], PCA [15], and ICA [14] are among the widely-used approaches which linearly transform data into a new space where data can be presented in a more structured way and more efficiently represented. Dimensionality reduction is an important byproduct of representation bases. Choosing a subset of coefficients corresponding to the representation can result in data compression and has been extensively used in the literature. As discussed earlier, our use of these methods is for the purpose of converting from the original data to a new space that captures the correlation between elements as well as providing an efficient representation for further processing. Therein lies the novelty of our work. As far as we know, this is the first work that conducts a comprehensive comparison at the intersection of generative models and representation bases while leveraging recent advances in adversarial learning.

## 3    Representation Bases

Finding a proper representation of random multivariate data is a key to many domains [14]. Linear transformations have specifically been of interest due to their conceptual and computational simplicity. The following techniques have been used in our work:

1. **Principal Component Analysis (PCA):** PCA linearly transforms the data by discovering orthogonal projections of high variance. Given a set of vectors $\{x_i\}_{i=1}^N$, $x_i \in \mathbb{R}^D$, a correlation matrix is computed as $C = \Sigma_{i=1}^N x_i x_i^T$, which has the following eigen decomposition: $C = E\Lambda E^T = E\Lambda^{\frac{1}{2}}\Lambda^{\frac{1}{2}T} E^T = E\Lambda^{\frac{1}{2}}(E\Lambda^{\frac{1}{2}})^T$, where $\Lambda$ is a diagonal matrix of eigenvalues, and their corresponding eigenvectors constitute the columns of $E$. Dimensionality reduction is performed by projecting data onto eigenvectors corresponding to the first $d$ maximum eigenvalues, which captures the maximum variance and is scaled with corresponding eigenvalues, i.e., $y_i = Fx_i$, where $F$ is the top-left block of $(E\Lambda^{\frac{1}{2}})^T$ with dimension $D \times d$. Data reconstruction is performed via the operation of $F^{-1}$ on the obtained coefficients.

2. **Independent Component Analysis (ICA):** ICA attempts to decompose multivariate data into maximally independent non-Gaussian components. Such a representation seems to be able to capture the essential structure of the data and provide a suitable representation which can be taken advantage of in neural networks [14]. FastICA, used here, introduced a different measure for maximizing the non-Gaussianity of rotated components [13].

3. **Tucker Decomposition:** The Tucker decomposition decomposes a tensor $T$ of order $N$ into a core tensor with the same order and $N$ unitary matrices.

It is viewed as a higher order singular value decomposition (HOSVD). If we consider an image dataset as a tensor $T \in \mathbb{R}^{d_1 \times d_2 \times d_3}$ of order 3, its Tucker decomposition is $T = \mathscr{T} \times_1 U^{(1)} \times_2 U^{(2)} \times_3 U^{(3)}$, where $\mathscr{T} \in \mathbb{R}^{d_1 \times d_2 \times d_3}$ is the core tensor which, as a lower rank approximation of $T$, gives a representation basis for it. Unitary or factor matrices are two-dimensional matrices which help in projecting $T$ into bases $\mathscr{T}$. The Tucker decomposition is widely used in compression by considering a subset of coefficients which carry most of the information in the dataset and eliminating lower rank coefficients, which typically has no adverse affect on tensor reconstruction.

We also utilize the Discrete Wavelet Transform (DWT) as a representation basis for a "held out" model. We use the DWT to set up a probabilistic model which can act as a basis for comparison for all generative approaches. The DWT offers a suitable and general basis for image representation which captures both frequency and location information. Therefore, it is highly viable as a benchmark model. We calculated DWT coefficients of datasets with a symmetric and biorthogonal 1.3 scaling function. We trained a Gaussian mixture model on all DWT coefficients (DWT-GMM) except the block of high frequency coefficients. The DWT-GMM is used as a benchmark for all generative models and is not used as a separate generative approach (but we plan to explore this possibility in future work).

## 4    Methodology

Our two stage approach comprising representation basis projection and deep learning is applicable to general 2D datasets. Below, we set up a cross-product of approaches wherein representation bases are paired with deep generative models. While we have elected not to explore variational autoencoders (VAEs) in the present work, this can be easily accommodated in the future.

1. Data Projection: We begin by projecting images and two-dimensional datasets into a representation basis space introduced in the previous section. Depending on the nature of the dataset, generative model, or representation basis approach, data preprocessing steps and some model customization are required to improve the results. In Sect. 5, we explain the preprocessing steps or model specifications adopted for the datasets used in this study.

2. Generative Modeling: Generative models are applied to learn the distribution of a *subset* of transformed coefficients obtained via one of the dimensionality reduction procedures detailed in Sect. 3. This is an efficient use of the compression aspect of the representation basis which makes the generative process fast and efficient. This way, the focus of generative modeling shifts from learning the distribution of data in pixel space to that of the distribution of coefficients in a more informative and structured space.

The generative models used in this work for structured image generation are GANs, NFs, and GMMs. The reason for this choice of models is the different approaches they take towards learning the data distribution. These models are briefly outlined below. For detailed explanation of generative models and their variants, please see [9,19].

**GANs** are deep generative models which have shown promising results in generating high-resolution images [9]. GANs are composed of two building blocks: generator $(G)$ and discriminator $(D)$ networks which are trained in an adversarial fashion to defeat each other. A GAN is formulated as a minimax zero-sum game in which the generator and discriminator try to optimize the value function $V$ from their own perspective:

$$\min_{G} \max_{D} V(G, D) = E_{y \sim p_y}[\log D(y)] + E_{z \sim p_z}[\log(1 - D(G(z)))], \quad (1)$$

where $p_z$ is a predefined prior for the input noise variable $z$, and $p_y$ is the true distribution of the data. Despite their impressive results on learning complex data distributions and generating natural-looking images, GANs cannot perform inference and evaluation of the probability density of new images and datasets—especially important in the domain of scientific datasets.

**NFs** were proposed as a generative model based on random variable transformations to approximate a tractable probability distribution such that sampling and inference is exact and efficient [22]. The basic idea of NFs is to transform a simple probability distribution (typically Gaussian) into a complex one via learning a sequence of invertible and differentiable mappings (bijectors). This is the generative direction. Applying a chain of mappings (bijectors) $f_k$, $k = 1, 2, \ldots, K$ on the random variable $\mathbf{z}_0 \sim p_0(z_0)$ results in a random variable $\mathbf{z}_K = f_K \circ f_{K-1} \circ \ldots \circ f_1(\mathbf{z}_0)$ with probability distribution $p_K$:

$$p_K(\mathbf{z}_K) = p_0(\mathbf{z}_0) \prod_{k=0}^{K} \left| \det \frac{\partial f_k}{\partial \mathbf{z}_{k-1}} \right|^{-1}. \quad (2)$$

In order for these transformations to be practical, determinants of their Jacobians should be easy to compute. Some of the suggested approaches are RealNVP [7], Glow [17], and FFJORD [10]. To implement NFs, we used the probability library of TensorFlow [1] and its distributions module. Bijectors were also trained by the FFJORD module in TensorFlow.

**The GMM** is a parametric method for probability density function estimation. The density function is represented as a weighted sum of Gaussian components [21]. The Gaussian mixture model represents data as normally distributed subpopulations with a hidden, unknown digital membership. The density of $X$ is formulated as a weighted sum of $K$ Gaussian distribution $N(\mu_k, \Sigma_k)$ as follows:

$$p(x | \pi, \mu, \Sigma) = \sum_{k=1}^{K} \pi_k N(x; \mu_k, \Sigma_k); \quad \text{with} \sum_{k=1}^{K} \pi_k = 1. \quad (3)$$

The parameters of the GMM model are estimated by maximum likelihood estimation (MLE). Typically, an iterative Expectation-Maximization (EM) algorithm [6] is applied which turns out to be reasonably efficient for this MLE problem.

# 5    Experimental Results

In this section, we detail the experimental evaluation of the two-step process described in the previous section on two different datasets, one from image processing and the other from scientific computing. To compare the performance of generative models in representation bases, we executed a set of experiments on the cross product of models and representation bases for these datasets.

With most image datasets, the pixel intensities range from 0 to 255 and are frequently normalized to a different range like $[0, 1]$ for training. Unlike image datasets, scientific datasets are not visually meaningful to human perception. Hence, measures like FID [11] developed for image quality of GANs based on the Inception v3 model are not immediately applicable to scientific datasets like XGC, where each two-dimensional slice has a different range, so *there is no unified range* in this dataset like there is in typical image datasets. Based on this observation, we propose a likelihood-based metric that we believe will be more suitable for this and other similar scientific datasets.

**Datasets.** We experimented with two datasets: Fashion MNIST [24] and XGC [5]. Fashion MNIST is a standard, curated and widely used dataset consisting of ten classes of clothing items. XGC consists of 16 planes corresponding to a doughnut's cross-sections. Each plane consists of 12,458 nodes with each node representing a histogram of perpendicular and parallel velocities of photons at specific checkpoints (please see Fig. 1). The histograms are not necessarily normalized. The velocity histogram of one of these nodes is depicted on the left in Fig. 1. The goal is to derive a generative model to simulate the two-dimensional velocity histograms of particles which are represented as images in a compressed and efficient way.

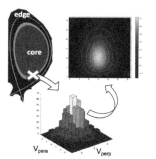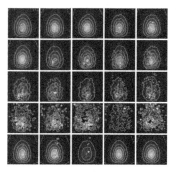

**Fig. 1.**    Depiction of a node in the XGC dataset (left). The $x$ and $y$ axes of the histogram represent the perpendicular and parallel velocities of photons, respectively. Samples from dataset (right).

**Preprocessing.** Slightly differing approaches were taken for the two datasets for projection to the PCA/ICA basis. Since the ICA bases generate an unconstrained range of pixel values, for the Fashion dataset, we first project the image intensities from a discrete range of $[0, 255]$ to the continuous range $[0, 1]$ and then project these intensity values to a wider range using an inverse sigmoid function $y(x) = \log \frac{x}{\beta(1-x)}$, where $\beta$ is a gradient slope factor. PCA/ICA is then applied to this new range of values. Since the inverse sigmoid is not defined at 0 and 1, we map all intensities to the interval $[\epsilon, 1 - \epsilon]$ for some value of $\epsilon$ and then apply the inverse sigmoid before applying PCA and ICA. In our experiments, $\epsilon$ is set to 0.001. The inverse sigmoid is used because the last nonlinear activation function in the generator of the GAN architecture for this dataset is sigmoidal, and therefore, we can match the intensities to the training data.

For the XGC dataset, the values are normalized numbers of particles in simulation which have a specific perpendicular and parallel velocity at a checkpoint. These values are normalized by the mean and standard deviation of each image separately (essentially a per image $Z$ score). Because each image has a different range, it impacts the choice of architecture and activation function in generative models.

**Generative Models Architecture.** Figure 3 depicts the architecture of a GAN for the XGC dataset. We used upsampling (conv2DTranspose) layers in the generator with a linear activation function in the last layer to allow for the range of generated images to be chosen freely for each image. This way, the generator is constrained to learn coefficients such that, after image reconstruction (via the transformation matrix), the values follow an acceptable range that is similar to the training set. The GAN architecture for Fashion is very similar to XGC, except for the number of filters and the use of sigmoidal activation instead of linear activation at the last layer of the generator.

The advantage of representation bases and dimensionality reduction is more tangible in NFs because these models are computationally expensive: when input/output dimensions are increased, the number of training parameters grows rapidly. We considered four layer of bijectors and 50 additional nodes in the hidden layers of bijectors.

**Dimensionality Reduction.** Our goal is to learn the distribution of a subset of coefficients as an efficient approach to data generation. The number of top eigenvalues and corresponding eigenvectors for each dataset was determined based on the $\ell_2$ distance between the training dataset and reconstructed images. For Fashion MNIST, more coefficients were needed to meet a certain error threshold: 324 and 400 coefficients were chosen respectively for XGC and Fashion datasets. We compare the performance of generative models in learning the distribution of a subset of coefficients for each method via different measures. We observed that for XGC, PCA, and ICA have similar performance across the board. For Fashion however, ICA had better performance than PCA, and therefore, we only focused on the performance of ICA-GAN for this dataset.

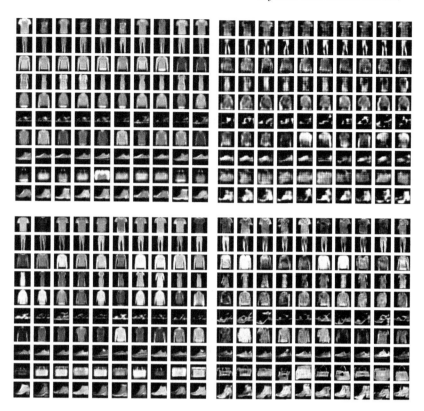

**Fig. 2.** Fashion generated images via ICA-GAN (left) and pixel-GAN (right) at epoch 10 (upper row) and epoch 50 (lower row). Image samples are randomly drawn and not cherry-picked. ICA-GAN generates plausible images close to the dataset from early iterations, with much fewer artifacts in terms of shape and texture. Pixel-GAN takes many more iterations to converge, with some images having artifacts.

**Metrics.** Many qualitative and quantitative measures have been proposed to evaluate generated images and learned probability distributions of generative models [4]. We consider two conventional and widely-used quantitative metrics—Frechet inception distance (FID) and average log-likelihood (entropy) of samples in kernel density estimation (KDE) [9] for evaluating the learned distributions and generated samples from different models. FID was proposed as a

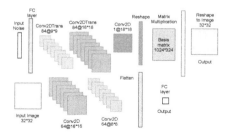

**Fig. 3.** The GAN architecture for the XGC dataset; generator upper row and discriminator lower row. A subset of representation bases is chosen.

statistical metric to measure the similarity between two distributions. First, by running the Inception v3 net on real and generated images, high level features (pool3 layer) are extracted as an embedding for images, and then a separate multivariate Gaussian distribution is fitted to real and generated embeddings. FID does not seem to be a suitable metric for evaluating scientific dataset generation. The features extracted from a deep learning network trained on real images which are perceptually meaningful to human vision *are not necessarily appropriate* for scientific data (where perceptual quality is not used). Furthermore, FID only provides a single scalar measure for the entire dataset and does not take the actual likelihood of the training set or generated images into account. For these reasons, we resort to metrics based on probability distributions and the likelihood of generated samples with respect to a reference model. KDE directly fits a probability density model to the generated images. We calculated the average of the negative log-likelihood (NLL) i.e. entropy of images sampled from learned distributions with respect to this reference density model (Table 1). However, as mentioned above, it is much more efficient to learn probability distributions in the space of a representation basis than in pixel space. These considerations affect our choice as described below. As mentioned in Sect. 3, we consider a reference model which is essentially a GMM on DWT coefficients. This model serves as a benchmark and is *not used* for generation or sampling. The number of coefficients used is $3 \times 256$ and $3 \times 324$ coefficients for Fashion and XGC datasets, respectively. To assess the learned density distributions via different models, we use the average of NLL values of sampled images from learned distributions via GANs, GMM, and NFs in the DWT-GMM space—essentially the DWT entropy. Furthermore, we compute the $\ell_1$ distance between the density curves obtained via KDE of the NLL values of generated images in the DWT-GMM model (see Figs. 4 and 5). Essentially, this distance is computed between the density curve of each model and the density curve of the real dataset on the interval that contains most of its density volume.

**Results and Discussion.** Experimental results for different combinations of modeling and generative bases are provided in Table 1 for the two datasets. These results show that ICA-GANs preserve the statistical properties of each dataset despite higher FID scores compared to equivalent pixel-GANs. The *very high entropy* of pixel-GAN for the XGC dataset shows that the learned distribution of data via pixel-GAN is far from the true distribution despite generating images which are visually similar to the training set. This indicates that generating a scientific dataset in pixel space may not be a reasonable approach. ICA-GAN (at epoch 50) had the best performance on the Fashion dataset which is a curated dataset with images being approximately registered within classes. Note that we cannot expect scientific data to be pre-registered. The better performance of the pixel-GAN on Fashion compared to XGC is partly because of the unified range of pixel intensities for Fashion allowing for the use of a single sigmoid activation function which confines the generated pixel values within $[0, 1]$. Overall, the results also show that GMMs with a representation

**Table 1.** Image generative models using representation bases with dimensionality reduction (324 and 400 coefficients: PCA, ICA, Tucker for XGC and Fashion datasets respectively). Numbers 10 and 50 in the 4$^{th}$ column denote the learned distribution at that epoch number. Metrics: DWT and KDE entropies (DWT-E and KDE-E respectively), FID and the $\ell_1$ distance (scaled by $10^{-2}$). For all metrics, lower is better.

| Dataset | Model | Loss | Target Dist. | DWT-E | KDE-E | FID | $\ell_1$ |
|---------|-------|------|--------------|-------|-------|-----|----|
| XGC | GAN | ADV | ICA | $-2,239$ | $-82$ | 5.6 | 4.0 |
|     |     |     | PCA | $-2,261$ | $-76$ | 5.6 | 4.0 |
|     |     |     | Tucker | $25,745$ | $-33$ | 13.9 | 5.0 |
|     |     |     | Pixel | $311,895$ | $207$ | 2.8 | 5.0 |
|     | NF | MLE | ICA | $3,241$ | $477$ | 6.0 | 4.8 |
|     |     |     | Tucker | $1,682$ | $1,105$ | 26 | - |
|     | GMM | MLE | ICA | $-1,096$ | $39$ | 5.5 | 4.3 |
|     |     |     | Tucker | $-2,474$ | $-455$ | 2.4 | 3.0 |
| Fashion | GAN | ADV | ICA 10 | $-2,451$ | $-453$ | 4.9 | 2.7 |
|     |     |     | ICA 50 | $-2,550$ | $-450$ | 2.2 | 2.2 |
|     |     |     | Pixel 10 | $-1,576$ | $-307$ | 5.0 | 3.5 |
|     |     |     | Pixel 50 | $-1,841$ | $-346$ | 1.3 | 2.6 |
|     |     |     | Tucker | $-1,146$ | $-333$ | 2.2 | 4.4 |
|     | NF | MLE | ICA | $-1,078$ | $-329$ | 2.9 | 8.9 |
|     | GMM | MLE | ICA | $-1,033$ | $-361$ | 2.3 | 5.7 |
|     |     |     | Tucker | $-2,660$ | $-480$ | 21 | 2.6 |

basis (after preprocessing) are powerful generative models for two dimensional datasets, regardless of whether the data arise from standard imagery or from scientific simulation.

Figure 2 shows that with a reasonable and simple architecture of GANs for learning the distribution of ICA coefficients of the Fashion dataset, it is possible to generate plausible looking images which are mostly texture and shape artifact-free from early iterations. Furthermore, Fig. 4 (and the $\ell_1$ distance in Table 1) also indicate that the generated images by ICA-GAN has the closest entropy to the Fashion dataset in both DWT-GMM and KDE benchmark models among deep generative models and representation bases. The pixel-GAN on the other hand does not produce close-to-dataset images until later iterations (with an identical discriminator) while many of the images have artifacts in terms of shape and texture. From Fig. 5, it might seem that the GMM has a better performance compared to the ICA-GAN for XGC data. However, it is important to note that less than $\frac{2}{3}$ of the ICA-GMM samples fall in the negative range of NLL while ICA-GAN shows a more homogeneous behaviour and hence lower entropy.

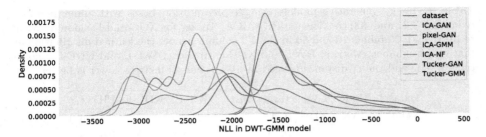

**Fig. 4.** Fashion negative log-likelihood (NLL) density distributions in the DWT-GMM benchmark model. For better demonstration, only samples with negative NLL are plotted (data density concentration). ICA-GAN samples depict NLL values near NLL of Fashion dataset.

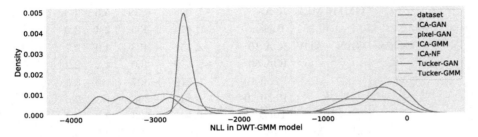

**Fig. 5.** XGC negative log-likelihood (NLL) density distributions in the DWT-GMM benchmark model. ICA-GMM seems to have better NLLs (lower entropy) however, GANs perform better on average since ICA-GMM has only part of samples (7K out of 12K) in negative range.

## 6    Conclusions

We proposed a framework for fast and efficient image generation that combines a representation basis approach with deep generative modeling. Our rationale was that learning a basis for data which preserves the statistical structure and correlation among image pixels can be a useful preprocessing step for the development of generative models. Furthermore, representation bases can be deployed for data compression during generation which is a boon for computationally intensive generative modeling frameworks. Immediate future work will focus on using over-complete dictionaries and coefficient compression within generative modeling.

**Acknowledgments.** This material is based upon work supported by the U.S. Department of Energy, Office of Advanced Scientific Computing Research, Scientific Discovery through Advanced Computing (SciDAC) program under Award Number DE-SC0021320.

# References

1. Abadi, M., et al.: TensorFlow: a system for large-scale machine learning. In: 12th USENIX Symposium on Operating Systems Design and Implementation (OSDI 2016), pp. 265–283 (2016)
2. Agustsson, E., Tschannen, M., Mentzer, F., Timofte, R., Gool, L.V.: Generative adversarial networks for extreme learned image compression. In: Proceedings of the IEEE/CVF International Conference on Computer Vision, pp. 221–231 (2019)
3. Bojanowski, P., Joulin, A., Lopez-Paz, D., Szlam, A.: Optimizing the latent space of generative networks. arXiv preprint arXiv:1707.05776 (2017)
4. Borji, A.: Pros and cons of GAN evaluation measures. Comput. Vis. Image Underst. **179**, 41–65 (2019)
5. Cole, M.D., et al.: Verification of the global gyrokinetic stellarator code XGC-S for linear ion temperature gradient driven modes. Phys. Plasmas **26**(8), 082501 (2019)
6. Dempster, A.P., Laird, N.M., Rubin, D.B.: Maximum likelihood from incomplete data via the EM algorithm. J. Roy. Stat. Soc. B **39**(1), 1–22 (1977)
7. Dinh, L., Sohl-Dickstein, J., Bengio, S.: Density estimation using real NVP. arXiv preprint arXiv:1605.08803 (2016)
8. Gal, R., Cohen, D., Bermano, A., Cohen-Or, D.: SWAGAN: a style-based wavelet-driven generative model. arXiv preprint arXiv:2102.06108 (2021)
9. Goodfellow, I.J., et al.: Generative adversarial networks. arXiv preprint arXiv:1406.2661 (2014)
10. Grathwohl, W., Chen, R.T., Bettencourt, J., Sutskever, I., Duvenaud, D.: FFJORD: free-form continuous dynamics for scalable reversible generative models. arXiv:1810.01367 (2018)
11. Heusel, M., Ramsauer, H., Unterthiner, T., Nessler, B., Hochreiter, S.: GANs trained by a two time-scale update rule converge to a local Nash equilibrium. arXiv preprint arXiv:1706.08500 (2017)
12. Hoshen, Y., Li, K., Malik, J.: Non-adversarial image synthesis with generative latent nearest neighbors. In: Proceedings of the IEEE/CVF Conference on Computer Vision and Pattern Recognition, pp. 5811–5819 (2019)
13. Hyvärinen, A.: Fast and robust fixed-point algorithms for independent component analysis. IEEE Trans. Neural Netw. **10**(3), 626–634 (1999)
14. Hyvärinen, A., Oja, E.: Independent component analysis: algorithms and applications. Neural Netw. **13**(4–5), 411–430 (2000)
15. Jolliffe, I.T., Cadima, J.: Principal component analysis: a review and recent developments. Philos. Trans. Roy. Soc. A Math. Phys. Eng. Sci. **374**(2065), 20150202 (2016)
16. Kang, B., Tripathi, S., Nguyen, T.Q.: Generating images in compressed domain using generative adversarial networks. IEEE Access **8**, 180977–180991 (2020)
17. Kingma, D.P., Dhariwal, P.: GLOW: generative flow with invertible $1 \times 1$ convolutions. arXiv preprint arXiv:1807.03039 (2018)
18. Kingma, D.P., Welling, M.: Auto-encoding variational Bayes. arXiv:1312.6114 (2013)
19. Kobyzev, I., Prince, S., Brubaker, M.: Normalizing flows: an introduction and review of current methods. IEEE Trans. Pattern Anal. Mach. Intell. (2020)
20. Li, K., Malik, J.: Implicit maximum likelihood estimation. arXiv:1809.09087 (2018)
21. Reynolds, D.A.: Gaussian mixture models. Encycl. Biometrics **741**, 659–663 (2009)
22. Rezende, D., Mohamed, S.: Variational inference with normalizing flows. In: International Conference on Machine Learning, pp. 1530–1538. PMLR (2015)

23. Tucker, L.R.: Some mathematical notes on three-mode factor analysis. Psychometrika **31**(3), 279–311 (1966)
24. Xiao, H., Rasul, K., Vollgraf, R.: Fashion-MNIST: a novel image dataset for benchmarking machine learning algorithms. arXiv preprint arXiv:1708.07747 (2017)
25. Xiao, Z., Yan, Q., Amit, Y.: Generative latent flow. arXiv preprint arXiv:1905.10485 (2019)

# Towards Compressing Efficient Generative Adversarial Networks for Image Translation via Pruning and Distilling

Luqi Gong, Chao Li$^{(\boxtimes)}$, Hailong Hong, Hui Zhu, Tangwen Qian, and Yongjun Xu

Institute of Computing Technology, Chinese Academy of Science, Beijing, China
{gongluqi,lichao,honghailong,zhuhui,qiantangwen,xyj}@ict.ac.cn

**Abstract.** Deploying GANs (Generative Adversarial Networks) for Image Translation tasks on edge devices is plagued with the constraints of storage and computation. Compared to some methods like neural architecture search (NAS), filter pruning is an effective DNN (Deep Neural Network) compressing method. It can compressing DNNs in a short time. The filter importance is measured by the filter norm, the filters with low norm are pruned. As for image classification, the filter with larger norm has larger influence on the final classification scores. However, as illustrated in Fig. 4, the filter with large norm don't always have a big impact on the quality of generated images for GANs. Based on the observation that the filter close to the filters' center in the same convolution layer can be represented by others in [8], we develop a distance-based pruning criterion. We prune the filters which are close to the filters' center in a convolution layer. KD (Knowledge distillation) trains the compressed model and improves its performance. The most common KD method ignores the transformation information across the feature maps, which is important for GANs. We take them as additional knowledge and transfer it from the uncompressed GAN to the pruned GAN. Our experiments on CycleGan, Pix2pix, and GauGan achieved excellent performance. Without losing image quality, we obtain $\mathbf{51.68\times}$ and $\mathbf{36.20\times}$ compression on parameters and MACs (Multiply-Accumulate Operations) respectively on CycleGan. Our code (We will open source within one week after the paper being received) will be made available at github.

**Keywords:** GAN Compression · Pruning · Knowledge distillation

## 1 Introduction

In recent years, GANs (Generative Adversarial Networks) [6] are frequently prescribed for image generation, image translation, text generation and style transfer. With the development of GANs for image translation tasks, their parameters and MACs become very large. However, some applications require interaction

© Springer Nature Switzerland AG 2021
I. Farkaš et al. (Eds.): ICANN 2021, LNCS 12892, pp. 637–647, 2021.
https://doi.org/10.1007/978-3-030-86340-1_51

with humans and demand low-latency on-device performance for better user experience. Edge devices (VR headsets, mobile phones, tablets, etc.) are tightly constrained by hardware resources. Deploying the GANs for image translation tasks on edge devices is limited by the device memory and inference speed. As an example, the frequently-used CycleGan [22] has 11.37M parameters and 56.83G MACs, making it difficult to deploy directly on edge devices.

With the observation that DNNs have a large parameter redundancy, model compression methods have been widely studied to reduce the number of parameters and MACs in neural networks. The most frequently used methods include human-designed, neural architecture search (NAS) [4], pruning [7–9,13], and KD (knowledge distillation) [15,17,18], etc. The above methods mainly compress the model for image classification and object detection. However, the network architecture and principle of GANs are different from classical CNN models. As for GAN compression, the human-designed method can not get rid of a large number of attempts. NAS consumes large computational complexity due to the huge search space. However, the pruning method compresses model quickly with a small amount of manual intervention.

Filter norm is mostly taken as the criterion for CNN model pruning methods known as the norm-based criterion. For the classification task, neurons with larger activation contribute more to the final classification scores. This assumption is not suitable for GANs because the GAN's output is image instead of classification score. Figure 4(b) verifies that the filter norm can't represent the filter importance for GANs. Existing CNN model pruning methods fine-tune the model by conventional training to improve the model performance. This only improve part of the compressed model's performance, which is still far from the uncompressed model. With the difficulty in restoring the performance of compressed model to the uncompressed by direct training, KD is proved to be an effective fine-tuning method for GAN in [14,19]. [14,19] transfer the uncompressed GAN's knowledge to the compressed GAN. This way is also performance limited as they simply make the compressed GAN to mimic the feature maps of the uncompressed GAN. However, mimicking the generated features of the uncompressed GAN is only a hard constraint in these works. How the output images are generated layer by layer from the input is very important implicit information for GANs. These works ignore transferring this kind of transformation information.

To address the problems mentioned above, we introduce a general GAN compression framework consisting of distance-based filter pruning and KD guided by transformation information across feature maps in different layers. In our GAN pruning method, we calculate the filter center in a convolutional or deconvolutional layer. Then the filters whose distance to the filter center less than the threshold are removed. The rest of the filters can achieve the same feature extraction effect as all the filters because the removed filters are deemed to be represented by other filters. Our pruning method is used for compressing a small GAN architecture. After that, the KD is applied to fine-tuning the pruned GAN. We regard the transformation information across the feature maps as the knowledge and transfer it from the uncompressed GAN to the compressed GAN. This kind of knowledge can guide compressed GAN to learn how to generate feature maps and output images layer by layer.

In summary, the contributions of our paper are summarized as follows:

– **Pruning**: We propose a filter distance-based pruning method for compressing efficient GANs. It can correctly measure the importance of the convolutional and deconolutional filters in GANs.
– **Distillation**: In order to restore the quality of the images generated from the GANs after pruning, the feature maps and their transformation information are transferred from the original GAN to the pruned GAN. We run the Pruning-Distillation process iteratively.
– We evaluate our proposed method on three image translation models trained on four benchmark datasets. We got 51.68× and 36.20× compression on parameters and MACs respectively without performance dropping for Cycle-Gan. We compressed the Pix2pix parameters by 22.31×, MACs by 12.46× at most. The GauGan got 16.49× parameter compression from 93.0M to 5.64M, meanwhile, the MACs were dropped from 281G to 25.63G with a slight performance decrease.

The rest of the paper is organized as follow. In Sect. 2, we introduce related methods of GAN compressing, including stacking human-designed modules, pruning, neural architecture search, and knowledge distillation. Then our proposed method are detailed in Sect. 3. We conduct comparative experiments and perform extensive analysis of experimental results in Sect. 4. Finally, we conclude our paper in Sect. 5.

## 2  Related Work

Generally, existing methods compress a meticulous model architecture with high performance by stacking human-designed CNN modules, pruning the over-parameterized network, or neural architecture search. After that, they promote the compressed network's performance by training or KD.

**Stacking Human-Designed Modules.** ShuffleNet [21], SqueezeNet [11], and MobileNet [10] compress the model by using the efficient modules designed manually. They stack the well-designed modules to get an efficient CNN network easily in this way. But they need to design the whole architecture including the number of layer and filter.

**Pruning.** Pruning methods remove the redundant connections or convolution filters. As for connection pruning, it leads to sparse networks. This needs specific hardware or acceleration library for deployment. Filter pruning methods are widely used in compressing meticulous CNN model. The most common criterion to calculate the filter importance is the filter norm. [20] compresses GANs by pruning filters with low filter norm. This criterion is effective for the classical CNN model because neurons with larger activation contribute more to the final classification scores. However, GANs have different kind of modules such as the deconvolutional layer. They are used for image generation whose outputs are images instead of classification scores.

**Neural Architecture Search.** NAS has been applied to design networks that are on par or outperform hand-designed architectures. Methods for NAS can be categorized according to the search space, search strategy, and performance estimation strategy used. [19] compresses GANs by developing a co-evolutionary approach. Generators for two image domains are encoded as two populations and synergistically optimized for investigating the most important convolution filters iteratively, obtaining portable architectures of satisfactory performance. However, this method is designed for specific GANs. GANs compressed by this method generate images with a poor performance. With the increase of compression ratio, the metric (FID) drops severely. [5,14] introduce neural architecture search (NAS) to GAN compression, and transfer knowledge of multiple intermediate representations from the original model to its compressed model. The large search space leads to big computing resource consumption which is hard to use in industry.

**KD (Knowledge Distillation).** KD is used to improve the performance of compressed model. It extracts the feature maps or outputs and transfers them from the uncompressed model to the compressed model, aligning them two by loss function. This method is proven to be effective for GAN compression in [1,2,5,20], but the insufficiency of knowledge makes the compressed GAN difficult to restore the performance to the uncompressed model. They simply transfer feature maps from the predesigned student GAN to the teacher GAN. Their success also depends on the appropriate design of student network architectures. [1,2] require us to design the compressed GAN's architecture including the number of layer and filter manually. However, setting a GAN architecture with an accurate model capacity is difficult in a trial-and-error fashion.

## 3   Method

Our method consists of convolution kernel pruning and KD illustrated in Fig. 1. For one step, we prune the GAN model according to a certain step compression ratio which means the pruning ratio for this step. Then KD is applied to the pruned GAN. We run the Pruning-KD step iteratively until the accumulated pruning ratio reaches the target pruning ratio or KD can't restore the performance of the pruned GAN.

### 3.1   Notations

Formally, we introduce symbols and notations in this subsection. We assume that a GAN network has $L$ layers. Input and output channels are represented as $N_i$ and $N_{i+1}$ respectively for the $i_{th}$ convolutional or deconvolutional layer. $\mathcal{W}_{i,j} \in \mathbb{R}^{N_i \times K \times K}, i \in [1, L], j \in [1, N_{i+1}]$ represents the $j_{th}$ filter of the $i_{th}$ layer, where $K$ is the kernel size. We regard $\mathcal{F}_i \in \mathbb{R}^{N_{i+1} \times w \times h}$ as the output feature maps of the $i_{th}$ layer, where $w$ and $h$ are the width and height, respectively. $f$ and $f_{step}$ are the target and step compression ratio, respectively. $\mathbb{G}$ and $\mathbb{G}'$ are the generators for uncompressed GAN and compressed GAN. Their outputs are $G(x)$ and $G'(x)$.

## 3.2 Filter Distance-Based Pruning Method

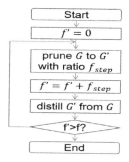

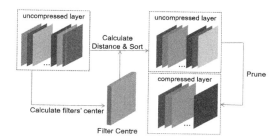

**Fig. 1.** The whole pipeline of our method. $f$ means the target compression ratio

**Fig. 2.** The filter distance-based pruning method for compressing GANs

As showed in [14,20], some filters are redundant due to their representation ability can be achieved by other filters. Thus these filters can be pruned. After pruning, the rest filters can play the same role and get the same performance in feature extraction as all filters remained.

As illustrated in Fig. 2, We take one pruning step as an example. We calculate the filter center $\mathcal{W}_i^*$ for the filters $\mathcal{W}_i = [\mathcal{W}_{i,1}, \mathcal{W}_{i,2}, ..., \mathcal{W}_{i,N_{i+1}}]$ in the $i_{th}$ layer, i.e.,

$$\mathcal{W}_i^* = \arg\min_{x \in \mathbb{R}^{N_i \times K \times K}} \sum_{j \in [1, N_{i+1}]} ||x - \mathcal{W}_{i,j}||_2. \tag{1}$$

The distances between the filters $\mathcal{W}_i$ and their center $\mathcal{W}_i^*$ are used to measure the importance of filters. They are calculated as $\boldsymbol{d} = [d_1, d_2, ..., d_{N_{i+1}}]$ where

$$d_j = ||\mathcal{W}_{i,j} - \mathcal{W}_i^*||_2^2. \tag{2}$$

$Top(\boldsymbol{d}, N)$ is a function that can get the top $N$ values in $\boldsymbol{d}$. It returns an ordered decreasing list whose length is $N$. This operation can evaluate and sort the filter importance. We note the last value in $d$ as the threshold $th$ by Eq. 3. The

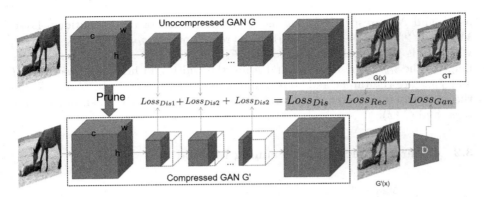

**Fig. 3.** Our KD loss consists of three parts: regular KD loss, paired learning KD loss, novel KD loss guided by the transformation information

threshold's index is $N - 1$. For one step, we set $N = (1 - f_{step}) \times N_{i+1}$. This achieves pruning the filters in the ratio of $f_{step}$.

$$th = Top(\boldsymbol{d}, N)[N - 1]. \tag{3}$$

Finally, we remove the filters in the $i_{th}$ layer whose distance to the center $\boldsymbol{W}_i^*$ is less than the threshold $th$. The pruned generator for this pruning step are parameterized with the remaining filters $\boldsymbol{W}_i' = [\boldsymbol{W}_{i,1}', \boldsymbol{W}_{i,2}', ..., \boldsymbol{W}_{i,f_{step} \times N_{i+1}}']$. We replace the original convolutional filters $\boldsymbol{W}_i$ with the pruned convolutional filters $\boldsymbol{W}_i' \in \mathbb{R}^{f_{step} \cdot N_i \times K \times K}$. The filters and their parameters are pruned to the ratio $(1 - f_{step})$ of the original.

We run the pruning step some times until the cumulative compression ratio reaches the target compression ratio $f$.

### 3.3   Fine-Tune Compressed GAN via KD

As illustrated in Fig. 3, we introduce transformation information into KD loss as the additional supervised information. The transformation information can be defined by the relationship between two intermediate feature maps. The intermediate feature maps are from two different layers in GAN. This kind of relationship can be represented as the inner product of these two vectors' directions. The vectors are flatten from the feature maps of two different layers.

For a GAN framework, assuming $\boldsymbol{\mathcal{F}}_i \in \mathbb{R}^{N_{i+1} \times w \times h}$ and $\boldsymbol{\mathcal{F}}_j \in \mathbb{R}^{N_{j+1} \times w \times h}$ are the feature maps for the $i_{th}$ and $j_{th}$ layer, respectively, where $N_{i+1}$ and $N_{j+1}$ are the number of output channels for the $i_{th}$ and $j_{th}$ layer, and $N_{i+1} = N_{j+1}$. $\boldsymbol{\mathcal{F}}_{i,m,n} \in \mathbb{R}^{N_{i+1}}$ and $\boldsymbol{\mathcal{F}}_{j,m,n} \in \mathbb{R}^{N_{j+1}}$ are the $(\cdot, m, n)$ entries of $\boldsymbol{\mathcal{F}}_i$ and $\boldsymbol{\mathcal{F}}_j$. Then, the transformation information matrix $\boldsymbol{M} \in \mathbb{R}^{N_{i+1} \times N_{j+1}}$ is calculated by

$$\boldsymbol{M} = \sum_{m=1}^{w} \sum_{n=1}^{h} \frac{\boldsymbol{\mathcal{F}}_{i,m,n} \times \boldsymbol{\mathcal{F}}_{j,m,n}^T}{w \times h}. \tag{4}$$

For a GAN compression task, we can assume that there are $N$ transformation information matrices denoted as $\boldsymbol{M}_i^T, i \in [1, N]$, which are generated by the uncompressed GAN, and $N$ transformation information matrices denoted as $\boldsymbol{M}_i^S, i \in [1, N]$, which are generated by the compressed GAN. For each pair of matrices between the teacher and student GANs $(\boldsymbol{M}_i^T, \boldsymbol{M}_i^S), i \in [1, N]$ with the same spatial size, we align them by the $l2$ norm where

$$L_T = \sum_{i=1}^{N} ||\boldsymbol{M}_i^T - \boldsymbol{M}_i^S||_2^2. \tag{5}$$

We also consider the loss of KD proposed in [14] as $L_F$. In the same way, we transfer the information of the feature maps $\boldsymbol{\mathcal{F}}_j^T, j \in [1, M]$ in the uncompressed GAN to the feature maps $\boldsymbol{\mathcal{F}}_j^S, j \in [1, M]$ in the compressed GAN by

$$L_F = \sum_{j=1}^{M} ||\boldsymbol{\mathcal{F}}_j^S - \boldsymbol{\mathcal{F}}_j^T||_2^2. \tag{6}$$

Paired image translation task consists of examples $\{x_i, y_i\}_{i=1}^{N}$, where the correspondence between $x_i$ and $y_i$ exists. Unpaired doesn't have this kind of correspondence. For the unpaired image translation task, we can view the uncompressed generator's output $G(x)$ as ground-truth and train our compressed generator $\mathbb{G}'$ with an objective $L_{rec}$. For the paired setting, we train our compressed generator $\mathbb{G}'$ with ground-truth $\boldsymbol{y}$. This objective is formalized as:

$$L_{rec} = \begin{cases} \mathbb{E}_{x,y}||G(x) - \boldsymbol{y}||_2^2 & \text{if paried GANs,} \\ \mathbb{E}_x||G(x) - G'(x)||_2^2 & \text{if unpaired GANs.} \end{cases} \tag{7}$$

The final loss is a multi-objective loss as showed in Eq. 8 where $\alpha_1, \alpha_2, \alpha_3$ are the coefficients, $L_{GAN}$ is the original loss for adversarial training.

$$L = L_T + \alpha_1 L_F + \alpha_2 L_{rec} + \alpha_3 L_{GAN}. \tag{8}$$

## 4  Experiments

### 4.1  Experimental Settings

**Models.** CycleGan [22] is an unpaired Image-to-Image translation model. It transforms the image from a source domain to a target domain. Pix2Pix [12] is used for supervising Image-to-Image translation. U-Net is the backbone of its generator which can better retain the pixel-level detail at different resolutions. GauGan [16] proposed a spatially-adaptive normalization method which can better protect semantic details.

**Datasets.** Cityscapes has 5000 images of driving scenes in 50 cities. Horse $\longleftrightarrow$ Zebra collects 1187 horse images and 1474 zebra images from ImageNet. Edges $\longrightarrow$ Shoes consists of 50025 images from UTZappos. Map $\longleftrightarrow$ Aerial has 2194 images downloaded from the Google map.

**Experimental Evaluation Metrics.** Frechet Inception Distance (FID) [3] uses the 2048-dimensional activations from the Inception intermediate layer. Then it models the activations from the real and generated images using the multivariate Gaussian distribution with mean $\mu$ and covariance $\sigma$. These statistics are then used for calculating the FID. The Lower FID is better.

**Implementation Details.** We first train a generator from scratch, then we prune it with the step compression ratio 5% and fine-tune it by our KD method. We carry out the pruning-distillation step above iteratively until the performance of the compressed GAN can't restore to the uncompressed GAN or the total compression ratio reaches the pre-set target compression ratio. For the Pix2pix and CycleGan, we use 0.0002 as the learning rate through the training procedure. The batch size is 1 for Cityscapes, Map $\longleftrightarrow$ Aerial, and Horse $\longleftrightarrow$ Zebra as well as 4 for Edges $\longrightarrow$ Shoes, 16 for GauGan. We adopt the Adam optimizer, keeping the learning rate constant before it linearly decays from the initial learning rate to 0. We set constant epoch as 100 while decay epoch is 100, 200, 300, or 400 depending on different datasets. Epoch set for compression is the same as from-scratch training. We use the generator with the best evaluation performance during training. We adjust $\alpha_1, \alpha_2, \alpha_3$ to ensure the three loss items are in the same order of magnitude.

## 4.2  Detailed Compression Results

**Table 1.** Experiment results on Pix2pix,GauGan, CycleGan

| Model | Dataset | Method | Parameters | MACs | mAP/FID |
|---|---|---|---|---|---|
| Pix2pix | cityscaps | Original | 11.38M | 56.80G | 35.62 |
| | | Li *et al.* [14] | 0.71M(16.02×) | 5.66G(10.04×) | 29.27 |
| | | Ours | **0.58M(19.62×)** | **3.69G(15.4×)** | **35.03** |
| | edges→shoes | Original | 11.38M | 56.8G | 24.18 |
| | | Li *et al.* [14] | 0.70M(16.25×) | 4.81G(11.81×) | 26.60 |
| | | Ours | **0.51M(22.31×)** | **4.56G(12.46×)** | **25.96** |
| | map→arial photo | Original | 11.38M | 56.8G | 47.76 |
| | | Li *et al.* [14] | 0.75M(15.17×) | 4.68G(12.14×) | 48.02 |
| | | Ours | **0.51M(22.31×)** | **4.56G(12.46×)** | **47.32** |
| GauGan | cityscaps | Original | 93.00M | 281.00G | 58.89 |
| | | Li *et al.* [14] | 20.40M(4.56×) | 31.72G(8.86×) | 56.75 |
| | | Ours | **5.64M(16.49×)** | **25.63G(10.96×)** | **54.40** |
| CycleGan | horse→zebra | Original | 11.37M | 56.83G | 61.53 |
| | | Shu *et al.* [19] | – | 13.40G(4.24×) | 96.15 |
| | | Fu *et al.* [5] | 0.98M(11.60×) | 6.39G(8.89×) | 83.60 |
| | | Li *et al.* [14] | 0.34M(33.44×) | 2.67G(21.28×) | 64.95 |
| | | Ours | **0.22M(51.68×)** | **1.57G(36.20×)** | **60.49** |

As shown in the Table 1, our method obtained better model performance and compression ratio.

For CycleGan compressed on horse $\longrightarrow$ zebra dataset, we achieved 51.68× compression on parameters and 36.20× compression on MACs. It is worth mentioning that, different from other methods [14,19], our method compressed the CycleGan without FID decreases.

For Pix2pix, we conducted experiments on three datasets. The mAP in Cityscapes drops only 0.1 with a compression ratio of 19.62×. For Map $\longleftrightarrow$ Aerial and Edges $\longrightarrow$ Shoes, we compress their model size by 22.31×, MACs by 12.46×.

GauGan is hard to be compressed in [14] which compressed it 4.56×. We compressed it 16.49× from 93.00M to 5.64M on parameters, 11× from 281.00G to 25.63G on MACs with small FID decrease.

### 4.3   Ablation Study

**Table 2.** Ablation Study For KD: Train, KD, and Ours mean fine-tuning the compressed GAN by normal training, the method in [14], and our KD method, respectively.

| Model | Datast | FID | | |
|---|---|---|---|---|
| | | Train | KD | Ours |
| CycleGan | horse→zebra | 67.721 | 63.5 | **60.488** |
| Pix2pix | edges→shoes | 27.37 | 27.46 | **25.96** |

**The Effectiveness of Our Pruning Method.** As illustrated in Fig. 4(b), we calculate the distances between some filters in GAN's certain layer and their filter center, we remove each of them. Then the normal training is applied to them as a fine-tuning process. Experiments show if we remove the filter with a large distance to the filter center, the GAN's performance is difficult to restore to the original GAN. This is because the filters far away from the filter center can't be represented by other filters. Such filters should not be removed. The Fig. 4(a) shows that the FID after pruning and fine-tuning is not clearly affected by the L1 norm of the filters, which indicates the norm-based pruning method is not suitable for GANs.

**The Advantage of our KD Method.** Table 2 shows that if we fine-tune the generator after pruning with the normal training method, the generator can't recovery to the original uncompressed performance. When we apply the KD method in [14], it can get a better generator while our KD method achieves the best results.

**Influence of Step Compression Ratio in Our Experiment Setting.** We set the step compression ratio to 3%, 5%, 7%, and 10% showed in Table 3. The FID fluctuation along with the different step compression ratio is less than 3, which means the performance of pruning is not sensitive to this parameter.

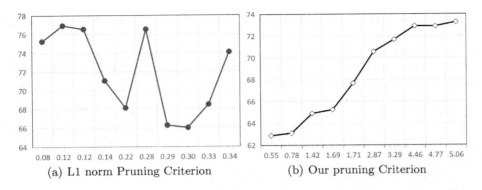

(a) L1 norm Pruning Criterion          (b) Our pruning Criterion

**Fig. 4.** The effectiveness of our pruning method

**Table 3.** Influence of step compression ratio

| Step compression ratio | 3% | 5% | 7% | 10% |
|---|---|---|---|---|
| FID | 60.20 | 60.49 | 62.87 | 60.45 |

## 5    Conclusion

In our work, we propose a general GAN compression framework. We apply a filter distance-based pruning method to design a small GAN architecture and use the KD method guided by transformation information across the feature maps to improve its image generation ability. Experimental results on different datasets and models showed that our method compresses GANs to a smaller size than other methods with minimal model performance dropping.

## References

1. Aguinaldo, A., Chiang, P.Y., Gain, A., Patil, A., Pearson, K., Feizi, S.: Compressing GANs using knowledge distillation. arXiv preprint arXiv:1902.00159 (2019)
2. Chen, H., et al.: Distilling portable generative adversarial networks for image translation. In: Proceedings of the AAAI Conference on Artificial Intelligence, vol. 34, pp. 3585–3592, April 2020. https://doi.org/10.1609/aaai.v34i04.5765
3. Dowson, D., Landau, B.: The fréchet distance between multivariate normal distributions. J. Multivar. Anal. **12**(3), 450–455 (1982)
4. Enzo, L.-A., Eduardo, L., Vasty, Z., Claudia, R., John, M.: Neural architecture search with reinforcement learning. Intelligence of the Total Environment (2019)
5. Fu, Y., Chen, W., Wang, H., Li, H., Lin, Y., Wang, Z.: AutoGAN-distiller: searching to compress generative adversarial networks. In: International Conference on Machine Learning, pp. 3292–3303. PMLR (2020)
6. Goodfellow, I., et al.: Generative adversarial nets. In: Advances in Neural Information Processing Systems, pp. 2672–2680 (2014)
7. Han, S., Pool, J., Tran, J., Dally, W.: Learning both weights and connections for efficient neural network. In: Advances in Neural Information Processing Systems, pp. 1135–1143 (2015)

8. He, Y., Liu, P., Wang, Z., Hu, Z., Yang, Y.: Filter pruning via geometric median for deep convolutional neural networks acceleration. In: Proceedings of the IEEE Conference on Computer Vision and Pattern Recognition, pp. 4340–4349 (2019)
9. He, Y., Zhang, X., Sun, J.: Channel pruning for accelerating very deep neural networks. In: Proceedings of the IEEE International Conference on Computer Vision, pp. 1389–1397 (2017)
10. Howard, A.G., et al.: MobileNets: efficient convolutional neural networks for mobile vision applications (2017)
11. Iandola, F., Han, S., Moskewicz, M., Ashraf, K., Dally, W., Keutzer, K.: SqueezeNet: AlexNet-level accuracy with 50x fewer parameters and <0.5mb model size (2016)
12. Isola, P., Zhu, J., Zhou, T., Efros, A.A.: Image-to-image translation with conditional adversarial networks. In: 2017 IEEE Conference on Computer Vision and Pattern Recognition (CVPR), pp. 5967–5976 (2017). https://doi.org/10.1109/CVPR.2017.632
13. Lee, N., Ajanthan, T., Torr, P.: Snip: single-shot network pruning based on connection sensitivity. In: International Conference on Learning Representations (2019)
14. Li, M., Lin, J., Ding, Y., Liu, Z., Zhu, J.Y., Han, S.: Gan compression: efficient architectures for interactive conditional GANs. In: Proceedings of the IEEE/CVF Conference on Computer Vision and Pattern Recognition, pp. 5284–5294 (2020)
15. Mirzadeh, S.I., Farajtabar, M., Li, A., Levine, N., Matsukawa, A., Ghasemzadeh, H.: Improved knowledge distillation via teacher assistant. In: Proceedings of the AAAI Conference on Artificial Intelligence. vol. 34, pp. 5191–5198 (2020)
16. Park, T., Liu, M., Wang, T., Zhu, J.: Semantic image synthesis with spatially-adaptive normalization. In: 2019 IEEE/CVF Conference on Computer Vision and Pattern Recognition (CVPR), pp. 2332–2341 (2019). https://doi.org/10.1109/CVPR.2019.00244
17. Romero, A., Ballas, N., Kahou, S.E., Chassang, A., Bengio, Y.: FitNets: hints for thin deep nets. In: ICLR (2015)
18. Sau, B., Balasubramanian, V.: Deep model compression: Distilling knowledge from noisy teachers (2016)
19. Shu, H., et al.: Co-evolutionary compression for unpaired image translation. In: Proceedings of the IEEE International Conference on Computer Vision, pp. 3235–3244 (2019)
20. Wang, H., Gui, S., Yang, H., Liu, J., Wang, Z.: GAN slimming: all-in-one GAN compression by a unified optimization framework. In: Vedaldi, A., Bischof, H., Brox, T., Frahm, J.-M. (eds.) ECCV 2020. LNCS, vol. 12349, pp. 54–73. Springer, Cham (2020). https://doi.org/10.1007/978-3-030-58548-8_4
21. Zhang, X., Zhou, X., Lin, M., Sun, J.: ShuffleNet: an extremely efficient convolutional neural network for mobile devices. In: Proceedings of the IEEE Conference on Computer Vision and Pattern Recognition, pp. 6848–6856 (2018)
22. Zhu, J., Park, T., Isola, P., Efros, A.A.: Unpaired image-to-image translation using cycle-consistent adversarial networks. In: 2017 IEEE International Conference on Computer Vision (ICCV), pp. 2242–2251 (2017). https://doi.org/10.1109/ICCV.2017.244

# Author Index

Printed in the United States
by Baker & Taylor Publisher Services